S. H. IRVINE

SOCIAL PSYCHOLOGY

SOCIAL

PSYCHOLOGY

PAUL F. SECORD, *Professor of Psychology*

CARL W. BACKMAN, *Associate Professor of Sociology*

University of Nevada

McGRAW-HILL BOOK COMPANY

New York
San Francisco
Toronto
London

Social Psychology

LIBRARY OF CONGRESS CATALOG CARD NUMBER: 64-22958
55912

6789101112 HD MM 7543210698

To my mother and to Professor George J. Dudycha -- P. F. S.

To my parents -- C. W. B.

Our decision to write a textbook in social psychology was prompted by several considerations. First, the rapid expansion and change in the field has not been adequately reflected in other textbooks, including the revisions of earlier texts. Perhaps this inadequacy arises because the earlier books were originally written within a framework that no longer encompasses present trends in social psychology. Recent activities, in particular, require a new organizational frame if they are to have their proper place alongside some of the older, more traditional topics. Research areas being emphasized today include the interaction process and the phenomenon of emerging structure in small groups; social-psychological analyses of ongoing social systems, such as hospitals or other work units; and social and person perception. In addition, several theoretical frameworks have emerged and are gradually bringing order to large areas of empirical findings. A textbook which adequately covers these developments must differ in structure from earlier books.

A second consideration is that social psychology can no longer be adequately surveyed by a person trained in only one of its parent disciplines. It is difficult enough for a psychologist or a sociologist to keep up with the social-psychological literature in his own area. To stay fully abreast of the literature in both areas has become an impossibility. We hope that through the collaboration of a psychologist and sociologist, the field can be adequately covered. The order of authorship does not signify any difference in the relative contributions of the two authors or in the overall contributions of their respective disciplines, psychology and sociology. Some parts of the book place greater stress on psychological research and thought; others stress sociological studies and ideas. These varying emphases reflect the empirical literature of the field: certain lines of inquiry have been of greater interest to the psychologically trained researcher and other lines to the sociologically trained. Moreover, in dealing with a specific topic or problem, we have considered the work done on it in both psychology and sociology and have attempted to weave together the contributions of both fields.

The text is organized topically rather than in terms of a single theoretical system. At the same time, each major topic has been organized in terms of what appears to be the most promising theoretical orientation. For instance, the topic of attitude organization and change has been treated largely in terms of dissonance theory, whereas exchange theory has been used extensively in the discussion of group structure and process.

This topical treatment should enable the instructor to use the book in a highly flexible fashion. He may vary the order of chapters, emphasize some subjects, omit others, etc. Asking the student to master the entire text in a three-hour semester or a five-hour quarter course would probably be too great an imposition. Since the book is comprehensive in coverage, it is assumed that most instructors will wish to omit or spend less time with certain portions, according to their own ideas of what is important or essential. In spite of its range, therefore, the book is regarded as suitable for a one-semester course.

While it is neither possible nor desirable in a textbook to cite all the literature in the field, we have attempted to be more comprehensive in this respect than most texts, in the hope that our volume will serve as a useful guide to the literature. Between four and five thousand references have been reviewed in a fashion ranging from a cursory examination to careful study, and many of these references have been cited. In order to achieve as extensive a coverage as possible, only a small number of experiments have been chosen for detailed presentation. Many others have been summarized as briefly as possible. Consequently, detailed quantitative data are seldom presented, and only a small number of tables have been included.

Two topics often given specific treatment in social-psychology texts have been omitted. Collective behavior, which traditionally has included the study of crowds, publics, and social movements, has not been explicitly dealt with, although some topics treated by us, such as the collective resolution of structural strain and social influence processes, bear at least tangentially on collective behavior. While we believe that collective behavior is an important area, it has been relatively neglected by social psychologists in recent years.

The second topic, culture and personality, has been omitted for a different reason. This area, along with the study of national character, appears to have become a distinctive field in itself rather than an integral part of social psychology. However, in discussing topics closely related to culture and personality, such as socialization, we have included some material pertaining to culture and personality.

We believe that the first course in social psychology should be upgraded. We have experimented with "toughening" introductory social psychology at Nevada, and the results, even for students of average ability, are encouraging. The mass of empirical research needing integration, the sophistication of experimental and field methods, and the recent theoretical developments all require considerable effort by the student if he is to adequately grasp the field. In our opinion, a course which presents "watered-down" material, which emphasizes practical affairs at the expense of scientific knowledge and methodology, and which omits the more difficult literature does a disservice to the student and to the field of social psychology. Upgrading the subject as this book does should produce a course which is no more difficult than many others taught in the junior year, such as advanced courses in the natural sciences.

In an attempt to encourage the student to read actively with maximum comprehension, study questions have been inserted immediately following each block of text material. These have not been formulated necessarily to stimulate interest or to require the student to apply his knowledge, but merely to encourage him to find the main ideas that have been presented in the preceding discussion. This departure from the frequent practice of placing them at the chapter end represents an attempt to apply what is known about learning theory and the habits of college students.

We are indebted to many persons for assistance in the preparation of the book. Numerous helpful suggestions and criticisms were made by the following psychologists and sociologists who read portions of the manuscript: Professors Carl W. Eriksen, Neil Gross, A. Paul Hare, William McGuire, Robert R. Sears, Michael Wertheimer, Robert F. Winch, Charles Wright, and Alvin Zander. We are especially grateful to Sidney Rosen and Neil J. Smelser, who read the entire manuscript and whose excellent criticisms led to significant improvements. The final responsibility for any inadequacies of the book remains our own, however. Finally, for assistance in typing and other clerical tasks, we are indebted to Karen Ayon, Betty Gwilliam, Carol Hackney, Hazel Hoelker, Norma Klenakis, Dee Krechmeier, Alma Smith, and Eileen Tibbetts; and for preparing rough drafts of most of the figures, we thank Don Schweitzer.

PAUL F. SECORD
CARL W. BACKMAN

CONTENTS

Social Psychology

THE NATURE OF
SOCIAL PSYCHOLOGY

The most distinctive feature of human life is its social character. People do things in concert; they work together and play together. Moreover, people in interaction share an understanding of their various acts. And they react to one another in terms of these meanings.

The social psychologist studies the behavior of individuals in social contexts. Thus his business differs from that of the general psychologist, who often isolates the individual from his social environment; and it differs from that of the sociologist, who often studies the patterns of social interaction separately from the acting individuals.

DISTINCTIVE CHARACTERISTICS OF INTERACTION

The behavior of an individual in the presence of another person is at once a response and a stimulus to that other person. Because the other person (O) reacts to the behavior of an individual (S), the behavior of S is likely to be tempered by the presence of O. S may consciously or unconsciously behave so as to elicit a particular response from O. His subsequent behavior depends upon his success or failure in eliciting certain behaviors from O.

But the matter is more complex than a simple sequential patterning of stimulus and response, action and reaction. Under ordinary circumstances, the behavior of persons in interaction flows quite smoothly, as in the case of two housewives chatting over the back fence. This occurs because each party to the interaction has learned to anticipate the response that an action on his part will elicit, as well as to anticipate the responses he will make toward the actions of the other party. Such interactions only flow smoothly, however, when both parties share the same definitions of their own and each other's acts, as well as a common understanding of the structure of their relation to each other. When two men in our society are introduced, each extends his hand and expects the other to extend his hand. But if one of the men is from a society where the handshake is not known as a symbol of greeting, this action is likely to falter. Such *mutual expectations* govern much everyday behavior. If the individual were studied only in isolation from other individuals, many of these controlling features of everyday interpersonal behavior would not be discovered.

TYPES OF ANALYSIS

The behavior of individuals in interaction may be analyzed in terms of three systems: the personality system, the social system, and the cultural system. Analysis in terms of *personality* considers properties of individuals such as attitudes, needs, traits, and feelings, as well as processes like learning or perception. For example, individual members of a delinquent gang might be studied. Such an analysis might reveal that they have stronger aggressive impulses than nondelinquents and that they perceive society as a rather difficult and threatening place to live. Analysis in terms of the *social system* focuses on relations among persons. Typically, each person is thought of as occupying one or more positions in these relations. Associated with each position are expectations as to how a person in that position should think, feel, and act.

For example, one position in our delinquent gang might be that of gang leader. Closely related to that position might be two others occupied by the gang leader's "lieutenants." Gang members expect a leader to suggest and initiate group activities, to guide the progress of ongoing activities, and to evaluate their success. His lieutenants are expected to provide support and aid to the leader in carrying out the activities. We might think of the remaining gang members as occupying the position of "follower." Thus, much of the behavior of the gang members is a function of the group structure, consisting of the positions of leader, lieutenants, and followers, and the relations among these positions.

Central to analysis in terms of *culture* are the agreed-upon ideas about the social and nonsocial world. These include complex systems of beliefs as well as the values that members of a society place upon various kinds of activities. The juvenile gang is unknown in some societies, a fact which suggests that certain aspects of our culture are relevant to gang formation. These include belief patterns favoring late marriage, which leave a large number of males unaffiliated, and the complex technological nature of employment in our society, which prevents the early entrance of a sizable number of young males into adult employment.

Psychologists as psychologists are concerned primarily with analysis in terms of individual behavior; sociologists as sociologists are interested primarily in analysis in terms of the social system. Anthropologists are concerned with cultural systems. Social psychologists, however, while using as basic data the behavior and characteristics of individuals, try to understand individual behavior in terms of variables from all three systems. While analysis in each of the systems is kept distinct, individual behavior provides the focal point for relating these systems to each other.

Thus certain aspects of the personality of individuals may result from properties of the social system. When the social system called the family is structured in a certain way, for example, it produces individuals who are strongly motivated to achieve wealth, success, and status in a society, and when structured in other ways, it produces a much weaker need for achievement. Similarly, certain personality variables may affect the functioning of social system. For example, the personality makeup of members of individual families produces marked variation in the functioning of this social system. Families in a whole society may be structured so as to encourage strong needs for achievement in children, because such behavior is related to the central values of the culture of the group. For the most part, social psychology deals in this fashion with the interplay between personality, social system, and, to a lesser extent, culture.

Methods of Social Psychology

The methods used by the scientist determine both the truth and the range of applicability of his conclusions. There is no certainty in science. Some generalizations are only more probable than others. Certainty about an interpretation depends on the extent to which methods of investigation exclude alternative interpretations. Certainty is always a matter of degree; some generalizations may be held with an extremely high degree of confidence, while others may be more tentative. Similarly, the range of applicability of a scientific generalization is a matter of degree. Few, if any, scientific generalizations apply to all situations other than the one in which they were first formed. This does not mean that nature, human or otherwise, is capricious and unpredictable, but rather that nature is complex. While the scientist may arrange a situation in simplified form so to observe the interaction of only a few variables at a time, in everyday situations these same variables are being affected by a host of others.

Social psychologists, like other scientists, attempt to state their findings in terms of cause and effect or in terms of antecedents and consequents. To make statements like "A causes B," or "B follows from or is the consequent of A," the following kinds of evidence must be provided:

1. The variables in question must be shown to vary together in some systematic fashion.
2. There must be some basis for inferring that the hypothesized consequent did not precede the hypothesized antecedent.
3. Evidence that rules out an interpretation in terms of other determining conditions must be provided.

The first of these, covariation or correlation, may easily be illustrated. The height and weight of persons are found to covary; within certain limits, the taller a person, the more he weighs. Covariation in this example is imperfect; taller persons are not heavier than all persons who are shorter than they are, but only heavier than most of them.

Difficulties in determining which of two associated variables is the antecedent are illustrated in the following example. A finding that persons married to each other have similar personalities could be explained by assuming that persons who are similar are more likely to choose each other as a mate. But it could also be explained by assuming that, in time, the personalities of persons married to each other change in the direction of greater similarity. Which of these variables is the antecedent cannot be ascertained from knowledge of covariation alone.

In some instances, the investigator has no difficulty in determining which variable is the antecedent. Members of a marital pair are more likely to have the same religious background than are unrelated persons. Since a person's religious background is determined long before marriage, similarity in this respect could not be a function of marital interaction, and it may safely be identified as the antecedent variable. Often the identification of the antecedent and consequent variables can be determined by a properly designed experiment. The experimenter who wishes to test the effects of knowing the religion of another group member on a person's choice of associations would introduce such knowledge prior to allowing his subjects to make choices. Finally, cause-effect relations are not always one-way relations in social psychology. Sometimes A can be demonstrated to be the antecedent of B, *and* B the antecedent of A! For example, similarity of personalities might lead two persons to select each other as marital partners, and the marriage relation may bring about further similarities.

Even though two variables are shown to be associated, and one is clearly the antecedent of the other, a cause-effect relation cannot be inferred until evidence is provided showing that other factors could not have brought about the association. A statistical association between smoking and lung cancer has been demonstrated; moreover, smoking is clearly the antecedent variable. These facts alone are insufficient to prove a cause-effect relation. Other plausible determinants that could produce this relation must be ruled out. For example, if it were true that urban dwellers smoke more heavily than rural dwellers, the actual cause-effect relation might be that polluted urban atmospheres cause lung cancer. This alternative hypothesis could be eliminated, however, if rural dwellers (or urban dwellers) considered separately were shown to reveal an association between lung cancer and smoking.

These three criteria are met in varying degree by the major research designs used in social psychology. Two broad types may be distinguished: experimental and nonexperimental. In the *experimental* method, the investigator manipulates a situation so that different groups of persons will represent in varying degree the condition whose effect is to be assessed. He also measures with as much precision as possible the behavior that he believes will vary with this manipulated condition. Also essential to the method is the control of all remaining variables so that they cannot affect the relevant behavior of the subjects. In this way, any effects upon behavior can be attributed to the manipulated variable. As a simplified illustration of these essential characteristics of an experiment, suppose that an investigator is interested in determining the effects of the size of a group on its ability to solve problems. He might set up several groups that are equivalent in all respects but size and proceed to test the efficiency of each in solving problems.

Nonexperimental or field methods cover a considerable variety of procedures. Most field methods involve making observations in the more complex situations of everyday life. Such observations may be gathered through interviews or by directly observing subjects. These observations may be highly structured, as when an interviewer asks each subject identically worded questions in the same order, allowing for a minimal variation in responses. Or they may be relatively unstructured, as when the investigator participates in the activities under observation and simultaneously attempts to identify in his own terms the important determinants of the ongoing activities. The structured interview is commonly used in survey or opinion research. Participant observation may involve living with a group for a year or more, taking copious field notes, as William F. Whyte (1943) did in his study of a street-corner gang. Where field techniques are employed, behavior is often studied in a completely natural setting. Sometimes, however, a field situation may be arranged so as to bring out behaviors relevant to the investigator's hypotheses. For example, an observer who wishes to study the aggressive behavior of preschool children may place them in nursery school settings designed to elicit more than the usual amount of aggressive behavior.

Field methods and experimental methods each have their advantages and disadvantages. The experimental method generally employs more precise measurement techniques, exercises greater control over conditions that might complicate interpretation of the findings, and is more likely to meet the three requirements for demonstrating a causal relation. But generalization from experimental situations to everyday ones is often difficult. Field methods usually permit more ready generalization to everyday situations. But meeting the three requirements for inferring cause-effect relations is more difficult with these techniques.

Differences between these two approaches are a matter of degree; moreover, they vary with the nature of the problem. Some experiments create conditions like those of everyday situations, and some field observations are made in atypical situations. In some field situations, the three requirements for inferring a cause-effect relation are met rather well. Some experiments, moreover, fail to meet these requirements. Behavioral science is replete with many experiments where some uncontrolled factor, rather than the supposed independent variable, has later been shown to account for the results. The degree of control exercised in experiments also raises the danger that the phenomenon observed is a product of the special conditions of the laboratory itself. Not only the very simplified nature of the situation but additional elements, such as the expectations of the subjects as to how the experimenter wants them to behave, may create behaviors that have no meaning outside the laboratory. Much has yet to be learned about the effects of the unique culture of the laboratory.

Both laboratory experiments and field studies in natural settings are needed for an adequate social psychology. Studies in natural settings often suggest alternative explanations of observed behavior that can be tested for validity in the laboratory. The much larger number of variables in nonlaboratory settings also precludes any direct generalization from the laboratory to the field situation. For maximum understanding, all the relevant conditions that affect behavior in a natural setting must be known. A laboratory experiment, which usually deals with only a few variables, cannot readily be applied to field settings unless such settings are carefully studied to discover the additional variables that might operate to influence the behavior in which the behavioral scientist is interested. This is another reason why the combined contributions of the sociologist and the psychologist yield a more adequate social psychology. Although there is much overlap in the activities of the two professions, the psychologist more frequently performs laboratory experiments and uses highly selected samples of subjects, such as college sophomores. The sociologist more frequently collects observations from natural settings and more often uses representative samples. By combining the knowledge and insights gained from both fields, the social psychologist is in a better position to predict the behavior of individuals in everyday situations.

Where possible, we have cited both field and experimental studies in support of our generalizations. To achieve clarity and to make social-psychological concepts and ideas meaningful, however, we have often cited commonplace experiences or observations. These anecdotal comments are made for purposes of exposition only and should not be confused with scientific evidence.

Plan of the Book

Part One consists of two chapters that deal with the perceptions, thoughts, and feelings of the individual. One topic is the influence of personal and social factors on these experiential processes, and another is experiences concerning social objects. Part Two moves to a larger individual unit, the concept of attitude, which includes perceptions, thoughts, and feelings, as well as behavioral dispositions. This series of four chapters is concerned with the processes, both individual and social, that influence a person's attitudes toward aspects of his environment. The influence processes discussed here are fundamental to interaction processes discussed later in other contexts.

In Part Three, the focus shifts to group structure and process, stressing features of interaction that lead to regular and stable relations between persons and groups. The observation of small groups enables the investigator to study the emergence of various group structures. Four structures are treated in some detail. These pertain to four aspects of relations among group members: liking, social power or influence, status, and communication. Also treated in these chapters is group process: the changing pattern of relations between elements of structure over time. Such processes may best be understood in terms of a theoretical conception that views interaction as an exchange of rewards and costs by individual members.

In Part Four, the relation of institutional structures to individual behavior is taken up. Institutional structures are analyzed in terms of the concept of social role. Various structured relations that constitute a social system are described. Depending upon the position he occupies in such a system, a person is treated in certain ways and is likely to exhibit behavior appropriate to his position. Special attention is given to sources of strain that disturb the smooth functioning of these systems, as well as to various means of resolving such strains.

Part Five, containing the final three chapters of the book, is concerned with the processes by which individuals learn the norms and behaviors appropriate to their groups.

PART ONE

Social Factors in Perceptual-Cognitive Processes

A vital part of everyday life is man's inward experiences. His perceptions, cognitions, and feelings about the world around him and the objects in it make his life rich and full. The origins of psychology lie in attempts to study this conscious experience. Today, the majority of psychologists and sociologists, and some other behavioral scientists, still consider perceptions, thoughts, and feelings to be an important object of study. Unlike the early introspective psychologist, who studied his own experience, modern behavioral scientists make inferences about the experiences of other persons from their verbal reports or from their responses to carefully structured situations.

Much of this subjective experience is inevitably shaped by the social nature of the world and by the personality of the perceiver. Perceptions and cognitions of many aspects of the stimulus field are modified through social experience and formal education. Feelings such as love and hate could not be experienced by a person living in complete isolation from other humans. In addition, the personal motives and emotional states of the perceiver affect his perceptions. When he is anxious or tense, he is likely to perceive some objects differently from occasions when he is happy and relaxed. The study of such experiences and their determinants is known as *social perception*.

Social perception includes essentially two topics. One is the influence of personal and social factors on experiential processes, and the other, experiences about social objects. Chapter 1 deals with such topics as the effects of emotional states on the ease or difficulty with which objects are perceived and the influence of motives and values on judgments of size.

Often the stimulus objects, such as words, pictures, or symbols, have social meaning. The principles governing the perception of persons as social objects, however, are reserved for Chapter 2. The focus of interest there is on how impressions of other persons are formed and how such impressions are shaped by the characteristics of the stimulus person, his position in the social structure, and the relation between him and the perceiver.

An individual's impressions of those persons with whom he interacts are important determinants of his behavior. Thus, an understanding of person perception is basic to social psychology. The principles outlined in this section will be referred to frequently in other parts of the book, and some studies relevant to person perception not presented in this part will be discussed later in connection with other topics.

chapter one

SOCIAL PERCEPTION

Traditionally, perception is concerned with the problem of correspondence between the nature of the physical world and the character of perceptual experience. How is it, we ask, that we can see or hear what is "out
there"? For example, we see objects in approximately their true size, regardless of their distance from us, even though more distant objects cast
smaller images on the retina. Another example is the perception of depth
and solidity, which occurs in spite of the fact that the retinal image has
only two dimensions, not three. Objects do not appear to be flat, as might
be expected from the nature of the image; they are seen as extended in
depth. Thus the basic task of perceptual studies is to define the properties
of experience or response, on the one hand, and the properties of stimulation, on the other, and to specify the correspondence between these two
sets of variables.

Perception is most appropriately defined in terms of experiences that
stem directly from sensory stimulation: the patterns of light and dark
emitted by the television screen are perceived as the figure of a man walk-
ing along a street. But much experience closely related to perception is
more remote from sensory stimulation. The man on the screen is liked or
disliked; he is known to be a hero or a villain; his intentions are guessed
at. Thus, feelings and cognitions related to perceptual objects may also
be a matter of interest. These cognitive and affective processes are important in social interaction. Much interaction, for example, is verbal in
nature: persons interact by exchanging knowledge, judgments, and feelings expressed in language terms.

The social psychologist has two specific interests in such processes.

One is in the effects of social and personal factors on these processes. For example, such questions as these have been asked: Do personal motives affect perceptions and cognitions? Does anxiety interfere with the perception of fear-arousing stimuli? Do we distort perceptions in the direction of what we want to see? The other interest of the social psychologist is in our perceptual, cognitive, and affective experiences concerning social objects. What principles govern the perception of minority group members, for example? What determines liking and disliking for people? How do we arrive at judgments about the characteristics of other persons?

These two interests are conventionally included under the rubric social perception. The effects of social and personal factors will be considered in this chapter, and the perception and evaluation of people will be deferred until Chapter 2.

Basic Processes Affecting Perceptual Response

To provide a foundation for later discussion of experimental work on social perception, the following basic processes affecting perceptual responses will be identified:

1. The selectivity of perception and characteristic ways of organizing stimulus patterns. At any given moment, the perceiver responds to only a small portion of the sensory information provided by his environment, and he organizes it in certain ways.
2. The frequency of previous experience with particular stimulus patterns and responses. Later perceptions are affected by these previous experiences.
3. Experiences with stimuli and responses that have been positively or negatively reinforced. This reinforcement history also influences later perceptions.
4. The contemporary factors prevailing at the moment of perception. Certain current conditions, such as hunger, fatigue, or anxiety, may affect what is perceived.
5. Indicators of perception. A person's sensory experiences cannot be directly observed by the scientist; thus, his conclusions about perception are partly a function of the indirect means he uses to study it.

ORGANIZING FACTORS IN PERCEPTION

That perceptual experience differs from the photographic registry of a camera is obvious. One basic difference lies in the selectivity of perception. Only a small portion of the stimulus energies reaching sensory receptors are translated into experience at any given moment. While you are reading this page, you are relatively unaware of that portion of the visual field extending away from the page, particularly at the periphery of the field; you are not aware of various sounds that are present; nor are you aware of the pressure of your shoes and other clothing on your body. Enter a room full of people with many conversations going on simultaneously; when you attend to one conversation, the others become background noise, only dimly perceived.

Similarly, the organism groups aspects of the stimulus field in certain ways so as to perceive objects against a background. In social interaction, where the behavior of another person provides rich information that we may use to form a judgment concerning him, we are likely to select and group only a few elements of information from the overload that is available to us. These principles may be applied to any familiar social-psychological problem.

For example, the manner in which prejudice against a minority group, such as the Negro, is maintained in the face of some pressure to the contrary may be partly explained in terms of these principles. A prejudiced person perceives selectively certain aspects of the behavior of the Negro: those that fit in with his preconceived ideas concerning the Negro. Thus he observes and notes behavior incidents that demonstrate stupidity, laziness, irresponsibility, or superstition; he overlooks other incidents that might contradict his prevailing ideas. The behavior of the Negro as he observes it thus supports his prejudiced beliefs.

FREQUENCY OF PREVIOUS EXPERIENCE: RESPONSE DISPOSITION

The previous experience of the organism with particular stimuli affects the way they are perceived in any contemporary situation. For example, *familiar* words presented in dim illumination are more readily recognized than *less familiar* words. We will assume that the more frequently a person has experienced a particular stimulus-response sequence under conditions that facilitate learning, the greater the probability that he will respond in a similar manner when the stimulus is again presented.

POSITIVE AND NEGATIVE REINFORCEMENT: AVOIDANCE LEARNING

Certain learning experiences do not increase the probability of occurrence of response, but actually decrease it. If responses are followed by negative or punishing consequences under certain circumstances, the strength of a response disposition may be *reduced*. For example, when stimulus materials are presented and immediately followed by the delivery of an electric shock to a person, the materials are likely to be less readily perceived on later occasions. When the subject has the option of avoiding the punishment by making a response that substitutes for the original response with which punishment has normally been associated, this learning to make the substitute response instead of the punished one is referred to as *avoidance learning*. In the case of perceptual responses, it is possible that avoidance learning results in failure to perceive a stimulus which, prior to learning, was readily perceived. Thus, it is clear that, depending upon the kind of experience which the organism has with a particular stimulus-response sequence, response disposition may be strengthened or weakened, or for that matter, may remain unchanged.

CONTEMPORARY DETERMINANTS: RESPONSE SALIENCE

The previous experience of a person with particular responses is not the only factor that determines its likelihood of occurrence at a given moment. Certain *contemporary* conditions predispose the organism to make certain responses. Given several responses which have been equally practiced, a particular one may be elicited by experimental instructions, by an immediately preceding sequence of behavior, by the presence of a motivated state, or by some aspect of the immediately present stimulus situation. Certain factors, particularly those involving cognitive expectations, fall under the familiar term *set*. Because this term has not always been used in a consistent manner, however, the more neutral term *response salience* will be used in the present discussion.

Response salience is illustrated in the following examples: A frightened person is more likely to perceive fearful objects; an experimental subject instructed to watch for animal forms in a set of ink blots is more likely to see them; and a hunter who has just perceived a deer among some distant trees is likely to anticipate seeing another. Other contemporary factors may *decrease* response salience; for example, persons in an anxious state might avoid certain perceptions. In short, response salience applies to *contemporary factors* that facilitate or interfere with particular perceptual responses.

In a given stimulus situation, the readiness with which a particular response will occur is a function of both contemporary factors and the previous experience of the organism with that response. Thus, the response in a particular situation depends upon both response salience and response disposition. For example, in one study (Bruner & Postman, 1949) ordinary playing cards and certain "trick" playing cards were presented starting with exposures so brief that they could not be recognized. Exposure time was gradually increased to the point where recognition occurred. It was found that such ordinary cards as the 5 of hearts and the 7 of spades were recognized far sooner than were such trick cards as a *black* 3 of hearts and a *red* 6 of spades.

This result, in our terms, is due to the strong response disposition developed through long experience with playing cards. On the other hand, the operation of response salience is shown in the fact that after two or more trick cards had been seen, subsequent trick cards were much more readily seen at brief exposures than they had been initially. Once the person became aware of the presence of trick cards in the experiment, he anticipated that further similar cards would be shown—i.e., this response became more salient.

INDICATORS OF PERCEPTION

The perceptual response to a stimulus is essentially subjective: if a photograph is projected on a screen before a person, his experience of that stimulus object is inherently private. The experimenter becomes aware of another person's perceptions only through his observation of the behavior of that person. Very commonly, the perceiver reports in words what he sees. Sometimes the perceiver is asked to draw what he sees, to manipulate some device (such as adjusting a variable disk to match the size of a disk which is presented as a stimulus), or to make a choice from several responses provided by the experimenter. Naturally all such procedures are imperfect measures of the perceiver's subjective responses. This inability to observe perceptual experiences directly means that it is often difficult to determine precisely what perceptual experience has occurred.

STUDY QUESTIONS

1. *Explain what is meant by response disposition and how it is related to frequency of a perceptual experience.*
2. *What is avoidance learning?*
3. *Explain what is meant by response salience.*
4. *Both response disposition and response salience may affect the probability of occurrence of a response. How may these two processes be distinguished from each other?*
5. *Distinguish between a perceptual response and a behavioral response indicator.*

Experiments Involving Impoverished Stimulus Conditions

Experimentation in social perception has dealt largely with two classes of dependent variables. One class consists of perceptual responses made under "impoverished" conditions: The subject is presented with ambiguous or blurred stimulus patterns or with stimulus objects presented for only a fraction of a second under conditions of low illumination. Impoverished conditions have been thought to maximize the influence of social factors on what is perceived and to be comparable to the many casual and fleeting observations made in everyday life. The other class of dependent variables consists of judgments of magnitude made in circumstances where social factors may distort judgment. Changes in judgment of size, weight, or other magnitudes may occur as a result of differences in value, emotional states, reward and punishment, or other complex factors. Experiments conducted under conditions of impoverished stimulation will be considered first.

An understanding of responses to rather indefinite stimuli has considerable practical importance. For example, in wartime, early identification of approaching aircraft as friendly or hostile is of great importance; hence accurate identifications are attempted at great distances. Similar problems confront the radar operator, who must distinguish between blips representing aircraft and those that result from atmospheric phenomena or from mechanical aberrations of the apparatus. Unobtrusive stimuli are also important in person perception. If a hostess invites us to stay for dinner, we seek subtle cues to tell us whether she really means it or is just being polite. In interview situations, the interviewer may often be influenced by stimuli which are at the periphery of his awareness. Some interaction situations, such as a developing romance between boy and girl, involve much behavior based upon responses to extremely subtle cues.

EFFECTS OF INCREASED RESPONSE SALIENCE

In this section, experiments that appear to involve an *increase* in response salience as a result of a motivating state will be included. The main series of experiments dealing with a possible *decrease* in response salience will be discussed later, under the heading of *perceptual defense*. The demonstration that response salience is heightened as a result of need arousal would have considerable theoretical significance. For example, the increase in need or motive, up to a point, would then have considerable adaptive significance, for the stronger the need or motive of a person to perceive certain goal objects, the more sensitive he would become to slight cues pertaining to such objects.

Also of interest here is the possibility that, when need or motive surpasses a certain strength, perceptual distortion occurs, and the individual "sees" objects that are not really there. Examples of the latter are familiar to most of us from the reports of hallucinations by persons who are starving and dehydrated while lost on the ocean or desert.

In a pioneer experiment (Levine, Chein, & Murphy, 1942) on the effects of bodily needs upon perception, subjects who had been deprived of food for different lengths of time were shown a variety of ambiguous drawings of objects, including some picturing food. The drawings were viewed through a ground glass screen, which made them difficult to see clearly. Subjects were asked to think of a word which could be associated with each drawing. The expectation was that the longer the subject had been deprived of food, the more likely he would be to report food words for the drawings. In our terms, the arousal of the hunger would be expected to increase response salience for food objects.

Results were mainly in accord with the hypothesis. Up to a point, the longer a subject had been deprived of food, the more often he would mention a food word in connection with a drawing. In general, this early experiment appears to demonstrate increased response salience, in the form of increased availability of food-related associations to food stimuli. In a similar experiment, McClelland and Atkinson (1948) obtained fairly comparable results.

Two qualifications should be offered: (1) At longer periods of deprivation the expected increases in food responses do not take place; (2) responses are in terms of associations with the drawings and do not necessarily represent a direct perceptual experience of the drawings as food objects. The experimenters had no way of proving that a food response, such as "apple," was provoked by a particular stimulus configuration to which the subject was exposed. In other words, it is possible that hunger increases the tendency to make food responses independently of the stimuli presented. This result would still be important, of course, but would not represent the change in *perceptual* response that the experimenters were trying to demonstrate: *perceptual* responses must always be linked to the stimulus.

In several subsequent experiments, the relation between food deprivation and *recognition threshold* was studied. The latter was determined by presenting stimulus materials in a tachistoscope, a device for exposing stimuli for a brief fraction of a second. Initial exposures are unrecognizable, and then they are gradually increased to the point where the perceiver clearly recognizes them. Thus, a low threshold means recognition at a brief exposure, and a high threshold recognition at a somewhat longer exposure. In one experiment (Wispé & Drambarean, 1953) using words relating to food and water, it was found that thresholds were lower for food and water words under conditions of greater deprivation and that neutral words did not differ for perceivers having different degrees of deprivation. In a similar experiment (Taylor, 1956), however, no difference in the recognition thresholds of satiated and deprived subjects was found.

What is probably the best-controlled study (Lazarus, Yousem, & Arenberg, 1953) included a free-choice experiment and a forced-choice experiment on the recognition of photographed objects. In the free-choice investigation, slides representing food and nonfood objects, such a bunch of grapes, pancakes, a cigarette lighter, a typewriter, etc., were exposed tachistoscopically under varying illumination. In the free-choice condition, subjects not aware of the purpose of the experiment, and for whom varying times had elapsed since their last meal, were asked to name the objects, using whatever words they wished to choose. The results were similar to those obtained in the previously cited experiments. With increasing deprivation up to four hours, food objects were recognized at lower levels of illumination. The hungrier the person, the more likely he was to recognize food objects. As in several of the earlier experiments, however, this sensitivity decreased with still greater deprivation, in this case at five to six hours.

The forced-choice investigation was conducted with additional subjects, in the same manner, except that instead of being allowed free guesses as to what the slide represented, the subject had to choose from a list of sixteen items which included the ten actually pictured. Results were strikingly different under these conditions: There was *no change* in recognition thresholds with varying degrees of hunger.

Taken together, these various experiments are very suggestive with respect to the perceptual mechanisms operating. In those experiments where the subject is free to choose from all possible identifying responses he might make to a pictured object, response salience is allowed to operate: hunger makes food-related responses more salient. But under forced-choice conditions, the subject must choose his response from a small list of words furnished by the experimenter. The correct responses to both the food and *nonfood* objects are thus made extremely salient, and it is unlikely that four hours of hunger deprivation can further increase the salience of the food objects to a point appreciably above that for the nonfood objects. Consistent with this reasoning is the point that, in this study, the threshold is lower under forced-choice than under free-choice conditions for three of the four degrees of deprivation. Presumably, increased response salience is responsible for this increased sensitivity.

The failure of increasing food deprivation to affect the recognition threshold beyond a certain point has several possible explanations. One is the cyclical nature of hunger. Studies have shown that physiological concomitants and subjective feelings of hunger are at a peak during the periods when a person normally takes his meal. Thus, a drop in hunger would be expected after this period has passed, even though the person has not eaten. Other possible explanations concern the changing reaction of the organism to increasing deprivation. Some experiments (McClelland & Atkinson, 1948; Wispé, 1954) have indicated that during the earlier phases of deprivation, responses pertaining directly to need satisfaction (e.g., food names) are most frequent, while later, more instrumental responses occur (e.g., words associated with cooking). McClelland (1951) has suggested that the organism may be goal-oriented in the earlier stages of deprivation, but that with increasing deprivation the individual stops making direct goal responses, and that when the strength of the hunger drive reaches a certain point, he *avoids* perceiving unattainable goal objects.

A study (Brozek, Guetzkow, & Baldwin, 1951) in which conscientious objectors volunteered to embark on a semistarvation diet for a period of six months is also relevant. The experiment was conducted during World War II, primarily in the hope of obtaining valuable information that might be applied to malnourished persons in war-ravaged countries. In this study, however, recognition thresholds were not tested. Instead, subjects were asked to respond with the first word that came to their minds as stimulus words were presented. Descriptions of dreams and responses to ink blots were also obtained. Unlike the earlier experiments, little relation between food deprivations and word associations was found, nor was there any relation to other imaginative content, such as dream content and responses to ink blots. Again, strong response dispositions to certain words must be considered as possibly having masked any effects of response salience due to hunger. For example, the word list contained such common everyday words as white, light, and woman. These stimulus words have strong linkages to such words as black, dark, and man, respectively, and it is probably not reasonable to expect even severe hunger deprivation to lead to replacement of these responses by food-related words. Similarly, the structure of the Rorschach ink blots may be such as to render food responses highly improbable. Thus, even though severe hunger may make food responses more salient, this greater salience will appear only in stimulus situations that have a reasonable probability of eliciting food responses.

Another result from a different report (Guetzkow & Bowman, 1946) on the above study yields some very important information, however. Individual differences in the manner in which persons reacted to severe food deprivation were readily apparent. At one extreme, for example, some persons persistently attempted to deny and ignore their hunger. If others talked of food, they angrily left the room. They tried to occupy themselves with activities that would not remind them of their hunger. At the other extreme, some persons shared fantasies of delicious dinners that they would eat if they could. One person stayed up until 5 A.M. reading the recipes in a cookbook, an activity that he would never think of engaging in under normal circumstances. Thus, for some subjects, food deprivation makes food-related responses highly salient, but for others, responses are less salient than normal. These individual differences may be due not only to psychological mechanisms such as active denial but also to differences in metabolic rates or other physiological conditions.

Summary: Need arousal and response salience

Where the structure of the experimental situation permits response salience to operate, arousal of the hunger need may be expected to make food responses more likely to occur. This increased salience may be expressed in the form of a greater number of food associations to food stimuli, in a lowered recognition threshold, or in a variety of other ways. The main condition facilitating response salience is a large repertory of responses from which the perceiver may select his response. Even where responses related to the main experimental variable are made more salient by experimental conditions, however, these salient responses may not appear as perceptual effects if other responses have a still higher probability of occurring because of strong response dispositions or because of salience for nonfood responses produced by incidental experimental conditions.

Where the structure of the situation prohibits the operation of response salience, the arousal of the hunger need may be expected to have little effect on the responses made. Such a situation is one where the response repertory is severely restricted by providing in advance a limited number of responses from which the subject must choose. Another relevant situation is one where *no* stimulus information is provided, as where the stimulus is well below threshold. Here the number of responses may be so large that food-related responses are still not sufficiently strong to compete with certain highly probable responses. Individual differences in reactions to need arousal are evident: some persons may respond to increasing deprivation by increased response salience, whereas others

may respond with decreased salience. More research on individual reactions and their causes is needed.

STUDY QUESTIONS

6. *What is meant by the phrase "impoverished stimulus situation"?*
7. *Why does the study of word associations under various experimental conditions have limited implications for an understanding of the* perceptual *process?*
8. *What is meant by a recognition threshold, and what is a tachistoscope?*
9. *How does response salience affect food responses in hungry subjects under
(a) free-choice conditions and (b) forced-choice conditions?*
10. *Why doesn't the recognition threshold for food objects continue to decrease
as subjects get hungrier and hungrier?*
11. *What is the likelihood that individuals differ from each other in their response
to hunger deprivation?*

EXPERIMENTS IN WHICH RESPONSE DISPOSITION OPERATES

The tendency of the individual to make certain responses rather than
others is a fundamental property of behavior. In more common-sense
terms, we speak of habits rather than response dispositions. In the present
instance, we are interested in the effects of social factors upon "perceptual
habits." To the extent that social factors can be identified as having an
important role in shaping the way in which the world around us is perceived, understanding of many aspects of our everyday life is enhanced,
for our day-to-day behavior is largely guided by the way in which we
perceive our immediate environment.

Effects of value upon response disposition

An early experiment appeared to demonstrate a relation between
"perceptual sensitivity" and the strength of an individual's values (Postman, Bruner, & McGinnies, 1948). Value was conceived of as a "sensitizing" factor. Like the tuner of a television receiver that selects certain channels, values were thought to "tune" the perceiver in on certain
value-related stimuli. In our terms, of course, this tuning process would
be a form of response salience; other things being equal, value makes
value-related responses occur more readily. As we will see, however,
subsequent analysis and further experimentation suggest that the
observed effects are due largely, if not entirely, to differences in response
disposition.

In this experiment, the strength of the various values of the individual
person was determined by administering the Allport-Vernon Study of
Values (Allport & Vernon, 1931). This inventory measures the strength
of a person's interest in six areas: theoretical, economic, aesthetic, social,
political, and religious. Certain words representing each of the six interest
categories were presented at brief exposures. These words were presented first below threshold and then at increased exposures on successive
trials until they could be clearly perceived. As expected, the higher the

value to the individual of the category represented by the word, the shorter was the exposure time at which the word could be recognized. The experiment was repeated (Vanderplas & Blake, 1949) using intensity of sound to vary the recognizability of the spoken word, and a similar result was obtained.

Although at first thought the lowering of a recognition threshold for valued stimuli may appear to represent convincing evidence of an increased perceptual sensitivity to valued words (or, in our terms, increased response salience), an alternative explanation in terms of greater response dispositions for valued words may be offered. The more ready perception of value-related words may be a function of the frequency with which these words have been experienced in the past. The frequency or repetition explanation is quite different from saying that value is operating to sensitize the perceptual system of the perceiver at the time that perceptual responses are being made. The alternate response-disposition explanation in terms of frequency takes a variety of forms, as follows:

1. In an independent study (Solomon & Howes, 1950), the briefness of duration of visual-perception thresholds for words was shown to be positively related to the frequency of occurrence of the words in ordinary language usage. Thus the assumption that value "sensitizes" the perceptual system for value-related words is unnecessary. Instead, the original findings may be explained by assuming that an individual has a lot of experience with words related to his high-value areas and little experience with words in low-value areas. Thus, a minister would most frequently encounter religious words and in a tachistoscopic recognition test would have the lowest thresholds for these words because of his frequent experience with them.

2. Another experiment (Postman & Schneider, 1951) offers a somewhat different explanation. The suggestion was made that *both* frequency of word usage and the duration of thresholds for words were *a function of the values of the individual*. This experiment confirmed the finding that thresholds were influenced by frequencies, but also demonstrated that thresholds for uncommon words varied according to the value which was attached to them.

These problems of interpretation have been recently clarified by further investigations (Johnson, Thomson, & Frincke, 1960). A series of experiments demonstrated that word frequency and word value are closely associated with each other. Several forms of statistical analysis revealed that the more frequently a word occurs in the English language, the more pleasant (or valued) it is likely to be. Also, the more frequently a nonsense word was experienced under experimental conditions, the higher the value rating it received. Thus frequency of experience with words raises their value. Finally, in order to answer the question concerning the effects of frequency and value upon word-recognition thresholds, lists of words matched in frequency but varying in value, and lists matched in value but varying in frequency, were presented. Value was found to lower recognition thresholds when frequency was held constant, and frequency lowered recognition thresholds when value was held constant.

In conclusion, the frequency of experience with a word and its value are normally closely associated, and any interpretation which identifies one of these factors as affecting the perceptual process is likely to be open to explanation in terms of the other factor. The fact that frequency of experience with words leads to higher values may have important social consequences, as Johnson, Thomson, and Frincke (1960) have noted. Possibly ideas and personal values may be manipulated through varying frequency of experience. Thus, those who sponsor the censorship of "evil" ideas have some support in the above findings, in that more frequent experience with these ideas is likely to increase their value—lessen their evil. Similarly, advertising by means of repetition should increase the value of those perceptual experiences associated with the advertising. A word of caution may be in order, however; for an individual's reaction to various experiences often depends upon the context in which the experience takes place. Frequency of experience under certain circumstances may *increase* distaste for the experience, as in the response of some persons to repeated television commercials.

STUDY QUESTIONS

12. *What is the meaning of the statement that "value operates to sensitize the perceptual mechanism"? Is there adequate experimental evidence to support this statement?*
13. *In what sense is there a relation between frequency and value?*
14. *What is the explanation for the influence of value upon recognition thresholds?*

Response disposition and the effects of reward and punishment

Another way in which psychologists thought they might demonstrate that perception is influenced by social factors was to prove that rewarding or punishing certain perceptual responses alters recognition thresholds. If perception is merely a function of the perceptual-visual mechanisms of the organism, they reasoned, accuracy of perception should in no way be affected by motivational factors. Therefore, a variety of experiments were carried out in the social-perception tradition to demonstrate that perceptual responses could be altered by the systematic application of rewards or punishments. The effects of positive or negative reinforcement upon perceptual responses is essentially a problem in perceptual learning—a highly technical and complex topic beyond the scope of this text. A few simple principles will be outlined and illustrated here, and the interested reader should refer to other sources (Brown, 1961; Wohlwill, 1960).

The concept of shifts in response disposition with reinforcement,

PART A

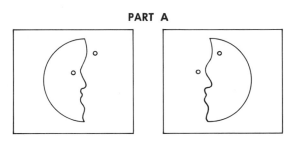

PART B

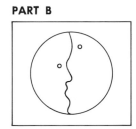

Figure 1–1
Reversible figure-ground faces. (Adapted with permission from E. Schafer & G. Murphy. The role of autism in a visual figure-ground relationship. *J. exp. Psychol.*, 1943, **32**, 335 – 343.)

particularly a strengthening of response disposition with positive rein-forcement, appears best to explain some of the results that have been obtained. The problem of negative reinforcement is more complex, as will be shown. Before experiments are cited, an experimental design com-monly used in perception should be described. This is a design consisting of a *training series* and a *test series*. During the *training* series, the experi-mental subjects are exposed to certain conditions, and others (the control subjects) are not exposed to them. The effects of such exposure or train-ing are determined by a subsequent *test* series in which all subjects are re-quired to make perceptual responses under the same conditions. The difference in performance between the experimental and control groups on the test series may then be attributed to the experimental conditions established in the training series.

A pioneer experiment (Schafer & Murphy, 1943) used as stimuli figures that could be seen in two different ways through a reversal of the figure-ground relationship. A figure similar to theirs is shown in Figure 1–1. Part A of the figure consists of two separate profiles which may readily be seen as faces. In Part B the two faces are juxtaposed, creating a whole in which, at any given moment, one face is normally seen as a figure on a circular background. In the training series the two faces were presented separately to subjects under different conditions. For a given group of subjects, one face was always rewarded and the other punished. Reward and punishment consisted of giving or taking away small sums of money. Proper controls were established by using two pairs of faces and by varying the punished and rewarded faces for the two groups of subjects.

After the training period, a test was made of the effects of the experi-mental training. For this, the pictures were joined and shown as a whole figure in a tachistoscope with an exposure too brief to permit a perceptual alternation of figure and ground; i.e., only one face could be seen. Subjects more frequently perceived the face that had been rewarded during the training series. In other words, they perceived this face as "figure" while the other portion of the circle was not experienced as a face but only as background.

This experiment differs from those previously cited in that readiness to respond is tested for only two alternate stimulus patterns. A wide variety of stimuli are not available to the subject, nor are a wide variety of responses. Response is "fixed" in that it takes the form of recognition of one or the other of the two faces. Thus the results cannot be explained in terms of a shift in response salience, as we have defined it. Because of the subject's recent experience with the faces, both are equally salient. But these results might be interpreted as demonstrating that repeated reinforcement of a particular stimulus pattern will strengthen the response to that pattern, so that it will be more readily perceived under marginal conditions, and that punishment or negative reinforcement will have the opposite effect.

Drawing firm conclusions, however, is not possible. Several different investigators have repeated the experiment with conflicting results. In one experiment (Smith & Hochberg, 1954), punishment was shown to modify recognition thresholds, but in two others (Rock & Fleck, 1950; Beatty, Dameron, & Greene, 1959), negative results were obtained. Two other experiments (Smith, Parker, & Robinson, 1950; Rigby & Rigby, 1952) involving the following perceptual tasks resulted in decreased recognition time as a result of reward: estimation of the number of dots in clusters, and recognition time for capital letters. Punishment or negative reinforcement, however, has not always produced consistent results (Lazarus & McCleary, 1951; Reece, 1954). In one instance, punishment resulted in a *lowered* recognition threshold (Pustell, 1957).

STUDY QUESTIONS

15. *Why are social psychologists interested in whether or not perceptual responses may be influenced by rewards and punishment?*
16. *Explain the training-test series design of a perceptual experiment.*
17. *Why isn't it possible to explain the changes in perceptual response to the figure-ground profiles in Figure 1-1 in terms of response salience?*
18. *In what ways do the effects of punishment on perceptual responses differ from the effects of rewards?*

Perceptual Defense

One of the most dramatic findings of the social-perception enthusiasts concerns the phenomenon of perceptual defense. Perceptual defense comprises three processes: (1) Emotionally disturbing or threatening stimuli have a higher recognition threshold than neutral stimuli; (2) such stimuli are likely to elicit substitute perceptions that are radically altered so as to prevent recognition of the presented stimuli; (3) these critical stimuli arouse emotional reactions even though the stimuli are not recognized. The student familiar with psychoanalytic theory will recognize similarities between perceptual defense and psychoanalytic mechanisms involving distortion of thought processes, such as the substitution of an innocent symbol for an anxiety-laden one in a dream.

EXPERIMENTAL CHARACTERISTICS OF PERCEPTUAL DEFENSE

An early experiment on perceptual defense presented a series of words tachistoscopically beginning with exposures well below threshold and increasing by small intervals until correct recognition occurred (McGinnies, 1949). For each presentation, the subject gave his opinion concerning what the word was. Eleven of the words were of a "neutral" character, and seven had an unpleasant or socially tabooed quality—for example, "bitch," "whore," "raped." A physiological measure of emotion aroused was used. This was the galvanic skin response (abbreviated GSR), a measure by an electronic device of the drop in the electrical resistance of the skin that occurs when an emotional reaction is aroused in a person.

A striking result of the experiment was that GSRs occurred while the tabooed words were still being exposed so briefly that the subject was not reporting recognition of these words. Also discovered was that recognition thresholds were higher for tabooed words than for neutral ones; that is, taboo words were more difficult to recognize. A third finding was that, at brief exposure times, incorrect responses or guesses for the neutral words were often structurally *similar,* as in the substitution of "trace" for "trade," whereas for taboo words, these guesses were structurally *dissimilar,* as in the substitution of "roared" for "belly."

At first thought this experiment appears to provide dramatic evidence for all three facets of the mechanism of perceptual defense. But it also presents a paradox: How can a person avoid perceiving a stimulus object before he has actually perceived what it is? Because of this paradox, other interpretations of the results have been sought. One simple explanation is that the subject may be failing to report taboo words even though he clearly perceives them. Probably a female college student who, in experiencing a brief flash before her eyes, thinks she sees a word not used in polite society is going to be absolutely certain of what she is seeing before she reports it. Failure to report would explain the GSRs to "subthreshold" taboo words, the defensive structuring of response words, and the "higher threshold" for taboo words.

There are also two other interpretations that might explain the higher thresholds, although they do not account for the GSRs or the defensive structuring of response words. One of these postulates that response salience is low for taboo words: a college student in a psychological laboratory is unlikely to anticipate being exposed to "dirty" words. The other invokes the factor of frequency (response disposition): probably taboo words occur less frequently in print, hence the higher threshold.

Further experiments have supported all the above alternate interpretations of the early "perceptual defense" findings. Two experiments (Postman, Bronson, & Gropper, 1953; Whittaker, Gilchrist, & Fischer, 1952) where settings were designed to encourage or discourage reporting taboo words demonstrated that subjects frequently withheld reporting taboo words under ordinary experimental conditions. Other experiments (Bitterman & Kniffin, 1953; Freeman, 1954, 1955; Kleiner, 1959; Lacey, Lewinger, & Adamson, 1953; Zigler & Yospe, 1960) have confirmed the importance of response salience in determining recognition threshold. Another form of response salience has also been noted: after exposure to the *first* taboo word, subjects more readily perceived subsequent taboo words. Some investigators (Aronfreed, Messick, & Diggory, 1953; Kleiner, 1959) have replicated the original experiment and have failed to obtain either GSR reactions prior to recognition of the stimulus words or higher thresholds for taboo words. Prior to most of these publications, however, the experiment had led other psychologists to take a variety of different approaches to perceptual defense. One such approach was to explain the experimental results in terms of learning principles rather than in terms of perceptual defense; this is taken up in the next section.

STUDY QUESTIONS

19. *What three processes characterize perceptual defense?*
20. *Briefly describe an experiment designed to demonstrate the phenomenon of perceptual defense.*
21. *To what extent do each of the following provide alternative explanations for the early perceptual-defense findings: (a) failure to report taboo words, (b) frequency or response disposition, and (c) response salience.*

MODIFICATION OF RECOGNITION THRESHOLDS BY LEARNING FACTORS

Postman (1953*a*) has suggested that *competing response dispositions* might explain higher recognition thresholds for taboo words. To illustrate, suppose the elements "wh--e" are perceived. Even though the stimulus word is actually "whore," "where" is a more likely response because of its stronger response disposition. Experimental variation of the number of elements common to taboo words and substitute responses has shown that such an explanation is quite plausible (Postman & Crutchfield, 1952). Other theories (Brown, 1961, pp. 315–319) based on response competition have also been suggested, but will not be discussed here.

Another possible explanation of differential thresholds for taboo and neutral words that does not involve a paradox is the principle of *avoidance learning.* Avoidance learning may be characterized as follows: The probability of occurrence of a response increases if it results in *avoidance of punishment.* In a classical demonstration of this type of "instrumental" learning, a sheep resting one of its legs on an electric grid learned to lift it in response to a buzzer, in order to avoid the shock that otherwise would have followed from the activation of the grid subsequent to the sounding of the buzzer. This principle might be extended to learning in social situations. For example, a child may learn to say that he is sorry for having committed some mischievous act whenever his mother reaches the point of threatening to punish him. This apologetic act is reinforced if his mother follows it by withholding punishment.

Some support for this view is provided in an experiment (Eriksen & Browne, 1956) where stimulus words conditioned to anxiety were found to have higher recognition thresholds. Another investigation (Dulaney, 1957) has demonstrated that such avoidance learning can, under appropriate conditions, produce either *defense* or *sensitization* to threatening stimuli. In the first instance, the perceiver has a higher recognition threshold; in the second, a lower threshold. A defense effect was accomplished by a training series in which recognition of a stimulus figure was followed by an electric shock, resulting in a higher recognition threshold in a later test series. Sensitization was produced by a training series in which selection of the stimulus figure (instead of one of several others) resulted in avoidance of the shock. In both instances, subjects were *not aware* of the shifts in recognizability that had taken place.

STUDY QUESTIONS

22. *Explain how competing response dispositions might account for higher thresholds for taboo words. What is the limiting condition which must prevail in order for this explanation to be valid?*
23. *Show how avoidance learning might account for perceptual-defense findings. What evidence is available in support of this interpretation?*

STIMULUS EMOTIONALITY AND RECOGNITION THRESHOLD

Many studies have demonstrated that stimuli with emotional connotations raise recognition thresholds.[1] A similar number of investigations indicate that stimuli with emotional connotations lower recognition thresholds.[2] The former phenomenon has been termed perceptual *defense* and the latter is called *sensitization*.

Brown (1961) has suggested that these conflicting results are quite reasonable if we assume a curvilinear relation between the emotionality of a stimulus and the recognition threshold. By this he means that, compared with neutral stimuli, stimuli having some emotional connotations raise the recognition threshold, but that at still stronger levels of emotionality, sensitization occurs instead of defense, and the threshold is *lowered*.

---

[1]Bruner & Postman, 1947; Eriksen, 1951, 1952; Lazarus, Eriksen, & Fonda, 1951; Postman & Leytham, 1951; DeLucia & Stagner, 1953; Gilchrist, Ludeman, & Lysak, 1954; Neel, 1954; Zukerman, 1955; Kissin, Gottesfeld, & Dickes, 1957; Levy, 1958; Mathews & Wertheimer, 1958; Davis, 1959; Miller, Scott, & Waters, 1959.

[2]Bruner & Postman, 1947; Lazarus, Eriksen, & Fonda, 1951; Eriksen, 1952; Postman & Brown, 1952; Kates & Klein, 1954; Neel, 1954; Osler & Lewinsohn, 1954; Smith, 1954; Daston, 1956; Greenbaum, 1956; Levy, 1958.

Since most experiments on perceptual defense have not obtained more than two different measures of emotionality of a stimulus, sufficient data are not available to prove or disprove this suggestion. His own experiment on the topic was regarded by him as only a preliminary test, and it provided only partial support for this interesting and reasonable hypothesis.

INDIVIDUAL DIFFERENCES IN PERCEPTUAL DEFENSE AND SENSITIZATION

Many studies of perceptual defense do not pay sufficient attention to individual differences, according to Luchins (1950). Because a word is socially taboo does not mean that it is taboo for all individuals. Some persons utilize taboo words calmly; others may be shocked when they are confronted with them, and still others, because of personal dispositions or motives, may have special attitudes toward some taboo words but not others. Moreover, individuals may have different ways of handling the arousal of anxiety or emotion. Persons have been shown to be consistent in their defense or sensitization reactions to pictures of people in aggressive or neutral scenes (Stein, 1953). They reacted to successive pictures which had aggressive content with either a consistently high threshold (defense) or a consistently low threshold (sensitization). These various individual differences are uncontrolled factors in many of the perceptual-defense experiments which simply compare group means.

One series of studies (Allport & Kramer, 1946; Lindzey & Rogolsky, 1950) at first appeared to demonstrate sensitization in anti-Semitic judges. Photographs of Jewish and non-Jewish persons were shown to anti-Semitic and nonprejudiced judges, and it was found that anti-Semitic judges appeared to be more accurate in identifying the ones that were Jewish. Later studies (Carter, 1948; Elliot & Wittenberg, 1955; Scodel & Austrin, 1957; Himmelfarb, 1960), employing more rigorous controls and better methods of analysis, however, demonstrated that there was no difference in accuracy between prejudiced and nonprejudiced judges. One finding repeatedly confirmed in virtually all these studies, though, was that anti-Semitic judges identified a larger number of photographs as Jewish, even though many of these identifications were incorrect. Thus, prejudice appears to be a motivational factor affecting responses. Possibly this response bias occurs because of the importance to a prejudiced person of identifying Jews. He errs on the "safe" side, putting a picture in the Jewish category if there is any likelihood that the person might belong there. Similar behavior occurs when he identifies names that are Jewish from a list of Jewish and non-Jewish names (Secord & Saumer, 1960).

Eriksen (1951) has emphasized the need for selecting for each individual in an experiment those stimuli likely to arouse defenses. Some studies (Bruner & Postman, 1947; Chodorkoff, 1954; Carpenter, Wiener, & Carpenter, 1956) have thus taken pains to do this by pretesting the stimuli for each individual. In general, such stimuli require longer tachistoscopic exposures for recognition. Another approach has been to place persons in various diagnostic categories by means of psychological tests and to make predictions from knowledge of these categories as to whether the person will react in a defensive or vigilant manner to "threatening" stimuli. A variety of studies (Lazarus, Eriksen, & Fonda, 1951; Eriksen, 1952; Petrovich, 1960) has shown that whether or not a person reacts with delayed recognition or accelerated recognition is partly predictable from knowledge of the individual's personality, although not all experiments have been successful in making such predictions (Kurland, 1954; Bitterman & Kniffin, 1953).

Of greatest interest are those studies that have focused upon the characteristic defenses of the individual. One study (Spence, 1957) created some anxiety by arranging for subjects to fail in an anagram-solving exercise. In a subsequent perceptual task, some anxious subjects were expected to respond with a higher recognition threshold, others with a lower recognition threshold. This hypothesis was supported; perceivers did show characteristic responses of defense or sensitization. One limitation of this experiment, however, is that we do not know how much anxiety was created by failure. Possibly, defense or sensitization reactions may be associated with the degree of anxiety aroused rather than with particular individuals. This question is resolved in the following experiment.

In this study the hypothesis was tested that "individuals who use sensitizing or 'alertness' defenses in a particular conflict area will more quickly perceive stimuli in that area than will individuals who use repressive or avoidant defenses in that area" (Carpenter, Wiener, & Carpenter, 1956, p. 380). Clinical psychologists evaluated test protocols to determine whether a subject's characteristic manner of handling verbal materials pertaining to sexual or aggressive impulses was defensive or vigilant. Defensive persons were labeled "repressers" and the others "sensitizers." By presenting at brief exposures critical words with sexual or aggressive content and also control words irrelevant to these contents, the thresholds of individuals were tested. Although there proved to be little difference between critical and control words for sensitizers, for the repressers there was a marked difference between the control and critical words for both sex and hostility content. Thus, those persons who handle threatening content by repression and avoidance have high recognition thresholds for threatening material.

STUDY QUESTIONS

24. *To what extent are individuals consistent in their use of sensitization or defense in reaction to threatening stimuli?*
25. *What is meant by the personal relevance of stimuli? How may it be determined?*
26. *What are "repressers" and "sensitizers" and how do these individuals differ in their recognition thresholds for anxiety-arousing stimuli?*

SUMMARY: PERCEPTUAL DEFENSE

With respect to the raised threshold for taboo or other threatening stimuli, a variety of explanations are available, none of which require that the perceiver "defend against" stimuli of which he is not aware. In some instances, the higher threshold for taboo words is more apparent than real; the subject has simply withheld reporting such words until he is absolutely sure. Certain experimental conditions can raise or lower the response salience of the taboo words. Where frequency is not controlled, differential learning is often sufficient to explain the phenomenon. A related explanation involves a partial perception of the stimulus: certain letters of a word or syllable are perceived, and since they are associated more frequently with a common word than with a taboo word, the common word is the response given.

In some instances the higher recognition threshold for anxiety-arousing words is perfectly genuine. Here avoidance learning appears adequate to explain the higher threshold. As Eriksen and Browne (1956) have suggested, the experimental situation is essentially a guessing game where the subject is provided with partial cues (such as the recognition of a few letters from a complete word) that he fills in by providing a complete response. Those words that have been associated with punishment or anxiety have low response dispositions and thus are not used as "guesses" of what the exposed word is.

The most interesting findings and those especially worthy of further investigation are the ones demonstrating that persons differ greatly in the way in which they react to threatening stimuli. Some appear to be more sensitive and vigilant and actually have lower thresholds for such stimuli, while others react with repressing or controlling mechanisms and have higher thresholds. Such tendencies have been shown to vary with diagnostic categories, experimentally produced failure, reactions to sex and hostility content in sentence-completion tests, and distortion of self-perception.

Drawing some general implications from these findings, it appears that people can learn to avoid perceiving certain threatening, dangerous, or anxiety-provoking aspects of their environment. A second general implication of the findings pertains to the understanding of the individual person. The psychological defenses of the person may, in part, take the form of heightened thresholds for stimulus materials that have a special significance for him because of his past experience. Other persons may respond quite differently—with vigilance or sensitization to stimuli which represent danger signals for them. Possibly such tendencies represent fairly general modes of adjustment for the individual.

Subliminal Perception

The word *subliminal* comes from *limen*, which means threshold. Any stimulus can be varied in intensity or duration to the point where it is so weak or so brief that it cannot be perceived. When this is the case, it is said to be subliminal. Experiments have suggested that although a person does not consciously perceive a stimulus, he may nevertheless be influenced by it.

In the 1950s a public furor arose over the possibility of using subliminal perception in advertising. One claim made was that by flashing subliminally at repeated intervals the words "Eat popcorn" and "Drink Coca-Cola" on the screens of movie theaters, substantial increases in the amount of popcorn and Coca-Cola consumed were brought about.[3] In general, however, such reports did not follow the requirement necessary for serious consideration by behavioral scientists: that the conditions and findings of such procedures be published for scrutiny by other investigators. Moreover, the idea of subliminal perception is by no means new. Hundreds of experiments relevant to the problem of subliminal perception have been conducted over a period of many decades, both in psychophysics and in the study of "extrasensory perception," commonly known as ESP.

Subliminal perception, if it existed, would have obvious practical importance, not only in advertising, but also as an essential principle underlying certain types of behaviors. For example, Freud and other analysts place great stress upon the importance of unconscious processes in behavior dynamics and in neuroses and psychoses. If it could be demonstrated experimentally that the organism could indeed have unconscious perceptions of aspects of its environment, the case for psychoanalysis would be greatly strengthened. This would permit responses to aspects of the environment not readily visible to observers other than the individual responding and thus would explain some behaviors that often seem bizarre or puzzling.

RESPONDING WITHOUT AWARENESS

The previous discussion of perceptual defense set aside, for the moment, the paradoxical nature of the notion of "defense"; i.e., the implication that somehow a threatening word presented below threshold is reacted to emotionally so as to prevent conscious recognition at that level of exposure. This, of course, is a form of subliminal perception. Although early findings in support of perceptual defense were not confirmed by more recent experimentation, a variety of investigators conducted experiments designed to resolve the apparent paradox in the concept of perceptual defense.

In one experiment (McCleary & Lazarus, 1949), nonsense syllables were used in place of meaningful words in order to eliminate the effects of associations that might have been formed in everyday experience with words. During the training period the GSR, showing emotional disturbance, was conditioned to each of the critical syllables by using electric shock as the unconditioned stimulus. A test period followed, during which these syllables and some control syllables were presented without

[3]For a critical evaluation of these claims, see McConnell, Cutler, and McNeil (1958, p. 229).

shock at exposures that ranged from well below to approximately threshold level. The GSR was measured each time, between the instant of exposure of the word and the subject's report of what he saw (the report being delayed sufficiently to permit the recording of the GSR).

Considering only syllables that were *wrongly* perceived; i.e., that were reported as *subthreshold* exposures, it was found that the GSR was greater for the conditioned syllables than for the control syllables. Even though the exposure was too brief to permit a correct perception, the syllable elicited the emotional response that had been conditioned to it. Thus the individual appears capable of making perceptual discriminations at two different levels, one at the level of conscious awareness (reporting the word seen), and the other at an emotional level, and these two kinds of responses appear to be independent of each other.

LIMITATIONS OF THE RECOGNITION THRESHOLD

Subsequent experiments, however, emphasized the statistical nature of thresholds and its implications for interpreting these experiments. The *absolute threshold* is the degree of intensity or exposure at which the stimulus is correctly perceived 50 percent of the time. In the experiments reported above, however, this traditional definition was not adopted; instead, the recognition threshold was used. This is the degree of exposure on that trial at which a word is correctly reported for the first time. From psychophysical experiments, it is well known that the threshold is never at an absolute point; it varies with experimental conditions and the state of the organism. Moreover, in recent years, there has been a movement in the direction of regarding thresholds as essentially nonexistent. Postulated instead is the concept of a range of exposure bounded at one end by a stimulus intensity providing zero information to the perceiver, and at the other by a stimulus providing maximum information. The recognition threshold is near the end of the range where maximum information is provided. Thus, exposures just below this point convey some information, even though the stimulus is not fully recognized.

Several subsequent experiments demonstrated directly that incorrectly perceived tachistoscopic stimuli often convey some information. In one experiment (Bricker & Chapanis, 1953), subjects who failed to recognize nonsense syllables at the first attempt were permitted to guess. Guesses were definitely not random; they were more often correct than would be expected by chance, even though the syllables were not recognized. This is demonstrated by Figure 1–2, which shows that for all the subjects in the experiment, the mean number of guesses required to identify correctly the experimental stimuli was smaller than the number required to identify the control stimuli.

In another experiment (Murdock, 1954) ten stimulus syllables were presented tachistoscopically. On each presentation subjects were asked to rank a list of them from 1 to 10, according to what syllable they thought had just been presented. Once again, the correct syllable was ranked

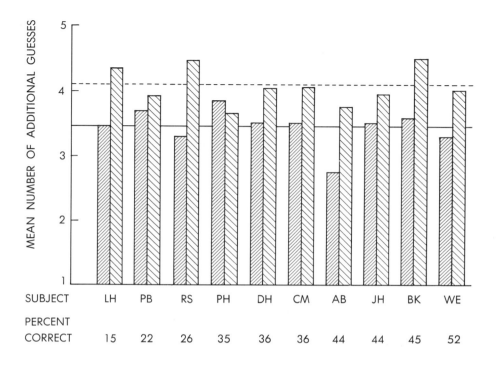

Figure 1–2
Guesses for control and experimental stimuli made by ten subjects. Dark bars show the mean number of additional guesses needed to identify experimental stimuli after an initial wrong response; light bars show mean number of additional guesses needed to make correct response after control stimuli. Solid horizontal line is the mean of dark bars; dashed line, the mean of light bars. (Adapted with permission from R. S. Lazarus & R. A. McCleary. Autonomic discrimination without awareness: A study of subception. *Psychol. Rev.,* 1951, **58**, 113–122.)

higher than would be expected by chance, even when the first-ranked syllable was not the correct choice. An introspective study (Hoisington & Spencer, 1958) was also made of the partial information which subjects obtained from brief tachistoscopic exposures. Subjects reported the following types of information: "In 'Building,' I got a block pattern." "At the beginning and ending, there is a jutting out that makes the external form easier to identify." References were made to "pattern of black and white"; "relative openness"; "the shading"; "the color of the print." Other experiments (Goldberg & Fiss, 1959; Wiener & Schiller, 1960), using a variety of different methods, are consistent with these results.

All these investigations also support the point that when exposure is so brief as to *exclude* partial information, correct guesses do not exceed chance. But exposures just below the recognition threshold allow the perceiver to obtain partial information, leading to guesses which are correct more often than would be expected by chance. Moreover, another experiment (Voor, 1956) has succeeded in showing that the more information the subject has concerning a subthreshold stimulus, the more likely he is to give a GSR.

STUDY QUESTIONS

27. *What are the disadvantages of using the recognition threshold in attempts to demonstrate veridical perception below the level of conscious awareness?*
28. *What evidence is available to the effect that subjects obtain partial information from stimuli that they cannot recognize?*

STIMULUS FOR THE GALVANIC SKIN RESPONSE

Where subjects respond differently to experimental and control stimuli, partial information is available to them, even though they are not able to report the stimulus words to which they were exposed. No suggestion has been made, however, to the effect that subjects make deliberate inferences from these stimulus fragments to arrive at the emotional or nonemotional meaning of the stimulus. Instead, it appears that, without actually recognizing the stimulus when partial stimulus information is available, the person does respond with a higher threshold and, in some instances, with significant GSRs. Thus, it remains to explain how GSRs representing an emotional reaction can be made in the absence of recognition of the word.

The most likely explanation has been offered by Eriksen (1956, 1958), who suggests that in the training series an emotional response is conditioned not only to the whole stimulus, but also to elements of the stimulus (e.g., letters or syllables of the word) that can be perceived below threshold. This is consistent with many learning-theory experiments on the phenomenon of stimulus generalization[4] and with the fact that as the partial information is reduced by making the perception of the stimulus increasingly difficult, GSRs cease to occur. Essentially, as both Postman (1953*b*) and Eriksen (1960) have suggested, different classes of responses may be made to the same stimulus through linkages which are quite independent of each other. In this instance, it appears that verbal response and GSR are linked to the stimulus by quite different mechanisms and that a GSR does not require any knowledge of the emotional connotations of the stimulus.

VERBAL REPORT AND GALVANIC SKIN RESPONSE

The idea of subliminal perception has aroused great interest mainly because of the possibility that the organism has some hitherto unknown mechanism for responding to threatening stimuli that is actually more

[4]*Stimulus generalization* means that after the organism has learned to respond to a given stimulus, it will also respond to perceptually similar stimuli. Thus, a dog conditioned to respond to a 1,000-cycle tone will also respond to tones having adjacent frequencies.

sensitive than ordinary perceptual responses reported verbally. If it existed, this mechanism would be of great significance in behavior sequences where a person is faced with emotionally threatening circumstances. It would particularly provide an explanation of the dynamics of behaviors resulting in the avoidance or nonrecognition of threatening situations. Goldiamond (1958), however, has presented an intensive discussion of methodological problems involved in determining perceptual response from overt behavioral responses and has made abundantly clear that such a mechanism cannot be inferred from the experimental evidence on subliminal perception.

Eriksen and his various colleagues[5] have addressed themselves to the question of whether or not GSR is more *sensitive* than verbal report. They have shown that GSR and verbal report are somewhat independent of each other in the sense that they are linked to the stimulus in different ways. Eriksen (1956) notes that requiring the subject to report the whole word or syllable which is presented places severe restrictions on the sensitivity of the verbal report. If the subject were permitted to give a verbal response for any perceptual discrimination (such as perception of a few letters of a word), sensitivity would be greatly increased. Contrary to the earlier findings of Dixon (1958), Eriksen (1960) concludes that the GSR is *not* more sensitive than verbal report when the proper experimental controls are used.

UNCONSCIOUS RESPONSE TO ABOVE-THRESHOLD STIMULI

The discussion of subliminal perception should not be confused with all behavior for which an individual is unable to identify the initiating stimuli. In other words, a person may respond to an *above-threshold* stimulus without realizing that he has been influenced by the stimulus. A great many of our everyday actions take place at a very low level of awareness. The clearest examples, perhaps, lie in the area of motor skills. Thus in playing the piano or in typing, we respond to many stimuli which are potentially recognizable, but which in the performance of the act are not noticed. This phenomenon is well established and is quite different from the concept of subliminal perception, which involves a response to stimuli which cannot be recognized even when the perceiver makes maximum efforts to identify them.

STUDY QUESTIONS

29. *Since partial recognition of stimulus material presented below threshold does not by itself account for the emotional reactions of the subject, what other explanation may be offered for the GSR responses which occur when the subliminal material is anxiety-arousing?*

30. *Which is the more sensitive response: GSR or verbal report?*

31. *Distinguish between subliminal perception and behavior without awareness.*

[5]Dulaney & Eriksen, 1959; Eriksen, Azuma, & Hicks, 1959; Fuhrer & Eriksen, 1960; Eriksen, 1960.

SUMMARY: SUBLIMINAL PERCEPTION

That the threshold is a statistical concept has been strongly emphasized. The individual may receive varying degrees of information from a stimulus to which he is exposed, information that ranges from zero to a maximum amount. Failure to understand that partial information may be gained from briefly exposed stimuli accounts for a good deal of confusion concerning subliminal perception.

The response of being able to report a stimulus word verbally to the experimenter and the emotional response represented by the GSR are largely independent of each other. Either can occur in the absence of the other, since they are linked to the stimulus word by different mechanisms. The suggestion that the GSR is conditioned to the stimulus word, and that, through sensory generalization, it occurs when fragments of the word are perceived, is a reasonable explanation that does away with the paradox in subliminal perception. The GSR, moreover, is not a more sensitive indicator of the presence of a stimulus than verbal report when the proper experimental controls are introduced.

In general, the experimentation on subliminal perception demonstrates the rather remarkable capacity of the human organism for responding to partial information contained in subliminal stimuli. At the same time, the process by which this is accomplished has become much less mysterious than it had at first seemed to be. Responsiveness to partial stimulus information, as well as responsiveness to stimuli that are above threshold but not recognized under certain circumstances, may well play important roles in our everyday lives and may provide explanations of a variety of behaviors which otherwise might seem quite puzzling.

Size Judgments and Value

Another facet of the movement to demonstrate that social factors may affect the perceptual process dealt with the distortion of judgments of magnitude under various experimental conditions. The man on the street thinks of perception as highly accurate—that we see what is actually out there. In most experimental work, moreover, the psychologist has shown that except under highly restricted or artificial conditions, perception *is* veridical.[6] Consequently investigators felt that if social factors could be clearly demonstrated to distort judgments which are normally veridical, the case for the importance of social factors in perception would be proved beyond doubt. A variety of investigators proceeded to demonstrate that the judgment of the size of objects, known to be highly veridical under normal conditions, could be shown to vary systematically with the value of the objects to the perceiver.

In these experiments on the distortion of judgments of magnitude,

---

[6]*Veridical* is a term commonly used by psychologists to describe accuracy in perception.

the mechanisms of response salience and response disposition are not adequate to explain the results. Here, we do not have difficult perceptions at the threshold level, nor do we have other marginal conditions making perception confusing and difficult. Instead, simple size judgments are made of various stimulus objects clearly in view.

PERCEPTUAL ACCENTUATION

In an early experiment (Bruner & Goodman, 1947), ten-year-old children estimated the size of coins by adjusting a circular spot of light so that its area seemed to them to be equal to the size of the coin. In order to do this, the child turned a knob on a box which controlled the size of a spot of light thrown from behind on a ground-glass screen. Coins used were the penny, nickel, dime, quarter, and half-dollar, and as control objects, gray cardboard disks of the same sizes were employed. It was found that the estimated size of every coin was larger than its true size, and that the overestimation increased with the value of the coin from 1 to 25 cents, but dropped with the half-dollar. These effects were not found with a control group which estimated the size of the cardboard disks.

In order to test for individual differences in the value placed upon coins and their effects upon perception, size estimates were also made by children from well-to-do homes and from poor homes. In the case of every coin, the "poor" children overestimated its size on the average more than the "rich" children. Finally, subjects were not given a coin to match but were asked to imagine one and to match its size from memory. With this procedure, overestimations similar to those made when the coins were present were given by the poor children, but to a lesser degree. Such overestimations were given by the rich children only for the half-dollar. Bruner and Goodman labeled this tendency to overestimate the size of valued objects *perceptual accentuation*. Thus, at first glance this experiment appears to be one more piece of evidence for the view that need or motive may affect perception; in this case, in the form of a distortion of perception from the veridical.

Some investigators have raised questions concerning whether or not some other uncontrolled difference between rich and poor children might not have accounted for the difference between them in judging coins. One experiment (Ashley, Harper, & Runyon, 1951) used subjects as their own controls; i.e., states were created in which the *same* subjects were sometimes rich and sometimes poor. Hypnosis was used to suggest to these adult subjects that they were either rich or poor. Each subject was tested at different times in both "rich" and "poor" states. Results were consistent with the previous experiment, both for judgments made with coins present and for judgments made from memory. In another experiment (Lambert, Solomon, & Watson, 1949), varying degrees of value of "poker chips" were created by exchanging them for candy in varying amounts. As anticipated, estimates of the size of the chips were accentuated according to the value of the chips at the time judgments were made.

Not all experiments have supported the hypothesis of perceptual accentuation. One repetition (Carter & Schooler, 1949), using more rigorous controls, failed to confirm the earlier findings except in the non-perceptual area of *memory* for coin size. Although in one experiment (Bruner & Postman, 1948), accentuation similar to that found for coins was also found to occur for a dollar sign and a swastika, other investigators (Klein, Schlesinger, & Meister, 1951) obtained accentuation only for the dollar sign, not for the swastika. Another study (Lysak & Gilchrist, 1955) of judgments of the size of dollar bills of varying denominations failed to find any systematic overestimation.

One experiment (Secord, Bevan, & Katz, 1956) has extended the notion of perceptual accentuation to dimensions other than size. In this study, persons prejudiced against Negroes, when compared with neutral judges, exhibited exaggerated judgments of the skin color and other Negroid dimensions of facial photographs of Negroes. Thus the concept of perceptual accentuation may well apply to many types of variables.

COMPARATIVE EFFECTS OF POSITIVE AND NEGATIVE VALUE

Up to this point, our discussion has not attempted to differentiate the effects of *positive* and *negative* value on size estimation. Do positive and negative value both produce overestimation to an equal degree? Different experiments are sometimes not compatible with each other on this question. As already noted, a swastika was accentuated in only one of two experiments using it, but a dollar sign was accentuated in both studies. In an experiment (Beams, 1954) on judging the sizes of food objects projected by Kodachrome images, children overestimated the size of strongly liked foods but not of strongly disliked foods. An early experiment (Proshansky & Murphy, 1942) examining the effects of re-ward and punishment on the lengths of lines and heaviness of weights produced overestimation and underestimation according to whether or not responses were rewarded or punished.

Perhaps the most convincing experiment involving the effects of both positive and negative values on size judgment is the following. In this experiment (Bevan & Dukes, 1952), ten students participated in a raffle-like gambling game, making estimates of small *equal-sized* rectangular cards differing in monetary value. Value was indicated on each card by a number, which ranged from 0 to $3 in units of 10 cents. Depending upon whether the number had a plus or a minus before it, it represented the amount that the subject was to win or lose. Each subject drew cards one at a time from a bag, briefly looked at the number, turned it over to the blank side, and made a size judgment by choosing one of twelve blank cards varying slightly in size and spread out on a table before him. The subject went through a thirty-minute session on each of five days, each card selected contributing to or subtracting from what he had previously earned. His standing at the end of each day was announced, but settlement was reserved for the last day.

Under these experimental circumstances, positive and negative value proved to be equivalent in producing size accentuation, and further, the greater the value, the greater the overestimation of size. In sum, this experiment is a convincing demonstration of the effects of value upon judgment of magnitude, and it suggests that when other things are equal, positive and negative values will have symmetrical effects on size judgment.

STUDY QUESTIONS

32. *What is meant by the concept of perceptual accentuation?*
33. *What is the major evidence in support of perceptual accentuation?*
34. *To what extent do positive and negative value play equivalent roles in affecting judgments of magnitude? Under what conditions do they fail to produce equivalent effects?*

PERCEPTUAL ACCENTUATION AND ITS EXPLANATION

If one considers all the experiments on judgment of magnitude which have been cited, a variety of perplexing and contradictory results is apparent. The following are some questions that might be raised:

1. Why does value affect the judgment of the size of an object?
2. Why does perceptual accentuation occur in some instances and not in others?
3. Why do positive and negative value sometimes produce equivalent effects and at other times quite different results?
4. Is there a way of explaining the experimental findings and answering the above questions in terms of principles or mechanisms which apply to traditional perceptual experiments?

A critical discussion by Tajfel (1957) makes considerable progress in answering questions 1, 2, and 4, and his ideas may also be used to answer question 3. The key to understanding the inconsistencies among the various studies is the fact that experiments on perceptual accentuation have involved two quite *different classes of stimulus objects:*

1. Those in which object dimensions are *relevant* to value. These are objects that in normal experience are more valued if they are larger. Thus, the larger a coin, the greater its value; the larger a gold nugget, the greater its value; the larger a food object, the greater its value.
2. Those in which object dimensions are *irrelevant* to value. These are objects that in normal experience are valued equally regardless of their size, or are valued independently of their size. For example, in the experiments using symbols, the size of the swastika should have little to do with its value—whether it is large or small, it is just as negative for those who felt strongly opposed to the Nazis. Similarly, stamps of different value are generally the *same* size, as are dollar bills.

When value is *relevant* to stimulus dimensions, it has two kinds of effects. First, it results in overestimation of the larger stimuli in the series and underestimation of the smaller stimuli. Thus, when a judge guesses the size of coins, he judges the quarter and half-dollar to be larger than they are and the penny, nickel, and dime to be smaller than they are. In a sense, he uses an exaggerated scale of measurement. Tajfel has called this the *intra*serial effect, a term stemming from the fact that the relations *within* the series of objects on the judged dimension are changed. Figure 1–3 illustrates the effect in exaggerated form. The intraserial effect by itself does not explain the various experimental results. To do this, it is necessary to postulate a second property of the judgment of *relevant* stimuli.

Under the condition where value is relevant, the difference in magnitude between a valued stimulus object and a neutral one tends to be more accentuated than would be the case between two comparable neutral stimuli. Tajfel has termed this effect the *inter*serial effect. This is illustrated by the experiments on coins where a coin is judged larger than a valueless metal disk of the same size. Thus, in those instances where value is relevant to the physical dimension being judged, as in the case of coins,

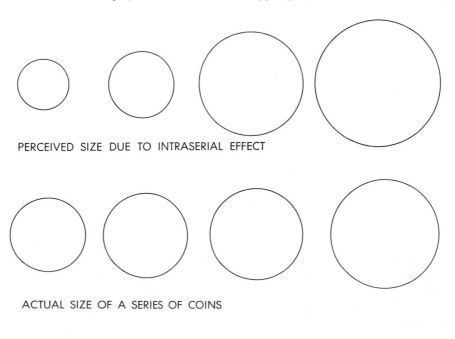

PERCEIVED SIZE DUE TO INTRASERIAL EFFECT

ACTUAL SIZE OF A SERIES OF COINS

Scale in millimeters

Figure 1–3
An illustration of the intraserial effect.

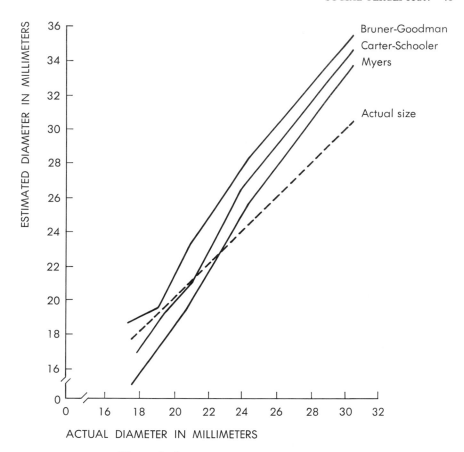

Figure 1–4

Accuracy of memory for size of coins as shown by three independent studies. (Adapted with permission from H. G. McCurdy. Coin perception studies and the concept of schemata. *Psychol. Rev.*, 1956, **63**, 160–168.)

both the intraserial and the interserial effect may be expected to occur, resulting in accentuation of the relative differences *within* the stimulus series, and accentuation of the differences *between* the valued stimuli of the series and the nonvalued control stimuli—here taking the form of overestimation of the valued stimuli.

These principles are illustrated by Figure 1–4, which plots the judgments of coins made *from memory* for a number of different experiments. In an old experiment on the judgment of coins performed by Myers (1913), the dime, penny, and nickel were underestimated and the quarter and half-dollar overestimated, providing an excellent example of the intraserial effect. The more recent experiments also show an intraserial effect, but they show the interserial effect as well—all the coins are overestimated.

In the case of *irrelevant* stimuli, where the physical dimension of the stimuli being judged is not regularly associated with value, neither the intraserial nor the interserial effect should occur. Bills of larger denominations do not have larger sizes; hence a dollar bill should not be seen as larger than a rectangle of the same size and general appearance. Table 1–1 summarizes the various experiments on value and judgment of magnitude, as well as classifying them according to whether the stimulus objects judged are relevant or irrelevant to value. An examination of the table makes clear that this classification is the crucial condition accounting for perceptual accentuation or the lack of it: only three studies are contra-

Table 1–1
Relevance of a Stimulus Dimension and the Occurrence of Perceptual Accentuation

STUDIES USING DIMENSIONS RELEVANT TO VALUE	STUDIES USING DIMENSIONS NOT RELEVANT TO VALUE
Myers (1913). Larger coins overestimated; smaller coins underestimated.	*Klein, Schlesinger, & Meister (1951).* Overestimation did not occur for a swastika.
Proshansky & Murphy (1942). Lines and weights overestimated or underestimated according to positive or negative value.	*Beams (1954).* No overestimation for disliked food objects.
Bruner & Goodman (1947); Tajfel & Cawasjee (1959). All coins overestimated; overestimation greater for larger coins.	*Bruner & Postman (1948).* Overestimation occurred for a swastika.
Bruner & Postman (1948). Overestimation occurred for a dollar sign enclosed in a circle (relevant if seen as coin).	*Lysak & Gilchrist (1955).* Dollar bills were not overestimated with increasing denominations.
Carter & Schooler (1949). For memory judgments only: all coins overestimated; overestimation greater for larger coins. With coins present: no overestimation occurred.	*Solley & Lee (1955).* The swastika was not overestimated.
Ashley, Harper, & Runyon (1951). Coins overestimated to a greater extent by S's believing themselves poor (in a hypnotic state).	*Dow & Gordon (1957).* Line figures having pleasant and unpleasant associations were not overestimated.
Klein, Schlesinger, & Meister (1951). Overestimation occurred for dollar sign enclosed in circle (relevant if seen as coin).	*Bevan & Dukes (1952).* Cards overestimated or underestimated according to their value in a gambling game.
Beams (1954). Overestimation occurred for liked food objects.	*Lambert, Solomon, & Watson (1949).* Token chips overestimated when they could be exchanged for candy.
Secord, Bevan, & Katz (1956). Negro faces judged more Negroid by prejudiced subjects.	

*These results are inconsistent with Tajfel's theory (1957).

dictory, whereas a large number of otherwise puzzling findings are consistent with the predictions. In the case of the Bevan and Dukes experiment, certainly blank cards do not vary in value with size in real-life situations; however, a characteristic of this experiment is that all cards are the *same* size, hence the perceiver has only their value to use in making size judgments.

The question of why positive value and negative value sometimes produce equivalent effects and at other times quite different results may now be answered simply. Under those circumstances where the size of an object is normally associated with positive value but not with negative value, accentuation will occur only for positive value. An example is the experiment (Beams, 1954) on liked and disliked food objects, where accentuation occurred only for liked objects. Up to a point, the larger a strongly liked food object, the greater its desirability; hence overestimation may be anticipated. But if a food object is strongly disliked, there is no particular reason why a larger portion of the disliked object will be even more negatively valued. The value of the liked object is connected with the consequences of eating it: under everyday conditions of free choice, liked objects will be eaten in varying amounts, with different-sized portions corresponding to different values, but disliked foods are unlikely to be eaten at all and therefore have a single value.

STUDY QUESTIONS

35. *Into what two classes does Tajfel divide the experiments on perceptual accentuation?*

36. *Explain what is meant by the* intraserial *effect and give some examples. How does value alter the intraserial effect, and what are the necessary conditions for such alteration?*

37. *Explain what is meant by the* interserial *effect and give some examples. Under what conditions does value produce the interserial effect?*

38. *Under what conditions may perceptual accentuation be expected to occur for both positive and negative values?*

SUMMARY: PERCEPTUAL ACCENTUATION

Considering in retrospect the various experiments concerning the effects of value on judgments of magnitude, one major contribution appears to be that value must be taken into account if the judgmental process is to be adequately explained. A second even more important contribution pertains to the manner in which value influences judgment. An aspect of the process already familiar from general experimental psychology, namely, the intraserial effect, has been shown to play an important role. If value varies systematically with the physical dimension being judged, the intraserial effect is accentuated. A likely explanation of this fact is that valuing the stimuli makes them more distinctive with respect to each other. This explanation would be consistent with other experimental findings that any factor which makes stimuli more distinctive will accentuate the intraserial effect. Thus, we again find that these social-perception findings can be closely integrated with general experimental psychology.

A somewhat more parochial contribution of this line of research is found in the *inter*serial effect: When value is regularly associated with a stimulus series, these stimuli are judged larger in magnitude than stimuli from a corresponding series that has no consistent association with value. This facet of the judgmental process deserves further research; perhaps it will even be found that any factor (not only value) which is correlated with a series of stimuli and which makes them more "distinctive" than a corresponding series will produce the interserial effect.

Finally, intraserial and interserial effects may apply not only to a series of physical stimuli but also to any abstract dimension, opening the way for the exploration of many variables that have great social importance. Such dimensions as the beauty of a painting, the warmth of a musical composition, and the judged intelligence of a person may be subject to the same kinds of principles. In conclusion, we once again find that value is capable of modifying our perception of the world around us.

Summary and Conclusions

The major focus of this chapter has been on the role of social factors in the perception of objects. The perception of objects is influenced by the selectivity of perception, by characteristic ways of organizing stimulus patterns, by frequency of previous experience with particular stimulus patterns and responses, by the extent to which such experiences have been reinforced, and by contemporary factors prevailing at the moment of perception. The probability of occurrence of a response due solely to previous experience is referred to as the response disposition. Response salience applies to contemporary factors that facilitate or interfere with perceptual responses. In a given stimulus situation, the readiness with which a particular response will occur is a function of both contemporary factors and the previous experience of the organism with that response.

Where the structure of the experimental situation permits response salience to operate, arousal of a need may be expected to make need-related responses more likely to occur. The main condition facilitating response salience is a large repertory of responses from which the perceiver may select his response. In situations where the structure of the situation prohibits the operation of response salience, the arousal of a need may be expected to have little effect upon the responses made. These are situations where the response repertory is severely restricted by providing in advance a limited number of responses from which the subject must choose. Individual differences in reactions to need arousal are evident: some persons may respond to increasing deprivation by increased response salience, whereas others may respond with decreased salience.

Rather complex methodological issues arise in experiments involving response disposition. The frequency of experience with a stimulus and its value are normally closely associated, and any interpretation which identifies one of these factors as affecting the perceptual process is likely to be open to explanation in terms of the other factor. Drawing firm conclusions on the several experiments that used reward and punishment to affect response disposition is not possible: experimental results have not always been consistent.

Perceptual defense comprises three processes: (1) Emotionally disturbing or threatening stimuli have a higher recognition threshold than neutral stimuli; (2) such stimuli are likely to elicit substitute perceptions that are radically altered so as to prevent recognition of the presented stimuli; (3) these critical stimuli arouse emotional reactions even though they are not recognized. With respect to the raised threshold for taboo or other threatening stimuli, many explanations are available, none of which requires that the perceiver "defend against" stimuli of which he is not aware. Many of these are artifacts of the methodology used; a higher recognition threshold is not really demonstrated. In some instances the higher recognition threshold for anxiety-arousing words is perfectly genuine. Here the experimental situation is essentially a guessing game where the subject is provided with partial cues that he fills in by providing a complete response. Those words that have been associated with punishment or anxiety have low response dispositions and thus are not used as "guesses" of what the exposed word is.

Individuals vary greatly in the way they react to threatening stimuli. Some are more sensitive and vigilant, and others react with repressing or controlling mechanisms. Apparently individuals can learn to avoid perceiving certain threatening, dangerous, or anxiety-provoking aspects of their environment. The psychological defenses of the person may, in part, take the form of heightened thresholds for stimulus materials that have a special significance for him because of his past experience. Other persons may react quite differently—with vigilance or sensitization. Possibly such tendencies represent fairly general modes of adjustment for the individual.

Experiments have suggested that, although a person does not consciously perceive a stimulus, he may nevertheless be able to respond as if he had perceived it. This is the phenomenon of subliminal perception. Some of the studies on subliminal perception led to faulty conclusions because they used recognition as a criterion for determining whether the stimulus had been perceived. This criterion ignores the fact that threshold is actually a statistical concept: the individual may receive varying degrees of information from a stimulus to which he is exposed, information that ranges from zero to a maximum amount. Failure of the experimenter to recognize the partial information gained from stimuli accounts for a good deal of the confusion concerning subliminal perception. The response of being able to report a stimulus word verbally to the experimenter and the emotional response represented by the GSR are largely independent of each other. The suggestion that the GSR is conditioned to the stimulus word, and that, through sensory generalization, it occurs when fragments of the word are perceived, is a reasonable explanation that does away with the paradox in subliminal perception. In general, the experimentation on subliminal perception demonstrates the rather remarkable capacity of the human organism for responding to partial information contained in subliminal stimuli.

Perceptual accentuation is the phenomenon that valued stimuli are likely to be perceived as larger than comparable neutral stimuli. A major contribution from the research on perceptual accentuation is the demonstration that value must be taken into account if the judgmental process is to be adequately explained. A second important contribution is the discovery of the means by which value influences judgment. This occurs as a result of the intraserial and interserial effects, both of which are involved when value varies systematically with the physical dimension being judged. The intraserial effect pertains to the overestimation of the larger stimuli in a series and the underestimation of the smaller stimuli. The interserial effect pertains to the accentuation of a valued stimulus object in comparison with a neutral one. When the conditions producing these two effects are taken into account, virtually all the experimental evidence on perceptual accentuation becomes consistent.

In general, results of experiments in social perception that at first appeared to represent distinctive social-psychological processes have turned out to be much less distinctive than they at first appeared. Many of the principles of general psychology have ultimately been used to explain the results of these experiments. Research in social perception, however, has made marked contributions to our understanding of individual differences in the perception of objects and has added to our understanding of perceptual processes in general.

chapter two

PERSON PERCEPTION

For many of us the most interesting objects of perception in our environment are other people. Much social conversation is an exchange of opinions and feelings about other people. In our everyday interaction with other persons, we frequently assess their intentions and motives with respect to us. We determine whether or not a person likes us, and our judgment of his feeling guides our own reaction to him. In situations where another person is attempting to influence us, we try to fathom his intentions and his sincerity. All these activities are relevant to the topic of person perception.

Nature of Person Perception

Person perception focuses on the process by which impressions, opinions, or feelings about other persons are formed. Although the term has come into common usage, *perception* (as we learned in Chapter 1) implies the use of direct sensory information, and hence it is not completely appropriate in the present context. Often an opinion concerning the other person is not based on direct observation of him but on statements by others or on knowledge of who he is. Moreover, opinions, evaluations, or feelings involve subjective judgment and inference that go beyond the kind of direct sensory impressions that characterize perception. Because of its wide acceptance, however, we will continue to use the term *person perception* to refer to these diverse phenomena.

Social psychologists are interested in person perception mainly because of its relevance for understanding human interaction. Since inter-action is mediated by the feelings, thoughts, and perceptions that indi-viduals have about each other, these subjective processes must be taken into account. In particular, person perception is important to under-standing the interaction processes of communication, influence, and change. Specific topics to be discussed in this chapter are the structuring of the stimulus environment by society, the shaping of the person cate-gories the perceiver uses, the relation between the perceiver's personality and his perception of others, the effects of his relation to other persons on his perceptions of them, and the effects of the interactional context on perceptions.

In everyday life, impressions and judgments of other persons are formed in widely varying situations. These situations vary in three major respects: (1) the amount of information available to the perceiver for purposes of forming a judgment concerning the other person, (2) the extent of interaction between the perceiver and the other person, and (3) the degree to which the relation between the perceiver and the other person is a well-established one. When we are introduced to a person, our information is often very limited, our interaction is restricted, and no established relation exists. We obtain only a brief glimpse of his appear-ance and hear him speak only a few conventional phrases, yet we may form a definite impression of his personality. At the opposite extreme in terms of information, interaction, and definiteness of the relation are impressions of personality based on a lifelong acquaintance with another person, as a friend or parent.

The complexity of the process of person perception is illustrated in Figure 2–1. The left block shows the various forms of stimulus informa-tion provided. The middle block lists factors that affect the perceiver's reaction to information, such as his previous experience, the implications of the stimulus person's actions, the association of the information with certain categories of persons (implicit personality theory and stereotypes), and the perceiver's conception of himself. The right-hand block lists facets of the impression formed: The perceiver attributes specific traits to the stimulus person, he forms feelings of like or dislike, respect, etc., and finally, he also forms impressions concerning whether they are caused by some situational factor or whether they are intentionally performed. These various determinants of person perception will be discussed in more detail in subsequent parts of this chapter.

The first portion of this chapter will deal with person perception under limited conditions, where amount of information and interac-tion are highly restricted and an established relation does not exist. Form-ing impressions of personality from limited verbal information about a person, or from such nonverbal information as appearance, inflections and quality of voice, facial expressions, gesture, and posture, will be briefly discussed. Somewhat more space will be devoted to impressions formed in situations where the basic information available is knowledge

Figure 2–1
Factors in forming impressions of personality.

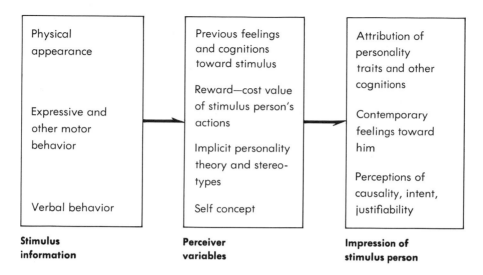

Physical appearance	Previous feelings and cognitions toward stimulus	Attribution of personality traits and other cognitions
	Reward—cost value of stimulus person's actions	
Expressive and other motor behavior		Contemporary feelings toward him
	Implicit personality theory and stereo-types	
		Perceptions of causality, intent, justifiability
Verbal behavior	Self concept	

Stimulus information **Perceiver variables** **Impression of stimulus person**

of the category a person belongs to; for example, a Negro, a surgeon, a teacher, a wealthy businessman. Later portions of the chapter will discuss situations where stimulus information is more abundant, where the relation between the perceiver and the other person is well established, and where various types of ongoing interaction between the perceiver and the other person take place.

STUDY QUESTION

1. *State three general dimensions or factors which may be used to classify the variety of conditions under which person perception occurs. Give examples of person-perception situations from everyday life which illustrate the varying circumstances under which person perception takes place.*

SOME DESCRIPTIVE MATERIALS

Perceptual experiences concerning persons around us may be introduced by examining the way in which two college girls, whom we shall call Sandra and Jane, describe certain acquaintances. These data were collected by the authors through interviews in which the girls were encouraged to talk freely and spontaneously. Sandra described her *best friend* as follows:

Ruth is my roommate and she's very interested in life. She has a very nice personality . . . well, when I say she's easy to get along with, I mean that's for people that she likes. Now, if she doesn't like anyone, she makes no bones about it. She's got that personality that sometimes causes trouble in the girls. Oftentimes there's a feeling of tension when a certain girl she doesn't like comes into the room and there are other girls in there. But otherwise she's fairly easy to get along with. She has several different moods. She is either real happy or she's real depressed.

   She dates fairly much but she can't seem to go toward one boy, and when she does like one boy she sort of falls hard and then if the boy doesn't like her as much as she likes him, she has a real rough time, and so personally I think that she should try to spread it around a little bit, but that's the only thing that kind of bothers me because of course then I have to help her along. She's not overpowering or demanding of a boy, and she plays sort of cool, I guess. She's just sort of more casual. She does have a feeling of—how can I say it? She's worried all the time that a boy is going to drop her. She does have that problem. She's sort of insecure that way. For that reason I think she is sort of real casual about the way she acts with a boy. She's real good on a date.

   I think she has a feeling of . . . well . . . not jealousy toward me. There's something between us—I can't quite put my finger on it, and oftentimes she'll leave me to do the . . . well, cleaning of the room; or she's afraid that I'm talking about her, which I don't talk about her. And there's this little tension between us. She has the tendency to go from one girl to another. While she's with one girl, the others are just completely out of the picture. She's been moving around ever since school started among different girls.

Sandra's description of Helen, *a girl she dislikes,* is quite in contrast to the description of her best friend:

   Well, I don't know Helen very well. The only reason I dislike her is because from what I've seen of her, she is petty. She is catty. I've heard her start stories about other girls that aren't true. I don't like that. She walks around as though she's carrying the whole world on her shoulders and it doesn't impress me at all.

Sandra's descriptions may be contrasted with those given by Jane, another college girl. These represent her *best friend,* Mary, and June, a *girl she dislikes:*

   Mary is a girl friend back in _____. We went to school together for one year. She is about 5 feet 6 inches, and has red hair. She's a lot of fun. She has a real good sense of humor; she's fun to be with; she's real smart. She plays musical instruments.

   I don't like June too well because she talks constantly about nothing in particular—just talk, talk, talk. Right now she likes my brother; he doesn't like her. Every time she sees me she goes out of her way to ask me how he's doing and for me to tell him to call her up. I don't know her too well.

   What can we learn from these descriptions? Perhaps most striking is the very great difference between the way in which Sandra and Jane describe their best friends. Sandra is able to grasp the complexity of her friend's personality, noting the various moods that characterize her, the way in which her casual behavior toward boys conceals her feelings of insecurity with respect to them, and her shifting attitudes toward Sandra herself. By way of contrast, Jane's description of her best friend is very superficial. She gives Mary's height and, the color of her hair and says that she is a lot of fun, is smart, and plays musical instruments.

The difference between the descriptions given by Sandra and Jane are not produced by differences in willingness to talk about their friends. The interviewers were careful to establish good rapport with the interviewees, who were encouraged to talk freely. In the unpublished study from which this material was taken, each subject described twelve persons whom he knew. Sandra's descriptions were consistently discerning, but from Jane's descriptions the interviewer got the impression that she went through life relating to others and perceiving others in an extremely superficial fashion. For example, Sandra described her boyfriend as intelligent and serious, but also went into some of his psychological difficulties in relating to others. She took a somewhat maternal, supportive attitude toward him and at the same time was able to admire some of his qualities. Jane, in contrast, spoke of her boyfriend as good-looking, a wonderful dancer, and lots of fun at parties. These diverse ways of perceiving others suggest a number of fundamental points about person perception:

1. The level of complexity at which persons are perceived varies from one perceiver to another. For example, one perceiver may classify others in terms of rather superficial characteristics, and another, in terms of less readily observable traits of the person, as in the case of our two perceivers.
2. Each perceiver has certain *central* traits or characteristics that he emphasizes in describing others. The other person is always sized up with respect to the degree to which he possesses or lacks those traits. One perceiver may emphasize security-insecurity, another, intelligence, and another, mood.
3. The centrality of traits in forming impressions of others is probably a function of the perceiver's own personality. From reading how they describe others, one gets the impression that Sandra and Jane are very different kinds of persons.
4. Others are often described in "relational" terms; that is, how the other relates to the perceiver and to other persons. For example, Sandra speaks of her friend's jealousy toward her and of Ruth's difficulties with boys. For the total sample of 120 tape-recorded descriptions of other persons, this predisposition to describe persons in relational terms rather than abstract traits was predominant.

As our discussion unfolds, we will find that these observations are supported by experimental studies.

MODES OF PERCEIVING OTHERS

The different modes of perceiving others may be described in terms of a dimension varying from the simple to the complex. Since perceptual experiences are private—no one can directly perceive the experience of another individual—we will assume that the use of language in describing others roughly parallels the perceptual experiences themselves.[1] The modes of person perception are as follows:

1. A person is described simply in terms of outward appearance or superficial characteristics; e.g., his body build, facial features, and mannerisms.

2. A person is described mainly in terms of a central trait and its immediate ramifications; e.g., a withdrawn person may be described by such closely related terms as *shy, quiet, retiring, ingratiating,* etc.

3. A person is described in terms of a cluster of *congruous* traits; i.e., traits which seem to belong together. For example, a large, strong man may be described as having a powerful voice and as being aggressive, self-confident, and forceful.

4. A person is described in terms of a variety of traits, including some which are *incongruous*; i.e., traits which seem *not* to belong together. To illustrate, a person may be described as kind, thoughtful, dishonest, and unsociable.

Watts, a linguist who has made extensive studies of the development in children of the language by which persons are described, has noted that children under the age of seven are seldom able to advance beyond the first mode: description in terms of outward appearance. He states:

> Up to the age of six and one-half or seven, children usually limit their descriptions of strangers to outstanding visible features. When a child has said that a man is *tall* or *short* . . . *fat* or *thin, strong* or *weak,* and *old* or *young,* he is usually brought to a stand unless some remarkable oddity of gait or of gesture, of demeanor or of dress fixes attention or provokes comment. (Watts, 1944, p. 174)

The second perceptual mode, the description of a person in terms of a single dominant trait, may be illustrated by a literary reference. This mode of description was developed over 2,000 years ago, as shown in the well-known characterizations written by Theophrastus, who was a student of Aristotle. One of his sketches follows.

> Grumbling is complaining too much of one's lot. The Grumbler is this sort of man. A friend sends him part of a feast and he says to the bearer: "I suppose your master grudged me his soup and wine since he didn't invite me." His mistress smothers him with kisses: "I should be surprised," says he, "if they came from your heart." He gets angry with Zeus not because it does not rain, but because it rains too late. He finds a purse on the road; "Ah!" he says, "but I never found anything worth having." If he has bought a slave cheap by coaxing the seller, he remarks: "It is much too cheap to be good." The happy news of the birth of a son is announced to him: "You should add,"

[1]The present treatment is not intended to deny the importance of vague or ill-defined feelings toward others, or such conditions as "unconscious hostility," but recognizes that such factors are probably best investigated within some framework other than a perceptual one.

he says, "that my property is now halved, and you would be telling the truth." When he has won a law-suit by an unanimous verdict he reproaches the composer of the speech for omitting several points. His friends club together to lend him money without asking interest. "Come, cheer up," says one of them. "Cheer up?" says he, "When I have to pay it back to every one of them and be grateful into the bargain!" (Aldington, 1924, pp. 40–41)

Although the literary writer may take the liberty of exaggerating the extent to which the various aspects of a person's behavior and appearance are expressions of a single dominant trait, the popularity of the thirty character sketches by Theophrastus, and the extent to which his approach has been used by many other successful authors throughout the intervening centuries, suggests that people often think of other persons in terms of a central trait. The reader will recall that the previously quoted descriptions given by Sandra and Jane of girls they dislike were limited to one or two central characteristics.

The third perceptual mode, that of describing another person in terms of a cluster of congruous attributes, is illustrated by well-known character descriptions by La Bruỳere, one of which follows:

I hear Theodacte from the ante-chamber: he raises his voice the nearer he comes; he enters, he laughs, he shouts, he roars; we close our ears, it is like thunder. He is no less dreadful from the things he says than from the tone in which he speaks. He only calms down and abandons this enormous clamour to splutter out vanity and folly. He has so little regard for time, persons and good manners, that everyone has a share without his having meant to give it; before he has sat down he has unintentionally offended the whole company. At dinner he sits down first and on the first seat; the women are at his right and left. He eats, he drinks, he tells stories, he jokes, he interrupts, all at the same time. He has no discernment of persons, neither the host nor the guests; he abuses people's silly deference to him. Is the dinner given by him or by Euthydeme? He absorbs all the authority of the table; and it is less troublesome to yield it to him than to dispute it. Wine and food add nothing to his character. If he gambles, he wins; he tries to jest at the loser, and offends him; yet the laughers are on his side; he is forgiven any fatuity. At last I yield and disappear, unable to endure any longer either Theodacte or those who endure him. (Aldington, 1924, p. 488)

Probably no one perceives another individual in a manner which embraces all the facets of his personality and character. On the other hand, the fourth perceptual mode is often approached, in the sense that many perceivers recognize incongruities in another's personality or behavior and often are able to characterize him aptly. Little is known about the factors that enable a person to be more insightful in his evaluation of others, in spite of the fact that such knowledge is extremely important in certain aspects of life.

SUMMARY: THE NATURE OF PERSON PERCEPTION

When given free rein in describing another person, perceivers refer to concrete behavior and to the ways that the other relates to them. Four perceptual modes were suggested. A person is described in terms of (1) outward appearance or superficial characteristics, (2) a central trait and its immediate ramifications, (3) a cluster of congruous characteristics, and (4) a variety of traits, including some which are incongruous. Perceivers differ in their use of the more complex mode; presumably, this is a function of the complexity and maturity of their personality. Most adults probably use one of the less complex modes on some occasions, and possibly many immature adults frequently fail to use the most complex mode.

STUDY QUESTIONS

2. *What differences have been noted in the ways in which different perceivers describe other persons?*
3. *What differences are apparent between the description of a friend and of a disliked acquaintance?*
4. *State the four perceptual modes in terms of which others may be described. Describe some of your acquaintances and determine which perceptual mode fits each of the descriptions.*

Varieties of Inference

INFERENCE FROM VERBAL CUE TRAITS

Many situations in everyday life provide us with verbal information about another person concerning whom we have little other information. On the basis of the verbal information alone, we often imagine what he looks like or make inferences about other aspects of his personality. The counterpart of this real-life situation has been studied in the laboratory by using the technique of presenting verbal information about a hypothetical person and requesting the perceiver to form an impression of him.

In a now classic study performed by Asch in 1946, groups of college students were told that a list of characteristics belonging to a particular person would be read to them and that they should try to form an impression of the kind of person described. A sample cue-trait list representing a stimulus person is as follows: "energetic, assured, talkative, cold, ironical, inquisitive, and persuasive." Following this, they were asked to write a brief characterization of the person in just a few sentences. Asch found that his subjects readily accepted the task, in spite of the sparsity of information about the hypothetical person.

Written impressions obtained in this manner differed greatly, in spite of the fact that all subjects were exposed to an identical list of traits. Asch found that many persons organized the list of traits into a relatively integrated, consistent picture of a person. In this process, certain traits were made central aspects of the person's character, while others were relegated to a minor role—or even ignored entirely, suggesting a preference for elementary modes of description. For example, when the cue traits *warm* or *cold* were used, they usually dominated the impression formed. In some instances, the impression formed included new qualities not in the original stimulus list. Occasionally the perceiver went so far as to give a physical description of the person. Those new qualities, physical or otherwise, were usually congruous with other elements of the written sketch. In another study (Kastenbaum, 1951), where several recorded statements supposedly directed toward another person in a conversation were presented as stimulus material, results were similar to those of Asch: The stimulus person was usually described in a congruous manner, and certain themes were emphasized over others.

Another type of study, in which subjects were told only the groups to which a person belonged and were then asked to describe the person, also illustrates attempts to resolve incongruity. Some of the stimulus persons were presented as belonging to four groups normally associated with wealthy businessmen and also to a fifth group—the Communist Party. In describing these persons, most of the subjects made definite attempts to resolve this incongruency in memberships. The following are some examples illustrating this process (Pepitone & Hayden, 1955):

> His political views are at variance with the whole capitalist pattern. He probably professes to be a socialist to ally himself with his workers, but is probably a Republican at heart. . . .
>
> As for his aims, ideals, etc., they are wrapped up in the party, and his cocktail conversation re: free enterprise, voting the Republican ticket was just so much B.S. to fool his friends and to do his job better for the party. (P. 304)

Other investigations (Haire & Grunes, 1950) similarly demonstrate modes of resolving incongruency.

The original experiment by Asch has been repeated with the same procedure, and comparable results have been obtained (Mensh & Wishner, 1947; Veness & Brierley, 1963). It has also been repeated using a live stranger. In one experimental variation (Kelley, 1950), the class instructor introduced a guest speaker by describing him prior to his appearance with the stimulus words from Asch's experiment, using *warm* or *cold* to describe the central trait in different classes. In another variation (Veness & Brierley, 1963) a person representing himself as a veterinarian described his activities in terms calculated to fit the peripheral terms from Asch's list. Warm and cold were represented in two different groups by the tonal qualities of the voice of the speaker, who was a speech expert. Both of these experiments were successful in replicating the essential results of Asch's study.

Luchins (1948) and others (Dinnerstein, 1951; Gollin, 1958) have noted that not all perceivers respond by elaborating upon the word list presented. Some merely repeat the list or give synonyms of words in the list. A few do not even think of the traits as belonging to a single person.

In general, however, the various repetitions of Asch's experiment have confirmed his original results, and it appears that most perceivers, at least, form impressions that go well beyond the stimulus information presented.

One particular facet of Asch's results emphasizes that stimulus words interact, with the central traits greatly influencing the meaning that is given to the peripheral words. A study (Bruner, Shapiro, & Tagiuri, 1958) that appears to contradict this point presented cue traits singly and required the perceiver to select from a list of traits those that seemed to go along with the cue trait. Then various combinations of traits were presented, and appropriate traits were again chosen from the list. A comparison of these single and combined presentations suggested that perceivers use stimulus information in an additive fashion. That is, each bit of information concerning another person presumably leads to a certain inference about his character. When many bits are presented, the perceiver simply adds up his inferences from each bit and arrives at a total impression. While the results of this study are indisputable, the maximum number of stimulus words presented was only three, as compared with Asch's seven. It might be that as the number of words is increased, the perceiver is increasingly inclined to give unequal weight to different words.

Two other studies (Wishner, 1960) demonstrate that a stimulus word may be either central or perhipheral depending upon the responses that the subject is permitted to make. These may be controlled by providing the subjects with different kinds of checklists on which they indicate their responses. Thus, one investigation has shown that the centrality or peripherality of a cue trait depended upon the content of the judgments made about the stimulus person. That is, warmth-coldness was a central cue trait when the experimenter required the perceiver to make decisions about such traits as generosity, wisdom, happiness, good nature, sociability, or their antonyms. Such a pair was not central if inferences were made about traits having little relation to warmth-coldness. Thus, judgments required of the subject by the experimenter can determine what cue traits are central and which are peripheral.

In everyday situations, however, as in one portion of Asch's experiment, the perceiver is completely free to use what terms he pleases to describe stimulus persons. Under these circumstances, he may be expected to emphasize in his perception of others descriptive categories that he is accustomed to using or that reflect his important values. Whenever he receives stimulus information concerning another person which is related to these values, his impression will be strongly influenced by the information. On the other hand, when stimulus information has no clear relevance to his characteristic descriptive categories, his impression of the person will be vague. These values, of course, may stem from personality characteristics of the perceiver as well as from various cultural sources.

Summary: inference from verbal cue traits

When a person is described in terms of trait words and individuals are asked to describe their impression of him, they usually write a relatively integrated, congruent sketch of that person. In this process, certain traits are selected as central, and others are relegated to a minor position or ignored entirely. Sometimes new qualities appear in the sketch. Individuals differ widely in the descriptions they give; some of them describe the stimulus person in terms that are fairly close to the original list of trait words, without increasing the congruity of the terms in which he is described. Presumably the selective emphasis upon certain cue traits is a reflection of the social or personal values that the perceiver attaches to the traits.

ORDER OF PRESENTATION

Many people believe that first impressions of a person are important and lasting. One experimental approach to this question examines the effects on impression formation by successively presenting adjectives providing information about a stimulus person. Both Asch (1946) and Anderson and Barrios (1961) found that adjectives presented first had a greater impact on the impression formed than those presented later. Another experimental approach presents blocks of stimulus information in different orders, and compares the impressions formed for each arrangement.

One extensive study of this kind (Luchins, 1957a; 1957b; 1960) achieved dramatic results strongly favoring stimulus information presented first. If the initial stimulus information suggested a friendly person, even though it was immediately followed by additional information suggesting that the same person was unfriendly, a large majority of the perceivers judged him to be friendly. Just the opposite was true when the initial stimulus information suggested unfriendliness and was followed by information suggesting friendliness.

Certain additional conditions introduced into the experiment, however, completely nullified this *primacy* effect. These included such procedures as warning the subject not to form an opinion until he had heard all the information, as well as separating the two blocks of information by an unrelated task. The fact that other experiments (Ostrander & Steger, 1960; Gollin, 1958) have not always resulted in a strong primacy effect suggests that the effect is very sensitive to the conditions under which judgments are made.

STUDY QUESTIONS

5. *When a perceiver is exposed to a list of traits describing a person and forms an impression of his personality, in what ways does his impression differ from the list of discrete traits?*

6. *In what way do the responses of the perceiver determine whether a cue trait*

describing a stimulus person is central or peripheral? What factors are likely to determine centrality in an everyday situation?
7. *What perceptual mode characterizes the impressions formed from limited verbal information?*
8. *What experimental evidence supports the popular notion that first impressions tend to be lasting? State some conditions under which primacy effects are weakened and recency effects favored.*

FORMING IMPRESSIONS FROM NONVERBAL INFORMATION

In some situations involving minimal information, minimal interaction, and lack of a structured relation, nonverbal cues may contribute to the impression formed. Thus, impressions may be based on facial features, appearance, body build, expressive movements, etc. An understanding of how person perceptions are formed from nonverbal cues may be important for a number of reasons.

First, in those everyday situations where stimulus information is very limited, nonverbal cues may be used as a basis for judgment. Such judgments may well lead the perceiver to draw erroneous conclusions concerning the stimulus person. For example, the interview behavior of patients depicted in a silent film is judged very differently from the same behavior when written transcripts, sound recordings, or sound films are used (Geidt, 1955). Second, in a face-to-face situation where the verbal behavior of a person may readily be observed, persons often present themselves so as to conceal their true feelings or characteristics. Sometimes nonverbal cues may reveal these feelings or characteristics to the observer. Finally, another reason for studying such limited situations is that they enable the investigator to identify with precision significant variables that are obscured by the complexity of the face-to-face situation.

Photographs as stimulus information

As a source of impression formation, probably physiognomy has been studied more thoroughly and systematically than other forms of nonverbal stimulus information, particularly by Secord and his colleagues. Judgment of personality from physiognomy is to be distinguished from the judgment of emotional states from facial expressions. The latter depends more upon transient aspects of the face, although in studying physiognomy it is obviously impossible to ignore completely the expressive aspects of the face. An even more important distinction is that studies of the recognizability of emotional expressions have emphasized accuracy, whereas the present emphasis is on the perceptual experience or impression of personality which is formed and on the stimulus cues that evoke it.

One finding repeatedly confirmed is that judges show marked agreement in attributing certain personality impressions to faces with particular physiognomic characteristics.[2] For example, one study (Secord & Muth-

---

[2]Thornton, 1943, 1944; Secord, Bevan, & Dukes, 1953; Stritch, 1954; Secord & Muthard, 1955*b*; Secord & Bevan, 1956; Beck, 1957.

ard, 1955*b*) demonstrated that facial photographs of women who had narrowed eyes, a relaxed and full mouth, a smooth skin, and considerable lipstick were perceived as more feminine and sexually attractive than women lacking these features. Another investigation (Secord, Dukes, & Bevan, 1954) demonstrated that men with a dark complexion, a coarse, oily skin, heavy eyebrows, and a straight mouth were perceived as hostile, boorish, quick-tempered, sly, and conceited.

Appearance and body build

The idea that personality and temperament are related to physique has a long history extending back to the ancient Greeks. A frequently quoted passage from Shakespeare's *Julius Caesar* (Act 1, Scene 2) illustrates the point:

> Let me have men about me that are fat;
> Sleek-headed men and such as sleep o' nights:
> Yon Cassius has a lean and hungry look;
> He thinks too much: such men are dangerous.

In modern times, extensive studies of the relation between personality and physique have been conducted. Although these studies focus upon the accuracy of judgments of personality from physique alone, they also contribute information about the formation of personality impressions that are not necessarily valid. Kretschmer (1925) observed that schizophrenics tended to be tall and thin, and manic-depressives, short and fat. He generalized this observation to normal persons differing in body build, and suggested that tall, thin persons were usually sensitive, withdrawn, and reserved, and short, fat persons, sociable and forceful. He has continued to refine his early ideas for many years, and the above statement is a considerable oversimplification of his typology. In a general sense, however, it does accord with what appear to be widespread lay notions concerning thin and fat persons.

Sheldon and his colleagues (Sheldon, Stevens, & Tucker, 1940; Sheldon & Stevens, 1942) offered a somewhat different system of describing body build and relating it to personality. The interesting point about his ideas for our purpose is that his evaluations of temperament (or personality) were based upon ratings made by himself or by others who were thoroughly familiar with his system of body typology. It is generally accepted that the correlations which Sheldon found between physique and personality were somewhat inflated because of failure to rate personality independently of knowledge of the stimulus persons' body build. But the presence of this "error" suggests the potency of body build in contributing to personality *impressions*, whether the impression is correct or not. Instead of explaining this relation as an error, we might suggest that the very choice of traits for describing personality produced relations between physique and personality through a kind of reasoning by analogy. For example, heavy, fat persons were characterized as "loving physical comfort," "slow to react," and "relaxed." Persons of athletic build were described as "energetic," "assertive of posture and movement," "needing and enjoying exercise," and "loving physical adventure." Thus, these "personality traits" may be arrived at through a process of direct inference from the nature of the body structure.

Expressive movements, gestures, posture, and voice qualities

To some degree, expressive movements and gestures are shaped by cultural factors, as well as by training; momentary states such as fatigue; and certain characteristics of the physical environment. It has been shown, for example, that Italians are much more expansive and free in their use of gestures than Americans, and further, that assimilation to American ways includes modification of these Italian patterns of expressive movements (Efron & Foley, 1947). Some of these factors, to the extent that they produce uniformity in expression, may mask individual differences. On the other hand, there are measurable individual differences in expressive movement (Allport & Vernon, 1932). Our interest here is in the question of whether or not expressive movements are used as cues in the judgment or evaluation of individuals.

Although it appears reasonable that expressive movements would occasionally be used as a basis for judgment, the experimental evidence is scanty. Common-sense psychology suggests that a person with a slumped posture who moves slowly would be judged dull, lifeless, and depressed in the absence of other cues to the contrary. A flabby handshake may suggest lack of warmth; jerky, erratic movements may indicate nervousness; sweeping, expansive gestures may suggest force and vigor; and constraint of movement with accompanying stiffness of manner may imply aloofness and reserve. As in the case of body build, these ideas are conjectural, for experimental studies which have been carried out on expressive movement have focused not on personality *impressions*, but on the veridical relation between expressive movements and personality traits.

One exception is an interesting experiment (Sarbin, 1954) in which postures were represented by "stick figures." These were figures in which the neck, trunk, limbs, hands, and feet were each represented by a single line, and the head by an oval. Subjects showed considerable consensus in choosing terms representing some feeling, attitude, or trait of the subject which seemed to be clearly suggested by the posture.

Other recent research by Ekman (1964a) presented inexperienced judges with photographs of the body posture of persons being interviewed and also excerpts of verbal behavior from the actual interviews. Photographs to which the verbal excerpts belonged were not identified; judges were asked to put together the photographs and the excerpts which, in their judgment, were from the same segment of the interview. They were able to match the body photographs and verbal excerpts correctly to an extent considerably greater than might be expected by chance. Several other experiments by Ekman (1964*b*) indicate that the body provides especially useful cues to judgments of the degree to which a person is relaxed or tense, while the head provides cues about the pleasantness or unpleasantness of his feelings.

Movement of the entire person along some particular path has also been investigated (Tagiuri, 1960). Line figures were presented, together with the information that they represented the path through which a person moved. Subjects were asked to describe in their own words the kind of person represented. For example, one figure was a straight line, another was a regular curve, and another was a very erratic path. For many of the "paths," the subjects agreed upon the type of person who might exhibit such movement. One common means for drawing inferences was the use of analogy; for example, a straight, direct path was often described as representative of a direct, straightforward, honest person. A meandering path was described as characteristic of a vacillating, undependable, wavering person. Also common were inferences more remote from the characteristics of the path; these were often more difficult to explain.

Certain qualities of the voice have been shown to be adequate cues in the judgment of social class (Pear, 1931, 1957; Crider & Lasswell, 1960). Emotions have been judged from the tonal qualities present in pronouncing such material as letters of the alphabet (Dusenbury & Knower, 1939), and various stereotyped, consistent judgments have been yielded by voice quality as a source of stimulus information (Allport & Cantril, 1934). Voice alone is sufficient to produce a high degree of agreement among judges on the personality traits of the stimulus person (Taylor, 1934; Fay & Middleton, 1936, 1941). In another study (Kastenbaum, 1951), perceivers described stimulus persons in terms appropriate to whether their voices in recorded conversations were warm, neutral, or cold. In this investigation, however, both voice quality and content or meaning served as stimulus cues. Research on judgments from nonverbal qualities of speech has been ably reviewed by Kramer (1962). Interesting observations obtained from extensive interviews have also been reported concerning the influence of the clothing a person wears on how he is perceived (Stone, 1959; 1962).

STUDY QUESTIONS

9. *Under what circumstances are nonverbal cues likely to influence the impression that a perceiver forms of a stimulus person?*

10. *What is the significance of the fact that judges may be shown to reach marked agreement on the traits they attribute to persons on the basis of nonverbal cues?*

Summary: Impressions from nonverbal information

In those situations involving minimal information, minimal interaction, and lack of a structured relation, nonverbal cues are likely to be used to form an impression of another person. The usual criterion for determining whether or not a particular bit of stimulus information is used as a cue is whether or not judges agree that a person presenting that cue has certain attributes. This criterion has been met in judgments of persons from photographs, body build, expressive movements, posture, voice qualities, and clothing.

NATURE OF INFERENCE PROCESSES

Research has repeatedly shown that when perceivers make judgments from very limited stimulus information in a context where interaction is restricted, they usually show marked agreement on the characteristics of the persons depicted. Since it is unlikely that this consensus arises from accuracy of judgment, some explanation of how perceivers arrive at consensus is needed. When faced with such minimal information as that contained in a few descriptive words, a photographed face, a voice, a body build and general appearance, or some expressive gestures, and *instructed to come up with an impression,* the perceiver is likely to use reason and imagination in order to satisfy the experimenter. A variety of inference processes are suggested by intensive observation and analysis of experimental situations involving person perception (Secord, 1958).

Temporal extension

One of the most widespread perceptual-cognitive processes operating in impression formation is *temporal extension.*[3] This takes place when a perceiver regards a momentary characteristic of the person as if it were an enduring attribute. For example, a smile usually means that the stimulus person is momentarily responding in a friendly fashion, but the perceiver may infer from this expression the enduring attributes *good-tempered* or *easygoing.* Or a single action by another person may lead to judgments of lasting characteristics.

Resemblance to a familiar person

Occasionally someone we meet reminds us of someone else we know well, and we attribute the characteristics of our familiar acquaintance to the stranger. In fact, in many instances we do this without being aware of the connection between the person currently being perceived and some figure from our past. In psychoanalytic theory this process is termed *transference.* The transference concept emphasizes the extent to which certain other persons are unconsciously perceived as having the attributes of one's father or mother.

Categorization

The process of *categorization* was briefly referred to in Chapter 1. Since it is impossible for a perceiver to respond to all the aspects of a person, he resorts to a classification system. More specifically, he uses available

---

[3]This process or a similar one has been described by Icheiser (1949); Heider (1958*a*); Secord (1958); Kaminski (1959); Fromm (1960).

information to place the person in a category associated with certain personality attributes. For example, the perceiver may estimate the age of the person from facial cues. If he believes that older persons are more responsible, more patient, and less energetic, he forms an impression which includes these characteristics. Some evidence for this view is found in a study showing that persons having different ages and occupations were assigned quite different traits (Kogan & Shelton, 1960).

Inference through analogy

The term *metaphorical generalization* has been applied to instances where analogy is used to bridge the gap from stimulus information to personality impression by Secord, Stritch, and Johnson (1960) as follows:

> Several lines of evidence converge to illustrate the use of analogy in forming impressions of people. Asch (1958) has demonstrated that metaphorical terms describing both human characteristics and physical properties of things or events are used in a parallel manner in many languages. In a variety of tongues, persons are referred to as warm or cold, deep or shallow, bright or dull, rigid or elastic. If qualities may apply to things and people, then it is only a short step to the suggestion that qualities inherent in stimulus information may be generalized to personality judgments. For example, a person who has a coarse skin or who uses coarse language may have attributed to him lack of sensitivity or a "coarseness" of personality; a person who dresses poorly may be thought of as uncouth. (P. 329–330)

In another form of inference by analogy, the perceiver makes an inference from the *function* of some observed attribute of the person. For example, the mouth is used for talking and for expressive communication; thus, persons with thin, compressed lips are rated low on the trait "talkativeness" (Secord & Muthard, 1955b). Also, persons seen in face-to-face relations are likely to be perceived as more intelligent, dependable, and industrious when wearing glasses than when not wearing them (Thornton, 1943; 1944). Possibly the popular notion that individuals with a high forehead are especially intelligent may be a functional inference; a high forehead is wrongly believed to mean more brain capacity, which implies greater intelligence. Further examples readily come to mind: A woman with full lips may be judged as more sexually attractive because lips are used for kissing, a man with an athletic build may be judged as more energetic and forceful, and another with a loud, powerful voice may be thought to be persuasive. As noted previously, a perceiver may make judgments of this kind without being clearly aware of how he arrived at them.

STUDY QUESTIONS

11. *Explain the following inference processes: temporal extension, resemblance to a familiar person, categorization, and inference by analogy.*

12. *What evidence exists for the position that the formation of inferences through the use of analogy is a rather general characteristic of the judgmental process?*

Summary: Nature of inference processes

Research has repeatedly shown that when perceivers make judgments from very limited stimulus information in a context where interaction is restricted, they usually show marked agreement on the characteristics of the persons depicted. Often it is unlikely that these judgments represent the true characteristics of the stimulus person, so a problem arises as to how to explain consensus. Several inference processes apparently are brought into play as a result of the perceiver's interest in arriving at an impression of the stimulus person.

Temporal extension is one such process: the perceiver regards a momentary characteristic of the person as if it were an enduring attribute. Sometimes, because he resembles a familiar person, the stimulus person may be assigned some of the traits of that person. A very common process is categorization or classification of the stimulus person according to certain identifying characteristics. The person is then assigned all the attributes which are considered to belong to that class of persons. Finally, under some circumstances, inference by analogy is used. This takes two forms. One, metaphorical generalization, leaps from a physical characteristic to a direct inference about some personality attribute. The inference is made possible by the direct applicability to the personality attribute of the meanings attached to the physical characteristic. The other, functional inference, bases a conclusion about personality on the function of some physical attribute.

SUMMARY: VARIETIES OF INFERENCE

Many situations in everyday life provide a minimum of information about a stimulus person; yet it appears that clear impressions of him are often formed. Laboratory investigations have dealt with such limited-information situations in order to study the processes by which the perceiver forms impressions of personality. When a person is described in terms of verbal cue traits, perceivers are likely to "process" these traits in their own characteristic manner, usually making them more congruous by changing their meanings, omitting some traits, and adding others. Studies of first impressions suggest that they are more important than later impressions, under certain limited conditions. Other conditions may weaken the effects of first impressions. Perceivers have also been shown to agree on certain personality attributes associated with nonverbal cues, such as facial features, body build, expressive movements, posture, voice qualities, and clothing.

Apparently, consensus among perceivers concerning the attributes of the stimulus person that are associated with stimulus information arises by means of a variety of inference processes. These processes include temporal extension, resemblance to a familiar person, categorization of the person, and two forms of reasoning by analogy.

Culturally Provided Categories: The Social Stereotype

In everyday life, we often find ourselves having only categorical information concerning a person. We know only that he is a Jew, a policeman, a teacher, or an old man. Where other information about him is minimal, such knowledge strongly affects our perception of him. This action of assigning attributes to a person solely on the basis of the class or category to which he belongs is known as *stereotyping*.

THE NATURE OF STEREOTYPING

Stereotyping has three characteristics: the categorization of persons, a consensus on attributed traits, and a discrepancy between attributed traits and actual traits. Each of these is discussed at length below.

Categorization of persons

Persons have many attributes differing greatly in visibility or distinctiveness. Society selects certain attributes as means of identifying various categories of persons, and ignores others. These attributes may be physical—such as age, sexual, or racial characteristics; they may involve membership in a group, organization, or society—as in occupational, church, or national affiliation; or they may even be based on certain distinctive behavior patterns. In other words, a stereotype is a special form of categorical response; membership in a category is sufficient to evoke the judgment that the person possesses all the attributes belonging to that category.

Two studies (Secord, Bevan, & Katz, 1956; Secord, 1959) using photographs varying in "negroidness' from markedly Negroid to markedly Caucasian tested this notion of categorical response, simply by determining whether the degree of stereotyping was reduced for the more Caucasian photographs. Both studies found that, as long as the individual is recognized as a Negro, stereotyping does not decrease as the pictures become increasingly Caucasoid. This is illustrated in Figure 2–2. Photographs *I* through *K* were almost always perceived as those of Negroes. As indicated by the height of the curve, they were more stereotyped than the Caucasian-appearing Negro photographs *C* and *D* and than the white photographs. Persons both high and low in prejudice assign these stereotype traits to photographs *recognized as Negro* regardless of the extent to which they contain Caucasian features. But persons more highly prejudiced stereotype all such photographs to a greater degree.

Finally, the responses of those few judges who identified the most Caucasoid of the photographs (*J, C,* and *D*) as Negro were examined. Even these pictures were stereotyped, by these judges only, to an extent at least equal to that of the average Negro photograph.

Consensus on attributed traits

The class of persons having some form of common identification is thought to share certain personal attributes. For example, we may group all unmarried women over a certain age into a single class, call them spinsters, and believe that they are very prim, lonely, and own pet cats which they greatly indulge. Or Americans may be considered industrious and materialistic; elderly persons may be regarded as old-fashioned, conservative, and cantankerous; Negroes may be perceived as happy-go-lucky, lazy, superstitious, and dishonest; and professors may be thought

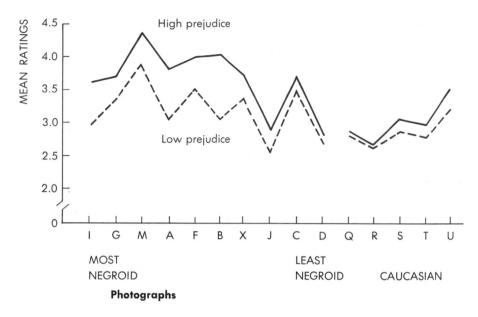

MEAN RATINGS

High prejudice

Low prejudice

I G M A F B X J C D Q R S T U

MOST
NEGROID

LEAST
NEGROID

CAUCASIAN

Photographs

Figure 2–2
Stereotype scores by photograph for high-and low-prejudice judges. (Adapted
with permission from P. F. Secord. Stereotyping and favorableness in the perception of Negro faces. *J. abnorm. soc. Psychol.,* 1959, **59**, 309-315.)

of as absentminded, impractical, idealistic, and eccentric. By definition
it is implied that those who hold the stereotype are in reasonable agreement with each other on the identifying characteristics of the category of
stereotyped persons and also on the attributes they possess.

An early study by Katz and Braly (1933) repeated by Gilbert (1951)
illustrates this consensus for ethnic stereotypes. A list of ethnic groups,
together with 84 words describing personal attributes (e.g., "aggressive,"
"intelligent") were presented to 100 Princeton students. Students checked
all those attributes that seemed to be characteristic of each ethnic group
and then went back over the checklist to identify the 5 attributes they
thought most characteristic of each ethnic group. Tabulations for both
studies, for the most common trait assignments among the 5 top choices,
appear in Table 2–1.

Consensus among the students is striking. If a student were to select
5 traits at random, the chances of assigning any one trait to an ethnic
group would be only 5 in 84. For 100 students selecting traits at random,
only 5/84 of 100, or approximately 6 students, would pick any one trait.
Yet we find that in 1932, 48 percent of the students and in 1950, 30 percent of the students declared that Americans were industrious, and as
many as 84 and 41 percent, respectively, designated Negroes as superstitious. Particular traits, then, were chosen by such large numbers of
students that we can assume the existence of stereotyping for these ethnic
groups.

Consensus varies considerably for different ethnic groups, indicating

Table 2–1
**Percent of Princeton College Students
Assigning Traits to Ethnic Groups**

	YEAR			YEAR	
	1932 (N = 100)	1950 (N = 333)		1932 (N = 100)	1950 (N = 333)
Americans			**Germans**		
Industrious	48	30	Scientifically minded	78	62
Intelligent	47	32	Industrious	65	50
Materialistic	33	37	Stolid	44	10
Ambitious	33	21	Intelligent	32	32
Progressive	27	5	Methodical	31	20
English			**Japanese**		
Sportsmanlike	53	21	Intelligent	45	11
Intelligent	46	29	Industrious	43	12
Conventional	34	25	Progressive	24	2
Tradition-loving	31	42	Shrewd	22	13
Conservative	30	22	Sly	20	21
Negroes			**Chinese**		
Superstitious	84	41	Superstitious	34	18
Lazy	75	31	Sly	29	4
Happy-go-lucky	38	17	Conservative	29	14
Ignorant	38	24	Tradition-loving	26	26
Musical	26	33	Loyal to family ties	22	35
Jews			**Irish**		
Shrewd	79	47	Pugnacious	45	24
Mercenary	49	28	Quick-tempered	39	35
Industrious	48	29	Witty	38	16
Grasping	34	17	Honest	32	11
Intelligent	29	37	Very religious	29	30
Italians			**Turks**		
Artistic	53	28	Cruel	47	12
Impulsive	44	19	Very religious	26	6
Passionate	37	25	Treacherous	21	3
Quick-tempered	35	15	Sensual	20	4
Musical	32	22	Ignorant	15	7

SOURCE: Reprinted by permission from G. M. Gilbert. Stereotype persistence and change among college students. *J. abnorm. soc. Psychol.*, 1951, **46**, 245–254.

that some stereotypes are definite and others are vague. Also, stereotypes in 1950 are much less definite than those in 1932, with the possible exception of stereotypes of the Germans, English, and Chinese, who are only slightly less definite in 1950. Stereotypes of the Japanese and the Turks, in particular, have become very weak. It appears that, among Princeton students at least, stereotypes have faded during the years intervening between the two studies.

Stereotypes are not confined to Princeton students. Many studies using similar procedures indicate that the general population, not only in this country but in others as well, has similar stereotypes concerning various ethnic groups. For example, one study sponsored by UNESCO

(Buchanan, 1951) carried out an opinion survey in nine countries: Holland, Italy, Australia, France, Germany, England, Mexico, and the United States. Stereotyping was prevalent in all these countries. Most agreement was obtained on the stereotype of the Russians and the Americans, but some agreement was obtained on the other countries as well.[4]

Consensus on stereotypes is only partial, even for the most definite stereotypes. That this is true even in the case of a stereotype as definite as that of the Negro may be illustrated by some unpublished data collected by the writers and shown in Table 2–2. Subjects differ even in assigning the *physical* attributes judged to be characteristic of the race. Thus, while 94 percent of a group of eighty-four students say that dark skin is *very characteristic* of Negroes, 6 percent say that it is only *somewhat characteristic*. With respect to the attribute "wide nose," 71 percent say it is *very characteristic*, but 27 percent say it is only *somewhat characteristic*. Much more variation occurs, of course, in the personality traits ascribed to Negroes. No personality trait is considered *very characteristic* by as many as 50 percent of the subjects.

Particularly notable is the point that identifying attributes and personality traits included in the checklist but *not* believed by the experimenter to belong to the stereotype were checked in every instance by at least a small minority of the judges as *very characteristic* of Negroes. Thus, with considerable justification, we may speak of a *personal stereotype* as characterizing a single individual's opinions and a *social stereotype* as representing the consensus of the majority of a given population of judges.

Discrepancy between attributed and actual traits

Almost always, stereotypes are thought of as at least partly false. A stereotype may be false in the sense that the traits attributed are an oversimplification of the true characteristics of the stereotyped individuals, or the traits may have little basis in fact. In one sense, it would seem that the inaccuracy of a social stereotype follows from one of the elements of its definition — namely, that all persons in a given class possess the traits assigned to that class. Since individuals universally vary in the kinds of traits which make up a social stereotype, it is obvious that the stereotype traits do not apply in the same degree to each member of the class. If a perceiver makes known what traits he believes are possessed by the *average* member of a class of persons, and at the same time recognizes the existence of individual differences, there is nothing necessarily inaccurate about his judgments. On the other hand, if he attributes exactly the same characteristics to each *individual* member of the class, his stereotype is necessarily a departure from reality.

Much misunderstanding of stereotypes has occurred because of failure to distinguish between statements about a class of persons in the abstract and perceptions of persons whom one knows and interacts with.

[4]Some other studies showing the universality of stereotyping include Vinacke (1949), Prothro (1954), Prothro and Melikian (1954, 1955), Jahoda (1959), Sinha and Upadhyaya (1960*a*, 1960*b*).

Table 2-2
Identifying Attributes and Trait Characteristics of the Negro Stereotype

IDENTIFYING ATTRIBUTE	RESPONSES (IN PERCENT*)			PERSONALITY TRAIT	RESPONSES (IN PERCENT*)		
	Very characteristic	Somewhat characteristic	Not characteristic		Very characteristic	Somewhat characteristic	Not characteristic
Curly hair	96	2	1	Deeply religious	46	48	6
Dark skin	94	6	0	Superstitious	33	52	14
Thick lips	87	13	0	Happy-go-lucky	26	50	24
Wide nose	71	27	1	Stubborn†	21	49	30
Low eyebrows†	14	51	34	Patient†	18	52	30
Protruding eyes†	13	49	38	Lazy	15	54	31
Prominent cheekbones†	14	44	42	Boastful†	23	36	42
Small ears	11	48	42	Moody†	12	54	34

*Percentages are based on an N of 84.

†These traits were included in the list but were not thought to belong to the Negro stereotype.

When provided only with an ethnic identification and no other information, as in most studies of stereotyping, the perceiver is *forced* to ignore individual differences and to respond to the group as a class of persons. This is illustrated by a study (Hartley, 1946) where three fictitious national groups were invented and college students were asked to rate these "Danerians," "Pirenians," and "Wallonians," along with thirty-two other known ethnic groups. Many of them showed no hesitation in rating these groups, and they generally assigned unfavorable traits. Another study (Bruner & Perlmutter, 1957) suggests that when objects differ in only one characteristic, such as ethnic identification, differences associated with that one characteristic are exaggerated.

That a person readily assigns traits to a class of persons does not mean that he will do so to the same degree when confronted with individual representatives of that class in face-to-face relations. In the latter situation, the perceiver is confronted with many differences among individuals besides ethnic identification. Moreover, interaction between the stimulus person and the perceiver often is a prominent factor affecting how the stimulus person is perceived, so that interaction diminishes categorical responses. The effects of forcing a perceiver to attribute the same characteristics to all members of a group may be illustrated by contrasting this procedure with one that permitted the judge to recognize subgroups within an ethnic group (Bayton, McAlister, & Hamer, 1956). When judges were asked to characterize "upper-class Negroes" and "lower-class Negroes," they were found to stereotype only the lower-class Negroes.

There is another side to this issue, however. The request to respond to ethnic identification alone does not force *consensus* among perceivers. Consensus reveals that social forces are shaping the perceptions of a class of persons in a given direction. One might say with considerable justification that a stereotype exists if there is marked consensus among judges on the traits assigned to a person category. Moreover, as has been stressed previously, there are many situations in everyday life where we respond to others mainly in terms of their group identification rather than reacting to them as individual persons. For most college students, for example, there are certain remote figures on the campus with whom they have little direct experience. Frequently students may have stereotyped conceptions of them. Among such figures are the university president, certain deans and professors, campus policemen, and building janitors.

STEREOTYPING AND PREJUDICE

Stereotypes need not consist wholly of unfavorable attributes. Many stereotypes are a composite of favorable and unfavorable traits, and some are predominantly favorable. Thus the question may be raised concerning whether prejudice toward a group results in the stereotyped assignment of unfavorable traits to that group. The previously mentioned UNESCO study of nine nations did demonstrate a relation between the "feeling of friendliness" toward a country and the extent to which the stereotype of that country contained favorable traits. The greater the feeling of friendliness toward a country, the more favorable were the traits in the stereotype, and the more negative the feeling, the more unfavorable attributes the stereotype contained. But even the country toward which feelings were extremely negative (Russia) was assigned certain favorable adjectives, such as "hardworking," "brave," and "progressive." Thus a stereotype does not simply consist of the assignment of a set of attributes to a category of persons on the basis of consistency with a positive or negative feeling toward that person category.

This point has received further support in another study (Secord, 1959) showing that, in evaluating photographs of Negroes, judges prejudiced against Negroes did not assign unfavorable traits in greater degree than neutral judges, provided these traits were not part of the stereotype. Prejudiced judges, moreover, assigned *favorable* traits in greater degree than neutral judges if the traits were part of the stereotype.

STUDY QUESTIONS

13. *Under what conditions is stereotyping likely to play a major role in perceiving the other person?*

14. *State and explain the three major characteristics of the social stereotype.*

15. *Discuss the problems involved in characterizing stereotypes as false or true. How does consensus on particular stereotypes relate to this question?*

16. *Explain what is meant by the following statement: "Membership in a category is sufficient to evoke the judgment that the stimulus person possesses all the attributes belonging to that category." Cite some evidence in support of this statement.*

17. *Criticize the following statement: "Stereotyping is simply the assignment of attributes or traits to a class of persons in accordance with the favorableness or unfavorableness of the attitude that one holds toward that class." Cite some experimental evidence in support of your criticism.*

ORIGINS OF STEREOTYPES AND FACTORS IN CHANGE

The processes by which stereotypes arise and undergo change will be discussed in Chapter 13 on Intergroup Relations. In addition, the general processes that shape the attitudes, thoughts, and feelings of the child, which are discussed in Chapters 17, 18, and 19, have some relevance to the development of stereotypes.

SUMMARY: THE SOCIAL STEREOTYPE

Stereotyping has three characteristics: (1) Persons are categorized according to certain identifying attributes; (2) perceivers agree on the attributes that the persons in the category possess; (3) A discrepancy exists between attributed traits and actual traits. To some extent, the inaccuracy of a social stereotype follows from one of the elements of its definition; namely, that all persons in a given class possess the traits assigned to that class. When a perceiver is provided with nothing more than an ethnic identification of a person, he is forced to ignore individual differences in making a judgment about him. For most familiar minority groups, however, consensus among perceivers is very much above the level that would be achieved if traits were chosen at random. Some stereotypes are more definite than others, judging by the varying amounts of consensus.

Stereotyping is not simply the assignment of favorable or unfavorable traits to a class of persons as a function of whether the perceiver has a positive or negative attitude toward the category. While those perceivers who are prejudiced against a class of persons may stereotype them in greater degree, this is evidenced in the assignment of both unfavorable and *favorable* traits. At the same time, under some circumstances negative feeling is associated with the assignment of a high proportion of unfavorable traits.

The Perceiver in Person Perception

The treatment of person perception to this point has dealt largely with a variety of principles characterizing the perceptions of all perceivers, without regard to individual differences among perceivers. This section will consider the problem of differences among individuals in the way they perceive others. Although a number of investigators have explored this topic, considerable research needs to be carried out before a systematic explanation of the role of the perceiver in person perception can be given. The present discussion, therefore, is largely tentative and speculative.

MODES OF PERCEIVING OTHER PERSONS

Earlier in this chapter we suggested that as children develop, their perceptions of others become increasingly complex, and further, that adults vary in the complexity of their perceptions of other persons. This complexity might take a number of forms, such as the ability to attribute contradictory traits to another person, or the number of dimensions or concepts used in describing others. Several lines of research pertain to this topic.

Concreteness – abstractness

The most sophisticated view of how individuals vary in their conceptualizations of their world and the persons in it has been expressed by Harvey, Hunt, and Schroder (1961). A major dimension in their system is *concreteness-abstractness*. Greater concreteness in a person is represented in many ways, some of which are the following: He makes more extreme distinctions: good-bad, right-wrong, black-white, etc.; he depends more on authority, precedent, and other extrapersonal sources as guidelines for action; he is intolerant of ambiguous situations; he has a low capacity to act "as if," to take the role of the other person. The more abstract person behaves in the opposite of these ways. Later, in Chapter 18, we will discuss the developmental experiences that produce variations in concreteness-abstractness. Here, several person-perception studies that seem relevant to this dimension will be described, although they were not originally formulated in terms of it. Gollin and Rosenberg (1956) asked whether or not persons who usually integrate diverse behavior elements of a stimulus person into a relatively congruous description also show this capacity for nonperson stimuli, particularly in a concept-formation task. First, the ability of the subjects to group diverse words under a single conception was tested. This was done by presenting ten words to the subjects: Buddhism, capitalism, Catholicism, Christianity, communism, democracy, fascism, Judaism, Protestantism, and socialism. Five of these are religious terms and five are political-economic terms. The subjects then wrote a paragraph showing how the terms might be related. These paragraphs were rated on the degree to which the subject had integrated these terms under the appropriate subconcepts and also on the extent to which an overall term, such as *social institutions* or *methods of group control,* covering all ten of the words had been used.

Next, a film was presented depicting a young woman who behaved in two incongruous ways, one set of actions representing a theme of kindness, and the other, promiscuity. Subjects wrote out their impressions of the young woman. In general, those who managed to relate the themes of kindness and promiscuity in describing the girl also used integrating terms on the concept-formation task; and conversely, many subjects who did not use integrative concepts for the ten words did not use them in describing the young woman. These results suggest that the extent to which a person is integrative in the way he handles concepts includes both nonperson and person concepts.

Another investigation (Bieri, 1955) attempted to measure the "cognitive complexity" involved in an individual's perceptions of others. Taking three persons at a time from the subject's environment, he was asked to indicate the way in which two of them were alike and different from the third. By repeating this process over and over for different combinations of persons, he provided a matrix of judgments that could be analyzed statistically to determine whether he used many dimensions or few in making these distinctions among persons. The investigator found that perceivers varied markedly in the complexity or simplicity of their judgments and that this variation was directly associated with the accuracy of their perceptions and inversely associated with their tendency to assume that other persons were similar to themselves.

A recent study has shown that cognitive complexity in a perceiver, assessed in the manner just described, is associated with the ability of a perceiver to attribute traits having opposite values to the same person (Mayo & Crockett, 1964). In a tape recording, different speakers described a person as possessing the positive traits *considerate, intelligent, humorous,* and *well-liked,* and the negative traits *immature, bad-tempered, dishonest,* and *sarcastic.* The impression of the stimulus person formed by perceivers low in complexity was dominated by the traits presented last (which were negative for some groups and positive for others), but perceivers high in complexity achieved an ambivalent impression, making use of both positive and negative traits.

Finally, an unpublished study has shown that where individuals have formed impressions of two different persons from a set of adjectives having opposite meanings, the more abstract individuals are better able to later integrate these into an impression of a single person when instructed to do so (Harvey & Schroder, 1963, p. 117).

STUDY QUESTION

18. *What is meant by the dimension of concreteness-abstractness as a characteristic of persons? In what ways has this characteristic of perceivers been related to person perception?*

Implicit personality theory

Another general question pertaining to perceptual modes is whether or not a perceiver has certain biases in his perception of others. All of us are familiar with the "perpetual grouch," who has little good to say about any person or even most events. The "trusting soul" is another person who should show bias in his perception of others. In comparison with other perceivers, he should rate persons higher in honesty, sincerity, and similar traits. The idea that perceivers generally have a relatively fixed set of biases in judging others has been referred to as the *implicit personality theory* of the perceiver (Bruner & Tagiuri, 1954). That is, without realizing it, the perceiver has a "theory" about what other people are like, and this "theory" influences his judgments.

An important study (Gross, 1961) has directly tested the notion of implicit personality theory. College students rated various traits for fifteen men and fifteen women ranging in age from twenty to forty years and differing widely in superficial characteristics. Each was shown in a thirty-second film. These data were subjected to an intensive statistical analysis in order to learn whether or not the ratings showed consistent bias on the part of the individual perceiver. For example, a tendency to rate stimulus persons consistently higher (or lower) on a trait than other perceivers do would be identified by this analysis as a form of bias. While some evidence was found suggesting that subjects did have systematic biases, such biases were extremely slight. Variations in the stimulus materials themselves influenced the judges' ratings to an overwhelming extent, compared with the biases of the perceivers. With this kind of stimulus material, then, response bias in the form of deviant averages for certain traits and certain perceivers is not very evident. The possibility remains that somewhat more complex stimulus objects might yield larger biases.

Another form of bias is that individual perceivers might associate certain traits with one another. For example, an individual might believe, through his experience, that a person who is friendly is also honest. Other perceivers might associate different traits. In other words, the ratings made by each perceiver would show certain correlations among the traits rated, regardless of who he is rating. A recent study (Koltuv,

1962) has demonstrated that such correlation patterns do characterize trait ratings of individual perceivers. Correlations were greater for ratings of closer acquaintances and for traits that a perceiver considered important in his thinking about other persons.

In another investigation (Secord & Berscheid, 1963), hypothetical persons were characterized in terms of a number of cue traits on two occasions, once in which they were described as Negroes and once as whites. Perceivers were then given a list of other traits and asked to estimate the probability that these persons were likely to have each of these traits. Statistical analyses of the traits belonging to each perceiver's personal stereotype of Negroes demonstrated that the traits on the list retained the same probability relation to the cue traits, whether the stimulus person was Negro or white and whether the perceiver was prejudiced or not. This finding demonstrates that relations among traits are a vital element in the perception of other persons and that these relations are relatively fixed for widely different stimulus persons as well as for perceivers having markedly different feelings toward the stimulus persons.

Another aspect of implicit personality theory that has been little studied, but that might well be an extremely important difference among perceivers, lies in the dimensions they use to describe other persons (Hastorf, Richardson, & Dornbusch, 1958). All too often, studies in person perception require the subject to use dimensions provided by the experimenter. Such a procedure prevents the investigator from obtaining knowledge of what dimensions the perceiver uses when left to his own devices, as he is outside the laboratory. One study (Richardson, Hastorf, & Dornbusch, 1960) of ten- and eleven-year-old children, who were asked in an interview to describe other children they knew, illustrates the point. Interviews were coded to determine the frequency of usage of the various descriptive categories. The main conclusions were that (1) perceivers consistently differed from each other in the categories they used in describing others, (2) some shifts in category use occurred as the same perceiver described different persons, and (3) some perceivers shifted more than others when describing different persons.

A somewhat different way of showing differences in use of dimensions in describing others is shown in two other studies. In one investigation of such perceiver differences (Rommetveit, 1960), subjects ranked hypothetical persons as potential friends. These stimulus persons were presented by showing their picture and a report of an interview supposedly conducted with them. Stimulus information was presented for each person suggesting that he was either high or low on each of three traits: intelligence, honesty, and looks. Thus materials on eight hypothetical persons having various combinations of these three traits were available. For example, one person was depicted as intelligent, honest, and good-looking and another as unintelligent, dishonest, and not good-looking. Other persons possessed one or two of these traits and lacked the remaining ones. Subjects ranked these stimulus persons according to how much they would like them as friends.

By examining the association between these friendship rankings and the presence or absence of each of the traits suggested by the stimulus material, it was possible to determine whether a person was especially oriented toward any one or more of the three traits. For example, if a perceiver was highly oriented toward whether or not a person was honest, and if he had no interest in the other traits, he would prefer as friends those stimulus persons depicted as high in honesty and would therefore rank them 1 to 4. He would rank those depicted as dishonest 5 to 8. As anticipated, preference ranks differed for different perceivers in a manner suggesting that they placed differing emphases on intelligence, honesty, and good looks.

Subjects also made judgments of the degree of similarity among the eight stimulus persons (Rommetveit & Svalheim, 1959). They were presented with three stimulus persons at a time and asked to state which two were most similar and most different from the third.[5] Again, if a trait was central for a perceiver, he was expected to be influenced most strongly by it in assessing similarity among other persons. An analysis of the rankings supported the idea that perceivers making similarity judgments of others vary in the emphasis they place on traits of others.

Another way of looking at differing emphases on traits by different perceivers is related to the intraserial effect, discussed in Chapter 1. There the intraserial effect was described as the tendency, when judging a series of stimuli, to overestimate the largest stimulus objects and underestimate the smallest ones. This occurred only when the objects were valued by the perceiver. More generally, this phenomenon may be described as a tendency to emphasize the extremes of a scale or continuum when the dimension in question is important to the perceiver. Tajfel and Wilkes (1964) tested this interpretation in a person perception study. Allowing college students to describe photographs of young men in their own words, they assumed that descriptive terms mentioned early and frequently would be most important to the perceiver. Each perceiver later rated another set of photographs on four descriptive terms highly important to him, and four unimportant to him, as selected by the experimenter from the free descriptions of each perceiver. They found that perceivers gave more extreme ratings to the important traits, confirming the hypothesized relation between the value of a dimension and emphasis on its extremes.

One of the reasons for the sparsity of research on implicit personality theory is the inadequacy of methodologies commonly employed in evaluating persons. A recent report (Jackson & Messick, 1963) has noted the inadequacies of these procedures and has suggested some new methods for evaluating a stimulus person that make adequate provision for variations in the dimensions used by perceivers. Applying these procedures, the investigators had judges rate the similarity or dissimilarity of various well-known political figures. They were able to demonstrate that one type of judge was apt to evaluate politicians along a single good-bad dimension, another type used a good-bad dimension but also a Republican-Demo-

---

[5]This is an adaptation of a procedure introduced by Kelly (1955).

cratic distinction, and a third type made many subtle distinctions, presumably reflecting a complex set of dimensions.

Accuracy in person perception

Throughout this chapter, little emphasis has been placed on whether person perception is accurate or not. We might expect, for example, that some persons are better judges of people than others. Also, we should be interested in how much discrepancy there is between an impression of a person formed under various conditions and what he is really like. Unfortunately, the assessment of accuracy has raised such difficult methodological problems that the definitive research necessary to provide conclusive answers to these questions has not yet been carried out (Gage & Cronbach, 1955; Cronbach, 1955, 1958; Altrocchi & Shrauger, 1964).

STUDY QUESTIONS

19. *What is meant by the concept of implicit personality theory? Describe the ways in which the implicit personality theory of one perceiver might differ from that of another.*

20. *What experimental evidence is there for and against the concept of implicit personality theory?*

PERCEIVER CHARACTERISTICS AND PERSON PERCEPTION

Attempts have been made to relate perceptions of persons to specific traits possessed by the perceiver. An examination of a few of these studies will indicate, however, that there is no simple relation between perceiver traits and how the other person is perceived. A number of studies have shown that the person perceptions vary systematically with the age and sex of the perceiver. In one study (Kohn & Fiedler, 1961), subjects rated their favorite teacher, father, mother, best male friend, best female friend, and a younger sibling on 6-point trait scales. The hypothesis that older persons would vary more in describing different stimulus persons than younger perceivers was supported for the several adult stimulus persons. In other words, the older the perceiver, the more differently he rated his father, mother, and teacher. Male and female perceivers also differed consistently in their perceptions of the various persons. Females perceived the several adult figures in a less differentiated and more favorable manner than did males. The investigators suggest that perhaps women, to a greater degree than men, use stereotyping in describing others, and that perhaps this is consistent with the common belief that women react "intuitively" to others and are not able to find logical reasons for their personality impressions. Other studies of the effects of age and sex of the perceiver support these findings in some respects.[6]

Various investigations have attempted to show that person percep-

---

[6]Secord & Muthard, 1955*a*; Wertheimer, 1960; Beach & Wertheimer, 1961; Fiedler & Hoffman, 1962.

tions are affected by the "authoritarian" traits of the perceiver. Intensive studies (Adorno et al., 1950) have identified a syndrome[7] of traits representing what psychologists term the *authoritarian personality.* An individual of this type rigidly adheres to conventional middle-class values and has an exaggerated concern with such values, is submissive toward the moral authorities of his ingroup, condemns and rejects people who violate conventional values, is preoccupied with power and status considerations, tends to identify with powerful figures, and is generally hostile toward members of outgroups. These traits are thought of as belonging together. A person high in some of them tends to be high in the remaining ones, and similarly, a person average in some of them tends to be average in the remaining ones, etc.

Several investigations (Scodel & Mussen, 1953; Scodel & Freedman, 1956; Crockett & Meidinger, 1956) placed subjects in two-person groups for approximately a twenty-minute period, instructing them to discuss with each other the topics of radio, television, and the movies. This was done in order to provide each subject with stimulus information about the other person. In some instances, two persons high in authoritarianism were paired, in others, two persons low in authoritarianism, and finally, pairs consisting of one high-authoritarian person and one low. The investigators were interested in the impressions formed of the other person in the dyad and wanted to find out how these would vary with the subject's own authoritarian traits. After completing the discussion period, the subject filled out a questionnaire as he thought the other person would fill it out. Items on the questionnaire were from the F scale, which is used for assessing the extent to which a person possesses authoritarian traits. In later studies (Jones, 1954; Kates, 1959; Lipetz, 1960), instead of having the subject actually interact with another subject, recordings of mock interviews with high- and low-authoritarian persons were presented. The latter technique has the advantage of presenting more precisely controlled and structured stimulus information to the subject. The results of these various studies are consistent with the following generalizations:

1. The perceiver usually assumes that the other person is a peer; that is, he is not thought of as having any especially significant characteristics that might set him apart from others.

2. The high-authoritarian perceivers assume that the other person has values like their own, and consequently they place him high on most of the authoritarian traits.

3. The low-authoritarian persons do not rate the other person as low authoritarian but usually rate him as average on authoritarian traits.

These results provide adequate evidence to the effect that the perceiver's own characteristics will affect the manner in which he perceives others. Such perceptions would presumably be quite different, however,

---

[7]A *syndrome* is a cluster of characteristics believed to be associated in the same person and to have a common basis.

if the perceiver did not regard the other person as belonging to the in-group. Moreover, these findings are subject to various interpretations. Several investigators (Scodel & Mussen, 1953; Scodel & Freedman, 1956; Lipetz, 1960) interpret them as supporting the view that the low-authoritarian perceiver perceives others more accurately (the high authoritarian even evaluates lows as high). Others (Crockett & Meidinger, 1956; Rabinowitz, 1956) have suggested that the high and the low authoritarians are simply reflecting their experience with other persons in everyday life and are little influenced by the stimulus information. This view is based on the assumption that the high authoritarian will mostly associate with others like himself, but the low authoritarian will frequently encounter persons having high-authoritarian traits. Thus, each could be regarded as making a kind of probability judgment about the traits of a complete stranger.

This explanation is made especially plausible by a study (Rabinowitz, 1956) in which subjects were given no stimulus materials but were asked to estimate how the "typical college student" would respond to F-scale items. Results closely parallel those of the previously cited investigations using stimulus materials.

Self- and person perception

Many studies have presented data showing that perceivers assume persons they like to be more similar to themselves than persons toward whom they feel neutral or whom they dislike,[8] although a few studies (Altrocchi, 1959; Rodgers, 1959) fail to support this notion. That is, when asked to describe themselves and, on another occasion, to describe their friends, persons are likely to assign many of the same traits to their friends that they assign to themselves. The degree to which such similarity is assumed and the significance of this phenomenon is somewhat obscured by certain complicated methodological problems encountered in collecting and interpreting such data (Cronbach, 1955; 1958). Just one such problem will be illustrated here.

Descriptive traits vary in social desirability. Most persons in our society consider such traits as intelligence and honesty to be highly desirable, and others, like shyness and hostility, to be highly undesirable. If we assume that persons like and approve of themselves, then they should assign desirable traits to themselves as well as to their friends and should avoid assigning undesirable ones either to themselves or to their friends. This in itself would produce similarities in ratings of self and friend—similarities that stem not from the specific content or nature of the trait, but simply from its desirable quality. Thus, assumed similarity between self and friend would have quite a restricted meaning if it were only due to the social desirability of traits.

[8]Fiedler, Blaisdell, & Warrington, 1952; Lundy et al., 1955; Lundy, 1956a, 1956b; Smith, 1957; Alfert, 1958; Morton, 1959; Vroom, 1959; Kipnis, 1961; Newcomb, 1961; Broxton, 1963.

An analysis of several types of self-friend data by the writers has indicated, however, that even after the effects of social desirability are controlled or corrected for, assumed similarity occurs to a greater extent than would be expected by chance (Secord, 1964). These data included a study of the attribution of undesirable traits to self and to friend and demonstrated clearly that individuals are more likely to attribute to their friends the undesirable traits that they believe they themselves possess, although they do not attribute these traits to persons whom they dislike.

Two other studies are also quite convincing demonstrations of assumed similarity. Both involve experimental manipulation of the self concepts of the subjects by providing them with false reports of personality tests they had taken. One of these investigations (Bramel, 1962), led subjects to believe that they had latent homosexual tendencies. Subsequently, they attributed homosexuality to the experimental partner. The other study (Secord, Backman, & Eachus, 1964), dealing with fifteen different traits, demonstrated that those traits changed in self were changed, in the same direction, in one's best friend. On the whole, although there are pitfalls in interpreting any single study, it appears that in general, assumed similarity between self and friend is a genuine phenomenon not explainable solely by the tendency to endorse socially desirable items.

STUDY QUESTIONS

21. *Explain how perceivers may differ in the emphasis they place on various traits in describing other persons.*

22. *What relations have been found between perceiver traits and the perception of other persons?*

23. *To what extent is person perception affected by the individual's concept of himself?*

SUMMARY: THE PERCEIVER IN PERSON PERCEPTION

This section has emphasized individual differences among perceivers in their perceptions of other persons. Very probably the cognitive structure and processes that characterize a perceiver are also related to the way in which he perceives other persons. One example was given of this: Perceivers capable of subsuming diverse concepts under a single broad term were also found to be able to see the diverse traits of a person as congruous with each other. Another question raised was whether perceivers have their own implicit personality theories about the nature of other persons. Although little tendency was found to rate persons consistently higher (or lower) on particular traits, perceivers did appear to have definite ideas about traits that go together in other persons. These traits seemed to be consistently associated for widely different stimulus persons and for perceivers having positive or negative feelings toward them.

Evidence was also presented demonstrating that different perceivers emphasize different traits in describing other persons. A study of children indicated that they use somewhat different categories from each other and that they differ from each other in the way they use these categories when describing different persons. When a stimulus person is rated on a trait that is especially important to a perceiver, he is more likely to use the extremes of the scale. Perceptions of stimulus persons have also been shown to vary with the age and sex of the perceiver. One aspect of personality widely investigated is the authoritarian personality. The following generalizations on this characteristic were drawn: Authoritarians assume stimulus persons to be peers, to have values like their own, and to be high on authoritarian traits. Those low in authoritarianism do not make this assumption or rate stimulus persons in this fashion. Another general finding is that persons assume that those they like are similar to themselves. While this could be due in part to the assignment of socially desirable traits to self and others, analyses have shown that assumed similarity occurs even when social desirability is controlled.

Perception in Ongoing Interaction

In person perception in face-to-face relations where the stimulus person has frequently engaged in interaction with the perceiver, a great many factors must be taken into account. Unlike inanimate objects, persons are engaged in continuous activity and are seen performing different actions in different situations. The perceiver must grasp extended temporal sequences and reduce these to some kind of order. The actions of other persons, moreover, have effects upon the perceiver. Here the task confronting him is vastly different from that discussed so far, where judgments were made from a photograph or from a few traits describing a hypothetical person. In a face-to-face relation, the perceiver is confronted with an overload of information which somehow has to be processed and reduced to manageable size. Certain general processing systems for perceiving others may therefore develop. Although no systematic program of empirical research has been conducted on the topic, it seems clear that perceivers exhibit certain "economizing processes" that make the perceptual task more manageable. These are discussed in the following section.

ECONOMIZING PROCESSES IN PERSON PERCEPTION

The adequate perception of nonsocial objects requires that the perceiver respond to *invariances* in his environment. For example, an object seen under varying degrees of illumination reflects differing amounts of light, but nevertheless is usually perceived as having a constant brightness. A white shirt looks white, not gray, even in dim illumination. This "brightness constancy" is experienced only because the perceiver is able to respond to an invariant aspect of the stimulus. In this instance it is the fact that any surface reflects a *constant proportion* of the light which falls on it. Whether in dim or bright illumination, a given surface may reflect, say, 40 percent of the light which illumines it. Such invariances characterizing many aspects of the stimulus field enable us to perceive our physical environment adequately.

Thus, it is only one step further to the assumption that the individual responds to invariances in perceiving the *social* environment. In person perception, the problem presented by the fluid, constantly changing, complex stimulus field may lead the perceiver to ignore certain of its important aspects and to exaggerate its stability. This would simplify the perceptual process, although it would also produce certain biases or misperceptions.

One of the most fundamental biases in person perception is that other individuals tend to be seen as constant, unchanging entities. Although in reality, an individual is never exactly the same person at any two moments in time, and in some instances is markedly different, he is usually seen as an enduring entity. He is the same person this week as he was last week; he is the same person even when behaving very differently in different situations. This is obviously an economy; it eliminates the necessity for perceiving behaviors of the other which deviate from his assumed character. This bias may be recognized as a form of temporal extension, discussed earlier in this chapter.

A second form of bias is the *tendency to see persons as origins of actions* (Heider, 1958*a*). It is simpler to interpret a hostile act as a natural expression of a malevolent person than to understand the situational and circumstantial factors that led him to commit the act. The average man exaggerates the role of the person as causal agent. Thus he fails to see the situational factors contributing to neurotic behavior; or he sees the businessman as having made a fortune by virtue of some special personal characteristic, overlooking the contribution of the economic system or certain fortuitous factors contributing to his success.

A third form of bias is the tendency to organize our perceptions of other persons around an *evaluative* factor. Other persons are reacted to negatively or positively; moreover, we are likely to see *all* properties belonging to the same individual as positive or all as negative (Heider, 1958*b*). This is the most common way of achieving congruous perceptions of others in terms of the simpler perceptual modes referred to earlier. This general tendency is expressed on rating scales as the familiar "halo effect": in various statistical analyses of ratings, the evaluative factor is nearly always a dominant one (Osgood, Suci, & Tannenbaum, 1957).

Finally, the process of categorization, mentioned previously, achieves a tremendous economy in apprehending others. We no longer need attend to the unique aspects of each individual person; instead we place him in a category along with many others. Placement of an individual in a person category involves attributing to him all the characteristics that belong to that group. Categorization involves two steps: (1) learning the identifying characteristics associated with a class of persons, and (2) learning the attributes associated with that class. Thus, the American child exposed to prejudice learns that persons with dark skins and thick lips are Negroes, and that Negroes are lazy, superstitious, happy-go-lucky, etc. The simplification achieved by such "coding" procedures is obvious; instead of observing complex behavior sequences, the perceiver may simply note skin color in order to arrive at conclusions concerning the attributes of the other person.

STUDY QUESTIONS

24. *Contrast person perception under limited conditions with person perception in everyday face-to-face relations.*
25. *Explain what is meant by the statement that the "perceiver responds to invariances in his environment."*
26. *Explain the four forms of biases or "economizing processes" that simplify the task of the perceiver in face-to-face relations.*

EFFECTS OF STRUCTURE ON PERCEPTION

In the case of someone with whom we frequently interact, a structured relation develops, and perception of the other person must be examined within this context. For example, the student has a special relation to such persons as his mother, his teacher, and his roommate, a relation that colors and shapes his perception of them. These relations have several structural aspects that affect perceptions. These include the role structure, liking or *affect* structure, and the status and power structures. Since these structures will be discussed fully in later chapters of the book, their relation to person perception will be only briefly treated here.

Effects of role

Two ideas normally associated with the role concept are that persons occupy a *position* in a relation, and that certain *expectations* are held as to the attitudes and behavior that should characterize a person in that position. Both the role occupied by the stimulus person and the role occupied by the perceiver are important. With respect to the stimulus person, our later discussion of role learning in Chapter 17 and of occupational socialization in Chapter 19 will show how, as a person occupies a new position, appropriate role expectations are applied to him. These include personal attributes appropriate to the position as well as expectations concerning behavior. For example, as they progress through medical school, medical students are increasingly perceived as having the attributes of doctors, particularly by the patients that are assigned to these students.

The importance of the role occupied by the perceiver is well illustrated by a study (Jones & deCharms, 1957) in which naval air cadets were asked to assume different roles in judging a sergeant who had admitted signing propaganda materials while a prisoner of war in Korea. Stimulus materials consisted of supposed recorded interviews with him. Role assumed by the perceivers were those of a psychologist, a member of a court of inquiry, and a soldier like the sergeant. The role assumed markedly affected the traits that were attributed to the stimulus person.

Liking

Liking for other persons is relevant to person perception in two senses. First, like or dislike for others has certain effects on the perceptions of those persons. Second, liking is itself a way of perceiving other persons. This section deals with the effects of well-established patterns of like and dislike on person perception; in other words, with liking as a structured aspect of the relation. Liking as a perceptual effect will receive some attention in a later section.

Well-established feelings of liking for another person affect the way he is perceived. The perceiver is more likely to attribute favorable traits to him and to avoid assigning him unfavorable traits. A person who is disliked is likely to have more unfavorable traits attributed to him and fewer favorable ones (Pastore, 1960*a*; 1960*b*). In an earlier discussion, we also noted that liking a person is associated with the assumption that he is similar to oneself. This is a correlational finding in which it is difficult to demonstrate whether liking or the assumption of similarity comes first. It seems probable, however, that each of these variables has the potential of bringing about the other, so that cause-effect relations may be two-way. Also demonstrated is that when we like another person, we assume that he likes us (Tagiuri, 1958), and perceiving another as liking us has been shown to cause us to like him (Backman & Secord, 1959).

Status and power

Two other aspects of structured relations that may be singled out are status and power. Where the statuses and relative powers of perceiver and perceived are markedly different, certain consequences for person perception evolve. Certain characteristic, rather undesirable traits are often attributed to the high-status, high-power stimulus person. This process appears to stem from fears and insecurities that the perceiver experiences. Thus a high-status person, such as one's foreman or supervisor, may be seen as arbitrary, capricious, or, on occasion, even malevolent, especially if he has performed some action detrimental to the perceiver. On the other hand, a high-status person performing some benevolent action may well be liked to a greater extent than if he were of equal status with the perceiver (Pepitone, 1958).

Some interesting interactions between status characteristics of the stimulus person and authoritarian characteristics of the perceiver have been demonstrated. Individuals in two-person groups who were confederates of the experimenter behaved in an irritating manner calculated to arouse hostility in the perceiver. Those persons high in authoritarianism were less rejecting of the high-status stimulus person and more rejecting of the low-status person than were individuals low in authoritarianism.

Often in everyday situations we encounter circumstances where another person behaves so as to increase or decrease our power and status. For example, another person might be instrumental in getting us promoted or in electing us to a position of power. The effects of this kind of action on our perception of him, particularly on our liking or disliking, have been studied experimentally (Horwitz, 1958). The following results have been obtained: (1) When *O* was perceived as reducing *S*'s power, *S* felt less attracted toward *O* or developed hostility toward him; (2) when *O* was perceived as enhancing *S*'s power, *S* felt more attracted toward *O*. Also, the effects of such shifts in power are not necessarily directly expressed in one's conscious feeling of like or dislike; they may be expressed in a number of other ways.

STUDY QUESTION

27. *Show how each of the following may affect perception: (a) role relations between perceiver and perceived, (b) positive or negative feeling toward the stimulus person, and (c) a differential status or power relation between perceiver and perceived.*

LOCUS OF CAUSE

In everyday situations, a perceiver usually interprets the behavior of another person in terms of the context of their interaction. Most of the experimentation discussed to this point has ignored interactional contexts. In ongoing interaction, however, these contexts are especially important. One of the most general contexts applying to many situations is *locus of cause.* Another person may be seen as responsible for a given action, or his action may be perceived as caused by the situation or an external agency. Intimately related to this idea are such notions as whether or not a person performs an action intentionally and whether or not an action performed by another is "justified." The effects on person perception of these various assumptions made by the perceiver have been studied experimentally.

In one experiment (Jones & deCharms, 1958), a problem-solving situation was arranged so that the perceiver was deprived of a reward as a result of the actions of the stimulus person. Under the special circumstance where the stimulus person was seen as failing the problem due to lack of effort and thus depriving the perceiver of a reward, the stimulus person was evaluated less favorably on a variety of traits. This is a situation where the "cause" of deprivation is seen as lying in the stimulus person — he didn't try to solve the problem, though he could have. In another condition, where he was perceived as unable to solve the problem even if he tried, he was *not* evaluated unfavorably. Here the "cause" is seen as external to the stimulus person.

Another experimental situation (Thibaut & Riecken, 1955) involved acceptance by the stimulus person of an attempt by the perceiver to influence him. Under one condition, the stimulus person had high status and power relative to the perceiver (he was presented as a university instructor or a Harvard law student with a superior background). Under another, the stimulus person had low status (he was presented as a college freshman with an inferior background).

This situation again involves internal and external loci of cause. If a person has high status and power relative to you, he does not have to accept your attempt to influence him. If he nevertheless accepts it, you are likely to believe that he does so voluntarily because he is a "nice guy." On the other hand, if a person has an inferior status relative to yours, he may accept your influence simply because of the pressure he feels. The general hypothesis tested by this experiment, then, was that if a person seemed to accept influence of his own volition, the perceiver who influenced him would experience an increase in liking for him. If, on the other hand, the cause of his acceptance was perceived as external to him — was perceived as lying in the status relations between him and the perceiver — the perceiver would not like him more than he did before the influence attempt. This hypothesis was confirmed: a large majority of the subjects who influenced the high-status person increased their liking of him to a greater extent than those who influenced the low-status person.

In another investigation, each participant served as a supervisor of the work of two other individuals who, unknown to him, were confederates of the experimenter (Strickland, 1958). The situation was arranged so that the participant supervised the work of one confederate more closely than that of the other. In time, he came to believe that the work of the less closely supervised individual sprang from an internal cause: interest in the work. When later given an opportunity to exercise equal supervision over both confederates, he continued to maintain a closer watch over the individual he had been supervising all along, suggesting an assumption of external cause: the supervision itself.

Finally, in another experimental situation (Hastorf, 1964), an individual who talked a great deal during a group discussion was perceived as having good ideas and as the group leader by persons who heard a tape recording of the discussion. But he was not perceived as having good ideas or as a group leader by persons who heard the tape recording and who were also shown that the experimenter had rewarded this individual for talking and discouraged the other group members from making contributions to the discussion. The latter group saw his behavior as externally caused rather than springing spontaneously from his good ideas and leadership qualities. These various experiments illustrate a principle: interpreting an action of another person as having an internal or external cause leads to quite different perceptions of his action.

Although they have somewhat different shades of meaning, the responsibility and justifiability of actions may also be interpreted in terms of loci of cause. If a person is seen as the cause of an action he performs, he is assumed to be responsible for it. If his action is not within his control, he is not assumed to be responsible. An action performed because of powerful external pressures is likely to be seen as justifiable. Here the locus of cause lies outside the person. Intentionality is also related to loci of cause; here, however, both loci are often found within the person. An individual may injure another person maliciously, or he may do it by accident. In one case the cause lies in his malicious intent, in the other case it may lie in his clumsiness or inattention to what he was doing.

Pepitone (1958) has summarized a series of experiments investigating these variables. In one study (Pepitone & Sherberg, 1957), by presenting recordings of supposedly authentic conversations among students like those serving in the experiment, intentionality was varied experimentally. Subjects were asked to put themselves in the place of one of the individuals in the conversation and to judge the other as if he had behaved toward them in that way. In these "overheard" conversations, O insulted S by disparaging his intelligence. Under one condition, O had good intentions: trying to get S to study. In the other, he had bad intentions: trying to impress his instructor. The experimenters found that O was less disliked when he had good intentions than when he had bad ones. An attempt to vary responsibility in a similar fashion was unsuccessful.

Justifiability may be illustrated by common experience. The extent to which another person's actions toward you are justified has much to do with your feeling toward him. For example, you might be angry with a girl who has broken a date for no apparent reason; whereas if she has broken it because of illness, you are unlikely to feel angry. Justifiability was successfully varied in another experiment (Pepitone, 1958), and O's attractiveness to S was shown to vary with the degree of justifiability of O's actions: the more justifiable the action, the more the person was liked. In further experiments, Pepitone (1958) also investigated the conditions which govern the attribution of such variables as responsibility and intentionality to other persons. He found that the higher the status of the other person, the more likely he was to be seen as having responsibility for his actions, as possessing good intentions, and as engaging in actions which are justified.

It has also been shown that under certain circumstances, judgment of the stimulus person is related to the justifiability of the *perceiver's* actions. In an experiment (Strickland, Jones, & Smith, 1960) where the stimulus person made hostile, critical remarks about the perceiver's ideas, some perceivers were led to believe that their ideas were supported by a group of persons like themselves. Others had no such support. It was found that the perceivers having the group-supported ideas were likely to regard them as more justifiable, and likely to show more dislike toward the stimulus person because of his critical remarks, than perceivers whose ideas were unsupported.

STUDY QUESTIONS

28. *Explain what is meant by locus of cause. Show how responsibility, intentionality, and justifiability may be interpreted in terms of locus of cause.*
29. *What are the effects on the perception of a stimulus person when the stimulus person is responsible for the perceiver getting a reward? What is a necessary condition for such effects to occur?*
30. *Consider the intentionality and justifiability of a stimulus person's actions and show how they are related to his being liked or disliked.*
31. *How can the justifiability or unjustifiability of the perceiver's actions affect his perceptions of a stimulus person?*

SUMMARY: ONGOING INTERACTION

The complexity of person perception in ongoing interaction is likely to produce a number of processes that simplify the problems of the perceiver. These include the tendency to see persons as unchanging entities, the tendency to see the cause of a person's actions as lying in him rather than in the situation, the coloring of perceptions by favorable or unfavorable evaluations of the stimulus person, and the placing of persons in ready-made categories associated with sets of personal attributes.

Interaction between persons takes place within structured relations which affect how they perceive each other. Several structural aspects of relations to person perception are the role structure, the liking structure, and the status and power structures. Role relations place each participant in a role category having attributes associated with it that are likely to be applied to all persons in that role category.

Established feelings of liking for another person bias other perceptions of him in a favorable direction. Liking a person is also associated with the assumption that he is similar to oneself. When we like another person, we assume that he likes us, and perceiving another as liking us leads to liking him. Under certain circumstances persons having a higher status and more power than the perceiver are apt to be perceived unfavorably. Similarly, another person who reduces the power of a perceiver is apt to be disliked.

Of various interactional contexts that may affect person perception, one of the most important is the perceived locus of cause. Such notions as responsibility, justifiability, and intentionality can be interpreted in terms of the locus of cause of the action. In general, a benevolent action toward the perceiver which is internally caused—that is, voluntarily performed by the stimulus person—leads the perceiver to like him better. No change in liking occurs if the benevolent action is externally caused. On the other hand, a hostile action leads to disliking if it is internally caused, but the stimulus person is excused if his action is externally caused. Actions performed with good intentions lead to liking; actions with bad intentions, to disliking. Actions that deprive the perceiver have little effect if they are seen as justified; if they are seen as not justified, they lead to dislike. When the actions of a perceiver are justified, he is more likely to resent criticism of them than when they are not justified.

Summary and Conclusions

Person perception focuses on the process by which impressions, opinions, or feelings about other persons are formed. It includes subjective judgments and inferences that go beyond direct sensory information. Several modes of perceiving other persons have been identified. At one extreme, a person may be described in terms of outward appearance or superficial characteristics; at the other, his description may include traits some of which are incongruous with each other. Modes of perception are likely to vary with the perceiver. They also vary with the amount of information available concerning the stimulus person, the extent of interaction between perceiver and perceived, and the degree to which the relation between them is well established.

Many situations in everyday life provide a minimum of information about a stimulus person but often produce a clear impression of him. In laboratory investigations, perceivers have been found to process such limited information to produce a more congruous impression than is implied by the information itself. Perceivers also agree in the personal qualities they associate with verbal and nonverbal cues. Various inference techniques are used to process limited information about the stimulus person, and in a general way, these techniques account for consensus among perceivers on the qualities they attribute to stimulus persons. Inference techniques include temporal extension, assumptions based on resemblance to a familiar person, categorization of the person, and two forms of reasoning by analogy.

Stereotyping, a form of categorization, has three characteristics: (1) Persons are categorized according to certain identifying characteristics; (2) perceivers agree on the attributes that the persons in the category possess; (3) a discrepancy exists between attributed traits and actual traits. The inaccuracy of a stereotype follows in part from the context in which persons are asked to describe others: They are given only identifying information about a class of persons, which forces them to ignore differences among individuals in the class. On the other hand, the widespread consensus on the traits attributed to various stereotyped classes of persons suggests that, to some degree, people do think in stereotyped terms. Stereotyping includes the assignment of both favorable and unfavorable traits to a group; it cannot be explained solely in terms of favorable or unfavorable attitudes toward a class of persons.

Individuals vary greatly in the way they perceive other persons. To some extent, the processes by which an individual perceives other persons are related to his more general cognitive processes. Each perceiver also appears to have his own "implicit personality theory" of what other individuals are like, particularly in the way he characteristically associates traits. Perceivers emphasize different traits in describing other persons. Perceivers of different ages and sexes, as well as those varying in authoritarian traits, perceive other persons quite differently. Persons exhibit a general tendency to assume that others are similar to themselves.

Because of the complexity of person perception in ongoing inter-action, the perceiver adopts a number of processes that simplify his per-ceptions. These have been described in detail. Interaction between per-sons takes place within structured relations which affect how they perceive each other. Aspects of relations which pertain to person perception and which have been discussed here are the role structure, the liking structure, and the status and power structures. Of the various interactional contexts that may affect person perception, one of the most important is the per-ceived locus of cause. Perceptions have been shown to vary markedly depending upon whether the action of a stimulus person is seen as caused by factors internal to him or lying outside him.

PART TWO

Social Influence Processes

Part One has analyzed perceptual and other responses to specific stimulus objects, with considerable attention being given to the properties of the stimulus object that determine the response of the individual. There is need, however, for a definitive concept that deals more broadly with the behavior of the individual and that is capable of encompassing a larger portion of his environment than the stimuli ordinarily used in perceptual studies. This broader unit of analysis should combine perceptual, cognitive, and affective responses occurring over a period of time to some aspect of an individual's environment. The concept *attitude* is used for this purpose. The term refers to certain regularities in feelings, thoughts, and predispositions to act on the part of an individual toward some aspect of his environment. While an attitude might pertain to a specific object, more often rather abstract entities like foreign aid or war are the focus of interest.

Part Two is concerned with the various processes that shape and influence a person's attitudes toward aspects of his environment. Two types of influence are simultaneously treated: the effect of the mass media and face-to-face communication with other persons. These two sources of influence are inseparable aspects of a single influence process.

Chapter 3 defines the concept of attitude, describes some methods by which attitudes of individuals may be assessed, and introduces some theory pertaining to an individual's need for consistency between the affective, perceptual, and cognitive components of his attitudes.

Chapter 4 discusses the role of the communicator in the influence process, with particular attention to factors determining the extent to which he is believable and the degree to which communications from him are accepted. The relative effectiveness of various types of communications are discussed, and some attention is also given to the structure of the communication situation.

Chapter 5 considers individual differences in susceptibility to influence as well as various individual processes that are sources of resistance to attitude change. Chapter 6 points up the importance of the social structure in determining the relative effectiveness of the influence process. Whether or not an individual is successfully influenced depends in large degree upon his position in the social structure and the relation of his position to that of the communicator.

chapter three

ATTITUDE ORGANIZATION AND BEHAVIORAL CHANGE

The previous section has dealt with behaviors largely governed by stimuli that impinge upon a person from his surrounding environment. But many behaviors appear to be relatively independent of the stimulus field. Persons often react in a consistent fashion under widely varying stimulus conditions. For example, a person may vote for the Democratic candidate in election after election, regardless of the personal characteristics of the particular candidate running for office that year. Some psychological concept is needed to account for this consistent behavior of individuals toward objects in their environment. The concept of *attitude* represents one method of treating this consistency.

Nature and Measurement of Attitudes

NATURE OF ATTITUDES

The term *attitude* refers to certain regularities of an individual's feelings, thoughts, and predispositions to act toward some aspect of his environment.[1] Feelings are often referred to as the *affective* component, thoughts as the *cognitive* component, and predispositions to act as the *behavioral* component. One may hold attitudes toward concrete objects, such as Coca-Cola, or toward abstract entities, such as democratic government. Attitudes may pertain to remote, impersonal entities, such as

[1]The definition of attitude has received extended technical treatment: See Sherif & Cantril (1945); Krech & Crutchfield (1948); Katz & Stotland (1959).

foreign aid, or they may be extremely personal, such as feeling that one's nose is too big.

The three components may be illustrated by an individual's attitude toward foreign aid. (1) The affective component of the attitude is his vigorous emotional feeling against foreign aid: this component is inferred from the fact that his blood pressure rises when he reads of large appropriations for this purpose, or when he encounters someone who stoutly defends foreign aid; or it is inferred from his angry behavior when he argues with a proponent of aid. (2) The cognitive component of his attitude consists of his ideas about foreign aid: this component is inferred from what he says he believes; for example, he may say that giving money to foreign countries impoverishes Americans, that the money is mainly siphoned off in the form of graft to officials of the foreign government, and that his country will receive nothing in return. (3) The behavioral component consists of action tendencies. These are inferred from what he says he will do or what he actually does: he writes his congressman telling him to vote against foreign aid bills, he denounces aid in conversations with friends and associates, and he reads articles written by persons who are against foreign aid.

An attitude is usually thought of as a *hypothetical construct*, not directly open to observation but inferred from verbal expression or overt behavior. A hypothetical construct is "an entity or process that is inferred as actually existing . . . and as giving rise to measurable phenomena, including phenomena other than the observables that led to hypothesizing the construct" (English & English, 1958, p. 11). Attitude belongs in this category if measurements from a limited set of observations are used to make inferences about attitude which in turn give rise to predictions about behavior that has not been measured. For example, from a set of statements that a person makes about Jews, we may infer that he has a strong negative attitude toward them. From this measure of attitude and from hypotheses about the effect of attitudes on the ability to make cognitive discriminations, we might also predict that if he is given a list of people's names, he will be better able to discriminate Jewish from non-Jewish names than a person less prejudiced against Jews will. As noted in Chapter 2, however, this reasonable hypothesis was not confirmed, a fact that should lead the investigator to reexamine the logical relations between the hypothetical construct and the predicted behavior.

Brief mention should be made of a distinction commonly made between attitude and *opinion*. An opinion is a belief that one holds about some object in his environment. It differs from attitude in being relatively free of emotion—it lacks the affective component central to attitude. The cognitive component or element of knowledge is prominent in opinion: it may take the form of a factual statement about the environment. For example, a man may believe that the earth is spherical, or that women drivers are less capable than men. If to him these are matters of fact, they are regarded as *opinions* or *beliefs*. They lack the affective component common to attitudes.

Another distinction of some importance is that between attitudes and value systems (Katz & Stotland, 1959). Attitudes are thought of as pertaining to a single object, even though that object may be an abstract one. Value systems, on the other hand, are orientations toward whole classes of objects. Individual attitudes are frequently organized into a value system. For example, a person whose value system has humanitarianism as a central value would have favorable attitudes toward democratic government, social welfare, labor unions, and equitable distribution of wealth, and unfavorable attitudes toward war, monopoly, dictatorships, and capital punishment.

Attitudes are often functional, in the sense that they may be emotionally satisfying for the individual. For example, an individual with considerable hostility may find an outlet for its expression in prejudiced attitudes toward minority groups. To some degree, he finds support from other persons of like mind and thus is enabled to express hostility with social approval. Attitudes may also be used to justify particular behaviors: prejudice toward minority groups provides an employer needing a cheap supply of labor with an excuse for paying low wages to members of minority groups. Some attitudes, however, are functional only in the limited sense that the individual may gain some satisfaction in holding attitudes similar to those of his neighbors and friends.

In a broader sense, an individual's entire personality structure and hence his behavior may be thought of as organized around a central value system comprised of many related attitudes. The authoritarian personality discussed in the previous chapter is an example. His personality is organized around power, status, authority, and moral values. By studying in great depth the attitudes and personalities of a small number of men, Smith, Bruner, and White (1956) have shown a variety of other ways in which attitudes and personality are interwoven. For example, a brief excerpt from materials provided by one of their subjects who had obtained a position with a small firm of patent attorneys and who attended law school at night reveals his attitudes toward his work and toward law school and shows how these attitudes relate to his personality:

> The school is wonderful. For the first time in my life I find myself looking forward to classes. I believe that I am at or near the head of my class. The case method was made for me. I am in my element when it comes to tearing a case apart and finding out what makes it tick. And, as you know, I am not unaffected by the sound of my own voice, and therefore I get a big kick out of the class discussions.
>
> As though that weren't enough, I am equally enthusiastic about my work. One day it may be a helicopter, the next day paint, the next electronics, the next an abstruse point of law. Here, rolled into one, are the ancient wisdom of the law, calling for scholarship; the fringe of scientific development, to stimulate the imagination; and constant strife and argument to exact care and method from my disorderly soul. I think you might have had to go far afield to prescribe a better dose for me than this one. (Pp. 94–95)

The concept of attitude is also useful in studying certain broad factors in a given society that mold attitude and behavior in particular directions. Thus, sociologists and others study the association of geographical region, urban-rural area, religion, race, and other demographic classifications with particular attitudes, for such diverse purposes as predicting voter preferences in an election or making inferences about the social forces producing particular attitudes. An example of the latter is found in the work of Kohn, who attempts to show that the different conditions of life experienced by the middle class and the working class generate quite different attitudes toward economic security, self-control, relations with authority, and preparation for the future (Kohn, 1959*a*, 1959*b*, 1963; Kohn & Carroll, 1960).

STUDY QUESTIONS

1. *Define the concept of attitude and discuss its component parts. What is meant by the statement that attitude is a hypothetical construct?*
2. *Distinguish between attitude and opinion, and attitude and a value system.*
3. *What are the uses to which the concept of attitude may be put?*

Summary: The nature of attitudes

The term *attitude* refers to certain regularities on the part of an individual in feelings, thoughts, and predispositions to act toward some aspect of his environment. Attitudes have three components: affective, cognitive, and behavioral. Objects toward which attitudes are directed may be concrete or abstract, personal or remote. Attitudes cannot be directly observed; they are a hypothetical construct that must be inferred from verbal expression or overt behavior. They are distinguished from opinion and belief in that the latter two lack an affective component. Individual attitudes are often organized into larger value systems, which are orientations toward whole classes of objects. Attitudes are often emotionally satisfying to a person and serve a variety of social motives. In addition to contributing to understanding an individual's behavior, the concept of attitude is useful in studying broad factors in society that mold attitude and behavior in particular directions.

MEASUREMENT OF ATTITUDES

Attitude measurement is a highly technical process that will not be treated intensively in this book.[2] Instead, some general indication of the variety of means by which attitudes might be measured will be indicated.

The Thurstone-type scale

Typically, attitudes are assessed by a series of carefully constructed, standardized statements, although more indirect techniques are sometimes used. The respondent is given a set of fixed responses from which he must choose, such as by specifying *agree* or *disagree*. Usually statements

---

[2]For a technical discussion of attitude measurement, see McNemar (1946), Green (1954), or Edwards (1957*a*).

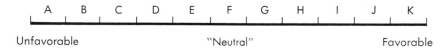

Figure 3–1
Thurstone equal-appearing interval continuum.

are assigned *scale values* in some fashion, so that a quantitative index of the attitude may be obtained. Basically, two quite different methods of scoring such statements may be used.

One procedure developed by Thurstone and Chave in 1929, is illustrated on page 102, which presents a scale for measuring attitudes toward war. A scale value is assigned to each statement at the time that the attitude scale is constructed. To accomplish this, a large number of judges, usually about two hundred, are presented with each statement and asked to place it on a scale containing eleven categories that appear to cover equal portions of the scale. One end of this eleven-category scale is designated as meaning that the statement is strongly favorable toward the attitude object, and the other end of the scale, strongly unfavorable toward the attitude object. The middle point is designated as neutral. An example is shown in Figure 3–1.

Each judge places the item in the category that he considers appropriate to the extremity and direction of the statement. Note that the judge does *not* express *his* attitude in making a judgment of the statement; he simply decides the degree to which it is favorable, unfavorable, or neutral. For example, given the item "Negroes and whites should attend separate schools," a judge might decide that this statement expresses an unfavorable attitude toward Negroes and so might place it toward the unfavorable end of the eleven-category scale, in category *C*. The categories *A* to *K* are commonly assigned the values from 1 to 11. The final scale value for a given item is determined from the values assigned by all the judges. Typically, they will differ from each other, assigning a range of values. If an item effectively measures an attitude, however, most of the judges will place it in a relatively small number of categories. The median of all the judgments becomes the value assigned.

Typically, an attitude scale constructed by the Thurstone method has about fifteen to twenty statements. From the statements on which judgments were made, final items are selected from the larger pool according to two criteria: (1) Items having the greatest agreement among judges on scale values are chosen, and (2) items are chosen so that their scale values range in approximately equal intervals all the way along the 11-point scale. The importance of this last criterion may be seen by drawing an analogy between an attitude scale and a 12-inch ruler. If certain regions of the attitude continuum are not represented by items, this is comparable to having a ruler with some of the markings missing.

When a scale constructed by the Thurstone method is used to assess a person's attitude, that person simply selects those items with which he agrees. Then his attitude score is the median of the scale values of the items with which he agrees. For example, suppose that he agrees with three items having the following scale values: 3.2, 4.5, and 5.8. His attitude score is 4.5, indicating that he is slightly favorable toward the attitude object, since 6 is the midpoint of the 11-point scale. If a respondent agrees with items having widely varying scale values, his median score should be looked at with suspicion. Since the items are carefully scaled, a person should agree only with those fairly close to his own position. Agreement with items having widely varying values may indicate carelessness in marking items, a failure to understand instructions, a misreading of certain items, or the lack of a definite position toward the attitude object. For purposes of illustration, a scale for attitudes toward war developed by this method is shown below. Scale values for each item are given.

SCALE OF ATTITUDE TOWARD WAR

Put a check mark (✔) if you agree with the statement.
Put a cross (×) if you disagree with the statement.

SCALE
VALUE*

SCALE VALUE*			
7.5 (	)	1.	Under some conditions, war is necessary to maintain justice.
3.5 (	)	2.	The benefits of war rarely pay for its losses even for the victor.
9.7 (	)	3.	War brings out the best qualities in men.
0.2 (	)	4.	There is no conceivable justification for war.
6.9 (	)	5.	War has some benefits; but it's a big price to pay for them.
8.7 (	)	6.	War is often the only means of preserving national honor.
0.8 (	)	7.	War is a ghastly mess.
5.5 (	)	8.	I never think about war and it doesn't interest me.
1.4 (	)	9.	War is a futile struggle resulting in self-destruction.
8.3 (	)	10.	The desirable results of war have not received the attention they deserve.
4.7 (	)	11.	Pacifists have the right attitude, but some pacifists go too far.
2.1 (	)	12.	The evils of war are greater than any possible benefits.
6.8 (	)	13.	Although war is terrible it has some value.
3.7 (	)	14.	International disputes should be settled without war.
11.0 (	)	15.	War is glorious.
6.5 (	)	16.	Defensive war is justified but other wars are not.
2.4 (	)	17.	War breeds disrespect for human life.
10.1 (	)	18.	There can be no progress without war.
3.2 (	)	19.	It is good judgment to sacrifice certain rights in order to prevent war.
9.2 (	)	20.	War is the only way to right tremendous wrongs.

*Scale values are provided here for purposes of information and do not normally appear on the scale.

SOURCE: Reprinted by permission from Ruth C. Peterson. *Scale of attitude toward war*. Chicago: University of Chicago Press, 1931.

Likert-type scale

Another procedure which yields similar results in terms of the reliability and validity of attitude measurement but which uses a quite different method of construction has been devised by Likert (1932). In this procedure, a large number of judges indicate *their own attitudes* by responding to carefully constructed statements thought to pertain to the attitude in question. They choose one of five possible responses to each item. These are *strongly agree, agree, undecided, disagree,* and *strongly disagree.* Weights of 1, 2, 3, 4, and 5, respectively, are assigned to the responses.

Consider, for example, the following item: "Negroes should be allowed access to public playgrounds and golf courses." Strong agreement indicates the most favorable attitude and hence receives the lowest weight, 1. Strong disagreement indicates the least favorable attitude and receives the highest weight, 5. Other response categories receive appropriate in-between weights. The total score for an individual is the sum of the weights for each response he makes to the statements. When an item is stated so that agreement indicates a con attitude, the weights are reversed. In other words, a prejudiced response always receives a higher weight and a pro response a lower weight, at least in the present example. Thus, for a group of persons having widely different attitudes, high total scores represent anti-Negro attitudes, and low total scores represent pro-Negro attitudes.

In constructing a scale by the Likert method, a large number of items is used at first. In order to reduce these, so that the final form of the scale may be taken by a respondent in a brief period, an *internal consistency* analysis of the items is made. Essentially, this is accomplished by determining the extent to which the responses of the persons in the standardization group to a particular item are consistent with their total scores. That is, the difference in responses to an item among those persons making the highest total scores and among those making the lowest total scores should be at a minimum. At the same time, the difference between the average response of the high and of the low group should be a maximum. For example, if those persons with the highest total scores all chose *strongly agree* for an item, and those with the lowest total scores all chose *strongly disagree,* persons within each group would be perfectly consistent with each other, and that item would be an effective one in discriminating between those with high and low scores. Such consistency, of course, is extremely rare, and in actual practice items retained for the final scale are the ones that best differentiate between persons with high and low total scores.

Single-question techniques

When an investigator is interested in obtaining quantitative measures on a considerable variety of attitudes from the same respondent, as is often the case in opinion polling, he may use only one or a few questions to assess each attitude or opinion. One type of question requires the respondent to choose one of several possible answers to a question. For example, he may be asked to choose the election candidate he prefers from those listed. Another type of question uses a scaled set of responses to obtain a crude quantitative score. For example, in attempting to measure willingness for combat during World War II, the following questions were used. The responses are worded to represent decreasing willingness to enter combat, and they may be weighted accordingly (Stouffer, Lumsdaine, et al., 1949, p. 45).

1. Which of the following best tells the way you feel about getting into an actual battle zone?
_____I want very much to get into it just as soon as possible
_____I'm ready to go any time
_____I'd like to go before it's over but I don't think I'm ready yet
_____I hope I won't have to go but if I do I think I'll do all right
_____I hope I won't have to go because I don't think I would do very well

2. Which of the following best describes your own feeling about getting into combat against the Germans?
_____I'd like to get into the fight as soon as I can
_____I'm ready to go when my turn comes
_____I'd just as soon stay out of combat if possible
_____I don't want to get into combat at all

The unidimensional scale

A question often raised concerning attitude scales constructed by the Thurstone or Likert methods is whether or not they measure a single attitude. Both techniques begin with a large pool of items. This pool might consist of items that represent several different attitudes instead of one, and nothing in the method of selecting the final items ensures that this heterogeneity will be removed. Apparently, the attitude object is largely specified by the judgment of the investigator in his selection of the original pool of items. The possible mixture of attitudes may be illustrated by reference to the Thurstone scale for attitude toward war shown on page 102. The statement "The benefits of war rarely pay for its losses even for the victor" could be interpreted as having to do with the economics of war; the statement "war brings out the best qualities in men" apparently has to do with individual bravery and heroism; and finally, the statement "War breeds disrespect for human life" appears to relate to a humanitarian value. So it could be argued that this scale is a complex of attitudes toward war and that it would be much better to measure economic, individual-achievement, and humanitarian attitudes toward war by means of separate scales confined to single dimensions.

Several different methods of determining whether or not a set of items lies in a single dimension are available. Of these, the best known is scale analysis, or the scalogram method, devised by Guttman (1950*a*, 1950*b*). To describe the elements of this procedure in a relatively nontechnical fashion, an attitude scale is considered unidimensional if *on every item* a person with a more favorable attitude gives a response more favorable than, or equally favorable to, a person with a less favorable attitude. In this case his response to every item is perfectly consistent with his overall position on the attitude dimension: he has a more favorable attitude and gives a set of responses more favorable than, or equally favorable to, a person with a less favorable overall position. The items yielding equally favorable responses for the two individuals are considered consistent because it is assumed that not all items will discriminate between these two individuals.

A hypothetical illustration may help to clarify the nature of a unidimensional scale in the sense described. Consider an attitude scale consisting of three items. Individuals could make four possible scores on this scale: 3, 2, 1, and 0, representing agreement with all three items at one extreme and disagreement with all three at the other. If ten persons were to take this scale, the scores and the pattern of responses obtained if it were unidimensional might take the form shown in Table 3–1. The symmetry of the response pattern reveals that the items are perfectly consistent. Scores of 2, for example, are made only by agreeing with items 1 and 2 and disagreeing with item 3, which apparently is a more extreme statement. No one makes a score of 2 by agreeing with items 1 and 3, or with 2 and 3, both events that would violate unidimensionality. Similarly, a score of 1 is made by agreeing with item 1, not with 2 or 3. Another sign of consistency is the observation that everyone who agrees with item 3 also agrees with items 2 and 1 and that everyone who agrees with item 2 agrees with item 1.

The essential characteristic of a unidimensional scale is that the *pattern of responses is reproducible from knowledge of the scale score.* Thus, in our example we know that every person who has made a score of 2 has agreed with items 1 and 2 and disagreed with item 3. For every other score, we can reproduce the pattern of responses. In practice, perfect consistency is seldom if ever achieved; a certain measure of "error" is allowed. One criterion suggested by Guttman (1950*a*, 1950*b*) is that the pattern of responses must be 90 percent reproducible in order for a

Table 3–1
Hypothetical Unidimensional Scale

PERSON	SCORE	AGREES WITH ITEM		
		1	2	3
1	3	x	x	x
2	3	x	x	x
3	3	x	x	x
4	2	x	x	
5	2	x	x	
6	1	x		
7	1	x		
8	1	x		
9	1	x		
10	0			

scale to be considered unidimensional. In other words, 10 percent of the responses may fall outside the unidimensional pattern.

The scalogram method and the problem of unidimensionality have been a controversial subject, and the technical issues involved are beyond the scope of this book. A few general comments may be made, however. First, an authoritative source (Selltiz et al., 1959) on methodology in social psychology has argued that if we wish to predict complex behavior, we need to measure a complex attitude, not a unidimensional one. From a practical point of view this appears to be a sound comment; however, theoretically, if both the attitude and the behavior could be measured unidimensionally, prediction would certainly be enhanced. Second, a scale may be reproducible when taken by one group of persons and not when taken by another. In general, however, the method has appeared to be useful for certain kinds of scaling problems.

Free-response method

The formal attitude scales constructed by the methods described are used when an investigator wishes to obtain a quantitative score for each person that he studies. These methods stress the affect component of the attitude, regarding it as a single continuum or dimension. But an attitude is much more than a point on a continuum. It often has extensive cognitive content. Two persons could have the same attitude score but very different cognitive content concerning the attitude object.

Investigators are sometimes more interested in getting a description of the cognitive content of an attitude than a quantitative measure of affect, and they frequently use some *free-response* technique for that purpose. The term comes from the nature of the questions asked, which leave the respondent free to answer in his own words. We often learn a great deal about the content of attitudes from our everyday interaction with other persons. Attitudes may be gauged from what a person says and does or even from subtle nuances of expression in his face or voice or gestures. One of the most commonly used techniques for obtaining rich information about the attitudes of individuals is the open-end interview. The term *open end* comes from the fact that the questions are worded so as to leave the answer open to the respondent. He has a wide variety of ways in which he might reply. This method not only brings out the extensive content of an attitude, but may also suggest relations between different attitudes and between attitudes and personality. In this procedure, a skilled interviewer asks questions that lead a person to talk freely about topics that are relevant to the attitude object. Because the person is free to say as much or as little as he pleases, and to express himself with vigor and emotion or to respond in a perfunctory fashion, it is also possible to judge how important or *salient* the attitude is for him.

A portion of a typical interview is shown below. The interview was conducted in 1942 with a college graduate working as a mailman who showed general dissatisfaction with many aspects of his life and who was not in sympathy with the war effort. The portion shown was preceded by questions about the role of the government in the war effort and about the extent to which the government had public support. Particularly noticeable in the excerpt are a number of inconsistencies in the respondent's attitude (Campbell, 1947, p. 526).

Q. Do you think the Jewish people are doing their share? How do you mean?
A. They're trying to get out of it, but so are all of us. They're richer than the rest of us and probably succeed a little better — and they have less principle and easier conscience. What great art has the Jew given the world except that of making money? I'm not anti-Jewish — I can't be because I'm Roman Catholic. They're hated by all alike — must be something wrong with them. There's something the matter with them when they are driven out of every country in the world.
Q. Do you think that in general there is any feeling against the Jews here in Brooklyn, apart from the war?
A. Sure, people just don't like them.
Q. Why do you think people feel that way?
A. If I could answer that I would become a great man. A lot of it's just instinct — like a dog that whirls around three times before he lies down. He had to do it in the brush to mash down a bed for himself, but still does it in the city — just instinct. We dislike Jews because that's the way we grow up to feel toward them.
Q. Do you have much contact with Jewish people from day to day?
A. I work with a few and they're regular fellows — they never make themselves superior and never sneer — but others are not like that. Most of them think they have superior intellects. How come 90 per cent of the communist parades are made up of Jews?

Various other free-response methods may also be used (Campbell, 1950). Almost any set of verbal statements by a person may be used for attitude assessment. Usually, however, some technique is employed to ensure that the statements of the person will be directed toward the attitude object. Methods include instructing a person to write a story in response to pictures, to complete incomplete sentences, or to write an essay on topics relevant to the attitude object. The problem of quantifying such verbal statements, including interview material, is solved by having independent judges assign quantitative values to elements of these verbal expressions. An important criterion for adequacy of such procedures is that quantitative judgments made independently by different persons must be in substantial agreement.

STUDY QUESTIONS

4. *Distinguish between formal scales and free-response methods of measuring attitudes.*
5. *Explain the Thurstone method and the Likert method of constructing attitude scales. What is a unidimensional scale?*
6. *What is the open-end interview? How may quantitative data be obtained from it?*

Summary: Attitude measurement

Two basic methods of assessing attitudes are the attitude scale and the free-response technique. The three most commonly used formal scales are the Thurstone, Likert, and Guttman scales. A Thurstone scale is constructed by having a large number of judges assign scale values to attitude statements, indicating the extent to which the items represent a pro or con position. By pooling this information, a scale value is assigned to each item. The final form of the scale includes statements having a wide range of scale values and eliciting maximum agreement from the judges. A respondent whose attitude is to be assessed selects the items with which he agrees, and his attitude score is the median scale value of the items he has selected.

A Likert scale is constructed by having a large number of judges express their attitudes on statements according to a five-choice response ranging from *strongly agree* to *strongly disagree*. These responses are weighted to obtain a total score, taking direction of attitude into account. From this information, the extent to which each item discriminates between persons having high and low scores is determined, and the items that best discriminate between them are retained in the final form of the scale. Investigators wishing to measure a large number of attitudes may use only one or a few questions for each attitude. Each question has scaled choices from which the respondent must choose.

A method of determining unidimensionality proposed by Guttman has been quite widely used. Unidimensionality is achieved if, within the limits of error, on every item a person with a more favorable attitude gives a response more favorable than, or equally favorable to, that of a person with a less favorable attitude.

The most representative technique in the free-response method is the open-end interview, where the subject is encouraged to talk freely about topics relevant to the attitude. Free-response techniques are especially useful where a rich description of the cognitive content of the attitude is desired.

Theories of Attitude Organization

In their enthusiasm for the new measurement techniques introduced by Thurstone in 1928 and Likert in 1932, investigators often studied attitudes almost apart from their relation to anything else. Today, psychologists and sociologists realize that the concept of attitude is most useful when studied in context: as a component of the personality of individuals, as serving functional or adjustive ends, or as a descriptive concept characterizing a prevailing mode of thought of the members of a category or subgroup. Context relating attitude to other variables is provided by theory. The years since World War II have seen the gradual development of theory appropriate to the study of attitude change. While none of the theories developed is as yet adequate, they nevertheless serve to integrate many investigations that formerly appeared to be unrelated. Moreover, much current research is generated by these theories.

Most of the theories are intrapersonal: they pertain to the relations of the three attitude components within an individual and specify various conditions that control these relations and produce changes in them. The remainder of this chapter will be devoted to a discussion of several representative theories in order to gain a perspective on the various empirical studies to be discussed in the chapters following.

CONSISTENCY AS AN ORGANIZING PRINCIPLE

One of the prevailing characteristics of human thought and behavior is its tendency to be consistent. If we like a person, we tend to attribute "good" traits to him, and we resist any suggestion that he might possess undesirable traits. We also have beliefs that are consistent with our behavior. Thus, after many news releases about the relation between lung cancer and smoking, a sample of respondents in Minneapolis were asked whether or not they believed the relation had been proved. Only 7 percent of the heavy smokers believed that it had, compared with 20 percent of the light smokers and 29 percent of the nonsmokers (Osgood, 1960). A good party Democrat is likely to give a friendly reception to speeches by any Democratic politician and an unfriendly reception to speeches by any Republican politician.

Serious thinkers throughout the ages have often referred to the consistency in human thought, feelings, and behavior, but only in recent years have behavioral scientists given serious attention to this concept. Perhaps the first behavioral scientist in this century to use the concept was the sociologist Sumner (1906) with his notion that the folkways are subject to a strain toward consistency. In a very broad sense, the Gestalt psychologists Max Wertheimer (1912), Wolfgang Kohler (1940), and Kurt Koffka (1935), with their emphasis on unity and organization, and Kurt Lewin (1935, 1936) in his field theory, contributed to the development of psychology along these lines.

In 1945 Lecky published a small book in which he attempted to explain much thought and behavior in terms of a single principle: the tendency of the individual to be self-consistent. He suggested that this single principle might substitute for the many principles of human behavior that had been developed for dealing with diverse areas of cognition and behavior. For example, he attempted to show how learning could be explained as well by a consistency principle as by conditioning. The process of forgetting was also explained by consistency: inconsistent elements drop out of memory. He even developed a theory of pleasure, based upon the idea that pleasure is experienced when the organism finds a way to make consistent some experience which is at first inconsistent.

Perhaps the father of modern consistency theory is Heider, who published an important paper on the topic in 1946 and in 1958 published a book-length monograph devoted to his "balance theory." In just the last decade, widespread interest in the principle of consistency has been evident. Many behavioral scientists are now assiduously devoting themselves to developing systematic theories based upon the principle, and many active research programs are in progress. Table 3–2 lists some of these individuals and their theoretical developments based on consistency, as well as several other theories of attitude organization of a more general nature.

Table 3–2
Theories of Attitude Organization

Heider (1946, 1958). A theory of balance. A positive or negative affect toward another person tends to be in a state of balance with an individual's affect toward an attitude object toward which the other person is also oriented. A state of balance is achieved either when the three signs of the relations are all positive or when two are negative. Balance and imbalance are related to cognitive structure, affect, person perception, influence, and attitude-change processes.

Newcomb (1953). A theory of symmetry in interpersonal communication. A person's attitude toward an object may be positive or negative; persons may be positively or negatively attracted to each other. These relations may also vary in intensity. Symmetry between two persons exists when signs of attraction are alike, signs of attitude are alike, and intensities are equal. Dissimilar but complementary relations of two persons toward an object may also be symmetrical. A variety of group processes are treated in terms of the theory.

Osgood and Tannenbaum (1955). A theory of congruity. Cognitive elements have positive, negative, or zero valence of varying intensity. Elements relevant to each other may also be positively or negatively related. Congruity exists when signs are all zero, or two are negative, and when intensities are equal. Cognitive structures and attitude change are treated in terms of the theory.

Cartwright and Harary (1956); Harary (1959). A formalization and elaboration of Heider's theory in terms of the mathematical theory of linear graphs. Takes into account more than three elements.

Festinger (1957). A theory of cognitive dissonance. Two cognitive elements are dissonant with respect to each other if the obverse of one element follows from the other. The existence of dissonance gives rise to pressures to reduce it. Processes of dissonance reduction are related to cognitive or behavioral changes.

McGuire (1960). A two-process theory of consistency. "Wishful thinking" is the tendency for the subjective probability of a proposition to be consistent with its desirability, and "logical thinking" is the tendency for a person's beliefs to relate to each other in the accord with the rules of formal logic.

Rosenberg and Abelson (1960). An extension of Heider's theory which provides for positively and negatively signed elements as well as positively and negatively signed relations, and which takes into account more than three elements. The theory is very similar to Cartwright and Harary's system, but is expressed in terms of matrix theory.

Katz and Stotland (1959). A theory of attitude change based upon four motivational bases for attitude: the adjustive function, the ego-defensive function, the value-expressive function, and the knowledge function. Only the value-expressive function and the knowledge function make direct use of a consistency principle.

Kelman (1961). A three-process theory of attitude change. Compliance occurs as a result of reward or punishment by the influence agent, identification occurs through formation of a satisfying relation to the influence agent, and internalization occurs when the change is congruent with one's values. Only internalization makes use of a consistency principle.

Only four of these theoretical approaches will be treated in any detail in this chapter: Rosenberg's theory of affective-cognitive consistency, Festinger's theory of cognitive dissonance, Katz and Stotland's motivational theory of attitude change, and Kelman's three-process theory of attitude change. Although Rosenberg's theory is not as broad as some of those listed in Table 3–2 and has not produced as much extensive empirical study, it is chosen for discussion because it contributes to a better understanding of the nature of affective-cognitive components and the relation between them. Festinger's theory of cognitive dissonance has led to extensive research and has the special merit of demonstrating the relations between cognitive elements and behavior. The approaches of Katz and Stotland and of Kelman are discussed briefly in order to gain a broader perspective on approaches to attitude change other than consistency theory. In addition, theories other than these four will be referred to in Chapters 4 and 5 in discussions of the specific research they have generated.

STUDY QUESTIONS

7. *Explain why attitude studies are more useful when placed in a theoretical context.*

8. *Give a general statement of what is meant by consistency theory.*

ROSENBERG'S THEORY OF AFFECTIVE-COGNITIVE CONSISTENCY

Rosenberg (1960*a*, 1960*b*) has concerned himself primarily with conceptualizing what happens *within the individual* when attitudes change. He is particularly interested in the relation between affective and cognitive components of an attitude. In general, past treatments have recognized both of these components, but have been unconcerned with specifying in any precise way how they are organized with respect to each other. Rosenberg attempts to remedy this deficiency. In addition, he extends the cognitive component of an attitude to include not only cognitions about the attitude object, but also *beliefs about the relations between that object and other important values of the person.* The affective component is defined in the usual manner as the positive or negative feeling that the individual has toward the attitude object. Thus, a person might have a negative feeling toward Republican congressmen. He also has certain beliefs about them that relate to other positively or negatively valued conditions. He might believe that Republican congressmen obstruct progress, that they hamper the economy, that they have outmoded views on taxation, and that their views on social welfare are inappropriate in a democratic nation.

Rosenberg's principal hypothesis is that the nature and strength of the feeling toward an attitude object are correlated with the cognitions associated with the attitude object. He makes the following statement:

> Strong and stable positive affect toward a given object should be associated with beliefs that it leads to the attainment of a number of important values, while strong negative affect should be associated with beliefs that the object tends to block the attainment of important values. Similarly, moderate positive or negative affects should be associated with beliefs that relate the attitude object either to less important values or, if to important values, then with less confidence about the relationships between these values and the attitude object. (1960*b*, p. 18)

Rosenberg (1953, 1956) has developed a procedure for determining the cognitive components of attitudes. He uses a set of thirty-five value statements, such as "all human beings having equal rights," "people being well-educated," "making one's own decisions," and "attaining economic security." The subject first categorizes each item in terms of its *value importance,* that is, how satisfying it is to him. To do this, he considers each value statement separately and rates its value importance by placing it in a category ranging from "gives me maximum satisfaction" (+10) through "gives me neither satisfaction nor dissatisfaction" (0) to "gives me maximum dissatisfaction" (−10). For example, if he values education highly, he might give a rating of +8 to "people being well-educated."

Second, the subject rates these value statements with respect to how well a particular attitude contributes to their realization. Suppose, for example, that the attitude concerns Federal aid to education. Taking the first value statement, "people being well-educated," he would rate Federal aid to education on a scale from +5 to −5, positive ratings implying that Federal aid to education contributes to the attainment of the value "people being well-educated," and negative ratings implying that Federal aid interferes with its attainment. Ratings of the value statements obtained in this fashion are termed the *perceived instrumentality* of the attitude object.

From ratings of value importance and perceived instrumentality, a *cognitive index* for the attitude object "Federal aid to education" may be obtained. This index represents the subject's pattern of beliefs about the extent to which Federal aid to education results in the attainment of or interference with the individual's values, weighted according to their importance.[3] It is a quantitative measure of the extent to which a person's attitude is consistent with his values.

A principal finding by Rosenberg (1956) is that the index of cognitive

---

[3]The index is obtained by algebraically summing the importance-instrumentality products for each of the values. Thus, if "people being well-educated" is ranked 9 in importance, and Federal aid to education receives an instrumental rating of 4, the product of these is 9 × 4, or 36. Similar products are obtained for each of the other thirty-four value statements as they pertain to Federal aid to education and are summed to obtain a cognitive index for the attitude object.

structure is consistent with the affect of an attitude, as measured by an attitude scale. That is, if a subject has strong positive affect toward an attitude object, he is likely to have a high cognitive index for that attitude, believing it to be instrumental in attaining his positive values and in blocking negative values. The association between the affective component of an attitude and the cognitive index has been found to be greatest for the person's most salient values. A person's attitudes, then, are anchored in his important values in a highly consistent manner.

Of particular importance are the implications of Rosenberg's theory and methodology for understanding attitude change. Many earlier studies[4] have shown in a somewhat less refined fashion the consistent association between the affective component of attitude and one's values. A basic proposition in his theory is as follows (Rosenberg, 1960*b*):

> When the affective and cognitive components of an attitude are mutually consistent the attitude is in a stable state; when the affective and cognitive components are mutually inconsistent (to a degree that exceeds the individual's present tolerance for such inconsistency) the attitude is in an unstable state and will undergo spontaneous reorganizing activity until such activity eventuates in either (1) the attainment of affective-cognitive consistency or (2) the placing of an "irreconcilable" inconsistency beyond the range of active awareness. (P. 22)

From this proposition it follows that if certain external forces bring about a change in either the affective or cognitive components of a previously stable attitude, pressures will arise to change the remaining component. Most studies previous to Rosenberg have emphasized change in cognitive components as a cause of change in affective components, stressing *rational* processes in attitude change. A good illustration is provided by certain attempts to change racial prejudice. Some attempts to change prejudice toward the Negro use communications designed to convince the individual of the unfavorable consequences of prejudice and of the lack of evidence concerning racial differences on important attributes. But if the person changes his beliefs in response to direct attempts of this kind, his new beliefs would be inconsistent with his negative affect, hence, according to this theory, he resists such approaches. To be successful, such pressures toward change would have to be strong and persistent, creating strong inconsistency between affect and cognition.

While most attitude studies have stressed change in cognitive components as a cause of shifts in affective components, Rosenberg has concentrated on demonstrating that a change in *affect* will produce cognitive changes (Rosenberg & Gardner, 1958; Rosenberg, 1960*c*). In one experiment, eight subjects who were in favor of the United States policy of giving economic aid to foreign nations were placed under deep hypnosis and their positive feeling reversed to a negative one. This was accomplished by giving each subject the following instructions while under deep hypnosis (Rosenberg, 1960*a*):

[4]Woodruff, 1942; Woodruff & DiVesta, 1948; Cartwright, 1949; Smith, 1949.

After you awake, and continuing until our next meeting, you will feel very strongly opposed to the United States policy of giving economic aid to foreign nations. The mere idea of the United States giving economic aid to foreign nations will make you feel very displeased and disgusted. Until your next meeting with me you will continue to feel very strong and thorough opposition to the United States policy of economic aid to foreign nations. You will have no memory whatsoever of this suggestion's having been made . . . until the amnesia is removed by my giving you the signal at our next session. (P. 327)

Before and after hypnotic manipulation, subjects indicated the value importance and the perceived instrumentality on Rosenberg's thirty-two value statements with respect to their own attitude toward foreign aid and two other attitudes used as controls. As predicted, subjects made large-scale changes in both perceived instrumentality and value statements involving foreign aid. Since affect was not manipulated for the control attitudes, no appreciable changes occurred with respect to them. Typically, a subject changed from a position extremely supportive of foreign aid to one of extreme opposition. At the same time, many of his related beliefs changed. For example, if before the affect manipulation he believed that foreign aid would help to maintain such positive values as "the prevention of economic depression," he later believed that *abandonment* of foreign aid would prevent economic depression.

Sometimes, instead of changing the *instrumental* relation between attitude and value, a subject altered the strength or even the direction (positive or negative) of his values, to make them more consistent with the experimentally produced affect. For example, if a subject continued to believe that foreign aid would prevent economic depression, but shifted from extreme support of foreign aid to extreme opposition, he might change the value of economic depression from a negative one to a positive one, arguing that economic depression had certain beneficial effects upon the country. The effects observed in this experiment persisted in most instances for an entire week, at the end of which period the experimenter removed the affect change and explained the entire experiment to the subjects.

Summary: Affective-cognitive consistency

Focusing on the relation between cognitions and affect and its consequences for attitude change, Rosenberg has linked cognitions about the attitude object with the person's values. Strong, positive affect toward an attitude object should be associated with beliefs that it leads to the achievement of important values, and negative affect toward an object suggests that it blocks the attainment of these values. Studies by him have demonstrated such linkages. With respect to attitude change, he postulates that if either affect or cognition shifts markedly, inconsistency arises and produces a force toward changing the remaining component. In experimental studies using hypnosis to shift affect, he has demonstrated striking changes in the associated cognitions and their relation to values.

STUDY QUESTIONS

9. *Explain what Rosenberg means by the cognitive and affective components of an attitude, and give an example of each.*

10. *State in your own words Rosenberg's major proposition concerning the relation between the cognitive and affective components of an attitude.*

11. *What is meant by the statement that the index of cognitive structure (based on value importance and perceived instrumentality) is closely related to the affect of an attitude? Explain this in terms of a concrete example.*

12. *According to Rosenberg, what necessary condition must exist in order for an attitude to change?*

13. *What are the consequences of producing experimentally a change in affect toward an attitude object? How do they support Rosenberg's theory of affective-cognitive consistency?*

FESTINGER'S THEORY OF COGNITIVE DISSONANCE

The theory of cognitive dissonance, developed by Festinger (1957), has the great merit of linking attitude to overt behavior, a problem that has been troublesome throughout the history of attitude research. Critics often argued that the concept of attitude was useless, because no one could be sure that a person would behave in accordance with his verbally expressed attitudes. Dissonance theory recognizes this shortcoming and helps to remedy it by specifying the conditions under which attitudes and behavior do correspond.

Festinger introduces his theory by noting that the attitudes of an individual are normally consistent with each other, that he behaves in accordance with his attitudes, and that his various actions are consistent with each other. For example, if a person believes in democracy, he does not believe in fascism. If he believes a college education is a good thing, he tries to send his children to college. If he behaves conscientiously in doing his college assignments, he is likely to behave conscientiously on a job. Of particular interest is the question of what happens when inconsistencies occur.

By the term *cognitive element* is meant any knowledge, opinion, or belief about the environment, about oneself, or about one's behavior. The term *dissonance* is introduced to represent an inconsistency between two or more cognitive elements. Two cognitive elements are in a dissonant relation if, considering these two alone, *the obverse of one element would follow from the other.* For example, if a person knew that the most he could afford to pay for a new automobile was $2,500 and that he had just been persuaded to sign a contract to purchase one costing $3,000, there would be a dissonant relation between these two cognitive elements. On the other hand, two cognitive elements are consonant with one another if one follows from the other. Thus, the knowledge that you are getting wet is consonant with the knowledge that it is raining.

Relations between cognitive elements may be either relevant or irrelevant. Dissonance and consonance may only exist between relevant elements. Many cognitive elements have nothing to do with each other. A person may know that the cost of first-class mail is 5 cents an ounce and may also know that spark plugs ignite the gasoline in an engine. These elements are irrelevant to each other.

The magnitude of dissonance is a function of the proportion of all relevant cognitive elements that is dissonant. These elements are generally weighted according to their importance. Thus, the magnitude of dissonance may be expressed in terms of the following ratio:

$$\text{Dissonance} = \frac{\text{importance} \times \text{no. of dissonant elements}}{\text{importance} \times \text{no. of consonant elements}}$$

From this ratio,[5] it is clear that the more nearly equal the relative proportions of consonant and dissonant elements, the greater the dissonance is. If there are only a few dissonant elements and many consonant elements, dissonance is relatively low. The number of dissonant elements can never exceed the number of consonant elements, for this would lead to a change, removing the dissonance. Hence the maximum value that dissonance can reach is 1, which is approached when the proportions of dissonant and consonant elements are equal.

Actually, the magnitude of dissonance is represented in terms of a ratio in order to clarify the concept rather than to offer a measuring device. Dissonance cannot be directly measured, and in actual practice in experiments, conditions are compared only with respect to whether or not condition *A* represents a greater or a lesser amount of dissonance than condition *B*. At best, a series of conditions may be rank-ordered, but the exact quantities of dissonance present are not measured.

Reduction of dissonance

Several propositions in dissonance theory have been stated as follows (Festinger, 1957):

> The existence of dissonance, being psychologically uncomfortable, will motivate the person to try to reduce the dissonance and achieve consonance. (P. 30)
>
> When dissonance is present, in addition to trying to reduce it, the person will actively avoid situations and information which would likely increase the dissonance. (P. 3)
>
> The strength of the pressures to reduce the dissonance is a function of the magnitude of the dissonance. (P. 18)

[5]Strictly speaking, not even the ratio presented is correct. If there are relatively equal proportions of trivial dissonant and consonant elements, dissonance should be smaller than in the case of relatively equal proportions of highly important dissonant and consonant elements. But the formula shown would yield equal amounts of dissonance in these two special cases. Thus the ratio should be further weighted by the mean importance of all of the relevant elements. But this is mainly an academic point, since the ratio is not used to actually measure dissonance.

Three ways of reducing dissonance are:

1. *Change of a behavioral cognitive element.* When knowledge of one's own behavior is dissonant with a belief, it is often simplest to change one's behavior. Thus if a person smokes but thinks it is bad for his health, he may stop smoking. Or if he realizes that "goofing off" instead of studying is inconsistent with knowledge that he intends to apply for medical school, he may stop goofing off.

2. *Change of an environmental cognitive element.* Sometimes the behavior of a person is dissonant with some environmental factor that can be changed. For example, he may reduce the dissonance between his knowledge that smoking causes cancer and his use of cigarettes by changing to a filter-tip brand. Perhaps the easiest aspect of the environment to change is the social or interpersonal environment. Thus a smoker bothered by dissonance may seek support from other persons who also smoke and who can present arguments and reassurance against the view that lung cancer is caused by smoking. He may, for example, point to the fact that many doctors smoke.

3. *Addition of new cognitive elements.* Sometimes it is difficult to change any of the cognitive elements that are involved in dissonance. Under these circumstances it is often possible to add new elements to outweigh the dissonant ones. A person who has purchased an automobile he cannot afford may convince himself that he is likely to get a substantial raise in pay, that he can readily borrow the additional money, or that he has probably overestimated his expenses and underestimated his income. The smoker worried about lung cancer may tell himself that smoking is relaxing and thus beneficial to his health.

IMPLICATIONS OF DISSONANCE THEORY

Many studies have explored various facets of dissonance theory, and more are in progress. One of these will be described to illustrate the usefulness of the theory in predicting attitude change. The experiment (Festinger & Carlsmith, 1949) chosen is of particular interest because it bears out predictions from dissonance theory opposite to those of common sense. From dissonance theory, the following hypothesis may be derived.

1. If a person is induced to say or do something opposite to his private attitude, he will tend to modify his attitude so as to make it consonant with the cognition of what he has said or done.

This is clear and obvious, but a second hypothesis is as follows:

2. The greater the pressure used to elicit the behavior contrary to one's private attitude (beyond the minimum needed to elicit it), the *less* his attitude will change.

To illustrate, if a person having a strong preference for Democratic candidates in an election were paid $5,000 to go out and persuade other persons to vote for Republican candidates, he would be less likely to switch his personal political preference than if he were to perform the same behavior for a fee of only $100. If $100 were just sufficient to elicit his acceptance of the task, this degree of reward would be more likely to result in a change in his own political preference than any other amount of reward. A greater amount of reward would appreciably strengthen the elements involved in working for a Republican victory and thereby would result in less dissonance and less pressure to change. It is at the point where the pressure to comply and one's political leanings are in approximately equal opposition that dissonance is at a maximum.

The following procedure was used to test the two hypotheses stated above. After completing a dull, boring "experimental" task, subjects were informed that a student helper usually brought in the next experimental subject and told him how enjoyable the experiment was. It was implied that this helper had failed to show up, and the student who had just completed the task was asked to serve in this capacity. Two magnitudes of reward for serving in this role were used for different groups of students: $1 and $20.

Here, then, is an experimental situation where the subject forms a strong private opinion that the task he has just engaged in is dull and boring, but where for a price (and presumably other considerations, such as his desire to cooperate with the experimenter), he agrees to tell a new subject that it is an enjoyable task. After they had served as helpers, subjects were interviewed and asked to rate their opinions concerning the experiment on an 11-point scale from maximum negative opinion to maximum positive opinion. As predicted, those who had received a reward of only $1 rated the experiment higher in terms of its enjoyability than those who had received $20.

In other words, if monetary reward is used as the pressure to win such compliance from a person, the prediction is that the more money he receives for complying, the less his attitude will change. The key to understanding the second hypothesis is the point that *dissonance is at its maximum* when the opposing cognitive elements are equal in strength and importance. Since the amount of attitude change is a function of the amount of dissonance, it is at the point where these opposing elements are equal that the greatest attitude change will occur. If opposing elements are made unequal by appreciably strengthening one set of elements but not the other, dissonance will be somewhat less, and attitude change will be smaller.

Summary: Dissonance theory

Festinger (1957) provides a useful summary, describing the basic theory as follows.

The core of the theory of dissonance which we have stated is rather simple. It holds that:

1. There may exist dissonant or "nonfitting" relations among cognitive elements.

2. The existence of dissonance gives rise to pressures to reduce the dissonance and to avoid increases in dissonance.

3. Manifestations of the operation of these pressures include behavior changes, changes of cognition, and circumspect exposure to new information and new opinions.

Although the core of the theory is simple, it has rather wide implications and applications to a variety of situations which on the surface look very different (P. 31)

STUDY QUESTIONS

14. *Explain the following: (a) cognitive dissonance, (b) relevant relations between cognitive elements, and (c) irrelevant relations between cognitive elements.*

15. *What are Festinger's three propositions concerning the reduction of cognitive dissonance?*

16. *Present three ways in which cognitive dissonance may be reduced.*

17. *Explain why, in Festinger's terms, an excess of pressure to perform dissonant actions brings about less attitude change than is accomplished by just enough pressure.*

A FUNCTIONAL THEORY OF ATTITUDES

Katz (1960), and Katz and Stotland (1959) in a somewhat more formal presentation, have offered a functional approach to the study of attitudes. From their point of view, the motivational basis of an attitude is the key to understanding change and resistance to change. They note that situational factors and the communication directed toward attitude change will have different effects depending on the motivational basis of the attitude. The motivational basis is conceptualized in terms of the function which an attitude performs for the person. Katz has described four major functions of attitudes as follows:

1. *The instrumental, adjustive, or utilitarian function.* By this is meant that the individual strives to maximize the rewards and minimize the penalties which he experiences. Thus, he develops favorable attitudes toward those objects which result in reward and unfavorable attitudes toward those which lead to punishment.

2. *The ego-defensive function.* Attitudes may function to protect the person from acknowledgment of unpleasant truths about himself or of the harsh realities in his environment. For example, a person with considerable insecurity about his own worth may develop strong prejudice against minority groups so that he can regard himself as superior.

3. *The value-expressive function.* A person may derive satisfaction from expressing himself in terms of attitudes that are appropriate to his personal values and to his self concept. Thus, an individual with strong democratic-liberal values may receive much gratification by engaging in actions that foster such values.

4. *The knowledge function.* The individual is presumed to have a basic drive to understand, to make sense out of, to "structure" his experience. Elements of experience that are at first inconsistent with what a person knows are rearranged or changed so as to achieve consistency.

The value-expressive function and the knowledge function tie in closely with Festinger's theory of cognitive dissonance, as well as other consistency theories. The value-expressive function concerns consistency between values (a form of cognitive element) and cognitive elements representing behavior. The knowledge function resembles Festinger's proposition that a person is motivated to reduce dissonance and achieve consonance. Katz and Stotland apply the consistency principle primarily to single attitude objects: They suggest that affective, cognitive, and behavioral components involving a single attitude object move toward consistency. In their system, different attitudes often may be inconsistent with each other without creating strain.

The instrumental, adjustive, or utilitarian function and the ego-defensive function represent some elements of attitude theory not yet discussed, and they deserve further elaboration here. Katz (1960) notes that to change an attitude that serves an adjustive function, one of the following two conditions must prevail:

> (1) The attitude and the activities related to it no longer provide the satisfactions they once did, or (2) the individual's level of aspiration has been raised. The Chevrolet owner who had positive attitudes toward his old car may now want a more expensive car commensurate with his new status. (P. 177)

Shifts in the satisfactions obtained from various behaviors, then, result in associated changes in attitudes. When new behaviors which are somewhat inconsistent with current attitudes are rewarded, existing attitudes are modified. Similarly, experiences which are punishing lead to unfavorable attitudes toward the communicators or objects which incite the punishment. As will be seen in Chapter 4, communications that arouse considerable anxiety or fear are likely to create unfavorable attitudes toward the communicator and his communication, a result consistent with theory.

Ego-defensive attitudes are readily aroused by any situation that threatens the individual. Prejudice toward minority groups is an example of an attitude that is sometimes ego-defensive. This attitude would be aroused by excessive competition, derogatory remarks by others, or any other threat to a person's status. Other factors[6] arousing such attitudes include the direct encouragement of their expression by other persons, especially those who hold authoritative positions, and the building up of inhibited drives or impulses in the person such as sexual or aggressive feelings.

Most important is the point that persuasive communications that are effective with attitudes having other motivational bases are often in-

[6]See Katz (1960, pp. 180–181) for a more extended discussion.

effective with ego-defensive attitudes. Thus, communications that provide a great deal of information in support of changing an attitude may not work because such a change deprives the person of an attitude that serves to bolster his ego-defenses. To take one example, an individual whose prejudice toward the Negro is rooted in his own sense of inferiority and his hostile feelings resulting from emotional conflict will be highly resistant to information supporting the view that there is no innate difference between white and Negro. Similarly, promise of rewards for change or the threat of punishment are unlikely to have much effect, unless they are more powerful than the ego-defense motives. Threat of punishment in particular, because it increases defensiveness, may boomerang, that is, effect a change opposite to that intended by the communicator.

Not content with the conclusion that ego-defensive attitudes are more resistant to change than other kinds of attitudes, Katz identifies the conditions and types of persuasive communications which should be effective with ego-defensive attitudes. Two necessary conditions are the reduction of threat and the ventilation of feelings. The communication must come not from a threatening or anxiety-arousing person, but from one who creates a relaxed atmosphere. Opportunities to "blow off steam" reduce the strength of impulses that otherwise provide strong support for ego-defensive attitudes. Communications that help the person to acquire insight in a nonthreatening way into his own mechanisms of defense have the best possibility of changing ego-defensive attitudes.[7]

STUDY QUESTIONS

18. *What are the similarities and differences between the theoretical approach to attitude change taken by Katz, on the one hand, and Festinger and Rosenberg on the other?*
19. *Explain each of the following motivational bases for attitudes: (a) the instrumental or adjustive function, (b) the ego-defensive function, (c) the value-expressive function, and (d) the knowledge function.*
20. *Why does Katz expect individuals to react differently from one another toward a communication aimed at changing their attitude?*

Summary: Katz's functional theory

The key to understanding change and resistance to change, according to this theory, is the motivational basis of an attitude. Attitudes may be utilitarian in that they lead to reward and avoidance of punishment, they may function to protect the person from acknowledgment of unpleasant truths about himself or of the harsh realities in his environment, they may provide satisfaction in expression of self and one's central values, and to the extent that they are consistent, they may satisfy a basic drive to structure one's experience. This view emphasizes the fact that shifts in the satisfactions associated with various behaviors, such as obtaining new rewards or receiving punishment, may bring about associated changes in

[7]This topic will be discussed in more detail in Chapter 5.

attitudes so that these attitudes continue to maximize the person's adjustment to his environment. The theory also discusses situational factors that arouse attitudes having different motivational bases and the types of influence approaches that are effective or ineffective with these different attitudes.

KELMAN'S THREE-PROCESS THEORY OF ATTITUDE CHANGE

The last theory to be discussed is one proposed by Kelman (1961). His conception of the various means by which attitudes may be changed is particularly useful because the theory itself suggests the conditions under which attitude change will be manifested and those under which it will not, and because it also identifies the conditions leading to temporary change and those producing permanent change. His ideas have some resemblance to those of French and Raven (1959) on power, to be discussed in Chapter 8. Kelman (1961) suggests that there are three distinct processes of social influence: *compliance, identification,* and *internalization.*

1. "*Compliance* can be said to occur when an individual accepts influence from another person or from a group because he hopes to achieve a favorable reaction from the other" (p. 62). Here the expression of opinion, even though the person privately disagrees with what he is expressing, is instrumental to gaining some reward or avoiding punishment. Thus an employee aware that his boss is proud of the jokes he tells may laugh heartily at them even though he does not think they are funny. In this way he avoids incurring his boss's displeasure. As might be expected, opinions of this sort are expressed only when they may be observed by the influencing agent.

2. "*Identification* can be said to occur when an individual adopts behavior derived from another person or a group because this behavior is associated with a satisfying self-defining relationship to this person or group" (p. 63). This is a means of establishing or maintaining a desirable relation to the other person or group and of supporting the self-definition that is part of the relation. One form which identification takes is shown in attempts to be like the other person or to actually be the other person. This is commonly observed in children who copy the behavior and attitudes of their parents or other models. In another form of identification, the individual does not attempt to be like another person, but forms a relation to him that demands behavior quite different from his. The individual behaves in terms of the expectations that the other person has with respect to his behavior. For example, a patient behaves in accordance with the expectations of his doctor and adopts his advice and suggestions. A final form of identification[8] maintains the individual's relation to a group in which his self-definition is anchored. Thus, a physician adopts the attitudes and behavior expected of him by his fellow physicians.

[8]Identification will be discussed in more detail in Chapter 17.

Identification, like compliance, does not occur because the behavior or attitude itself is intrinsically satisfying to the individual. It occurs because of the satisfying relation to another person or group, and it requires the activation of the relation in order for it to occur. Thus, in particular settings, an individual performs his role as a doctor, but there are some situations to which this role is not relevant, as for example, situations relating to his wife or children. Unlike the compliance situation, however, the individual actually believes in the attitudes and actions that he adopts as a result of identification.

3. "*Internalization* can be said to occur when an individual accepts influence because the induced behavior is congruent with his value system" (p. 65). Here the content of the induced attitude or behavior is intrinsically rewarding. The attitude or behavior helps to solve a problem or is demanded by the values of the individual. Thus a person with a liberal political attitude is likely to support a government program for medical care of the aged because one of the values to which he subscribes is that government should promote the public welfare.

Which of these various processes are likely to occur depends in part upon the *source of power of the influencing agent.* If he has strong control over rewards and punishment that the individual might receive, compliance is likely. For example, a child may often comply with the strictures of a stern parent even though his private feelings are in other directions. If on the other hand, the relation to the influence agent is a satisfying one, identification is likely to occur. Thus a daughter enjoying an affectionate relation to her mother may adopt many of her attitudes and behaviors. Finally, internalization occurs when the communicator is highly credible or believable. The recommendations of an expert are accepted if they appear to be congruent with one's values.

In a similar fashion, the conditions leading to the reaction of the individual vary for the different influence processes. When the influencing agent is in a position to closely observe an action or a statement of opinion, compliance is likely to occur. The child behaves well when the stern parent is watching him. Identification requires that the relation to the influence agent be a salient one: the situation must be dominated by the relation. The daughter adopts her mother's attitudes, for example, when playing the mother role toward her younger sister. Finally, attitudes or actions that have been internalized are likely to be expressed only when the values that were relevant to the initial acquisition are activated. The values with regard to honesty become particularly salient when the individual is taking an examination, for example.

These processes have somewhat different implications for permanence of the attitude change. An attitude adopted through compliance is likely to be abandoned if the agent exerting the initial influence loses control over the individual. Such attitudes are also likely to remain isolated from other attitudes and values. Behavior or attitudes initiated as a result of identification are maintained only so long as the relation to the influencing agent remains a satisfying one—and so long as the agent himself retains the attitude. Internalized attitudes are likely to persist as long as the values relevant to their adoption are maintained. A final point of importance is that particular situations are not necessarily pure examples of just one of these processes. Often two or more processes occur simultaneously, or all three may operate together. Thus, if an agent has powerful control over a person, but the relation is also a satisfying one, both compliance *and* identification are likely to occur. In addition, if the attitudes or actions required by this situation are also congruent with other attitudes held, internalization may take place.

STUDY QUESTIONS

21. *Explain what is meant by each of the following processes of social influence: (a) compliance, (b) identification, and (c) internalization.*
22. *State the conditions under which each of the above types of influence is likely to be successful and unsuccessful.*

Summary: Kelman's three-process theory

Compliance occurs when a person accepts influence from another individual or a group because he expects to obtain a favorable reaction from the other. With this process private attitudes are unlikely to change, and compliance is likely to occur only when it may be observed by the influencing agent.

Identification occurs when a person adopts certain actions or attitudes because they are associated with a satisfying self-defining relation to another individual or group. These actions may closely resemble the behavior of the other person, or they may be based on a relation to him that demands quite different behavior. The continuance of the actions or attitudes depends upon maintaining a continued relation to the influencing agent.

Internalization occurs when a person accepts influence because the induced behavior is congruent with his value system. In this case, but not in the cases of compliance of identification, the attitude or behavior is intrinsically rewarding. The theory takes into account the source of power of the influencing agent, the various conditions that control each of the influence processes, and their implications for permanence of attitude change.

Summary and Conclusions

Rosenberg's approach provides an explicit means of relating affective and cognitive components and demonstrates that attitude cognitions are instrumentally related to values. Unlike Festinger, however, he explicitly limits himself to "internal consistency," excluding from consideration behavioral elements as well as the various external conditions that might facilitate or block attitude change. The strength of Festinger's dissonance theory is the linkage it provides between behavior and attitude. This is especially evident in the forced-compliance situation, where behavior discrepant with existing attitudes is experimentally elicited.

Although Katz accepts consistency as the basis of the value function and knowledge function, he believes that consistency has certain limits. Along with his collaborator Stotland, he suggests that the principle is especially applicable to single attitude objects: the affective, cognitive, and behavior components toward a *single* object move toward consistency. Much inconsistency, however, may exist among different attitudes, according to Katz and Stotland. In a sense, dissonance theory provides for this by declaring that many cognitive elements are irrelevant to each other. But perhaps a theoretical system is needed that handles irrelevant as well as relevant elements. Katz stresses the importance of motivational factors conceived in terms long familiar to psychologists. In a wider sense, his adjustive and ego-defensive functions stress a broader consistency principle, embracing motivation and action.

Kelman, like Festinger, Rosenberg, and Katz, recognizes the role of internal consistency in attitude change. Like Katz, he suggests two other processes by which attitudes may be changed. He differs from all the other theorists in making a sharper distinction between overt and covert behavior—between public expression and private opinion. His three-process theory treats these two aspects of behavior as relatively independent of each other.

In contrast, Festinger is very explicit about the relation between these two facets of behavior. Speaking of compliance brought about by reward or threat of punishment, he states that if the compliant behavior is at variance with private attitudes, "dissonance inevitably follows from such a situation." It is likely, but not inevitable, that such dissonance will move the individual in the direction of private conformity in order to reduce the dissonance.

Kelman's approach attempts to specify conditions under which situations produce public conformity with little "dissonance" and others that produce more "dissonance" and probably lead to changes in private attitudes. His approach seems best suited to understanding long-term shifts in attitude occurring as a result of ongoing associations with other persons.

These four theories are only a sample chosen from a larger number of theories that have many points of similarity but some important differences. As a group, they make major contributions to the problems of attitude organization and change. Perhaps the most important general contribution of attitude theory is that it helps to solve the problem of *validity*. Throughout the history of attitude research, some psychologists and sociologists have been skeptical because, they asserted, the concept of attitudes was of doubtful validity. By this was meant that, unless it could be demonstrated that a person holding a particular position on an attitude continuum behaved in accordance with that position, the measurement of attitude was invalid. It was more or less assumed that there should be a direct correspondence between a person's overt behavior and his feelings and thoughts as indicated by his responses to an attitude test.

The relation between attitude and behavior is no longer conceptualized in such simple terms. Today we understand that it is necessary to have a theoretical structure that defines the conditions and the manner in which cognitive, affective, and behavioral elements do correspond to each other. The various theories permit us to devise experiments to study the manifold relations between cognitive, affective, and behavioral elements and the conditions that affect these relations. Thus, these theories enable us to make sense out of a great many otherwise unrelated phenomena. Present-day attitude theory, however, is by no means complete. The very existence of so many competing theories suggests that many problems remain to be solved. For example, a recent review of the early research on dissonance theory offers alternative interpretations of findings and points up many inadequacies in experimental design and analysis (Chapanis & Chapanis, 1964).

In the following three chapters, the various research findings on attitude change will be described, and the theories already discussed will often be referred to in the attempt to explain the results of the various experiments. It will also become apparent that consistency theories are not entirely representative of attitude theory. Some investigators have attempted to apply learning theory to attitude research. Such theory assumes a greater diversity of motivation underlying attitude change than simply the need to restore consistency. The learning-theory approach also emphasizes attitude change as a process covering a broader span of time than is generally dealt with by consistency theories. To some extent, the theories of Katz and Stotland and of Kelman take learning theory into account, but further applications of learning theory to attitude change will be introduced from time to time in the chapters which follow.

chapter four

PROCESSES OF ATTITUDE CHANGE

The first of the major topics to be discussed in this chapter is the role of the communicator in influencing attitude change, particularly the relative efficacy of communicators who vary in credibility. Second, some attention is given to the effectiveness of communications that emphasize threat. This is a common technique in advertising such products as automobile insurance, mouthwashes, and deodorants. The threat is intended to arouse some anxiety over potential financial loss in the case of insurance, or over personal unpopularity in the case of mouthwashes and deodorants. A third topic is the organization of the communication. Communications may present one side or both sides of an argument. They may also have various sequential arrangements that are more or less effective. The last section of the chapter treats the effects on attitude change of committing oneself to a particular choice or line of behavior. Dissonance theory is particularly useful in explaining the consequences of such commitment for changes in attitudes.

Credibility of the Communicator

Long before behavioral science developed, the importance of the communicator in the influence process was recognized. History calls attention to the many public figures who were notable for their skill in persuading the masses—sometimes in inflaming them to riot and other forms of violence, sometimes in calming them and preventing hasty action.

Certainly the prestige or status of the communicator affects the acceptance or rejection of his communications. Some of the early experiments in psychology demonstrated the importance of the communicator's prestige simply by presenting the same communications to separate but similar groups of students, in one instance with the communication represented as coming from a prestigious figure, and in another from an unknown person or from a person toward whom the students had negative attitudes. More recently, Hovland, Janis, and Kelley (1953) have discussed in a more systematic fashion the role of the communicator in the process of persuasion.

These authors note that a communicator can accomplish change in a variety of ways. If he has a striking personality, he may well command considerable attention, adding to the effectiveness of his message. If he has high status in a group, his position may suggest group approval — in which case he derives his power not so much from his own personality as from his position. Thus, messages to the people from the President of the United States command their attention and also, because of the high prestige of his office, are likely to be accepted. Another type of communication may call for an expert communicator — one who knows the answers to technical questions because of his training and experience. In general, Hovland, Janis, and Kelley identify two major components of what they term the *credibility* of the communicator — that is, how believable he is. The characteristics of the communicator are *expertness* and *trustworthiness*.

Expertness may derive from special training or education, from experience, and from somewhat more general attributes such as age, position, or social background. The determinants of trustworthiness are more difficult to identify. Again, position or status may evoke a feeling of trust. Certain personality characteristics, particularly physical appearance, ways of expressing oneself, and other mannerisms, may be associated with trustworthiness. One of the marks of a successful confidence man is that he appears to be so honest and straightforward (Sutherland, 1937). Another factor in trustworthiness is the perceived intent of the communicator. If he stands to gain through acceptance of his message by other persons, he is usually considered less trustworthy. Many people therefore are skeptical of the communications of publicity agents, salesmen, politicians, and purveyors of television and radio commercials.

EXPERIMENTATION ON COMMUNICATOR CREDIBILITY

In experiments assessing the impact of communicator credibility, two kinds of effects are important. One is the audience's *evaluation* of the communicator and his message, and the other is the amount of *attitude change* (or behavioral change) produced by the communication. Experiments use a variety of different communications: (1) magazine articles on different topics purported to come from communicators of high and low credibility, (2) a recording of a radio program on appropriate treatment for delinquents variously attributed (for different listening groups) to a judge of a juvenile court, a layman, and a speaker discovered to be a former delinquent, and (3) a recorded communication on the devaluation of currency, in one case presented by an economics professor likely to be considered unbiased, and in the other, by an importer (whose business would be markedly improved by devaluation).

Typically, such experiments use attitude questions before and after presentation of the communication. The questions generally have multiple-choice answers to which the experimenter can assign numerical values, so that he can obtain a quantitative index of the amount of attitude change occurring as a result of the communication. More recently it has been shown quite clearly (Lana, 1959) that the testing prior to the communication can be eliminated and that postcommunication assessment of attitude is quite adequate and in some instances preferable for testing various hypotheses. In this procedure, subjects are assigned at random to experimental and control conditions, so that their initial attitudes are known to be equivalent except for random variation. The experimental group is exposed to the communication, but the control group is not. Any difference in attitude between the groups over and above random variation may safely be attributed to the persuasive communication.

Another objective of design is the avoidance of the "guinea-pig effect." This phenomenon is illustrated by the tendency of persons to cooperate with the experimenter: If they understood that he was interested in whether or not they had changed their attitudes in accord with the communication, they might well slant their answers in the desired direction. Such answers might not be representative of their behavior in nonexperimental situations. A second consequence that might result from knowledge that they were being studied is that they would tend to be more consistent in their "before" and "after" responses than if they were unaware of the connection between the two questionnaires. To avoid the guinea-pig effect, care is usually taken to embed the relevant questions in a larger questionnaire, which ostensibly has some purpose other than to assess the effects of the communication on opinion change. Often the questionnaire and the communication are temporally separated (as when the prequestions are given one week before the communication) so that when they receive the communication, the subjects do not see its relation to the earlier questionnaire. The guinea-pig effect is also less likely to occur if only postcommunication attitudes are assessed.

STUDY QUESTIONS

1. *What are the factors that lead to the communicator being perceived as a highly credible person?*
2. *Distinguish between the* evaluation *of a communication and the* acceptance *of a communication.*
3. *What is meant by the "guinea-pig effect" in experimentation on attitude change? How may it be controlled?*

FINDINGS CONCERNING COMMUNICATOR CREDIBILITY

In three experiments reported by Hovland, Janis, and Kelley (1953), evaluation of the communicator was determined by asking such questions as these: Was the author (of the magazine article) fair in his presentation? Are the conclusions of the communicator justified by the facts? Did the program do a good job of giving the facts? Answers to the questions indicated that the reactions to the communications were definitely affected by the audience's perceptions of the communicator's intentions, expertness, and trustworthiness. When it had been presented by a communicator of high credibility, a communication was judged more favorably than the same message presented by a person of low credibility.

With respect to attitude change, the results were not quite so consistent. Only two of the three experiments produced greater attitude change for the highly credible communicator than for the communicator of low credibility. Also worth noting is that even communicators of low credibility brought about some attitude change in the direction of the communication. Moreover, when attitudes measured immediately after the presentation of the communication were compared with attitudes persisting three or four weeks later, it was found that the effects of communicator credibility had disappeared during this period. Possibly this may result from a dissociation of the source of the communication from the communication itself—the individual recalls some of the communication, but does not spontaneously associate it with a particular communicator.

Interaction between communicator credibility and the communication

The total communication process should be kept in mind when considering the effects of persuasive communications. It may be thought that credibility effects occur because the communicator "attaches his prestige" to the message, leading to its acceptance. Asch (1952) has noted, however, that the process is not this simple. He found that the *meaning* of the communication is partially determined by the reputation of the person who makes the statement. By presenting to various groups of students the same statements attributed to different authors, Asch was able to demonstrate alterations in the perceived meaning of the message. Take, for example, this quotation from Jefferson: "I hold it that a little rebellion, now and then, is a good thing, and as necessary in the political world as storms are in the physical." Following are interpretations by one student who was told that Jefferson was the speaker and by another who was told that Lenin was the speaker:[1]

Jefferson probably meant rebellion as an upheaval in personal political opinions within a party, rather than a	Lenin based his statement on the Marxian dynamic concept of society. He implied that the world is ever

[1]Reprinted by permission from S. E. Asch. *Social psychology*, pp. 420–421. Copyright 1952. Prentice-Hall, Inc., Englewood Cliffs, N.J.

revolutionary turnover of one party by another.

changing and that rebellions were necessary, now and then, to ensure the progress of society. He also implies that individuals can influence their destinies by their own actions.

These quotations clearly indicate a change in the cognitive content of the statement. Each student assimilates the passage to his understanding of the assumed author. There is an interaction between the context, comprised of the communicator and the respondent's knowledge of him, and the respondent's understanding of the communication. Thus, if a respondent is distrustful of a communicator, he may interpret an otherwise credible message to make it less believable.

Interpretations of the effects of credibility

Hovland, Janis, and Kelley asked why a highly credible communicator is more effective than a communicator with low credibility. One possible explanation they considered was that people will not listen to a communicator of low credibility; certainly they are not likely to in a nonexperimental situation. In an experimental situation, the audience is a captive one and cannot escape; but even there, respondents might pay less attention to a communicator of low credibility and might make fewer attempts to understand the communication. A second possible explanation of the difference in effectiveness was that respondents are more inclined to *accept* a communication from a source with high credibility than from one with low credibility.

It was possible to rule out the first of these explanations—that low credibility lowers attention. In all three experiments reported by Hovland, Janis, and Kelley, information tests were given to determine the degree to which the audience had learned the communication, and it was found that the credibility of the communicator made no difference in this respect.[2] Thus it seems unlikely that there could have been differences in attentiveness toward the different communicators. This leaves the second explanation as the more likely. Apparently, messages presented by communicators of low credibility are less likely to be accepted.

The effects of credibility deserve examination from another point of view. Let us assume that the communications used in the experiments reported were fairly persuasive—a reasonable assumption, since even the communications delivered by communicators low in credibility produced *some* attitude change. From the point of view of consistency theory, the two situations differing in credibility are quite different. The situation involving the highly credible communicator and the persuasive communication is consonant, balanced, or congruous; but the situation involving the low-credibility communicator and the persuasive communication is dissonant, unbalanced, or incongruous.

[2]In one experiment (Kelman & Hovland, 1953), there was greater recall for a neutral communicator about whom no information was given.

The most likely resolution of this incongruity in the experiments discussed would be that the communicator is perceived as somewhat more credible than he would be had he delivered a less persuasive message, and also that the message is perceived as somewhat less persuasive than it would be had it been delivered by a more credible communicator. Incongruity is resolved by a compromise process in which both communication and communicator are reinterpreted. This is in accordance with our previous discussion of the tendency of respondents to reinterpret the meaning of communications to make them more consistent with their knowledge of the communicator. It is also consistent with Osgood and Tannenbaum's congruity theory (1955), which predicts that where a listener is inclined to favorably evaluate both the communicator and his communication, but to a different degree, the difference will be resolved by shifting both evaluations toward each other. Evidence is consistent with this view (Tannenbaum, 1956).

STUDY QUESTIONS

4. *What is meant by the statement that the communicator and the communication* interact *to produce an effect?*
5. *What are three ways in which the effects of communicator credibility on evaluation and acceptance of the communication may be interpreted? Are all these interpretations equally valid?*

Fear-arousing Appeals

In considering persuasion through communication, one's attention is often focused on the communication itself. It is natural to think of the communication as the primary force for change. If the communication is effective, one thinks, the desired influence or persuasive effect will take place. In line with this view, many students of the communication process have studied the content of various communications in the attempt to discover what it is that makes them effective or ineffective.

One problem concerns the relative merits of "emotional" versus "rational" appeals. Can the orator skilled at playing upon the emotions of his audience sway it more effectively than the statesman who appeals to its intelligence and good sense? Behavioral scientists have subjected the question of emotional versus rational appeals to controlled experimentation. The early approaches to this topic have been reviewed by Hovland, Janis, and Kelley. Experimental findings are quite contradictory; some support rational appeals and others emotional appeals.

Unfortunately, as Hovland and his colleagues note, the problem was not clearly defined in these early experiments. For one thing, the identification of a communication as having a rational or an emotional appeal is not always clear-cut. A rational appeal may arouse certain emotions; an emotional appeal may make a person think. One experiment (Ruechelle,

1958) has demonstrated quite clearly that both naïve and expert judges were unable to agree on the classification of materials intended by the experimenter to have either a rational or an emotional appeal. Even more serious is the fact that the aspects of a communication which account for its effectiveness or ineffectiveness could not be identified in the early types of experiments conducted. Finally, these early approaches did not clarify why and how emotional or rational appeals lead to an audience response, although knowledge of this is necessary for complete understanding of the problem.

One type of emotional appeal is the "fear appeal," which has been studied in a manner designed to avoid some of the problems just raised. Many mass communications use fear appeals. Government officials, for example, may try to gain support for national defense activities by stressing the dangers inherent in failure to prepare for emergency situations. Health organizations, both public and private, may emphasize disease and pain in an attempt to promote better health. Advertisers sometimes employ fear appeals: A common approach taken by insurance companies is to picture a serious accident in a strange town, emphasizing that "this could happen to you!" Witness also the widespread use by toothpaste and deodorant advertisers of the threat of being unpopular for failure to practice oral or body hygiene by using their products.

In essence, all such appeals "threaten" the individual with unfortunate consequences unless he follows the advice of the communicator. Thus, the terms *threat appeal* or *fear appeal* are commonly used to refer to them. Such threat appeals deserve study because of their widespread use and because of the theoretical problems they raise in connection with understanding persuasive communications.

STRENGTH OF A FEAR APPEAL AND ITS EFFECTIVENESS

A well-known experiment on this topic (Janis & Feshbach, 1953) was designed to examine the effects of three different intensities of fear appeal in a standard communication on dental hygiene. A fifteen-minute illustrated lecture was prepared in three forms, identical in their treatment of the causes of tooth decay and their recommendations on oral hygiene, but differing in the nature and amount of threat material included. The three presentations may be briefly characterized as follows:

1. *The strong appeal.* Here, decay, pain, and disease were stressed. Photographs vividly portraying tooth decay and mouth infections were employed.
2. *The moderate appeal.* Fewer references were made, in a less dramatic manner, to consequences of neglect of oral hygiene. Less serious cases were used as illustrations; photographs involved only mild cases of oral pathology.
3. *The minimum appeal.* Still fewer references were made to the consequences of poor oral hygiene. Instead of photographs involving oral

pathology, X-ray prints were used. Only photographs of healthy mouths were employed.

Some feeling for the nature of the strong appeal may be gained by the following excerpt:

> If you ever develop an infection of this kind from improper care of your teeth, it will be an extremely serious matter because these infections are really dangerous. They can spread to your eyes, or your heart, or your joints and cause secondary infections which may lead to diseases such as arthritic paralysis, kidney damage, or total blindness. (Janis & Feshbach, 1953, p. 79)

Investigators were interested not only in the amount of attitude change, but also in evaluation of the communications — in whether or not the three types of appeal actually created three degrees of anxiety or feelings of threat, as they were designed to. To determine this, the following questions were asked, the respondent being given the choice of five answers to each ranging from *very worried* to *not at all worried*.

> 1. When you think about the possibility that you might develop diseased gums, how concerned or worried do you feel about it?
> 2. When you think about the possibility that you might develop decayed teeth, how concerned or worried do you feel about it?

These questions were asked one week before the communication and immediately thereafter. A tabulation of the responses revealed very clearly that the greatest amount of worry was produced by the strong appeal and that considerably less worry was evoked by the moderate and minimum appeals (these two were not very different in the amount of anxiety aroused).

The experimental subjects had also been asked five questions pertaining to the central issue of the experiment: Did the different communications produce changes in oral hygiene — such as the kind of toothbrush used, methods and frequency of brushing teeth, etc. The most effective appeal proved to be the *minimum appeal*, which brought about a net increase in conformity to accepted practices on the part of 36 percent of the subjects,[3] as compared with no change in a control group not exposed to any communication, and a net change of only 8 percent in the strong-appeal group. This finding is consistent with another study (Nunnally & Bobren, 1959) demonstrating that respondents were less willing to attend to mental health communications arousing high anxiety and presented in a personal manner ("this could happen to you") than they were to less anxiety-arousing, more impersonally presented statements.

The relative effectiveness of the three appeals on dental hygiene was also tested by measuring the subjects' resistance to a later communication opposite to the initial message. One week after the initial communication,

---

[3]In the minimum-appeal group, 50 percent of the subjects increased conformity to accepted practices, 14 percent decreased conformity, and 36 percent showed no change, yielding the net change of 36 percent in the direction of the influence attempt.

all the groups received a countercommunication from another authority who stated that it doesn't matter what kind of toothbrush one uses or how one brushes one's teeth. Presumably, the stronger the initial influence, the more resistant the subjects would be to such countercommunications. After the countercommunication, additional questioning showed that the group which had originally heard the minimum appeal proved most strongly resistant to the countercommunication. Of this group, 32 percent remained unaffected by it, 54 percent became more firmly convinced than ever of the importance of using proper oral hygiene, and only 14 percent shifted their position in the direction of the countercommunication. This represents a net shift of 40 percent *away from* the countercommunication (reiterating the position of the initial communication even more firmly). By way of contrast, in the group which originally heard the strong appeal, a net shift of only 8 percent away from the countercommunication occurred.[4]

In an unpublished study by Janis (described in Hovland, Janis, & Kelley, 1953, pp. 73–74), two printed selections supposedly from popular magazines discussing the dangers of excessive cigarette smoking were presented to some forty adult subjects of varying educational levels. Both versions made the same recommendations and the same threats regarding the consequences of smoking. But in the stronger of the fear-arousing appeals, the threats were elaborated in detail, especially the unpleasant aspects. In the case of this strong fear appeal, the subjects made many spontaneous comments concerning the intent of the communicator and expressed doubts concerning his sincerity. Samples are as follows:

> I was mostly amused by this propaganda effort. I felt this guy is an alarmist and I wondered what his real purpose is. Why is he so aroused about it?

> I think it was written to scare people—to scare them out of the habit of smoking—because it is so extreme. . . . I think he is probably a smoker himself.

> It is overdone. I realized that it might be unpleasant to other people but my reaction was humor. . . . I think he is a crusader, someone who ballyhoos an idea and he may not really believe in it himself; he may not have humanitarian motives. (Hovland, Janis, & Kelley, p. 74)

A number of the more sophisticated subjects who had "discounted the communicator and his communication" indicated elsewhere in their interview that they were somewhat disturbed by what he had said. There is a suggestion here that the fear appeal arouses strong emotion, but the individual reduces his anxiety by a denial mechanism. An alternative interpretation, however, is that the high-pressure tactics of the fear appeal are offensive and arouse resistance. This interpretation has some relation to the dissonance explanation offered below.

[4]In the strong-appeal group, 32 percent remained unaffected by the countercommunication, 38 percent shifted away from the countercommunication in the direction of the original communication, and 30 percent moved in the direction of the countercommunication.

A dissonance interpretation of fear appeals

The strong fear appeal differs from the minimum appeal in that it is *dissonant with a larger number of cognitive elements that the subject already believes.* Some examples of these elements in the dental-hygiene experiment are:

1. I know of no one who has suffered dire consequences from not brushing his teeth.
2. Many people I know well do not brush their teeth regularly and seem to get along all right.
3. I feel perfectly healthy even though I have not been brushing my teeth.

Thus, in the strong fear appeal, the elements presented by the communicator are relevant to and dissonant with a fairly large number of elements that are consonant with existing attitudes and behaviors of the respondent.

By way of contrast, the elements in the minimum fear appeal are dissonant with only a few elements to which the respondent subscribes, and the two sets of elements are more evenly balanced. In the grossly imbalanced situation represented by the strong fear appeal, the easiest mode of reducing dissonance is to reject or discredit the communicator and his communication. This is consistent with Rosenberg and Abelson's (1960) balance theory, which states that the smaller proportion of elements, not the larger, is most likely to be changed. The minimum fear appeal, however, is more balanced. For many respondents, acceptance of the communication may be the easiest way of resolving dissonance.

This discussion may be summarized in a general proposition concerning resistance to a communication: Resistance to a communicator and his communication is a function of the ratio of existing cognitive elements to relevant dissonant elements in the communication. The greater the number of existing cognitive elements relative to dissonant elements in the communication, the greater the resistance.

STUDY QUESTIONS

6. *What is the relation between the strength of a fear appeal and its effectiveness in changing opinion?*
7. *What types of reactions occur commonly when persons are presented with strong fear appeals?*
8. *Explain the reaction to fear appeals of varying strengths in terms of dissonance theory.*

Effects of prior communications on fear arousal

Just as prior attitudes are important in determining the effects of a given communication, earlier communications may also affect the response to later ones. This was clearly illustrated in an experiment (Janis, Lumsdaine, & Gladstone, 1951) conducted before there was any public knowledge that the Soviet Union had produced an atomic bomb. In another connection, an experimental group had been given a pessimistic communication about the atomic bomb—that Russia already had an atomic bomb, had atomic factories, etc. Control groups were available which had not received this communication. Some months later, President Truman announced that Russia did in fact have the atomic bomb. The reaction of the experimental group to this announcement was immediately studied and compared with reactions of the control groups. The group that had already been told Russia had the atomic bomb did not react to Truman's message with as much concern or worry as the groups whose first knowledge came from the President's message.

The investigators suggested that a form of "emotional innoculation" takes place when a fear-arousing communication is first presented and that later communications become less effective as a result. Apparently, various defensive reactions of the individual come into play as a result of the arousal of fear. Studies of the intensive and persistent bombing raids in Britain, Germany, and Japan during World War II similarly suggest that, although at first the average citizen is greatly frightened, he later becomes relatively inured to subsequent raids (Janis, 1951). An intensive study (Janis, 1958) of pre- and postoperative anxiety among surgical patients also suggests that, particularly for patients who would otherwise have low preoperative anxiety, providing information which increases the amount of "worrying" they do prior to the operation reduces the emotional problems often experienced after the operation.

Although alternative interpretations are possible, these findings may be explained in terms of the dissonance principle previously stated. If a communication arouses some dissonance but is unsuccessful in eliciting attitude change, the individual is likely to reduce this dissonance by adding new cognitive elements consonant with his existing cognitive structure. Thus, on a later occasion, a communication similar to the original one will be dissonant with a larger number of elements than was originally the case; and the individual will be even less likely to accept the message than he was earlier. For example, persons receiving a pessimistic communication about Russia having the atomic bomb might well produce such additional elements as "They won't deliver it because we have many more bombs than they have," "They probably have too few bombs to do much damage," etc.

STUDY QUESTIONS

9. *To what extend may a prior communication on the same topic affect a later fear appeal?*
10. *Explain how dissonance theory may be used to interpret the results of experiments with fear appeals. State the major principle for applying dissonance theory to such experiments.*

Organization of the Communication

The way in which a communication is organized and presented may also affect its reception. Many aspects of organization have been studied.

One question concerns the effect of one-sided versus two-sided communications. Should a communicator present just the arguments in favor of the conclusion he wants the audience to adopt, or should he acknowledge and elaborate some of the counterarguments? Another question is whether the message should draw its own conclusion or whether this should be left to the audience. Experiments have also been conducted on the so-called *primacy-recency* problem: Is information presented first or information presented last more effective? Another aspect of message structure is the sequential arrangement of two kinds of elements: (1) those that arouse a need or motive, and (2) those that offer a means of satisfying the need. Many communications must include both pro and con arguments; the most effective ways of arranging these have also been studied. Finally, the effects of the individual's desire for knowledge and its relation to the structure of the communication have been investigated. Each of these topics will be considered in this section.

ONE-SIDED VERSUS TWO-SIDED COMMUNICATIONS

Everyone is familiar with the high-pressure salesman who presents a wealth of overextended arguments in favor of his product and who will not accept any suggestion that the product might have its limitations. Such a communicator represents the extreme of the one-sided case. To what extent is a one-sided presentation effective? Can the introduction of some arguments opposed to the communicator's position improve his effectiveness in persuading others to accept his influence attempt?

One of the best-known experiments (Hovland, Lumsdaine, & Sheffield, 1949) on this topic was conducted during World War II. When Germany surrendered, the military command feared that soldiers in general would fail to appreciate the extensive efforts yet to be expended in defeating Japan.[5] Most soldiers, they thought, might expect to go home long before they actually could be discharged.

In the process of preparing an information program designed to convince soldiers that a long and hard war with Japan was yet to be fought, social psychologists devised an experiment to compare a one-sided program with a two-sided program. The one-sided program mentioned such arguments as the great length of supply lines to our Pacific forces, the resources and stockpiles of Japan, the size and quality of the Japanese army, and the determination of the Japanese people. The two-sided program discussed these same points, but also acknowledged some factors which would favor a short war, such as our naval victories and superiority, the previous progress made in a two-front war, Japanese shipping losses, and future damage from air war. Such arguments for the other side were merely acknowledged; both programs still predicted a long war of at least two years' duration. These communications were presented in recorded form to different groups of soldiers,

[5]The sudden capitulation of Japan resulting from the atomic bombing was not anticipated at that time.

whose opinions were determined before and after the communication. Care was taken to eliminate the guinea-pig effect. A control group received no communication but took the initial and final questionnaires.

The interesting result of this experiment was that neither the one-sided nor the two-sided program had any overall superiority in changing the attitudes of the soldiers. Both programs lengthened the estimate that soldiers generally made of the duration of the war.

More important was the discovery that the two communications had different effects on different groups of soldiers. Of the soldiers who had not completed high school, a larger proportion was influenced by the one-sided communication than by the two-sided communication; conversely, of those who had graduated from high school, a larger proportion was influenced by the two-sided communication. Differences were also apparent according to the initial opinions of the soldiers before exposure to the communication. Those who had originally thought the war would be a short one were more effectively influenced by the two-sided communication, and those who had thought the war would last at least two years were more effectively influenced by the one-sided communication.

Advertising is typically one-sided and rarely contains a negative comment on even a minor aspect of the product. The inclusion of some negative material in an overall favorable context might well produce higher credibility. One rare example is found in the caption in an ad for the English Ford: "Here's the car with 'the inside door handle too far back—but everything else is wonderful'" (Faison, 1961, p. 14). In an experimental attempt to apply the two-sided approach to advertising, Faison prepared one-sided and two-sided commercials on automobiles, gas ranges, and floor wax. These were tested on approximately five hundred high school, vocational school, and college students, and it was found that the two-sided commercials produced significantly more attitude change in favor of the product. This change was still present when tested six weeks later.

Dissonance in one- and two-sided communications

The previously stated principle that resistance to change is a function of the proportion of existing cognitive elements that are dissonant with elements in the communication provides a reasonable interpretation of the results of the experiment cited above. Less educated soldiers presumably had less familiarity with the logical arguments for and against a lengthy war. When exposed to a one-sided communication, they therefore had fewer preexisting elements that were dissonant with the communication, and consequently they were able to accept it.

The better-educated soldiers were presumably more familiar with the various logical arguments opposed to the communication. For them, a one-sided communication ignoring such arguments was dissonant with more existing cognitive elements. These men could reduce the dissonance by adding new consonant elements, such as those questioning the communicator's expertness or his intent. On the other hand, the more complete set of arguments in the two-sided communication was less dissonant with the cognitive elements possessed by the better-educated soldiers. The reader may work out for himself an interpretation based on similar principles that explains why the two-sided communication was more effective for the men who had originally thought the war would be short and the one-sided communication was best for those who had thought the war would be long.

"Innoculating" effects of two-sided presentations

One-sided and two-sided communications also differ in their ability to "innoculate" the respondent against later counterpropaganda. In one experiment (Lumsdaine & Janis, 1953), the two-sided communication was shown to be dramatically effective in innoculating the audience. Different groups of subjects who had heard the argument that Russia would not be able to produce atomic bombs in quantity for at least five years were exposed to a countercommunication at a later date. They differed radically in their receptiveness to the countercommunication, depending upon whether or not the initial message had been one-sided or two-sided. Only 2 percent of those who had initially been exposed to a *one-sided* communication retained the position advocated by that communication, whereas 67 per cent of those who had initially been exposed to a *two-sided* communication retained its position in spite of the counter-communication.

In other words, the effect of the one-sided communication was entirely wiped out by the countercommunication, but the two-sided communication retained its effect.[6] The investigators suggest that the presentation of opposing arguments in a context that rejects them weakens their future effectiveness. Here again, the dissonance principle also fits if we assume that the two-sided presentation is more likely than the one-sided to generate new cognitive elements in support of the communication. These elements later help to resist the counterpropaganda.

Effects of acknowledging counterarguments versus actively refuting them

Another question concerns the manner in which opposing arguments should be handled. Such arguments may merely be acknowledged, as in the experiments already described; or they may be both acknowledged and actively refuted; or they may be acknowledged and actively refuted, with evidence offered to support the refutation. In one sense, the active refutation of opposing arguments makes the communication somewhat more one-sided than it otherwise would be, and thus one might make

---

[6]This is demonstrated by the fact that the acceptance of the initial communication by a control group not exposed to the countercommunication was roughly equal to that for the group exposed to the two-sided communication followed by the countercommunication; namely, 69 percent.

predictions based upon the *degree* of two-sidedness rather than the mere existence of two-sidedness. For example, since simple acknowledgment of opposing arguments represents the most two-sided communication, one would predict that this form of presentation would be most resistant to countercommunications. While this prediction has not been tested, several experiments have been conducted in which the degree of refutation was varied (Thistlethwaite & Kamenetsky, 1955; Thistlethwaite, Kamenetsky, & Schmidt, 1956; Ludlum, 1958). Unfortunately, the findings are ambiguous and contradictory and do not permit drawing a conclusion.

DRAWING THE CONCLUSION VERSUS NOT DRAWING IT

Another problem concerns the effects on attitude change of having the communicator explicitly draw the conclusion of his message for the audience versus having him leave it up to the audience to draw its own conclusion. Logical arguments may be presented in favor of either approach. For example, it might be argued that the audience may draw the wrong conclusion if left to its own devices, or on the contrary, it might be argued that an audience which has made up its own mind will be more likely to accept the communicator's message. Results of experiments on this topic, unfortunately, are inconclusive. In one experiment (Hovland & Mandell, 1957), more change in attitudes was accomplished when the communicator drew the conclusion for the audience. In another experiment (Thistlethwaite, de Haan, & Kamenetsky, 1955), which took greater care to separate comprehension of the message from the effect of the message upon opinion change, there was no difference in acceptance between persons who heard the conclusion drawn and those left to draw their own. The former group, however, did show greater comprehension of the communication.

STUDY QUESTIONS

11. *Describe the circumstances under which (a) one-sided communications are more effective; (b) two-sided communications are more effective.*

12. *Interpret the differential effects of one-sided and two-sided communications in terms of dissonance theory.*

13. *Compare one-sided and two-sided communications with respect to their "innoculation" effects.*

ORDER OF PRESENTATION OF SEPARATE COMMUNICATIONS

Two other questions concerning organization of the communication are (1) What is the most effective order of presentation of separate communications? (2) What is the most effective ordering of the elements in a communication? A typical example of the first question is the separate presentations of their positions by two political candidates appearing on the same television program. Which has the advantage, the first or the second speaker?

The second question has many ramifications. To illustrate one, if a single communication has arguments the audience wants to hear (e.g., taxes can be reduced) and also arguments they are less receptive to (e.g., national defense is weak), in what order should they be arranged?

An entire volume (Hovland, 1957) has been published on order of presentation, and many individual experiments are scattered throughout the research literature. Only the highlights of this topic will be discussed here. The problem has already been introduced in Chapter 2 in connection with the effects of first impressions in judging personality. In that instance, the question was whether information presented first has a stronger effect than information presented last (the so-called primacy-recency issue). With some qualification, experimental results favored information presented first; first impressions were stronger than later ones. In this section we are interested in the primacy-recency question as it applies to successive persuasive communications, as well as to the elements of a single communication.

The so-called "law of primacy"

The question has been raised as to whether or not a "law of primacy" applies to persuasive processes. Do initial communications, like first impressions, have a stronger impact than later ones? In 1957 Hovland and Mandell found that although some experiments have yielded significant results in favor of primacy, others failed to confirm these results and in some instances favored recency. They suggest that primacy is more likely to occur in an experiment where the classroom instructor is the experimenter. Students may receive the first communication as something to be learned, and the prestige of the instructor is likely to command its acceptance. In this context, the second communication, having a content opposite to the first, is likely to be confusing and therefore is less likely to be accepted. A more recent review by Lana (1964) points out that primacy occurs only under certain conditions and that with our present knowledge incomplete, primacy-recency is not entirely predictable from experimental conditions.

Several discussions (Bateman & Remmers, 1941; Hovland, Janis, & Kelley, 1953; Miller & Campbell, 1959) suggest another reason why primacy-recency investigations of communication often do not yield consistent results. The temporal arrangement of the communications and of the tests measuring the subject's knowledge of the communications is likely to have marked effects upon recall and acceptance of the messages. From extensive experimentation on forgetting, we know that if two communications are equally well learned, the more recent of them will be better remembered. But this difference varies with the interval between presentations and with the interval between the last presentation and the test of recall. As every student studying for his final examination knows, material that he learned well early in the term is not re-

'called as easily as material well learned at the end of the term. He also knows that at the end of the term, there is little difference in his recall of material learned in the second and third weeks of the term, even though the latter was more recently learned. Two factors, then, favor recency: (1) a longer interval between successive communications, and (2) presentation of a test for retention of the materials immediately after the last communication.

As far as recall is concerned, learning theory predicts a recency effect in the typical experiment on successive persuasive communications. Communications are typically presented in immediate succession, followed by an immediate recall test. Although the successive presentation does not favor either primacy or recency, the immediate recall test favors recency. Thus it is surprising that primacy effects have been attained at all. It is possible that if these experiments had used delayed tests of acceptance and recall, results would have favored primacy to a greater extent than they have. A recent experiment (Miller & Campbell, 1959) with persuasive communication confirms a maximum interval between communications and immediacy of the *recall* test as favoring recency. It further demonstrates that a primacy effect occurs on *acceptance* (not recall) of the communication under conditions that minimize recency.

A final caution should be added. Under nonexperimental conditions, where individuals are not a captive audience and are free to attend to or reject whatever communications they please, communications that reach them initially may be more effective because the individual may elect not to attend to later communications that oppose those he has accepted. This points up the desirability of being the first to get your message across in a practical situation, but it does not, of course, mean that later communications are "weaker." A possible reason why initial communications may have more effect in a nonexperimental situation is that individuals may make commitments to a given position after hearing the communication and thus may feel compelled to reject contrary communications. Although one experiment (Bennett, 1955) supports the view that commitment strengthens an attitude, three other studies (Hovland, Campbell, & Brock, 1957; Luchins, 1957; Anderson, 1959) specifically concerned with primacy and recency provide no support for this suggestion.

ORDERING OF ELEMENTS WITHIN A COMMUNICATION

We turn now to another aspect of presentation: the arrangements of the elements of a single communication in order to maximize attitude change. The following topics will be discussed: (1) the effects of ordering elements so that they first arouse a need and then present information calculated to satisfy the need, (2) the optimal sequential arrangement of arguments pro and con, and (3) the arrangement of elements having desirable and undesirable consequences in order to achieve maximum acceptance.

Ordering of elements pertaining to need arousal and its satisfaction

A common practice in advertising is to arouse a need and then to offer a means of satisfying the need. An advertisement, for example, may attempt to arouse a desire to drink something and then suggest that the advertised product will best fit the need. One study has examined the problem of sequence here, testing the following hypothesis: "A communication situation in which information assumed to satisfy aroused needs is placed after need arousal will bring more acceptance of that information than a situation in which the information is placed before need arousal" (Cohen, 1957, p. 81).

College students were presented with communications on grading practices calculated to arouse some apprehension lest grading be stiffened. One communication presented information arousing apprehension followed by information resolving the apprehension, and the other presented the same information in reverse. The results strongly favored the hypothesis. Worth noting, however, is that individuals who had strong needs to structure (or make sense out of) the communication were equally influenced by both communication sequences. The hypothesis was confirmed, then, mainly for those persons who had low needs to structure communications. Apparently, when presented with information relevant to need satisfaction before arousal of the need, they are unable to use it for need satisfaction after the need has been aroused. The group with low needs for structure also showed a significant decrease in acceptance when tested three months later, an effect not found in the other respondents. Another study (Nunnally & Bobren, 1959) is consistent with the main findings. When anxiety was aroused by a communication on mental illness, acceptance was increased if solutions to problems raised by the communication were also given.

STUDY QUESTIONS

14. *Explain what is meant by the statement that order of presentation of material may be studied with respect to separate communications or a single communication.*
15. *What is the law of primacy? How valid is this law?*
16. *When a communication contains two kinds of elements, one tending to arouse a need and the other providing information leading to the satisfaction of the need, what is the most effective sequence in which these elements should be arranged?*

Sequence of pro and con arguments

The familiar two-sided communication discussed previously can be studied from another angle, namely, in what *sequence* should the pro and con arguments be presented?[7] Probably every reader has experienced a situation where he has been led to commit himself to some action or opinion against his real wishes. How does this happen? One means of

---

[7]*Pro* arguments are those which favor the communicator's position; *con* arguments are those opposed.

accomplishing it is to present him with a series of communications with which he agrees, and only at the end, after acceptance has been assured, to present the remaining elements, with which he disagrees. One study (Janis & Feierabend, 1957) examined the relative effectiveness of two communications: one in which pro arguments were followed by con arguments, and another in which con arguments were followed by pro arguments. The presentation of the pro arguments first was found to lead to greater acceptance of the communication in two experiments with high school students on the topic of civil defense.[8] The reason for this, it was suggested, is that at a certain point in the communication process before he hears the con arguments, the individual accepts the communicator's message and from that point on tends to be less influenced by the opposing arguments which follow. On the other hand, if an individual hears con arguments first, he is likely to avoid conflict by ignoring or disputing the pro arguments which follow.

The investigators were careful to note that their hypothesis is likely to hold only for *nonsalient* con arguments, that is, arguments that the individual is not likely to think of himself. The reason for this is easy to see. If the respondent hears a whole succession of pro arguments but has clearly in mind certain con arguments which are not mentioned by the communicator, the extreme one-sidedness of the communication to that point is likely to lead him to reject the communicator or communication. At the very least, his acceptance will be relatively weak, and the presentation of the con arguments at the end of the communication will do little to strengthen acceptance. The logical argument for the pro-con sequence is based primarily on the assumption that by the time the pro arguments have been presented, the individual has strongly accepted the communication, thus weakening the impact of the subsequent con arguments. Also worth noting is that the pro-con sequence is probably superior only when the audience contains a substantial proportion of persons who differ from the communicator. Where the audience is already on the communicator's side, the pro-con sequence is unlikely to be superior to the con-pro.

Learning successive elements

Another study applies learning theory to order of presentation of elements. The learning-theory interpretation is as follows: "If, for example, the source remains the same for a series of messages, the receipt of each message can be considered a separate conditioning trial on which the source constitutes a stimulus to which the response of agreement is being conditioned (or extinguished)" (McGuire, 1957, p. 98).

This idea was tested experimentally by having a communicator transmit a series of communications each arguing for the likelihood of some

---

[8]Although the two communications resulted in different degrees of favorableness toward civil defense, few students hearing either communication actually volunteered for civil defense work.

future contingency which was either pleasant or unpleasant. Acceptance of the communication could be thought of as either rewarding or punishing. For example, suppose a communicator argued that the scheduling of 7 A.M. classes was to be markedly increased in order to relieve the classroom shortage. A college student who accepted this message and who disliked early morning classes would, of course, experience displeasure ("punishment") at the thought of having to go to class at 7 A.M.

The major hypothesis tested by the experiment was the following:

> When those messages supporting the likelihood of pleasant contingencies were presented first and those supporting the likelihood of unpleasant contingencies offered later, a greater total amount of agreement with the message contents would be evoked than when the messages were presented in reverse order, i.e., with the undesirable messages followed by desirable ones. (Pp. 99–100)

The reasoning underlying this hypothesis is that when pleasant contingencies are presented first, responses of paying attention, comprehending, and accepting conclusions will be progressively strengthened. These strong responses will also occur when the communications involving unpleasant contingencies are subsequently presented, and thus these communications will also be learned and accepted. On the other hand, when messages referring to unpleasant contingencies are presented first, the responses of paying attention, comprehending, and accepting will be weakened by punishment. The individual will learn to withhold attention and comprehension, so that by the time the messages involving pleasant contingencies are presented, he will have developed a habit of ignoring or not accepting them.

After preliminary questioning had determined the desirability and undesirability of various events, as well as the estimated likelihood of their occurrence, persuasive communications pertaining to them were presented in either of two sequences: (1) two messages arguing for the probability of two desirable events followed by two messages pertaining to two undesirable events, and (2) the reverse order. Acceptance of the communications, as measured by postexperimental questionnaires, proved to be significantly greater for the persons exposed to the desirable-undesirable sequence than for the reverse sequence. Moreover, an information test demonstrated that learning was greater for the desirable-undesirable sequence, while evaluative responses indicated that this effect was not the result of greater credibility of the communicator in the desirable-undesirable sequence.

Thus, it appears that even in a captive audience, individuals are capable of selectively exposing themselves to different communications according to the pleasant or unpleasant consequences of the messages. When a series of messages are presented by the same source, their effects in terms of reward or punishment are progressive: Responses to later messages are affected by experiences with earlier ones.

STUDY QUESTIONS

17. *Describe the most effective sequence for pro and con arguments in a communication, and give the reasons why this sequence is optimal. To what type of argument does this sequence apply?*

18. *What ordering of communication elements having pleasant and unpleasant contingencies leads to maximum attitude change? Explain why this is so.*

SUMMARY: ORGANIZATION OF THE COMMUNICATION

Many aspects of the organization of the communication have been studied. One question is whether one-sided or two-sided communications are more effective. No general answer to this has been provided: the relative effectiveness of the two types of communications varies with different conditions. One-sided communications appear to be more effective than two-sided messages if the audience is already in substantial agreement with the communicator or if the audience lacks knowledge concerning the issues and arguments. Both of these conclusions are consistent with the principle that resistance to a communication is a direct function of the number of existing cognitive elements that are dissonant with elements of the communication. Two-sided communications also appear to "innoculate" the person against later counterpropaganda to which he may be exposed.

Although communications that draw the conclusion for the audience have been compared with communications that allow the audience to draw its own conclusion, no clear-cut findings in favor of either have emerged.

Two additional questions concerning organization of the communication are (1) What is the most effective order of presentation of separate communications? (2) What is the most effective order of elements in a communication? The first question has led to a number of experiments to determine whether a communication was more effective when it was presented prior to another communication or after another communication. This is commonly referred to as the primacy-recency question: If the first communication is more effective, the result is referred to as a primacy effect; if the last is more effective, as a recency effect.

A number of methodological problems were encountered in this experimentation that made it difficult to determine whether primacy or recency of communication had the advantage. In the typical experiment, both communications are presented in immediate succession and are followed by an immediate test of recall and of attitude change. Presenting both communications in immediate succession provides little advantage to recency; presenting the test immediately after the last communication clearly favors recency. These effects hold true with respect to the amount of learning of the communication that takes place. They also apply to attitude change resulting from acceptance of the communication, although for acceptance, primacy may be somewhat stronger than recency. Under nonexperimental conditions, primacy is likely to have advantages over recency.

When a communication contains two kinds of elements, one tending to arouse a need and the other providing information leading to the satisfaction of the need, the most effective arrangement presents the need-arousing elements first and the elements providing need satisfaction last.

Communications often contain some arguments (called pro arguments) that favor the communicator's position and other arguments (called con arguments) that are opposed to his position. If the con arguments are nonsalient (not likely to be thought of by the respondent), the most effective sequence in which they may be presented is pro arguments first, con arguments last. This finding is consistent with approach-avoidance concepts derived from learning theory. Another experiment viewed arguments as reinforcing if they led to favorable consequences for the respondent and as punishing if they produced unfavorable consequences. Presentation of the favorable arguments first was found to be more effective, a result consistent with the hypothesis that a "habit" of acceptance or rejection is built up, depending upon the order in which arguments are presented.

Commitment and Attitude Change

Dissonance theory has been used to interpret a variety of phenomena. Many of them, however, may be explained by other theories. The present section discusses phenomena that are particularly amenable to dissonance theory interpretations and difficult to explain by other methods. A recent book (Brehm & Cohen, 1962) reviewing research in this field cites approximately fifty articles directly devoted to dissonance theory. It is inevitable that such great activity would lead to a reevaluation of the theory and new perspectives on it. One contribution of this research is clarification of the circumstances under which dissonance is clearly aroused and under which predictions are relatively unique to dissonance theory. These circumstances are best established when an individual *commits* himself either to choosing one of two or more alternatives, or to engaging in actions contrary to his attitudes.

TWO FORMS OF COMMITMENT PRODUCING DISSONANCE

One of the commonest forms of choice made in everyday situations is commitment to one of two or more alternative actions, where commitment to one path requires giving up alternate actions. Usually the various alternatives possess both positive and negative aspects. For example, a person may decide between two automobiles, two houses, or two girls. Dissonance should arise as a result of this choice if the chosen object has some negative qualities or if the forsaken object has some positive ones. The presence of the dissonance should then lead to efforts to reduce it. Often these take the form of attempts to add cognitive elements that augment the positive values of the chosen object and detract from the forsaken object.

For example, evidence has been presented to the effect that new car owners, many of whom presumably considered another make of automobile before making their selection, attempted to reduce dissonance after their purchase by reading advertisements about the make of car they had bought (Ehrlich et al., 1957). Since advertisements contain a large number of favorable elements, this behavior may be interpreted as an attempt to reduce dissonance arising from a commitment that required abandonment of the advantages of the alternate purchase.

A second form of commitment that creates dissonance requires a person to behave in a manner opposite to his attitudes. Brehm gives a good example of this kind of situation:

> Suppose a town mayor privately believed that taxes should be raised though his party took the official stand that taxes should be lowered. Suppose further that his party would not support him for re-election unless he spoke out in favor of lower taxes, and party support was necessary to be assured of election. Thus to keep on good terms with his party in general and to keep his job of mayor in particular, the individual would have to argue against his private attitude on the issue of taxation. Clearly his verbal behavior would be discrepant from his private attitude. (Brehm, 1960*b*, pp. 165–166)

This type of situation is termed a *forced-compliance* situation, or the behavior is referred to as *attitude-discrepant behavior*. Many other illustrations of behavior contrary to attitudes can be given. Every employee, for example, has to do his work in a manner prescribed by his superiors, a manner sometimes different from what he would choose if left to his own devices. Often in the course of his work he is required to carry out a variety of tasks which are disagreeable to him because they run counter to his attitudes. In the family, each individual member cannot do as he pleases and must show some regard for the wishes of the other members: this produces much attitude-discrepant behavior. The housewife and mother, for example, often resents some aspects of her role, particularly if she has a strong inclination to follow some occupational career.

The process by which an individual becomes a member of a group is also relevant. When he joins a group, it is unlikely that he possesses to the fullest extent the same attitudes as the typical group member. Having joined, however, he behaves in accordance with the demands of the group, and to the extent that his behavior is discrepant with his attitudes, he is likely to shift them so as to conform to the group norms.

Since dissonance theory is formulated to suggest fairly complete resolution of dissonance by changing one of the two sets of opposing elements, it is especially suited to irrevocable-choice situations or to attitude-discrepant behavior. Once an expensive object like a car or house has been purchased, the decision cannot be reversed without considerable cost. Thus dissonance cannot be resolved through some sort of compromise: one cannot enjoy the advantages of both objects and avoid the negative aspects of the one possessed. Similarly, in the forced-compliance situation "something has to give" in order to achieve consonance: A compromise is not sufficient. Our town mayor, pressed by his party to lower taxes and by his private convictions to raise them, cannot resolve his dissonance by recommending no change in taxes, for that would satisfy neither his party nor his own convictions. Some of the other balance theories are constructed to allow resolution through changes in both sets of elements, but this compromise type of resolution does not apply very well to irrevocable-choice situations or to attitude-discrepant behaviors.

STUDY QUESTIONS

19. *What are the advantages of commitment situations for studying dissonance theory?*

20. *What are two major forms of commitment situations that produce dissonance?*

EXPERIMENTAL FINDINGS ON CHOICE SITUATIONS

A typical dissonance experiment (Brehm, 1956) on a choice situation was presented to the subjects as if it were experimental work being done on a contract basis for a group of manufacturers. College women (mostly sophomores) were asked to make judgments on an 8-point rating scale of the desirability of eight different objects, such as an automatic coffee maker, a sandwich grill, a desk lamp, etc. By desirability was meant the attractiveness, quality, and usefulness of the object to the girl herself. The experimenter explained to the subjects that they would be paid for their participation by being given one of the eight objects, but that it was not possible to give everyone her choice. Each girl was to make her selection from a pair "chosen at random" by the experimenter. In actuality, the experimenter presented each girl with a pair suited to the degree of dissonance he wished to create. The choice of the pair presented to each subject depended upon her previous ratings. For one group of subjects, the experimenter created high dissonance by presenting a pair of objects both of which had been rated high in desirability, to a relatively equal extent. For another group, objects having moderate or low and not quite so equal desirability were presented in order to create low dissonance. A control condition was also used where the subject was given one of the objects without having made a choice.

After having made their selection, a portion of the subjects was presented with new information as a source of additional cognitive elements that might be used to reduce dissonance. The experimenter explained that four manufacturers had expressed an interest in knowing what customers thought was good or bad about their product. Subjects were asked to read brief "research reports" for four products, including the two that they had made their choice from. He then asked various questions about the opinions formed by the girls. Following this, he said that the manufacturers were interested in reactions that customers might have after leaving the store with their product, and all subjects were asked to rate the eight products again.

A main hypothesis of the experiment was that when subjects had been provided with new information after having made a choice, in the high-dissonance situation the desirability of the chosen product would be increased and the desirability of the rejected alternative decreased. This was confirmed. The overall change in desirability for the two items combined was statistically significant for the high-dissonance group but not for the low-dissonance group.[9] Additional findings are of interest. In the condition where subjects were not provided with new information from which they might draw additional cognitive elements, the difference between the high- and low-dissonance groups was not significant. Also, in the control condition, where the subject did not have a choice of two alternatives, no appreciable change in desirability ratings occurred. Hence, *choice* appears to be crucial in creating dissonance.

In order to demonstrate that the findings on choice in laboratory experiments might be applied to highly important decisions in real-life situations, a study (Cohen, 1962) was made of thirty Yale college students who were considering becoming engaged during the Christmas vacation. Prior to the vacation, they were asked questions intended to measure the positive and negative aspects of becoming engaged, such as the following: "How important an issue is loss of freedom to you in considering engagement?" "How much difference in 'social levels' would you say there is between you and your fiancée?" Before and after the vacation, they were also asked questions aimed at assessing the degree of positive affect toward the prospective fiancée.

The greater the number of negative aspects of engagement perceived by the student prior to the engagement, the more dissonance he would feel if he became engaged. Since aspects of engagement are relatively objective and difficult to change, and positive affect is more subjective and more readily changed, it was expected that dissonance aroused would be resolved by an increase in positive affect. Thus the main hypothesis was that the greater the number of negative aspects of engagement perceived by the student prior to the engagement, the more he would increase positive affect toward his fiancée.

To test the hypothesis, the twenty students who actually became engaged during the vacation were divided into two groups, one consisting of those who had indicated a larger number of negative aspects of engagement (high dissonance), and the other of those who had indicated a fewer number of negative aspects (low dissonance). As predicted, the high-dissonance group showed a significantly greater increase in positive affect toward the fiancées than did the low-dissonance group. Because of its correlational design and lack of laboratory controls, the investigation is subject to alternative interpretations, but nevertheless it suggests how dissonance theory may be applied to real-life situations.

[9] All ratings were corrected for a possible artifact due to statistical regression.

The research literature on choice situations has been nicely summarized by Brehm and Cohen (1962, p. 303). Each of the following principles is supported by one or more experiments:

1. When the person chooses between attractive alternatives, the *more attractive* the rejected alternative, the greater the dissonance.
2. When the person chooses between two courses of action, the *more negative* the characteristics of the chosen alternative, the greater the dissonance.
3. When the person chooses between attractive alternatives, the *greater the number* of rejected alternatives, the greater the dissonance.
4. The *less similar* the attractive alternatives, the greater the dissonance.
5. The *more recent* the choice between attractive alternatives, the greater the dissonance.
6. The *more important* the relevant cognitions pertaining to a decision, the greater the dissonance.

COMMITMENT TO ATTITUDE – DISCREPANT BEHAVIORS

It is important to understand the factors that determine the magnitude of dissonance aroused when a person's behavior deviates from his attitudes. In Chapter 3 we noted that one experimental condition can usually be specified to arouse more dissonance than another condition. This idea can be applied to a situation where behavior is contrary to attitude. An illustration is the experiment cited in the previous chapter (Festinger & Carlsmith, 1959), where a student who had just worked on a dull, boring task was required to inform the next participant that it was very interesting. The relative amounts of dissonance in the two experimental conditions can be illustrated by the following ratios:

Greater dissonance	Lesser dissonance
$\dfrac{\text{Feeling that task is dull and trivial}}{\text{Pressure by } E + \text{payment of \$1}}$	$\dfrac{\text{Feeling that task is dull and trivial}}{\text{Pressure by } E + \text{payment of \$20}}$

In the numerator of the ratios are the cognitive elements associated with the private attitude—the feeling that the task is dull and insignificant. These elements are dissonant with engaging in the behavior. In the denominator are the cognitive elements consonant with engaging in the behavior—these derive from the pressure to conform to the experimenter's request and the desire for the monetary payment. A more general expression of the ratio would be the following:

$$\text{Dissonance} = \frac{\text{cognitive elements dissonant with the behavior}}{\text{cognitive elements consonant with the behavior}}$$

The magnitude of dissonance as a function of this ratio is shown in Figure 4–1. One caution to keep in mind in using the ratio is that dissonance cannot be directly measured; the usual approach is to compare

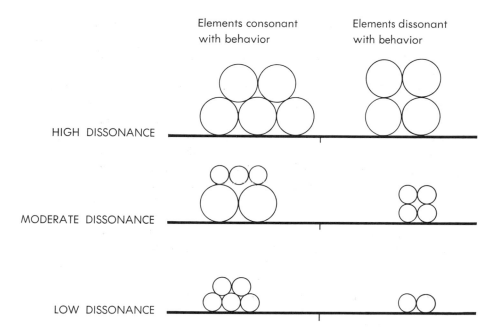

Figure 4–1

Magnitude of dissonance as a function of the number and importance of elements and the relative balance of opposing elements. Large circles represent important elements; small circles, less important elements.

two or more ratios that differ in only one cognitive element or complex of elements. Another caution is that the ratio should be weighted by some measure of the importance of the two sets of elements. Two ratios can be numerically equal, but if the overall importance of the elements in one is greater than those in the other, dissonance will be greater in the first. A final obvious point is that the ratio must always be less than 1; *otherwise the discrepant behavior will not occur.* In this case, the elements dissonant with the behavior outweigh those consonant with the behavior, inhibiting its expression.

STUDY QUESTIONS

21. *What factors affect the amount of dissonance in choice situations?*
22. *Explain how two experimental situations may be established so that we can infer that dissonance aroused will be greater in one than in the other.*

Need discrepant behavior be persuasive?

Brehm (1960*b*) and Cohen (1960) have asked whether, in order to create dissonance and subsequent attitude change, the discrepant behavior must be some form of action which aims to have a persuasive effect on other people, or whether other forms of discrepant behavior will also produce dissonance and change. In the experiment with the student who had the dull task, for example, was it his active attempt to convince the next subject that the experiment was interesting and significant which changed his attitude in a favorable direction?

According to dissonance theory, dissonance should be aroused whether or not the discrepant behavior involves an attempt to persuade others. This question is important. If dissonance and accompanying attitude change occur only for *persuasive* discrepant behavior, the results can readily be explained in terms of learning theory. Attitude shifts would result from a change in habit strengths due to rewards following the discrepant verbal responses (Hovland, Janis, & Kelley, 1953).

Several studies document the point that discrepant behavior which is *nonpersuasive* also produces dissonance and consequent attitude change. In one experiment (Brehm, 1960*a*) eighth-grade boys and girls were induced to eat a vegetable that they disliked intensely. Cognitive elements *dissonant* with eating the vegetable are those associated with the intense dislike. These were held constant for two groups. Cognitive elements *consonant* with eating the disliked food were varied in order to create different degrees of dissonance for the two groups. The low-dissonance group was told that the vegetable was nutritious, increasing the extent to which consonant elements outweighed dissonant ones. The high-dissonance group was told that food value was low. Thus the following dissonance relation was produced:

Greater dissonance	Lesser dissonance
Dislike of vegetable	Dislike of vegetable
Pressure by *E*	Pressure by *E* + nutrient value

As predicted, those in the high-dissonance group who ate the vegetable reduced their intense dislike to a greater extent than those in the low-dissonance group.

In one part of another experiment (Mills, 1958), arranged so that it was easy to cheat without detection, cognitive elements consonant with cheating were varied by offering two different incentives to win a prize. A low- and a high-dissonance group were created by offering the former a $5 prize and the latter a 50-cent prize. The following is the dissonance relation created here:

Greater dissonance	Lesser dissonance
Moral cognitions against cheating	Moral cognitions against cheating
Desire to win + 50¢ prize	Desire to win + $5 prize

As anticipated by dissonance theory, those persons who cheated for only a 50-cent prize shifted in the direction of a more lenient attitude toward cheating than those who were offered a $5 prize.

Another investigation (Aronson & Mills, 1959) held constant the elements consonant with joining a discussion group on sex attitudes. Two degrees of dissonance were created by varying the elements dissonant with joining. Female college students in the low-dissonance group were required to read to a male experimenter a list of words pertaining to sex but not obscene (e.g., prostitute, virgin, petting), and those in the high-dissonance group were required to read a list of obscene sex-related words. The relevant relations created are the following:

Greater dissonance	Lesser dissonance
$\dfrac{\text{Reading highly embarrassing sex words}}{\text{Pressure by } E + \text{desire to join group}}$	$\dfrac{\text{Reading less embarrassing sex words}}{\text{Pressure by } E + \text{desire to join group}}$

The group reading the more embarrassing words experienced more dissonance and consequently shifted to a greater extent in the direction of a favorable attitude toward the group.

From the results of these studies of nonpersuasive discrepant behavior, as well as many additional studies cited by Brehm and Cohen (1962), it is clear that attitude-discrepant behavior need not be persuasive in order to bring about dissonance and consequent attitude change.

Role of decision in attitude change: Commitment without behavior

Brehm (1960*b*) and Cohen (1960) have also raised the question as to whether discrepant *behavior* is actually necessary in order to bring about attitude change. Possibly, they note, a *decision* to engage in discrepant behavior creates dissonance and consequent attitude change, whether or not the behavior is actually engaged in. Several studies (Rabbie, Brehm, & Cohen, 1959; Brehm & Cohen, 1959) demonstrate that a mere decision to engage in discrepant behavior without actually proceeding to perform the new actions is sufficient to arouse dissonance and bring about attitude change. In Cohen's words, "A person who *chooses* [italics supplied] to behave in a way he would ordinarily avoid experiences dissonance; the more unpleasant the induced behavior, the greater the magnitude of dissonance and the greater the consequent attitude change in order to reduce it" (Cohen, 1960, p. 305).

Effects of a decision not to comply

So far our discussion of attitude-discrepant behavior has been restricted to situations where the subject commits himself to engage in the behavior. Now suppose that a person is subjected to a similar situation but *decides not to comply.* As before, the ratio of dissonant to consonant elements determines the amount of dissonance. However, if one decides *not* to comply, elements that were formerly dissonant become consonant, and vice versa. For the experiment on cheating previously described, the relevant ratios would be as follows:

Greater dissonance	Lesser dissonance
$\dfrac{\text{Desire to win} + \$5 \text{ prize}}{\text{Moral cognitions against cheating}}$	$\dfrac{\text{Desire to win} + 50 \text{¢ prize}}{\text{Moral cognitions against cheating}}$

If a person decides not to cheat, his cognitions about the prize to be gained from cheating are dissonant with his decision not to cheat. Thus, other things being equal, the stronger the elements associated with cheating, the more dissonance he will experience if he decides not to cheat. A subject who has decided not to cheat is likely to reduce dissonance by valuing honesty to a greater extent than he did before his decision. The more he was tempted, the greater will be his attitude change favoring honesty, provided he manages to resist the temptation. Experimental findings (Mills, 1958) are consistent with this interpretation.

Postcommitment arousal of dissonance

Another question is whether, at the time of commitment, a person must be aware that his behavior will be discrepant with his attitude. Often in everyday circumstances, an individual commits himself to some behavior only to discover *later* that he has committed himself to a line of action that conflicts with certain of his attitudes.

An experiment (Brehm, 1959) bearing on this point has ascertained whether or not greater dissonance occurs when an act of choice is followed by an unforeseen event which is potentially dissonant with the commitment made. This was accomplished by inducing junior high school students to eat a small portion of a disliked vegetable and later informing them that a letter would be written to their parents stating that they had eaten the vegetable. The direct implication of this additional information was that they might have to eat more at home. It was found that this information did indeed create greater dissonance and a greater change in liking of the vegetable, particularly for those who reported in a questionnaire that they ate the vegetable at home less frequently than it was served. Thus, under these experimental conditions at least, an event outside the control of the individual may produce dissonance because of a previous commitment and may consequently lead to changes in attitude.

STUDY QUESTIONS

23. *Attitude-discrepant behavior sometimes takes the form of attempting to persuade others of something one does not believe in. To arouse dissonance, is it necessary that the behavior take this persuasive form? Why or why not?*

24. *To what extent can commitment alone, without the corresponding behavior, produce dissonance?*

25. *What are the effects on dissonance arousal of a decision* not *to engage in attitude-discrepant behavior?*

26. *To what extent can subsequent events produce dissonance with respect to a commitment that was not dissonant at the time it was made?*

THE EFFECT OF VOLITION ON DISSONANCE

The research of Brehm and Cohen has led to what amounts to a major revision of Festinger's theory of cognitive dissonance. We have just discussed a number of experiments involving some pressure by the experimeter plus other incentives to engage in behavior at variance with one's attitudes. They make clear that it is not primarily engaging in the behavior that produces the dissonance; instead, dissonance seems to arise from having *committed* oneself to discrepant behavior. Brehm and Cohen carry this point one step further, suggesting that not all kinds of commitments produce dissonance but only *voluntary* ones. To the extent that the person feels compelled to engage in the discrepant behavior, dissonance should not occur, according to their view.

Several experiments suggest that the more freedom a person has in deciding whether or not to commit himself to attitude-discrepant behavior, the greater the dissonance aroused (Brehm & Cohen, 1959; Cohen, Terry, & Jones, 1959; Davis & Jones, 1960). Unfortunately, these particular experiments do not prove conclusively that freedom of choice is independent of other factors that might determine dissonance. A possible interpretation of these studies is that freedom of choice simply represents the individual's awareness of the degree of balance or imbalance between opposing cognitive elements and his consciousness of the direction of the forces they represent. Thus as the elements associated with engaging in the behavior approach in strength the elements associated with not engaging in the behavior, dissonance should be at a maximum. It would seem that when the two sets of elements are evenly balanced in this fashion, the individual would also be more likely to perceive that he had freedom of choice than he would when elements associated with engaging in the behavior were strong relative to those associated with not engaging in the behavior. If a man who easily yields to temptation is offered a million-dollar bribe to commit perjury, he will undoubtedly feel that he has no choice but to accept; also, dissonance will be low. But if he is offered only a small bribe, a sum that just barely motivates him to perjure himself, he will feel that he is quite free to take it or leave it; also, dissonance will be high. In other words, in most dissonance situations, perceived freedom of choice appears to be *directly* associated with the relative balance of the two sets of opposing elements, a factor that itself determines the magnitude of dissonance.

A critical test of whether volition is important in producing dissonance requires the creation of differences in volition that vary *inversely* with the relative balance of the two sets of elements. Thus the question raised is whether dissonance arises from the relative balance between the cognitive elements dissonant with engaging in the action and the cognitive elements consonant with engaging in the action, or whether it arises from the inconsistency of voluntarily committing oneself to engage in an action one does not believe in.

Brehm and Cohen (1962, pp. 206–210) have created this situation in an ingenious experiment. They reasoned that if the cognitive elements consonant with the attitude-discrepant behavior represented *illegitimate* pressures, subjects would feel that they did not have to participate if they did not wish to. To create this condition, through the cooperation of fraternity pledgemasters they obtained thirty undergraduates who had been told that they were to help out in some research for a *short* period of time. Upon their arrival, however, the experimenter demanded that the pledges sign up for a boring and profitless task that would take three to four hours. Moreover, to make the situation completely illegitimate, the professor, who had no connection with any of the fraternities, threatened to have the pledges' fraternities penalize them if they failed to participate in the unexpectedly long task. Two conditions, one of high coercion and one of low, were established through the following instructions (Brehm & Cohen, 1962, p. 207):

> *High coercion.* Now we need your cooperation, and if you don't cooperate, I'm afraid we'll have to report you as uncooperative to your pledgemaster and the other fellows and really push for some severe penalties. This can have very bad effects; we'll try to see that it has very strong consequences for extending your pledge period considerably and even for keeping you out of the house permanently.

> *Low coercion.* Now we need your cooperation, and if you don't cooperate, I'm afraid we'll have to report you as uncooperative to your pledgemaster and the other fellows and see that you get some hours of extra duty as a pledge.

The high-coercion condition is more illegitimate than the low; ejection from the fraternity is even threatened. Thus the subject should feel freer to refuse to participate. Essentially, these manipulations of coercion and volition create the following two conditions:

More even balance and less volition	More imbalance and greater volition
Sacrifice of several hours	Sacrifice of several hours
Low coercion to participate	High coercion to participate

This arrangement of the ratio of elements dissonant with the activity to those consonant with the activity is similar to previous experiments discussed: Balance is more even where coercion is low. In the case of volition, however, the intent of the experimenter's manipulations was to reverse the usual relation. Normally, close balance and high volition would be associated, as would imbalance and low volition. But because the force used in this manipulation was *illegitimate,* the investigators anticipated that the inverse association would be created. Of course, it was necessary to build into the experiment a method of checking on the success of this manipulation, as described below.

All but one of the subjects, in the low-coercion condition, committed themselves to participation. Immediately after participation, ratings were taken on the amount of threat perceived (to determine the perceived degree of coercion), on the perceived freedom of choice (to measure volition), on the amount of annoyance aroused by the request to participate (to determine illegitimacy), and on evaluation of the experimental task (to measure attitude change).

The results of this experiment are reported in Table 4–1. First, we may determine whether or not the inverse relation between volition and balance was in fact created. We find that the experiment was successful in this respect: The evenly balanced (low-coercion) group is characterized by *low* volition, and the imbalanced (high-coercion) group is characterized by *high* volition. Second, we turn to the crucial question: Which factor was more successful in producing attitude change, the balance of the elements toward and against performing the behavior, or the inconsistency in the voluntary performance of a distasteful task?

Examining the ratings on satisfaction with the experiment, we find that high satisfaction scores (mean = 1.09) are associated with high volition and imbalance and that low satisfaction scores (mean = −0.70) are associated with low volition and balance. Thus the greatest attitude change occurs where volition is high and there is a relative *imbalance* of elements. This greater attitude change suggests that highly voluntary commitment produces more dissonance than less voluntary commitment and even outweighs the effects on dissonance of the balance of the elements toward and against engaging in the behavior.

DISSONANCE AND PERSUASIVE POWER: A DILEMMA

One question that has received little attention is whether structuring a communication situation in terms of dissonance theory effectively increases one's persuasive powers as expressed in terms of the *number* of participants who comply. Dissonance approaches a maximum when elements dissonant with engaging in the desired action are approximately equal to elements consonant with the action. But the same communication will not produce exactly the same degree of balance for all recipients. Some individuals will be aware of additional consonant or dissonant elements not mentioned by the communicator. Thus, if a communicator

Table 4–1
Mean Ratings of Postquestionnaire Items by Experimental Groups

	SEVERITY OF THREAT	ANNOYANCE	VOLITION	SATISFACTION
High coercion (N = 10)	4.00	2.88	3.14	1.09
Low coercion (N = 10)	2.18	1.61	2.04	−0.70
Control (N = 10)	1.46	2.64	0.95	−1.58

In all cases, the higher the mean figure, the greater the response in question. The first three variables were rated on an 8-point scale; satisfaction was rated on a scale from 4 to −4.

SOURCE: Reprinted by permission from J. W. Brehm & A. R. Cohen. *Explorations in cognitive dissonance.* New York: John Wiley & Sons, Inc., 1962.

aims to create a balanced ratio, for some recipients the dissonant elements will outweigh the consonant ones, and these persons will not be influenced. The communicator faces a dilemma: in creating dissonant elements, he runs the risk of failing to obtain the attitude-discrepant behavior necessary for producing attitude change.

This dilemma has not been encountered in our previous discussion because we have dealt only with situations where the great majority of participants have engaged in the attitude-discrepant behavior. But outside the laboratory, such situations are probably difficult to create.

Two experiments with military personnel are relevant to this neglected problem (Torrance, 1959; Smith, 1961), although additional research is needed for conclusive answers. These investigations suggest that "low-pressure" techniques elicit compliance from a larger proportion of the participants than do other techniques, and also that they produce an appreciable amount of attitude change. Smith's experiment provides an example of the low-pressure situation: In an attempt to persuade Army reservists to accept unusual foods, they were presented with fried grasshoppers and with a rationale for eating them and similar foods in terms of emergency situations they might later encounter. No direct pressure was applied to make them eat them: the choice was their own. About 89 percent of the participants ate grasshoppers under this condition, as compared with only 50 percent in another condition where a dissonance-arousing persuasive communication was used.

Such low-pressure methods create a minimum of dissonant elements, and thus avoid the risk of generating noncompliance. Perhaps such techniques are also effective because participants who comply have a greater feeling of volition in complying than they would have if more pressure were applied.

LIMITATIONS OF PRESENT KNOWLEDGE

Although dissonance theory has generated much interesting research it should not be accepted uncritically. Some of the key experiments are receiving intensive reanalysis, and various alternative interpretations to dissonance theory are becoming apparent (Chapanis & Chapanis, 1964). The present section on attitude-discrepant behavior has discussed several experiments where greater rewards, because they generate less dissonance, produce less attitude change. Rosenberg (1964) has offered alternatives to the dissonance interpretation and, by repeating this type of experiment with slight modifications, has successfully produced a direct relation between the amount of reward and the degree of attitude change, instead of the usual inverse one.

He notes that subjects generally come to a psychological experiment with some apprehension that they are going to be evaluated — with respect to their mental health, intelligence, personality, or some unknown attribute. Given this attitude, what reaction would be expected from a student who had just been offered a large sum of money for performing a simple task? Rosenberg suggests that he may assume that the situation is testing his independence or his honesty, his ability to resist a "bribe." Another possible reaction is one of suspicion and covert hostility toward the experimenter. Under these circumstances a subject may adopt an uncooperative attitude and evaluate the experiment more negatively than he otherwise would.

Rosenberg reasoned that apprehension about being evaluated or hostility toward the experimenter could not affect the subject's responses to an attitude questionnaire if the dissonance-creating activity appeared to be part of one experiment, and the attitude assessment, part of another, entirely independent experiment. In his study, subjects were given rewards ranging from 50 cents to $5 for writing an essay setting forth reasons why their university football team should not participate in the Rose Bowl game even though their team had won the Big Ten championship. Students were overwhelmingly in favor of such participation.

After writing the essay, subjects participated in an apparently unrelated experiment conducted by a different experimenter in a different location. Only one item in a questionnaire given at that time was pertinent to the Rose Bowl game. The results were that the *greater* the reward they had received for writing the anti-Rose Bowl essay, the *less* favorable their attitude toward participation became. This result, of course, is directly contrary to dissonance theory, which assumes that the *smaller* the reward, the greater the dissonance and concomitant attitude change.

Considered as a whole, the support for dissonance theory is fairly impressive. Such contradictions as have just been described, however, suggest that the theory requires further modification and development, and perhaps that it applies only under a somewhat more limited set of conditions than at first had been thought.

STUDY QUESTIONS

27. *The following two variables are associated or correlated in many dissonance experiments on commitment: (a) the ratio of dissonant to consonant elements, and (b) the amount of volition. What is the usual direction of association between these variables?*
28. *Describe the crucial experiment which demonstrated that volition may be a critical factor in producing dissonance.*

Summary: Commitment and attitude change

Dissonance theory is best applied to situations where an individual has committed himself either to choosing one of two or more alternatives or to engaging in behavior contrary to his attitudes. Under these circumstances, dissonance is most clearly identified, and predictions are relatively unique to dissonance theory and often opposite to common sense. Another reason why these situations are most appropriate to dissonance theory is that they confront the person with an either-or choice of modes of reducing dissonance. Compromises are seldom possible, and the individual must move along some definite path to reduce dissonance. The amount of dissonance aroused in choice situations is dependent upon many factors: the positive or negative characteristics of the chosen and rejected alternatives, the similarity between the alternatives, the number of rejected alternatives, and the importance of the cognitions pertaining to a decision.

The relative dissonances in two experimental conditions can be determined by examining the ratio of dissonant to consonant elements in each. The situation in which these elements are more closely balanced arouses greater dissonance. Thus, in forced-compliance situations, the amount of force just sufficient to persuade the individual to engage in attitude-discrepant behavior will arouse the greatest dissonance and produce the most attitude change. Behavior discrepant with attitudes need not be in the form of attempting to persuade other people; moreover, it need not actually be engaged in. Apparently it is commitment as such to discrepant behavior that produces the dissonance.

Under certain circumstances where a person has been pressured to perform some behavior not consonant with his attitudes, if he decides *not* to comply he may be regarded as having committed himself to resisting the pressures. Dissonance may arise in this situation because of the opposition between commitment to resistance and the positive cognitive elements associated with compliance. Dissonance may also be aroused some time after a person has committed himself to a position that he discovers only later is in opposition to his own. Recent experimentation not only stresses commitment, but goes one step further to suggest that dissonance is aroused primarily by commitment that is voluntary rather than involuntary.

Dissonance has limitations when used to increase persuasive power over the number of persons who comply: creating dissonant elements may cause their total to outweigh consonant ones. A low-pressure technique is probably safest, to insure that elements consonant with compliance outweigh dissonant elements for all target persons. Much research on dissonance theory is subject to alternative interpretations, suggesting that the theory needs further modification and that better experimental control must be achieved.

Summary and Conclusions

The credibility of a communicator affects both the evaluation of the communication he presents and the amount of attitude change. Moreover, the communication may affect the interpretation of the communicator's intentions, and the audience's feelings toward the communicator may in part determine how the communication itself is interpreted. Findings concerning communicator credibility are readily interpretable in terms of dissonance theory, although alternative explanations are possible.

Strong fear-arousing appeals are likely to be ineffective; the anxiety they create produces suspicion of the communicator's motives or arouses other types of defense in the individual. On the other hand, a relatively impersonal appeal arousing a small amount of anxiety is likely to be effective. Fear-arousing communications may also have the property of "immunizing" the individual against future anxiety-arousing appeals of a similar nature, so that later communications of this type have little effect. The greater attitude change for mild fear appeals may be explained in terms of dissonance theory as follows: The cognitive elements in strong fear appeals are dissonant with a large number of elements to which a person already subscribes, while minimum fear appeals are dissonant with only a few. The more balanced ratio of dissonant to consonant elements in the latter situation produces greater attitude change.

The manner in which a communication is organized and presented may also affect its reception. One-sided communications are more effective for people who already agree with the communicator, but people who disagree with the communicator do not change their opinions in response to one-sided communications. Just the reverse is true for two-sided communications. Moreover, a two-sided communication is more effective than a one-sided communication in innoculating the audience against countercommunications. Whether the communicator draws the conclusion implied by his message or leaves it up to the audience does not seem to make a distinct difference in the audience's acceptance of it.

Initial communications are not more effective than subsequent ones, although an initial communication might possibly produce selective exposure to subsequent messages. For maximum effectiveness, elements of a communication should be arranged first to arouse a need and then to present information which leads to its satisfaction. The reverse sequence is less effective for most persons. For nonsalient arguments, pro arguments should be presented first in order to create acceptance of the communicator and his message before the con arguments are introduced. It has also been demonstrated that elements of a communication having pleasant contingencies tend to produce an attitude of acceptance which persists through the presentation of subsequent elements.

A special class of situations is those where an individual has committed himself to choosing one alternative to the exclusion of others or to engaging in behavior contrary to his attitudes. Under these circumstances, dissonance is most clearly identified, and predictions are relatively unique to dissonance theory and often opposite to common sense. The amount of dissonance aroused in choice situations is dependent on certain characteristics of the alternatives. The relative dissonances in two experimental conditions can be determined by examining the ratio of dissonant to consonant elements in each: the closer the balance, the greater the dissonance. Behavior discrepant with attitudes need not be persuasive; moreover, it need not actually be engaged in. Apparently it is commitment to potential behavior discrepant with attitudes that produces the dissonance. Recent experimentation not only stresses commitment, but goes one step further to suggest that dissonance is aroused primarily by commitment that is voluntary rather than involuntary.

chapter five

PERSUASIBILITY AND RESISTANCE

$\mathbf{P}$ersons differ markedly in their susceptibility to persuasive communications. That some people, but not all, are "pushovers" for sales pitches is common knowledge. Advertising is more likely to be believed by some people than by others. In interpersonal situations, some persons may be readily persuaded to go along with the suggestions of their friends or associates, while others stubbornly "stick to their guns." Many students accept uncritically virtually everything their professor tells them; others critically examine his ideas. Why some persons are highly resistant to persuasive communications and others are easily persuasible is one question we will attempt to answer in this chapter.

A related topic concerns specific techniques that individuals use to resist influence. Although these vary from one person to another, some forms of "defense" are common. One illustration which has already been discussed is found in certain forms of resistance conceptualized in terms of dissonance theory. For example, if a persuasive communication creates sufficient dissonance because its elements are not consonant with many of a person's existing beliefs, he may disbelieve the communicator or the communication. A final topic in the chapter deals with reactions that vary depending upon certain relations between the communication and the attitudes of the respondent.

Generality of Persuasibility

Persuasibility, in the sense used here, refers to the tendency of the individual to accept or reject persuasive communications. The assumption is made that some individuals are more susceptible to persuasive communications than others. Before discussing research pertaining to this assumption, two related concepts should be mentioned: *conformity* and *suggestibility.*

PERSUASIBILITY AND RELATED CONCEPTS

For convenience, we will make a rather arbitrary distinction between persuasibility and conformity. In one sense persuasibility is more general than conformity, and in another it is less general. In the first sense, persuasibility pertains to the acceptance or rejection of persuasive communications of any kind, but conformity is limited to the general tendency of an individual to conform to group norms and standards. If an individual's behavior deviates from that of other members of his group, pressures are generally exerted to force his conformity to the desired norm. Individuals differ greatly in their response to such pressures, ranging all the way from those who yield readily to those who are staunchly independent.[1] *Conformity*, then, refers to acceptance or nonacceptance of some norm or standard. Persuasibility refers to the response to any kind of influence attempt by a communicator, whether or not his position is a normative one.

But in the second sense, persuasibility is a more limited concept. It pertains to the individual's response to *persuasive* communications; in other words, to rather direct influence attempts. Conformity is broader in that it includes behavior complying with norms even when no direct influence attempt has occurred. While the two concepts are closely related and cannot be treated entirely apart from each other, this chapter will deal primarily with persuasibility, and conformity will be discussed mainly in Chapter 10.

Interest in the other concept, *suggestibility*, extends back to the origins of psychology, and studies of it are numerous. Suggestibility is an even broader term than persuasibility. It includes not only the individual's susceptibility to persuasive communications, but also his propensity for responding to various communications or actions of other persons that have no persuasive intent. For example, a "suggestible" person might adopt some of the mannerisms of a person he admires. This facet of suggestibility has some relation to *identification*, a topic to be discussed in detail in Chapter 17. The term suggestibility is often applied to situations where the subject is unaware that the actions he performs have been "suggested" by others or where he is unaware of the actions themselves. This chapter is limited to a discussion of susceptibility to persuasive communications and will not discuss the broader issues pertaining to suggestibility.

---

[1]For a review of the experimental literature on conformity, see Blake and Mouton (1961*a*).

IS PERSUASIBILITY TOPIC-FREE?

Before persuasibility can be associated with personality, we must determine whether persons differ in susceptibility to persuasive communications in a way that can be measured. A discussion by Janis and Hovland (1959) examines persuasibility from this point of view. They point out that a person might possibly be highly persuasible on certain topics but not at all persuasible on others. His susceptibility might also vary with different forms of appeal, different communicators, different media, or other aspects of the communication situation. For example, a person who is prejudiced against minority groups might be extraordinarily resistant to any attempts to shift his attitudes on that score, but quite persuasible on other issues. One individual might be especially susceptible to communications from persons in authority, and another might be especially resistant to fear appeals but not to other forms of persuasive communications. The question of whether a person is consistently persuasible in situations varying in these respects needs empirical study.

Several aspects of the communication situation that have been investigated are the communication topic, the form of appeal, the amount of knowledge the individual has, and whether the communication is in accord with or counter to the attitudes of the recipient. One study (Janis & Field, 1956) has asked whether the susceptibility of a person to persuasive communications remains constant in situations that vary in these respects. Persons were found to be persuasible to a similar degree on five different topics, in their response to five types of appeals, and in reacting to initial communications and countercommunications.

In this experiment the consistency of response to initial communications and countercommunications was demonstrated by showing that persons who were more susceptible to an initial message were also more susceptible to a subsequent message advocating an opposite position. Topics were chosen on which individuals would have quite different amounts of knowledge, in order to test for consistency in that factor. The appeals were based on the following different approaches: logical arguments, fear-arousing statements, idealized heroes or exaggerated villains, the desire for social approval, and the prediction of a pleasant event.

On the other hand, individuals were not perfectly consistent in responding to these five aspects of the communication. To some degree their responses differed depending upon the topic and appeal used. Thus, these findings provide support for both consistency and specificity in the individual's response to persuasive communications. The investigators refer to a tendency to be persuasible to roughly the same degree in the different situations as *topic-free* persuasibility. This term emphasizes that their communication situations were varied primarily in the topics chosen and other conditions related to these topics, such as the appeal used and the amount of knowledge possessed by the individual.

That persuasibility is both topic-free and topic-bound at the same time is illustrated schematically in Figure 5–1. Person 3 is obviously the most persuasible and person 4 the least. Person 4, however, is more persuasible on topic C than person 2, who in other respects is more persuasible than person 4. Similarly, although person 1 is generally more persuasible than person 2, he is somewhat less persuasible on topic B.

Further support for the idea that persons are similarly persuasible in different situations is provided in a study (Abelson & Lesser, 1959*b*) of first-grade children, where persuasibility was defined as the tendency to seek agreement with the attitudes of the communicator. This definition of persuasibility has some relation to the previously discussed notion of conformity, in that it emphasizes agreement with an authority figure, who is likely to emphasize behavior norms. In the investigation children were consistent in their susceptibility to different communicators. For example, if a child agreed with attitudes represented as those of his mother, he was likely to agree with the attitudes of the experimenter; if he was a boy, he was likely to agree with the attitudes of his teacher. Boys were generally more consistent than girls in the degree of persuasibility they displayed in different situations. Finally, a study (Linton & Graham, 1959) of college students, using measures quite different from those in the other studies, also obtained some evidence for consistency in persuasibility on different communication topics.

In general, we may conclude that the degree to which a person is persuasible is somewhat consistent for different topics and appeals, in-

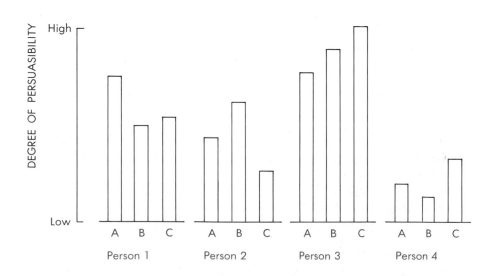

Figure 5–1
Topic-free and topic-bound persuasibility of individuals.
A, B, and C represent different communication topics.

cluding those that agree with or run counter to his attitudes and those on which he has considerable knowledge or little knowledge. At the same time, individuals vary considerably in their susceptibility to these different aspects of communication situations. While a person's *average* level of persuasibility in many situations may be appreciably higher than the average level of most persons, he shows a fairly wide range of responsiveness to communication situations differing in the respects that have been enumerated. Because of this variability, measures intended to represent individual levels of persuasibility should consist of a composite score for each person based on a variety of topics and appeals.

STUDY QUESTIONS

1. *Distinguish between persuasibility, conformity, and suggestibility.*
2. *What are some of the major ways in which communication situations differ from one another?*
3. *What is meant by the term* topic-free persuasibility?

Correlates of Persuasibility

INTELLIGENCE AND SUSCEPTIBILITY TO PERSUASION

Common sense suggests that the more intelligent person would be less susceptible to persuasive communications. Presumably the more intelligent person would be more critical of a propaganda message, for example, because he is usually more informed and because he has a superior understanding of the logic of arguments and an ability to weigh evidence. Yet, early studies reported up to 1937 showed almost a zero correlation between resistance to persuasive communications and intelligence level (Murphy, Murphy, & Newcomb, 1937).

A review by Hovland, Janis, and Kelley (1953) of more recent studies indicates, however, that for some types of communications, intelligence is positively associated with resistance and for other types, negatively associated. These reviewers suggest that studies are contradictory or inconclusive because the various components of intelligence have different implications for reaction to persuasive communications. They offer the view that different components will be used in different degrees when communications have quite different content, as illustrated in the following quotation.

> Two general hypotheses can be inferred concerning the conditions under which general intelligence is predictive of responsiveness to persuasive communications:
> 1. Persons with high intelligence will tend—mainly because of their ability to draw valid inferences—to be *more* influenced than those with low intellectual ability when exposed to persuasive communications which rely primarily on impressive logical arguments.
> 2. Persons with high intelligence will tend—mainly because of their superior critical ability—to be *less* influenced than those with low intelligence when exposed to persuasive communications which rely primarily on unsupported generalities or false, illogical, irrelevant argumentation. (P. 183)

A similar position is taken in a more recent publication (Hovland & Janis, 1959). So far as the present writers are aware, however, these hypotheses have not been tested by experiments specifically designed for the purpose. The conclusion must be drawn that there is little correlation between general intelligence and resistance to persuasive communications, but that substantial correlations might possibly be found if the reactions of individuals varying in separate components of intelligence were compared for certain types of communications.

PERSONALITY CORRELATES OF PERSUASIBILITY

Only the most recent studies of persuasibility have attempted to measure the persuasibility of individuals with methods that can be generalized to different topics and appeals. Earlier studies have usually measured the extent of acceptance by an individual of a single persuasive communication. Generalizations to other communication situations cannot be drawn from such studies, because individuals are known to vary in persuasibility depending upon the communication topic. Thus, this section will deal primarily with studies employing topic-free measures of persuasibility. In addition, studies investigating the same personality trait that have been repeated by various investigators in different communication situations will be used as a source of information concerning associations between persuasibility and personality traits.

Self-esteem and persuasibility

One common-sense proposition is that a confident, competent person should be less persuasible. The personality variable most generally representing this type of person is self-esteem. Although a considerable number of studies have demonstrated an inverse association between self-esteem and *conformity*, only a few have examined the relation between self-esteem and *persuasibility*.

One study using self-ratings by high school juniors yielded significant correlations, for male subjects only, between high persuasibility and feelings of inadequacy and social inhibitions (Janis & Field, 1956). Feelings of inadequacy were measured by ratings on such questions as "How often do you feel inferior to most of the people you know?" and social inhibitions by questions such as "Do you prefer to work with others rather than alone?" In another investigation, a somewhat higher correlation between persuasibility and feelings of inadequacy was found for mental patients (Janis & Rife, 1959). These associations between self-esteem and persuasibility receive indirect support from studies demonstrating that *conformity* is also associated with similar personality characteristics (Blake & Mouton, 1961*b*).

Certain studies of the association between self-esteem and conformity have other implications for persuasibility (Campbell, 1961). They suggest that persons with a history of success should be less persuasible and those with many failures should be more so. For example, Mausner (1954) contrived a situation involving judgments of lengths of lines so that one set of individuals working alone generally made incorrect judgments and another set made correct judgments. Later, two-person groups were formed with one member who had a history of failure and another who had usually been successful. They were chosen so that their previous judgments were quite different from each other's. When asked to make a new set of judgments in a situation where each could observe the other's judgments, the member with the history of previous failure changed his estimates markedly toward those of his partner who, unknown to him, had previously been successful.

Further implications for persuasibility are suggested in a review by Cohen (1959) of various studies relating self-esteem to conformity. He notes that individuals with high self-esteem make active efforts to maintain esteem, and those with low self-esteem exert less effort. He suggests that in a mass communication situation, communication sources and messages that threaten a person's self-esteem will be rejected more by those with high self-esteem than by those with low self-esteem, while sources and communications that enhance self-esteem will be accepted to a greater extent by high self-esteem persons than by those with low self-esteem.

STUDY QUESTIONS

4. *Discuss the relation between intelligence level and susceptibility to persuasion. In your discussion mention factors that make study of this problem difficult.*
5. *What is the nature of the relation between self-esteem and persuasibility? To what extent is this relation determined by a person's past experiences of success or failure?*

Aggressiveness and persuasibility

As in the case of the relations of intelligence and self-esteem to persuasibility, a common-sense hypothesis is readily available for aggressiveness. One would expect that the more aggressive person would be less persuasible. Yet Janis and Field (1959), using three measures of aggressiveness from a self-inventory and one from a projective test,[2] found no significant correlations for either males or females between aggressiveness and persuasibility for any of the measures. Janis and Rife (1959), using the same self-inventory, reported no relation among mental patients.

These investigators offer a plausible explanation as to why little correlation was found between persuasibility and a measure of aggressiveness based on a self-inventory. Aggressive items in an inventory generally refer to socially undesirable feelings and behaviors, and the aggressive

[2] A *projective* test is one which does not require the individual to describe himself. The subject responds freely to an ambiguous situation, producing material which can be used to draw inferences about his personality.

individual tends to be a defensive person who is unlikely to admit to having undesirable traits. Therefore, because of his defensiveness, he is unlikely to endorse the very items which yield a high score on aggressiveness. When aggressiveness was determined from clinical records of the subject's antisocial *behavior*, the incidence of aggressiveness was highest among the patients of low persuasibility, a finding which supported the original common-sense hypothesis. In other studies, an inverse relation was found between rebelliousness and persuasibility among adolescent boys (King, 1959), and between aggressiveness and one measure of persuasibility among first-grade children (Lesser & Abelson, 1959).

More aggressive individuals are not more resistant to persuasive communications under all circumstances. Weiss and Fine (1955) report that where the communication advocates aggressive actions, aggressive persons more readily accept the communication. In this study, persons found to be aggressive on various personality measures were more influenced than less aggressive persons by a mimeographed article on juvenile delinquency recommending that offenders be punished. The same investigators later performed another variation of the experiment in which aggressiveness was deliberately induced in selected subjects. As a result, the subjects showed greater acceptance of the aggressive communication. This outcome is consistent with findings discussed in the previous chapter indicating that individuals are more likely to be influenced by communications which are in basic agreement with their attitudes than by communications opposite to their attitudes.

Persuasibility and other differences among individuals

A variety of other personality characteristics have been studied to ascertain their relation to persuasibility. In most instances, however, correlations are very low, results of different studies are contradictory, or there is only one study upon which conclusions might be based. The traits studied include "neurotic defensiveness" (Janis, 1954, 1955; Janis & Field, 1959); "perceptual dependence," "inner- and other-directed attitudes" (Linton & Graham, 1959; Witkin, et al., 1962); authoritarianism (Linton & Graham, 1959; Harvey & Beverley, 1961; Witkin, et al., 1962); "social isolation," "interpersonal attractiveness (Lesser & Abelson, 1959);" and "richness of fantasy" (Janis & Field, 1959; Janis & Rife, 1959).

Some interesting but not completely consistent sex differences in persuasibility have been found. Two studies (Janis & Field, 1959; King, 1959) have indicated that high school girls are more persuasible than boys, but a third (Abelson & Lesser, 1959a; 1959b) revealed no overall difference in persuasibility for first-grade boys and girls. One would expect differences in persuasibility between the two sexes to occur as a result of the socialization process: Females gradually adopt the woman's role, which calls for more docility and cooperativeness. Some support for sex differences in persuasibility comes from the fact that traits in which men and women differ are often those that have some relation to persuasibility (Hovland & Janis, 1959). For example, females are less aggressive than males, and since aggressiveness is associated with resistance to persuasibility, a difference in the persuasibility of males and females should be found.

STUDY QUESTIONS

6. *What is the relation between persuasibility and aggressiveness? What problem is encountered in using self-inventories to assess this relation?*
7. *What sex differences are there in persuasibility, and how might these be accounted for?*

CAUSAL EXPLANATIONS OF THE RELATION
BETWEEN PERSUASIBILITY AND PERSONALITY

In the instances where substantial correlations between personality traits and persuasibility have been found, three causal explanations have been suggested by Hovland and Janis (1959); (1) Persuasibility of a given level may produce the behavior representing the personality trait; (2) the behavior representing the personality trait may produce a particular level of persuasibility; (3) both persuasibility and the personality trait may be produced by some third factor.

To illustrate the first causal sequence, a person who is highly susceptible to persuasive communications may feel embarrassed and helpless about his submissiveness, feelings which would produce a general low level of self-esteem. The second causal sequence is illustrated by a person with low self-esteem who feels impelled to avoid social disapproval and therefore to conform to persuasive attempts of others. To illustrate the third type of causal association, a person with intense feelings of guilt may have both low self-esteem and sensitivity to public opinion, traits which in turn produce high persuasibility (Rickman, 1950). Hovland and Janis suggest that the next phase of research on persuasibility and personality might well consist of controlled laboratory experimentation aimed at discovering the relative importance of these causal sequences.

A good deal of controlled experimentation has already been performed on the relation between *conformity* and personality. If we assume that conformity and persuasibility are closely associated, then it seems safe to conclude that low self-esteem as represented by a feeling of failure can definitely cause greater persuasibility. Many experiments create situations where one set of subjects fails and the other succeeds; the former have been shown to conform to a greater extent.

In these experimental situations there is no doubt about the causal sequence, because those who fail are chosen at random by the experimenter, and failure occurs prior to the conformity situation. Also, one of the experiments on aggressiveness *induced* aggressiveness in the experimental subjects. As a result they showed greater responsiveness to a communication recommending aggressive actions. Here the cause-effect sequence is clearer than where the only data consist of a correlation between a personality trait and a response to a communication. It is quite possible, of course, that this is not the only valid causal sequence: in everyday situations one or more of the three types of explanations could apply simultaneously.

LIMITATIONS OF THE APPROACH

In sum, although marked individual differences are the rule in studies of responses to persuasive communications, associations between personality traits and topic-free measures of persuasibility have been found to be rather low. In the case of a few traits, such as self-esteem and aggressiveness, investigations have been fairly consistent in producing moderate correlations between these traits and persuasibility. Many other traits, however, seem to have only low or zero correlations with persuasibility.

Such findings do not lend themselves to any statement of a general principle. Their inconclusiveness could be due to the inadequacy of the personality measures used, although in some instances such measures represent the best of our present knowledge of personality appraisal. It could also result from the fact that persuasibility is inevitably in large part a function of the communication situation. While it is true that Janis and Field (1956) have demonstrated that persuasibility is to some extent topic-free, it is not perfectly topic-free, and many other aspects of the communication situation that have not been studied might also cause variation.

Katz (1960) has emphasized the point that, depending upon the motivational basis of a person's attitude, a given communication may be effective or ineffective. For example, a person may be prejudiced against Negroes because prejudice provides an outlet for strong hostilities generated by emotional conflicts. He is therefore unlikely to respond to a communication calculated to reduce prejudice by emphasizing that there are no innate differences between Negroes and whites; such an attitude shift would deprive him of his outlet for hostility. But when an individual's prejudice is based primarily upon the need to conform to the normative standards of those around him (prejudice being the norm), he might well respond to such a communication, particularly if it came from those whom he perceives as setting norms.

This kind of process emphasized by Katz is not taken into account by the approaches just reviewed, where persuasibility is measured across varied communication situations. Measurement in that fashion prevents the investigator from examining intraindividual differences in reactions to different kinds of communications. A portion of the next section will examine studies which contribute to an understanding of the interplay between individual characteristics and the nature of the communication situation.

STUDY QUESTIONS

8. *Give several causal explanations for the relation between persuasibility and personality.*

9. *In general, how much overall correspondence between personality and persuasibility has been demonstrated? How do Katz's ideas about attitude organization account for this conclusion?*

Processes in Resistance to Change

Some authorities who have considered the tremendous barrage of communications reaching the average person on every side in the twentieth century have expressed serious doubts that the individual will be able to retain his identity and independence. While it is probably true that modern man is subjected to many more influence attempts than his predecessor, the individual has many resources at his command for resisting influence. The remainder of this chapter will discuss the various means by which the individual maintains the integrity of his attitudes in the face of strong pressures to change. The discussion immediately following will deal with individual defenses, and after that, some attention will be given to the interplay between the nature of the communication and the individual's responses to it.

INDIVIDUAL PROCESSES IN RESISTANCE TO CHANGE

Whether or not a communication is effective depends in part upon certain factors within the individual. These include selective exposure to communications, the immunizing effects of exposure, motivational resistance to changing certain attitudes, and cognitive balance as a source of resistance.

Selective exposure

Anyone who has been irritated by a radio or television program and who has switched to another station or channel has selectively exposed himself to a communication. The term *selective exposure* includes seeking exposure to certain communications and avoiding others. Similarly, in reading newspapers and magazines, and even in listening to people in face-to-face situations, individuals may attend to communications in which they are not interested or which offend or repel them.

As Katz and Lazarsfeld (1955) note, the persons whom the communicator most desperately wishes to reach are the very ones who are most likely to avoid exposure to his message. For example, studies of the behavior of voters in election campaigns demonstrate clearly that voters who are already heavily committed to a partisan position are the ones most likely to hear and read campaign speeches (Lazarsfeld, Berelson, & Gaudet, 1948; Berelson, Lazarsfeld, & McPhee, 1954; Campbell et al., 1960). The "independent" voter is not a person who weighs the issues carefully and rationally before making up his mind; he is a person who has little interest in politics and who pays least attention to election campaigns.

Several other studies illustrate the importance of selective exposure in reducing the effectiveness of mass promotional campaigns. During World War II, a pamphlet on the importance of purchasing defense bonds was distributed to almost every household in the United States. A survey was made in one city, Baltimore, to determine the reaction to the pamphlet (Cartwright, 1949). It was found that 83 percent of the persons in the sample contacted did not remember seeing it. Of the 17 percent who recalled seeing it, one-third did not even look inside the cover. Altogether, only 11 percent of the sample interviewed had read any part of the pamphlet. The main reason why the pamphlet tended to be ignored appeared to be that it looked like commercial advertising or Sunday supplement material. The selective aspect of exposure is also illustrated by the fact that when, in Bridgeport, a free movie about the bond drive was shown, only 5 percent of the population attended. Moreover, *those who came were those who believed most strongly in buying bonds.*

Another study involved an intensive educational campaign over a six-month period, aimed at providing people in Cincinnati with information about the United Nations. It demonstrated clearly that only those who were already interested in the United Nations welcomed the information (Star & Hughes, 1950). Intensive efforts to get people interested in the United Nations were unsuccessful.

These studies make abundantly clear that individuals expose themselves to communications selectively, depending upon their interest in the communication topic and situation. But not all these studies strongly support the idea that a person exposes himself only to those communications he agrees with. In a test of dissonance theory, Feather (1963) found that smokers were *more* interested than nonsmokers in information linking smoking with lung cancer, and that they did not avoid information about the harmful effects of smoking. He suggested that dissonance does not affect exposure, but modifies the evaluation of information received.

Evidence is also available demonstrating that loyal party voters may pay considerable attention to the opposition. One intensive voting study, for example, obtained quantitative measures of the number of items read or heard that were favorable to each of the presidential candidates in the 1948 election (Berelson, Lazarsfeld, & McPhee, 1954). Although 54 percent of the Republicans heard or read more items favorable to Dewey, the Republican candidate, 46 percent of them heard or read more items favorable to Truman. Similarly, 43 percent of the Democrats heard more items favorable to Dewey, and 57 percent heard more items favorable to Truman. While these figures indicate a slight bias in exposure, they suggest that by and large partisans are likely to expose themselves to opposition arguments.

A study of the Nixon-Kennedy television debates conducted during the 1960 election also indicates surprisingly little avoidance of opposing arguments (Carter, 1962). Since both candidates appeared on the same program, of course, opposing arguments might be somewhat more difficult to avoid than in the case of a program presented by a single candidate. Nevertheless, it would be possible for viewers to attend closely to their candidate and turn their attention to other matters when the opposition candidate appeared. Selective exposure may take place, even when the communicator and respondent are in close communication—as every college professor knows through his classroom experience with students! A comparison of the extent to which arguments presented by opposing candidates in the television debates were recalled, however, suggested a minimum of selective exposure, since viewers recalled arguments from both sides equally well. This was true for viewers who said that both candidates made effective arguments and for those who said that only their own candidate made effective arguments. Only the viewers who said neither candidate presented effective arguments recalled appreciably more of the arguments of their own candidate than of the opposition.

Because of the nature of survey methods, it is extraordinarily difficult to prove that persons *actively avoid* exposure to arguments in which they are not interested. For this reason, a variety of laboratory experiments have studied selective exposure. Perhaps the best controlled is one conducted by Festinger (1957, pp. 162–176) as a test of a hypothesis from dissonance theory.

According to dissonance theory, a person seeks out information if he expects it to reduce dissonance and avoids information expected to increase dissonance. In Festinger's experiment, subjects were invited to participate in a gambling game and were required to choose one or the other of two sides. Records were kept of the extent to which a person was winning or losing. At the end of twelve trials, he was shown a graph which purported to depict the probability that his side was winning or losing. His motivation to examine this graph was thought to be a joint function of three factors: (1) the amount of dissonance he was experiencing at the end of the twelve trials, (2) the extent to which he expected the information to reduce or increase his dissonance, and (3) the fact that, if he changed sides, he would have to pay a penalty.

Dissonance at the end of the twelfth trial was a function of the degree to which a person's choice of sides had led to a consonant or dissonant outcome in terms of winning or losing. Table 5–1 indicates the several degrees of dissonance and their relation to the subject's motivation to examine the graph. For example, if a person is winning, he should experience little dissonance and thus should have little motivation to examine the graph. If he is breaking even or slightly losing, he is likely to be hopeful that the probability graph will confirm his choice as the side that will eventually come out ahead. As dissonance increases, however, he becomes fearful that the probability information will confirm his fears that he has chosen the wrong side, and he avoids looking at it. Once he decides to change to the other side in spite of the penalty, he expects the probability information to reduce dissonance by confirming his contemplated choice, and therefore he is interested in examining it.

In his experiment, Festinger measured the time in seconds that the

Table 5–1
Dissonance and Selective Exposure

CONDITIONS AT END OF 12TH TRIAL	DISSONANCE AROUSED	SELECTIVE EXPOSURE
S is winning.	No dissonance	No interest in graph; would confirm choice of side.
S is breaking even or slightly losing.	Mild dissonance	Considerable interest in graph; would confirm choice of side and reduce dissonance.
S is losing substantially but sticking to choice.	Considerable dissonance	Graph is avoided because it would confirm wrong choice, increasing dissonance.
S is experiencing great loss; thinking of choosing other side.	Great dissonance	Considerable interest in graph; with change of side would be dissonance-reducing.

SOURCE: Based on data presented in L. Festinger. *A theory of cognitive dissonance.* New York: Harper & Row, Publishers, Incorporated, 1957.

participant spent looking at the graph. These varying amounts of voluntary exposure coincided with the hypothesized relations outlined in Table 5–1, thus providing support for the dissonance theory interpretation of selective exposure. His experiment has been repeated by Cohen, Brehm, and Latane (1959) with an additional condition: The choice of one or the other sides was confidential and private in one case and was to be made public in the other. Both conditions produced results comparable to those in the original experiment, with the public condition accentuating dissonance and consequent selective exposure.[3]

This dissonance interpretation, which stresses the point that a person avoids exposing himself to communications he disagrees with *only if he believes they arouse dissonance*, may well explain why partisans often expose themselves to the opposition. The experimental situation was one where the communicator (a graduate student) was highly credible, and his probability data were likely to be believed. But an election campaign situation is quite different. A loyal Democrat or Republican probably has little fear that listening to a candidate from the opposing party will change his own views. In fact, he may enjoy listening to an opposition candidate because he can deride and refute his arguments. He is particularly able

[3]Recently, Chapanis and Chapanis (1964) report a common-sense interpretation of these findings by F. E. Emery as an alternative to a dissonance interpretation: A person examines the graph when he needs more information to help him decide whether he should change sides.

to do this when the candidate is on television and cannot talk back. Casual observation by the authors of a few friends viewing the Nixon-Kennedy television debates revealed that when the opposition candidate was speaking, they talked out loud, refuting his arguments. This may well have been a widespread phenomenon, but it does not appear to have been systematically investigated.

STUDY QUESTIONS

10. *Explain what is meant by selective exposure to communications. What are its consequences?*
11. *Under what circumstances may individuals pay some attention to communications with which they do not agree?*
12. *Explain selective exposure in terms of dissonance theory, outlining the conditions under which a person will pay attention to or avoid a communication.*

Immunizing effects of exposure

Early work on one-sided and two-sided communications suggested that when a person has been exposed to both sides of an argument, the belief he accepts will be more resistant to change than if he has been exposed only to communications agreeing with his beliefs (Hovland, Lumsdaine, & Sheffield, 1949). A series of recent experiments extends this idea in the following way. When a belief is widespread in a society, so that the individual is unlikely to encounter contradictory evidence or opinions, the belief will yield readily to a strong persuasive attack. The reasoning behind this is that under such circumstances the individual has had no occasion for developing resistance to countercommunications or for thinking of arguments in support of his belief. But if, prior to an attack upon it, arguments against the belief are presented in weakened form, he should develop some resistance to future attacks. The more such arguments lead to active formulation of defenses against them, the more the individual will be immunized against further attacks.

In the first study (McGuire & Papageorgis, 1961) designed to examine these ideas, four beliefs about health were chosen, such as the following: "The effects of penicillin have been, almost without exception, of great benefit to mankind." "Most forms of mental illness are not contagious." Each person was put through two experimental sessions — first an immunizing session, and second a test session. In the first session, persons in the control group received no treatment; others received various forms of treatment intended to immunize them against later attack. Immunization procedures included active defenses such as writing an essay providing arguments in support of the belief or refuting arguments against the belief, and passive defenses such as reading an essay provided by the experimenter which either defended the belief or supplied weak arguments refuting the belief.

In the test session, strong arguments against the belief were presented. The results were in accord with the predictions. When the initial beliefs had not received any immunization treatment, they were appreciably weakened by the strong counterarguments in the test session. Initial beliefs that had received *supportive* arguments in the immunizing session were further strengthened by these arguments; but when they were subsequently exposed to counterarguments, the initial beliefs were weakened virtually as much as if they had received no supportive treatment. In contrast, initial beliefs that had been immunized by exposure to weak counterarguments were not influenced to the same extent by subsequent strong counterarguments—a result demonstrating that the beliefs had acquired some immunity to countercommunications.

A further experiment determined that exposure to weak counterarguments created resistance not only to the specific counterarguments later presented in a stronger form, but also to alternative arguments not introduced as a part of the immunization procedure (Papageorgis & McGuire, 1961). This effect occurs presumably because exposure to *any* counterarguments is likely to lead the recipient to think up a variety of supporting arguments for his belief, including some which will enable him to resist counterarguments he has not yet heard. This defensive process is probably effective also because it produces lower credibility toward later countercommunications—that is, it produces a larger number of cognitive elements dissonant with the later communication.

That active defense produces the most general immunization is indicated by another condition varied in this and a subsequent experiment (McGuire, 1961). When a recipient exposed to weak counterarguments was required to compose an essay actively defending his belief, the immunization process applied to novel counterarguments as well as to the original ones. But when the individual was required only to read an essay defending his beliefs, the immunization effect did not generalize to new arguments. Finally, a study by McGuire (1962) demonstrated that active refutation also establishes resistance that persists over a longer period of time than resistance established by mere exposure to supporting arguments, and that this persistence also applies to counterarguments other than the ones explicitly refuted. Thus exposure that generates an active process of defense rather than a passive one is likely to provide the most general form of immunity to counterarguments.

If we may assume that these findings hold generally, they have very important implications. The most central values of our culture might be readily susceptible to change, should forcible exposure to counterarguments occur, simply because no effort has been expended in developing defenses against attacks which never occur. Thus, belief in a democratic government, virtually universal among Americans, might well be susceptible to a concerted attack in a situation where an American is isolated from his fellow believers and exposed to counterarguments—as in Korean prison camps where the Chinese Communists used intensive brainwashing procedures. The experimental work just described suggests that the way to build resistance to such attacks is to challenge somewhat the concepts and principles of democracy, forcing the individual to develop defenses.

STUDY QUESTIONS

13. *What previous exposure conditions make a belief particularly susceptible to attack by counterarguments?*
14. *What factors are most likely to immunize a belief against future counter-arguments?*

Motivational resistance to change

The discussion of attitude theory in Chapter 3 mentioned that some attitudes might be particularly resistant to change because they have an "ego-defensive" basis. An attitude may serve to keep from awareness motives that are socially unacceptable. This effect is achieved either when the attitude facilitates ego-defensive responses or when it facilitates responses that permit satisfaction of the unacceptable motive in a socially acceptable way, thus reducing the tension experienced.

According to Freud, stimuli that threaten to arouse sufficient anxiety to disrupt the effective functioning of cognitive processes must be kept from consciousness. Sarnoff (1960) suggests that certain attitudes serve this function. According to him, one type of attitude helps to reduce or eliminate threatening external stimuli. This attitude takes the form of denial. An illustration is found in the common expression "it can't happen to me." Thus, heavy smokers may resist communications warning of the dangers of lung cancer by developing attitudes supporting their immunity to this disease, stressing other more imminent dangers, and so on. The net effect of such reactions is to reduce the threatening character of the communication.

Another type of attitude may reduce or eliminate threatening internal stimuli — stimuli stemming from unacceptable motives or impulses. The well-known mechanism of *repression* is an example: repression is a process by which material is excluded from conscious awareness. Another mechanism is *projection:* the attribution of unacceptable motives to other persons instead of oneself. The hostile individual justifies his hostile behavior by perceiving others as hostile toward him. Another familiar mechanism is *reaction formation:* responses directly contrary to those required for tension reduction occur, but in this way the individual is kept from recognizing the unacceptable motive. For example, a mother who resents her child and who is unable to accept this fact smothers her child with affection in order to hide from herself her resentment.

Such attitudes as these, Sarnoff stresses, are not readily amenable to change through ordinary methods. Direct persuasive communications either are ineffective or, in some instances, result in a strengthening of the attitude. This follows from the fact that acceptance of the communication would eliminate an attitude that protects the individual against an unacceptable motive or that fosters behavior which satisfies the unacceptable motive.

Cognitive balancing as a defensive process

Resistance to attitude change may be conceptualized in terms of the necessity of the organism to retain a state of consonance, cognitive balance, congruity, or consistency. In this view, any persuasive communication that is dissonant with existing attitudes will arouse defensive reactions. Most of the psychologists who have a theory based on consistency have dealt with this problem of defensive reactions. A number of processes suggested by Abelson (1959) may be used for illustrative purposes. These have been further elaborated and formalized by Rosenberg and Abelson (1960).

The essentials of their system are as follows. Cognitive elements have either a positive or a negative value. In addition, the relation between elements may be either positive or negative. Thus, such concepts as mother, money, and God have positive values for most persons, and death, injury, and imprisonment have negative values. Positive relations between elements are illustrated by such terms as *likes, helps, is consistent with;* while negative relations are depicted by such terms as *dislikes, fights, opposes, is inconsistent with.* A *balanced* state exists under the following conditions:

1. Two positive elements have a positive relation. Example: The United States (+) helps (+) her Latin American neighbors (+).
2. Two negative elements have a positive relation. Example: Russia (−) and the Chinese Communists (−) are working together (+).
3. A positive element is negatively related to a negative element. Yugoslavia (+) has resisted domination (−) by the Soviet Union (−).

An *unbalanced* state exists under the following conditions:

1. One positive element is negatively related to another positive element. Example: Latin America (+) is not supporting (−) the United States (+).
2. Two negative elements have a negative relation. Example: The Soviet Union (−) and the Chinese Communists (−) are highly critical (−) of each other.
3. A positive and a negative element have a positive relation. Example: The United States (+) and Russia (−) have entered into a trade agreement (+).

States of imbalance are regarded as disturbing and are likely to be resolved by various means. Some modes of resolving belief dilemmas suggested by Abelson include the following:

1. *Denial.* This is the simplest and most often used mode of resolving a belief dilemma. The value of the object is denied or declared to be opposite, or the sign of the relation is explained away, as illustrated in

ORIGINAL IMBALANCED STRUCTURES   BALANCED STRUCTURES

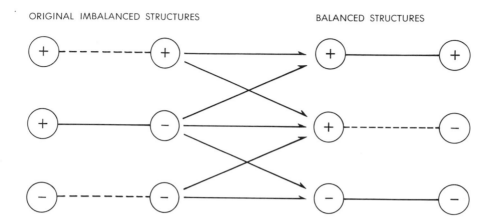

Figure 5–2

Achievement of balance through denial. An imbalanced
structure may be converted to a balanced one by changing
one of the elements or the relation between them. (Adapted
with permission from R. P. Abelson. Modes of resolution
of belief dilemmas. *J. conflict Resolut.*, 1959, **3**, 343–352.)

Figure 5–2. For example, the heavy cigarette smoker values smoking
positively but lung cancer negatively. A communication linking smoking
with lung cancer is likely to be resisted because it creates imbalance.
Denial can be used to explain away the positive relation between lung
cancer and smoking by suggesting that this correlational finding does not
demonstrate cause and effect, or that the evidence for the relation is insufficient. Another less likely mode of resolution through denial shifts
the value of smoking from positive to negative.

2. *Bolstering.* One of the two objects is additionally supported by relating
it to other cognitive objects in a balanced way, as illustrated in Figure
5–3. For example, the smoker who is anxious about lung cancer may tell
himself that smoking is extremely enjoyable, soothes his nerves, and adds
to his social life. The imbalance between lung cancer and smoking is not
eliminated, but the total balance in the entire system of related elements
is improved. This mechanism is very similar to Festinger's notion, discussed in Chapter 3, of adding new cognitive elements to reduce dissonance.

3. *Differentiation.* Denial and bolstering are defenses that preserve the
identity of the elements. Differentiation restores balance by splitting an
element into two parts that have a negative relation to each other, as
illustrated in Figure 5–4. For example, hydrogen bomb testing is positively valued for many people as necessary for defense, but poisoning of
the atmosphere is negatively valued. For a person with these values, there
is imbalance in the belief in bomb testing. This can be resolved by differ-
entiating the attitude object into two parts: testing "dirty" bombs that

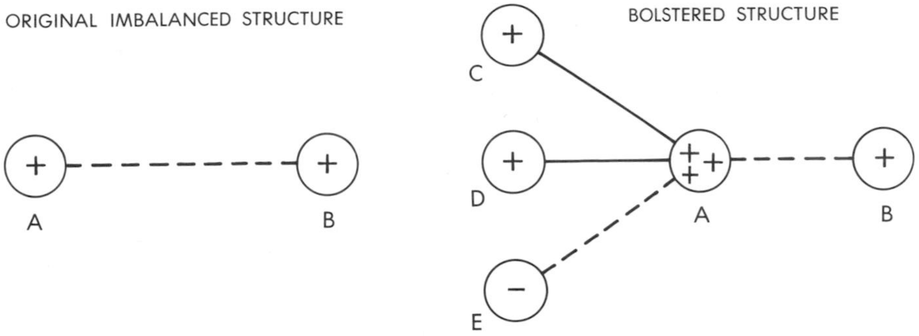

ORIGINAL IMBALANCED STRUCTURE

BOLSTERED STRUCTURE

Figure 5–3
Reduction of imbalance through bolstering. In the bolstered structure the units AC, AD, and AE are all balanced.
The relative effect of the imbalanced unit AB is thus reduced. (Adapted with permission from R. P. Abelson.
Modes of resolution of belief dilemmas. *J. conflict Resolut.*,
1959, **3,** 343–352.)

ORIGINAL IMBALANCED STRUCTURE

BALANCED DIFFERENTIATED STRUCTURE

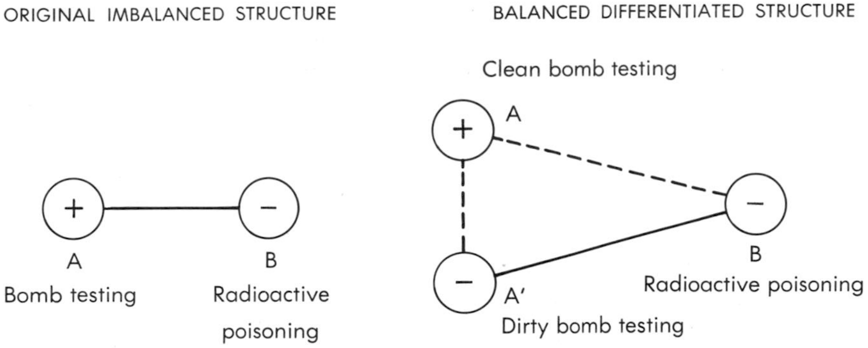

Figure 5–4
Achievement of balance through differentiation. One
element is split into two which have opposite signs, both
possessing balanced relations with the remaining element.
(Adapted with permission from R. P. Abelson. Modes of
resolution of belief dilemmas. *J. conflict Resolut.*, 1959,
3, 343–352.)

poison the atmosphere and "clean" bombs that do not. A similar example
can be applied to the lung cancer problem: smoking can be differentiated
into smoking ordinary cigarettes and smoking filter cigarettes. If the person believes that filter cigarettes protect against lung cancer, he can
restore balance by smoking them.

Thus, when cognitive balance or consistency is threatened by a persuasive communication, the individual has a variety of resources for

restoring balance without yielding to the pressure exerted by the communication.

STUDY QUESTIONS

15. *Explain how attitudes may have an ego-defensive function and how this makes them more resistant to change.*
16. *What three sets of signs constitute a balanced state? What three sets are unbalanced?*
17. *Describe several mechanisms by which an unbalanced state may be restored to a balanced one.*

Summary: Individual processes in resistance

Individual processes contributing to resistance to change include the following: selective exposure, immunizing of beliefs, motivational resistance to changing certain attitudes, and cognitive balancing as a defensive process.

Selective exposure includes seeking exposure to certain communications and avoiding others. Studies of mass promotional campaigns indicate that only a very small proportion of the potential audience is exposed to the communications. In general, the persons exposed are those who are most interested in the issues and who are generally favorable to the communicator's position. Survey studies, however, have not demonstrated clearly that persons actively avoid communications representing a position they disagree with. Laboratory experiments designed to test this proposition have been somewhat more successful in supporting it.

A series of experiments has demonstrated that beliefs which have seldom been challenged are readily susceptible to attack by strong counterarguments. These beliefs may be partially immunized against such attacks by presentation of counterarguments in weakened form. Under certain conditions, the resistance generated by this method extends not only to the specific arguments used for immunization, but also to new arguments. Immunization is most effective when it requires the individual to engage in an active rather than a passive defense of his beliefs.

Attitudes vary in the manner in which they are motivationally supported. Certain attitudes probably serve to defend the individual against various forms of threat or anxiety. Anxiety may stem from external dangers or from one's own unacceptable impulses. The attitudes that help relieve anxiety aroused by such threats are likely to be strongly resistant to change. These attitudes often operate in the manner of the classical Freudian defense mechanisms.

Finally, the tendency to maintain a balanced cognitive state provides some resistance against attitude change. Examples of mechanisms used to maintain balance are denial, bolstering, and differentiation. In denial, the value of the object that creates imbalance is denied or declared to be opposite, or the sign of the relation that creates imbalance is explained away. Bolstering does not completely restore balance, but adds additional cognitive elements having values that increase overall balance. Unlike these two mechanisms, differentiation restores balance by changing the identity of one of the elements, splitting it into two parts that have a negative relation to each other.

INDIVIDUAL PROCESSES AND THE COMMUNICATION

As was mentioned when the topic of persuasive communications was introduced, to consider separately each of the components of the communication process (such as the communicator or the recipient) may result in the neglect of important effects resulting from the interplay between these components. The point will be made more evident in this section, which treats several aspects of the relation between individual processes and the nature of the communication. Topics include the relation between the motivational basis of the recipient's attitude and the type of communication, differential forgetting over time of aspects of the communication (leading to the "sleeper effect"), and the effects of the distance between positions of the communicator and the respondent.

The communication and motivational bases of attitudes

The discussion of attitude theory in Chapter 3 referred to the thesis of Katz and Stotland (1959) that persuasive communications affect attitudes differently depending upon the relation of the communication to the motivational basis which supports the attitudes. A variety of experimental work corroborating this view has been carried out. One problem attacked in several studies[4] contrasted the effects of a communication designed to increase insight into the sources of prejudice with a communication based on the thesis that the characteristics of any group are relative to the cultural influences to which they are subjected. To increase insight, the first communication presented a case history explaining the psychodynamics of prejudice. The other communication presented descriptive material showing how Negroes were subjected to unfavorable circumstances in the United States and how their characteristics have resulted from this treatment. The extent to which subjects were ego-defensive was also measured.

Since prejudice is thought to have some motivational basis, particularly in persons with moderate and high ego-defensiveness, the "insight" approach was expected to be more effective in reducing prejudice than the appeal presenting information about historical circumstances. This expectation was supported, particularly for persons who were moderately ego-defensive. Those who were strongly ego-defensive were presumed to be too resistant to accept the insight approach, and those who were low in ego-defensiveness were presumed to have little motivational basis for their prejudice and thus little "insight" to gain.

---

[4]Katz, Sarnoff, & McClintock, 1956; Katz, McClintock, & Sarnoff, 1957; McClintock, 1958; Stotland, Katz, & Patchen, 1959.

Another study has demonstrated that individuals with an authoritarian personality (see Chapter 2) respond differently to different forms of communications intended to reduce prejudice (Wagman, 1955). Since power and status are central values for the authoritarian person, he might be expected to be more responsive to communications from strong authoritative sources. A nonauthoritarian individual might be expected to be less susceptible to influence from this kind of communicator. To test these hypotheses, a nonauthoritarian communication making an objective appeal against prejudice and two communications appealing to authority were presented to a group of persons high in authoritarianism and a group of persons low in it.

The nonauthoritarian communication stressed the lack of prejudice toward the Negro in some cultures, the poor adjustment value of prejudiced attitudes, and a review of the forward progress made by the American Negro. One authoritarian communication was a booklet reporting that the great majority of military leaders and business executives supported discrimination, and the other was a booklet stating that these authorities were opposed to discrimination.

Results were in accord with expectations. The nonauthoritarian communication slightly reduced prejudice among nonauthoritarian subjects, but boomeranged with authoritarian individuals (increased prejudice slightly). The authoritarian communication advocating less discrimination toward Negroes was fairly successful in reducing prejudice of both the authoritarian and nonauthoritarian individuals. Finally, the authoritarian booklet aimed at increasing prejudice produced some increase for extreme authoritarians, but boomeranged for extreme nonauthoritarians (produced a reduction in prejudice).

The sleeper effect and persistence of change

Many of the studies cited in earlier chapters have measured attitude change not only immediately following the communication, but also at various intervals of time thereafter. As might be expected, in many instances opinion change was greatest immediately following the communication, and the individual gradually moved back in the direction of his initial position as time passed. In a number of well-documented instances, however, the amount of attitude change was *greater* after a lapse of time, most often a period of weeks. This latter finding has been termed the *sleeper effect* by Hovland, Lumsdaine, and Sheffield (1949) and has been discussed further by Hovland, Janis, and Kelley (1953). One explanation of the sleeper effect is that if the recipient of the communication has some doubt concerning the credibility of the communicator, this will initially produce less acceptance; but over a period of time, the recipient will dissociate the contents of the communication from the source. Thus his resistance to acceptance will be lowered, resulting in a greater amount of opinion change in the direction of the communication.

This notion was tested in a series of experiments. In one study, the

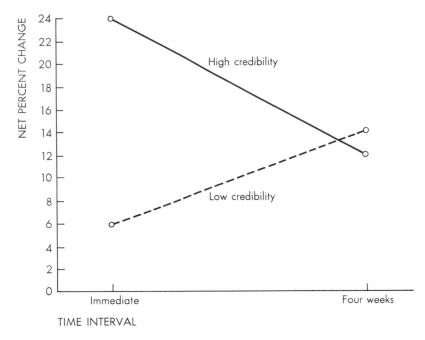

Figure 5–5
Retention of attitude change and the sleeper effect. (Adapted with permission from C. I. Hovland, I. L. Janis, & H. H. Kelley. *Communication and persuasion.* New Haven, Conn.: Yale University Press, 1953.)

same communications were presented by a source which had high credibility and by another which had low credibility (Hovland & Weiss, 1952). Although immediately after the communications there was more acceptance of the one presented by the trustworthy person, four weeks later the amount of acceptance was approximately equal for the two sources. Opinion change had declined for the high-credible source and increased for the low-credible source. The results of this experiment are illustrated by Figure 5–5.

In a different investigation, information about the communicator was reintroduced at the time of delayed testing for opinion change, thus reminding the recipients of his low (or high) credibility (Kelman & Hovland, 1953). Under these circumstances, opinion change remained low for the low-credible source. Finally, another experimenter first had high school students learn a communication on the effects of smoking, and then immediately presented to a subgroup of these students a counter-communication discounting the truth of the original communication (Weiss, 1953). As might be expected, acceptance of the initial communication was greater for those who had not received the countercommunication. Six weeks later, however, the difference between the two groups

had disappeared, a result which again suggests that the skepticism introduced experimentally with respect to the initial communication becomes
dissociated from the source, leading to greater acceptance of the source
after the passage of time.

Watts and McGuire (1964) have investigated in a comprehensive fashion the relation between persistence of attitude change and retention of
various aspects of the communication. From their data we may infer
that a person who has changed his attitude as a result of a communication
is likely to move back toward his initial position at a steady rate. On the
other hand, recall for various aspects of the communication drops off
rapidly in the first week following exposure, and thereafter is forgotten
at a much slower rate. They also find that six weeks after exposure, those
persons who are unable to remember the *topic* of the communication
retain their changed attitude to a greater extent than those who remember the topic. This is similar to the sleeper effect discussed above
and has a similar explanation.

Quite a different finding occurs with respect to recall of specific
arguments: recall is best for those persons showing the greatest attitude
change. Finally, those persons initially exposed to a communication
from a positive source who recall the *source* after an interval of one, two,
or six weeks show a greater attitude change than those who do not recall
the source. No such difference is found for those persons initially exposed
to a communication from a negative source.

STUDY QUESTIONS

18. *How does the motivational basis of an attitude determine its susceptibility
to different kinds of communications?*
19. *What approach is theoretically most effective with ego-defensive attitudes?*
20. *To what kinds of communications are high-authoritarian and low-authoritarian persons most responsive? To what kinds are they resistant?*
21. *What is meant by the sleeper effect in acceptance of communications? How is
this process explained? Relate retention of attitude change to recall of various
aspects of the communication.*

Distance between positions of communicator and respondent

The discussion of one-sided communications (see Chapter 4) noted
that individuals who are initially opposed to the position taken by the
communicator are more influenced by a two-sided communication. Conversely, those who are in essential agreement with the position of the
communicator are more influenced by a one-sided communication. Thus,
the reaction of the recipient of a communication is markedly affected by
the discrepancy (or correspondence) between the communicator's position and his own.

The most recent book (Sherif & Hovland, 1961) in the Yale studies of
communication series has presented systematic analysis of the various
effects of discrepancies between the position of the communicator and

that of the recipient. In the first place, the position of the communicator as perceived by the respondent is not necessarily the same as his position as determined by social consensus. The experiments reported demonstrate the operation of systematic biases. Two major processes are *assimilation* and *contrast*.

A respondent whose own position is relatively close to that of the communicator is likely to perceive the communicator's position as even closer than it is: this is the *assimilation* effect. But a respondent having a position rather distant from that of the communicator is likely to see the communicator's position as even more distant: this is the *contrast* effect. These effects have been confirmed by experimental work. Thus the respondent's *perception* of the position of the communicator must be taken into account in determining the potential effect the communication might have upon the respondent.

The evaluation of a communication is related to the distance between the position of the communicator and that of the respondent. For each respondent and each issue, there is a range within which the position of the communicator can differ from that of the respondent and still be evaluated as fair and unbiased. Positions outside that range will not be favorably evaluated by the recipient. A similar range exists for rejection of the communication.

This is illustrated by the previously cited experiment in which a non-authoritarian communication intended to reduce prejudice slightly increased prejudice of individuals high in authoritarianism, and an authoritarian communication intended to increase prejudice slightly reduced prejudice of individuals extremely low in authoritarianism. Authoritarianism is highly correlated with prejudice. Thus in both cases where the respondent moved in a direction *opposite* to the communication, his own position and that of the communicator were at a considerable distance from each other.

The relation between an individual's own stand and his evaluation of a communication is also well illustrated by an experiment (Hovland, Harvey, & Sherif, 1957) conducted in a region where prohibition was a lively topic of discussion. It had recently been submitted in a referendum to the voters of Oklahoma, where legal prohibition of alcoholic beverages was optional for each county. The term *dry* will be used to refer to a stand favoring prohibition and the term *wet* to a stand favoring unrestricted sale of alcoholic beverages. The sample of persons tested included some with extremely dry positions, such as the members of the Woman's Christian Temperance Union. Comparable extremes at the wet end of the attitude continuum were more difficult to obtain, but the investigators selected some individuals, mostly college students, through personal acquaintance.

Each individual's own position was assessed by means of a set of attitude statements ranging from extremely dry positions to extremely wet positions. Then a five-item scale was used to determine each respondent's evaluation of the fairness and impartiality of communications having three different positions. A very close relation was found between the evaluation of a statement and its distance from the position of the respondent. For example, the extremely wet statement was evaluated most favorably by the respondents who themselves favored an extremely wet position. As the stand of the respondent deviated from an extremely wet position, the statement was less favorably evaluated. Those having extremely dry positions, for example, regarded the extremely wet statement as completely unfair and biased. Similar results were obtained for an extremely dry statement: The closer the respondent's own stand to that of the statement, the more favorably he evaluated it. Finally, a statement having a moderately wet position was most favorably evaluated by respondents holding a similar position.

Latitudes of acceptance and rejection vary depending upon whether the issue is a familiar or unfamiliar one, whether the issue is one in which the respondents are especially interested and involved, whether the communicator has high or low credibility, and whether the facts on the issue are ambiguous or clear. In the study just discussed, ranges of acceptance were relatively narrow because of high involvement and familiarity. These same factors *broaden* the range of *rejection*.

The voting studies referred to previously (see the section on selective exposure) also illustrate the effect of high involvement. Most voters feel very strongly on the issue of party affiliation and vote accordingly. Because of this high involvement, the latitude of acceptance of political communications that deviate from one's own position is very narrow and the latitude of rejection is broad. These concepts are consistent with the findings from the voting studies indicating that political communications produce very little change in the positions of the voters.

The implications of these ideas are that on issues of great personal concern to individuals, and in circumstances where the credibility of the communicator is not great, the communicator's message must not deviate very far from the position held by his respondents if he is to be successful at all. If he wishes to change their position markedly, he apparently will be able to do so only in a series of communications, each moving the respondent a small distance at a time. On the other hand, if an issue is of little concern to a recipient, and the communicator is highly credible, a communicator is likely to induce change more effectively if his position is more distant from that of the respondent.

A laboratory experiment was designed to test this notion (Hovland & Pritzker, 1957). Because of the laboratory setup, the communicator was highly credible; and issues such as the desirability of compulsory voting and the adequacy of five hours' sleep per night were chosen, so that subjects would not feel high personal involvement. It was found that the greater the discrepancy between the position of the communicator and that of the recipient, the more the recipient was influenced. In other words, the greater the amount of change advocated by the communicator, the greater the change in the respondent's attitude. This conclusion applies only where all conditions favor a very wide latitude of acceptance, as in this experiment. A study by Aronson, Turner, and Carlsmith (1963) demonstrates that the latitude of acceptance is narrower for a communicator of moderate credibility than for one of high credibility, and offers a dissonance interpretation of this fact. We may conclude that where personal involvement in the issue is high, where the issue is familiar, where the stimulus situation is clear, and where the communicator does not have high credibility, the latitude of acceptance is apt to be very narrow.

Summary: Individual processes and the communication

This section has emphasized the relation between individual processes and the communication. Experimental work indicates that communications which are designed to take into account the motivational basis underlying an attitude are somewhat more successful than communications which are not. Further research on this topic is needed for more definite conclusions.

The passage of time after a communication is often accompanied by a dissociation of the source from the ideas presented, a phenomenon demonstrated by the sleeper effect. This effect accounts for the observation that when a communicator has relatively low credibility, attitude change is sometimes greater after the passage of time than immediately following a communication. A person who has changed his attitude as a result of a communication is apt to move steadily back toward his initial position with the passage of time. The persistence of his initial attitude change, however, varies with several recall conditions. Attitude change is more persistent when a person is (1) unable to remember the communication topic, (2) able to remember specific arguments, and (3) able to recall the source, if it was positive.

Several principles have been developed with respect to the effects of the distance between the position of the communicator and that of the recipient. The position of the communicator as perceived by the respondent is not necessarily the same as the communicator's position as determined by social consensus. Two major forms of systematic bias are assimilation and contrast. The assimilation effect occurs when a respondent whose own position is relatively close to that of the communicator perceives the communicator's position to be even closer than it is. The contrast effect occurs when a respondent having a position rather distant from that of the communicator sees the communicator's position as even more distant than it is.

The evaluation of a communication is related to the perceived distance between the position of the communicator and that of the respondent. For each respondent and each issue, there is a range within which the position of the communicator can differ from that of the respondent and still be evaluated as fair and unbiased. These latitudes of acceptance and rejection vary depending upon whether the issue is a familiar or unfamiliar one, whether it is one in which respondents are especially interested and involved, whether the communicator has high or low credibility, and whether the facts on the issue are ambiguous or clear. Thus, if a communicator is to be successful he must make sure that his position is within the respondent's range of acceptance.

PERMANENCE OF INDUCED CHANGES

The extent to which a change in opinion or behavior is permanent depends upon the dynamics of the influence process. An analysis by Kelman (1962) suggests some of these dynamics and their implications for transitory or permanent change. He has had some tentative success in devising experiments to test his ideas.

Chapter 3 noted Kelman's three processes of attitude change: compliance, identification, and internalization. Since compliance is a process where the change is brought about through reward or threat of punishment, and since active surveillance by the influence agent is necessary, it might appear that the change would be temporary. We have, however, already noted Kelman's suggestion that action contrary to his opinions may require the individual to reexamine them and bring them into line with the new behavior, a process also suggested by dissonance theory. A second possibility is that "action may provide the occasion for the occurrence of new experiences in relation to the object (Kelman, 1962, p. 86). These may be favorable or rewarding and so may result in a shift in attitude to conform to the new experience.

Action may also create a new "psychological situation." A psychological situation may be characterized in terms of approach-avoidance tendencies toward the attitude object. For example, as a person approaches the attitude object prior to action, his tendency to avoid it may increase more sharply than his tendency to approach it, so that under ordinary circumstances he would not engage in action with the object. But if through added external pressures he is forced to engage in the action, his tendencies to avoid the object may be outweighed by his tendencies to approach it. Once the action is engaged in, resistance to it may fall permanently below the tendency to perform the action; thus, the change becomes permanent. A simple illustration is found in the initial resistance to performing some anxiety-arousing action for the first time, such as diving from a height or making a public speech. Usually such initial actions are followed by a considerable drop in resistance to further enactment.

To the extent that a change takes place as a result of identification or internalization, the change is more likely to be permanent. In the case of identification, the change occurs through the formation of a satisfying relation to the communicator. While this relation persists, the accompanying attitude changes are maintained. In internalization, the induced opinion or behavior is consonant with the individual's value system and persists as long as he does not make any basic changes in his values.

STUDY QUESTIONS

22. *Explain what is meant by assimilation and contrast.*

23. *For each of the following two cases, state the conditions under which the communication is likely to be accepted: (a) when the position of the communicator is close to that of the respondent, and (b) when the position of the communicator is distant from that of the respondent.*

24. *Discuss the factors likely to make a change of attitude permanent.*

Summary and Conclusions

The two major topics of discussion in this chapter have been the personality correlates of the persuasibility of individuals and the processes that result in individual resistance to change. Experiments have shown that the persuasibility of individuals has some consistency for different topics and appeals, but individuals also vary systematically in their responses to specific topics and appeals. It has been found that topic-free persuasibility has some relation to self-esteem and aggressiveness. Probably relations between persuasibility and personality are markedly attenuated by variations in persuasibility from one communication situation to another. In addition, certain forms of interplay between the nature of the communication situation and the characteristics of the individual have been shown to operate: such findings limit the extent to which persuasibility tendencies generalize across communication situations for a given individual.

Of the various defenses that an individual may display in the face of communications dissonant with his attitudes, selective exposure is one of the simplest and most effective. This has its dangers, however, for when the individual has not previously been exposed to counterarguments, then exposure to strong counterarguments may have telling effects upon attitudes that he has always accepted without question. Resistance to such a contingency may be developed by exposing him to a weak form of the counterarguments, particularly if he is stimulated by them to actively defend his beliefs.

Several types of resistant attitudes serve to reduce threat or anxiety by denying the existence of external dangers or by keeping socially unacceptable motives out of the awareness of the individual. Attitudes that are strongly consonant with other cognitive elements subscribed to by the individual are also highly resistant to change. Balance theory provides a variety of defenses whereby the imbalance or dissonance created by a persuasive communication can readily be repaired without changing the attitude. Communications that take into account the motivational basis of the respondents' attitudes are more likely to be successful.

The passage of time after a communication is often accompanied by a dissociation of the source from the ideas presented, a phenomenon demonstrated by the sleeper effect. This effect accounts for the observation that, where the communicator has relatively low credibility, attitude change is sometimes greater after the passage of time than immediately after a communication. Memory for various aspects of the communication also make attitude change more or less persistent.

The perceived position of the communicator relative to that of the respondent is an important determinant of the evaluation and acceptance of the communication. Where the issue is one in which the respondent is highly involved, where the communicator is not highly credible, and where the issue is familiar and unambiguous, the respondent is likely to accept the communication only where the communicator's position is relatively close to his own. In the opposite conditions, the communicator is likely to achieve more attitude change the more distant his position from that of the respondent.

At the end of the chapter a topic requiring more research was briefly discussed: the conditions that make for temporary or permanent changes in attitudes.

chapter six

PERSUASIVE COMMUNICATION
AND THE SOCIAL STRUCTURE

To this point we have focused primarily upon the individual, discussing the organization and structure of his attitudes, his responses to varying aspects of the communication situation, his persuasibility and its relation to his personality, and the processes by which he resists influence. This treatment may have created a picture of persuasive communication as a process that goes on between a single communicator and a single recipient. Such indeed was the early conception of mass communication held by many observers in the decades before World War II, a conception well characterized by Katz and Lazarsfeld (1955):

> Their image, first of all, was of an atomistic mass of millions of readers, listeners and movie-goers prepared to receive the Message; and secondly, they pictured every Message as a direct and powerful stimulus to action which would elicit immediate response. In short, the media of communication were looked upon as a new kind of unifying force—a simple kind of nervous system—reaching out to every eye and ear, in a society characterized by an amorphous social organization and a paucity of interpersonal relations. (P. 16)

Thus, in the older view, each individual was visualized as sitting before his television set or reading his newspaper and responding to the message in a manner having little to do with the rest of his life or his relations to other persons and groups. As noted in the introduction to Part Two, however, this is a false image of the communication process. Research over the past two decades has made abundantly clear that the effects of a communication depend upon the place of the communicator and the respondent in the structure of society and upon their immediate relations to other persons and groups. These two views of mass communication are presented schematically in Figure 6–1.

Survey versus Laboratory Studies

The importance of the social structure in the communication process can be illustrated by comparing survey studies of the effects of the mass media such as radio and television with investigations of the communication process in the experimental laboratory. Laboratory studies have several characteristics: They use communications constructed to suit the experiment, the issues they cover are not of vital concern to the respondents and sometimes are not current, and the audience is a captive one, frequently consisting of college or high school students.

Survey studies, on the other hand, attempt to determine the effects of actual communications in the mass media, such as the effects of a political campaign upon voter preferences, and they use a representative sample

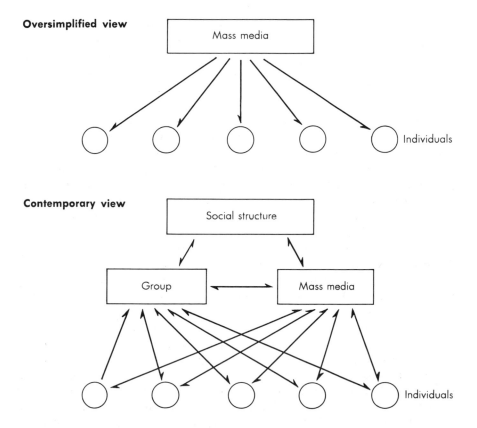

Figure 6–1
Two views of mass communication.

of the population. For example, one common procedure used in survey studies of voting is the panel technique (Lazarsfeld, Berelson, & Gaudet, 1948; Berelson, Lazarsfeld, & McPhee, 1954). A sample of voters is chosen as a "panel." They are interviewed a number of times during and just after an election campaign. This procedure allows the investigators to discover how voters make up their minds to vote one way or the other and how a wide variety of factors—including the mass media—influence the decision process.

The differences in the survey and laboratory methodologies have resulted in widely divergent effects of persuasive communications in the two settings. While one-third to one-half of the respondents in the typical laboratory experiment change their attitudes in the direction advocated by the communicator, only about 5 percent of the respondents in survey studies shift in the desired direction. The limitations of mass campaigns have been well documented. One experiment (Hartmann, 1936), conducted in Allentown, Pennsylvania, used leaflets to influence the citizen to vote for the Socialist party (in the 1930s the Socialist party was much stronger than it is today). Although propaganda leaflets were judged to be above average in their appeal, it was estimated that it took approximately 10,000 of them to win only 72 additional votes for the Socialist party. The experimenter estimated further that about half of these 72 votes would probably have been obtained without the aid of the leaflets, because of certain other factors having nothing to do with the experiment.

A later study (Star & Hughes, 1950), already discussed in Chapter 5, covered a six-month educational campaign designed to acquaint the people of Cincinnati with the United Nations. Hundreds of movies were shown, radio stations carried 150 spot broadcasts per week, newspapers played up the United Nations, 2,800 clubs were reached by speakers, and 59,588 pieces of literature were distributed. Yet the percentage of citizens who had heard of the veto power of the United Nations Security Council increased only 3 percent, from 34 percent to 37 percent. The percentage of those who could explain how the veto power worked (7 percent) did not change at all.

A number of plausible reasons for the marked discrepancy between the effectiveness of persuasive communication in the laboratory and in survey studies are as follows. Most of them have been suggested by Hovland (1959).

Selective exposure accounts for a part of the difference obtained in the two approaches. High school or college students in a classroom make a compact audience forcibly exposed to the experimental communications. But when a communication is distributed to the general population through television, radio, leaflets, or some other mass medium, the individual has freedom of choice in electing to listen to or read it. A large number of those opposed to the position of the communicator and many who are neutral will choose to ignore the communication and thus will not be influenced by it.

Unlike the laboratory situation, in the survey method respondents are not segregated from communications that may conflict with the communication under study. In assessing the effectiveness of an advertisement channeled through the regular mass media, for example, it is impossible to isolate the respondent from all other competing advertisements before the survey interviewer reaches him to obtain his reactions. But in experimental studies where opinion is assessed before the respondent leaves the laboratory, he has had no opportunity to be exposed to subsequent countercommunications. Of course, many laboratory experiments have an interval of a week or more between the communication and the test of opinion change, and in those instances the respondent may well be subjected to various countercommunications. Even here, however, if the topic of the laboratory communication is quite unlike those appearing in the mass media, the respondent may be safe from countercommunications.

Often the communicator in the laboratory or classroom is more credible than the communicator in everyday communication situations. He is usually implicitly sponsored by the instructor of the class and by the educational institution in which the experiment takes place. On the other hand, the communicator in mass media is frequently anonymous, as he is in most newspaper articles, and sometimes he is definitely suspect. Influence attempts often come from advertisers, politicians, salesmen, and many others who are likely to gain personally from acceptance of their message; hence the respondent may heavily discount their influence attempt.

Still another difference is that communications in survey studies are frequently of considerable interest to the respondent. He becomes personally involved in such matters as the election of local, state, or Federal officials, and he may have strong feelings about national or international issues. As a result, he often has a vested interest in *not* changing. Topics used in laboratory studies have less often aroused strong feelings, although there are some exceptions. By its very nature, the laboratory experiment makes the communication one in which the student is less involved—it is often not a communication that he can go out and act upon.

Finally, unlike the everyday setting, the laboratory audience is relatively isolated, and conditions are such that interaction among its members is highly restricted. In contrast, communication via the mass media may be talked over with friends, relatives, and other associates, who are likely to share the same opinions as the respondent himself and to help him resist attempts to change his attitudes. When interaction is restricted in the laboratory, acceptance or rejection is more likely to be an individual matter.

These many differences between the laboratory setting and communication in everyday life require that the role of the social structure in mediating communications be discussed. The rest of this chapter will be devoted to that topic. It should be noted, however, that even though results obtained in the laboratory often differ from those obtained in survey studies, laboratory studies have their merits. They have provided a useful framework for conceptualizing attitude organization and change in the individual, and they have pointed to the various sources of resistance that may arise. The general principles pertaining to organization, change, and resistance in the individual continue to apply to communication in the social structure.

STUDY QUESTIONS

1. *How does the focus of the present chapter modify the picture of the persuasive communication process that has been conveyed by the earlier chapters?*
2. *Indicate the differences in effectiveness of communications in laboratory studies and in survey studies. Enumerate the reasons for these differences.*

SUMMARY: SURVEY VERSUS LABORATORY STUDIES

In general, attitude change has been much greater in laboratory studies than in surveys. This difference is accounted for by the individual's greater selective exposure to survey issues, the presence of competing communications in survey situations, the lesser credibility of the nonlaboratory communicator, the greater vested interest which respondents often have in survey issues, and the support in resisting change which the individual receives from other persons in the survey situation. In spite of the considerable differences between the results of laboratory and survey studies, the combination of the two methods provides the most adequate information concerning the influence process.

Functions of Groups in the Communication Process

On several occasions we have noted that groups may reinforce or interfere with the effectiveness of a communication. This section discusses the ways in which such processes operate. Because investigations in this area have studied the relationship of small groups to the communication process in two different contexts, discussion will be divided into two overlapping parts. One of these is concerned primarily with the functioning of the groups themselves and is based to a greater extent on research with laboratory groups. The other has a somewhat broader framework encompassing the associations of the respondent with other persons and his place in larger social structures. This topic is more often represented by survey studies. The sections which follow deal first with the role of small groups in the persuasion process as (1) agents for resistance to change, and (2) agents of change. Later sections will be concerned with the place of the individual in larger social structures and the effects of this place upon his reception of communications.

GROUPS AS AGENTS FOR RESISTANCE TO CHANGE

Groups may reinforce or interfere with the effect of a communication from some media source in three general ways: (1) through the effects of group structure on exposure, (2) through determining the credibility of various communicators, and (3) through providing social support for attitudes.

Effects of group structure on exposure

The group structure may affect the manner in which a communication is filtered as it passes from one person to another. This filtering process determines the degree to which group members are exposed to the various elements in the communication. In a manner analogous to the way a radio or television tuner selects certain wavelengths or channels, the communication structure of the group generally filters out communications that are dissonant with group opinion and focuses on those that are consonant. Studies of voting, for example, have shown that people talk politics primarily with members of their family and friends. Since these other persons usually have similar political attitudes, the chances of encountering dissonant views through interpersonal channels are reduced.

The degree to which family members have similar political attitudes is emphasized by a study of a panel of voters in one county where it was found that only 4 percent of the voters had relatives voting differently from themselves (Lazarsfeld, Berelson, & Gaudet, 1948). Moreover, discussion with those who disagree with one's opinions is likely to be actively avoided; thus one Republican says, "All of my neighbors are Democrats, so there's no use talking with them about it [politics]" (Berelson, Lazarsfeld, & McPhee, 1954, p. 102).

Brodbeck (1956; 1960) has attempted to demonstrate a form of selective exposure within the group. She reasoned that members of a group whose confidence in their own beliefs had been shaken by an exposure to a countercommunication would seek discussion partners who agreed with their beliefs. From a comparison of disagreers whose confidence had been shaken with subjects who agreed with the communication, she concluded that her experiment with a number of small groups confirmed her hypothesis. Steiner (1962), however, has pointed out that the number of disagreeing subjects with shaken confidence choosing a discussion partner with the same attitude did not exceed chance: only 9 of the 27 subjects made such a choice, whereas 11 would have been expected to do so if all members had chosen purely at random. Considerably more than 11 members would have had to choose partners with the same attitude if the hypothesis was correct.

In Brodbeck's studies the choice in question was of a partner whom one might *listen* to over a one-way telephone. Unwillingness to *listen* to people who disagree should not be confused with the individual's interest in *talking* to them. Under certain circumstances, considerable communication is directed *toward* a person who deviates from group opinion, as will be discussed later in this chapter and in Chapter 10.

Credibility of communicators

The members of a group are likely to have not only similar opinions on a variety of issues but also similar opinions regarding the credibility of various communicators. For a highly religious group, for example, a minister of their faith has high credibility and an atheist low credibility. For a group of physicians, a surgeon has high credibility, but an athletic coach talking about health has much lower credibility. In general, communicators likely to transmit messages consonant with group attitudes and values are assigned high credibility, and those with dissonant communications are assigned low credibility. A factor multiplying the effectiveness of highly credible communications directed toward groups is that key positions in the group's communication structure are held by members who personify group values: They are apt to relay communications consonant with their values and filter out dissonant ones.

The group as a source of social support for attitudes

Groups are not so homogeneous, nor are the communication channels so uniform, that people are never exposed to contrary communications. A person in a modern society is continually bombarded with a great variety of messages, many of them contrary to his attitudes. Perhaps the most dramatic source of resistance to the continual pressure is found in the social support provided by his group. This support is one of the most important reasons why his attitudes do not constantly shift in the direction of each new barrage of communications. Essentially, the support of the group may be characterized in the following terms.

Persons are attracted to others who have attitudes similar to their own. When confronted with a person whose attitudes are at variance with theirs, they exert pressure on him to change. Festinger (1954) has suggested that these tendencies arise out of a need to validate one's attitudes—to find support for them in social reality. The resulting pressures toward uniformity are particularly effective in small, intimate groups, because persons in such groups are normally highly dependent on each other for the satisfaction of their emotional needs, such as the needs for affection, companionship, and encouragement. Such groups have been traditionally referred to as *primary* groups. The processes by which group members exert influence on each other to bring about conformity will be treated in more detail in Chapter 10. At this point, the manner in which the group supports resistance to communications from the outside will be illustrated.

An excellent example of how membership in a primary group may produce strong resistance to persuasive communications is provided by an analysis of Wehrmacht in World War II (Shils & Janowitz, 1948). According to this study, the most important factor accounting for the strong resistance of German troops to Allied propaganda, in spite of the hopelessness of their situation toward the end of the war, was the loyalty of a soldier to his own unit. The unit met his physical needs, providing him with food, clothing, shelter, and protection, and also offered him affection, esteem, and support. Allied propaganda disseminated among German troops in the form of leaflets urging surrender had little effect upon soldiers belonging to such units. Asking the soldier to surrender had small chance of success if it meant that the soldier must desert his comrades. Even less effective were Allied communications attempting to cast doubt on the Nazi ideology—most soldiers did not concern themselves with politics, and devotion to Nazism was *not* a basis for their resistance to Allied propaganda.

On the other hand, once the primary group was broken up, or its functions were disrupted by lack of food or ammunition, the need for physical survival often became so strong that persuasive communications urging surrender and guaranteeing safe-conduct were frequently effective. Thus, either the virtual dissolution of the primary group or group agreement on surrender was a necessary condition for the effectiveness of Allied persuasive communications. Similar feelings of loyalty to the primary group existed among American soldiers, who, when asked what factors enabled them to keep going when things were tough, stressed that they couldn't let their outfit down, that "buddies" depended upon them, etc. (Shils, 1950).

Other examples of how the group helps the individual to resist influence come from the study of prisons and of delinquent gangs. Although prisons are supposed to rehabilitate the criminal, influences in that direction are usually effectively blocked by the formation of strong informal groups among prisoners. These groups support and perpetuate attitudes that are favorable to continuation of criminal activity after release. Similarly, members of delinquent gangs are strongly resistant to reform efforts of police, social workers, and other community workers.

According to several authorities, attempts of the Chinese Communists to brainwash American prisoners captured in the Korean conflict were successful in destroying resistance and obtaining minor cooperation in part because primary groups were deliberately broken apart (Committee on Government Operations, U.S. Senate, 1956; Schein, 1958). The Chinese captors segregated leaders or resistors, instituted an informer system, gave special privileges to those who cooperated, and removed all recognition of military rank. As a result, the average American stood alone against his captors, although he was physically in the midst of his fellow prisoners.

On the other hand, virtually all the Turkish prisoners successfully resisted attempts by their captors to obtain cooperation. Although the lack of success of the Chinese Communists in manipulating Turkish prisoners may have been due in part to the fact that only one Chinese interrogator spoke Turkish fluently, it also appeared to be due to certain group factors among the Turks. They maintained a high level of discipline and organization, the highest-ranking Turk remaining in charge of the unit and receiving full support from other Turkish prisoners.

A laboratory experiment has shown that placing a high value on one's group is associated with resistance to communications running counter to the group's values (Kelley & Volkart, 1952). The experiment was performed with boy scout troops, using a communicator who suggested that boys in the modern world would profit more from learning about their cities and from various activities in town than they would from the typical boy scout activities. Measures of attitude before and after the communication revealed that those who strongly valued their membership in the group reacted against the communicator's critical message and took an even more favorable position on scout activities. Boys who valued the group less highly either were not influenced by the communicator or were influenced to adopt slightly less favorable attitudes toward scout activities.

So far, the group has been shown to support members in resisting communications that run counter to shared attitudes representing the central values of the group and strongly sanctioned by it. Another question is whether attitudes that are shared by the members but which are *not particularly relevant to the goals of the group* are also resistant to change because of group support. While a study directly applicable to the question has not come to the attention of these writers, several studies show that, even on issues of low relevance, the group *does* exert some pressure on persons who deviate.

One experiment (Schachter, 1951) established laboratory groups that varied in two ways: (1) in the power of the group to hold its members, and (2) in the relevance or importance of the activities over which the power of the group extended. By prearrangement with the experimenter, certain paid participants deviated from established group attitudes. Results showed that when the activities were less important to the group, it exerted some pressure on the deviate to conform, but not as much as it exerted for more relevant activities. In a study of friendship associations, it was found that attitudes having little relevance to friendship (opinions about big business) were nevertheless frequently adopted because individuals perceived their friends as exerting pressure for adoption (Steiner, 1954).

STUDY QUESTIONS

3. *Explain how groups intensify selective exposure.*
4. *What role is played by communicator credibility in group resistance?*
5. *What are the sources of attraction of a group for its members?*
6. *What is a primary group?*
7. *To what extent are issues having low relevance to the group supported against pressures to change?*

Summary: Groups as agents for resistance to change

Groups may interfere with the effect of a communication from some media source in several ways. One of these is through the communication structure existing in the group, which serves to filter out dissonant communications. Another is through determining the level of credibility of communicators according to the degree of consonance or dissonance between their attitudes and those of the group. Finally, groups furnish social support for the attitudes of their members by providing rewards for conformity and sanctions for deviation. The degree to which sanctions are exercised against deviators varies directly with the power of the group and the relevance of the attitude to the group's central values.

GROUPS AS AGENTS OF CHANGE

The group may facilitate change in several ways, each of which will be discussed in turn: (1) indirectly, by removal of support for an attitude, (2) by generating discussion that leads to clearer and somewhat different conceptions of what attitudes are shared by group members, and (3) through *group-decision* processes.

Removal of support for an opinion

If the group is weakened by external or internal stresses, it may abandon its shared attitudes and accept new ones that would otherwise have been strongly resisted. We have already noted the role of the small combat unit in maintaining the fighting spirit of the German army in World War II. At first Allied propaganda urging surrender had little effect upon these troops. Near the end of the war, however, when the primary groups were disorganized and scattered by Allied forces, these soldiers surrendered readily. Many of them mentioned that the safe-conduct leaflet urging surrender which was distributed as propaganda warfare played a significant role in bringing about their decision (Herz, 1954). A similar pamphlet appeared to have little effect prior to this time. Similarly, North Koreans who were separated from their military units were readily influenced by United Nations propaganda which, before separation, had little effect upon them (Riley, Schramm, & Williams, 1951).

The fact that perceived support for a contrary opinion leads to change is also illustrated by an experiment (Kelley & Woodruff, 1956). College students who listened to a recorded communication contrary to their norms and who heard applause from an audience supposedly like themselves were more likely to accept the counternorm communication than students who believed that the applause came from anonymous outsiders.

Role of discussion in promoting change

Klapper (1961) calls attention to the role of communication and discussion among group members in bringing about change. Various problems or crises confronting the group may stimulate intensive discussion that clarifies group attitudes. Members who previously had perceived the group attitudes incorrectly may not agree with them once the misunderstanding is cleared up; the attitudes become targets for change. According to Katz and Lazarsfeld (1955), such discussion may also reveal the presence of hitherto unsuspected minority group support for opinions contrary to the norms. Thus individuals who had privately held dissident opinions are now encouraged to bring them into the open.

The group-decision process

A somewhat more direct use of the group as an agent of change involves a process commonly known as group decision. It was first studied in a series of experiments conducted during World War II by Lewin (1958) and his colleagues. In the light of present knowledge, the term *group decision* is not too appropriate, for the process includes quite a number of elements in addition to the making of a decision by the group.

The steps commonly taken in bringing about change by group decision include the following: (1) An issue is presented which involves a course of action that can be associated with existing motivations of the audience. (2) Members of the audience are asked to discuss their feelings about cooperating with the communicator, including any objections that they might have. (3) The group leader recognizes and accepts objections without disapproval, supporting the rights of members to raise objections. (4) Requests for information are complied with by the group leader. (5) The leader encourages discussion among the members that will to some extent answer as many of the objections as possible. (6) At the end of the discussion, members are asked to make a decision as to whether or not they will carry out the desired actions (a procedure referred to as *individual commitment*). (7) Members are given the opportunity to see how many others agree to try out the new actions (a procedure known as *perceived group consensus*).

Many of these elements have been familiar for a long time as practical means of influencing a person. Requiring him to take a pledge or an oath or to swear on the Bible is a method of eliciting individual commitment which has been practiced since ancient civilization. Slightly newer forms of the same method are involved when he signs a pledge card to donate a certain amount to charity, responds to an advertisement by clipping a coupon and sending it in, signs a preliminary sales contract, etc. The techniques used by the organization Alcoholics Anonymous are good examples of the combined use of individual commitment and group consensus. The new member pledges not to drink again, and he also gains support by becoming acquainted with other members of the chapter who have made similar commitments: thus the force of group consensus is placed solidly behind his new resolve to stop drinking.

In the experiments reviewed by Lewin, the objective was to persuade housewives to make more use of certain unpopular meats, such as sweetbreads, beef hearts, and kidneys, in order to alleviate the meat shortage and help the war effort. Three groups used as controls were exposed to conventional techniques of persuasion, consisting of attractive lectures that linked the problem of nutrition with the war effort, emphasized the vitamin and mineral value of the three meats, and stressed health and economic values. Recipes were also distributed. Three other groups were handled by the group-decision process, which consisted of the seven steps listed above. At a later time, women from the two kinds of groups were asked whether or not they were now using these meats. Of those who had never before served them, only 3 percent of the persons who had heard the lectures were using them, but 32 percent of the persons who had participated in the group-decision process were serving them. Similar experiments aimed at increasing the home consumption of fresh and evaporated milk and encouraging the feeding of orange juice and cod liver oil to infants also yielded results in favor of the group-decision process (Lewin, 1958).

Lewin interpreted group-decision procedures as a three-step process: "unfreezing" the group attitudes that ordinarily serve to resist change, establishing a new set of attitudes, and "freezing" these. This appears to be a reasonable interpretation of what happens. What is not clear, however, is what elements of the group-decision process are responsible for these changes. A glance at Table 6–1 indicates that quite a variety of factors might account for the difference in the relative effectiveness of the propaganda lecture and the group-decision procedure.

Fortunately, one experimenter later undertook to determine the relative effectiveness of these various aspects of the group-decision process (Bennett, 1955). She used a large number of groups so that the effects of each factor could be separately assessed and the remaining factors controlled. The experiment investigated the importance of the following conditions: decision versus no decision, discussion versus no discussion, public commitment versus private commitment, and high perceived group consensus versus low perceived consensus. The experimenter attempted to influence college students to volunteer for participation

Table 6–1
**Possible Effective Factors in Group Decision
as Compared with Lecture**

GROUP DECISION	LECTURE
Audience actively participates and is likely to become personally involved.	Audience is passive; does not participate.
Members perceive willingness of some other members to unfreeze attitudes.	Audience is silent; members cannot perceive inclinations of others.
Leader's permissive attitude toward objections may strengthen desire to help him by behaving in the manner suggested.	Audience does not participate; hence leader cannot win support by being permissive.
Members are required to commit themselves on the desired action.	Audience is not required to make decision on desired action.
Members perceive others committing themselves to desired action.	Audience is unable to perceive private decisions of others.

in various psychological experiments which were to be conducted during the semester. The criterion of effectiveness was the number of students in each experimental condition who did volunteer.

The investigation led to the following conclusions: Group discussion was *not* found to be a more effective inducement to action than a lecture. Also, a decision involving public commitment was *not* more effective than one made less publicly or made anonymously. On the positive side, a decision regarding future action was found to be more effective in bringing about that action than no decision on it. Also effective was a high degree of actual or perceived group agreement on performing the desired action.

An earlier experiment suggests that additional conditions affecting the group-decision process need to be identified (Schachter & Hall, 1952). Although it also demonstrated that more subjects volunteered when they perceived others were willing to volunteer, its results were unlike Bennett's in that the opportunity to make a private decision led to more volunteering than a decision requiring public commitment.

An experiment by Kipnis (1958) takes into account the type of relation the leader has to his members. His investigation compared participatory with a lecture style of leadership under three conditions: (1) where the leader offered to reward subjects for compliance, (2) where the leader threatened to punish those who did not comply, and (3) where no sanctions were exercised by the leader. One result was that, when the leader had either reward power or exercised no sanctions, participatory leadership induced more private attitude change than lecture leadership. Threat of punishment resulted in more change under lecture leadership than under participatory leadership: group discussion in the participatory condition reinforced resistance to change.

STUDY QUESTIONS

8.   *Suggest ways in which a group may indirectly contribute to attitude change.*
9.   *Explain what is meant by the group-decision process.*
10. *Summarize conclusions concerning which aspects of the group-decision process are effective and which are ineffective*

Summary: Groups as agents of change

The group may facilitate attitude change in indirect ways. Any actions or processes that weaken the group open the way for change. Also, extensive discussion may clarify group attitudes so that they become targets for change. Discussion may also reveal minority group support for members secretly holding attitudes at variance from the group norms and may thereby strengthen their deviant attitudes.

A process known as *group decision* has frequently been used as a deliberate means of bringing about change. In it a leader encourages discussion of an issue involving a course of action that can be associated with existing motivations of the group members. He recognizes objections to the proposed action and complies with requests for information, but allows the group to make its own decision as to whether it will adopt the action. At the present time, it appears that the elements in this process which effect change are (1) the making of a decision or commitment by the members, (2) the perception that a large proportion of the other members have committed themselves to change, and (3) group discussion in situations where the leader either has reward power or does not exercise any form of sanction.

Position in the Social Structure

REFERENCE GROUPS AND THE COMMUNICATION PROCESS

So far discussion has been primarily about the effect of small, intimate groups on communication processes. The place of the individual in the larger social structure is also relevant to his acceptance or rejection of a communication. A person need not even be a member of a group in order for it to influence him; if he merely aspires to become a member, the attitudes held by that group may serve as a guide to his opinions and behavior. The same is true where a person has just joined a group and is not yet accepted as a member in the fullest sense.

Thus, in World War II, "green" replacements assigned to veteran combat units which had been temporarily removed from the battlefront rapidly shifted their initial attitude of eagerness for combat to acceptance of the attitude that "combat is hell." Replacements with initially similar attitudes assigned to *inexperienced* units did not undergo the same shift in attitude toward combat (Merton & Kitt, 1950). Presumably, the replacements assigned to veteran units wanted to be accepted by the veterans and thus shifted their opinions to conform.

The concept of reference group

The influence of a group on the attitudes of an individual is often treated in terms of the concept of *reference group* (Hyman, 1942, 1960). A reference group is a group the individual takes as a frame of reference for self-evaluation and attitude formation (Merton, 1957*b*). Such a group may have one or both of two functions. First, it may set and enforce standards of conduct and belief: this has been called the *normative* function of a reference group. Second, it may serve as a standard or comparison point against which persons compare themselves and others: this has been called the *comparison* function (Kelley, 1952).

To illustrate the comparison function, studies during World War II indicated that drafted married men comparing themselves with such groups as their unmarried fellow draftees or their unmarried civilian friends felt that induction involved greater sacrifices on their part (Stouffer et al., 1949). Comparison processes will be treated in more detail in the discussion of status in Chapters 9 and 12. The discussion here will be limited to the normative function of reference groups.

One further restriction will be placed on the present treatment. The term *reference group* as originally used was applied to both the single individual and the group, but reference individuals have been more recently referred to as opinion leaders. While much of the discussion of reference groups here applies also to opinion leaders, the leaders will be discussed separately in a later section.

A reference group may be a membership or a nonmembership group. Usually, of course, groups to which a person belongs are reference groups for him. Although a reference group is usually a group whose acceptance and approval is desired, in some instances an individual may be influenced by a group that he dislikes. In this case he is motivated to adopt attitudes opposite to those of the group and the group is termed a *negative reference group*. For example, while the family is normally a positive reference group, two studies of political attitudes demonstrate that it can be a negative reference group in that those who rebel against it often adopt a political position opposite to that of their parents (Newcomb, 1943; Maccoby, 1954).

Reference groups as social support

Reference groups often play a role in the communication process similar to that already discussed for small, intimate groups. They may establish various levels of credibility for the communicator, thereby creating selective exposure, and they may provide social support for the individual's attitudes. This social support often takes the form of providing a frame of reference or a context within which the communication is received and interpreted. An example is the finding that persons moving up the socioeconomic ladder are more likely to be Republican than Democratic, a phenomenon which suggests that they are using groups to which they aspire to belong as a frame of reference for their political attitudes (Maccoby, 1954).

Many communications in everyday life call up an anticipated audience — some individual or reference group to whom we might relay the message, or with whom we might talk it over. An experiment demonstrates clearly that such anticipated audiences may affect the manner in which the communication is received (Schramm & Danielson, 1958). Two groups were given a two-sided set of arguments for and against lowering the voting age to eighteen years. These groups were told that they were to prepare speeches in competition for a prize. For one group, the prize was to be given by "The Society for Constitutional Government — dedicated to preserving the U.S. Constitution unchanged"; for the other, it would be awarded by "The Association for Lowering the Voting Age to 18 — if they can fight, they can vote." These groups, together with a control group that received no communication, were given attitude tests before and after the communication. Each group was found to remember more arguments consonant with the aims of the organization giving the prize. A related experiment obtained similar results (Zimmerman & Bauer, 1956). Thus, it seems that when positive reference groups or persons are tied in with the receipt of a communication, they are likely to lead us to interpret the message in a direction consonant with their attitudes.

Several studies make clear that voting preferences are strongly influenced by reference groups (Lazarsfeld, Berelson, & Gaudet, 1948; Berelson, Lazarsfeld, & McPhee, 1954). For example, the individual who early in an election campaign favors a candidate not preferred by his family or by his close associates frequently casts his final vote for their candidate, not his. That this shift is probably due to actual pressures from the group is suggested by the fact that most of a voter's discussion of politics takes place with his friends, coworkers, and family.

Salience of reference groups

All of us have many reference groups, but these are not always relevant to communications we receive. For example, the church group to which a person belongs is unlikely to be a salient group when he is watching a sports broadcast on television. Several experiments have stressed the point that a reference group must be made salient before it affects attitudes (Festinger, 1950a; Kelley, 1955; Charters & Newcomb, 1958). This has also been recognized by groups in a practical sense and has stimulated the development of devices likely to make the group salient, such as uniforms, badges, pins, insignia, and certain rituals, like the salute. More study is needed to define the conditions under which a reference group is salient to a communication situation.

Kinds of reference groups

Many investigations provide definite evidence that the effects of a communication on the respondent vary with the kinds of reference groups he has, although the exact nature of the process is not always clear. One study, for example, assesses the effects of the mass media on preadolescents and adolescents in terms of two reference groups: their parents and their friends or peers (Riley & Riley, 1951). The subjects were classified according to whether their family was their only reference group, or whether they had both their family and their peers as reference groups. Definite differences were discovered between the two classifications in preferences for certain types of comics, radio programs and television programs. Younger children having only the family as a reference group liked the "Bugs Bunny" type of comic and action programs such as Westerns to a greater extent than children who had both family and peer reference groups. Among the adolescents, those having only the family as a reference group had stronger preferences for action and violence programs. To some extent, differences in preference for various mass media may be a direct reflection of peer-group values, because those who had the strongest drive toward peer-group values also had the strongest preferences for media reflecting such values as sports, popular music, popularity with the opposite sex, and association with the gang. The data appear to support the view that the type of group membership may influence the impact of the mass media on individuals. An alternative interpretation, however, is that program preferences are a reflection of individual personality characteristics which also determine the individual's group memberships.

STUDY QUESTIONS

11. *What is a reference group? Explain the two functions it may have. What is a negative reference group?*
12. *Suggest several ways in which reference groups may determine reactions to the mass media.*

Summary: Reference groups

A reference group is a group taken as a frame of reference for self-evaluation and attitude formation. It may have two functions: A normative function and a comparison function. The normative function is that of setting and enforcing standards of conduct and belief. The comparison function is that of establishing it as a standard or comparison point against which persons may compare themselves and others. This discussion has been limited to the normative function; the comparison function will be discussed in Chapters 9 and 12.

A person need not be an actual member of a group to use it as a reference group. Reference groups establish various levels of credibility for communicators, support selective exposure to different communications, and provide social support for a person's attitudes. By using the position taken by his reference group, a person will readily accept communications that advocate a similar position, but will be likely to reject those that run counter to it. The effects of a reference group depend on its salience relative to a particular communication. Some evidence has been presented showing that the kind of reference groups a person has affects his response to various communications.

INTERPERSONAL COMMUNICATION NETWORKS

We have already stressed the role of the group as a comparatively stable communication structure or system of channels through which communications move. Communications that run counter to group opinions may never travel through the entire network to reach all members of the group, whereas those that are in agreement with group attitudes are likely to be freely transmitted. No reference has been made, however, to communication channels extending beyond the group, except perhaps in the sense that the group establishes the levels of credibility of various communicators. We now turn to the larger communication process by which messages travel from the mass media or other general sources to ultimately reach the respondent.

The two-step flow of communications

Much of what has been said emphasizes the function of groups in the influence process as they affect both exposure to and acceptance or rejection of a communication. Such emphases suggest the conclusion that influence attempts through secondary sources like the mass media are relatively ineffective. Yet communications through the mass media apparently do modify or reinforce opinions, although often in an indirect manner known as the *two-step flow of communications.*

In their analysis of the 1940 presidential election, Lazarsfeld, Berelson, and Gaudet (1948) observed that personal contacts were more effective than the mass media in influencing voter decisions. They suggested that ideas flow from the mass media to certain key persons and from these *opinion leaders* to less active individuals. Thus, they visualized the mass media as exerting influence mainly through the mediation of the opinion leader. Other studies have also stressed the importance of interpersonal channels of communication. Klapper (1961) notes that in totalitarian countries, the contents of such radio programs as Voice of America and Radio Free Europe spread freely by means of person-to-person contact among certain segments of the population. Additional studies to be referred to later have shown the importance of interpersonal channels in contexts including public affairs, moviegoing, marketing, fashions, the adoption of a new drug by physicians, and changes in agricultural practices adopted by farmers.

More recent studies have also suggested that the two-step flow hypothesis needs further modification (Katz, 1957; Menzel & Katz, 1956; Rogers & Beal, 1958). In particular, investigations of the process of diffusion or spread of new elements through a population have added considerable detail to the notion of a two-step flow. They have provided a better understanding of the conditions under which mass communications are disseminated through interpersonal channels, as well as of the conditions under which mass communications reach the respondent directly. First, more than two steps may sometimes be involved. Opinion leaders may have their opinion leaders, who in turn may have theirs. Thus, a chain of interpersonal links rather than a single link may connect the original source with its recipients. Second, the flow is not necessarily from the mass media through interpersonal contacts to the persons ultimately affected. The flow may be reversed: Interpersonal communication channels may stimulate persons to consult the mass media. In a study of the diffusion of information in an industrial firm, many employees who received word of an impending reorganization from personal contacts turned to such media as the company newspaper for further information (Wager, 1962).

Whether a person obtains information directly from the mass media or indirectly from other persons depends in part on his position in the social structure. Doctors who were more integrated into the medical community—in terms of the number of other doctors who designated them as friends and as persons whose advice was valuable—were more influenced by interpersonal channels of communication (Menzel & Katz, 1956). In a group like the medical community where norms and values favor innovations, such highly integrated doctors are more apt to lead the way in the adoption of a new drug. But in groups where the norms are unfavorable to innovation, as in certain agricultural communities which have been studied, highly integrated persons are not likely to lead in the adoption of an innovation (Marsh & Coleman, 1956). The degree to which a new practice is diffused through interpersonal channels and the speed of diffusion are largely dependent on whether adoptions of the practice are made by integrated persons or isolated ones. Where the practice is taken up by integrated persons, and norms are favorable to innovation, the innovation is likely to spread rapidly through the group.

Whether persons are more apt to be influenced directly through the mass media or indirectly through interpersonal communications depends on the stage of the adoption process, as well as on whether persons are early adopters or late adopters. Rural sociologists (Rogers & Beal, 1958) studying the adoption of new farming practices have postulated a process consisting of the following five stages:

1. *Awareness stage.* The individual is initially exposed to the new practice but lacks details about it.
2. *Information stage.* He secures more information about the new practice.
3. *Application stage.* He considers the advantages and disadvantages of the new practice and makes a decision whether or not to try it.
4. *Trial stage.* He tries out the innovation on a limited and temporary basis.
5. *Adoption stage.* He makes the decision either to continue or discontinue the new practice on a permanent basis.

In a study of the adoption of a new type of agricultural spray, it was found that the mass media were more important in the early phase of making persons aware of the product (Rogers & Beal, 1958). In the later phases of acquiring additional information and deciding whether to use the product for a trial period, interpersonal influences predominated. Also, persons who adopted the product relatively late were more influenced by interpersonal communications than the early adopters. These findings add support to the distinction emphasized by Katz (1961) between obtaining information and *legitimation.* By legitimation is meant sanction by the group in favor of the innovation.

Katz draws a similar conclusion from a comparison of two diffusion studies. In both cases commercial or formal sources played an important role in disseminating information about the innovation; but in its trial and adoption, personal communications with friends, neighbors, and colleagues played the crucial role of legitimizing its use. Farmers gained information about a new hybrid corn primarily from salesmen and agricultural bulletins; doctors gained information about a new drug from salesmen or medical journals. Farmers were most influenced to try out or adopt the product by their neighbors; doctors by their colleagues and by medical journals.

STUDY QUESTIONS

13. *What is meant by the two-step flow of communications? What other forms does the flow of communication take?*

14. *Describe the stages in the adoption of an innovation. Indicate the relative predominance of the mass media or interpersonal sources during each of the various stages.*

Opinion leaders and the flow of information

A number of studies have shown that opinion leaders are specialized: they are leaders in one content area and not in another (Merton, 1949; Katz & Lazarsfeld, 1955). Depending on the area, both the opinion leaders and the persons they influence have certain characteristics. For example, in the area of fashions, younger and more gregarious women are likely to be leaders, but in public affairs, the opinion leader is likely to be older, higher in status, and better educated.

Although opinion leadership varies with content, Katz (1957) has noted some consistent characteristics of opinion leaders: (1) They personify certain values, (2) they are competent, and (3) they have a strategic social location. With respect to the first of these, opinion leaders often represent the values and attitudes of their group more closely than anyone else. Thus, for the members, an opinion leader personifies their values, and they identify with him and support him. In a study of boys' camps, for example, it was shown that the leader represented the important group values—fighting ability and campcraft (Lippitt et al., 1952). Boys imitated these leaders even when the leaders had made no attempt to influence them.

With respect to the second characteristic, competence often means that the leader has more expert knowledge than others. Thus the leaders in the boys' camps were the most competent at fighting and campcraft. Physicians who led in the adoption of new drugs were more in touch with the professional literature and with research information disseminated at medical conventions (Coleman, Katz, & Menzel, 1957). Similarly, the farmers who made more trips to the city were leaders in adopting a new hybrid corn seed (Katz, 1961).

With respect to the third characteristic, location in the communication structure, opinion leaders have a wider range of acquaintance than nonleaders, and they are "centrally located." For example, the doctors having the largest number of social contacts with other physicians were almost always those who influenced other physicians in the friendship group to adopt a new drug (Menzel & Katz, 1956). Similar findings were obtained for the doctors who were most often turned to for advice and for those with whom cases were most often discussed. Another aspect of social location characterizing opinion leaders is that they often form a link between outside media or agencies and the smaller communication system in which they are influential. Men are more often opinion leaders in politics because they circulate outside the home to a greater extent than women. Opinion leaders in politics also belong to a greater number of organizations than nonleaders do (Katz & Lazarsfeld, 1955). Doctors influential in the adoption of a new drug more frequently attend out-of-town meetings and have contacts more geographically remote than doctors who are not influential (Coleman, Katz, & Menzel, 1957).

Klapper (1961) has called attention to a neglected function of the opinion leader, that of *resisting* change. Since the leader is likely to conform most closely to the group norms, it would appear that most of his communications with others would be in the direction of the norms and he would be likely to resist outside communications reaching him that are counter to the norms. This pull in the direction of the norm is illustrated by the finding that voters who early in the campaign intended to vote differently from their family and associates more often than not finally changed their mind and voted with their primary group (Lazarsfeld, Berelson, & Gaudet, 1948). The fact that discussion of politics in such groups waxed strong in the later phases of the campaign suggests that opinion leaders played a part in the vote changes. This role of opinion leaders in stabilizing norms and resisting influence deserves further study.

The marginal person: Cross-pressures

Some persons occupy a position in the social structure subjecting them to opposing points of view. In an election, for example, the members of a person's family may support one candidate and his close friends another. An early study of voting revealed that these "marginal" persons were more likely to make up their mind later in the campaign, to change their vote intentions, and to make more frequent changes than others (Lazarsfeld, Berelson, & Gaudet, 1948). Such marginal persons have often been considered especially susceptible to persuasive communications. Indeed, it has often been argued that mass campaigns might well direct themselves primarily to undecided persons, since it has been repeatedly demonstrated that individuals with entrenched positions are unlikely to be readily influenced by the mass media. One problem in this connection, however, is the fact that marginal persons often escape from their dilemma by turning away from the issue. Voters subjected to cross-pressures, for example, have less interest than other voters in the election, and mass campaigns are therefore unlikely to reach them (Lazarsfeld, Berelson, & Gaudet, 1948).

Conditions affecting importance of personal influence

A note of caution should be given concerning the two-step flow hypothesis. Opinion leaders are not a *necessary* link between the mass media and the respondent. It has already been mentioned that the role of personal influence varies considerably depending upon the topic of influence. On some occasions, moreover, mass communications may reach the respondent directly. A study of the Kennedy-Nixon television debates prior to the 1960 election, for example, suggests that at least a minority of voters were influenced directly by the television program (Goeke, 1961). An experimental study (De Fleur & Larsen, 1958) of leaflet communications is consistent with this finding: It demonstrated that as the volume of information is increased, interpersonal channels of communication assume proportionately less importance.

Several studies of the spread of major news items also support the view that important news in the mass media reaches persons directly, although a majority of these persons then talk it over with other people (Larsen & Hill, 1954; Danielson, 1956; Deutschmann & Danielson, 1960). In other words, when a mass campaign is not very intensive and does not pertain to an important issue, its effectiveness might be amplified because of dissemination through personal channels; but where a campaign concerns an important issue and has the massive coverage achieved by the television debates, personal communications assume somewhat less importance as a means of receiving news.

In contrast to the television debates, the magnification of personal influence with diminished information flow is dramatized by a study of the small Greek village of Kalos, where the town's opinion leader was one of the only two villagers who could read (Stycos, 1952). He received a newspaper and relayed those contents that he felt worth conveying; obviously his function was of tremendous importance. An opinion leader in a strategic position like this is called a *gatekeeper* because he controls the flow of information (Lewin, 1958).

STUDY QUESTIONS

15. *What is meant by the statement that opinion leadership is to some extent specific to communication content?*

16. *What are some general characteristics of opinion leaders?*

17. *Why is the opinion leader thought to play a role in resisting change?*

18. *What is a marginal person? To what extent is he a desirable target for the propagandist?*

19. *How does the role of opinion leaders vary with the intensity and amount of communication?*

Summary: Interpersonal networks

Person-to-person communications play a very important role in dissemination of messages from the mass media. Mass communications sometimes follow a two-step flow pattern, from the communication to the opinion leader and from the opinion leader to other respondents. In this process the opinion leader serves not only to relay the information, but also is an influence agent. The flow pattern may sometimes be comprised of a chain of several opinion leaders. Also, the flow may be reversed: interpersonal channels may stimulate persons to consult the mass media.

A person's position in the social structure in terms of the frequency of his communication with others determines both followership and leadership in the adoption of innovations. The process by which innovations are adopted has several stages ranging from the acquisition of information about a new practice to a final decision to adopt it permanently. Information direct from the mass media plays an important role in the early stages, whereas in the later stages interpersonal influences predominate.

Opinion leaders are likely to be specialized: their leadership is often confined to a particular content area. Three general characteristics of opinion leaders that have been identified, however, are the following: (1) Opinion leaders personify the values of the group, (2) they are competent, and (3) they have a strategic social location. As representatives of the group norms, opinion leaders may also serve to resist change.

A particular kind of respondent is the marginal person, who is subjected to cross-pressures because he has membership in groups with opposing attitudes. Although he might be considered an easy target for change, he often lacks interest in or actively avoids issues related to the conflict between the groups.

SUMMARY: POSITION IN THE SOCIAL STRUCTURE

The importance of a person's position in the social structure with respect to his exposure and receptivity to communications has been illustrated by discussing the importance of reference groups and interpersonal networks. Reference groups provide support for existing attitudes; communications that advocate positions opposed to the norms of a person's reference groups are unlikely to be successful. The more salient a reference group is in a particular communication situation, the more likely it is to influence the acceptance or rejection of the communication.

Interpersonal networks are important aspects of the communication process. Most communications are transmitted through such networks, which may serve to filter out or distort dissonant messages and to reinforce consonant ones. The more centrally located a person is in such a network, the more likely he is to play an important role in the adoption of new ideas or practices. When the norms are favorable to change, he is likely to lead in the adoption of innovations; otherwise, he may help to resist innovations. Although opinion leaders are somewhat specialized, a number of general characteristics that they have in common have been enumerated.

Society and Persuasive Communication

For the most part, we have discussed the effects that the respondent's primary groups and immediate associates have upon his acceptance of communications. The greatest amount of research has been conducted on this aspect of the social structure, and it is undoubtedly paramount in the influence process. The larger society in which communication takes place, however, may also affect the communication process in various ways.

THE PRIMARY GROUP AND THE LARGER SOCIAL STRUCTURE

The function of primary groups in helping the individual to resist influence is often buttressed by the larger social systems to which they are related. For example, the previously mentioned role of the small combat units of the Wehrmacht in resisting Allied propaganda was augmented by aspects of the larger system (Shils & Janowitz, 1948). The German military was controlled by a small but dedicated core of Nazi officers, who served as links between the armed forces and the leaders of the Nazi party. Certain policies of this larger system strengthened the primary groups in their resistance to propaganda.

For example, solidarity was fostered by maintaining men in the same small units over a long period of time. Soldiers were warned of severe sanctions for desertion. In addition, letters from home which encouraged military efforts were approved, but strict controls were placed upon letters which mentioned deprivations at home and which might draw the loyalty of the soldier from his combat unit to his family.

OPINION LEADERS AS LINKS BETWEEN SOCIETY AND THE INDIVIDUAL

The larger social structure should also be considered with respect to its influence on the effectiveness of the opinion leader. In a study of the process of absorbing new immigrants into Israel, the opinion leaders who were initially most effective were community leaders such as rabbis, teachers, or local businessmen (Eisenstadt, 1951, 1952). A main function they performed was interpreting what economic, political, and occupational activities were most desirable for the immigrant to engage in — in general, interpreting the new society to the immigrant. This role of the opinion leader in linking the individual to the larger society is illustrated by the following quotation from an immigrant (Eisenstadt, 1951):

> Whenever we do not know what to do, we come and ask them . . . they are able to tell us what we have to do, how we can best get the work, to what schools to send our children. These parties and elections are also so confusing, and we do not know what they are for and how one should behave there . . . they explain it to us and advise what to do. If it were not for this, we would probably get lost and suffer a lot. . . . (P. 228)

At a later stage in the assimilation of the immigrants, however, the community leaders lost favor with those immigrants who gained a good understanding of the new country and its values. They came to regard their former leaders as overly conservative and not completely representative of the new society. Their shift in attitude was accompanied by a greater dependence on communications from the mass media. This study demonstrates that much of the strength of the opinion leader is dependent upon his relation to and his place in the larger social structure, as well as upon his relation to the persons he influences.

THE VALUE STRUCTURE AND THE COMMUNICATOR

The values prevailing in a society will affect the degree to which communicators will be motivated as well as permitted to structure the situation in order to facilitate persuasion. An excellent example of this can be seen in the attempt of the Chinese Communists to brainwash their captives in the Korean conflict. Such an effort was consistent with strong ideological elements that prevailed in the Chinese Communist society (Biderman, 1961; Chen, 1960). Communist ideology is based upon revolution or reform: somehow society and its members are to be transformed. This concept includes eliminating from the populace bourgeois and capitalist thinking and replacing it by the notion of the socialist state. Early in the Chinese revolution, this idea was put to work to reform and convert persons who had formerly been leaders in the vanquished society. Conquered Chinese Nationalist troops, for example, were encouraged to join the revolutionary forces and become loyal Communists.

Another noteworthy factor in the Communist ideology was that war with an enemy nation was "total": It included the concept of "reform" of the conquered. For the Chinese Communists, this concept invalidated the long-established tradition that captor nations should not exploit prisoners for war-related functions—as, for example, using confessions for propaganda purposes (Biderman, 1961; Biderman & Zimmer, 1961). Also invalidated by the concept of total war was the generally accepted international practice of allowing prisoners to keep their conventional military structure, with the senior officer remaining in charge. The destruction of this military structure was one of the most important factors in making individuals more susceptible to persuasive techniques.

Communicators in any society are likewise affected by the central values of that society. There is one important manner in which these values differ from society to society, however, and which is highly relevant to the communication process. This is the extent to which different societies permit free expression of diverse values. In the modern world we are often reminded of the fact that contemporary societies differ concerning the value of free speech.

Actually, all societies place certain limits on expression of opinion, but they differ with respect to the range of values that may be expressed and with respect to certain structural features that make such restriction effective. In a democratic society, where the range of expression is apt to be broad and restrictions less effectively implemented, some views receive wider expression than others. For example, in the United States, a citizen cannot advocate the overthrow of government without incurring penalties, although he may freely criticize the government in many ways. As will be seen in the following section, the narrower the range of values which are permitted expression, the more effective communication based on those values is likely to be.

STUDY QUESTIONS

20. *Why is the relation of the primary group to the larger social structure important in determining the effects of mass communications?*

21. *In what way does the opinion leader serve as a link between society and the individual?*

22. *What generalization can be drawn concerning the range of values permitted expression in a society and the effectiveness of communication based on those values?*

COERCIVE PERSUASION

The social structure and the values of society determine the effectiveness of communications in two general ways: (1) through control of exposure to communication, and (2) through the ability to manipulate reward and punishment. A number of studies have been made of environments in which values are permitted a very narrow range of expression and in which the social structure allows optimum control over communications and over reward and punishment. At the extreme, these include the investigations of brainwashing in civilian prisons in Communist China and in POW camps. Similar studies have been made of the less extreme conditions in convents, monasteries, mental hospitals, and military academies. These investigations delineate clearly the importance of the variables of exposure and reward and punishment. There is nothing particularly magical about brainwashing or its effects; similar processes and effects are found wherever similar conditions for persuasion exist.

Schein, Schneier, and Barker (1961) have adopted a term that aptly describes this influence process: *coercive persuasion.* It is to be preferred to brainwashing, for it emphasizes the complete control that the communicators have over the respondents with respect to both communication and the administration of rewards and punishment. Processes of control discussed by Schein, Schneier, and Barker include the following:

1. The captors exercise virtually complete control over reward and punishment. In the case of civilians imprisoned in Communist China, eating, sleeping, urination, defecation, and even free movement in cramped cells were controlled by the captors. In institutions such as mental hospitals, monasteries, and military academies, control of reward and punishment by the authorities is less extreme, but it is still much greater than in the case of a free citizen living at home.

2. Communications are controlled in a variety of ways. In the Communist POW camps, letters from home detrimental to morale were permitted to reach the captive; other letters were withheld. No access to mass media from the home country was permitted; in general, only Communist publications were available. An atmosphere of distrust was created by the establishment of an informer system among the prisoners and a spy system among the prison personnel. Varying degrees of control are exerted in similar ways in certain other institutional situations.

3. The individual is separated from his normal social contacts and daily routine and is thus deprived of sources that normally provide anchorage for his beliefs. This occurs in prison camps, mental hospitals, convents, monasteries, and military academies. In civilian prisons in China and POW camps in Korea, interpersonal liaisons that might interfere with institutional goals were discouraged and blocked. Such potential sources of stubborn resistance to change were handled by physical relocation of the members, by assignment of leaders calculated to create norms congenial to the prison authorities, and in POW camps, by encouraging mistrust and informing among fellow prisoners.

4. An individual with previous beliefs that might conflict with those of the authorities is "desocialized."[1] This is a process of stripping him of his previous attitudes and habits. Often it is accomplished through a "mortification of self."[2] Civilian captives in Communist China and some POWs were required to make "confessions" of "guilt." The monk takes vows of poverty and gives up his possessions, even his clothes. The civilian inducted into the military undergoes a similar process: the possessions he is permitted to have are severely restricted, and his former statuses (his occupation, social standing, etc.) are denied him. Similar but less severe steps occur when a person enters a hospital, a social fraternity, etc. (Goffman, 1961a).

5. Whenever possible, groups that support accepted values are formed, or at least encouraged. For example, study groups in which Communist ideology was emphasized were organized in POW camps in Korea and in the revolutionary war colleges in Communist China (Lifton, 1957; 1961).

The effects of coercive persuasion

Persuasion in a coercive context has produced some rather dramatic effects on the individual. These include *ritualization of belief* and *identification with one's captors*. Ritualization of belief is likely to occur in any group where there are relatively severe penalties for the expression of beliefs contrary to those approved by authority. This is true of certain totalitarian societies as well as institutional settings such as monasteries, nunneries, fraternal orders, and mental hospitals, although the degree to which it occurs varies in these institutions.

Schein, Schneier, and Barker point out that the ritualization of belief is characterized by profound changes in the functions of the belief system of the individual. Essentially, it takes the form of a movement away from the function of beliefs as a *means of appraising reality* toward their function as *mechanisms of social adjustment*. For example, beliefs may reflect an individual's experience with the world around him, and they may also be adopted to facilitate his functioning in that world. People appraise reality by classifying their experience into familiar categories: a person alone in a house at night hearing strange sounds is uncomfortable until he has attributed them to familiar sources. But some beliefs are adopted to facilitate effective functioning in one's environment: A person may adopt the same political opinions as his boss in order to get along well with him.

In the process of ritualization of belief, the individual gradually gains control over both his outward expression of beliefs and his private

---

[1]Socialization processes are discussed in detail in Chapters 18 and 19.

[2]This is a term used by Schein, Schneier, and Barker (1961).

thoughts, ultimately allowing only the "approved" expressions and thoughts to occur. Evidence that ritualization of belief took place among some persons who eventually defected from the Soviet Union comes from an intensive study (Bauer, 1957) of these defectors conducted by means of interview and life-history methods. Many Soviet refugees repeatedly characterize their earlier actions as "pushing doubts into the background." They report having come to regard their thoughts as dangerous property. One man complained of life aboard ship because of the "danger that you might say something against the regime while asleep." Another said of the doubts he had while still an officer in the Soviet army, "If you kept these things in your head they might come out some day. You were afraid that you might tell somebody. Therefore, very few people in the Soviet Union think about these things."

Ritualization of belief, then, is a process whereby the forceful control over the person's life exerted by the society or organization to which he belongs requires him to accept the "approved" beliefs and attitudes in order that he may function adequately or even survive, or as in the case of a mental hospital, in order that he may leave it. With regard to the latter, hospitalization may in some instances force the mental patient to put away his delusions in order to obtain release.

Identification with captors

Another striking effect of persuasion in a coercive setting is *identification with one's captors*. Several studies have noted its occurrence in some prisoners in Nazi concentration camps and in Communist Chinese prisons (Bettelheim, 1943; Schein, Schneier, & Barker, 1961). The identification process takes the form of adopting some of the attitudes and behaviors characteristic of the captors. Obviously this greatly increases the effectiveness of the captor in influencing and controlling the prisoners.

In Nazi concentration camps, many inmates who were imprisoned over a period of years copied their gestapo guards. They adopted their guards' contemptuous attitude toward the unfit prisoners, often torturing and killing them. They accumulated old pieces of gestapo uniforms and incorporated them into their dress. Like their captors, they prided themselves on their toughness and ability to stand at attention for long periods. They even copied the leisure activities of the gestapo guards, such as the "game" of finding out who could endure being hit for the longest time without uttering a complaint.

Some American civilians imprisoned for an extended period in Communist China also eventually identified with a cellmate or with their interrogator, gradually adopting his Communist ideology and in particular his belief that they had been guilty of "crimes against the people" and of "bourgeois thinking." Although these behaviors may strike the uninitiated as strange, the underlying motivation is probably the same as in the case of ritualization of belief: Behavior shifts in order to make a better adjustment to the prison situation.

These studies of prisoners point to two important factors in identification. One is the status of the person identified with: he tends to be relatively similar to the prisoner in certain respects. Thus, in Communist China he was often a cellmate who had at least partly moved from the initial prisoner status to a new one involving acceptance of Communist China and its ideology. The interrogator also was a person who talked freely and earnestly with the prisoner; often he was a Chinese who had been educated in the United States.

A second characteristic of these persons as objects of identification was the tremendous power they held over the captives. Probably both of these factors are essential for identification to take place. Such findings are consistent with theories of identification presented in Chapter 17.

Control in other contexts

As noted earlier, total institutional control should not be thought of exclusively in the context of brainwashing, alien ideologies, and concentration camps. For example, the idea of structuring a mental hospital for its maximum effect upon the individual has led to a new concept in treatment of the mentally ill, known as the *therapeutic community* (Greenblatt, York, & Brown, 1955). A mental hospital organized in this manner accepts the premise that the patient's attitudes and behavior are markedly influenced not just by the psychiatric staff, but also by nurses, ward attendants, orderlies, and fellow patients. Consequently an attempt is made to involve all these persons in helping the patient to get well. Such common institutional goals as security of custody, orderliness and docility, and smoothly functioning routine are subordinated to the larger therapeutic purpose. The activities of each member of the institution are therefore carefully structured to this end.

In lesser degree and in less deliberate fashion, postgraduate educational institutions operate in a similar way to accomplish the objective of changing the layman into a professional person. Most notable in this respect are the institutions which give professional training, such as military academies and medical, law, and theology schools, as well as graduate schools preparing students for the doctorate degree in various subjects (see Chapter 19).

Control of communication in free societies

Lest the reader be left with a false impression of the contrast between totalitarian societies and a democratic society, some comments should be made on the extent to which communication is controlled and channeled in democratic societies. In the United States communication is affected by such factors as the continually decreasing number of newspapers that manage to avoid bankruptcy, the frequency of newspaper mergers, the growth of newspaper chains, the dominant position of the news wire services, and the power of the radio and TV networks. These circumstances inevitably put the responsibility for presenting undistorted pictures of events into the hands of a fairly small number of individuals.

In the first place, the sheer volume of news is so great that only a small fraction of it can be widely disseminated. The gatekeepers of the mass media make the decisions on which items shall receive national coverage. One study of the flow of news from the Associated Press to four nonmetropolitan dailies in Wisconsin documents this point very clearly (Cutlip, 1954). About 100,000 to 125,000 words of news copy flow into the Associated Press in one news cycle. Editors select approximately half the copy for transmission over trunk lines. From this half, the Wisconsin AP bureau selects only one-fourth for transmission to Wisconsin dailies, adding, however, additional Wisconsin news. Four typical dailies printed from 55 percent to 87 percent of the copy they received. Thus only a small fraction of all the news is ultimately printed in these papers.

Second, and perhaps most important, is the fact that because of their nationwide audiences, the people who control the mass media will present material that in overwhelming proportion is consistent with the audience's dominant values and attitudes. Divergent views as a rule cannot attain a widespread sympathetic hearing even though there is freedom to speak. People whose views are not in accord with dominant values are limited to media having very small and specialized audiences. Thus the mass media in a free society, as in a totalitarian society, function largely to preserve the *status quo*.

Informal communication channels in a free society, however, are more divergent from those in a totalitarian society. Groups who have deviant attitudes and values within a rather wide range are permitted to communicate freely and to relay their views to others. A free society usually contains a great many groups and organizations with all sorts of aims and purposes that deviate from the society's central values. While some such informal channels exist in totalitarian societies as well, they are necessarily clandestine and greatly restricted in scope.

STUDY QUESTIONS

23. *What are two general ways in which the social structure and the values of society determine the effectiveness of communications?*
24. *Explain what is meant by the term coercive persuasion. List and explain the major processes of control used in coercive persuasion.*
25. *Explain the two effects of coercive persuasion: ritualization of belief and identification with one's captors.*
26. *What are some of the factors making for control of communications in a democratic society?*

SUMMARY: SOCIETY AND PERSUASIVE COMMUNICATION

Groups gain a part of their strength from their position in the larger society. Thus their relation to the larger society is an important determinant of the extent to which they support the individual in resisting attitude change. Similarly, the position of the opinion leader in the larger society often determines the effectiveness with which he influences his followers.

The social structure and the values of society determine the effectiveness of communications in two general ways: through control of exposure to communications, and through the ability to manipulate reward and punishment. Where these conditions are maximized, we may refer to the persuasive process as being coercive, a process that has been described in some detail.

Communication situations are structured in terms of the value structure of society. In particular, communication in totalitarian societies is likely to be more one-sided and more compelling than in democratic societies, where more dissent is permitted.

The Effectiveness of Mass Communications

No doubt most persons interested in the influence process would like to know exactly how effective the mass media are in disseminating information and obtaining desired actions. As this chapter has indicated, however, this is an almost meaningless question. Effectiveness varies with the nature of the communication, the situation, the communication channels, and the prevailing attitudes and behaviors of respondents.

Mass communications may be thought of as having several kinds of effects. One of these is to expose persons to information about various aspects of reality ranging from the latest happenings on the international scene to the recent trends in food preparation. A second effect is to persuade people—to vote, to buy, or to behave in other ways in accordance with the communicator's wishes. A third class of effects, which has little to do with persuasive intent, includes the many kinds of reactions to the entertainment content of the mass media. Each of these effects will be discussed in turn.

ACQUAINTANCE FUNCTION OF THE MASS MEDIA

There seems little doubt that the mass media, through providing repeated exposure to a commercial product, can acquaint large numbers of people with it. Many persons can readily repeat some radio and television advertisements from memory, for example. Whether or not such exposure to a product leads to acceptance of it depends upon many other factors. These include the person's attitude toward the use of the product, the degree to which his habits are already established, and the number of competing communications. If the individual's attitude is relatively neutral, if he does not have established preferences, and if competing communications are few, an intensive advertising campaign may be highly effective. This is particularly true in the case of products that are readily accessible and that are bought on impulse, as in the case of items on the shelves of a supermarket. Faced with a variety of labels for the same product, the consumer is likely to select the familiar one if such other matters as accessibility and price are relatively equal. But sometimes the desire for novelty and curiosity concerning the unfamiliar may lead him to try a new product.

Where communications run counter to important attitudes, however, quite a different result may be expected. The most intensive studies of the mass media have been in the area of voting, where the individual has firmly established attitudes highly resistant to change, and where he is strongly supported by group attitudes. A recent survey (Katz & Feldman, 1962) of thirty-one studies of the television debates between Nixon and Kennedy concluded that, although the debates reached a sizable proportion of the electorate, although they appeared to affect the information persons had, and although they increased the salience of certain issues, their overall effect was to reinforce prior voting inclinations rather than to change them.

Mass communications which attempt to bring about marked changes in attitude are unlikely to succeed. But communications that capitalize on attitudes and motives already existing in the population, and that produce facts leading to an easily available course of action serving these attitudes and motives, may be quite effective. Thus during World War II, Kate Smith's marathon radio drive to sell war bonds sold many millions of dollars' worth of bonds (Merton, 1946). Important here were well-established attitudes toward helping one's country and the war effort, the example of self-sacrifice on the performer's part, and the ease with which the respondent could take action — simply by calling in his pledge on the telephone. An example of a failure of a mass campaign has already been cited in the six-month educational effort in Cincinnati to acquaint persons with the United Nations. This campaign did not appeal to central attitudes; only people who were already interested in the UN were influenced. Moreover, it did not recommend any particular action.

We may conclude that intensive exposure is usually effective in acquainting a person with some topic or product, but whether or not he takes any action on it depends upon several factors: (1) the strength of his attitudes pertaining to the item, (2) whether his attitudes are conducive to or opposed to the action, and (3) whether action is clearly outlined in the communication.

NONPERSUASIVE EFFECTS OF THE MASS MEDIA

So far, the discussion in these chapters on social influence and attitude change has ignored a variety of effects which might result from persuasive communications, but which have little relation to the intent of the communicator. Some of these nonpersuasive effects are (1) the effects on human values of crime and violence in the mass media, (2) the effects of escapist media material, and (3) the effects of audience passivity in media attendance. The research literature on these topics has been carefully reviewed by Klapper (1961), and the discussion below draws heavily upon his conclusions.

Crime and violence

Parents, educators, and others have often expressed concern about the high proportion of crime and violence in mass media and its possible effects, such as to contribute to juvenile delinquency. The recent discussion on the effects of television are reminiscent of past concern over such older media as the movies and the comic book. All three sources have been charged with contributing to a rise in delinquency. Content analyses have confirmed the fact that the mass media do, in fact, devote much of their content to crime and violence, although it should be noted that almost all of this is in fictional form.

One cannot generalize from content to effect, however. While charges against the mass media have been made with considerable heat, the evidence presented in support of them is not scientifically adequate. In fact, the most careful studies suggest that the depiction of crime and violence has little effect on juvenile crime. This should not be surprising. The discussion earlier in this chapter of carefully designed persuasive attempts to influence actions such as voting has shown that political attitudes are strongly anchored by the relation of the individual to others and that they are highly resistant to change. One would expect that moral values relevant to crime and violence would be even more resistant to alteration through the mere depiction of behaviors opposite to the values.

Although children vary in the degree to which they expose themselves to such material, no cause-effect relation seems demonstrable. Most studies indicate that frequent viewers are no more delinquent than infrequent viewers. The minority of studies indicating that juveniles who already have criminal records do view more of such material are unable to demonstrate a causal relation between the media and criminal behavior. Klapper draws the following conclusions:

> In combination, these various findings strongly suggest that crime and violence in the media are not likely to be prime movers toward delinquency, but that such fare is likely instead to reinforce the existing behavioral tendencies, *good or ill,* of individual audience members. . . . (P. 165)

Escapist content of the mass media

Another criticism directed against the mass media pertains to the fact that much of it is escapist fare or fantasy material. This includes TV family comedy, much light fiction, daytime serials, and often even the very material considered serious drama by the communicators. Claims and counterclaims with respect to such escapist content are widely heard. Some critics maintain that listeners turn into addicts, become apathetic, and no longer "face the real world." Supporters, on the other hand, argue that such material provides relaxation as well as a harmless channel for aggressive impulses. Klapper notes that much content of the mass media is in fact escapist in nature, but concludes that such material does not *cause* any particular life pattern. It does, however, serve certain psychological needs and reinforce patterns already characteristic of the audience.

Passivity in receiving mass communications

A widespread criticism of the mass media, particularly of its fictional material, has been that consuming this material is a passive occupation which substitutes for more spontaneous and creative activities the individual might otherwise engage in. There appears to be little doubt that television in particular has preempted a considerable portion of the average child's day. One extensive study of television has estimated that in the early grades the average child spends two hours a day watching it and by the sixth or seventh grade spends three to four hours – a peak that falls slowly through the high school years (Schramm, Lyle, & Parker, 1961). This investigation also notes the dramatic changes that such extensive viewing has produced in leisure-time activities. It has cut deeply into moviegoing, radio listening, and comic book and pulp magazine reading, and it has reduced the time for play. In general, television dominates the child's leisure time. On the whole, however, these data suggest that television has not been substituted for active pursuits, but has displaced previous outlets of a passive nature. The most elaborate study relevant to this topic, conducted in Britain, also indicates that television does *not* produce passivity (Himmelweit, Oppenheim, & Vince, 1958).

The most general conclusion that can be drawn at the present time concerning these various nonpersuasive effects of the mass media is that such media are selectively used by different individuals according to already existing predispositions and attitudes. It seems that their effect, if any, consists of further reinforcement of existing characteristics rather than induction of new and undesirable ones.

STUDY QUESTIONS

27. *Summarize the factors determining whether or not intensive exposure to a communication leads to the desired action.*
28. *Provide arguments for and against the charge that crime and violence in the mass media materially increase delinquent behavior.*
29. *What effects do fantasy or escapist material in the mass media have on the individual?*

SUMMARY: EFFECTIVENESS OF MASS COMMUNICATIONS

No simple statement can be made concerning the overall effectiveness of the mass media. Intensive exposure is usually successful in acquainting a person with some topic or product, but whether or not he takes action on it depends upon several factors: (1) the strength of his attitudes pertaining to the item, (2) whether his attitudes are conducive to or opposed to the action, and (3) whether action is clearly outlined in the communication.

Various nonpersuasive effects of the mass media include the effects on human values of crime and violence in the mass media, the effects of escapist material, and the effects of audience passivity. A general conclusion drawn from many studies is that the mass media are selectively used by different individuals according to already existing predispositions and attitudes. Any effect they have takes the form of reinforcement of existing characteristics rather than the induction of new ones.

Summary and Conclusions

The much smaller amount of opinion change occurring in survey studies as compared with laboratory studies of persuasive communication can be explained by such factors as the role of groups in attitude change, the flow of communication, and certain other conditions characterizing persuasive communication in everyday life. Evidence has been presented to show that primary groups provide strong anchorages for many opinions. A person need not be a member of a group in order to derive support from it: groups which he identifies with serve as a frame of reference for his attitudes.

Groups may also serve as agents of change. Factors that create dissension or weaken the group prepare its members for accepting counternorm communications. In particular, the perception that other members are committing themselves to a change and the making of a decision to change are effective factors in bringing about attitude shifts.

Person-to-person communication has been shown to play an important role in mass communication. Mass communications sometimes follow a two-step pattern, from the communication to the opinion leader and from the opinion leader to other persons. In this process, the opinion leader serves not only to relay the information, but also as an influence agent. The communicator may sometimes be linked with the respondent through a chain consisting of several opinion leaders. Sometimes interpersonal contacts lead the respondent to seek further information in mass media. In general, opinion leaders personify group values, possess expert knowledge, and occupy a strategic social location. As representatives of the group norms, they may serve to resist change as well as to bring it about.

The total setting in which it takes place is an important determinant of a communication's effectiveness. Institutions and societies vary in the range of values permitted expression. The narrower the range, the more effective communications in accordance with these values are likely to be. Persuasive communication in certain institutions and in totalitarian societies is termed *coercive persuasion,* a phrase emphasizing the complete control that the authorities exert over reward and punishment and the channels of communication.

Mass communications accomplishing intensive exposure are usually effective in acquainting a respondent with some topic or product, but whether or not he takes any action with respect to it depends upon the strength of his attitudes about it, whether his attitudes are favorable or unfavorable, and whether action is clearly outlined in the communication. In general, the effects of the mass media on human values about crime, and the consequences of escapist media material and audience passivity, seem to depend on the individual's existing predispositions and attitudes.

PART THREE

Group Structure and Process

This section and the following one examine the emergence, maintenance, and change of regularities in interaction. In part, such regularities of thought, feeling, and behavior can be explained in terms of expectations, norms, or rules of conduct that guide behavior in social situations. This source of regularity, the institutional structure, will be treated in Part Four, using the concept of social role.

Part Three focuses on regularities whose source is subinstitutional: the direct exchange of primary rewards. Primary rewards are inherent in the interaction itself and not contrived to elicit certain behaviors. Examples are the pleasures of companionship experienced by friends and the enjoyment of social conversation between fellow workers. In contrast, institutional regularities are supported by secondary reinforcers, such as money or social approval. A worker is formally rewarded for his productivity through a complex payroll system.

Subinstitutional regularities, termed *elementary social behavior* by Homans, are better highlighted by some situations than others. For example, the behavior of a group of strangers in the small-group laboratory is less influenced by institutional controls than the behavior of a well-established, formally organized group. Similarly, interaction in informal situations, such as association between two friends or among a group of children at play, is more likely to illustrate elementary social behavior. By studying such situations, principles underlying elementary social behavior may be more readily identified.

Elementary social behavior is not confined to newly formed groups; moreover, these units are not free from institutional controls. The exchange of affection between two persons, an example of elementary social behavior, may occur between two children whose play is relatively free from institutional controls, but in other instances, such an exchange may be tightly interwoven with a host of institutional processes. An example of the latter is love between husband and wife, where the institution of the family is relevant. Thus, elementary social behavior and institutional behavior are separate largely in an analytical sense; most concrete behaviors illustrate both.

The concept of *structure* refers to patterned regularities in feelings, perceptions, and actions that characterize aspects of the interactions between members of a group. For example, the pattern of liking among group members has been called the *affect* or *sociometric* structure. This is portrayed graphically by a *sociogram,* where points representing each member are connected by arrows indicating the direction of liking from member to member. The organization and patterning of such sociograms portrays the idea of structure in a concrete fashion.

The term *process* refers to the changing pattern of relations between elements of structure over time. For example, in a newly formed group of strangers, the process by which friendships develop may be traced. The various stages of this process may be illustrated by showing the affect structures existing in the different periods of development. Such processes may best be understood in terms of a theoretical conception that views interaction as an exchange of rewards and costs by individual members. While exchange theory is recent, and few studies testing it have been published, it admirably performs one function of theory—that of organizing in a coherent framework many diverse empirical findings.

These chapters on group structure and process make abundantly clear that the relation between two people is a function of more than their characteristics as individuals. Even when the characteristics of both are taken into consideration, their behavior cannot be predicted without knowing something of the history of the relation between them and of their relations with other persons.

Chapter 7 begins with a discussion of interpersonal attraction. Its major topic, the sociometric or affect structure, was one of the first forms of elementary social behavior to be studied, and a great deal of research literature is available. It also treats processes that lead to progressive modification of the affect structure. In contrast, social power, treated in Chapter 8, has not been intensively studied, and the discussion is more speculative. Social power pertains to the relative ability of persons to influence other members of the group. As will be seen, power is dependent upon a variety of factors and takes several different forms. The exercise of different types of power over a period of time also has different consequences depending upon the type of power that is used. While *legitimate power,* a form stemming from the institutional structure, is given some attention, more discussion is devoted to the forms of power that are based upon a more direct exchange of rewards and costs.

One topic in Chapter 9 is status, which refers to patterns of differential evaluation or estimated worth of group members as judged by each other. As in the case of power, a variety of criteria may underlie status. The basis of such status rankings and the processes that maintain or underlie change in these rankings are considered. Since the relation between status and various patterns of communication in groups has frequently been a focus of empirical study, the other topic in this chapter is the communication structure of the group.

Chapter 10 deals with a phenomenon basic to the functioning of all groups: the emergence of norms. Continued interaction results not only in regularities of feeling and behavior, but also in perceptions and cognitions of the conduct of group members. Group members arrive at consensus on what feelings, perceptions, and behaviors are appropriate or inappropriate. A theory is presented offering an explanation of how and where such consensus occurs and the degree to which members conform to these norms. Chapter 10 is concerned primarily with how such normative structures emerge. Later, in Part Four, more attention will be given to the effects of well-established norms on the behavior of the individual.

Leadership, the focus of Chapter 11, has long been a popular topic with behavioral scientists. Their research has gradually led to abandonment of the lay view that leadership is an attribute of an individual. Leadership is currently conceived of by the behavioral scientist as a role or function that arises in a group and that is filled or met in varying degrees by a number of group members, according to the demands of the situation and the members' characteristics.

The chapters previewed so far have emphasized the determinants rather than the consequences of structures and processes emerging from interaction among groups of persons. Chapter 12 shifts to the most frequently explored consequences of variations in group structure and process: the effectiveness with which a group performs its tasks and its efficiency in providing satisfaction to its members. The effects of various structural and other variables, such as size of the group, on effectiveness and satisfaction are discussed. Chapter 13, the last in this portion of the book, deals with the emergence, maintenance, and change of prejudiced attitudes and behaviors on the part of one group toward another. The topic is included here because many theoretical principles presented in the other chapters apply to the diversity of findings on intergroup relations.

chapter seven

INTERPERSONAL ATTRACTION

Liking for other persons and their reciprocal feelings toward us are among the most important aspects of social life. Being liked by others can have significant effects upon a person's well-being, and having friends is important to everyone. Feelings of liking lead to increased association, and they shape the behavior of individuals in interaction. Groups are formed on the basis of attraction between persons. Even in large, formal organizations, liking determines to some extent mutual associations and communication patterns among individuals, as well as patterns of influence. This chapter discusses in some detail how feelings of liking play a part in social interaction and in structuring groups. Although feelings of dislike are also important, much less research has been devoted to them, and they will be discussed only occasionally.

Sociometry

Any group of persons observed over a period of time exhibits regularities in patterns of association. Where members can choose whom to associate with in a given activity, some persons are chosen more frequently than others. Each individual, moreover, regularly chooses certain persons and ignores others. In part, choices are based upon liking or *positive affect* toward the other person. The patterns of attraction characterizing regular associations among group members may be termed the *affect structure* of a group. Such regularities of association have been conceptualized in terms of *sociometric structure*. The phrase comes from sociometry, an intellectual movement within the behavioral sciences founded by Moreno (1953). Moreno developed the sociometric test and some of the early methods of analyzing data obtained from it. His followers and other behavioral scientists further elaborated upon this instrument and used it to study various group phenomena.

THE SOCIOMETRIC TEST

Essentially, a sociometric test is a means of obtaining quantitative data on the preferences of group members for associating with other members. Administration of sociometric tests is arranged so as to protect the privacy of the individual's choices. In a sociometric test, persons indicate their choices or rejections of other group members for association in some specified activity or context. The tests have essentially two components: (1) a prescribed procedure for making choices, and (2) a criterion by which choices are made. For example, a school child might be instructed to select the *one* person in his classroom that he would most like to have as a seat mate.

The instruction to choose the most-preferred person illustrates one procedure sometimes used. Many different procedures for determining sociometric choices and rejections have been developed over the years. In some instances each individual is allowed an unlimited number of choices or rejections; in other instances, a number is specified. Where more than one choice is allowed, a ranking of preference in terms of first choice, second choice, etc., may be requested. In fact, in one procedure, persons simply rank others in the group from first choice to last choice.

Almost any criterion for choice may be specified: the criterion in the example above is the desirability of another child as a seat mate. Individuals may indicate which persons they prefer as friends, or simply which they like or dislike. More often some more specific criterion is used, such as choice of a roommate by college students, choice of a flying partner by Air Force pilots, choice of a group leader in a fraternity, and choice of a work partner by employees. In early sociometric tests, it was considered important for the investigator to tell group members that their choices would be used to restructure the group and for him to actually effect such a rearrangement. This requirement, however, is rarely adhered to in contemporary research.

Recently a form of measurement known as *relational analysis* has added a perceptual dimension to sociometric measurement (Tagiuri, 1952; 1958). In a relational analysis a subject, besides making choices, guesses who will choose him. In addition, he may put himself in the place of the other group members in turn and guess whom they will choose and whom they will perceive as choosing themselves.

Before we examine the ways in which sociometric data may be analyzed, two facts should be recognized. First, patterns of choice vary depending on the criteria of choice. For instance, when choosing whom they would like to work with, persons do not make the same choices as when they are choosing whom they would like to spend their leisure time with. Second, patterns of choice revealed by a sociometric test reflect a person's *desire* for association. While desired patterns are generally similar to actual patterns, the correspondence is far from perfect.

STUDY QUESTIONS

1. *What is a sociometric test? To what aspects of group structure does it pertain?*
2. *Explain what is meant by relational analysis.*
3. *What are the effects of using different criteria of choice in a sociometric test? To what extent do sociometric preferences represent the frequency of actual associations among group members?*

ANALYSIS OF SOCIOMETRIC DATA

Responses to a sociometric questionnaire may be summarized in a number of ways. Perhaps the best-known method is a graphic presentation called a *sociogram*. A sociogram consists of points connected by lines or arrows, as in Figure 7–1. Each point represents a person. The solid lines in this particular sociogram represent choices and the broken lines rejection. Arrows indicate the direction of choice.

The points in a sociogram are arranged so that the distances between them represent the degrees of positive attraction between the persons in the group. For instance, the points representing two persons who choose each other will be placed closer together than points representing two persons only one of whom chooses the other. Those points in turn will be closer together than points representing two persons neither of whom choose each other. In Figure 7–1, the pair consisting of persons 2 and 3, where attraction is mutual, is closer together than the pair consisting of persons 3 and 9, where attraction is only one-way. Similarly, the pair 5 and 8, who reject each other, are placed a greater distance apart than the pair 8 and 9, involving one-way rejection.

The sociogram presents in easily discernible form a number of features of the sociometric structure. Some individuals are the focus of many solid lines. Such highly chosen persons are frequently referred to as sociometric *stars* (see person 5). Others, such as person 10, are relative *isolates*, receiving few choices and making few. *Cliques* or subgroups can be identified from the clustering of points located closely together and having lines indicating mutual choice. See, for instance, the clique composed of persons 1, 2, 3, 4, and 5. Cleavages between subgroups are represented by the distance between groups, reflecting the absence of choices between them, or by broken lines indicating rejection that connect members of two groups.

While a sociogram may readily convey a sense of structure, the construction of such a diagram is often a result of a trial-and-error process in which certain features may be missed in the attempt to achieve a simple structure. Moreover, if the number of persons in the group is

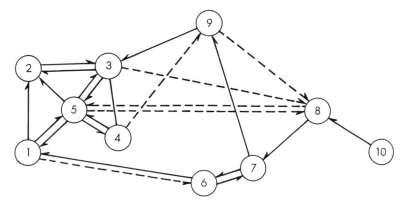

Figure 7–1

A sample sociogram. Each circle represents a group member. Solid arrows represent choices; broken arrows, rejection. [Adapted with permission from Marie Jahoda, M. Deutsch, & S. W. Cook (Eds.). *Research methods in social relations*. Vol. 2. New York: Holt, Rinehart and Winston, Inc., 1951.]

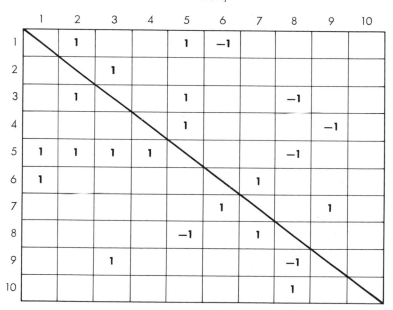

Figure 7–2

A sociometric matrix. Rows indicate the outgoing choices of each person, who is identified by a number, and columns indicate the choices received by each person [Adapted with permission from Marie Jahoda, M. Deutsch, & S. W. Cook (Eds.). *Research methods in social relations*. Vol. 2. New York: Holt, Rinehart and Winston, Inc., 1951.]

large, and if they are permitted to make many choices, such diagrams are unwieldy. For these reasons, other forms of analysis have been developed, most notably *matrix analysis* and *index analysis* (Forsyth & Katz, 1946; Festinger, 1949; Proctor & Loomis, 1951). In fact, the choices and rejections in a sociogram such as that in Figure 7–1 would normally be summarized in matrix form before the sociogram was constructed. A matrix is created quite simply by arranging persons as choosers on one axis, the vertical, and as recipients of choices on the other axis, the horizontal. Persons must be arranged in the *same order* on both axes.

Figure 7–2 presents in matrix form the choices of the various numbered persons presented in graphic form in Figure 7–1. A minus sign designates a rejection rather than a choice. The entries in the first *row* indicate, for instance, that person 1 has chosen persons 2 and 5 and rejected person 6. The entries in the first *column* indicate that person 1 has been chosen by persons 5 and 6. A variety of operations may be performed on such a matrix to identify the structural aspects of the sociogram in a more objective manner. These operations are too complex for presentation here; the interested reader can consult other sources (see Proctor & Loomis, 1951; Lindzey & Borgatta, 1954).

A third way of summarizing sociometric data is known as index analysis. A number of indices have been proposed to describe certain sociometric characteristics of either the individual or the group. An example of the former would be the index for the choice status of an individual. A commonly used index of choice status for a given person i is as follows:

$$\text{CS}_i = \frac{\text{number of persons choosing}}{N - 1}$$

where CS_i stands for choice status and N is the number of persons in the group (Proctor & Loomis, 1951, p. 571). This index ranges from 0 to 1, depending upon the proportion of persons in the group who choose person i. An example of an index of group structure is one for *cohesiveness,* expressed as a ratio of the observed number of mutual-choice pairs to the total possible number of such pairs.

$$\text{Cohesiveness} = \frac{\text{number of mutual pairs}}{\text{number of mutual pairs possible}}$$

Again the reader may wish to consult the previously cited sources for further details on index analysis and for an overview of statistical techniques for determining the statistical significance of various individual and group sociometric indices.

In sum, sociometric analysis is a means of describing the feelings of a group toward its own members and toward other groups. Through such analysis it is possible to identify by objective means persons in the group who are generally liked, disliked, or ignored. By using criteria more specific than liking or disliking, other kinds of key persons may also be discovered, such as leaders or followers, or persons who are important communication links in the group. Such analysis also makes possible the identification of cliques within a group and the kind of feeling existing between the clique and other subgroups or between the clique and the group as a whole. Various other social-psychological properties of groups may also be related to sociometric indices. For example, such indices as the number of in-group choices relative to the number of times members choose persons outside the group, and the number of times the leader is chosen relative to the number of rejections he receives, have been suggested as indices of the morale of the group.

STUDY QUESTIONS

4. *Identify the major elements and dimensions of a sociogram. What information about a group is yielded by a sociogram?*
5. *What is contained in a sociometric matrix?*
6. *What is a sociometric index? Give examples.*

Correlates of Choice Status

Investigations of sociometric structure have sought answers to a number of related questions. Some have focused primarily on the *determinants* of choice. A few studies, such as that of Criswell (1937), have identified such determinants by studying cleavages in groups. For example, if in a primary grade classroom, boys choose boys and girls choose girls as seat mates, this cleavage of the class into two groups indicates that sex is a determinant of choice. Most commonly, however, determinants of choice have been sought by comparing persons frequently chosen with those infrequently chosen. The classic study by Jennings (1950) of girls in a correctional institution, in which she identified the personal characteristics of girls of high and low choice status, illustrates this approach. Frequently chosen and infrequently chosen persons have also been identified in order to study the consequences of having high or low choice status.

In correlational studies of the sort just described, it is often difficult to decide whether a characteristic of a person produces his particular choice status, or whether he is perceived to have that characteristic because of his status. To illustrate this problem, one finding is that persons with low choice status are seen by group members as having unfavorable personality characteristics, whereas the overchosen are described in favorable terms. The choice status of a person may result from his possession of these traits. Possibly, however, a person may be seen to have these traits because of his choice status, when he does not in fact possess them. Even when the personality characteristics of a person are assessed independently, i.e., by a personality test, the question of which is a determinant and which is a consequence may still be raised. In many instances cogent arguments can be made for effects in either direction. Often the truth lies somewhere between, both variables being to some extent consequences and determinants of the other.

The remainder of this section will focus upon the determinants of choice and rejection, rather than the effects of choice. Chapter 11 on leadership, and Chapter 12, concerned with ongoing interaction in a problem-solving situation, will take up some of the consequences of choice status.

Over the years a wide variety of demographic, cultural and personality characteristics has been studied in relation to sociometric choice. Although most studies have focused on the characteristics of the over- or underchosen, some have employed a broader approach in which the characteristics of the choosers were also taken into account. Where this has been done, an attempt has generally been made to discover whether the chooser is similar to or different from the target of his choice in the characteristics studied. The results of these studies suggest a number of tendencies that affect the patterns of sociometric choice in the group.

First, persons choose those with whom they have the greatest opportunity to interact. One study of choice patterns in a married-student housing area revealed the effects on sociometric structure of sheer distance as well as the physical arrangements of the buildings and of the apartments within each building (Festinger, Schachter, & Back, 1950). Occupants who were physically close or who were likely to encounter each other frequently because of the arrangement of the apartments were more apt to choose each other.

Gullahorn (1952) has also demonstrated that nearness is a determinant of choice. Studies of propinquity in mate selection, where physical distance has been shown to be inversely related to marital choice, are consistent with this view.[1] Somewhat more indirect evidence has also been provided by a recent study of friendship formation in medical school (Kendall, 1960). A strong association between choice and the closeness in alphabetical order of medical students' last names was found. Since seating assignments to courses were made alphabetically, those with names close to each other had greater opportunity to interact. Similarly, the sociometric choices of college students are influenced by common domicile, college class, major scholastic interest, and socioeconomic status, with the first-mentioned factors being the most influential (Lundberg & Beazley, 1948). This finding again supports the interaction hypothesis, for persons who are in the same college class, who major in the same subjects, and particularly, who live in the same dormitory, would be expected to interact much more frequently.

Second, persons choose others having characteristics considered desirable in terms of the norms and values of the group. A wide variety of characteristics has been shown to be related to choice status. To illustrate,

[1] Winch, Ktsanes, & Ktsanes, 1954; Winch, 1955*a*; Winch, 1955*b*; Winch, Ktsanes, & Ktsanes, 1955; Ktsanes, 1955; Bowerman & Day, 1956; Winch, 1958; Murstein, 1961.

studies of both children (Bonney, 1944) and adults (Lundberg & Steele, 1938) indicate a positive correlation between choice status and socio-economic status. Studies of personality correlates, although sometimes difficult to interpret, generally show a correlation between choice status and desirable characteristics. Persons having such characteristics as high intelligence or marked abilities, as measured by various achievement tests, are also more frequently chosen (Bonney, 1944; Grossmann & Wrighter, 1948).

Perhaps the best documentation of the view that the overchosen have desirable characteristics comes from the study of attitudes. A now classic study of Newcomb (1943) showed that conformity to the dominant values and norms in a college community was positively correlated with choice status. In a small college for women, where the climate of opinion was liberal and where concern over national political and economic issues was marked, the girls who were most frequently chosen were usually the most liberal. These initial findings have been confirmed in a later study (Morton, 1959).

A third general trend is for persons to choose others who are similar to themselves. The evidence is strongest and most consistent for attitudes, values, and social-background characteristics. A recent study by Newcomb (1961), to be discussed in more detail later, has demonstrated the point made earlier by Winslow (1937), Richardson (1940), and Precker (1952) that a person chooses others similar to himself in attitudes and values. Similarity in social background has been related to choice in several investigations. An analysis of the sociometric choices of fifth graders has shown that they choose others similar to themselves in socioeconomic status (Bonney, 1946). Studies of sources of cleavages in the sociometric structure have also revealed the influence of religion (Goodnow & Tagiuri, 1952), race (Criswell, 1937), and ethnic group membership (Loomis, 1943).

A more recent study by Broderick (1956) provides evidence for similarity in values as well as social-background characteristics. He suggests that the degree to which similarity is predictive of friendship choice appears to depend on the following: (1) the particular class of similarity — whether it is a status characteristic, a value, or a personality trait; (2) the degree of similarity; (3) the significance of the similarity — in some groups, for instance, similarity in a particular value may be considerably more important than in others; (4) breadth of similarity — the number of different ways in which two persons are similar. Although they are not within the typical framework of a sociometric study, the findings on similarity in mate selection are also illustrative. Persons who marry each other generally reveal a certain degree of similarity in social-background characteristics (Winch, 1958) and in attitudes (Byrne & Blaylock, 1963). At least one study, however, found that among Dutch students attraction and similarity of values were not associated (Ramuz-Nienhuis & Van Bergen, 1960).

In contrast to similarity in social background or in values, the evidence for similarity in personality traits is less consistent. Some years ago, Richardson (1939) surveyed the evidence from about forty studies and concluded that friends are similar in personality. More recent evidence also supports the notion that persons seek to associate with others who are similar (Shapiro, 1953; Tharp, 1963; Secord & Backman, 1963; 1964). In contrast, a study of marital choice has provided general evidence of attraction between persons who are different in some respects rather than similar: At least, for certain personality needs, people whose need structures were complementary rather than similar chose each other (Winch, 1958). Some subsequent investigators (Kerckhoff & Davis, 1962) found support for this interpretation; others have not.[2] This suggests that similarity or complementarity in personality characteristics leads to attraction only under conditions not yet identified. For example, a study by Hoffman (1958) suggests that the association between the personality composition of a group and the level of attraction among members depends on the contribution of the personality makeup of the members to success in solving the group's problems.

In addition to the several determinants of choice already identified, other studies have suggested that persons choose others whom they perceive as choosing them. The techniques of relational analysis have been applied to a number of groups, and a strong tendency for a person to perceive that those whom he selects choose him in turn has been found (Tagiuri, 1958). Another study using a different procedure is also consistent with this finding (Newcomb, 1956). A third study demonstrates a causal sequence in which the perception of being liked by another person results in a liking for that person (Backman & Secord, 1959). These various studies of liking, taken together, suggest a two-way effect. In part, liking for other persons appears to be influenced by the perception we have of their feelings toward us, and our perceptions of these feelings are in part influenced by our liking for the persons.

A related principle is that an individual likes others whom he believes view him in a favorable light (Worchel, 1961; Deutsch & Solomon, 1959). Also, an individual likes others whom he believes see him as he sees himself (Deutsch & Solomon, 1959; Backman & Secord, 1962). These two principles would make opposite predictions for the case of the few individuals who have negative attitudes toward themselves. Current evidence suggests that for such persons, both principles continue to operate, somewhat counteracting each other (see Chapter 19 for further details). Finally, in situations where persons have achieved gratifications in each other's presence, as when the members of a group successfully accomplish a goal, liking increases (Sherif et al., 1954).

To summarize the determinants of choice on a sociometric test, a

[2]Bowerman & Day, 1956; Schellenberg & Bee, 1960; Murstein, 1961; Hobart & Lindholm, 1963.

person is likely to choose the following individuals: (1) those with whom he has a greater opportunity to interact, (2) those who have characteristics most desirable in terms of the norms and values of the group, (3) those who are most similar to him in attitudes, values, and social-background characteristics, and (4) those whom he perceives as choosing him or assigning favorable characteristics to him, (5) those who see him as he sees himself, and (6) those whose company leads to gratification of his needs.

STUDY QUESTIONS

7. *Explain why the demonstration of a correlation between choice status and some other factor does not prove that a one-way cause-effect relation exists.*
8. *Summarize the determinants of choice status. What types of similarity between chooser and chosen have the greatest effects on choice?*

Theories of Interpersonal Attraction

Although much early sociometric research was not guided by systematic theory, in more recent years the accumulation of empirical findings has led to the development of several theories of interpersonal attraction. No attempt will be made to include them all; only a few representative theories will be discussed. The theories are of two general kinds: those that focus on the characteristics of individuals, and those that focus on the rewards and costs experienced in the interactional process.

Theories of friendship which explain attraction in terms of the characteristics of the dyad go back to antiquity.[3] The basic question has been whether persons who are similar or those who are different are attracted to each other. Today it is known that this question greatly oversimplifies the matter.

NEWCOMB'S THEORY OF INTERPERSONAL ATTRACTION

Newcomb (1961), following Heider (1958*b*), has developed and tested a theory that persons with similar orientations (attitudes) are attracted to each other. Through long experience, an individual becomes dependent upon other persons for information about the environment. He uses this information to confirm and extend the impressions of his senses. Thus the individual is conceived to need support from others for his attitudes and beliefs. When he encounters a person with attitudes contrary to his own, a state of strain arises, particularly if he likes the person. This strain is uncomfortable, and the individual seeks to resolve it by finding agreement with other persons. This basic motivation has been called the need for *consensual validation* (Sullivan, 1947), which means that people attempt to validate their attitudes through seeking agreement with others.

[3]For excellent reviews of the history of these theories, see Grant (1951) and Broderick (1956).

The greater the importance and common relevance of the attitude object to the persons in a dyad, the stronger the attraction. By *importance* is meant the strength of the feeling, cognition, or behaviors toward the object in question. These may be positive or negative. By *common relevance* is meant the degree to which the object is perceived as having common consequences for the persons in question. The term *object* refers to any focus of perception, including physical objects, symbols, other persons, or one's own self. For example, for most married couples it is more important that they agree on whether or not they like children than on whether or not they like a particular make of automobile. Agreement on the former will lead to more attraction to each other than will agreement on the latter.

Newcomb's theory is couched in system terms. Each variable—attraction, orientation, perception of the orientation of the other person—is in part a consequent of and in part a determinant of each other variable. Not only is the attraction of A toward B affected by the similarity between A's attitude toward X and his perception of B's attitude toward X, but his own attitude and his perception of B's attitude are influenced by the degree to which he is attracted to B. For example, assume that A, who is attracted to B, discovers a discrepancy between his attitude and B's attitude toward an object of common relevance, such as another person, X. A likes person X; i.e., has a variety of affective and cognitive components of a positive or favorable nature with respect to X. He discovers, however, that B dislikes X and views many of X's attributes unfavorably. Given the attraction of A toward B, this discrepancy between A's attitude and his perception of B's attitude would give rise to strain and to a postulated force toward change in the relations between these three system components.

A change returning the system to a state of balance could take a number of forms. First, a shift could occur in A's perception of B's attitude: A might decide that he was mistaken in attributing to B a negative attitude toward X. Assuming that B actually has a negative attitude, this form of resolution would be labeled *misperception*. Second, A might change his own attitude in the direction of B's and develop a similarly negative attitude toward X. Third, A might attempt to convince B that he is mistaken about X. If B were attracted to A and experienced a similar strain, he might be amenable to such a persuasive attempt. Fourth, A might simply restore the system to balance by reducing his attraction toward B.[4]

This illustration suggests that, depending on the system variable focused upon, Newcomb's theory of strain toward symmetry can be viewed not only as a theory of interpersonal attraction, but also as a theory of social perception and social influence. Since our main concern here is

[4]In order not to complicate this illustration further, two other changes have been omitted. Since the degree of strain is in part a function of the importance and perceived common relevance of person X to A, changes might be made with regard to those two variables in order to reduce strain.

with explanations of interpersonal attraction, the theory will be considered mainly from that point of view.

From his theory Newcomb predicted that, as strangers in a new group begin to interact and thus to gain information concerning each other's attitudes, the bonds of attraction making up the affect or sociometric structure of the group form most strongly between those who hold similar attitudes toward objects of importance and common relevance. These predictions were tested in a study of two groups. Both were composed of male college students who were initially strangers and who lived together in a house provided by the experimenter. Their orientations toward a variety of objects, including each other, and the patterns of attraction that developed were measured at various points during a sixteen-week period.

The observations and the changes that occurred over the period observed were in accord with the theory. Preacquaintance similarities, measured by the experimenter from the students' responses to questionnaires on a variety of specific topics and from their rankings of certain values, led to the development of patterns of attraction between persons at a late stage in the sixteen-week period, but not at an early stage. Since these attitudinal values did *not* change to any extent over the period studied, it would appear that as persons became acquainted with each other's values, attraction formed between those who were similar. When two persons held relevant and similar orientations toward themselves and toward other house occupants, they were especially likely to be attracted to each other. As acquaintance increased, consensus between members of a pair in attitudes toward other house members increased, and there was a parallel increase in their attraction to each other.

If the assumption is made that persons positively value themselves, the theory would predict that a close association would be found between liking oneself and believing that other persons like one. Such was the case: A person liked others who had the same feeling toward him as he had toward himself. The association between attraction to a person and perceiving him as having similar attitudes was true for cognitive elements as well. Each subject described himself by checking a series of adjectives and then used the same adjective checklist to describe himself as he thought each of the others in the group would. A close association was found between attraction and agreement on such a self-description. This appeared to hold for unfavorable as well as favorable items: an individual was attracted to persons whom he perceived as seeing him the way he saw himself, in terms of both faults and virtues. These findings with regard to the self as an object have been confirmed by others (Tagiuri, 1958; Backman & Secord, 1959, 1962; Broxton, 1963). Also, a study conducted in another theoretical context to be described below showed that attraction was affected not only by perceived similarity but by actual similarity as well (Backman & Secord, 1962).

Finally, another study, while not concerned with attraction as the dependent variable, provides experimental evidence for strain toward symmetry. Using a confederate, Sampson and Insko (1964) created two balanced and two imbalanced conditions in a perceptual task situation. In one, subjects were led to like their partner and to perceive him as making judgments similar to their own. In the other, they were led to dislike their partner and to perceive his judgments as different from theirs. The two imbalanced situations were manipulated so that a disliked partner was seen as making similar judgments, and a liked partner, as making dissimilar judgments. The prediction that subjects would change their judgment more frequently in the *imbalanced* situations was confirmed. In another similar experimental situation, however, where judgments of the outcome of jury trials were made, the prediction that subjects would respond so as to be different from a disliked partner and similar to a liked partner received less conclusive support.

In summary, Newcomb's theory of strain toward symmetry postulates that individuals strive to achieve a state of balance. Balance is present when persons *A* and *B* are attracted to each other and hold similar attitudes toward objects of common relevance to them. When imbalance occurs, one or more of the component parts are changed to restore balance. These various components of the system are not independent, but have mutual effects upon each other. Attitudes toward the self and other group members are of particular significance for the determination of strain or balance. Studies of living groups[5] by Newcomb and by others are generally consistent with his theory.

STUDY QUESTIONS

9. *State the elements of Newcomb's theory of interpersonal attraction.*
10. *What is meant by the statement that the variables in Newcomb's theory constitute a system?*
11. *Describe the various means by which a state of strain may be resolved.*
12. *Describe the kind of evidence supporting Newcomb's theory.*

THEORY OF COMPLEMENTARY NEEDS

Perhaps the most widely known theory that stresses differences rather than similarities as a basis of attraction is the theory of complementary needs, proposed by Winch (1958). This theory, developed and tested largely in the context of mate selection, has been offered as a general principle of dyad formation, of which mate selection is a special case. While not denying that persons who fall in love and marry are similar in a number of respects such as social-background characteristics, Winch proposed that the need structure of persons attracted to each other is different or complementary rather than similar.

Winch suggested two general reasons why persons who differ in need

---

[5]The term *living group* refers to a group of persons who share a common domicile, such as occupants of a dormitory, members of a sorority living in the sorority house, etc.

structure are attracted to each other. First, each member of the dyad finds interaction mutually or reciprocally rewarding because his needs are expressed in behavior that is rewarding to the other member. For example, a person with strong nurturance needs behaves in a protective, nurturant manner toward another person who has strong needs to be dependent. In this way, each individual satisfies his needs and is in turn satisfied. Second, persons are attracted to others who have characteristics they once aspired to but were prevented by circumstances from developing. Instead, they have modeled themselves after the image of a person with the opposite traits. But they still retain a wistful admiration for individuals who possess the once-coveted traits. To illustrate (Winch, 1958):

> To tie these ideas together, let us dream up a little boy, Herbert, whose mother demanded "model" behavior and gave him to understand that neither she nor anyone else would ever have anything to do with him unless he did as she said. Let us imagine that little Herbert was frightened and conformed but realized that occasionally he had impulses to be "bad." Let us assume that he was worried about those impulses and subsequently became a very "good" and "controlled" boy—a bit of a sissy and not very popular. One of his ego-models—taken up, cherished, and abandoned—would probably be a swashbuckling exemplar of derring-do, mobilized at all times to run his sword through anyone who might cross his path. And as Herbert became an adult, we might expect that he would be attracted to expressive people, to people who talk back and don't take nonsense from others. This is something we might feel sure that he would wish he could do—just feel some aggression well up in his veins. We might expect him to draw vicarious gratification from seeing other people "blow their tops." We might even expect that he would marry a girl who would blow her top regularly. (P. 87)

Need complementarity may take either of two forms. Persons *A* and *B* may be regarded as complementary in needs because *A* is high and *B* is low on the *same* needs, or because *A* is high on one or more needs and *B* is high or low on certain *different* needs. To illustrate the former, which is called type I complementarity, a person who is very high in the need to dominate others and a person who is very low in this need would be mutually attracted. Type II complementarity is illustrated by the previous description of a nurturant and a dependent person attracted to each other.

Evidence for this theory is far from conclusive. Winch and his associates studied the need structure of twenty-five married couples and concluded that the bulk of the evidence supported his general hypothesis of complementarity. Since his initial investigations, a number of others have tested these ideas. Several studies[6] failed to confirm Winch's conclusions, but another recent investigation has supported them (Kerckhoff & Davis, 1962). Since the investigations differed from each other in the populations studied, the manner in which the needs were assessed, and a number of other respects, it is difficult to pinpoint the reason for such disparity in

[6]Bowerman & Day, 1956; Schellenberg & Bee, 1960; Murstein, 1961; Hobart & Lindholm, 1963.

findings. Yet, the preponderance of evidence casts doubt on the plausibility of this hypothesis, at least as originally formulated. Further refinements, however, may still result in specifying those conditions under which complementarity does in fact produce attraction.

Elsewhere, the present writers have outlined a theory of stability and change in behavior that has implications for interpersonal attraction (1961). While this theory will be discussed in greater detail in Chapter 19, it has certain implications for need complementarity. It proposed that persons will like others whose characteristics, behavioral and otherwise, aid them in maintaining *congruency*. Such a perceptual-cognitive state is achieved by an individual in a relation with another person when the other's characteristics or behavior contain implications congruent with elements of his own behavior and self concept. The present writers have made the following suggestions (Secord & Backman, 1961).

> Implications for self-definitions may take three forms: S may perceive O's behavior as directly confirming a component of self, O's behavior may enable S to behave in ways that would confirm a component of self, O's behavior may (by comparison) lead other Os to confirm a component of S's self-concept. Examples of each form are:
>
> An S who regards himself as mature and responsible perceives that Os respect him for these characteristics.
>
> An S who regards himself as nurturant encounters an O in need of help; this allows him to behave toward O in a manner which supports his nurturant aspect of self.
>
> A girl who regards herself as popular and well-liked keeps company with an unpopular girl; Os are viewed by her as judging her favorably by contrast.

Depending on the implications for congruency, this theory predicts that attraction between two persons is a function of *similarity* in certain traits and further, that certain combinations of dissimilar traits in a dyad result in attraction. Some predictions from this theory are the same as those of Winch, but others are opposite to his. To illustrate attraction through similarity, a person who regards himself as friendly and outgoing is expected to be attracted to others who are similar in this respect, since their behavior would allow him to behave in a manner congruent with this particular facet of his self conception. Attraction between a nurturant and a dependent person illustrates attraction based on dissimilar needs and is consistent with the notion of congruency.

In summary, Winch's theory of need complementarity proposes two forms of interpersonal attraction based upon the need structures of individuals in a dyad. In one, persons A and B are complementary in need structure because A is high and B is low in the same need. In the other, A is high on a need, and B is low on a different need. Both situations are believed to be complementary because each member finds the behavior of his partner rewarding. Empirical evidence is at present preponderantly negative.

In interpersonal congruency theory, the extent to which the other person is perceived as behaving in a manner congruent with the self concept is taken as a basis for need complementarity. This theory appears to provide a somewhat clearer rationale for need complementarity, but empirical findings in support of it must be regarded as tentative.

EXCHANGE THEORIES OF ATTRACTION

The theories of attraction examined so far have emphasized personality characteristics. Those which will be briefly reviewed here emphasize factors in the history of the interaction between persons. Recently Thibaut and Kelley (1959) and Homans (1961) have independently arrived at general theoretical formulations which are remarkably similar and which are consistent with the findings presented here. Both theories attempt to explain social behavior in terms of the rewards exchanged and the costs incurred in interaction. As such, both include a theory of interpersonal attraction. The following four concepts are basic to exchange theory: reward, cost, outcome, and comparison level.

The term *reward* is a familiar one. The review of other theories has taken note of rather important rewards that are achieved in interaction. For example, consensual validation about the world as well as about oneself is a kind of reward that theories such as Newcomb's suggest people exchange in interaction. Any activity on the part of one person that contributes to the gratification of another person's needs can be considered a reward from the standpoint of the latter person. The term *cost* is similarly a very broad concept. The costs of engaging in any activity not only include "punishment" incurred in carrying out that activity, such as fatigue or anxiety, but also, as Homans argues, include the value of rewards foregone by engaging in this activity rather than alternative activities. The term *outcome* refers to rewards less costs. If the outcome of an interaction is positive, it may be said to yield a *profit;* if it is negative, a *loss.* Because a person profits from an interaction with another, however, does not necessarily mean that he likes that person. For attraction to occur, the outcome must be above some minimum level of expectation or desserts, called the *comparison level.* This level is influenced by his past experiences in this relation, his past experiences in comparable relations, his judgment of what outcomes others like himself are receiving, and his perceptions of outcomes available to him in alternative relations.

This way of looking at interpersonal attraction has two advantages. First, it provides a general rationale for explaining why persons with certain characteristics receive more than their share of choices as well as why persons with one characteristic choose others with certain different characteristics. Second, it permits an examination from a process standpoint of the changes in attraction that occur among members of a group. These advantages will become clearer as each is examined in more detail.

Exchange theory and characteristics of the overchosen

The previous section on correlates of choice status indicated that persons whose characteristics were considered desirable in terms of the norms and values of the group received more than their share of choices. Exchange theory suggests a number of reasons why this would be expected. The behavior of persons who are chosen by many others must reflect characteristics that have considerable reward value to a variety of people in the group. A person's behavior may have widespread or general value for a number of reasons.

First, he may facilitate rewarding interaction for others. Certain characteristics of the overchosen girls in Jennings's study illustrate this point. She notes that each of these girls helps others, protects others, and increases the rewards and reduces the costs that other girls, particularly the less popular, experience in interaction with her as well as with others in the group. Referring to the overchosen as leaders, Jennings notes the following:[7]

> Each leader "improves" from the point of view of the membership, through one method or another, the social milieu. Each widens the social field for participation of others (and indirectly her own social space) by ingratiating them into activities, introducing new activities, and by fostering tolerance on the part of one member towards another. Each leader shows a feeling for when to censure and when to praise and apparently is intellectually and emotionally "uncomfortable" when others are "unhappy" or "left-out."

Second, the ability of the overchosen person to handle his own emotional problems minimizes the cost to others of interaction with him. Jennings notes further:[8]

> Moreover, each leader appears to succeed in controlling her own moods, at least to the extent of not inflicting negative feelings of depression or anxiety upon others. Each appears to hold her own counsel and not to confide her personal worries except to a selected friend or two; even among leaders between each other this very careful reticence is usual. Each appears able to establish rapport quickly and effectively with a wide range of other personalities and to win their confidence. Each appears to possess to a greater or less degree unusual capacity to identify with others to the extent of feeling solicitude for them and to act in their behalf. By one manner of behaving or another, each leader lightens the "burdens" of other members of the group.

For a quite different population, male college undergraduates, a similar picture of the overchosen emerges: They possess traits that increase the rewards and decrease the costs of others (Bonney, Hoblit, & Dreyer, 1953). A study of characteristics of people who are rejected sociometrically is also consistent with exchange theory (Kidd, 1951). Such persons have been shown to display domineering, belligerent, inconsiderate behaviors which raise the costs to other persons of interacting with them.

---

[7]Reprinted by permission from Helen H. Jennings. *Leadership and isolation.* (2nd ed.) New York: Longmans, Green & Co., Inc., 1950. P. 203. Copyright by David McKay Company, Inc.

[8]*Ibid.*, pp. 203–204.

Choice, group factors, and exchange theory

Characteristics of the overchosen mentioned in the previous section may account for consistencies among the choice statuses of an individual in the various groups to which he belongs, since the same characteristics will facilitate favorable reward-cost outcomes in virtually any group. But other observations indicate that many individual characteristics are related to choice status because of (1) special characteristics of other group members, (2) properties of the group, and (3) the general situation in which interaction occurs (Jennings, 1950; Bonney, Hoblit, & Dreyer, 1953).

Homans's analysis of some of Jennings's findings makes the point that the desirability of traits depends upon who judges them. During the study of these girls, who were incarcerated in a training school, housemothers were interviewed and the behaviors that housemothers approved and disapproved of in the various girls were noted. The girls had been divided on the basis of their choices into three classes: the overchosen, the average-chosen, and the underchosen. An analysis of the two sets of data suggested that in *most* instances, both the housemothers and the girls found the same characteristics rewarding. The girls overchosen by their fellow inmates were seen by the housemothers as possessing approved traits and those who were underchosen, disapproved traits. As Homans (1961) notes, the exceptions were consistent with exchange theory:

> The few kinds of behavior that the housemothers disapproved of but mentioned the overchosen most often as displaying these were just the kinds of behavior that the girls themselves were apt to have looked on much more favorably. Their rebellious behavior, described as "refusing to do what is requested by a person in authority," initiatory behavior ("behavior considered as too self-directive and too self-confident"), and reticent behavior ("does not bring personal problems to the housemother") were surely characteristic of independent girls, ready to lead and support their fellows in standing up to the housemother on occasion. If, in short, the housemothers found rewarding most of the activities provided by the overchosen, the girls themselves probably found all of their activities rewarding. And the more valuable to the other members of her group were the activities that a girl performed, the higher was the esteem in which they held her. (P. 160)

Further illustration of the point that the relation between choice status and individual characteristics is affected by the character of the group is the fact that a trait may be associated with choice status because its possession may facilitate the achievement of some goal which members share. Characteristics popularly associated with leadership, such as intelligence, knowledge, and aggressiveness, might lead to popularity in a situation where the accomplishment of some task was highly rewarding to the group.

When the individual characteristics are of an attitudinal character, those whose opinions and behavior correspond to group norms have high choice status. One of the major rewards people achieve in interaction is consensual validation. The person whose opinions and behavior correspond to the norms provides rewards to a great many others in the group at very low costs to himself. He does so since norms are by definition widely shared with respect to objects of importance to group members.

Similarity, mutual attraction, and exchange theory

The explanation in terms of exchange theory for the general finding of similarity between persons who choose each other requires analysis of the implications of similarity for costs and rewards in interaction. The similarities observed between friends on a variety of social-background and demographic characteristics, such as religion, rural-urban background, class in college, and age, may well be a product of two processes.

First, many such characteristics are related through the social structure to frequency of interaction. Other things being equal, persons in the same college class or in the same age category would be expected to interact more frequently because of the greater opportunity for interaction. As noted earlier, opportunity to interact is related to attraction. Thus the similarity of friends to each other may result simply from the fact that similar persons have more opportunities to interact and consequently to become friends. Second, similarity in background characteristics[9] is associated with similarity in values. Similarity in values is rewarding because each person, at very low cost to himself, can provide consensual validation to the other.

Similarity in abilities and personality traits is a more complex matter, since rewards and costs depend in part on the particular ability or trait. With certain traits or abilities, the attraction between similar persons may rest on the fact that the trait or ability allows them to engage in an activity which is mutually rewarding. This is most obvious in the case of abilities and skills. The possession of similar skills at bridge, for instance, allows persons to engage in an activity not possible with nonplayers. In this connection Festinger (1954) has presented a theory, and has cited considerable evidence consistent with it, involving the assumption that individuals have a need to compare their abilities with someone who has similar abilities. Since interaction with those who are similar would generally lead to satisfaction of this need for comparison, attraction should occur as a consequence.

Exchange theory also explains the contradictory findings with respect to personality traits. Persons who are similar in such traits as the need for order would be likely to find interaction most profitable. On some other traits, persons with different but complementary traits would probably provide each other with maximum reward at minimum cost. Again the combination of a nurturant and a dependent person may be cited as an illustration.

---

[9]Lazarsfeld and Merton (1954) have discussed similarity in background under the term "status homophily."

STUDY QUESTIONS

13. *Describe exchange theory, defining the following terms: reward, cost, profit, outcome, and comparison level.*

14. *Show how exchange theory explains the characteristics of the overchosen and the underchosen.*

Exchange theory and opportunity to interact

One of the most intriguing questions about interpersonal attraction is why propinquity and other factors that affect opportunity to interact are associated with liking. Although individual characteristics have been emphasized as important determinants of attraction, the mere ease and volume of interaction also has rather strong effects on attraction. As Homans noted some years ago, "You can get to like some pretty queer customers if you go around with them long enough (1950, p. 115).

Thibaut and Kelley (1959) have suggested a number of ways in which physical proximity may be related to attraction. First, those who are located close to each other are more likely to interact because of the ease of initiating such interaction. This in turn heightens the possibility that they will discover behaviors that are rewarding to both.

Second, persons who are physically close are often more similar than those who are physically distant. For instance, people who live in the same neighborhood usually have the same socioeconomic background and are often of similar ethnic and religious backgrounds. As has just been noted, similarities in status in turn are associated with similarities in value.

A third way in which interaction may be related to liking has been suggested by Newcomb (1956). As persons interact, or to use Newcomb's term, engage in communicative behavior, they exchange information. This in itself increases the degree to which they are similar and contributes further to attraction.

Fourth, with continued interaction each person is better able to predict the behavior of the other. Such predictability reduces the costs of interaction and increases the level of rewards exchanged. Such costs as the effort exerted in learning how the other person will respond to various behaviors or the anxiety generated over doing or saying the wrong thing are reduced as one gets to know another person well enough to predict his responses. Such predictability also allows one to elicit rewarding behavior more effectively from the other person. The net result is a more favorable reward-cost outcome.

A fifth factor, noted by both Homans and Thibaut and Kelley, is that interaction with those who are physically close costs less in time and effort than interaction with those more distant. Other things being equal, then, the profit experienced in relations with more accessible persons is higher. Thibaut and Kelley suggest that in view of this, relations maintained over some distance must be more rewarding than relations between persons who are physically close. They cite a study providing some support for this supposition (Williams, 1959). When residents of a suburban housing development had friends residing outside the immediate community, they had greater agreement with these friends on values than with persons residing in the same area. As observed earlier, an important reward that individuals gain in their interaction with others is support for their values.

Other findings cited previously fall conveniently into this framework of rewards and costs intrinsic or extrinsic to the relation (Sidowski, Wycoff, & Tabory, 1956; Sidowski, 1957; Kelley et al., 1962). Liking other persons who like us in turn, who see us in a favorable light, and who recognize both our virtues and our faults is consistent with a reward-cost viewpoint. If we assume, moreover, that the effects of rewards experienced in a given situation generalize to other aspects of the situation, including persons, then the finding that people who are present in rewarding situations are liked is also understandable within this framework (Kelley et al., 1962).

Summary: Exchange theories of attraction

Exchange theories view attraction as a function of the degree to which persons achieve in their interaction with others a reward-cost outcome in excess of some minimum level. Any activity on the part of one person that contributes to the gratification of the needs of another is considered a reward. Costs include punishments incurred and deterrents in interacting with another person, such as fatigue, anxiety, and fear of embarrassment, as well as rewards foregone because of the interaction. The reward-cost outcome must be at least slightly above some minimum level of what the person feels is his due. This level is influenced by past experiences in the relation and in comparable relations, perceptions of what others like oneself are obtaining, and perceptions of costs and rewards obtainable in alternative relations. These influence the comparison level, a standard against which satisfaction is judged.

Exchange theory provides an explanation of why persons in a group receive widely different number of choices: Some members provide high rewards at minimum costs to those they interact with, and others supply only small rewards at high cost. Exchange theory also offers an explanation of why similarity between persons leads to mutual attraction. Similarity in social background and in values provides high rewards at low cost to both members of the dyad. Similarity in abilities, and to a lesser extent in personality traits, has comparable effects. In some instances different or complementary traits may be the basis of a high reward-cost outcome in interaction. The fact that high opportunity for interaction leads to liking is also consistent with exchange theory, because of the lesser cost involved in such interaction. It may be concluded that exchange theory succeeds in integrating and making sense out of a wide variety of data on interpersonal attraction.

STUDY QUESTIONS

15. *How does exchange theory explain the fact that opportunity to interact increases the likelihood of choice?*

16. *What is accomplished by applying exchange theory to diverse findings on interpersonal attraction?*

Exchange theory and friendship formation

A major advantage of exchange theory is that it provides some integration between the diverse principles attempting to explain interpersonal attraction. Even more important, however, is that such a framework provides an explanation for the exceptions to these principles. Even a cursory examination of one's own friendships reveals exceptions. You may not like the person next door or someone whom you have had considerable interaction with. Your best friend and you may differ not only on some social-background characteristics but on a number of attitudes. He may on occasion criticize your faults or, even worse, your virtues. To account for these exceptions as well as to see better the principles previously set forth, let us turn to a *process* analysis of friendship formation.

This analysis will focus upon the sequential events and stages leading to the development of friendship, rather than the correlates of friendship that have already been discussed. These processes may be examined by describing them in terms of an imaginary group. Suppose that a group of students from various universities, all initially strangers to each other, meet for a weekend conference. The formation of dyads characterized by a relatively high rate of interaction and positive affect may be described in terms of the following sequence.

At the first meeting of the hypothetical group, beneath the hum of polite conversation a process termed *sampling and estimation* occurs. Each person explores, at varying degrees of cost to himself, the rewards available in potential relations with other persons around him. For example, although accidental factors operate at this phase, an important determinant of whether Mr. *A* will approach Miss *B* is his estimate of potential costs and rewards.

His estimate of cost will be affected by factors ranging from sheer distance — it takes less effort to talk to the girl standing close to him than to Miss *B*, who is across the room — to his estimate of how likely it would be that he could strike up a conversation with her. If she already is earnestly conversing with several others, he might be discouraged by the costs of breaking into the conversational circle and the likelihood that he would have to share with others the available rewards. These perceived costs and rewards are always weighed against estimates of reward-cost outcomes in other relations available at that time. As for estimation of rewards, a variety of cues might suggest to *A* that Miss *B* has possibilities in that direction. Perhaps her face, via processes discussed in Chapter 2 suggests that she has certain personality characteristics that *A* finds rewarding in others. She may, by her clothes or her manner, suggest that she would have the same interests as *A*, or perhaps she strikingly conforms to *A*'s ideas of beauty.

Assume that the approach is made and that *A* strikes up a conversation with *B*. The conversation, initially at least, may be governed by the dictates of politeness, but a certain amount of exploration may also be noted. For instance, one feature frequently characteristic of opening conversations is that each person attempts to discover what he has in common with the other. Inquiries are made about where the other comes from, whether he knows a mutual acquaintance, what his college major is, and perhaps what he thinks about the purpose of the student conference. What each person encounters in the other depends in large part on what aspects of himself each discloses. This is in part determined by the strength of his desire to continue interacting, which in turn depends on the costs and rewards being exchanged and the estimates that he makes of future costs and rewards relative to those anticipated in alternative relations. It also depends on the estimate he has of the effects of various disclosures.

At this point there begins another process, which for want of a better term we have labeled bargaining. The term *bargaining* may suggest a highly conscious and rational process, and in this respect the word is inappropriate. The process is not highly conscious; yet actions occur that have the character of the marketplace. Each person behaves in order to motivate the other to produce rewarding behavior.

In part, such attempts take the form of certain strategies whose common aim is to distort the other person's perception of what he is giving and receiving and what he may expect in the future. One may exaggerate one's value to others and the costs to oneself of what one is offering. Upon learning of Miss *B*'s interest in skiing, for example, *A* may exaggerate his own interest in this area. Or both persons may indicate that other alternatives are open to them and that they are incurring some costs in continuing to talk with each other rather than reaping rewards in alternative associations.

In part, however, attempts to elicit rewards from the other person take the form of giving progressively greater rewards that prompt the other to return in kind. At the same time, each person may also attempt to lower the costs of the other so as to improve the other's profit position and ensure the continuation of the exchange. Both may, for instance, discover a difference in views on some subject and tacitly agree to avoid the subject. Each recognizes that the costs of an argument might reduce the profit of the other person to the point where the rewards being currently received from him would be eliminated by termination of the relation. Where the bargaining process progresses in this fashion, a spiral effect can be observed. As each person is increasingly rewarded, he in turn is motivated to increase the profit of the other. This process would be expected to stabilize at the point where the costs of increasing the profit of the other person become so large that more can be gained from some alternative relation.

Although this discussion has focused on the dyad, the interaction of Mr. *A* and Miss *B* goes on against a background of alternatives. In fact, during the course of the evening each may sample alternatives and estimate possibilities in other relations. Such processes, however, have been attenuated by the developing relation between *A* and *B*, because interaction with one person necessarily reduces time spent with another. Other persons have also been forming subgroups. Such grouping progressively increases the costs of interaction with alternative persons. Mr. *A* might well have reaped a higher rate of profit with Miss *C*, but her involvement with other persons discouraged the processes of sampling and bargaining that might have resulted in attraction between them.

Another process is called *commitment*. Members of a pair progressively reduce sampling and bargaining with other persons. They commit themselves to a particular other person. Mr. *A* and Miss *B* stop casting a roving eye and settle down to an evening together. Should this association endure beyond the evening, and should the couple continue to associate on an increasingly exclusive basis, a final stage termed *institutionalization* is reached.

In institutionalization, shared expectations emerge recognizing the rightness or legitimacy of the exclusiveness of the relation and patterns of exchange that have developed. These expectations will be shared not only by members of the dyad but by other group members as well. Perhaps by the end of the conference Mr. *A* and Miss *B* are "going steady," a relation that has become institutionalized in our society.

The formation of a dyad may be summarized in terms of exchange theory as follows. When a group of strangers meet, each person samples interaction with various other persons and estimates the profit entailed in various alternative interactions. Generally he commits himself to the interactions yielding the highest profit. In a dyad he engages in a process of bargaining, by means of which he elicits rewards from the other person in exchange for his own rewarding behavior toward the person. Bargaining is characterized by an attempt to obtain maximum rewards at minimum cost. In part, the process may include some misrepresentation of one's own resources in order to encourage rewarding responses from the other person. As a whole, bargaining tends toward maximizing the rewards and minimizing the costs of both members of the dyad. As a relation develops, a stage called commitment is arrived at. In this stage, the process of sampling and estimating interactions with alternative persons is minimized or stopped altogether, and the members of the dyad focus on their interaction with each other. An end stage may be reached when the relation becomes institutionalized, as in engagement or marriage.

In the case of Mr. *A* and Miss *B*, the processes of sampling and estimation, bargaining, commitment, and institutionalization were telescoped into a relatively brief period. More typically, they would continue much longer. Also, in an attempt to present an overall view, certain details have not been mentioned. We now turn to some of these.

Changes in costs and rewards

As mentioned earlier, exchange theories view attraction as a function of the reward-cost outcomes that persons experience in relation to some level of expectation of what these outcomes should be (the *comparison level*). From this standpoint any change in affect in a positive or negative direction can be analyzed in terms of either a change in costs and rewards or a change in comparison levels. Thus, a person may be less attracted to another if his cost rises rapidly relative to his reward or if his comparison level rises.

Changes in the costs and rewards that persons experience in relation with others may stem from any of five sources. First, changes may occur simply as a function of past exchanges. As each person continues to exchange rewards, the behavior rewarding to the other may become increasingly costly to produce due to fatigue, embarrassment, or loss of alternative rewards. At the same time, the value of the reward may decrease as the relevant needs of each person become satiated. Or changes in the direction of a reduction in costs and an increase in rewards might occur similarly as a function of past exchanges. Dependencies may be established, and the needs created may be satisfied by behavior that, as a result of practice, is both more effective and produced at less cost.

To illustrate a decline in outcome, consider a hypothetical marital relation in which one partner makes continual demands for support of a precarious self conception. Such demands may be met by his partner at increasing costs in terms of feelings of loss of integrity, increasing disgust, loss of opportunities to engage in rewarding interaction with others, etc. To illustrate an increase in reward-cost outcomes, consider a marital relation in which the once self-sufficient bachelor becomes increasingly dependent on the domestic services of his wife, while she in turn becomes increasingly skilled at providing them. A related point is that the experience gained as a function of past exchanges makes the behavior of the other person more predictable. This in turn lowers the cost of uncertainty and increases the ability of each to elicit rewarding behavior from the other person.

A second source of change in costs and rewards arises from shifts in the characteristics of the dyad members. Although this may occur as a result of previous exchanges in the relation, frequently such changes come about in other ways. As a result of experiences in other relations and with the nonsocial environment, new opinions, attitudes, and self conceptions are developed that require consensual validation. In addition, other kinds of needs emerge and new goals are embraced. These changes alter both the reward value and the costs of a person's behavior to others and theirs to him. Such changes may lead to increased attraction between group members, as happens when one adopts a new attitude and finds that another person whose previous views were of little account is now a valuable ally because he holds a similar view. A decline in attraction may also occur. Behavior of the other person which formerly had high reward value may now carry less value, or perhaps the behavior demanded by the other which at one time was expressed with little cost now comes at considerable sacrifice.

A third source of change is modification of the external situation so that the behavior of persons in the relation acquires different reward-cost values. The sudden increase in the attraction toward the expert when the situation demands his skills or knowledge is a case in point. Another is the case of the successful executive whose wife was frugal and thus helpful during his struggling early days, but whose behavior is inappropriate and actually costly now that success has been achieved.

A fourth source of change lies within the relation itself. A person experiencing profitable interactions becomes increasingly motivated to ensure the continuation of such interaction by increasing the profit of the other. Such a cycle in which each person motivates the other and is similarly motivated in turn can also work in the reverse direction. A person whose reward-cost outcome is adversely affected may be motivated to reduce the profits experienced by the other, who retaliates and thereby continues the cycle.

A fifth form of change occurs through the association of behaviors having certain reward-cost values with behaviors having quite different values. One way in which this happens is that behaviors of each person which were initially neutral will, through association with an exchange of behaviors which are rewarding or costly, become rewarding or costly in themselves. A person may come to enjoy playing bridge because such play has been associated with other rewards exchanged during the game. Another way in which this association occurs is that the behavior of each person, which was initially rewarding to the other, may in time become rewarding to the actor himself because it has been regularly associated with rewarding responses of the other. A person may enjoy playing bridge because playing has been previously associated with appreciative responses from his partner. By a similar process of association, behavior that is costly to oneself or the other person may gradually become inhibited

In sum, costs and rewards may change as a function of (1) past exchanges which shift reward-cost values of current behaviors, (2) changes in the characteristics of the dyad members occurring through training, education, or other experiences, (3) changes in external circumstances that introduce new rewards and costs or modify the values of old ones, (4) sequential factors in the relation itself, such as the augmentation of satisfaction in current relations as a result of previously rewarding experiences in the dyad, and (5) associations with other behaviors having different reward-cost values.

STUDY QUESTIONS

17. *Explain the following processes: sampling and estimation, bargaining, commitment, and institutionalization.*

18. *Describe the five factors leading to changes in costs and rewards.*

Changes in comparison level

Costs and rewards might remain the same, yet affect in a relation might change through a lowering or raising of the persons' comparison level. The comparison level may be affected by a number of factors, including reward-cost experiences in the dyad, the perception of the experiences of others in relations like one's own, and what each of the participants estimates he might legitimately expect in alternative relations.

Thibaut and Kelley (1959) suggest that the comparison level will gradually rise as the outcomes of the dyad members become progressively better or decline as they become worse. This rise in comparison level relative to the profits received may underlie the generally experienced decline in noticeable satisfaction after the initial glow that characterizes many relations in their early stages, such as an infatuation with a member of the opposite sex. Similarly, the decline in comparison level when outcomes are reduced may well explain how persons find satisfaction in situations that they never thought they would. The common emotion of envy when another person's outcomes are improved relative to one's own may be seen as a rise in comparison level on perceiving the improved outcomes of the other. In particular, where the other is one's partner in an exchange, such envy may contain a strong element of feelings of injustice.

This discussion has identified factors that influence the level of affect, but has not specifically referred to the determinants of the permanence of a relation. Obviously, affect is important to permanence. In most relations, positive affect and permanence are associated, but in some this is not so. Persons may remain in them even though the outcomes they receive are below their comparison level and they are repelled rather than attracted to the other person.

The loveless marriage is a case in point. The couple may stay together even though the satisfactions received are below the level that would result in positive attraction. They do so because they perceive that in the alternatives available, the costs are greater or the rewards are less. If it is the wife whose outcomes are below the comparison level, she may feel that she has no chance of getting a better husband and that without one, the prospects for adequate support for her and her children are dim. Other costs that function to preserve such relations include guilt over depriving children of a loved parent, religious sanctions, and fear of loneliness. Thibaut and Kelley introduce the term *comparison level for alternatives* to handle such situations. As long as a relation provides outcomes above the comparison level for alternatives, it will endure even though such outcomes are below the comparison level and the persons are not attracted to each other.

In sum, a crucial element determining the amount of satisfaction gained in a dyadic relation is the relation of the reward-cost outcome to the comparison level. The comparison level is the level of profit that individuals in the relation feel entitled to by virtue of previous experiences, the observation of other dyads, or normative standards. As a relation develops increasing profits for both members, the comparison level itself also rises, making the increase in profit appear less substantial than it would be if the comparison level remained constant. Similarly, since the comparison level falls as profits in the relation decline, the relation continues to yield satisfaction even though it may appear unrewarding to outsiders with different comparison levels. Finally, the comparison level for alternatives relative to the profits gained determines the durability of the relation. A dyad may persist even though outcomes are below the comparison level because the potential for satisfactions in other dyads is even lower.

Using exchange theory as a framework, this section has focused on process and on the simplest structure, that of the dyad. Larger structures, and particularly the relation between such structures, will be discussed in Chapter 13 on subgroup formation and intergroup relations. The remaining pages of this chapter deal with certain aspects of structures larger than the dyad to which exchange theory may profitably be applied.

STUDY QUESTIONS

19. *Explain how satisfaction may change even though cost-reward outcomes remain unchanged.*
20. *What factors alter the comparison level?*
21. *What is the difference between the comparison level and the comparison level for alternatives?*
22. *How is the comparison level for alternatives related to the stability of a dyad?*

Elements of Structure

THE CHOICE CRITERION AND STRUCTURE

The affect structure revealed by a sociometric test depends in part on the choice criterion used in the sociometric questionnaire. In her early work, Jennings (1950) found that the choice pattern differed depending upon whether the choice was of persons to spend leisure time with or persons to work or live with. Her analysis of the reasons her subjects gave for choosing or rejecting persons suggested two bases for choice. On the criterion of spending leisure time, subjects chose a person on the basis of her ability to satisfy their social-emotional needs, such as the need for support for one's self conception, for consensual validation about the world, etc. Choices made according to the criterion of living or working together appeared to be based on the person's group role, her contributions to the smooth functioning of the group, her conformity to group standards, etc.

Jennings refers to the structure revealed by the use of a leisure-time criterion as a *psychegroup* and that revealed by the use of a working- or living-type criterion as a *sociogroup*. These two terms are simply analytic devices to emphasize two different bases of choice. A given choice in any situation reflects both to some degree. The distinction is nevertheless useful to keep in mind, because the basis of choice affects certain features of the structure.

Jennings found, for instance, that in contrast to a sociogroup, a psychegroup is characterized by higher mutuality: each person makes fewer choices, but choices are more frequently reciprocated. Among over four hundred girls in a state institution, about 70 percent of the choice on a leisure-time criterion were mutual. In contrast, on a living-working group criterion, approximately 35 percent of the choices were mutual. In addition, choices were more evenly distributed when a leisure-time criterion was used: fewer persons received a large number of choices, and more persons received at least one choice.

These findings might be expected from our discussions of interpersonal attraction and of the nature of the difference between the bases of attraction in a psychegroup and a sociogroup. When the criterion is a sociogroup one, choices of all members should be concentrated on a few persons whose group role is crucial. When the choice of another person is in terms of a psychegroup criterion, choices should be more widely distributed over the membership, since needs of members differ markedly. Mutuality would be higher also in a psychegroup since reciprocity of choice would be associated with the satisfaction of social-emotional needs.

MEMBER CHARACTERISTICS AND GROUP STRUCTURE

Given a particular criterion, the affect structure will be influenced by the distribution of the needs and resources of the persons involved. What characteristics will become relevant will depend in part on the individuals, their particular personalities, and the alternatives open to them for obtaining satisfaction, as well as the demands of the situation. The situation affects the resultant structure by determining the relevance of individual characteristics and the frequency and ease of interaction. In addition, what characteristics become relevant will depend in part on the past history of the group and values that have emerged in this historical process. One of Newcomb's (1961) groups very early began to differentiate along the lines of urban-rural background. This was accompanied by the development of stereotypes in terms of which members of each group saw the other. The stereotypes hastened the process of structural differentiation by providing the members with perceptions of similarities and differences which, as already noted, influence attraction.

STUDY QUESTIONS

23. *What is a psychegroup and a sociogroup? How do they differ in structure?*
24. *Explain the above differences in structure in terms of exchange theory.*
25. *How may group structure be affected by member characteristics?*

The compromise process

No analysis based on the characteristics of its members will provide a complete explanation of choice. One reason is that persons may not accurately assess the characteristics of others, and another is that the final structure which emerges is always a compromise. The group structure moves toward an equilibrium in which each person's position in the affect structure is the best he can obtain in terms of his reward-cost outcomes. Two individual features of the sociometric structure are a resultant of this compromise process or tendency toward equilibrium. These are the development of mutuality and the tendency to choose persons equal to oneself in choice status.

Over time, the attraction between persons becomes increasingly mutual. Newcomb, in the living-group study described previously, found that mutuality increased with increasing acquaintance, particularly among persons who were not excessively popular or unpopular.

Newcomb suggests that these findings are consistent with the principle that systems tend toward a balanced state. Assuming that the common focus of orientation in this case is the self, and further, that persons usually evaluate themselves positively, the perception that another person who is liked does not return the feeling would be strain-inducing. Such strain would be reduced by decreasing one's attraction toward this person. An individual would similarly experience strain if he perceived that another person toward whom he had little feeling had a warm regard for him. A more balanced state would be achieved by developing warm feelings toward that person.

Another way of stating these ideas is that persons choose others who are equal in choice status. According to Homans (1961), the finding that girls chose as leisure-time companions others who were equal to them in their work-living status is consistent with the proposition. Homans's reasoning is based on the relation between positions in two different sociometric structures, one representing personal liking or attraction and the other representing evaluations of contributions to the group. But the work of Newcomb (1961), as well as that of Backman and Secord (1964) who have also published evidence showing that pairs of mutually attracted persons in a group tend toward equality of choice status, suggests that on just the undifferentiated criterion of liking, those who are equal in attraction status are preferred. Mutuality and the choice of persons who are similar in choice status to the chooser may be thought of as an outcome of the stabilization of relations, where each person is obtaining his best available reward-cost outcomes.

An examination of certain departures from this state of equilibrium should identify the forces toward balance. Two assumptions are made. One is that the order of persons by choice status represents the order of value attached to their behavior and to their other characteristics. A second assumption, true by definition, is that the order of choice status reflects the quantity of alternative relations available to each member.

The greater the number who choose a given person, the greater the number who are willing to establish a relation with him.

Consider first the case where person *A* of low status is attracted to person *B* of high status. The chance for the development of a mutually satisfactory relation is low, because both are apt to experience outcomes that are lower than in some alternative relation. *B*'s profit in such a relation is apt to be relatively low because of the low value of *A*'s behavior. In this instance we would expect him not to continue the relation.

Under certain circumstances, *B* might be able to exact from *A* behavior that is of high value to him. But since *A* has low choice status, such valuable behavior is not typical of him and would normally be produced only at high cost to *A*. Were this the case, the outcomes to *A* would be low, and he would withdraw from the relation. Such a relation would be maintained only in instances where the initial assumptions stated above did not hold, as where some aspects of *A*'s behavior are of particular value to *B* but not to others, where this behavior can be produced by *A* at low cost, or finally, where *B* is prevented either through inaccurate assessment of his alternatives or by some force of circumstances from establishing more valuable alternative relations.

The fact that movements toward mutuality and equality of choice status between choosers are observable fairly early in a group, particularly at high levels of attraction, suggests that persons become relatively adept at gauging their chances of satisfactory outcomes in a relation. This undoubtedly stems from previous experiences in relations with persons of markedly different status, that led to poor outcomes. Probably "crushes" in early dating characterized by lack of mutuality and equality provide useful training, leading persons in the courtship process to select and fall in love with those whose value in the marriage market is roughly the same.

The compromise process, then, consists of adjustments in relations among group members in the direction of a state of equilibrium in which each person's reward-cost outcomes are maximized. This state of balance is characterized by many mutual choices, especially between persons equal in choice status.

STUDY QUESTIONS

26. *Describe what is meant by the compromise process. What is its relation to mutuality and choice status?*

27. *How does the compromise process contribute to the permanence of a relation?*

Cohesiveness

As previously noted, members of a dyad are attracted to each other to the extent that their reward-cost outcomes exceed their comparison levels. However, persons may remain in a relation even where the outcomes experienced drop below the comparison level and they are no longer attracted. They remain as long as the outcomes are above the comparison level for alternatives. In this instance, the binding force is not attraction but the awareness that the outcomes in the relation are better than can be obtained outside. With groups larger than a dyad, the term *cohesiveness* is employed to refer to the forces acting on group members to remain in the group. While cohesiveness is generally equated with attraction to the group, our previous analysis suggests that in some instances this interpretation may be inappropriate. Typically, discussions of cohesiveness distinguish between the following three bases of attraction to the group, each basis referring to different sources of rewards (Thibaut, 1950; Festinger & Kelley, 1951; Libo, 1953; Cartwright & Zander, 1960).

1. The basis of attraction to the group may lie in the interaction itself. In this instance the group is characterized as highly cohesive because the interaction results in high reward-cost outcomes to participants. This may occur because the needs of various members are complementary, their interests and attitudes are similar, or the organization of the group and the situation in which interaction takes place are conducive to cooperative, friendly interaction.

2. Members may be attracted to the group because each individual finds the group activities *inherently* rewarding. Groups formed to pursue a particular recreation or hobby, such as golf, tennis, or chess, are examples.

3. Members may be attracted to a group because membership is a means to achieving other ends. They may perceive that only through group action can they achieve a goal, such as getting a particular piece of legislation enacted. Or perhaps membership may be a source of favorable reward-cost outcomes in terms of the status one can achieve among persons outside the group.

While it has been amply demonstrated that these various sources of attraction contribute to cohesiveness (Cartwright & Zander, 1960, pp. 69–162), little attention has been paid to two points which exchange theory would underscore. First, attraction to the group is dependent on the *comparison levels of group members*. Second, the total force operating on group members to remain in a group is a function not only of attraction to the group, but also of the *outcomes available in alternative relations outside the group.*

Some groups are highly cohesive even though their members are experiencing low reward-cost outcomes. Low-status, underprivileged groups have been shown to have high cohesiveness both in and out of the laboratory (Pope, 1942; Thibaut, 1950). This reflects a higher level of attraction than might be expected on the basis of outcomes experienced by the members of such groups. But outcome must be considered in relation to comparison level. For underprivileged, low-status groups, the low quality of outcomes available in alternative relations, the low level of outcomes previously experienced, and perceptions of what other persons like oneself are obtaining all suggest a low comparison level. Since attraction to the group is a function of the degree to which outcomes are above the comparison level, attraction to the group in this instance may well be higher than would be expected from the relatively low outcomes alone. Persons may remain in a relation even when attraction is absent and their outcomes fall below their comparison level. This occurs, however, only if their outcomes remain above their comparison level for alternatives. They are held in the group by the realization that leaving it would result in even lower outcomes.

STUDY QUESTIONS

28. *Define group cohesiveness.*
29. *What are three kinds of rewards that persons gain through group membership?*
30. *What variables in addition to outcomes must be taken into consideration in explaining the cohesiveness of a group?*

Summary and Conclusions

By asking members of a group to indicate their preferences for association with other members, various graphical or quantitative descriptions of the affect structure of a group may be obtained. This technique is useful in identifying persons who are highly popular and who are relatively isolated. It is also useful in identifying cliques and other aspects of the group, such as its state of morale. Because of the importance of the affect structure, many investigators have studied the factors that determine choice. Empirical evidence indicates that members are likely to choose (1) those with whom they have a greater opportunity to interact, (2) those who have the most desirable characteristics in terms of the norms and values of the group, (3) those who are most similar to themselves in attitudes, values, and social-background characteristics, and (4) those who are perceived as choosing oneself or assigning favorable characteristics to oneself.

Several theories have been proposed to explain the attraction between members of a group. Newcomb's theory of strain toward symmetry postulates that individuals strive to achieve a state of balance. Balance is present when persons *A* and *B* are attracted to each other and hold similar attitudes toward objects of common relevance to them. When imbalance occurs, one or more of the component parts are changed to restore balance. The various components of the system are not independent, but have mutual effects upon each other. Attitudes toward the self and toward other group members are of particular significance for the determination of strain or balance. Studies of living groups by Newcomb and by others are generally consistent with his theory.

Winch's theory of need complementarity proposes two forms of interpersonal attraction based upon the need structures of individuals in a dyad. In one, persons A and B are complementary in need structure because A is high and B is low on the same need. In the other, A is high on a need, and B is low on a different need. Both situations are believed to be complementary because each member of such dyads finds the behavior of his partner rewarding. Empirical evidence is at present mainly negative.

In Secord and Backman's interpersonal congruency theory, the extent to which the other person is perceived as behaving in a manner congruent with the self concept is taken as a basis for attraction, but empirical findings in support of it must be regarded as tentative.

Exchange theories view attraction as a function of the degree to which persons achieve in their interaction with others a reward-cost outcome in excess of some minimum level. Any activity on the part of one person that contributes to the gratification of the needs of another is considered a reward. Costs include punishments incurred, such as fatigue, anxiety, and fear of embarrassment, as well as rewards foregone in other relations because of the interaction. For attraction to occur, the reward-cost outcome must be at least slightly above the comparison level, a standard against which satisfaction is judged. This level is influenced by experiences in comparable relations, past levels of satisfaction in this relation, perceptions of what others like oneself are obtaining, and perceptions of costs and rewards obtainable in alternative relations. Exchange theory succeeds in integrating the preceding theories and making sense out of a wide variety of data on interpersonal attraction.

Friendship formation is explained in terms of exchange theory as follows. When strangers meet, they sample interactions with other persons, estimate the profit obtained in each, and commit themselves to interactions yielding the highest profit. Through bargaining, they maximize rewards and minimize cost. When commitment becomes firm, sampling and estimation are reduced or eliminated altogether.

Once a dyad has been formed, the relation may change with changes in either reward-cost outcomes or the comparison level. Costs and rewards may change as a function of the following: (1) past exchanges that change reward-cost values of current behaviors, (2) shifts in cost-reward values because of alterations in the characteristics of the dyad members through training, education, or other experiences, (3) changes in the external circumstances that introduce new rewards and costs or modify the values of old ones, (4) sequential factors in the relation itself, such as the increasing development of mutually rewarding affect, and (5) associations with other behaviors having different reward-cost values. Changes in the comparison level may occur as a result of reward-cost experiences in the dyad or the observation of the outcomes of persons in other dyads.

The durability of the relation is determined by the comparison level for alternatives: the dyad persists as long as the outcomes achieved are greater than can be expected in alternative relations.

Variation in sociometric structure is based on a number of factors. When choice is based on a leisure-time criterion, structure is characterized more by mutual choice and an even distribution of choice. When choice is based upon a work criterion, choices are more concentrated on the few persons who play a crucial role in carrying out the task. The compromise process contributes to the group structure that emerges. This process consists of adjustments in relations among group members in the direction of a state of equilibrium in which each person's reward-cost outcomes are maximized. This state of balance is characterized by many mutual choices, especially between persons equal in choice status.

Cohesiveness is related to the affect structure of the group. The term refers to the forces acting on group members to remain in the group. In part, they may be represented by attractions having three different bases: (1) high reward-cost outcomes stemming directly from interaction between members, (2) group activities that are rewarding for their own sake, and (3) membership in the group as a means to attaining other ends. Attraction is also based upon the comparison levels of group members, and the total force operating on group members to remain in the group is a function not only of attraction to the group, but also of the outcomes available in alternative relations outside the group.

chapter eight

SOCIAL POWER

Social power, like affect, is also a pervasive aspect of social interaction. Considered on a large scale, it colors relations among nations. It plays an important role in government and political parties. Various types of organizations, large and small, are organized according to a power structure. In groups of any size, some members are more powerful than others, and this fact has important consequences for group functioning. Further, virtually all forms of interaction involve differences in the relative power of the participants to influence one another. Thus, power differences enter into relations between supervisor and employee, parent and child, salesman and customer, politician and voter, doctor and patient, and teacher and student.

An analysis of power is essential to an understanding of the flow of interaction in a group and is necessary to explain the distribution of rewards and costs among group members. In the popular view of power relations, the power differential is assumed to stem from the personal characteristics of the individuals involved. As this chapter will show, however, power does not arise solely from personal characteristics, but is dependent upon the relation between persons and groups and the place of that relation in the context of the larger social structure.

In spite of the importance of social power in everyday relations, students of small-group behavior have expressed substantial interest in it only recently. Consequently some of the principles outlined here must be regarded as tentative and subject to verification by further research. As these principles are introduced, the relative degree of their tenability will be mentioned.

Most contemporary discussions of power[1] focus on the direct exercise of power by one member of a dyad on the other. Analyses of power within the framework of larger structures, where one person may exercise indirect influence over many others, are infrequent in the literature on the small group (French, 1956; Harary, 1959). Hence, direct power will be considered first, and more space will be devoted to it. Similarly, the focus in small-group research has been largely on the relations between two or more individuals rather than on subgroups or larger units. Some attention will be given to power in the latter context in Chapter 13 on intergroup relations.

Determinants of Direct Power

Either explicitly or implicitly, most contemporary discussions of the determinants of social power recognize three classes of variables: resources, dependencies, and alternatives. A *resource* is a property of an individual — a possession, an aspect of his behavior, or merely his presence — which enables him to affect the rewards and costs experienced by another person. The value of such resources is not determined solely by the property of the individual, but also by the *dependency* of the other person on him. For example, the beauty of a girl is a resource only in relation to those males who are attracted by feminine beauty. In situations where beauty in unimportant, it is unlikely to be a resource. In general, dependencies originate either from internal states, such as personality needs, or from the situation. An example of dependency arising from a situation is the need of a group for the services of an expert to solve a problem posed by an emergency.

The potentialities for influence in a relation between two persons are, however, dependent on more than just the characteristics of each person and the situation. They are also a function of the availability of *alternative* sources of reward and means of reducing costs. The power of a beautiful girl to attract men depends in part upon the availability to them of other beautiful girls, as well as the degree of sacrifice (cost) the men need to make to gain their favor. These simple examples do not exhaust the determinants of resources, dependencies, and alternatives. The following discussion identifies them in more detail.

RESOURCES

French and Raven (1959) have delineated types or bases of social power. Each type has associated with it certain costs and rewards. In addition, these investigators have related the types of power to each other

---

[1]French, 1956; French & Raven, 1959; Levinger, 1959; Blood & Wolfe, 1960; Emerson, 1962.

as well as to other variables, such as the strength of the power, the range of behavior involved, and the degree to which changes induced continue to be associated with the original source of influence.

Reward and coercive power

The first type of power they distinguish is *reward power*. This type, exerted on another person O by person P, is based on the perception by O that P has the ability to mediate rewards for him. A supervisor has power over an employee because the worker knows that his supervisor can recommend wage increases or perhaps even get him promoted. Similarly, a second type of power is called *coercive power* and is based on O's perception that P has the ability to mediate punishments for him. A supervisor is perceived as capable of withholding wage increases or of arranging for the worker's discharge.

These two types of power are similar in a number of respects. In both, the range of power is limited to behaviors for which P can reward or punish O. The strength of both appears to be a joint function of the magnitude of the rewards or punishments involved and the perceived probabilities that these will be incurred. These perceived probabilities are a function of two factors. One is the extent to which O thinks he is being observed by P. The greater the surveillance by P, the more likely O is to believe that his behavior will be rewarded or punished. The other is the past history of O's relation to P. If a supervisor has seldom rewarded or punished an employee, either directly or indirectly, his reward and coercive power is likely to be weak.

Referent power

Reward power has a property which coercive power lacks: It may gradually be transformed into *referent power*. Referent power is based on identification, or the desire to be like another person.[2] We have already encountered essentially this notion in Chaper 3, where Kelman proposed that identification is one form of social influence. A possible explanation of this transformation of reward into referent power is that, first, the exercise of reward power by P makes him attractive to O, and, second, his attractiveness makes him an object for identification. That reward power makes P attractive is suggested by an experiment demonstrating that individuals whose power was based solely on reward were rated more favorably than those having no power or those whose power was based solely on punishment (Brigante, 1958). French and Raven suggest that the strength of the referent power of P over O, as well as the range of behaviors to which it applies, will vary with the attractiveness of P to O.

While changes in O that result from referent power are initially de-

---

[2]The bases of identification are more fully discussed in Chapter 17. Reward is only one of a number of possible determinants of identification.

pendent on O's relation to P, some of them may in time become independent of P. Unlike reward or coercive power, the continuation of such changes is not dependent on observability by P of the particular behavior involved. Herein lies a distinction between the powers of parents and police officers: Parental power is largely referent power, but police power is based mainly on coercion. Thus, children eventually behave well in the absence of their parents, but traffic laws are frequently broken when no police officers are around. The question of surveillance as a necessary condition for control will be treated in more detail in Chapter 10.

Expert power

Expert power[3] is based on O's perception that P has some special knowledge in a given situation, as in the case of a patient who is influenced by his physician to follow a particular regimen. The strength of this type of power varies with the degree of expertness attributed by O to P and is limited to behavior relevant to such expert knowledge. Whether or not behavior induced by such means will persist depends upon its continued association with the advice of the expert. Continuation is not dependent, however, upon the degree to which this behavior is observable.

Legitimate power

Legitimate power is based on the acceptance by O of internalized norms and values which dictate that he accept influence from P. Because of certain characteristics such as age, sex, class, or caste, or because of his position in some recognized hierarchy, or because he has been designated by some authority, P is perceived as having a legitimate right to dictate O's behavior, at least in certain areas. In part, this is a source of the power held by military officers, corporation executives, government officials, and parents. The continuation of behavior induced by the exercise of legitimate power depends not on its observability but on the persistence of the underlying values and norms involved. The strength of legitimate power depends upon the degree of O's adherence to the underlying norms and values. Although legitimate power may on occasion cover a broad area of behavior, more frequently it is narrow in scope. For example, a mother may exert legitimate power over a wide range of her child's behavior, but a department head in a business firm must restrict his legitimate power to job-related behavior.

Resources and exchange theory

Although power theorists have used the concept of resources in arriving at a classification of forms of power, they have not usually treated the concept from the standpoint of exchange theory. Such treatment is useful because, as will be discussed in more detail later, each exercise of

---

[3]A more extended discussion of the determinants of expert power is given by Thibaut and Kelley (1959, p. 101).

power is characterized by an exchange. The more powerful person may exact compliance from the less powerful, but in return he is expected to give his good will, his approval, or some other resource.

The notion of resources may thus be translated into cost and reward terms. In the case of reward and coercive power, translation is simple. When a person tries to influence another, he holds out the promise of either gratifying that person's needs if he complies, or frustrating his needs if he refuses to comply. His intentions are either to reward the person for compliance or to raise the person's costs for noncompliance. The rewards and costs in referent power are rather complex and arise out of internal processes such as, for example, the process by which the child rewards himself with the assurance that a loved parent loves him in turn. The rewards obtained in expert power involve feelings of confidence and assurance gained when following the advice of the expert. The costs to be avoided in this instance are the alternative feelings of uncertainty and fear of failure.

Rewards and costs in legitimate power appear to be both internal and external. Individuals are rewarded with feelings of satisfaction when their own behavior conforms to their values and norms, and they incur costs in the form of guilt feelings when their behavior does not conform. For example, a mother who realizes that she has punished her child because of some personal problem of her own and not because of any misbehavior on his part may feel guilty. Rewards and costs in legitimate power may also arise from external sources: individuals are rewarded and punished by other persons who share these values.

An important contribution from exchange theory is that a person uses his resources to influence another only at some cost (Harsanyi, 1962). Thus, the strength of his power over another person is a function not only of his resources, but also of the cost of using them. A child who controls his parents through temper tantrums or hunger strikes does so at the cost of an emotional upheaval or hunger pangs. The more costly the resource is, the less the net strength of P's power over O. A lover who threatens to commit suicide if his loved one deserts him is using a very costly resource, his own life, and is not likely to be effective. A legislator may have a number of favors owed to him by various other legislators; these debts provide him with some power over their votes. But use of this power is costly; once the favors are returned, his power is lost. Thus, he is likely to use them only for issues very important to him on which he expects a close vote.

Continued exercise of power

The types of power differ in the extent to which they may be continually exercised and still remain effective. A change in the power relation resulting from exercise of it may occur in two ways: (1) through its effects on rewards and costs, and (2) through creation of conditions that alter the bases of power.

The first of these changes occurs because continued use of power by *P* over *O* directly affects the rewards or costs experienced. Repeated use of the same rewards by *P* may make them less satisfying to *O* as his needs become satiated. For example, as a person's salary continues to rise, his major needs become relatively satiated, and the costs in terms of responsibility and demands upon his time continue to rise. The promise of a further salary increase is likely to be less effective as a means of control over his behavior. Some rewards, however, increase dependency and result in an increase in power. The rewards provided each other by lovers in the early stages of their relation and the relative absence of costs during this period are one illustration.

An example of a condition resulting from the continued exercise of power that eventually changes the power base was noted in our earlier comment that reward power may be transformed into referent power. Similarly, the continued use of coercive power is likely to diminish *O*'s affect for *P* and decrease identification with him, thereby reducing *P*'s referent power. In contrast to reward and coercive power, the continued exercise of legitimate power is not apt to lead to an increase or diminution of power except where it might lead to further affirmation or to questioning of norms and values. Similarly, expert power is not apt to be affected by continued use except where its continuation increases or decreases *P*'s stature as an expert or results in *O* picking up the knowledge upon which *P*'s expert power is based.

Summary: Resources

A resource is a property of an individual—a possession, an aspect of his behavior, or merely his presence—which enables him to affect the rewards and costs experienced by another person. The value of a resource is not determined by the individual alone, but also by the dependency of the other person on him.

Five types of power have been distinguished, each based on somewhat different resources. The first is reward power, based upon the perception by *O* that *P* can directly or indirectly reward him. The second, coercive power, is the counterpart of reward power and is based on *O*'s perception that *P* can directly or indirectly punish him. Both kinds of power apply only to the behavior that *P* can reward or punish, and their strength is a joint function of the strength of the reward or punishment and the probability that it will be incurred. Reward power, however, has a property which coercive power lacks: It may gradually be transformed into a third type of power, referent power. Referent power is based on the mechanism of identification. Unlike reward and coercive power, it does not require continued surveillance of *O* by *P* in order to ensure conformity of *O*'s behavior to *P*'s wishes. A fourth type of power, expert power, stems from special knowledge *P* has which *O* needs. Fifth, legitimate power is based on the acceptance by *O* of internalized norms and values which dictate that he accept influence from *P*.

These types of power differ in the extent to which they may be continually exercised and still remain effective. A change in the power relation resulting from continued exercise may occur in two ways: (1) through its direct effects on rewards and cost, and (2) through creation of conditions that alter the bases of power. Thus, the continual use of certain kinds of rewards may lead to satiation, or conversely, to increased dependency. The continued exercise of power may produce changes in identification, in norms and values, or in expert knowledge, similarly altering the power bases.

From the viewpoint of exchange theory, each exercise of power is an exchange of rewards and costs. Resources may be interpreted in such terms, and this view will be useful in the treatment of power processes later in the chapter.

STUDY QUESTIONS

1. *Distinguish between direct and indirect power.*
2. *Explain what is meant by a resource.*
3. *Discuss each of the five types of power. In what important way does reward power differ from coercive power?*
4. *Discuss the various effects of the continued exercise of power.*
5. *Explain how resources may be conceptualized in terms of exchange theory.*

DEPENDENCIES

The behavior or other characteristics of a person constitute a resource only if they have some relevance to the satisfaction of another person. An understanding of why person *P* is able to influence *O* requires as much knowledge of *O*'s dependencies as of *P*'s resources. As mentioned earlier, such dependencies may have their source in characteristics of the individual or the situation, or in some combination of both. Characteristics of a person take the form of social needs or other attributes that make the resources of *P* especially valuable to him. An individual with a strong need to please others is likely to be easy to control: he is dependent upon the good will of others.

Children are apparently dependent on the friendliness and helpfulness of other children. A study of power in children's groups suggests that children whose behavior facilitates the gratification of the social-emotional needs of other children have high power in a group. The investigator (Gold, 1958) summarizes his results as follows:

> The data show that the higher power children are in fact more friendly as a group, more likely to be helpful to their peers and more able in terms of their psychological adjustments to be outgoing in social relationships, while the low power children as a group are quite different, and are, for example, more likely to use physical force as a method of attempting to influence their peers and more likely to manifest behavior symptoms of deeper lying disturbances. (P. 59)

That this principle is not restricted to children's groups is suggested by another study (Rosen, Levinger, & Lippitt, 1961). The investigators found that characteristics associated with high power in a group of boys aged twelve to fourteen were also generally found among adult women. The order in which characteristics of boys were associated with high power was: helpfulness, fairness, sociability, expertness, fearlessness, and physical strength. For the women the order of the items was the same except that fairness was placed before helpfulness.

The relevance of the situation to varying strength of dependency is indicated by the fact that the more frequently situations requiring a particular resource are likely to recur, the greater will be the perceived importance of this resource as a source of power. The finding that fearlessness and physical strength were ranked low by both groups was attributed to the fact that relatively few situations call for these resources. A subsequent analysis in which the adult subjects ranked the importance of the characteristics in a variety of situations provided data consistent with these hypotheses. Such findings parallel those noted earlier in the discussion of the characteristics associated with high sociometric choice status. Both suggest a high correlation between popularity and power, particularly in small, informal groups, where satisfaction of social-emotional needs is dominant.

ALTERNATIVES

Power is determined not only by the resources of P and the dependency of O on P, but also by the consequence of not complying. O compares his reward-cost outcome for compliance with that for noncompliance. The greater the disparity between these outcomes, the greater P's power over O. Essentially this disparity is a function of the alternatives available to O. If O has a resource in sufficient quantity himself, or if he may gain the resource at lower cost in relations with persons other than P, it will be relatively ineffective as a source of P's power over O. This is most obvious in the case of expert power: the expert influences others by his possession of scarce knowledge. If everyone were an expert (a contradiction in terms), the expert would be powerless.

An experiment performed by Meyers (1944) and discussed by Tannenbaum (1962) supports the point that power is a function of the alternatives available to the person being influenced. Individuals had a large number of activities, such as solving Chinese puzzles, listening to jazz records, and reading poetry, to choose from. In different sessions, the number of activities was varied from two to a large number. Two kinds of influence attempts were made by the experimenter. In the positive attempt he instructed the subjects to engage in a single specified activity. In the negative attempt he instructed them not to perform a certain activity.

The results were in accord with the notion of alternatives. Compliance with the positive instruction varied inversely with the number of alternative activities available: the greater the number, the less likely the subject was to confine himself to the single specified activity. But compliance with the negative instruction varied directly with the number of alternative activities. It is less costly to forgo a particular activity when there are other attractive ones available.

The consequences of not complying have a special significance when *P*'s influence attempt is based upon threats. One possibility is that *P* will not carry out his threat anyhow. Thus, the extent to which *P*'s threat is convincing is a determinant of the power that *P* has over *O*. One of the most interesting forms of threat, that which is based on the promise of mutual harm, has been analyzed intensively by Schelling (1960). A furious driver may threaten to smash another car with his own if the right of way is not yielded. Or a union may threaten a strike costly to itself if management does not raise wages a few cents. Schelling notes that *P* really does not have much incentive to carry out the threat, regardless of whether *O* complies, because of its cost to himself. In the case of such threats, power appears to vary with the extent to which *P* can make *O* believe that he is committed to carry out the threat. A driver may speed up so that a collision cannot be avoided unless the other party yields the right of way. Any means by which *P* gives up his control over the exercise of the threat is a strategy likely to secure his power. The favorite of crime writers is the blackmailer who deposits a damaging secret paper with another person unknown to *O*, with instructions to release it in the event of his death.

In summary, it is clear that the power of *P* is a function not only of his resources, but also of the factors that make *O* dependent on him. An individual's dependencies arise from his own characteristics, such as the strength of his social motives, his resources, his previous experience in power relations, and so on. In addition, *O*'s dependency on *P* is a function of certain elements of *O*'s situation, especially the number and value of alternative relations he can form with persons other than *P*. Thus, *O* compares the reward-cost outcome of complying with the reward-cost outcome of not complying, and his dependency on *P* is a function of the disparity between these outcomes.

STUDY QUESTIONS

6. *Show how the power of* P *varies with the dependency of* O.
7. *Explain how the possibility of alternative relations makes it necessary to go beyond the dyad in gaining an adequate understanding of power.*

Power Processes

The previous discussion of the characteristics of persons who have considerable power should not lead us into thinking of power as an attribute of a person. The exercise of power is a function of characteristics of both the influencer and influencee, as well as of other people in the situation. Moreover, power must also be examined in the context of ongoing interaction processes.

From the point of view of exchange theory, a conception of power as a process whereby one person causes changes in the behavior of another is inadequate because it ignores the symmetry implied by the notion of exchange. Not one but both persons are influencing and being influenced. They are exchanging behaviors that result in their experiencing certain costs and certain rewards. What is exchanged differs depending upon the type of power exercised. When an employee complies with his supervisor's legitimate requests, he receives continued approval in exchange. Behind this approval, of course, lie salary increases or promotion. If power is based upon identification, the identifier obtains psychic satisfaction in modeling his behavior after that of the model.

If it is true that each person is influencing the other, why do we view one person as more powerful? The answer lies in the nature of the *bargain* made between the two persons. That person is more powerful who receives rather valuable behavior from the other in exchange for behavior that he is able to produce at low cost. A nod of approval for an arduous task well done illustrates the disparity in what each person gives. Another way of stating it is that the higher-power person can affect the outcomes experienced by the lower-power person to a greater extent.

ELEMENTS OF POWER PROCESSES

In a recent discussion Emerson (1962) defines power as follows: "Power (PAB), the power of actor A over actor B is the amount of resistance on the part of B which can be potentially overcome by A" (p. 32). This power lies in B's dependency on A, which is determined by the variables in the following proposition: "Dependency (DBA) the dependency of actor B upon actor A is (a) directly proportional to B's *motivational investment* in goals mediated by A, and (b) inversely proportional to the *availability* of these goals to B outside of the A-B relation" (p. 32). Thus, as previously emphasized, power is a function not only of A's resources, but also of B's dependencies and alternatives.

Since both parties in a relation have varying degrees of power over the other, Emerson demonstrates that a power-dependence relation between A and B can be described as a pair of equations:

$$PAB = DBA$$
$$PBA = DAB$$

These may be translated as follows: The power that A has over B is equal to the dependency of B on A. Similarly, the power that B is capable of exercising over A is equal to A's dependency on B.

Power relations described in this manner may vary in two independent ways. First, they may vary in the degree to which one person is capable of exercising power relative to the other. This depends on the strength of dependencies that exist between the two persons. They may be relatively independent, as in the case of two casual acquaintances neither of whom has much influence over the other, or highly dependent, as in the case of lovers each of whom has the power to strongly affect the outcomes of the other. A second manner in which power relations may vary is in the degree of equality that exists between the two persons. Emerson characterizes a relation as balanced where, regardless of the degree or level of dependency, the parties hold equal power over each other. In terms of his equations this is represented as follows:

$$PAB = DBA$$
$$= \qquad =$$
$$PBA = DAB$$

A relation is described as unbalanced when one actor has greater power than the other. Symbolically this could be represented as:

$$PAB = DBA$$
$$\vee \qquad \vee$$
$$PBA = DAB$$

In this instance, the power of A over B (PAB) is greater than the power of B over A (PBA) because the dependency of B on A (DBA) is greater than A's dependency on B (DAB).

CONSEQUENCES OF HIGH BUT EQUAL POWER: BALANCED RELATIONS

Where both members of a pair have high power over each other, one might think that each person's power is balanced by the counterpower of the other, thereby producing a minimum of mutual influence. It would seem that each would be reluctant to make demands on the other if he is highly dependent on him, since the other could impose equally costly counterdemands or interfere with his gratification by breaking off the relation. One might further suppose that the potentiality for conflict in such a situation is great. Yet everyday observation, as well as more systematic evidence, suggests that persons who are close friends exercise considerable influence on each other and at the same time maintain amicable relations (Back, 1951). This occurs because certain arrangements emerge to facilitate influence without conflict.

In one such arrangement, the two parties assign different values to various activities. Norms are established dictating that in one situation, one party will give way, and in another situation, the other will give way. For example, a husband may have the final word in the choice of an auto but leave to his wife final say on the living-room drapes. In a second arrangement, norms dictate some alternation of advantage, as when two children equally powerful and equally motivated to play with a particular toy agree to take turns. Many of the rules of "fairness" have as their function the avoidance of costs arising out of power struggles. Third, since two persons are unlikely to be precisely equal in power, conflict may be avoided by the regular acquiescence of the less powerful member. An example would be a marital pair where the wife ordinarily submits to the wishes of a more powerful husband. Of course, the parties themselves may not be aware of a condition of slight inequality, and hence the stronger of the two is unlikely to always get his way.

8. *Show that power and dependency are interdependent concepts—each must be defined in terms of the other.*
9. *In what two ways may power vary from one dyad to another?*
10. *What happens when both members of a dyad have high but approximately equal power? How is high cost avoided?*

To recapitulate, the power of *P* is defined in terms of the resistance which *O* has to *P*'s efforts to influence him; that is, it resides in the dependency of *O* upon *P*. *O*'s dependency is directly proportional to *O*'s interest in satisfactions provided by *P*, and it is inversely related to the availability of these satisfactions outside the relation. The power relations in a dyad may vary in two ways: (1) The amount of power each member exerts over the other may be great or small, and (2) the power of one member may be either unequal or approximately equal to that of the other. Where both members of a dyad have high power, several arrangements may emerge that avoid the costs of conflict. These include a division of areas in which each exerts the controlling power, an alternation in the exercise of power, or since perfect equality is probably rare, the regular acquiescence of the weaker partner.

MODES OF RESOLVING IMBALANCE

Emerson has argued that an unbalanced relation is unstable since it encourages the use of power, which in turn sets into motion processes that he has called cost reduction and balancing operations. These are illustrated in the following. (1962):

> Let actor *B* be a rather unpopular girl, with puritanical upbringing, who wants desperately to date; and let *A* be a young man who occasionally takes her out, while dating other girls as well. . . . Assume further that *A* "discovers" this power advantage, and in exploring for the limits of his power, makes sexual advances. In this simplified illustration, these advances should encounter resistance in *B*'s puritanical values. Thus when a power advantage is *used,* the weaker member will achieve one value at the expense of other values.
> In this illustration the tensions involved in an unbalanced relation need not be long endured. They can be reduced in either of two ways; (1) the girl might reduce the psychic costs involved in continuing the relation by redefining her moral values, with appropriate rationalizations and shifts in reference group attachments; or (2) she might renounce the value of dating, develop career aspirations, etc., thus reducing *A*'s power. (P. 34)

The first solution illustrates cost reduction. By changing her values, *B* is able to reduce the pains incurred in meeting the demands of *A*. This solution does not reduce her power disadvantage; *A* can still make painful demands in other areas. The second solution, however, by reducing her motivational investment in goals mediated by A (in this case, dating), erases her power disadvantage.

This solution by *withdrawal* occurs when the costs incurred by the less powerful member result in a reward-cost outcome that is below some alternative, including the alternative of no relation at all. In a voluntary relation, this places a limit on the degree to which the more powerful member of a pair may exploit the less powerful. The process of withdrawal is one of four balancing operations in which inequality can be corrected. In withdrawal, if B reduces his motivational investment in goals mediated by A, B's dependency on A can be reduced to where it is equal to that of A. Renunciation of the values of dating in the case just cited illustrates balancing of power through withdrawal.

In the second balancing operation, *forming alternative relations* (termed by Emerson *extending the power network*), B's dependency is also decreased so that it is equal to that of A. This occurs if B develops an alternative source of satisfaction in a relation with C. The illustration above precludes an example of this second balancing operation. Had the girl been more popular, however, she would have been able to form alternative relations in which she could have obtained gratification.

The third and fourth balancing operations require further comment, since they are related to a number of features of process and structure in interaction. Emerson derives the phenomenon of *status* or *differential evaluation* from the third balancing operation. The status given to the more powerful member is a source of satisfaction to him *which is provided by the less powerful person*. As the more powerful member becomes increasingly motivated to achieve positive evaluation from the less powerful, his dependency on the latter is increased and the power discrepancy between the two is decreased. Abuse of power on the part of the more powerful is discouraged by the prospect that such behavior will lead to loss of status.

The fourth balancing operation involves a process that has received considerable attention in recent years: *coalition formation* (Mills, 1953, 1954, 1956; Caplow, 1956; Vinacke & Arkoff, 1957). Ever since the observation of Georg Simmel (1950) in this regard, investigators have been intrigued with the tendency in three-person groups for a pattern to emerge which involves a pair and a third party. Emerson views this as a model of the process leading to the emergence of norms which ensure group functioning against the disruptive effects of abuse of power. The power of each member is restricted by the potential combination of other members that constrains him to behave in conformity to a norm.

It is difficult to illustrate this point, since such norms are an integral part of every group situation. Even in newly formed groups, members are guided by norms (such as those of courtesy) which control unrestricted use of power and which have been developed in other group contexts. Yet during a crisis created by an overuse of power, this process of coalition formation may readily be observed, as when workers combine and demand that a boss agree to rules restricting the requests that he can make of them. Perhaps a clearer illustration is the instance where two children threaten not to play with a third unless he stops being so bossy. In social situations where the male has a dominant role in relation to subordinate females, and where he might thereby exploit the relation for sexual purposes, norms placing limits on his power hold him in check. This is illustrated by norms against dating and other forms of association which develop in relations between a male supervisor and a female worker or between a female student and a male teacher. A more complete discussion of norm development in such situations will be offered in Chapter 10.

One final point not made by Emerson might be included. In general, continued interaction between two persons will increase the motivational investment of each in the goals mediated by the other *in the direction of greater equality* unless there are certain safeguards against this process. As noted earlier, in a dyad where both members have high but relatively equal power, continued interaction is accompanied by a decrease in costs and an increase in rewards and thus brings about an increase in the dependencies of both parties. Since the higher power member is able to exact more from the relation, his dependency should increase at a more rapid rate. Accordingly the balance of power moves toward equality. In addition, increased interaction between members of a pair decreases both the degree of dependency on, and the availability of, relations with other persons. These processes, together with the fact of inertia in human relations, go far to explain the continuation of a relation which appears, to the outsider at least, to be an exploitative one.

MAINTENANCE OF POWER DIFFERENCES

Where it is essential for power differences to be maintained, various features of the social structure operate to discourage the development of mutual dependency. In the military, officers and enlisted men are segregated to some extent and a degree of formality is maintained in their relations, as illustrated by the salute and the use of titles and last names. Similarly, in business organizations, high executives erect a variety of barriers between themselves and their underlings, such as separate lunchrooms and rest rooms. The most common form of dependency that threatens to develop between superiors and subordinates is friendship, which would upset the power differential required if the organization is to function properly. Other mechanisms with a similar function arise in other relations requiring a power differential, such as the teacher-student relation and the therapist-patient relation. In all these situations it is essential for the achievement of organizational goals that the more powerful person retain the power of decision and control of the relation.

PERCEPTION OF POWER AND INTERPERSONAL STRATEGIES

Power is such a pervasive and vital aspect of interaction that most persons seem to be quite sensitive to the facts about power. There is some systematic evidence that most people perceive fairly accurately the power structure in a group and their own relative position in the structure, and further, that their behavior toward other persons is consistent with such perceptions. In a study of power in two boys' camps, boys were found to perceive accurately the relative power of group members, including their own (Lippitt et al., 1952). Furthermore, the frequency and character of the attempts of each boy to influence another were consistent with these perceptions. Boys who perceived themselves as high in power made more attempts to influence others and in one camp were more directive in these attempts. A study of Air Force personnel provides similar evidence (French & Snyder, 1959). The amount of influence attempted by an airman was proportional to the extent that he was liked and accepted by the person he influenced.

Perhaps more striking are the results of another study (Levinger, 1959). The perception of the relative power of partners working together on a task was experimentally varied over a series of joint decision-making trials. Subjects were given different initial perceptions of their own resources and of their task ability relative to the partner, and the partner (who actually was the experimenter's assistant) varied the degree to which he accepted or rejected the naïve subject's attempts to influence him. Variations in initial information and in the feedback of information from the partner were expected to produce corresponding variations in the subject's perceived power, and he was expected to behave in accordance with his perceived power. For example, if he believed his power was low, he was expected to reduce his influence attempts, to decrease his refusals to concede to his partner, and to reveal less confidence when speaking to him. These hypotheses were confirmed. In particular, whether the partner acquiesced to or resisted influence attempts appeared to be the most important determinant of the perception of power and of power-relevant behavior.

Less systematic observation of everyday interaction reveals ubiquitous interpersonal strategies that are based upon an advantageous use of the balancing operations previously described. Such strategies either change the objective situation to the power advantage of one party, or simply alter the definition of the situation to the advantage of one of the actors.

As previously illustrated, a person may use withdrawal to reduce his motivational investment in goals mediated by another, as in the case where a girl decides that she does not want to date, or where she alters the feedback she gives to a boy so as to disguise her interest in dating. This strategy is so common that we have a name for it, "playing hard to get." In the marketplace we see this strategy used by the buyer who attempts to present an air of indifference to the wares of the seller.

With respect to the second balancing operation, forming alternative relations, one can attempt to develop alternative sources of gratification or one can merely give the impression that one has such an alternative.

The date who talks a good deal about her other dates is using the same strategy as the buyer who indicates that he can get the same article cheaper around the corner.

Flattery is the most obvious illustration of a strategy associated with the third balancing operation, raising another person's status in order to increase his dependency on us. The fourth balancing operation, the invocation of a norm, as when one demands "common courtesy," is based on the potential of coalition formation.

Summary: Power processes

The power of *P* is defined in terms of the resistance that *O* has to *P*'s efforts to influence him. Resistance is a function of the dependency of *O* upon *P*. *O*'s resistance is directly proportional to his interest in satisfactions provided by *P* and inversely proportional to the availability of these satisfactions outside the relation. The power relations in a dyad may vary in two ways: (1) The amount of power that each member exerts over the other may be great or small, and (2) the power of one member may be equal or unequal to that of the other.

Where both members of a dyad have high power, several arrangements emerge to avoid the costs of conflict. These include assignment of the controlling power to different areas for each member and a normatively governed alternation of power. If a slight difference in power exists, conflict may also be avoided by the regular acquiescence of the less powerful person.

Several modes of resolving imbalance are (1) withdrawal from the relation, (2) formation of alternative relations, (3) emergence of a status differential, and (4) coalition formation, leading to the formation of norms inhibiting the abuse of power. Continued interaction increases motivational investment in the goals mediated by the other person, thereby altering the relation in the direction of greater equality. When achievement of organizational goals requires that power differentials be maintained, features of the social structure emerge to discourage the development of mutual dependency. In particular, barriers are erected against the formation of personal friendships between superiors and subordinates.

Empirical evidence indicates that people accurately perceive their own power and the power of other persons with whom they interact. This sensitivity to power differences leads to the use of various interpersonal strategies calculated to shift the balance of power, either perceptually or in fact. These include disguising one's dependency, presenting the illusion of having many alternatives, increasing the dependency of the other by raising his status, or invoking norms that restrict the other person's alternatives.

STUDY QUESTIONS

11. *Explain each of the four ways in which an imbalance of power may be resolved.*

12. *Why does continued interaction decrease power differences? How are power differences maintained where they are essential to adequate functioning?*

13. *Describe interpersonal strategies that might be employed for altering power relations.*

Power Structures

Discussion so far has been concerned with direct power, that is, with power exerted by one person *A* on another person *B*. Another form of power is indirect. *A* may exert *indirect power* on *C* if *A* has control over *B* and *B* has control over *C*. Whereas direct power in a dyad can be discussed in terms of the resources, dependencies, and alternatives of the members of the dyad, the degree to which a group member exercises indirect power requires consideration of additional features of the power structure. In the previous chapter, the affect structure was conceptualized in terms of points connected by a series of arrows representing choices or rejections. The power structure may be similarly represented. In fact, French (1956) has suggested that by merely reversing the direction of the arrows of a sociogram, the power structure based on interpersonal attraction may be represented. Such a graphic representation he calls a *power digraph.*

Sociogram A of Figure 8–1 is a sociometric chain involving four persons in which *A* chooses *B*, *B* chooses *C*, and *C* chooses *D*. If a choice is assumed to indicate that the chooser is dependent on goals mediated by the chosen, then a reversal of the arrows in Sociogram A produces Digraph A, which depicts the fact that *D* has power over *C*, who has power over *B*, who has power over *A*. In Digraph A, *D* has direct power over *C* and, through him, indirect power over *B* and *A*. If *D* takes a particular position on some opinion continuum and attempts to influence the others to adopt his position, he will by virtue of his power over *C* cause *C* to move toward his position, which will result in similar movements on the part of

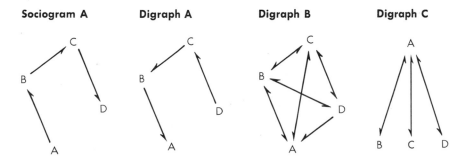

Sociogram A   **Digraph A**   **Digraph B**   **Digraph C**

Figure 8–1
Power digraphs. (Adapted with permission from J. R. P. French, Jr. A formal theory of social power. *Psychol. Rev.*, 1956, **63**, 181–194.)

B and finally on the part of *A*. Since in this illustration the possibility of counterpressure from other group members is excluded, the group would eventually move to the position advocated by *D*. In this structure *D* has maximum indirect power. While a power structure based on affect is unlikely to take this form, such a structure might be approximated in the chain of command of an organization.

A quite different structure with a relatively equal distribution of indirect power is shown in Digraph B. All members have both direct and indirect power over all the others. A group of close friends characterized sociometrically by mutual choice might have such a structure. In this structure no one person has more direct or indirect power than any other, and a group decision would be a compromise equally reflecting the views of the various members.

Digraphs A and B suggest that power structures vary with respect to (1) the degree of mutuality, (2) the number of levels of power, (3) the degree of connectedness, and (4) the proportion of direct to indirect influence. Mutuality is present to the extent that persons have counterpower over those who exert power over them. Digraph B illustrates high mutuality. In a friendship group, a high level of mutuality is common; in formally organized work groups, it is lower.

The levels of power may be determined by counting the number of links that separate the two positions which are farthest apart. Digraph B has only one level of power, since all members have direct power over each other. Since *A* and *D* in Digraph A are separated by three links, that structure has three power levels.

Connectedness is a function of the extent to which members have at least some form of power, direct or indirect, over each other. A structure in which every position is directly or indirectly connected with every other position would have high connectedness. If *A* were connected to *D* in Digraph A, the occupant of every position could exert influence directly or indirectly on every other occupant. On the other hand, if the arrows between *B* and *C* were removed, the network would be a disconnected one. In this instance the members of one pair would be unable to influence those in the other.

Finally, the proportion of direct power relative to indirect power is a function of the number of links that *separate* each member from every other member. The fewer such links, the more rapidly and the more directly members can exert influence on each other. In the completely connected network such as Digraph B, where each person can directly influence the other, twelve links separate the members. In contrast, in Digraph C, members are separated by a total of eighteen links. Each may communicate with *A* directly, and *A* may communicate with each. However, *B, C,* and *D* must exert indirect influence on each other via two links through *A*. Whether this increases or diminishes the power of each on the other depends on the power relation that exists between each person and person *A*.

Let us examine in more detail the determinants of indirect power. Take the simple case of a three-person network $A \rightarrow B \rightarrow C$. It is obvious that any power exerted by *A* on *C* will be limited by the changes that he can bring about in *B*. This in turn will be a function of the influence he can exert on *B*, as well as of *B*'s resistance to such influence. The previous discussion of power relations in the dyad noted that determinants of influence are the resources, dependencies, and alternatives of the dyad members; but determinants of resistance have not yet been mentioned.

Resistance to influence has two determinants, one internal and one external to the individual. Internal factors consist of the cognitive organization of the individual—including his value structures, which might be disrupted by change—as well as such psychological states as fatigue, anxiety, or other emotional inhibitors of action. External factors include pressures against change generated by persons other than *A* who have power over *B*. Discussion of the isolated dyad has ignored the fact that at any one time a variety of persons outside the dyad exerts influence on members of the dyad. Reluctance to engage in behavior desired by one person is often due to the pressures exerted against such behavior by others.

The degree to which pressures exerted by *A* can overcome resistance in *B* is one determinant of the influence that *A* may have on *C*. His influence also depends on the resources, dependencies, alternatives, and degree of resistance that characterize the relation between *B* and *C*. Under certain circumstances, the pressure that *A* causes to be exerted on *C* through *B* will be greater than pressure exerted directly. This occurs where *B*'s resistance is minimal and the power of *B* relative to *C*'s resistance is greater than *A*'s direct power over *C*. Everyday interaction abounds with illustrations, as the case where one sibling makes another act or refrain from acting in a certain manner by getting mother to speak to him.

Where the relative power of each person over the next in a network becomes progressively less, or where resistance becomes progressively greater, one can expect a rapid decline in influence as the number of links increases. Bureaucratic organizations have a structure of this kind. Typically the relations between the chief executive and those next in command are characterized by maximum power and minimum resistance. His immediate subordinates serve at his will without the protection afforded employees further down the chain of command. The former are chosen on the basis of how well their views and predispositions coincide with his. Without such "yes men" at the top of the hierarchy, the influence of the chief executive would be seriously impaired.

In short, the indirect power of person *A* on person *N* in a network depends on the number of links, the resistance at each link, and the relative power of the persons in each link. *A*'s indirect power over *N* will vary directly with the power advantage that each member has over the next member and with the degree to which such power advantages are greatest in the early portion of the flow of influence.

Summary: Power structures

Where the source of power is interpersonal attraction, power structures may be thought of as the inverse of a sociogram. The more attracted O is to P, the more power P has over O. Power digraphs, of course, may also be derived from other bases of power.

Structures vary markedly in the degree of direct or indirect power that each member has over the other. Some general properties of power structures include (1) the degree of mutuality, (2) the number of levels of power, (3) the degree of connectedness (the extent to which each member has influence over every other member), and (4) the proportion of direct to indirect power. The amount of indirect power that a person P may exert over another person O depends upon the number of intervening links, the resistance of each person serving as a link, and each one's relative power over the next person in the chain of power links leading to O. In some instances, the indirect power that P can exert over O is greater than his direct power.

STUDY QUESTIONS

14. *Show how a power structure based on interpersonal attraction may be derived from a sociogram.*
15. *Draw a digraph to illustrate indirect power. Draw another illustrating that two persons have the same amount of indirect power over a third person.*
16. *In what basic ways may power structures vary?*
17. *What factors determine indirect power?*

Summary and Conclusions

Three classes of variables are important in social power: a person's resources, dependencies, and alternatives. A resource is a property of an individual—a possession or an aspect of his behavior—which enables him to affect the reward-cost outcomes of another person. An individual's dependencies arise from his own characteristics, such as his resources, the strength of his social motives, his previous experience in power relations, etc. Dependency is also a function of the number and value of alternative relations with other persons.

Five types of power have been identified. Reward power is based upon the perception by O that P has the power to reward him. Coercive power, the counterpart of reward power, is based on O's perception that P can punish him. Referent power, which often develops out of reward power, is based on identification, the desire to be like another person. Expert power stems from special knowledge that P has which O needs. Finally, legitimate power is based on the acceptance by O of internalized norms and values which dictate that he accept influence from P. These bases of power differ in their permanence and the extent to which systematic changes occur over time. The continued exercise of power has different consequences depending upon the type being used: exercise may increase or decrease the amount of power available.

The power of *P* may be defined in terms of the resistance that *O* has to *P*'s efforts to influence him, which in turn is a function of the dependency of *O* upon *P*. *O*'s dependency is directly proportional to his interest in satisfactions provided by *P* and inversely proportional to the availability of these satisfactions outside the relation. Power relations in a dyad may vary in two ways: (1) The amount of power that each member exerts over the other may be great or small, and (2) the power of one member may be equal or unequal to that of the other.

Several modes of resolving imbalance are (1) withdrawal from the relation, (2) formation of alternative relations, (3) creation of a status differential, and (4) coalition formation, leading to the formation of norms inhibiting the abuse of power. Continued interaction results in the increasing equalization of power. When the attainment of organizational goals requires that power differentials be maintained, normative controls develop to discourage the growth of mutual dependency.

Research indicates that people accurately perceive their own power and the power of other persons with whom they interact. Various interpersonal strategies are employed to shift the balance of power either in fact or perceptually. People may disguise their dependency, pretend to have many desirable alternatives, increase the dependency of the other by raising his status, or invoke norms that restrict the other person's alternatives.

Where the source of power is interpersonal attraction, a power structure may be thought of as the inverse of a sociogram. A digraph may also be derived from bases of power other than interpersonal attraction. Some properties of these digraphs include the following: (1) the degree of mutuality, (2) the number of levels of power, (3) the degree of connectedness, and (4) the proportion of direct to indirect power. The amount of indirect power that a person *P* may exert over another person *O* depends upon the number of intervening links, the resistance of each person serving as a link, and that person's relative power over the next person in the chain of power links leading to *O*.

chapter nine

STATUS AND COMMUNICATION

Persons may be ranked on dimensions other than affect and power. Star athletes are idolized by sports fans; the successful business executive is admired by the average citizen; scientists, professors, and physicians are respected by most people; beautiful women are admired by males in a society; distinguished statesmen command deference from many; and heroes are honored by all. In small groups, the worth of each member is evaluated in an agreed-upon way by all the other members. All these evaluations may be classed as *status* evaluations. Just as the affect structure of the group may be identified and described, so may the status structure. The first half of this chapter will discuss the nature of status, identify characteristics of status structures found in groups, and describe processes associated with status.

In addition to affect, status, and power structures, a fourth kind of structuring in groups may be observed. Systematic observation reveals that some members of a group initiate communications more frequently than others. Also, communications are not addressed equally to all; some members receive communications more frequently. Thus the group may be thought of as having a communication structure. The last half of the chapter will describe a variety of processes associated with that structure.

Status

NATURE OF STATUS

Status is the worth of a person as estimated by a group or a class of persons. The estimate of worth is determined by the extent to which his attributes or characteristics are perceived to contribute to the shared values and needs of the group or class of persons. In this context, the terms *attribute* and *characteristic* have a very broad meaning, which includes not only personal qualities but also a person's activities, possessions, position in a group, and other more remote factors associated with him.

Which attributes contribute to status depends upon the persons making the status evaluation. Status attributes may relate to values and needs shared by only a small group or by a whole society. In our own society, examples of attributes widely regarded as signs of status are beauty, especially in a woman, or the possession of wealth. Examples of attributes whose contribution to status varies from group to group include the following. Among physicians, being a surgeon carries high status; among adolescents, the possession of a car confers status; and among professors, the publication of significant research contributes to status. Attributes are sometimes rather broad, as the beauty of a woman. In that case they may be broken down into more specific characteristics, in this instance perceptual ones, such as the shape and configuration of facial and bodily features.

Only those attributes that are similarly valued by group members contribute to status. If a person has some unique characteristic which is of value only to one or two other members of a large group, it does not contribute to his status. Suppose, for example, that only two members of a tennis club know how to play chess. Although this skill might be mutually valued by the two members, and each of them might value each other, possession of the skill would not confer any status upon them. On the other hand, the best tennis players in the club would have very high status.

DETERMINANTS OF STATUS

Among the several bases for status are the capacity of a person for rewarding those with whom he interacts, the extent to which he is seen as receiving rewards, the types of costs he incurs, and his investments.

Reward value of high-status persons

Persons are accorded high status to the degree that their attributes are rewarding to each group member and to the extent that their behavior is rewarding to all. The attribute that provides the greatest reward to the greatest number is associated with maximum social approval and thus with maximum status. But an additional element is that these rewarding attributes must also be relatively rare. Certain activities contributing to highly important values of the group are engaged in by all members, and thus no one member gains an advantage in terms of status. Only the attributes in scarce supply confer status. Thus members of a football team who are average in ability may confer high status on the one man who can save the game through his superior skill at kicking a field goal or completing a forward pass leading to a touchdown. Similarly, on a scientific research team the man with deep insight and brilliance is likely to have very high status because of his ability to solve difficult research problems regarded as insoluble by other members of the team.

Under some circumstances, as Homans (1961) notes, even conformity to group values can be rare. In the study by Jennings (1950) discussed in Chapter 7, those who had high choice status on the living-working criterion conformed most closely to the values of the group. Newcomb (1943), in his Bennington College study, reported similar results. If most persons realize group values to only a moderate degree, then close conformity is relatively rare and hence is particularly rewarding to the other members. In general, most studies support the view that leaders, who have high status, conform closely to the values of the group.

Rewards received and costs incurred

Persons are also accorded status depending on the extent to which they are seen as receiving rewards or incurring costs. Esteem is one such reward, and to the extent that a person is perceived as esteemed by other persons, he is ranked high in status by the perceiver. Thus, an individual who learns only that another person has received popular acclaim is likely to attribute high status to him. In general, to the extent that a person is a recipient of things valued by our society, such as high income, he is likely to be accorded status.

Persons may be similarly ranked in terms of costs which they experience. The great distinction conferred on a soldier who receives the Congressional Medal of Honor is in direct proportion to his personal sacrifice and disregard for his own safety: often the award is posthumous. Unlike rewards, not all costs contribute to status. Only those costs that assist in the realization of the values of the group and that are not incurred by almost everyone are associated with high status. The soldier who exposes himself to the enemy needlessly, without achieving an objective, is likely to be reprimanded instead of being given a medal. Similarly, such features of an occupation as responsibility and drudgery are both costs, but only the former contributes to high status.

Investments

Another feature associated with status is a person's investments (Homans, 1961), which are aspect of his past history or background. Whereas attributes have reward value, investments may have no intrinsic value, but acquire value through consensus of opinion. They confer upon a person a right to be accorded a certain status. Investments may include such features as race, ethnic background, family, age, sex, and seniority. Perhaps seniority best conveys the meaning of "investments." A factory worker who has been on the job a long time expects certain privileges not accorded to relatively new employees. For example, he expects to be paid a higher salary, to receive certain vacation privileges, and in the event of a slowdown in production, to be retained while newer employees are laid off. Similarly, seniority on a faculty carries with it certain privileges. Faculty members having full-professor rank are more likely to be able to specify the hours during which they will teach, to choose the more interesting courses, and to have larger, more private offices, as well as to be paid higher salaries.

STUDY QUESTIONS

1. *What is meant by status? What special meaning is attached to the term* attribute *or* characteristic *when used to signify status?*
2. *Discuss the several conditions that determine whether or not an attribute is a status attribute.*
3. *What are investments associated with status? How do they differ from attributes?*

In sum, status arises out of interaction. Persons are accorded high status to the degree that their attributes are rewarding to group members. To contribute to status, however, such attributes must be relatively rare: only those characteristics in scarce supply confer status. The more a person is perceived to receive rewards, the higher his status is likely to be. Similarly, high status is associated with the incurrence of relatively rare costs that contribute to the realization of the values of the group. A man's investments—his past history or background—also contribute to status.

COMPARISON PROCESSES AND STATUS

Basic to the phenomenon of status is the process of comparison. Persons compare themselves and others with respect to rewards received, costs incurred, and investments accumulated, and they are in varying degrees satisfied or dissatisfied with the comparisons. Homans has suggested that reactions to such comparisons can be understood in terms of two principles: distributive justice and status congruence.

Distributive justice and status congruence

Distributive justice is obtained when the outcomes or profit of each person—his rewards minus his costs—are directly proportional to his investments. Realizing that persons do not generally measure and compare outcomes in such an exacting manner, Homans suggests that in practice a person merely compares his standing relative to another person on these variables, thinking of himself as higher, lower, or equal to the other person.

This principle could be stated in terms of the following equation:[1]

$$\frac{\text{My investments}}{\text{His investments}} = \frac{\text{my rewards minus costs}}{\text{his rewards minus costs}}$$

[1]Homans recognizes two categories of cost: those which are rare and valuable, such as responsibility, and those which are commonplace and of no particular value, such as drudgery or boring routine. The equation given allows only for the latter type of cost, which should decrease with increasing investments. Rare and valuable costs, however, should increase with investments.

When equality prevails, distributive justice is achieved. Marked inequalities are perceived as unjust.

A study by Homans (1954) provides an illustration of how feelings of injustice arise where investments are not proportional to outcomes. Two groups of female employees in a utility company were the ledger clerks and the cash posters. Ledger clerks were superior in such investments as seniority and knowledge. Their costs in terms of responsibility were also greater than those of the cash posters. Although some of their rewards, such as the intrinsic interest and variety of their work, were also greater, the ledger clerks were only equal to the cash posters in such rewards as pay and autonomy. Consequently their outcomes were not sufficiently in line with their superior investments, and they complained about the injustice of being underpaid and not having sufficient independence.

Another investigation (Patchen, 1961), of workers in an oil refinery also supports the principle of distributive justice. For example, he found that if a comparison person who earns more than the respondent is superior in such investments and costs as seniority and education, only 14 percent of the respondents are dissatisfied when they compare their own wage with his. But if they regard themselves as equal or superior to the comparison person in investments and costs, 75 percent are dissatisfied with the fact that he earns more.

The principle of distributive justice also implies a definition of *status congruence* as that condition in which all the status attributes of a person rank higher than, equal to, or lower than the corresponding attributes of another person. Thus a faculty member of professorial rank expects himself to be not only a better teacher than a young instructor, but also a wiser committee member and a more accomplished scholar. Homans gives an example of a person who is established as another's superior in most status attributes, but who, when in danger of losing his superiority in one of them, extends himself to maintain his superiority. He notes that in certain supermarkets, full-time workers were paid more and held higher seniority than part-time workers. The attempt to maintain status congruence occurred when a full-time and a part-time worker were assigned the same job. It was well expressed by one of the full-timers: "A full-timer has got to show the part-timers that he can work faster than they can. It's better to work with them than against them, but he's got to show he's a better man" (1961, p. 252).

Status congruence also explains *status symbols*. Characteristics which initially have no status value but which are regularly associated with certain status levels eventually come to be perceived as symbols of status. The binding of women's feet in China had long been a symbol of status, but it had no intrinsic value beyond that of identifying the woman as belonging to a family of high status, one in which its daughters did not have to engage in physical labor. In an American business corporation, the status of an executive is often associated with such features as the privacy and size of his office, cost of office furnishings, number of secretaries and telephones assigned to him, etc. The importance of status symbols is illustrated by the report that in one corporation, when an executive of lesser rank moved into an office formerly occupied by an assistant vice president, a maintenance man was sent to the office to remove 1 foot of carpeting from the borders of the room. This was done so that the office would no longer have wall-to-wall carpeting, a status symbol reserved for higher-ranking officials (Hartley & Hartley, 1952, p. 575).

A question may be raised as to why the concepts of distributive justice and status congruence are both needed, when the end result is the same. The answer lies in the reasons behind the discomfort people feel when these two conditions are not obtained. With respect to distributive justice, persons are concerned when their profits are out of line with their investments because they have learned to expect that high investments will bring high rewards. When this expectation is not met, they feel cheated. In the case of status congruence, persons have learned that when the various stimuli they present to others are not consistent, others will behave toward them in an unpredictable manner — sometimes in a rewarding fashion and other times not. Thus the principles of distributive justice and status congruence have somewhat different functional bases. As Homans (1961) says:

> Distributive justice is a matter of the relation between what a man gets in the way of reward and what he incurs in the way of cost, here and now; status congruence is a matter of the impression he makes on, the stimuli he presents to, other men, which may affect their future behavior toward him and therefore the future reward he gets from them. (P. 250)

Thus, Homans's view of status congruence is that persons strive toward a state where they are ranked uniformly in all respects because such a state is associated with the rewarding certainty that others will behave consistently toward them.

Two studies provide support for this view. In one, the degree of status congruence among the dimensions of income, occupation, education, and ethnic position was determined for each individual in the group studied (Lenski, 1954). Persons having low status congruence were found to be politically liberal, a fact which suggests that they were dissatisfied with the present state of affairs, felt frustrated, and sought social change. Persons high in status congruence were less frustrated and more satisfied, and they were more conservative in their politics.

The other investigation indicated that where status congruence is lacking, interpersonal conflict is more likely to occur (Exline & Ziller, 1959). Members of groups were assigned the task of choosing six considerations from a list of fifteen that best answered the question whether movies or television are better educational aids. In some groups, status incongruence was created by assigning different voting weights to individuals who were informed that they were equal in ability. Status congruence was created in other groups by assigning voting weights according to the supposed ability of the members to perform the task. It was found that groups characterized by status congruence were more congenial and reached agreement more readily.

STUDY QUESTIONS

4. *State the principles of distributive justice and status congruence and explain how they work.*
5. *What are status symbols, and how does a characteristic become a status symbol?*
6. *Explain how the failure to meet conditions of distributive justice has different consequences from the failure to achieve status congruence.*

Interpersonal comparison

Basic to the phenomenon of status is the process of interpersonal comparison. It is through periodic comparison with others that an individual eventually develops a clear idea of his status. A person frequently compares himself with others with respect to income, possessions, skills, or other attributes. He does not, however, compare himself with just anyone. He may feel angry or embarrassed if certain persons make more money than he does, but the incomes of some other persons are of no interest to him. The people to whom a person compares himself and the degree to which he makes comparisons are determined by the principles of distributive justice, the person's perception of his power, and the conditions allowing for ease of comparison.

Thibaut and Kelley (1959) have noted several conditions under which status comparisons are likely to be made. First, each person must be able to observe the rewards, costs, and investments of others so that he can compare them with his own. Second, with respect to a more powerful authority, each person must have approximately the same power to obtain rewards or avoid costs, since this creates a rivalrous condition. Third, a person is more likely to compare himself with another whose rewards and costs are not too different from his own. The principle of distributive justice suggests a fourth condition: Comparisons are likely to be made with persons having similar investments, because they should experience similar costs and rewards. Many small face-to-face groups meet these conditions. Examples include men in prison, minority groups living in ghetto conditions, children of similar ages in a family, graduate students in an academic department, pledges in a fraternity, and various work groups in industry.

Thibaut and Kelley discuss sibling rivalry as a major example of status comparisons and their consequences (1959):

> With the triad and larger groups, status comparisons may be quite important, for it becomes possible for two (or more) persons to be receiving much the same kinds of rewards or cost cutting from a third person. The prime example, of course, is that of sibling rivalry. When two children require and receive pretty much the same sort of treatment from a parent, any difference in the quantity of rewards received will be highly visible. If the parent is to avoid sibling jealousy and being charged with favoritism, either he must be scrupulously equitable or he must create some sort of noncomparability be-

tween the children's outcomes by providing them with different kinds of rewards. If the two children are quite similar, the first is possible; if they are
quite dissimilar, the second is possible. Sewall's. . .data on jealousy as affected
by age difference between siblings is consistent with this analysis, although not
conclusive because of small numbers of cases. Jealousy was found to be greater
for intermediate age differences than for very small or large ones. On the
other hand, a difference between the children often renders one of them more
attractive to the adults, with the consequence that he is favored over the sib.
Koch. . .reports that among first-born children the wish to change places with
the younger sibling increases with the age difference between them. She
comments that, "The sib who is two to four years younger than a five-or-six-
year-old is at that adorable one-to-four-year age when it will probably be
showered with attention and affection by adults, both in and out of the family"
. . . .We suspect a similar explanation accounts for Smalley's. . .finding that
relationships between siblings are more frequently characterized by jealousy,
the larger the difference between their intelligence quotients. (Pp. 226–227)

Persons compare costs as well as rewards. This is well illustrated by
the child who becomes extremely indignant when his brother is *not* punished for something for which he himself has been punished. Similar
reactions occur in adults, although they may be clothed with pious decla-
rations. If we assume that persons incur costs in resisting temptations to
commit crimes, a similar comparison of costs may underlie the public
reaction of indignation over "easy" treatment of a criminal.

STUDY QUESTIONS

7. *Status comparisons are not made under all conditions. Explain what conditions are likely to give rise to status comparisons.*

8. *Indicate the role of rewards, costs, and investments in status comparisons.*

Summary: Comparison processes and status

Status arises out of comparisons of people's rewards, costs, and investments. Homans suggests that two principles explain reactions to such
comparisons: distributive justice and status congruence. Distributive
justice is obtained when the outcomes of each person are directly proportional to his investments. If a person's investments are more extensive
than those of another, then the reward he gets should be greater too; also,
his costs should be higher. Status congruence is a condition in which all
the stimuli presented by a person rank higher than, equal to, or lower
than all the stimuli presented by another person.

Although the two principles are closely related, they have a somewhat
different motivational basis. With respect to distributive justice, persons
are concerned when their profits are out of line with their investments because they have learned to expect that reward-cost outcomes should be
proportional to investments. When this expectation is not met, they feel
cheated. In the case of status congruence, persons have learned that when
the various stimuli they present to others are out of line, the other people
will behave toward them in an unpredictable manner, sometimes in a rewarding fashion and sometimes not. When status congruence is lacking,
interpersonal conflict is more likely to occur.

Status comparisons are more likely to be made under some conditions than others. Persons must be able to observe the rewards received and the costs incurred by others, they must have relatively equal power to obtain rewards or avoid costs, and the rewards and costs of different individuals must not cover too wide a range.

STABILITY IN THE STATUS STRUCTURE

A stable status structure and the stability of each group member's position in that structure are a product of a number of processes. Some of them ensure status congruence and distributive justice. Since such states are rewarding to individuals, changes that disrupt them will be resisted; hence processes that create congruence and justice lend stability to the system. A second set of processes contributes to stability by increasing the value consensus in a group. Since the attributes of members are evaluated in accordance with their rarity and their contribution to group values, the greater the consensus with respect to group values, the greater the stability of the system. Finally, a person's position in the status structure allows and encourages him to behave in a manner that validates his status.

In addition Benoit-Smullyan (1944) has called attention to *status conversion* processes, which lead to status congruency. In part such processes involve the manipulation of stimuli that a person presents to others so that the others will judge him similarly on various dimensions of status. A person may use resources associated with a position on one continuum to advance himself on another, as when a wealthy person uses his money to obtain power, or a teacher uses his disciplinary authority to silence a student who is asking questions he cannot answer. Or a person may carefully monitor his behavior and appearance so as not to emit incongruent stimuli. One such instance revolves around the exchange of help among workers. Workers avoid asking help from those whom they regard as their equals, since such requests would imply less competence and hence less esteem. Blau (1955) has noted this phenomenon among a group of employees in a governmental agency. Homans (1961) provides a good example from a 1956 study by Zaleznik, Christensen, and Roethlisberger:

> In a certain machine-shop, described by Zaleznik, there were two classes of workers, called by different job-titles: machinists and operators. As the titles suggest, the machinists ranked higher than the operators in seniority, pay, and reputed skill. Operators often borrowed tools from machinists and went to them for help in dealing with mechanical difficulties: their asking for help was congruent with their inferiority in other respects. But machinists hardly ever borrowed tools or asked help from other machinists, and when they did so tried to disguise their behavior. They pretended it was not help they wanted but only a chance to compare notes, to discuss with a fellow expert technical problems of interest to both. (P. 252)

Status congruence is aided by the tendency of perceptual processes to be balanced. Status is likely to be perceived in a global fashion: people who are high in one dimension are seen to be also high on others. Persons presented favorably in terms of one aspect are judged favorably in terms of other aspects. The general idealization of heroes is a more commonplace example: they are not expected to have traits or attributes for which they cannot be admired. These phenomena are consistent with balance theory as proposed by Heider and others (see Chapter 3).

Another tendency is to perceive persons who are seen together as having equal status. As Benoit-Smullyan (1944) notes:

> Those who regularly associate with a person of high prestige status, come, in some mysterious fashion, to "participate" in that prestige, at least to the extent of raising their own. For this reason even menial offices rendered to a king tend to ennoble, and the servants of the great assume a supercilious demeanor. . . . [On the other hand] close association with those of markedly lower prestige status tends to degrade. These facts explain in large part the ceaseless struggle of those of low prestige to lessen the physical, and . . . the social distance separating them from those of high prestige; and the no less determined efforts of those of high prestige to avoid . . . propinquity with those of lower prestige. Prestige contagion and prestige participation explain the various manifestations of the nearly universal phenomena of social climbing and snobbery. (Pp. 151–161)

STUDY QUESTIONS

9. *Explain how the desire to maintain status congruence and distributive justice produces stability in the status structure. What are status conversion processes, and how do they produce congruency?*

10. *How does the tendency of perceptual processes to achieve a balanced state contribute to a stable status structure?*

11. *Indicate how association between persons leads to enhancement of the status of the person in the lower position.*

So far various internal processes contributing to status congruence have been noted, and it has been suggested that the desire to maintain status provides internal resistance to change. Stability of the system is also in part a function of external factors that produce value consensus. While the determinants of value consensus will be more fully discussed in Chapter 10, their relation to the status structure should be noted here. Obviously those persons high on the various dimensions of status support values related to these dimensions. Not so obvious, however, is that low-status persons also support the same values, even though the values are related to dimensions on which these persons are ranked low. The impoverished person who ranks others in terms of wealth, or the Negro who ranks others in terms of lightness of skin color, are cases in point.

Thibaut and Kelley (1959) have suggested a number of reasons for this consensus on values. In part, those who are disadvantageously ranked perceive some prospect of achieving these values. Another support for the values, however, is that they are of functional importance in everyday life. Even though a poor person may maintain that money isn't everything, he knows full well that he would have difficulty getting along with less than he has.

Perhaps a more subtle reason cited by these theorists is that, when the low-status person acknowledges the superior attributes of the high-status person, he reduces the power of that person to some degree. This arises from the fact that the high status of a person is dependent upon the assent of the low-status persons to the values supporting his high status. Only if they recognize his status does he really have it. Thus the high-status person cannot abuse his position by misusing his power, for he may thereby lose his status. The dignitary given the best table and attentive service in a fine restaurant is in no position to register complaints; in fact, he must recognize that he has been accorded high status by generous tipping. This example illustrates another reason why low-status persons often support the high status of others; they may make direct gains from it. For example, high-status persons in a community must contribute much more of their time and money to charity. High-status persons in a business organization are expected to work overtime without extra pay if the work is needed. Thus, the low-status person often escapes many responsibilities and obligations that go with high status.

Several studies suggest that individuals behave so as to validate their status, thus helping to maintain the status structure of the group, as well as their own position. Whyte (1943), in his classic study of a street corner gang, noted that the bowling scores of the members consistently reflected their status when they were bowling with the group but deviated markedly in some cases when they were not bowling with the group. Whyte explained this consistency as a function of the correspondence between a member's confidence and his group status and also as a result of group pressures. When the scores of low-status persons momentarily rose out of line, they were often mercilessly heckled until their confidence was shaken and their performance suffered.

That confidence and status are associated is also suggested by another study. Harvey (1953) demonstrated that a subject's expectations concerning future performance in a dart-throwing game corresponded to his group status. Estimates of their own performance by high-status participants were higher than similar estimates by low-status participants.

The work of Brookover, Thomas, and Paterson (1964) suggests that a person's ideas of his performance in specific areas are related to more general aspects of self and also to evaluations of him by others. They found a substantial correlation between a person's performance in several areas of study and his self conceptions of his general ability and his ability in specific areas. They also obtained sizable correlations between these conceptions of ability and the ideas persons had concerning what others thought of their abilities.

STUDY QUESTIONS

12. *In what ways does value consensus contribute to a stable structure?*

13. *Explain why low-status persons support the values of their group.*

Summary: Stability of structure

Since status congruence and distributive justice are rewarding conditions, people will resist changes that disrupt them and by doing so will contribute to stability of the status structure. Status conversion processes contribute to status congruency: a person presents himself to others so that they judge him similarly on various dimensions of status, or he uses a resource from one status dimension to advance himself on another. Balance theory suggests that status will be perceived in a global fashion: there is a tendency to see all its dimensions in a favorable or unfavorable light. Association between a person of low status and one of high status is likely to improve the status of the former.

Certain external processes contributing to value consensus among group members also contribute to stability of the status structure. Obviously persons high on the various dimensions of status support values related to these dimensions. But low-status persons also support these values. In part this is because they perceive some prospect of achieving these values. The values are also functionally important in everyday life: they bring rewards and reduce costs. A more subtle factor is that, by acknowledging superior attributes of the high-status person, the low-status person reduces the power of that person. A high-status position is dependent on recognition of the relevant values by the low-status person. Thus the high-status person cannot abuse his position by misusing his power. Finally, persons are allowed and encouraged to behave in a manner appropriate to their position in the status structure.

CHANGE IN THE STATUS STRUCTURE

Status congruence, distributive justice, and value consensus have been discussed so far from the standpoint of stability, but these same variables together with a fourth, the need for self-enhancement, also have implications for an analysis of change. The need for self-enhancement, which is discussed in more detail in Chapter 19, is expressed in the use of various individual processes to maximize status. A person may present himself so as to increase his status on a particular dimension. He may also misperceive his own characteristics and those of other persons in order to convince himself that he occupies a higher status. Even though such actions may alter an individual's position, they do not interfere with the stability of the status system in a group unless competition for position becomes too disruptive.

Another type of reaction does upset stability, however, since it reduces value consensus. Of the dimensions upon which people are judged, some are more crucial than others. One way in which a person can increase his status relative to others is to perceive that the dimensions on which he is relatively high are the important ones and that those in which he ranks low are rather incidental. The findings from a number of studies suggest that persons do engage in this process. The older worker in industry emphasizes seniority more than education. Upper-middle-class persons emphasize wealth in overall class position and deprecate the importance of coming from an old family. When group members emphasize different values in this manner, the status structure becomes less stable.

Value consensus may also be weakened during a period when objective conditions are changing the value structure of a group. Attributes that at one time were important determinants of status, because they were associated with attaining important values and goals and were relatively rare, no longer carry as much weight. In the early period of a group's existence, for example, the abilities of a "promoter" may lead to high status, but after the group becomes established, administrative abilities may become more important.

Status congruence has been emphasized as a source of stability in the group structure, in that departures from such a state encounter resistance. At the same time, however, status congruence can spread the effects of changes in one dimension to other dimensions. As a new dimension emerges or becomes more important, the ranking on this dimension will exert pressure toward realignment of persons on other dimensions and will thus reestablish congruence at a new level. Similar effects occur as a result of the failure of distributive justice. These effects are all consistent with balance theory.

STUDY QUESTIONS

14. *What is meant by the need for self-enhancement, and how does it manifest itself?*

15. *What two factors may contribute to a weakening of value consensus?*

16. *How may status congruence contribute to changes in the status structure?*

DISTINCTIONS BETWEEN STATUS AND AFFECT STRUCTURES

Unfortunately, affect and status have not been clearly separated in studies involving sociometric measurement. Particularly where findings based on different criteria of choice have been lumped together, it is difficult to know whether conclusions drawn apply to the affect structure or the status structure, or both. Yet affect and status involve different sentiments and represent different group structures. There is a subtle but very real distinction between affection and admiration, which the disappointed swain well knows when told, "I admire you immensely but I do not love you."

One distinction between affect and status was established in the discussion of psychegroups and sociogroups. Choices on a psychegroup criterion tend to reflect the relatively idiosyncratic needs of the individual; those involving a sociogroup criterion reflect the shared needs of group members as influenced by task, group, and situational factors. As a result, the psychegroup structure is characterized by a more even distribution of choices and the sociogroup structure by a concentration of choices directed toward certain persons (Jennings, 1950). A recent study of popularity among adolescents found a much greater concentration of choice on a few persons where the criterion of choice reflected status, and a more even distribution where it reflected liking (Coleman, 1961). This difference between the two structures reflects a difference in the shared bases of evaluation. People accord status to others on the basis of values and needs that are *jointly held* by group members, but they like each other on the basis of relatively unique values and needs. This is not to say that affect is based on completely unique values. Certain persons are widely liked because their behavior meets common needs and coincides with widely held values. But liking includes a sizable unique component and status does not.

Because of this difference in consensus of values, the status structure is more hierarchal than the affect structure. In the status structure, persons are more uniformly ranked relative to each other, and since their positions are based on agreed-upon criteria, the positions are more readily associated with the shared attribution of worth. The shared nature of the criteria involved is crucial here. The moral element peculiar to status, as well as its importance to the individual, follow from this. Status comparisons always involve relative worth, because a person is judged on how well he measures up to values which, if widely shared, are generally important values. That the values are widely shared means that others will react uniformly to a person in terms of the degree to which his behavior is consistent with them. Whereas a person may find some persons but not others whose relatively unique needs and values result in their liking him, he will be accorded higher or lower status uniformly by all persons. Since persons are rewarded to the degree that their behavior coincides with the values of others, status becomes strongly associated with the rewards persons experience in interaction. Consequently, people learn to become crucially concerned about their status.

STUDY QUESTION

17. *Indicate the various points of distinction between the affect structure and the status structure.*

STATUS CONGRUENCE AND CONSISTENCY THEORY

Sampson (1963) has recently provided a theoretical scheme that links status congruence with notions of cognitive consistency discussed in Part Two of this book. He makes the assumption that social interaction requires some coordination among the actions of the person involved. This coordination is presumed to require a degree of anticipatory knowledge about one's own future behavior and the behavior that may be expected of the other persons in the situation. Such expectations enable persons to carry out the interaction with a minimum of confusion.

Through experience, each individual acquires a large number of such expectations which provide a kind of model of his social world. The more internally consistent they are, the less confusion and conflict he will encounter in social interactions. Therefore the individual strives to achieve this state of *expectancy congruence.*

These individual tendencies toward expectancy congruence motivate a person to present himself in a congruent manner. If he behaves inconsistently, he finds it difficult to maintain a consistent picture of himself. He also confuses and disturbs other persons, who put pressure on him to behave more consistently. Sampson gives an example of a nurse who felt not only that she must be a strict supervisor of a group of nursing trainees for whom she was responsible, but also that she must be a warm, compassionate counselor, helping the trainees with their personal problems. She found it very difficult to behave toward the trainees in these incompatible ways.

The general principle of expectancy congruence makes status congruence a special case: incongruency in status dimensions is only one way in which a person might present himself in an inconsistent fashion.

SUMMARY: STATUS

Status is the worth of a person as estimated by a group or a class of persons. The estimate of worth is determined by the extent to which a person's characteristics are perceived to contribute to the shared values and needs of the group or class. Persons are accorded high status to the degree that their attributes are rewarding to the group members. Only characteristics in scarce supply, however, contribute to status. Status may be analyzed in terms of the extent to which a person is perceived to receive rewards and incur costs, as well as with the extent of his investments—his past history or background.

Status arises out of the comparisons of rewards, costs, and investments of persons. The principles of distributive justice and status congruence explain reactions to such comparisons. Distributive justice is obtained when the outcomes of each person are directly proportional to his investments. Status congruence is a condition in which all the stimuli presented by a person rank higher than, equal to, or lower than than all the stimuli presented by another person. Distributive justice and status congruence have a somewhat different motivational basis. When distributive justice fails, the person feels cheated; when status congruence is violated, others do not behave toward him in a predictable manner. Status comparisons are most likely to be made by members of small face-to-face groups, where rewards received and costs incurred by others may be readily observed, where the power of different members is not too disparate, and where rewards and costs received are not too different.

Because of their tendency to maintain status congruence and distributive justice, people resist changes potentially disruptive of these states.

Such resistance contributes to the stability of the status structure. Persons present themselves to others so that they will be judged consistently on various dimensions of status; they also use resources from one status dimension to advance themselves on another. The tendency of perceptual processes to form balanced states contributes to perception of all the dimensions of status attributed to a person in an unfavorable or favorable light. High-status persons maintain the *status quo* by supporting values relevant to their status. Low-status persons do too—because they perceive some prospect of achieving these values, because these values are functionally important, and because, in conferring high status on other persons, they gain some measure of control over them. Finally, persons are allowed and encouraged to behave in a manner appropriate to their position in the status structure.

The individual's need for self-enhancement leads him to present himself in such a way as to maximize his status. It may also lead him to misperceive his place and the place of others in the status hierarchy. Differing emphases on different values produce stress toward change. These arise from differing investments or from changes in the group function occurring as a result of external factors. Disruption of status congruence or of a condition of distributive justice produces pressures to restore equilibrium, which under certain conditions may be established in a revised status structure.

Affect and status structures have frequently been confused, but they may be clearly distinguished on the basis of the following differences. Affect choices reflect the more idiosyncratic needs and values of the individual, whereas status choices reflect the shared needs and values of group members. Because of this difference in consensus on values, the status structure is more hierarchal than the affect structure. Positions in the status structure are based on widely shared evaluations having an element of moral approval. These evaluations more uniformly affect the rewards and costs that members experience, making status important to the group member.

Communication

If over a period time one were to observe systematically groups such as residents of a dormitory casually discussing campus events, a committee focusing on a neighborhood problem, or housewives exchanging gossip, he would note certain regularities in communication among group members. If each person's communicative acts were counted, a fair degree of consistency in their frequency would be discovered over time. If in addition to his initiation of communications, the number of times each person received a communication were recorded, certain persons would be observed to receive many more communications than others. The same persons would be likely to address various members, as well as the group as a whole, more frequently. If the content of communications were also taken into account, certain systematic differences would be perceived. Some group members would express opinions more often, and others would more frequently request opinions or express agreement or disagreement with the opinions stated.

OBSERVATION AND ANALYSIS

Bales has provided a method called *interaction process analysis* for observing communication in a systematic fashion. The heart of the method is a system of categories which is presented in Figure 9–1. The system is used to classify the interaction that takes place in a group. Each item of behavior, whether it is a verbal comment or merely a shrug or laugh is classified in one of the categories shown in Figure 9–1 and tallied on a moving paper. For each item, the person initiating it and the person (or persons) toward whom he directs it are identified. Bales (1950) provides a hypothetical running account of this recording procedure. Here is the first portion of his account:

> Let us imagine we are observing a group of five persons who are meeting together to come to a decision about a point of policy in a project they are doing together. Three or four of the members have arrived, and while they wait they are laughing and joking together, exchanging pleasantries and "small talk" before getting down to business. The missing members arrive, and after a little more scattered conversation the chairman calls the meeting to order. Usually, though not necessarily, this is where the observer begins his scoring. . . .
>
> The chairman brings the meeting up to date with a few informal remarks. He says, "At the end of our last meeting we decided that we would consider our budget before laying out plans in greater detail." The observer, sitting with the observation form in front of him, looks over the list of twelve categories and decides that this remark is most relevant to the problem of orientation, and specifically that it takes the form of an "attempted answer" to this problem, and so he classifies it in Category 6, "Gives orientation, information, repeats, clarifies, confirms." The observer has already decided that he will designate the chairman by the number 1, and each person around the table in turn by the numbers 2, 3, 4, and 5. The group as a whole will be designated by the symbol 0. This remark was made by the chairman and was apparently addressed to the group as a whole, so the observer writes down the symbols 1-0 in one of the spaces following Category 6 on the observation form.
>
> In this one operation, the observer has thus isolated a unit of speech or identified the member who performed the act, and the person or persons to whom it was directed. If he were writing on a moving tape instead of a paper form, as we do for some purposes, he would also have identified the exact position of the act in sequence with all others. (Pp. 259–260)

Observations recorded in this manner may be analyzed in a number of ways. One is to construct a "who-to-whom" matrix. In this matrix, shown

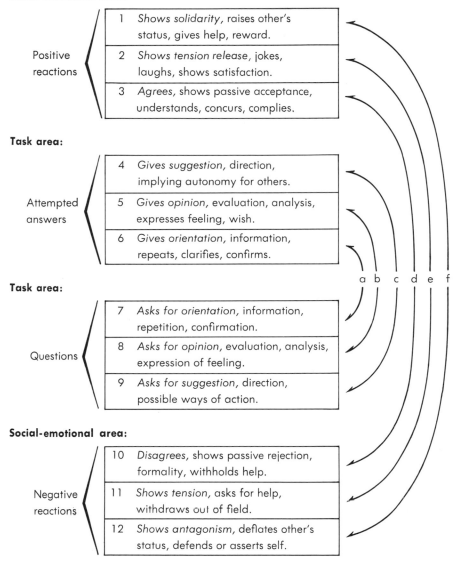

Social-emotional area:

Positive reactions
1. *Shows solidarity*, raises other's status, gives help, reward.
2. *Shows tension release*, jokes, laughs, shows satisfaction.
3. *Agrees*, shows passive acceptance, understands, concurs, complies.

Task area:

Attempted answers
4. *Gives suggestion*, direction, implying autonomy for others.
5. *Gives opinion*, evaluation, analysis, expresses feeling, wish.
6. *Gives orientation*, information, repeats, clarifies, confirms.

Task area:

Questions
7. *Asks for orientation*, information, repetition, confirmation.
8. *Asks for opinion*, evaluation, analysis, expression of feeling.
9. *Asks for suggestion*, direction, possible ways of action.

Social-emotional area:

Negative reactions
10. *Disagrees*, shows passive rejection, formality, withholds help.
11. *Shows tension*, asks for help, withdraws out of field.
12. *Shows antagonism*, deflates other's status, defends or asserts self.

a   b   c   d   e   f

Key:
a. Problems of orientation
b. Problems of evaluation
c. Problems of control
d. Problems of decision
e. Problems of tension-management
f. Problems of integration

Figure 9–1

The system of categories used in observation and their relation to major frames of reference. (Adapted with permission from R. F. Bales. A set of categories for the analysis of small group interaction. *Amer. sociol. Rev.*, 1950, **15**, 146–159.)

in Table 9–1, persons are arranged on one axis as initiators and on the other as the recipients of a communication. Many of the empirical studies discussed in the following sections make use of this type of matrix to analyze data.

STUDY QUESTIONS

18. *What major categories of communication are classified by means of inter-action process analysis?*
19. *Describe the main features of a "who-to-whom" matrix.*

THE COMMUNICATION STRUCTURE AND ITS CORRELATES

One investigation combined observations made on a number of groups in a variety of face-to-face situations and put them into one matrix (Bales, 1952). When participants were ranked according to the total num-ber of acts they initiated, it was found that they ranked similarly on the number of communications they received, the number they directed toward other individuals, and the number of acts they addressed to the group as a whole. Not only did high initiators differ from others in the volume and direction of their communications, but the content of their communications also differed. Those who most frequently initiated acts gave out more information and opinions to other persons than they re-ceived, while the remarks of the low communicators more frequently fell in the categories of agreement – disagreement and requests for informa-tion.

Table 9–1
Aggregate Matrix for 18 Six-man Groups

PERSON ORIGINATING ACTS	INDIVIDUAL RECEIVING ACTS						TOTAL TO INDI-VIDUALS	TO GROUP AS A WHOLE	TOTAL INI-TIATED
	1	2	3	4	5	6			
1		1238	961	545	445	317	3506	5661	9167
2	1748		443	310	175	102	2778	1211	3989
3	1371	415		305	125	69	2285	742	3027
4	952	310	282		83	49	1676	676	2352
5	662	224	144	83		28	1141	443	1584
6	470	126	114	65	44		819	373	1192
Total received	5203	2313	1944	1308	872	565	12205	9106	21311

SOURCE: Reprinted by permission from R. Bales, F. Strodtbeck, T. Mills, & Mary E. Roseborough. Channels of communication in small groups. *Amer. Sociol. Rev.*, 1951, **16,** 463.

These features of communication appear to be related to the size of the group, the physical arrangements of its members, the members' personalities, the group's normative structure, certain features of the communication process, and the affect, power, and status structures of the group. Each of these will be discussed in turn.

Size and physical arrangement

Group size has been related to several features of the communication structure and to several other communication variables (Thomas & Fink, 1963). Two studies suggest that, as size increases, the most active communicators become increasingly active relative to the other group members (Bales et al., 1951; Stephan & Mishler, 1952). The fact that in a different task situation Miller (1951) failed to obtain this result, however, casts some doubt on the generality of these findings.

The content of the communication also appears to vary with group size. Bales and Borgatta (1955) found that, as size increased, the frequency of communication increased in the categories of showing tension release and giving suggestions, and decreased in showing tension, showing agreement, and asking for opinion. On the basis of studies by Berkowitz (1958) and Slater (1958), Thomas and Fink (1963) conclude that smaller groups inhibit the expression of disagreement and dissatisfaction.

As to physical arrangement, a number of studies suggest that proximity, as well as other physical features which increase the probability of contact, also affects the frequency of communication between members and the amount of interpersonal attraction (Festinger, Schachter & Back, 1950; Wilner, Walkley, & Cook, 1952; Byrne & Buehler, 1955).

Individual differences in communication

While the personality characteristics which are associated with a high frequency of speech in a group have not yet been isolated, persons do have a characteristic rate of speech and of silences (Goldman-Eisler, 1951; Borgatta & Bales, 1953; Klein, 1956). Investigations suggest that a person has an upper boundary to his communication rate that he reaches if the situation allows. In fact, in connection with her observations of the frequency of participation of group members, Klein (1956) makes the following comment:

> Moreover, it seems as though each member has in mind a standard time which he feels entitled to fill, so that when he feels he has spoken too much, or too little, in the first half-hour of the meeting, he will modify his volubility during the second half in order to average on the whole his self-appointed allowance of communication. (Pp. 166–167)

This kind of self-allotment, of course, reflects more than personality factors. First, the amount of communication is affected by the extent to which an individual conforms to the norms of the group. In a classic study, Schachter (1951) was able to show that the degree a person's conformity to the norms for opinions in the group affects the frequency with which he is a recipient of communication from others. Schachter arranged for paid participants to adopt three different roles in a discussion group. One, called the *mode,* was instructed to champion a position which the greatest number of persons in the group took. A second, the *deviate,* was instructed to take and maintain an extreme position opposed to the modal opinion. A third, the *slider,* was asked to take the extreme position of the deviate and then, as the discussion continued, to move step by step to the modal position. It was found that members communicated most frequently with the person whose position was most deviant, at least until it appeared to them that he was not going to change his opinion.

Second, the amount of communication engaged in by the various members of a group has been related to the affect, power, and status structures. Empirical studies on this topic will be discussed in the next two sections.

Affect structure and communication

Bales (1952) reports that persons who are high on initiation are also high in popularity and status—their status being reflected by the fact that they are perceived to have the best ideas and to guide the discussion effectively. Other investigators report correlations between status and frequency of participation (Norfleet, 1948; Bass, 1949). In one study, however, the correlation between participating and being liked was considerably lower than that between participating and being chosen as most productive (Norfleet, 1948). This is consistent with Bales's initial findings (1953) that the relation between liking and frequency of initiation is curvilinear: the highest initiator in a five-man group was less liked than the person second or third in initiating communication; he was also more disliked than all others.

In Chapter 7, evidence was cited in support of the proposition that, other things being equal, an increase in interaction results in an increase in liking. Here the reverse might be noted: an increase in liking results in an increase in interaction. One investigator created two different types of two-person discussion groups (Potashin, 1946). In one the participants were friends, and in the other nonfriends. The discussion between friends was longer, and each member of the friend pair contributed a relatively equal amount to the discussion. Nonfriends had shorter discussions and less equal contributions. Since interaction leads to liking, and liking to further interaction, such sequential effects should over time increasingly restrict communication to group members who are friends. This is consistent with a discussion by Klein (1956), who suggests that in informal friendship groups, the affect structure provides a fairly accurate picture of the communication structure. A study of rumor transmission in a neighborhood group has provided empirical support for this suggestion (Festinger et al., 1948).

STUDY QUESTIONS

20. *How does the size of a group affect the communication structure? How many aspects of physical arrangements that affect communication can you suggest?*
21. *Describe the relation between the amount of communication directed toward an individual and the extent to which he conforms to norms.*
22. *What is the relation between frequency of communication and status? Between liking and communication?*
23. *Under what circumstances are the affect and communication structures likely to be markedly similar? Under what circumstances are they likely to be dissimilar?*

Power, status, and communication

The structural variable that has most frequently been investigated in relation to communication is status, although the situations studied often involve differences in power as well. Two studies pertaining primarily to the relation between power and communication will be cited first.

Husbands and wives were studied in a situation requiring them to reconcile differences of opinion (Strodtbeck, 1951). This provided evidence for an association between frequency of communication and power. The spouse having the highest frequency of communication most frequently won the arguments. More recently, further empirical support for the association between frequency of communication and power has been presented in an investigation of problem-solving groups (Riecken, 1958). After providing a hint about a uniquely good solution to a problem to persons variously ranked high or low in talkativeness, the investigator found that the more talkative persons were more influential in getting this solution adopted.

Three relations between communication and status may be proposed: (1) Communication is likely to be directed toward high-status persons, (2) communication is likely to be directed toward persons of equal status, and (3) where the equality of status of two persons is in doubt, they are likely to avoid communication with each other. Evidence for each of these points is presented in the following discussion.

A number of investigations suggest that communication is likely to move upward in the status and power hierarchies. In two studies status differences were created by telling subjects that their task was more important than that of another group with whom they were working (Kelley, 1951; Cohen, 1958). Cohen's experiment in addition created the impression of differences in power by telling low-status subjects that the high-status group would determine whether they would be allowed at a later time to join the high-status group. An analysis of written messages exchanged by the groups revealed a clear tendency in both studies for messages irrelevant to the task to be directed upward in the status hierarchy.

Other investigators studied communications between members of different professions attending a mental health conference (Hurwitz,

Zander, & Hymovitch, 1960). Prior to meetings of discussion groups, each subject was asked to estimate how must he felt various other persons would influence him. The individuals perceived to have the greatest potential influence were classified as high-power persons, and those perceived to have little potential influence were classified as low-power persons. Later observation of the frequency and direction of communications demonstrated that subsequent communicative behavior was consistent with these perceptions. The low-power persons more frequently directed communications to high-power persons.

Several studies document the second point—that persons who are equal in status are more likely to communicate with each other than with persons having higher or lower status. One study, on the basis of replies to questions asking ninth- and tenth-grade girls whom in their own grade they would like most to talk with on a number of designated topics, produced the matrix shown in Table 9–2. Subjects were arranged in order of status on the vertical axis as initiators of communications and on the horizontal axis as recipients of communications. The figures in the cells represent the proportion of topics they would like to talk about; in other words, the desired amount of communication. The matrix provides quantitative evidence that persons are most likely to receive communications from others having a status equal to their own, and also that persons at all status levels prefer to direct communications toward others having higher status. This evidence may be observed if the matrix is examined in the following way. First, from the increasing figures in each *row*, it is

Table 9–2
Status and the Desire to Communicate

STATUS OF INITIATOR	STATUS OF RECIPIENT					
	Low 0	1	2	3	4	High 5
Low 0	**0.07**	0.26	0.22	0.26	0.41	0.49
1	0.11	**0.26**	0.26	0.26	0.47	0.60
2	0.07	0.20	**0.38**	0.42	0.54	0.69
3	0.07	0.18	0.36	**0.62**	0.76	0.81
4	0.05	0.19	0.33	0.52	**0.81**	0.88
High 5	0.04	0.16	0.25	0.39	0.66	**1.36**

SOURCE: Reprinted by permission from Matilda W. Riley et al. Interpersonal orientations in small groups: A consideration of the questionnaire approach. *Amer. sociol. Rev.*, 1954, **19**, 715–724.

clear that persons at all status levels prefer to communicate with those having higher status: the higher the status of the recipient, the more communications are directed to him. Second, in each *column* except the first, the highest figure falls on the principal *diagonal* of the matrix. Thus the largest number of communications is received from persons having a status equal to that of the recipient.

The third point—that when the equality of status of two persons is in doubt, they are likely to avoid interaction—was a suggestion by Homans (1961). Interaction is potentially costly, because a person might come out of it with a demonstrably lower status. If he avoids interaction, he can at least preserve a precariously balanced subjective equality of status. One study of power relations and desire for interaction between professions provides some support for this idea (Zander, Cohen, & Stotland, 1959).

The finding that persons who are unambiguously equal in status communicate with each other more frequently will be discussed in a later section. Some additional comments will be made here, however, concerning the upward direction of communication. This upward flow is due in part to processes inherent in the communication and status structures and to processes that make the communication and status structures interdependent, so that a person's position in one is supported by his position in the other. We have previously commented on the mutually reinforcing relation between liking and frequency of interaction. Liking leads to more frequent interaction, and increasing interaction produces more liking. A similar relation between frequency of interaction and status appears. Those who frequently initiate communications are more frequently judged as having the best ideas and as doing the most to guide discussion: this should contribute to the status of the high contributor.

Similarly, high- and low-status persons differ in the content of their communications in a manner consistent with their respective statuses. High-status communicators more often give information and opinion, activities associated with high status, whereas the responses of the low-status persons are passive, involving such responses as agreement, disagreement, and requests for information (Bales, 1952). An analysis of the content of messages exchanged between high- and low-status members also indicated that the high-status members protected their position by not criticizing their job in messages sent to low-status persons (Kelley, 1951). At the same time the messages from low-status persons admitted confusion over the task, a communication content consistent with low status.

Further indirect evidence indicates that high status is associated with high rates of communication (Hurwitz, Zander, & Hymovitch, 1960). High-status persons direct their communication toward other high-status persons, while low-status persons, less at ease in interaction, inhibit their responses, and when they communicate, do so mainly to high-status persons. Since high-status persons are more often the recipients of communication, and since such communication normally requires a response, one would expect a high rate of return communication on their part. These various processes converge to account in part at least for the association between a high position in the status structure and an active position in the communication structure.

STUDY QUESTIONS

24. *What is the relation between frequency of communication and power?*
25. *State three relations between status and communication, and briefly describe the evidence for them.*

Summary: The communication structure

Groups existing for any length of time appear to have a definite communication structure. This is evidenced by the fact that individuals show consistency in the number of communications they receive, the number they initiate, and the content of the communications they initiate. Frequency of communication is associated with the degree of status a person has in a group: the higher his status, the more likely he is to initiate and receive communications. Normally, however, persons with the highest frequency of communication are not the best liked. The larger the group, the more disparity exists between the high and low communicators.

Individual differences in communication rates are probably associated with variations in personality, although precise relations have not been identified. In addition, communication rates are affected by the degree of conformity to group norms. Persons who deviate markedly from norms are likely to receive many communications if group members believe that they can enforce conformity. If a person is recognized as an incorrigible deviant, however, he is likely to receive a minimum of communications.

Positive affect toward others is likely to be associated with a high amount of communication: friends communicate more with friends than with nonfriends. In informal friendship groups the affect structure closely resembles the communication structure. Three relations between communication and status may be described: (1) Communication is likely to be directed toward high-status persons, (2) communication is likely to be directed toward persons of equal status, and (3) where the equality of status of two persons is in doubt, they are likely to avoid communication with each other. These relations follow from the processes inherent in the communication and status structures and from processes that simultaneously determine the communication, status, affect, and power structures.

COMMUNICATION STRUCTURE AND EXCHANGE THEORY

Many of the research findings reported in the area of communication structure and process are derivable from exchange theory. First, let us consider the rewards and costs that group members commonly experience as they communicate.

Rewards

One reward experienced by a person as a result of a series of communicative acts on his part or on the part of another is group locomotion: as a result of communication, he and other group members are likely to move closer to the goal that prompted formation of the group. As group members learn that some individuals have knowledge and skill that can be used to achieve group goals, the communication rate of these persons may be expected to rise. The content of their communication will also reflect this awareness. More frequently than others they will be targets of requests for information and opinion, and they will more often provide information, give suggestions, and express opinions.

Another group of rewards is related to obtaining conformity, both to norms of opinion and norms of behavior. In part such conformity is rewarding because it facilitates effective group action; in part, however, a condition of conformity is satisfying in itself. This is particularly the case with respect to opinions that cannot be validated directly against some aspect of physical reality. Some opinions can be checked: My opinion that the room we are sitting in is 10 feet long can be tested by measuring it. Most opinions, however, are not so readily validated: One may believe that if the loser in the last presidential election had been the winning candidate, the present rate of unemployment would have been lower.

Festinger (1950*b*; 1954) has suggested that in such cases powerful forces emerge to "validate" one's opinion by comparison with the opinions of others. When a person encounters another holding a contrary opinion, he attempts to change that opinion in the direction of his own. The fact that group members direct communications toward the person holding deviant opinions has already been noted. An individual does this because in the past such influence attempts have been rewarding: other persons have moved their opinions closer to his. When a deviate does not shift his opinion to the satisfaction of the group, however, communications directed toward him fall off and he is rejected. This general topic of validation of one's opinions by comparison with the opinions of others will be discussed in more detail in Chapter 10.

A wide variety of other social-emotional needs is rewarded in communicative activity. Some are related to the need for self-enhancement. On the basis of his study of communication in experimentally created hierarchies, Kelley (1951) suggested that communication upward in a status hierarchy is rewarding because it serves as a substitute for movement to a higher status. Another principle likely to operate in everyday situations, where a person has some control over whom he interacts with, is status contagion. According to this idea, when a low-status person is communicating with a high-status person, others are likely to classify him as an equal or near equal of the high-status person. Finally, other studies indicate that persons are motivated to communicate with high-status persons because the latter have power to provide low-status persons with rewards and to defray their costs (Cohen, 1958; Hurwitz, Zander, & Hymovitch, 1960).

Costs

The major costs experienced through communication are the reverse of rewards. These can be readily noted if one asks what inhibits people from speaking. Persons may recognize that their contribution might impede rather than expedite achievement of group goals. Similarly, they may withhold a communication because previous contributions in similar situations lowered their status or reduced affect toward them. Being rebuffed or publicly ignored is costly because it confirms low status. The feeling of anxiety engendered by previous experience with these costs is often sufficient to inhibit participation. This anxiety is particularly strong under conditions that make the likelihood of such costs highly salient. In groups where they are relatively low in popularity, status, and power, persons learn from sad experience that the balance of rewards and costs associated with their contributions is frequently negative. Since individual variability in power, status, and affect is greater as the size of the group increases, greater individual differences in communication should also occur.

A review by Hare (1962) of available data supports this idea:

> Not only does the average amount of participation per member diminish as group size is increased, but the distribution of participation also varies. . . . Generally, in discussion groups of sizes three to eight, all members address some remarks to the group as a whole, but typically only one member, the top participator, addresses more to the group as a whole than to specific other members. As group size increases, a larger and larger proportion of the participators have total amounts of participation under their "equal" share, that is, under the mean for the group. (P. 231)

Our analysis has suggested some of the rewards that motivate persons to communicate upward in the affect, status, and power hierarchies. The discussion of costs suggests why persons also are motivated to communicate with their equals. Communication upward is hazardous; persons are never sure that the high-status person will behave in a rewarding fashion. Among equals, however, each has sufficient counterpower to ensure equality of exchange. Evidence for such equality has been previously cited in the study of two-person discussion groups (Potashin, 1946). Members of each friend pair talked approximately an equal amount; in nonfriend pairs, one member talked more than the other. Finally, where there is uncertainty over equality of status, interaction may be costly because it might confirm low status instead of equality. Thus the tendency for those whose relative status is in doubt to avoid interaction is understandable from the standpoint of exchange theory.

Other previously described findings on communication structure are similarly derivable from exchange theory. It is not surprising that proximity as well as other factors affecting the frequency and ease of interaction facilitate the development of communication patterns in a group. These factors reduce such costs as time and effort in communicating. Similarly, individual differences in communication rates reflect not only the individual's position in the power, affect, and status structures, but also denote the significance of these rewards and costs in his psychic economy. For instance, some persons may tend toward high volubility because of strong status strivings.

STUDY QUESTIONS

26. *Summarize the rewards and costs that may be experienced by a person as a result of communicating with other members of his group.*

Summary: Communication and exchange theory

Rewards experienced by a person as a result of communicative acts on his part include moving the group toward its goals, validating his opinions or attitudes, and satisfying social-emotional needs such as the need for self-enhancement. Costs of communication include the possibility that his contributions may impede achievement of group goals or may lower his status. Exchange theory explains many of the observed relations between communication and status. Communication occurs among equals because each has sufficient counterpower to ensure equality of exchange. Communication is often directed upward because of the greater reward-cost outcomes that may be derived from communication with a high-status person. Factors such as proximity and other conditions affecting the frequency and ease of interaction facilitate communication because they minimize cost.

Summary and Conclusions

Status is the worth of a person as estimated by a group or a class of persons. This estimate of worth is determined by the extent to which a person's characteristics are perceived to contribute to the shared values and needs of the group or class. Status arises out of the comparisons of rewards, costs, and investments of persons. The principles of distributive justice and status congruence explain reactions to such comparisons. Distributive justice is obtained when the outcomes of each person are directly proportional to his investments. Status congruence is a condition in which all the stimuli presented by a person rank higher than, equal to, or lower than all the stimuli presented by another person. Status comparisons are most likely to be made by members of small face-to-face groups, where rewards received and costs incurred by others may be readily observed, where the power of different members is not too disparate, and where rewards and costs are not too different.

Various processes operate to maintain the status structure. These include people's inclination to present themselves in a manner compatible with status, the tendency of perceptual processes to form balanced states, and factors supporting the values that underlie status attributes. Forces toward changing status structures include the need for self-enhancement, differing emphases on values, changes in group function occurring as a result of external factors, and disruption of status congruence or distributive justice.

The status and communication structures are related to each other. Communication structures in existing groups are evidenced by the fact that particular frequencies of initiation and receipt of communications, as well as the content of communications initiated, are consistently associated with certain individuals in the group. Three relations between communication and status may be described: (1) Communication is likely to be directed toward high-status persons, (2) communication is likely to be directed toward persons of equal status, and (3) where the equality of status of two persons is in doubt, they are likely to avoid communication with each other. These relations follow from the processes inherent in the communication and status structures and from processes that simultaneously determine the communication and status, affect, and power structures.

Exchange theory explains many of the observed relations between communication and status. Communication occurs among equals because each has sufficient counterpower to ensure equality of exchange. Communication is often directed upward because of the greater reward-cost outcomes that may be derived from communication with a high-status person. Factors such as proximity and other conditions affecting the frequency and ease of interaction facilitate communication because they minimize cost.

chapter ten

EMERGING NORMS
AND CONFORMITY

Members of all groups exhibit certain regularities in their patterns of interaction. A close look at these patterns reveals that they often involve behavior which is considered desirable by group members. Further, they often involve behavior in which members exert pressures upon one another to conform to some recognized standard. Such regularities in group behavior have been explained in terms of *social norms*. A norm is a standard or behavioral expectation shared by group members against which the validity of perceptions is judged and the appropriateness of feelings and behavior is evaluated. The concept is broadly defined here to include perceptual, cognitive, and affective responses, as well as overt behavior. Thus the treatment by some writers (see Rommetveit, 1955) of frames of reference and behavior standards as two distinctly different kinds of norms is not adopted in this discussion. Shared frames of reference pertain simply to perceptual-cognitive behavior and are not basically different from behavior standards.

As an illustration, norms typical of a fraternity may be described. A fraternity is likely to consider the following appropriate: making moderately good grades, dating girls from certain sororities but not others, helping on fraternity projects, having feelings of loyalty toward the fraternity, being congenial with fraternity brothers, and believing that one's own fraternity is the best on the campus. Being placed on probation for poor grades, dating girls from the "wrong" sorority, refusing to cooperate on fraternity projects, disliking the fraternity, or fighting with fraternity brothers are clearly regarded as inappropriate.

Also closely associated with typical discussions of social norms are the mechanisms through which they are enforced. Of interest here are the means by which group members communicate to others the nature of appropriate and inappropriate behavior and the ways in which they exert pressure on other members to conform to the norms. Also important are the conditions that maximize or minimize these norm-defining and norm-enforcing processes. This chapter will focus primarily on these processes and conditions, while Chapters 14, 15, and 16 will focus upon norms as rules of conduct, in connection with the topic of social roles.

Norms and Norm Formation

The formation of a norm as a frame of reference against which perceptual judgments are made may be illustrated by a well-known laboratory experiment (Sherif, 1948). Three persons were brought into a dark laboratory room. They were told that a point of light would appear, move a short distance, and then go out. Their instructions were to call out the number of inches they thought the light had moved. The light was turned on repeatedly at intervals, and the subjects made a judgment each time. They were not asked to respond in any particular order; each gave his judgment as soon as he was ready.

Although subjects started out with somewhat different judgments in the experimental situation, after a number of trials the differences were narrowed down. Ultimately, judgments made by the three subjects were within an inch or two of each other. For example, on the first appearance of the light, one subject may make a judgment of 2 inches, another a judgment of 12 inches, and a third a judgment of 8 inches. But repeated presentations of the light result in a gradual shift in the judgments of all three until they stabilize around a mean, say, of 7 inches, with a range from 6 to 8 inches. Thus members of this small group eventually agree with respect to the distance that they believe the light moves on each trial.

The judgments in the experiment pertain to a well-known perceptual effect. A *stationary* point of light shown in a dark room will *appear* to move, a phenomenon known as the *autokinetic effect.* Thus the experimental subjects have no real basis for judging the amount of movement: the light is actually stationary. In the absence of clear perceptual cues upon which they might base their judgments, the participants apparently turn to each other for guidance. Many groups have been studied in this basic situation and in related ones, and the end result is nearly always consensus on some very narrow range of judgments (see Figure 10–1). This agreed-upon range has been referred to as a *social norm.*

Three further observations may be made about these laboratory norms. If an individual has formed a norm in the group situation and on a later occasion is tested alone, he still responds in terms of the norm. If subjects each form their norms in individual situations, however,

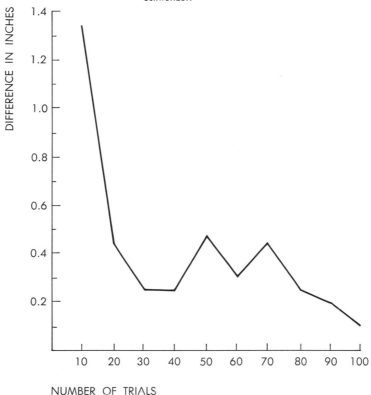

Figure 10–1

Convergence of judgments of the autokinetic effect in a two-person group. The difference between the mean judgment of two persons computed over each successive block of ten trials is shown. Data from which the figure was prepared were taken from an unpublished study by Don Schweitzer.

DIFFERENCE IN INCHES

NUMBER OF TRIALS

and are later placed together in a group, they will gradually change these individual norms to arrive at a common group norm. Another noteworthy fact is that most individuals in this laboratory situation state that they have *not* been influenced by the judgments of the other persons. Thus in this situation, at least, norms arise through processes of which the individual is not fully aware. Finally, the fact that actual pressures toward consensus are present in this situation has been demonstrated in several experimental variations. A naïve subject participated together with a high-status person who, by arrangement with the experimenter, established a norm at one point and then deliberately shifted to another. The naïve subject was observed to follow the high-status person's judgments. If norms were shifted too often and too radically, the naïve subject became very uncomfortable, presumably because he experienced a conflict over whether to conform to his subjective experience or to the judgments of the high-status person.

STUDY QUESTIONS

1. *Explain what is meant by a social norm.*
2. *What is the autokinetic effect? What are the main results obtained in experiments with individuals and groups in the autokinetic situation?*

FORCES TOWARD NORM FORMATION

That individuals in the laboratory who are confronted with the auto-kinetic situation will arrive at consensus has been clearly demonstrated. Moreover, consensus is arrived at in many other situations where individuals interact with each other, both in the laboratory and outside. A major aim of this chapter is to explain *why* persons in interaction gradually acquire certain uniformities in their behavior.

Pressures toward conformity in the behavior of group members arise whenever reward-cost outcomes are likely to be adversely affected by nonconformity. Such pressures are likely to arise for behavior relevant to the achievement of group goals. For example, rules against all members of a committee talking at once are obviously needed. Or in a squadron of military planes, strict conformity to carefully defined maneuvers is essential if accidents are to be avoided. These examples involving goal-relevant behavior are obvious; however, the necessity for having *opinions* conform to a norm, particularly opinions not relevant to group goals, is much less obvious. We may ask why pressures toward conformity of opinion arise.

Festinger has postulated a drive within human organisms to evaluate their opinions (Festinger, 1950*b*, 1954). He notes that having incorrect opinions can be punishing or even fatal. An example of punishing consequences would be the false belief that the girl you are dating is in love with you. This may lead to highly embarrassing, inappropriate behavior on your part. Fatal consequences are illustrated by the occasionally encountered opinion "I didn't think the gun was loaded."

PHYSICAL VERSUS SOCIAL REALITY

There are two sources that we rely on to determine the validity of our opinions: physical reality and social reality. We use our senses to obtain a good deal of information about the physical environment; to some extent, our opinions are validated by such information. But a second source of information is other persons. To a large extent, they interpret the world for us. Our parents warn us of dangers in the environment and explain away our unfounded fears. They also direct us toward rewarding aspects of the environment. Ultimately we learn to lean heavily on the opinions of others to validate our own. An important difference between physical and social sources of information is that social reality is often less certain: frequently there is little consensus among the opinions of other persons.

The relative weight of these sources of information varies with different circumstances. A series of experiments indicates the factors that account for variation in the extent to which a person may depend upon physical or social reality. In general, where clear stimulus cues are provided for a perceptual judgment, or where information is provided leading to an obviously correct answer, the individual is less influenced by the judgments of other persons. Where stimulus material is difficult or is structured so that the correct answer is not very clear, as in the autokinetic situation, the individual is more prone to rely upon judgments by other persons.

In one study a college student enters the laboratory along with seven other students and is seated at the end of the row. The experimenter explains that the investigation concerns the ability to make certain perceptual discriminations (Asch, 1956). Sets of lines of varying length are to be presented and compared with a "standard" line. In each set the particular line that equals the standard line is to be chosen. Individuals are to call out their judgments by identifying the correct line. A series of eighteen different sets are to be shown and judged.

During the first few trials, the student finds that the judgments are simple and obvious—any dolt could see which line is equal to the standard. To his great dismay, however, he discovers that on the next trial, the line that he sees as obviously correct is not chosen by the other students; they unanimously agree on a line that is unquestionably longer than the standard line. In fact, as the experiment continues, he finds that the rest of the group agrees with his perceptions on only one-third of the trials.

Most persons placed in these circumstances feel great pressure to disregard their own perceptions and to conform to the rest of the group. About one-third of them yield markedly to this pressure, conforming to the group on one-half or more of the trials. Others resist it to some degree, although not without great discomfort. What the subject does not know is that the other seven students are in the confidence of the experimenter, who has previously arranged with them to make wrong judgments. In this experiment, the powerful social pressure from the unanimous consensus of the seven other students frequently leads an individual to conform even though the stimulus situation is clear and unambiguous.

A variant of this experiment has been carried out with the aim of determining the extent of conformity when different types of stimulus materials are used (Blake, Helson, & Mouton, 1956). One might expect that judgments easily made from simple stimulus information would be less susceptible to conformity pressures than judgments having a basis only in social reality. Also, more difficult judgments should exhibit more conformity than easy judgments. In this study, each subject heard the responses of four other persons by means of earphones. He was under the impression that the other four were in adjoining rooms, although actually all their responses were tape-recorded. Since his judgments were made after he heard theirs, he was subject to their influence.

Each subject (1) responded to a simple task (the number of clicks of a metronome), (2) expressed attitudes having a basis only in social reality (answers to questions about war and peace), and (3) solved arithmetic problems varying in difficulty. The experimenter arranged matters so that the simulated group responses concerning the metronome and arithmetic items were frequently wrong and the attitude items were frequently unpopular (unpopularity was determined by the answers of a standardization group like the experimental subjects).

As might be expected, when presented with the metronome and arithmetic items, subjects were less prone to conform to the supposed group responses than they were when presented with attitude items. On the trials where the simulated group gave the wrong answer, 57 percent of the subjects nevertheless made the correct choice of metronome clicks, and 63 percent gave the correct answer to the arithmetic problems. But in the expression of attitudes, only 20 percent chose the answers preferred by the control group. A large proportion of the remainder chose the response unanimously presented by the simulated group on the tape-recording. Similarly, greater conformity to simulated group responses occurred for the more difficult arithmetic items than for the easier ones. Many other experiments, with different materials and situations, have yielded similar results.[1] There is some doubt whether matters of taste or preference, such as esthetic judgments of drawings, are subject to conformity pressures. One experiment (Crutchfield, 1955) failed to find conformity on such judgments; however, another investigation (Madden, 1960) requiring judgments of beauty did demonstrate conformity tendencies.

It may be concluded that the greater the anchorage of a judgmental situation in unambiguous stimulus information, the greater the resistance to conformity pressures will be. This resistance will be lower the more difficult the information is. Judgmental situations anchored only in social reality will exhibit more conformity behavior.

STUDY QUESTIONS

3. *What is meant by the need to validate one's opinions? In what ways is it satisfied?*
4. *Describe what is meant by the pressures of social reality. In what types of situations are the pressures toward social reality likely to be at a maximum?*

So far we have pointed to the consequences for reward-cost outcomes of conformity or deviation in opinions held by group members. Some opinions are closely linked to behavior. In that case, additional rewards and costs are involved, and the pressures toward conformity are increased. For example, opinions that are highly relevant to maintaining the

[1]Crutchfield, 1955; Weiner, Carpenter, & Carpenter, 1956; Kelley & Lamb, 1957; Coleman, Blake, & Mouton, 1958; Patel & Gordon, 1960; Radloff, 1961; Smith, 1961.

group or achieving its goals are subject to high conformity pressures. A group member's pessimism concerning ultimate achievement of the group goal may interfere with active efforts of the group to achieve its goal. On the other hand, opinions that have little relevance to maintenance of the group or achievement of its goals are likely to be subject only to weak conformity pressures. The importance of relevance has been demonstrated in an experimental investigation to be described in a later section (Schachter, 1951).

When only behavior and not opinion is involved, the rewards and costs of conforming or deviating are more prominent. Besides the obvious reward-cost outcomes that might occur, however, are certain more subtle consequences noted by Thibaut and Kelley (1959) as following from establishing norms to guide interaction. Consider two persons in a dyad who cannot achieve their best outcomes at the same time; for example, a husband who wants to go to the movies and a wife who wants to go dancing. This situation requires the use of power by a dyad member to extract desired behavior from the other member. But the constant use of personal power is not necessary if they can agree on a rule for trading, so that on one occasion they go dancing and on another to the movies. Ultimately agreement on this trade manifests itself in a regular sequence of behavior. If the sequence is interrupted, the injured party appeals to the rule to restore the appropriate sequence.

As Thibaut and Kelley note, such norms serve as excellent substitutes for personal influence. They make it unnecessary for a person to "spend" some of his power. A person may use his association with another to request a favor, but he is likely to feel obligated to return the favor. Moreover, the person who is asked to grant the favor may be unwilling to do so because for some reason he does not want the other person obligated to him. Both parties may relieve themselves of this psychological burden by establishing a norm to control the relevant behaviors. These ideas may be extended to include groups larger than two persons.

Some norms serve the purpose of identifying group membership. The satisfactions that persons experience when conforming to such norms stem from the feeling that one belongs to a group whose membership is valued. Conformity to rules of etiquette and to those governing correct speech signifies membership in polite, middle-class society, just as conforming to the norms of toughness may signify one's status in a lower-class boys' gang.

The rewards and costs in most forms of behavior subject to normative pressures are much more obvious than those discussed to this point. Often it is clear to all members that certain behaviors improve outcomes and others worsen them. In fact, the extent to which reward-cost outcomes are affected underlies the sociological principle of integration between norms and values. To the degree that a given rule of conduct establishes a valued state of affairs characterized by favorable outcomes, strong pressures will be exerted toward conformity to it. As discussed in more detail in Chapter 14, norms may be classified according to their relation to important values.

NORM-SENDING PROCESSES

According to Thibaut and Kelley, norms typically develop in a situation where persons would not ordinarily adopt the attitudes or behavior in question. There is no need for group controls where persons spontaneously produce certain behaviors of their own accord. But where the environment provides little structure, or where individuals have some resistance to performing particular actions that are necessary to group functioning, normative processes emerge to provide structure or to ensure that the behavior will be carried out. The operations by which norms are communicated and enforced have been termed *norm-sending* processes (Rommetveit, 1955). Norm-sending has three essential components: (1) defining the attitudes or behavior in question, (2) monitoring the extent to which the person conforms to the norm, and (3) applying sanctions (reward or punishment) for conformity or nonconformity.

Norm-sending may occur in many different ways. One example is that of direct, explicit norm-sending. The instructor in a class may indicate exactly what reading is expected of the class members, what kinds of examination questions must be prepared for, and what attendance is expected. Similarly, the parent in part transmits certain norms to his child in explicit verbal terms. He is not to tell lies, to make faces, or to break household furnishings. Much norm-sending, however, involves indirect communication. Norms for appropriate behavior on the part of a graduate student illustrate this process.

The graduate student is expected to be highly responsible and capable of independent study and work. Absence from seminars and failure to perform assigned tasks are violations of the norm. He is also expected to have a serious attitude toward his work and the profession for which he is preparing. If certain incidental behaviors on his part do not seem consistent with these expectations, faculty members are likely to have a low opinion of him. For the most part, however, these expectations are not conveyed to the new graduate student in so many words. Aside from evaluating the student's task performance through assignment of letter grades, the faculty communicates the norm by example and through various subtle sanctions.

In the first place, the professor sets an example of the proper attitude through his own enthusiasm and devotion to his work. He does not spare himself in attempting to advance his profession; in many instances this is apparent to the student. By giving heavy assignments, he makes clear that he expects a great deal of work from the student. In particular, he watches for signs of resistance to such tasks and ridicules typical objections or excuses commonly used by undergraduates. For example, the graduate student who asks how many pages an assigned paper should consist of is likely to be met with a raised eyebrow.

In the second place, most graduate students participate in some sort of professional employment under the supervision of professors. The assistant soon finds that his personal life is to be subordinated to his job. He is on call at any time, including weekends or holidays, should the work require it. He is likely to be given a brief period and a firm deadline for completing an arduous task. No questions are asked about other commitments that he might have—they are automatically assumed to be subordinate.

Thus, while normative expectations held by faculty members toward graduate students are not usually expressed in so many words, the "norms are sent" to the student through example, through assignment of tasks, and through indirect sanctions applied to inappropriate conduct. Incidentally, this illustration is not meant to imply that the faculty member is the only norm-sender. Other graduate students also serve an important function in this respect.

STUDY QUESTIONS

5. *In general terms, how does exchange theory account for normative pressures toward conformity?*

6. *What is meant by norm-sending processes?*

Summary: Norm formation

A basic human requirement appears to be the need for validation of one's opinions. Although clear information from the physical environment contributes to satisfaction of this need, the behavior of other persons also provides a source of validation. Particularly in situations where he is uncertain or confused—where he does not know how to react—a person can turn to the behavior of other persons to observe a stable world. This social reality provides him with a reference point for his own behavior. The more ambiguous the nonsocial stimulus situation, the more likely he is to depend on social reality for orientation.

To the degree that conformity in attitude and behavior improves reward-cost outcomes experienced by persons in interaction, pressures to ensure such action will be exerted. A wide variety of ways in which conformity or lack of it affects reward-cost outcomes will be cited in the remainder of this chapter.

Operations by which norms are communicated and enforced have been termed norm-sending processes. Norm-sending has three essential components: (1) defining the attitudes or behavior in question, (2) monitoring the extent to which the person conforms to the norm, and (3) applying sanctions (reward or punishment) for conformity or nonconformity. Norms may be communicated and enforced in a considerable variety of direct or subtle ways.

A Theory of Normative Behavior

Any theory that attempts to account for the normative character of social interaction must answer three questions. These concern the focus, extent, and distribution of conformity in a group.

1. What determines the kinds of behavior or attitudes that become targets of norm-sending? This question is dramatized by observations of the tremendous variability from group to group in the areas for which conformity is demanded. This is especially apparent for groups with widely different cultures; in fact, the fascination of the study of other societies lies largely in the differences between their norms and ours. But illustrations from our own society also make the point. In some areas, individual variability is little constrained by norms. It matters little which shoe we put on first in the morning; no one cares what color pajamas we wear or which side of the street we walk on; and we may assemble our meals from a wide variety of foods without being censured. In other areas, individual variability is severely curtailed. Men in our society are expected to shave daily. In certain occupations, they must wear a shirt and tie with a suit. When eating in the company of others, people must observe certain manners. An adequate theory must explain why some behaviors and attitudes are subjected to normative control and others are not.

2. Why is much greater conformity to norms found in some groups than in others? To illustrate, some religious groups conform much more strictly to the tenets of their faith than others. Similarly, the amount of discipline and obedience to orders is greater in some military units than in others. An adequate theory must explain these differences.

3. What determines the distribution of conformity *within* a group? To illustrate again with religious behavior, some members of the same church practice their religion more faithfully than others. Some college students carry out assignments and attend class more regularly than others in the same class. In any social group such as a fraternity chapter, certain members conform more closely to normative demands than others. Thus, some members do more than their share of committee and project work.

These three questions, then, deal respectively with the focus, extent, and distribution of conformity to norms. Again relying extensively on concepts from exchange theory, we can answer them in terms of the effects of four conditions: (1) the degree to which group members find the behaviors or attitudes of other persons rewarding or costly, (2) the power structure of the group, as determined by the distribution of rewards, dependencies, and alternatives, (3) the degree to which behavior in accordance with the norm is intrinsically rewarding or costly, and (4) the degree to which behavior is open to surveillance and to imposition of sanctions.

Focus, Extent, and Distribution of Conformity

The following three sections discuss the focus, extent, and distribution of conformity in terms of the four conditions outlined above.

AREAS IN WHICH NORMS EMERGE

Norms have a variety of *indirect* reward-cost outcomes, such as making the continued exercise of interpersonal power unnecessary, or helping to affirm a person's group membership. While a more extended discussion of conformity theory would include a consideration of these indirect outcomes, the present treatment will emphasize the more direct outcomes related to needs arising in the process of group formation and development.

Rewards and costs of conformity

Persons form groups to satisfy a variety of needs. Normative controls arise in the areas of behavior where members have become dependent upon the group for need satisfaction. These norms encourage behavior that maximizes member satisfaction and discourage behavior that might interfere with satisfaction. The prevalence and strength of the norms depend in part upon the extent to which members rely on the group for satisfaction of the particular needs aroused, and in part upon the strength of these needs.

Groups generally serve one or both of two types of needs: task-related needs or social-emotional needs. These relate to the sociogroup and psychegroup structures respectively, which were discussed in Chapter 7. Behaviors that contribute to accomplishment of a group task are likely to be subjected to normative control, for they lead to achievement of the group goals and member satisfaction, as well as to avoidance of failure. Thus norms develop to ensure cooperative action and to establish consensus on attitudes relevant to group goals. For example, members of a group must be required to attend meetings fairly regularly if the group is to survive. Members elected to office must be willing to serve; others must be willing to work as committee members. Consequently norms develop to encourage regular attendance and acceptance of service to the group, and sanctions are applied for failure to meet these task needs.

That the necessity for successfully achieving group goals leads to norm development is dramatized by Sutherland's (1937) classic study of the professional thief. Behaviors that would result in failure and arrest have strong negative sanctions, while those that are essential for success are mandatory. .For example, when thieves collaborate on a job, strict punctuality is a must. Failure to appear on the appointed time and place endangers the success of the enterprise and might even lead to arrest. Thus there is no waiting among thieves, and sanctions are likely to be applied to the person who fails to show. Similarly, professional criminals require each other to remain aloof from acquaintance with strangers or neighbors. A growing acquaintance with noncriminals lessens the anonymity of the criminal and might ultimately lead to detection and arrest of him and his associates.

Quite different needs are satisfied in psychegroups, leading to norms quite distinct from those of sociogroups. Psychegroups are formed largely for social-emotional satisfaction; they strongly emphasize obligations to meet certain individual needs of members, such as needs for friendship and love, for opportunities to share one's triumphs and defeats, and for belonging, acceptance, and support. Examples of this type of group are fraternities and sororities, which emphasize social needs like friendship and shared activities, and the family, which emphasizes emotional support. In such groups, norms arise to encourage fair treatment and to prohibit competition and aggression. Thus fraternity brothers are not supposed to compete with each other for the affection of the same girl. In the family, strong sanctions are applied for aggressive actions of the children toward each other or toward their parents.

The distinction between task-related and social-emotional needs should not be thought of as absolute; most groups in part satisfy both needs. For example, it has been shown that industrial work groups provide some emotional support to the individual worker that counteracts various anxiety-producing aspects of his work environment (Seashore, 1954; Roethlisberger & Dickson, 1939).

Power structure of the group

The attitudes and behaviors that are necessary to the satisfactions of the most powerful persons in the group are most likely to be subjected to normative control. As noted in Chapter 8, the amount of power possessed by a person depends upon the extent to which his resources satisfy the dependencies of others on him, and upon the number of alternative satisfactions available to these others. For example, in a family with small children, norms develop in directions desired by the parents rather than the children, because of the great discrepancy in power that exists between them. As the children reach adolescence and young adulthood, however, norms controlling the behavior of all the members change somewhat, in part because of the shift in balance of power toward a less unequal distribution. This occurs because of the increase in alternative satisfactions available to the young person, who finds increasing emotional satisfactions in his peer groups, and because of his reduced economic dependence on his parents when he obtains a job. These norm shifts are illustrated by the adolescent's criticism of some of the parents' behaviors and by the greater freedom he has in the hours he keeps and the activities he participates in which are not supervised by his parents.

Intrinsic costs and rewards

Certain behaviors are less susceptible to control than others by virtue of the fact that they are intrinsically associated with very high rewards or costs other than those derived from conformity. Thus, these behaviors produce rewards or costs that, compared with positive or negative sanctions from other members, have a relatively large effect on the total satisfaction experienced by the person. Any behavior associated with powerful biological or social motives may fall into the high-reward class.

Thus, smoking, which becomes a persistent habit difficult to break and which probably receives support from physiological drives, is unlikely to be successfully prohibited through legislative or other normative controls. Costly behaviors, too, are often exempt from normative control—other persons cannot reasonably *require* an individual to perform the behavior. For example, certain dangerous combat missions in wartime are not regarded by commanding officers as normative requirements, and only volunteers are assigned to them.

Where behavior is very costly, norms are likely to arise to reduce cost. For example, the medical student finds himself burdened with far more to do than he can possibly accomplish. Under these circumstances, he has to make decisions about what shall have priority. But this is a common problem for all medical students. In this instance, to avoid excessive competition from brilliant students, the group is likely to develop norms concerning how much work they will perform and what aspects of their work shall have priority, as well as norms ensuring cooperation with each other in sharing the work burden.

Similarly, where present normative behavior leads to unsatisfactory reward-cost outcomes, old norms may fade and new norms providing more satisfactory outcomes may arise. In recent years, a number of students of deviant subcultures have elaborated the process by which old norms are supplanted by new ones (Cohen, 1955; Merton, 1957*b*; Cloward & Ohlin, 1960). Fundamental to the initiation of this process is a lack of integration between the normatively approved means and goals in a group: behaving in the approved manner does not result in effective goal achievement. For example, the young, relatively untrained worker who adopts the middle-class norm that one should strive to move up the economic ladder through hard work may not find anyone willing to employ him. Where many individuals find themselves in this situation, they may in interaction with each other develop new normatively approved means of their own that do lead to goal achievement, or perhaps they may collectively develop new normatively approved goals that they can achieve with the means available to them.

Patterns of gang delinquency have been explained in this fashion. Lower-class boys or members of minority groups blocked in attempts to achieve the success goals of the dominant middle-class culture collectively fashion a set of normative expectations, a way of life containing means and goals that are functionally compatible. Such means as stealing and such goals as obtaining kicks from drugs, while disapproved by the larger society, become approved means and goals within this delinquent subgroup.

Surveillance and sanctions

Obviously, attitudes and behaviors that are difficult to monitor are less likely to be subjected to normative control. Sanctions cannot be applied unless transgressions are noted. Thus one's public or overt behavior is controlled by norms to a greater extent than one's private behavior or beliefs. The importance of surveillance may be illustrated by comparing open hostility with the indirect expression of aggression. The latter occurs much more frequently. Open hostility toward another person, such as physical violence, is easily observed and sanctions are readily applied; but various subtle forms of aggression, such as criticism in a context of pretended well-meaning, are difficult to detect and to punish.

STUDY QUESTIONS

7. *State three questions that must be answered by an adequate theory of conformity.*
8. *Explain how the types of needs satisfied by the group contribute to the behavior areas that fall under normative control.*
9. *What aspect of the power structure determines what behavior becomes subject to normative control?*
10. *How does the intrinsic reward-cost value of a behavior affect whether or not it becomes normatively controlled?*
11. *What part is played by surveillance and sanctions in subjecting behavior to normative control?*

Summary: The focus of conformity

Persons form groups to satisfy a variety of needs. Normative controls arise in the areas of behavior where members have become dependent upon the group for need satisfaction. In groups that have primarily a task function, for example, norms develop to ensure cooperative action and to establish consensus on attitudes relevant to goals. In groups that have predominantly a social-emotional orientation, behaviors providing emotional support, friendship, or love are more likely to be subjected to normative control. Attitudes and behaviors that are necessary to the satisfactions of the most powerful persons in the group are apt to be supported by norms.

Behaviors that are associated with powerful physiological drives or that are very costly are difficult to subject to normative pressures. In situations where costly behavior is necessary to achieve group goals, norms are likely to arise to minimize costs for members. Where present normative behavior has relatively unsatisfactory outcomes, norms are likely to be modified to produce more acceptable reward-cost outcomes. Finally, behaviors that are difficult to monitor are less likely to be subjected to normative control.

DEGREES OF CONFORMITY IN DIFFERENT GROUPS

The second question which any theory of normative behavior must answer is why much greater conformity is found in some groups than in others. Why, for example, are discipline and obedience to orders greater in a military unit than in a classroom group? The answers to this question are again found in the four conditions previously enumerated. The first is the degree to which members find the behavior of other persons in the group rewarding or costly.

Rewards and costs of conformity

Festinger, Schachter, and Back (1950) have suggested that the extent to which a group can exert pressure on its members to conform to some norm is limited by the cohesiveness of the group. In Chapter 7 cohesiveness was defined in terms of forces acting on a member to remain in the group. Several bases of attraction to the group were noted in Chapter 7: (1) high reward-cost outcomes stemming directly from interaction between members, (2) group activities that are rewarding for their own sake, and (3) membership in the group as a means to attaining other ends. Attraction is also relative to the comparison levels of group members, and the total force operating on group members to remain in the group is a function not only of attraction to the group, but also of the outcomes available in alternative relations outside the group.

Since the strength of the negative sanctions that a group can exert on its members is limited by the strength of the forces that hold members in the group, we might expect that the severity of negative sanctions that a group can impose on a recalcitrant member would vary with the strength of cohesive forces. Cohesion, in turn, depends on the degree to which the reward-cost outcomes of members exceed their comparison levels for alternatives. Casual observation of groups that are able to impose severe negative sanctions on their members supports this formulation. They are groups where membership involves high outcomes or groups where one would expect the members to have very low comparison levels for alternatives, either because they can command little in alternative relations or because alternatives are blocked. Certain adolescent groups illustrate the former, since they often provide satisfaction for powerful needs and are highly cohesive. Examples of groups whose members would be expected to have low comparison levels for alternatives are military units, religious sects, and prisoner groups. The alternative to conformity in a military situation is often a court martial and imprisonment. Members of religious sects, because they are often not accepted in other groups, have low alternative sources of satisfaction (Pope, 1949). Consequently the sect may very effectively control its members through such techniques as ostracism should they attempt to deviate from sect norms. Similar considerations apply to prisoner groups, since a prisoner is forced by assignment to prison blocks to associate with certain other prisoners, and he has no alternative associations.

A closely related point is that membership in groups besides the one in question may make conformity in that group costly. This is the case where the groups have conflicting norms. For example, if a person belongs to a fraternity which subscribes to the notion that the proper grade for a gentleman is a C, and if he also belongs to a campus group which stresses scholarship, he may find conformity to the norms of the latter group costly. From this line of reasoning it would seem that to the extent which a group discourages its members from association in other groups with conflicting norms, it would elicit a higher degree of conformity from its members because of reduced cost.

Various empirical studies have presented systematic evidence that pressures toward conforming behavior are stronger in a more cohesive group. One investigation determined the uniformity of attitudes and behaviors in campus housing groups which had various degrees of cohesiveness (Festinger, Schachter, & Back, 1950). It was found that the more cohesive the group, the more uniform the attitudes and behavior of the members. Moreover, in the more cohesive groups, those who deviated from the norm were less likely to be accepted as friends.

In a laboratory experiment already described in Chapter 9, certain participants were paid by the experimenter and by prearrangement adopted several different positions with respect to the norms in a group situation (Schachter, 1951). One person conformed closely to the norm, another (the slider) started from a deviant position but moved toward conformity to the norm, and the third maintained a nonconformist position. The experimenter analyzed the different ways in which these three types of persons were treated by naïve members. Although neither the conformer nor the slider was rejected by the other members, the deviant participant was rejected.

By forming groups in which activities differed in attractiveness, the experimenter had established differing levels of cohesiveness. He found that the greater the cohesiveness of the group, the greater the rejection of the deviant. This result was indicated by an initial high frequency of communications putting pressure on the deviant to conform and a subsequent marked reduction in communication, indicating rejection. Also, the more the deviation was relevant to the activity of the group, the more the deviant was rejected. Replications of the experiment generally support the findings (Emerson, 1954; Berkowitz & Howard, 1959). Members of high-cohesive groups are also more willing to accept influence than those of low-cohesive groups (Pepitone & Reichling, 1955; Lott & Lott, 1961). A study of high school teachers belonging to different subgroups of teachers also indicated that the more cohesive the group, the greater the conformity of the teacher to the norms of her subgroup (Rasmussen & Zander, 1954).

In another experiment, under one condition conformity was instrumental to being liked, and under another condition it was not (Walker and Heyns, 1962). This investigation is especially important for the exchange theory interpretation of conformity, for it emphasizes the rewarding consequences of conforming to norms. Subjects were informed that when persons agree with each other, they get along better and like each other more. To emphasize liking, subjects were also asked to rate each other on liking. Under this condition where conformity was instrumental to liking, the degree of conformity to tape-recorded opinions represented as coming from other subjects like themselves was much

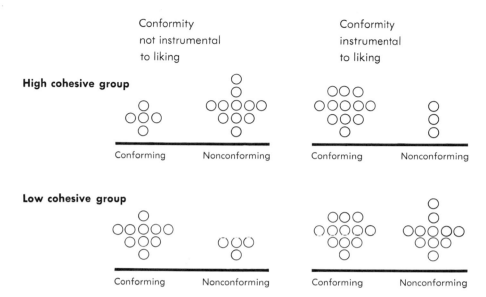

Figure 10–2
**Conformity as a function of cohesiveness and the
instrumentality of liking.** Each circle represents a
person. (Adapted with permission from E. L.
Walker & R. W. Heyns. *An anatomy for conformity.*
Englewood Cliffs, N.J.: Prentice-Hall, Inc., 1962.)

greater in high-cohesive groups than in low-cohesive groups. In a
control group, comparable except for the absence of instructions making
conformity instrumental to liking, conformity was somewhat higher in
the *low*-cohesive group. These relations are illustrated in Figure 10–2.
Thus, the degree of conformity to the opinions of others is a function
of the extent to which such conformity is thought to be rewarding.

STUDY QUESTIONS

12. *What determines the limit of the negative sanctions that can be exerted on
a group member to force him to conform?*
13. *Explain why groups such as military units and religious sects are able to
obtain relatively high conformity to norms from their members.*
14. *What is the experimental evidence in support of the view that group cohesiveness is associated with a relatively high level of conformity?*

Power structure of the group

From the discussion of power in Chapter 8, various features of a
group's structure might be expected to affect the extent of conformity
of the members. The connectedness of the power structure, the proportion of direct to indirect power, the number of power levels, and the
degree to which persons within each power relation have counterpower
over each other should be important. Greater conformity would be

expected with greater connectedness of the power structure, with a greater proportion of direct to indirect power, with fewer levels of power, and, in groups where many members exert influence over each other, with a greater number of members having counterpower over each other.

Since the degree to which persons in a group are able to influence each other is also dependent on the basis of power that exists between members, group conformity might be expected to vary with such bases. Some empirical studies are relevant to this issue.

The increasing use of coercive power not only increases the likelihood of conformity, but also arouses resistance to conformity. Resistance to conformity is reduced, however, if the person is attracted to the power figure. At the same time, exercise of coercive power reduces the level of attraction. One laboratory investigation relates the use of coercive and legitimate power to conformity (French, Morrison, & Levinger, 1960). To establish a basis for the legitimate and illegitimate exercise of power, subjects were informed what fines would be levied for working too slowly. When the supervisor levied fines outside this legitimate range, resistance to conforming to the norm increased. We might infer from these findings that an important condition for minimizing resistance to conformity to the norm is that the sanctions be perceived as legitimate by the member. Another study suggests that reward is more effective than punishment in bringing about conformity, mainly because of the resistance aroused by the use of punishment (Zipf, 1960).

From the discussion of power in Chapter 8, the basis of power might also be expected to determine the extent to which an influence attempt results in a permanent change. Influence through referent power is more apt to effect a permanent change in both public and private behavior. An influence attempt based on coercive power is likely to produce a temporary change persisting only as long as surveillance is maintained. The range of behavior is also likely to vary with the basis of power. Again, referent power should cover a broader range, whereas expert power is likely to be narrowly restricted to certain areas of behavior. Thus, groups in which normative control is based primarily on referent power are likely to exercise strong conformity pressures over a long period of time.

There are two main ways in which the continued use of power may result in an increase or decrease in the power of *A* over *B*. First, continued use of a particular form of power by *A* may directly affect the value of rewards or costs related to the power. To illustrate, the continual use of certain kinds of rewards by *A* will diminish in effectiveness as *B*'s needs for these rewards are satiated. A mother who controls her child by frequent rewards of cookies, candy, and other desired foods is apt to find that the efficacy of this control is greatly weakened as the child becomes accustomed to receiving these foods. At the same time, there are some kinds of rewards that, through creating further dependency, lead to an increase in power. In a relation where mutual attraction is initially low, for example, mutual attraction and dependence may gradually build up to the point where each member of the dyad has considerable power to gratify or inflict punishment on the other.

Second, continued use of a particular form of power by *A* over *B* may indirectly augment or reduce *A*'s power by creating side effects that broaden or reduce other bases of power in the relation. For example, continued use of reward power may foster identification that in turn increases referent power. In contrast to reward power, *A*'s continued exercise of legitimate power is not apt to lead to an increase or diminution of power except where it might cause *B* to further affirm or to question the values underlying it. Similarly, the continued exercise of expert power by *A* is not apt to be affected by continued use except in the case where such continued application either increases (or decreases) *A*'s status as an expert or results in *B* picking up the knowledge upon which it is based.

We have noted a laboratory experiment suggesting that the continual use of coercive power results in diminished affect toward the power figure, as well as decreased identification and reduced referent power. Coercion in a laboratory situation, however, is rather mild. Under extreme conditions of coercion and forced overt compliance, the basis of power may be converted to referent power. Chapter 6 described how some individuals imprisoned for a long time in concentration camps in World War II identified strongly with their captors. In Chapter 4, it was shown that various manipulations of dissonance through "forced compliance" brought about marked attitude changes. The dissonance experiments suggest the possibility that when coercion is made sufficiently powerful, the individual may decide to voluntarily commit himself to the position of the power figure. This commitment is likely to be followed by as full an acceptance of the position as possible, in order to reduce the dissonance brought about by the voluntary commitment.

To the extent that the power structure of the group takes forms that increase over time, the conformity level of group members may be expected to be high. Where the prevailing modes of control have bases that lose effectiveness over time, the level of conformity may be expected to be low.

STUDY QUESTIONS

15. *Describe the relations between conformity on the one hand and the use of reward power, coercive power, and legitimate power.*

16. *What types of power are likely to contribute to conformity over a period of time? Why?*

17. *In the exercise of power to elicit conformity, certain changes in the amount of power that A has over B occur. State what these changes are and explain why they occur.*

Intrinsic costs and rewards

In groups where behavior that happens to be in conformity with group norms is rewarding for its own sake, conformity is likely to be high. This is often characteristic of groups where satisfaction of social-emotional needs is dominant, or in task groups where the tasks themselves are enjoyable. Examples of the former are fraternities and sororities; of the latter, sports clubs. Where conformity involves behavior that is costly, however, as where tasks are boring, fatiguing, or dangerous, conformity is likely to be at a lower level, unless the costs of nonconformity are correspondingly increased. In work situations where sanctions for nonconformity are weak, the level of conformity to norms may be low. This line of reasoning is often used as an argument against seniority, tenure, and civil service systems, which protect the worker against severe sanctions.

Surveillance and imposition of sanctions

Similarly, in instances where conforming behavior is not intrinsically satisfying, surveillance becomes necessary. Unless behavior is monitored in some way and sanctions are imposed for failure to conform, the behavior is unlikely to occur. An obvious example is the military group, where many activities are not satisfying for their own sake. Similarly, most work situations have organized systems of surveillance and sanctions. Factory workers punch time clocks to provide a check on their working hours, whistles are blown to indicate the start and end of work shifts, and foremen and supervisors monitor the work operations to ensure a minimum interruption of work activities. Apparently, sixth-grade schoolwork is not too intrinsically satisfying. In an experiment where pupils were highly motivated to obtain a good grade, there was more cheating on examinations under conditions of low surveillance (Mills, 1958).

As the type of work becomes more intrinsically satisfying, surveillance and sanctions are much less evident. Various skilled crafts and professional work activities illustrate the point. For example, the skilled craftsman works with a minimum of supervision and control, and there is little monitoring of the teaching activities of the professor. If these people are not intrinsically motivated, they are unlikely to do a good job.

STUDY QUESTIONS

18. *What is the role of the intrinsic reward or cost value of behavior in determining the extent to which a group conforms to norms?*
19. *Under what conditions are surveillance and sanctions necessary to ensure conformity?*

Research suggests that another type of condition may make surveillance unnecessary. In a study where subjects felt that they were moderately accepted by other members of the group and that they had a possibility of becoming completely accepted, a high degree of conformity to the norms in *both* public and private behavior was found (Dittes & Kelley, 1956). On the other hand, subjects who had a very low degree of acceptance and who perceived the likelihood of being rejected by the group conformed very closely to the norm in their public behavior, but deviated markedly in private. Thus it appears that it is possible to create certain types of motivating conditions that will lead a person to conform both publicly and privately, without the necessity for surveillance. Where the major motive for conformity is insecurity over status or total rejection, public conformity is likely to be high, but conformity in private behavior is unlikely to occur.

Two other conditions require careful surveillance if conformity is to occur. These are the exercise of coercive power and nonlegitimate power. Under conditions of surveillance, these processes are likely to create public conformity accompanied by marked resistance to conformity, which expresses itself in sharp dissension in private attitudes. Several experiments support this conclusion (Raven & French, 1958a; French, Morrison, & Levinger, 1960).

Summary: Degrees of conformity in different groups

To the extent that conformity is costly, forces exerted toward it cannot exceed forces to remain in the group. Chapter 7 established that the latter forces are a function of the cohesiveness of a group. Several forms of attraction may contribute to cohesiveness: (1) high reward-cost outcomes stemming directly from interaction between members, (2) group activities that are rewarding for their own sake, and (3) membership in the group as a means to attaining other ends. Cohesiveness is also based on the comparison levels of group members, and the total force operating on group members to remain in the group is a function not only of attraction to the group, but also of the outcomes available in alternative relations outside the group. It is clear that the extent to which groups may exert negative sanctions for nonconformity depends upon their cohesiveness. Both casual observations and more formal investigations are consistent with this view.

Conformity also varies markedly with the power structure of the group and with the bases of power. Referent power is more likely to lead to relatively enduring conformity, while coercive power is likely to produce temporary conformity under conditions of surveillance only. Extreme coercion, however, may be converted to referent power. Referent power also controls a broader range of behavior compared with expert or coercive power. The exercise of coercive power leads to the accrual of resistance to conformity. Possibly the resistance arising to coercive power is essentially a weakening of other forms of power, such as referent power. Finally, the continued exercise of power may produce shifts in reward-cost outcomes that strengthen or weaken the power relation. Legitimate power and expert power are not likely to be weakened by continued use, but coercive power in moderate amounts is likely to weaken the power relation if long exercised.

Groups vary markedly in the extent to which the behavior relevant to their functions and goals is intrinsically satisfying. In groups where behavior that happens to be in conformity to group norms is rewarding for its own sake, conformity is likely to be high. This is often characteristic of groups where satisfaction of social-emotional needs is dominant, or in task groups where the tasks themselves are enjoyable. Where conformity involves behavior that is costly, as where tasks are boring, fatiguing, or dangerous, conformity is likely to be at a lower level, unless the costs of nonconformity are correspondingly increased. Finally, where conforming behavior is not intrinsically satisfying, surveillance becomes necessary. Unless behavior is monitored in some way, and sanctions are imposed by failure to conform, the behavior is unlikely to occur.

DISTRIBUTION OF CONFORMITY IN THE GROUP

The third question which must be answered by a theory of normative behavior is why there is variation among group members in the extent to which they conform to norms. While answers to the first two questions resided largely in group processes, the question of individual differences in conformity within different groups requires attention to both group processes and personality factors. Certain group conditions, such as the power structure of the group, may increase or decrease variation among members. But personality factors also play an important part in variation through their relation to structures or processes that characterize a particular group. This section considers both group and individual factors in explaining the distribution of conformity.

Rewards and costs of behavior

As already shown, where outcomes experienced in the group are high and those available in alternative relations are low, uniformity occurs in the behavior and attitudes of the members. Thus, all members conform to approximately the same degree. Where cohesiveness is low, however, a much wider variation in conformity is likely to occur. Those members who have important satisfactions outside the group will frequently deviate from the norm, as will members who do not find much satisfaction in the group. This is illustrated by a study of books on psychology written by ministers and books on religion written by psychiatrists (Klausner, 1961). The study showed how each person developed attitudes deviant from the norms of his group. For the ministers, psychology or psychiatry was an important nonmembership reference group; for the psychiatrists, religious groups were important reference groups. Thus allegiance to outside groups is likely to produce deviation from the norms of one's reference group. Another illustration is the previously cited study of pressures toward conformity in housing groups: The occupants showing least conformity to norms were found to have more affiliations with outside groups (Festinger, Schachter, & Back, 1950).

Another factor making for individual differences in conformity is the varying pressure exerted upon different persons in the group. As Festinger (1950*b*) has shown, when a member of a group begins to deviate from normative behavior, other members place increasing pressure on him to conform. In terms of exchange theory, we would say that this occurs because his deviant behavior has reduced the rewards and increased the costs of other members. If, however, he behaves in an increasingly deviant fashion, a certain point on a continuum of deviance is reached where pressures toward conformity are reduced, and he is rejected (Schachter, 1951). In part, this may be a function of another principle for which there is fragmentary evidence, namely, that pressures on a person toward conformity are associated with the perception of the likelihood that he will conform (Festinger, 1950b). If a person is thought of as a "hopeless" deviant, pressures to conform would be rather light; attempts to elicit conformity from him are too costly in time, energy, and frustration. Here, then, is a person who, if he remains in the group, has a very low status and at the same time experiences very little pressure toward conformity.

Another factor making for individual differences in conformity is that different persons vary in their susceptibility to conformity pressures. A review of the research literature on this topic indicates that persons who are likely to be more susceptible to conformity are more submissive, low in self-confidence, less inclined to nervous tension, more authoritarian, less intelligent, less original, low in need achievement, high in need for social approval, conventional in values, and high in need for inner conformity (Blake & Mouton, 1961b). To the extent that a group has members who vary markedly in these characteristics, it will have a greater variability in conformity.

Power, status, and conformity

As noted later in Chapter 11, a person in a position of leadership has two contrary demands placed upon him. One is to conform more closely to the norms of his group than the average member, and the other is to deviate from group norms by introducing changes in group goals and activities. A variable closely associated with leadership is status. Various studies support the view that the higher the status of a person, the more likely he is to conform to group norms. For example, high school students who are best liked are seen as having the greatest proportion of conforming traits (Riley & Cohn, 1958), campus leaders reflect most closely the values of the college community (Newcomb, 1943), high-status workers in an industrial work group conform most closely to the output norms of the group (Roethlisberger & Dickson, 1939; Homans, 1954), and politicians reflect the values of the voters (Fromm, 1941). Verba (1961) suggests that this demand for greater conformity on the part of leaders arises from their central role in the group, especially their function as representative and spokesman for the group. In this role they must represent group opinion, not their own desires.

Another facet of the role of leader, however, requires him to break away from the norms at times. He has the greatest contact with parts of the social system external to the group. Under some circumstances, the group must change if it is to function efficiently. Then it is the role of the leader to introduce changes in the norms. Hollander (1958) has pointed out that although this involves deviation from group norms on the part of the leader, it is at the same time *conformity* on his part to the expectations the group has toward his role. Hollander has made some further progress toward resolving the apparent paradox in findings that a leader is often both a conformist and a deviate. In the early phases of interaction, a leader is likely to conform in order to build up status and power. In this process, he acquires "idiosyncrasy credit," which is a balance of attitudes toward him on the favorable side. In later stages of interaction he can engage in some deviant behavior, using some of his favorable credit balance in the process.

This idea might also be expressed in terms of the "security" of the leader. One study has shown that when the security of the leader of a delinquent gang is threatened, he conforms closely to the group norms (Short, 1961). On the other hand, a leader whose position cannot be shaken may engage in deviant behavior at little cost. To a large extent, the security of the leader is a function of the basis of his power. For example, where he exercises leadership because he has expert knowledge or because his power is legitimate, he is freer to depart from the norms of the group.

Homans (1961) discusses at some length the amount of conformity exhibited at various status levels. He concludes from a number of studies (Kelley & Shapiro, 1954; Dittes & Kelley, 1956; Bartos, 1958) that both high- and low-status persons conform less than those intermediate in status.

In these studies, subjects with varying degrees of acceptance from the group had to choose between an answer which appeared to be correct but which differed from reported group judgments, and the apparently wrong answer, favored by group members. For persons at each status level (level of acceptance by members), Homans enumerates rewards that they might anticipate and costs that they risk incurring.

Whether he goes along with the group or whether he acts independently, a high-status person has little to lose if his choice is later shown to be wrong. He can spend some of his idiosyncrasy credit. But if he acts independently and his choice turns out to be correct, he validates his high status. Thus the balance of potential outcomes for high-status persons favors nonconformity in this situation.

Similarly, whether he goes along with the group or acts independently, a low-status person has little to lose if he turns out to be wrong. Since he is already at the bottom of the status hierarchy, he cannot be lowered further; moreover, wrong behavior on his part might even be ignored. If he conforms to the group and turns out to be right, little is gained: he has only behaved like other members. If he acts independently and is proved correct, he has the satisfaction of showing up the rest of the group. For him, the balance of outcomes favors nonconformity.

For the person of intermediate status, aspiring to move toward the top level, rewards and costs are otherwise. If he goes along with the group and turns out to be right, he adds a slight increment to his status. If he is wrong, he loses little in company with other members. But if he acts independently and is proved wrong, he suffers an appreciable loss of status: he does not possess the idiosyncrasy credit characteristic of the high-status member, and unlike the low-status person, he has plenty of room to move downward. This risk outweighs any benefits he might achieve through an independent, correct decision. The balance of outcomes in his case favors conformity.

A study of the relation between conformity and sociometric status in cliques of delinquent boys yields further evidence in support of this association between status and conformity (Harvey & Consalvi, 1960). When persons in first, second, and last positions in cliques of four or five boys were compared, nonconformity was found to be greatest for the highest-status boy, next greatest for the lowest-status boy, and least for the second-highest boy.

STUDY QUESTIONS

20. *What is the relation between the cohesiveness of a group and the individual differences in conformity among group members?*
21. *Indicate the roles of power and status in producing varying pressures toward conformity with respect to different members of the group.*

Intrinsic value of normative behavior for different persons

Some group members gain intrinsic satisfaction from the performance of normative behavior, not only because conforming brings rewards from other group members and leads to accomplishment of group goals, but also because the behavior satisfies certain needs that the person has. In a social-emotional group which has norms of friendly, cooperative behavior, persons with high needs for affiliation enjoy behavior that happens to conform to the norm. For some other members, normative behavior may be singularly unrewarding. For example, persons with marked hostility feelings may find it difficult to conform because of the need to express their hostility. In task groups, persons who have strong achievement needs and who are skilled in the appropriate group activities may experience pleasure in carrying out the tasks. But unskilled persons may experience too much difficulty and frustration in the task group.

Essentially, what we have described is an interaction between group processes and personality characteristics that produces different reward-cost outcomes for conforming behavior on the part of various group members. A number of studies support this view. For example, one investigation has shown that persons made to feel accepted by a group are more attracted to it if they have low self-esteem, and they conform to a greater extent (Dittes, 1959). Presumably these members have a greater need for acceptance, possibly because they have fewer alternatives. Two other studies have shown that persons with strong needs for social approval conform to a greater extent than those with less strong needs for approval (Moeller & Applezweig, 1957; Strickland & Crowne, 1962). Similarly, more self-confident persons in a task group are less dependent on the judgment of others and conform to a lesser extent (Bray, 1950; Hochbaum, 1954; Smith, 1961).

Another study has identified two patterns of reaction on the part of deviants (Dean, 1961). One represents a process of social accommodation, where a drive to maintain positive relations with people who are liked contributes to conformity. The other process is one of self-correction: the individual perceives a discrepancy between the opinions of others and his own as a piece of information that can be used to arrive at a "correct" opinion. These processes of social accommodation and self-correction resemble another suggestion: that conformity may be primarily a reaction to the source of the communication (a person) or to the communication itself (McDavid, 1959). Persons reacting to the source are thought to be motivated by a need for acceptance, those reacting to the communication, by a need for success.

The concept of alienation is relevant here. One writer suggests that alienation has three components: powerlessness, social isolation, and normlessness (Wilson, 1960). He found that scales measuring these components are highly correlated, indicating that deviation (normlessness) may frequently be a function of powerlessness and social isolation. Another investigation indicates that the extent to which a person conforms is a joint function of the strength of his need for affiliation with other persons and various conditions of social support (Hardy, 1957). Thus, when a person has a strong need for affiliation and is unanimously opposed in attitude by other members, he changes his attitude to join with the other members. When group members are divided, however, there is little change in his attitude. Or if the high-affiliation member has a single partner who supports his position in opposition to the majority, he does not shift toward conformity. Individuals low in the need for affiliation do not conform to the attitudes of a unanimous majority opposed to them. These findings are consistent with exchange theory, especially if the reasonable assumption is made that individuals with low needs for affiliation with other persons find satisfactions alternative to the feeling of being accepted. In some cases, such persons may even obtain some perverse satisfaction in *not* being accepted by others.

Surveillance and sanctions over various positions

The extent to which the position of a group member exposes him to public view would appear to be an important variable in determining conformity. Certain kinds of high-status positions are subject to monitoring and punitive action. For example, persons like school principals and civic or governmental officials feel strong pressures to conform to certain norms. Only in the sense that the position itself calls for behavior deviant from that of other persons are they relatively free not to conform. Certain other types of leadership positions, however, are less public in nature; hence the incumbent is less constrained by surveillance.

Whether or not persons having low status in a group are likely to be affected by surveillance and sanctions depends upon certain conditions. The behavior of a person with low status is likely to receive less attention, and he is less likely to be punished for norm violation. On the other hand, certain personal factors or characteristics of the group structure may expose him to public view. If he is especially interested in moving upward in the group, if he is anxious over the possibility that he may be rejected by the group, or if group conditions create feelings of insecurity, he may take pains to make his behavior public, hoping that conformity will be instrumental to upward mobility. A commonplace example is the relatively low-status executive who goes out of his way to agree with senior executives at committee meetings.

STUDY QUESTIONS

22. *Indicate how the nature of the group and the personality characteristics of its members contribute to variability in conformity on the part of different members.*
23. *Describe group or personality factors that produce variations in surveillance and sanctions over group members.*

Summary: Distribution of conformity in the group

Where cohesiveness is high, conformity in the behavior and attitudes of members is likely to occur. Where cohesiveness is low, a much wider variation in conformity will be present. Members who have important satisfactions outside the group will frequently deviate from the norm, as will members who do not find much satisfaction in the group. The varying pressure exerted toward different persons in the group also creates individual differences in conformity. The person who engages in moderate deviation from the norm is at first likely to experience strong pressures toward conformity. If he rarely conforms, however, pressures toward conformity may diminish; in a sense he may be regarded as a hopeless deviant.

The person high in the power structure who occupies a position of leadership has two contrary demands placed upon him. One is to conform more closely to the norms of his group than the average member, and the other is to deviate from group norms by introducing changes in group goals and activities. Empirical evidence is consistent in demonstrating that leaders may be both more conforming and less conforming, in appropriate circumstances. In a general sense, conformity and status are associated. The most conforming are those with moderate status, and the next most conforming are those with the lowest status. Those with the highest status conform least. With repect to persons having low status, this finding applies mainly where the low status is relatively permanent and there is little opportunity or hope of increasing status.

There is an interaction between group processes and personality characteristics that produces different reward-cost outcomes for conforming behavior on the part of various group members. In social-emotional groups, persons with high needs for affiliation are most likely to conform because conformity is compatible with their needs. Persons who are hostile or lacking in social skills, however, are likely to exhibit minimum conformity. In a task group, the need for achievement and the possession of skills relevant to group goals are likely to produce high conformity for some members. For members lacking these qualities, conformity is likely to be low. These ideas are well supported by empirical reasearch.

Finally, conformity depends upon the extent to which a person's position is exposed to public view. Also, conditions or personal characteristics that cause a person to make his behavior relatively public are likely to encourage conformity.

Summary and Conclusions

A basic human requirement is the need for validation of one's opinions. Although clear information from the physical environment contributes to satisfaction of this need, the behavior of other persons also provides a source of validation, particularly where stimulus cues from the physical environment are ambiguous. Pressures toward norm formation arise to the degree that conformity in attitude and behavior improves outcomes experienced by persons in interaction. Operations by which norms are communicated and enforced have been termed norm-sending processes, which have three components: (1) defining the attitudes or behavior in question, (2) monitoring the extent to which the person conforms to the norm, and (3) applying sanctions for conformity or nonconformity.

An adequate theory of normative behavior must answer the following three questions: (1) What determines the kinds of behavior or attitudes that become targets for norm-sending? (2) Why is greater conformity found in some groups than in others? (3) What determines the distribution of conformity among the individual members of the group?

Using concepts from exchange theory, these questions can be answered in terms of the effects of four conditions: (1) the degree to which group members find the behaviors or attitudes of other persons rewarding or costly, (2) the distribution of rewards, dependencies, and alternatives that determines the power structure of the group, (3) the degree to which behavior in accordance with the norm is intrinsically rewarding or costly, and (4) the degree to which behavior is open to surveillance and to imposition of sanctions.

Normative controls arise in the areas of behavior in which members have become dependent upon the group for satisfaction of their needs. Attitudes and behaviors that are necessary to the satisfactions of the most powerful persons in the group are most likely to lead to norm formation. Where behavior required to achieve group goals is especially costly, it may not be controlled by norms. If norms do arise for such behavior, they usually serve to minimize cost or distribute it evenly. Behaviors that are difficult to monitor are also less likely to be subjected to normative control.

The extent to which a group may exert negative sanctions for nonconformity depends upon its cohesiveness. Cohesiveness is based upon various sources of attraction to the group and upon the outcomes available to the members in alternative relations outside the group. Conformity varies markedly with the power structure of the group: certain types of power are more likely than others to produce sustained conformity to norms. Another factor affecting the level of conformity is the extent to which behavior relevant to group goals is intrinsically satisfying: the more satisfying it is, the more likely members are to conform.

Where cohesiveness is high, members are likely to conform. Where cohesiveness is low, individuals vary more in the extent to which they conform. Persistent deviants may be recognized as such, and pressures may not be applied to them. Persons high in power conform more closely to the norms of their group in some respects, but under some circumstances they are required by their role and function to conform less than other members. Persons with intermediate status conform to a greater extent than those with high or low status. The task-related or social-emotional function of the group interacts with the needs of the members to produce differing degrees of conformity in individuals who have need structures of varying relevance to the group functions. Members also conform to the extent that their position is open to surveillance and sanctions.

chapter eleven

LEADERSHIP

Leadership has played a vital role in the affairs of men since earliest recorded history. Historians emphasize heroes in battle and the importance of their deeds for the future course of history. They also give considerable attention to the role of politicians and statesmen in the development of empires, territories, and nations. In modern society, organizational and informal activities alike are characterized by a difference in the contributions of the participants. Some individuals contribute somewhat more of their energies or skills than others, and they vary in the extent to which they exert influence over each other. Business organizations, government, political parties, and nonprofit institutions illustrate this emphasis on leadership by providing unusually high rewards for their leaders, by conducting a continual search for men with leadership ability, and by stressing human relations or leadership training.

This widespread interest in leadership documents the point that it is an important social problem; however, the popular view of leadership overestimates the importance of the contribution of the individual leader. As we shall see, the early research of behavioral scientists on leadership suffered from a similarly misplaced emphasis. Current formulations of the problem take a quite different form. This chapter focuses on the nature of leadership behavior and its relation to individual personality, to the composition and function of the group, to the situation, and to the group structure. Chapter 12 discusses the relation of leadership to group productivity and member satisfaction.

The history of research on leadership reflects in capsule form the gradual evolution of social psychology into an increasingly complex and sophisticated structure. Like much early research in the behavioral sciences, the initial approach to leadership was to compare individuals, in this case to explore how leaders differ from nonleaders. This tactic is generally acknowledged to have failed: few stable differences were found. A later approach focused on leadership *behavior,* emphasizing those acts leading either to goal achievement or to the maintenance and strengthening of the group. In this approach all members of the group were seen as performing leadership acts in varying degree.

The focus on leadership behavior was accompanied by an interest in the effects of the situation and of the composition of the group on leadership behavior. Out of this line of investigation interest turned toward the structural determinants of leadership: it was believed that relatively permanent patternings of group interaction developed and provided a context within which leadership was exercised. An evolving view of leadership placed stress on the *leader-follower* relation, recognizing that the behavior of the leader depends upon the complementary behavior of followers. Finally, many present-day students of the topic regard leadership as the allocation of leadership roles to certain individual members of a group. Such role allocation may be readily interpreted by exchange theory, which analyzes the leadership process in terms of the reward-cost outcomes of leaders and followers. The present chapter will review the various approaches to leadership, placing emphasis upon the more current research strategies.

Nature of Leadership

Early research on leadership shared with the average man a fundamental bias referred to in Chapter 2: the tendency to see persons as origins of actions. Leadership behavior was believed to originate from the personal qualities of the leader, and insufficient attention was given to the contribution of the group structure and situation to such behavior. The extreme form of this bias is reflected in such statements as "a military officer is a leader of men," which implies that his personal qualities enable him to lead enlisted men in any and all situations.

Empirical studies compared leaders with nonleaders, focusing on personality traits in the hope of uncovering the bases of leadership. Unfortunately, the relation between personality traits and leadership proved more complex than originally assumed. After a review of the research on this topic, Gibb concluded that attempts to find a consistent pattern of traits that characterize leaders had failed. He pointed out that the attributes of leadership are any or all of those personality characteristics that, in any *particular situation,* make it possible for a person either to contribute to achievement of a group goal or to be seen as doing so by other group members. Gibb (1954) offers the following reasons for the failure to find distinctive personality patterns in leaders:

1. Appraisal devices for measuring the really significant aspects of personality may not yet have been developed.

2. Existing appraisal techniques may not be sufficiently reliable or valid.

3. The marked difference between groups investigated may mask similarities in leadership characteristics that might be discovered if leadership behavior in a given situation were studied in a series of similar groups.

4. Leadership is probably a complex pattern of functional roles. Because leaders take first one role and then another, certain invariant relations between personality and taking particular roles may have been overlooked.

As Cartwright and Zander (1960) noted, dissatisfaction with the trait approach has led to a new tactic focusing on leadership *behavior:*

> Dissatisfaction with the trait approach has, then, given rise to a view of leadership which stresses the characteristics of the group and the situation in which it exists. Research conducted within this orientation does not attempt to find certain invariant traits of leaders. Rather, it seeks to discover what actions are required by groups under various conditions if they are to achieve their goals or other valued states, and how different group members take part in these group actions. Leadership is viewed as the performance of those acts which help the group achieve its preferred outcomes. Such acts may be termed *group functions.* More specifically, leadership consists of such actions by group members as those which aid in setting group goals, moving the group toward its goals, improving the quality of the interactions among the members, building the cohesiveness of the group, or making resources available to the group. In principle, leadership may be performed by one or many members of the group. (Pp. 492–493)

As the above quotation suggests, a wide variety of acts depending on the situation and the character of the group could be classified as leadership behavior. There is growing empirical (Halpin & Winer, 1952; Fleishmann, Harris, & Burtt, 1955) and theoretical convergence (Parsons & Bales, 1955; Thibaut & Kelley, 1959; Cartwright & Zander, 1960) on considering as leadership behavior those acts that are functionally related either to goal achievement or to the maintenance and strengthening of the group. Acts in the former category, instrumental to achieving the goals of the group, include making suggestions for action, evaluating movement toward the goal, preventing activities irrelevant to the goal, and offering effective solutions for goal achievement. Acts serving to maintain the group through meeting the social-emotional needs of the group members include encouraging other members, releasing tension that builds up, and giving everyone a chance to express himself.

In short, the attributes of leadership are any or all of those personality characteristics that, in any particular situation, make it possible for a person to contribute to achievement of a group goal, to help hold the group together, or to be seen as doing so by other members. Our emphasis is placed on leadership behavior: those actions that are functionally related either to goal achievement or to the maintenance and strengthening of the group. Such behavior is engaged in to a varying degree by all members.

STUDY QUESTIONS

1. *What are the reasons for the failure to find a consistent pattern of traits possessed by leaders?*
2. *What types of actions or behaviors are performed by leaders? What implications does this have for the generality of leadership from group to group or situation to situation?*

Role Differentiation

The behavioral or functional approach to leadership emphasizes that leadership behavior may be performed by any group member; yet relatively early in the life of a group, certain persons engage in such behavior to a much greater degree than others. This specialization has been conceptualized as *role differentiation* (Bales & Slater, 1955). Since role differentiation is most readily observed in groups with a minimum of structure, most of the relevant research has been done on newly formed laboratory groups. While many of the findings may be applicable to well-established groups, some caution should be exercised in generalizing to such groups.

NATURE OF ROLE DIFFERENTIATION

As noted in Chapter 10 in the discussion of the communication structure, at a relatively early point in the development of newly formed, initially leaderless groups, the frequency, direction, and content of communication become established at different levels for different members. The individual who talked the most also received the most communication from others. He directed a larger proportion of his comments to the group as a whole rather than to individual members, and these comments were more often in the positive task-oriented categories—giving suggestions, information, and opinion. Other group members were more apt to consider the person most frequently initiating actions as having the best ideas and as doing the most to guide the discussion effectively. Such specialization of behavior, and the development of consensus in recognition of such specialization, is the substance of role differentiation.

Heinicke and Bales (1953), who observed the development of such consensus in groups over a series of sessions, describe it in terms of an early struggle between men with top status from which the victor ultimately emerges as the agreed-upon leader.

Although their groups had developed a high degree of status consensus by the end of the first session, during the second session this consensus declined, and a somewhat different hierarchy emerged. The second session was characterized by a status struggle, particularly between the two top men. Subsequently, however, the struggle was resolved, and consensus on the old structure reappeared, along with a more positive social-emotional atmosphere.

The roles of the two top-status individuals were critical. During the first two sessions, the number 1 man played a very active part, apparently in order to establish his position and defend it. He initiated many suggestions, and received many agreements and disagreements. His activity in the second session appeared to be a defense of his top position, challenged by the number 2 man. Since he was secure by the third and fourth sessions, however, he was able to permit other persons to play more active roles. Although he continued to receive the most responses, especially agreement, he no longer had to exert himself unduly to win his point.

Some of the groups studied by these investigators, however, did not show this trend toward consensus. For these groups, member agreement on the statuses of other members fluctuated in an erratic fashion. This appeared to be a function of the extent to which agreement was reached at the end of the first session. The high-consensus groups were characterized by high agreement among members on their relative ranking at the end of the first session. Those groups who failed to obtain any stability in agreement even in later sessions were characterized by low agreement from the beginning. This suggests the underlying reason for their failure to reach consensus: The groups reaching agreement early were high in initial value consensus, and the groups failing to agree contained members holding divergent values. Bales and Slater (1955) note the following:

> For the present, we suspect that the groups High on status consensus are those in which it happens, through original composition, that a fairly high degree of latent consensus in critical values exists. Given this common base, a common interpretation of the nature and importance of the task might reasonably follow, and the result is a high degree of consensus on who is producing the best ideas for task solution. Those so perceived are allowed or encouraged to specialize in the task area, and so build up their total amount of participation. (P. 297)

In sum, role differentiation is most clearly illustrated by emergent leadership. In initially leaderless groups, certain members increasingly initiate and receive communications and direct a larger portion of their comments to the group as a whole. These comments take the form of giving suggestions, information, and opinion. Other group members increasingly recognize these persons as having the best ideas and doing the most to guide the discussion. This role differentiation is most likely to occur where group members initially share important values relevant to group activities. In groups outside the laboratory, role differentiation is likely to be well established. The functions of the various members are likely to be prescribed with some degree of formality. Later chapters on social roles will treat the effects of such institutionalized structure in more detail.

TASK AND SOCIAL-EMOTIONAL SPECIALIZATION

Role differentiation between leader and nonleader is not the only kind of differentiation that occurs. Many small groups have a *task leader* and a *social-emotional leader*. The task leader is a person who supplies ideas and guides the group toward a solution. The social-emotional leader helps to boost group morale and to release tension when things are difficult. Bales and Slater (1955) provide evidence for such specialization. The task specialist was ranked high on initiation, receiving, and guidance, but was not ranked high on liking. The social-emotional leader was usually the best liked. Increasing specialization in these two functions appeared in successive sessions. In the first session, in slightly over half the groups the man who ranked first on ideas was liked best, but by the fourth session this held true for only 9 percent of the groups.

Role differentiation and equilibrium

Such role differentiation has been related theoretically and empirically to certain basic tendencies toward a state of equilibrium in groups (Lewin, Lippitt & White, 1939; Coch & French, 1958; Parsons & Bales, 1955). While this equilibrium problem will be treated in greater detail in Chapter 12 on group productivity and satisfaction, we might briefly note here that movement toward task accomplishment in groups frustrates needs and incurs other costs so that forces arise to direct group activities away from the task and toward dealing with these needs and reducing or compensating for costs. These diversionary activities, since they interfere with task accomplishment, eventually in turn give rise to forces directing the group back to task activities. The effect of the two sets of forces is to maintain a balance or equilibrium between meeting both the task and the social-emotional functions of groups. One manifestation of the forces toward equilibrium is the development of hostility toward the task specialist who is pushing the group toward task accomplishment. Bales and Slater (1955) describe this process for groups high on status consensus which have a clear-cut differentiation between task and social-emotional roles. According to these investigators, the task specialist initially generates liking because he satisfies needs of members for completing the task. But he arouses hostility because of his prestige, because he talks a large proportion of the time, and because he requires other members to focus on the task. The more he talks, the more ambivalent other members become toward him. Eventually they transfer some liking from him to another person who is less active and who expresses their negative feelings. This social-emotional specialist is best liked. He represents the values and attitudes that have been disturbed, deemphasized, threatened, or repressed by the requirements of the task.

Apparently, to the degree that such hostility occurs, differentiation between the two roles takes place. There are two grounds for this expectation. First, such hostility makes performance of both roles incompatible, and second, the personalities of the members attracted to and capable of playing the two roles are likely to be different (Thibaut & Kelley, 1959). The social-emotional specialist must like and be liked if he is to meet the social-emotional needs of others. In contrast, the task specialist must be emotionally detached. If he is to lead the group to accomplish its goals, he cannot become so emotionally dependent upon other members that he is unable to exercise power over them. Data on differences between the idea specialist and the best-liked person are consistent with this supposition (Bales & Slater, 1955). Best-liked persons like other group members strongly and about equally. The idea specialist differentiates his liking to a much greater extent: he likes some members much more than others.

Other research indicates that effective leaders differentiate between followers to a greater extent than ineffective leaders: they see the personalities of the members they like best and least as more dissimilar (Fiedler, 1960). Bales and Slater suggest that these differences also reflect personality differences between those who become social-emotional specialists and those who function as task specialists. Liking everyone strongly and to an equal degree may reflect a strong need to be liked on the part of those who become social-emotional specialists. Because of this need, they may have developed considerable skill in making other people like them. The task specialist, on the other hand, may well be one who is able to accept negative reactions from others.

STUDY QUESTIONS

3. *What are the differences in the behavior of group members which indicate that role differentiation is occurring? What special condition in initially leaderless groups must exist in order for role differentiation to occur?*

4. *Describe the different functions of the task specialist and the social-emotional specialist.*

5. *What two sets of forces give rise to a state of equilibrium in the functioning of groups?*

6. *What is the source of hostility toward the leader of a group? What type of leader is likely to be the target of such hostility?*

Leadership in different groups

Groups vary in the extent to which they emphasize task and social-emotional abilities as criteria for leadership. Bales and Slater (1955) recorded interactions taking place in discussion groups meeting for four successive sessions. After this period, they asked members to specify whom they thought most definitely stood out as a leader. Their laboratory groups, whose purpose was to solve a problem in human relations through discussion, emphasized the task function, and this criterion was most heavily weighted in determining who was perceived as a leader. Those seen as leaders were those who most frequently initiated and received communications and offered ideas and guidance. Their interactions were seldom social-emotional. Nevertheless, there were also observed differences among the various groups studied. The following quotation shows how the weighting of various leadership functions determines attribution of leadership to different individuals:

> Since different groups emphasize task and social emotional problems in varying proportions, the attribution of leadership will depend not only upon the choice of one person over another but also upon the differential stress placed upon these group problems by the group. The group problems might thus be conceived as factors, with weights assigned to them by the group according to some elementary kind of value consensus. One group, e.g., might attribute leadership on the basis of, say, .7 task ability, .3 likeability; another might reverse the weights. Consensus on leadership attribution according to this notion would depend upon (a) the amount of group agreement upon the weights to be assigned (value consensus), and (b) the amount of group agreement upon ratings given each member on each factor (rating consensus). Leadership would thus be thought of as tending to "bridge the gap" among the more specialized roles, and perhaps also to "shift in time," being attributed now to one sort of specialist, now to another, according to the most pressing problems or the major values of the group. (Pp. 290–291)

Conditions favoring maximum role differentiation

The reasoning to this point suggests that the degree of role differentiation would vary directly with the extent to which task functions are unrewarding or costly. The less satisfaction experienced in working toward a goal and the more costs incurred, the more likely task and social-emotional functions are to be centered in different persons. Rewards would be low where task success is unrelated to member needs. Costs would be high where members disagree on both the importance of the task and how it is to be accomplished. Similarly, costs are apt to be high to the degree that influence attempts among group members must be largely personal in nature. These conditions would prevail in groups where the affect, status, power, and communication structures are relatively undeveloped and where there is little consensus on values, on the appropriateness of activities, or on the facts of the situation and how facts are to be assessed.

These suppositions may be tested by examining cases both where role differentiation has occurred to the greatest degree and where it has not. Verba (1961) has argued that the temporary small experimental groups that Bales and his colleagues have studied provided conditions especially conducive to role differentiation. Having to arrive at a joint solution to a hypothetical problem in human relations could be expected to stimulate differences of opinion because of value differences. At the same time, the patently experimental atmosphere would not prompt high involvement in the task, and thus task efforts by a leader would not be well appreciated.

Moreover, these initially leaderless groups were composed of university undergraduates who, with few exceptions, were strangers with status characteristics (age, sex, etc.) providing little basis for differentiation, and hence attempts to assume leadership had little support from established status characteristics or from an established group structure. Experimental studies of emergent leaders and of leaders in groups with an established structure suggest that established leaders are less directive and evoke less resistance on the part of followers than emergent leaders. Verba (1961) draws the following conclusions:

> In the experiments, therefore, individuals who do not value highly interpersonal control by others are brought together in groups where the exercise of such control has no external backing from some extra-group hierarchy. The members are unknown to each other and have no apparent status differences such that one member would be expected to exert more influence in the group than another. Under these circumstances it is no wonder that the most active group member, even if he contributes the most to group performance, will tend to be rejected by the group on socio-emotional criteria. His control attempts are viewed as arbitrary and as direct personal challenges. And such directives are likely to arouse negative reactions. As Frank has put it, "Resistance to an activity is readily aroused if it involves submitting to an arbitrary personal demand of someone else, and it is thereby equivalent to a personal defeat." (Pp. 169–170)

These comments should not be interpreted to mean that role differentiation will not be encountered in established groups outside the peculiar culture of the laboratory. Everyday experience, as well as empirical studies, shows that role differentiation does occur in established groups under many circumstances (Zelditch, 1955; Grusky, 1957). In established groups in natural settings, bifurcation of roles might be expected where the leader and other group members differ sharply in task involvement and in their views on orientation to the task. In industrial groups, by virtue of his position in the managerial hierarchy, the supervisor is likely to be more involved in task accomplishment than the worker and to see the work situation differently from him. Under these circumstances it is not surprising that informal leaders are ones who mainly perform a social-emotional function. In fact, a wide range of circumstances can create differences in attitudes and values between a task leader and his followers, thus encouraging the emergence of a social-emotional leader.

On the other hand, any set of circumstances that reduces these differences increases the probability that one person will be able to carry on both functions. Several studies indicate that where conditions make either task accomplishment or solving emotional problems highly salient for all members of the group, the person who leads the way in solving the salient problem will be liked, and bifurcation of the two roles will be minimized (Marcus, 1960; Turk, 1961; Meile, 1962). Hostility toward the leader and role differentiation is also reduced where the style of leadership encourages a wide distribution of directive acts so that no one person becomes the sole target of hostility for reward-cost outcomes reduced by such acts. Thus the democratic leader who encourages division of responsibility and participation in decisions may well be able, as Thibaut and Kelley (1959) suggest, to carry on both a social-emotional and a task role.

LEGITIMACY OF LEADERSHIP

Our initial focus on laboratory groups has ignored a solution to the equilibrium problem which arises in groups that exist over a period of time. As previously noted, where costs incurred by group members are perceived to be due to the personal acts of the task leader, hostility is likely to be directed toward him. Thibaut and Kelley point out, however, that where group members perceive the directive attempts of the leader as legitimate, hostile reactions are not apt to occur. Verba (1961) makes the following comment on this point:

> One of the most effective ways in which the instrumental directives of a group leader acquire legitimacy and avoid being received as personal, arbitrary challenges to the group members is for the leader to be perceived as acting not as an individual but as the agent of some impersonal force, such as the "demands of the situation" or the group traditions and norms. The invocation of some external authority by the group leader relieves the follower of the burden of accepting the control of another individual. Thibaut and Kelley, in a study of power relations in the dyad, conclude that group norms have the effect of reducing the tension between the more powerful and the less powerful member of the group. The impersonalization of expectations of behavior through the adoption of norms makes the influence relationship between the more and the less powerful group member more stable and palatable for both of them. For the less powerful member, the use of controls without a normative base would make those controls arbitrary and unpredictable, and lead to resistance on his part. For the more powerful member of a dyad, the use of purely personal power would also be unpleasant. He must either reduce his attempted control (and thereby perhaps endanger the accomplishment of the group goal) or risk the negative reactions of the other member. Thus the exercise of control in the name of a set of norms that legitimizes the control is to the advantage of both leader and follower. (Pp. 172–173)

One way in which the leader's actions acquire legitimacy is through formal recognition of his leadership role. This is demonstrated in an experiment where one supervisor was elected and the other was assigned by the experimenter (Raven & French, 1958b). Under these circumstances, the elected supervisor, who is likely to be perceived as having more legitimate power, was shown to exert a greater influence over his work group than the nonelected supervisor.

Another investigation conducted in a classroom situation indicated that the arousal of hostility toward the instructor was a direct function of the extent to which he violated the legitimate expectations of the student by following his own inclinations rather than the student's desires

(Horwitz, 1963). In ROTC classes, instructions for making paper objects were given somewhat too rapidly to be grasped thoroughly. Votes were then taken to determine whether the procedure should be repeated or not. In the teacher-centered condition, students were led to expect that the instructor's vote would have twice the weight of the group. In the student-centered condition, students were led to expect that the instructor's vote would be weighted only one-fourth as heavily as that of the group.

Actual votes, which took the form of ratings of the desire for continuing or for going back over the instructions, were disregarded. Votes were announced by arrangement so that the instructor moderately favored going on to the next topic, but the group moderately favored repeating the instructions for making the paper objects. With these ratings, going on was legitimate in the teacher-centered group because of the extra weight given to the instructor's rating. In the student-centered group, however, going on meant that the instructor was arbitrarily reducing the weight given to the student's desires relative to the weight given his own, and this action was perceived as illegitimate. Considerably more hostility toward the instructor was expressed in this condition, as determined by student evaluations of him collected by the experimenter.

Another type of social norm protects the task leader from the damaging psychological effects of withdrawal of positive affect. In time, norms develop to encourage a degree of social distance between the leader and most of his followers, preventing the development of emotional dependence of the leader on all but a few of his followers. This allows him to carry out his task functions without experiencing too painfully the emotional rejections that he encounters.

As Homans (1961) notes, a distinction should be made between liking and esteem. Leaders are often respected, particularly if they have earned respect through skillful leadership; but they are less often liked. To the degree that a task leader is successful in providing the group with many rewards, he may be liked. In the long run, however, his control over the rewards and costs received by the members of the group and his superior status are likely to produce ambivalent feelings toward him.

STUDY QUESTIONS

7. *What conditions favor maximum role differentiation? What aspects of group structure give rise to these conditions? What is the relevance of rewards and costs to these conditions?*

8. *To what extent is role differentiation expected to occur in laboratory experimental groups? Why?*

9. *In groups outside the laboratory, what conditions make for considerable role differentiation? What conditions reduce role differentiation?*

10. *What is meant by the legitimacy of the leader's role? (See the section on legitimate power in Chapter 8 for a more complete discussion.)*

Summary: Task and social-emotional specialization

A frequently occurring phenomenon in groups is the emergence of a task leader or idea specialist and a social-emotional leader. The task specialist organizes and directs the activities of members so that they are focused on achieving group goals with maximum efficiency. The social-emotional specialist boosts morale and releases tension arising from the group's work activities. These two specialists help to maintain the group in a state of equilibrium. Movement toward task accomplishment in groups frustrates needs and incurs other costs, so that forces arise to direct group activities away from the task and toward dealing with these needs and reducing or compensating for costs. The social-emotional specialist, through joking, encouragement, or through generating *esprit de corps*, helps to dissipate these diversionary forces.

The task specialist is seldom the best-liked member of the group. His role in focusing the efforts of other members on achievement precludes this and occasionally generates some hostility toward him. For adequate functioning, moreover, he cannot become so emotionally dependent on other members that he is unable to exercise power over them. This is reflected in his highly selective liking for other members, as compared with the social-emotional specialist, who likes others strongly and equally well.

Role differentiation varies directly with the extent to which task functions are unrewarding or costly. It is likely to be maximized in groups where the affect, status, power, and communication structures are relatively undeveloped and where there is little consensus on values, on the appropriateness of activities, or on the facts of the situation and how these facts are to be assessed. In established groups, where the power of the leader has mainly a legitimate basis, hostile feelings and reactions toward him are somewhat reduced. His requests are seen not as stemming from some personal or arbitrary need, but from the demands of the situation or from the group norms.

Leadership is also less likely to be bifurcated where conditions make either task accomplishment or solving emotional problems highly salient for all members of the group. In that case the one person contributing to the salient function will probably be liked. Another factor reducing hostility toward the task leader is the distribution of responsibility for and participation in decisions, so that no one person becomes the sole target of hostility.

ROLE ALLOCATION AND EXCHANGE THEORY

Exchange theory suggests that whether a person assumes a leadership function depends upon the reward-cost outcomes experienced by him and by his followers. The rewards and costs would be a function of the requirements of the external situation, such as the nature of the task confronting the group; the characteristics of the person and his followers, and his and their needs, and his and their skills; his position in the power and communication structures; and in some instances, his position in the affect structure. These rewards and costs are considered in more detail below.

Rewards and costs experienced by the leader

The rewards of leadership are twofold. First are the satisfactions to be gained from successful task accomplishment. Second are the rewards gained from leadership activity in itself. These include satisfaction of needs for achievement and dominance, as well as other social-emotional needs.

Persons who assume leadership incur a number of costs. In addition to the effort directly expended in goal-related activities, the leader experiences costs in the form of strains stemming from the necessity of serving as a model for group behavior. Other costs include anxiety imposed by the everpresent possibility of failure, rebuffs in his attempts to lead and consequent loss of status, and blame as well as guilt when his direction is accepted but results in group failure. Finally, since his behavior is apt to affect adversely the reward-cost outcomes of other members, he faces the costs of losing their friendship. He risks not only his status but also his popularity. Closely related is the cost of loneliness. The leader is often avoided, not only because he may have incurred hostility, but also because of his power: others regard interaction with him as risky in terms of possible reward-cost outcomes.

Rewards and costs of followers

Following a leader has several rewards. First among these is goal achievement. Often followers are willing to be led because they recognize that without leadership, the goals of the group would not be achieved. Second, just as certain personality needs are met by leadership behavior, others are met by followership. Dependency needs are directly met by following a leader. If the leader has highly valued characteristics, other needs may be met vicariously through identification with him. This principle underlies the glorification of a leader which occurs in many groups. Finally, one of the rewards gained by the follower is a cost forgone. By accepting a follower role he escapes anxiety over the risk of failure in a leadership role and blame when failure occurs.

Among the costs of being a follower is the lower status he occupies. In some groups—for example, work groups—the worker-follower receives less pay as well. The follower also has less control over the activities of the group and of specific other members. Thus these activities may be less rewarding and more costly to him than they would be if he had a greater degree of control. He also forgoes the intrinsic satisfaction that might be gained from engaging in leadership tasks: he is more likely to be assigned the duller routine jobs.

Situational determinants of leadership

Rewards and costs associated with various leader and follower behaviors are in part a function of situationally imposed requirements. A number of studies suggest that if the costs of inaction in the face of situational demands are great enough, group members will respond with appropriate behavior. Thus, in initially leaderless groups studied in the laboratory, or in groups studied in a natural setting where established leaders fail to carry out leadership functions, certain members will rise to the occasion (Bales & Slater, 1955). What kinds of behaviors will occur and who will perform them are in part dictated by the demands of the situation. One investigator finds that the social-emotional specialist in a mental hospital group is more apt to exercise leadership when conflict develops between patients (Parker, 1958). Others have shown that as a group proceeds through the problem-solving process, members respond with behavior appropriate to the problem that the group faces at that particular phase of the process (Bales & Strodtbeck, 1951).

Who will respond depends on the rewards and costs arising out of the interplay between the demands of the situation and the characteristics of individuals. The distribution of skills affects the costs of members: those who have the required skills to a high degree can respond at less cost to themselves than those less skilled. Studies that show a shift in leadership with a change in the nature of the task document this point. For example, in one study, the same group was observed performing six different tasks and leadership ratings for each member in each task situation were obtained (Carter, Haythorn, & Howell, 1950). These were analyzed statistically to determine the basic task functions underlying the specific tasks. The analysis suggested that there were two families of tasks underlying leadership in the group. One was characterized by ability to lead in *intellectual* task situations and the other by ability to lead in situations where the task called for *manipulation of objects*.

Situations calling for different interests also yield varying reward-cost outcomes for members assuming leadership. Persons other than the designated leader emerge to perform a leadership function in connection with a specific problem in which they are especially interested (Crockett, 1955).

STUDY QUESTIONS

11. *What is the general relation between leadership and reward-cost outcomes?*
12. *What are the rewards and costs experienced by a leader? By a follower?*
13. *Explain how rewards and costs associated with a leader's or follower's function result in part from situational requirements. What is the relevance of individual characteristics here?*

Summary: Role allocation and exchange theory

Whether a person performs a leadership function and the degree to which he is allowed to do so depends on the reward-cost outcomes experienced by him and by others. The rewards experienced by the leader include satisfactions gained from successful achievement of group goals and satisfactions intrinsic to leadership activity itself. His costs include effort expended in goal-related activities and strains arising from the necessity of serving as a model for group behavior. He may experience anxiety because of the possibility of failure and criticism of his attempts to lead, and he constantly risks his status. Since his behavior tends to affect adversely the reward-cost outcomes of other members, he is likely to lose their friendship.

Rewards experienced in following a leader include goal achievement, satisfaction of dependency needs, identification with a strong leader, and freedom from the costs of assuming a leadership role. Costs of following include occupying a lower status, having less control over group activities, and forgoing rewards that a leader experiences.

Rewards and costs associated with leader and follower behaviors are in part a function of situationally imposed requirements. Who will respond to a particular situation depends on the rewards and costs arising out of the interplay between the demands of the situation and the characteristics of individuals. Those who have the required skills to a high degree can respond at less cost. Varying interests among group members affect their reward-cost outcomes differently in different situations.

PERSONALITY CHARACTERISTICS AND LEADERSHIP BEHAVIOR

At the beginning of the chapter we noted that the study of individual differences between leaders and nonleaders has not proved very fruitful. This conclusion should not be interpreted to mean that the distribution of leadership among members has no relation to their personality. While no personality trait guarantees leadership in all situations, studies of the relative frequency of various characteristics of both leaders and followers, and studies of the generality or specificity of leadership from situation to situation and group to group, suggest that certain personality characteristics increase the likelihood of a person's adopting a leader or follower role in a wide variety of situations. This is especially true if leadership *behaviors* are compared, in contrast to fixed traits thought to be relatively permanent characteristics of the person.

Several studies illustrate that leadership has some generality across different tasks (Carter & Nixon, 1949; Gibb, 1954; Katz et al., 1957). Another investigation shows that it has some generality across different groups performing the same task. The greatest amount of generality across tasks occurs when the tasks have a related content. This is demonstrated by a study in which the same groups performed six tasks emphasizing different activities: intellectual construction, reasoning, discussion, motor cooperation, mechanical assembly, and clerical activities (Carter, Haythorn, & Howell, 1950). A statistical analysis of leadership ratings indicated that these tasks fell into two different classes: One was characterized by intellectual activities and the other by manipulation of objects. Within any one class, the same persons usually served as leaders. In another study the composition of three-man groups working on the same task was varied (Borgatta, Couch, & Bales, 1954). Those who were high on task ability, individual assertiveness, and sociometric popularity in the first group ranked high in these respects in three subsequent group sessions where they interacted with different persons.

Some characteristics such as intelligence, or some general skills such as verbal fluency, may be associated with leadership in a wide range of situations, because persons high in these can successfully perform leadership activities at low cost. Leader or follower roles may be related to personality because the activities called for by these roles lead to the satisfaction of dominant personality needs. This is consistent with evidence that leaders are generally high in such traits as ascendance (Guetzkow, 1960) and dominance (Hunter & Jordan, 1939; Richardson & Hanawalt, 1943), and it is consistent with cogent arguments that those who readily take the follower role find in it satisfaction for strong dependency needs (Fromm, 1941).

Studies of a wide variety of groups in natural settings show that task leaders of more effective groups are able to differentiate to a greater degree among their followers than leaders of less effective groups (Fiedler, 1960). They see their best and poorest workers as more dissimilar than do less effective leaders. Since this perceptual characteristic relates to effective functioning of the group, it will be discussed in more detail in the next chapter. A closely related difference is the more selective liking expressed by the task leader. Comparisons of the task specialist with the social-emotional specialist by Bales and Slater indicate that the latter likes everyone strongly and equally, while the former likes others more selectively. Bales and Slater (1955) interpret this difference, as well as the greater rigidity and absolutism implied by the social-emotional specialist's high F-scale scores (see Chapter 2), as indicating a strong need to be liked on the part of the person who is a social-emotional specialist:

> These best Liked men, then, say in effect, "I like everyone." In connection with their high F-score, this suggests the possibility of a certain rigidity in the attitudes of many best Liked men toward interpersonal relationships. They may "have to be liked" and may achieve prominence in this respect because of the ingratiating skills they have acquired during their lives in bringing this desired situation about. Their avoidance of differentiation in ratings may be an expression of the compulsive and indiscriminate nature of this striving. (Pp. 294–295)

They interpret the task specialist's lower F scores and more selective liking for other group members as indicating ability to face a certain amount of negative feeling:

> It would seem to be important for the task specialist to be able to face a certain amount of negative feeling toward him without abandoning his role, and his apparent willingness to make differentiated Liking choices may be indicative of at least a minimal ability of this kind. Not to have to like everyone implies an awareness and acceptance of the fact that everyone may not have to like him. (P. 295)

Finally, some characteristics may be associated with leaders because their possession leads others to allow them to assume leadership. The nature of these characteristics depends upon the reward-cost outcomes they provide for followers. Sanford's (1952) study of the types of leadership preferred by authoritarian and equalitarian individuals provides an illustration. Gibb summarizes Sanford's findings as follows:[1]

> In summary, it is found that authoritarians and equalitarians differ in the kind of leadership they demand and in their responses to leader behavior. Authoritarians prefer status-laden leadership, strong authority and direction on the part of the boss. Toward weak leaders they express open hostility. Equalitarians, on the other hand, are able to accept strong leadership if the situation demands it, but they have no need for powerful authorities. Authoritarians care little for personal warmth in their leader but they do demand that he contribute to their locomotion toward group and individual goals. Equalitarians are inclined to evaluate leaders in terms of their "human relations" behavior and their group process, rather than goal orientation. The possibilities of frustration and conflict are clear. Authoritarians are dissatisfied and uncomfortable under a nondirective leader. A group of equalitarians could be expected to go into a decline under a rigid and directive leader.

14. *Under what circumstances is leadership likely to be general across different groups?*
15. *What kinds of individual characteristics, if any, are likely to be possessed by leaders? What differences are there between task and social-emotional leaders in this respect?*
16. *How may followers determine the attributes that a leader is likely to have? Give an example.*

Summary: Personality and leadership

Leadership has some generality across different tasks, especially if the tasks are similar in content. Also, when the composition of groups performing the same task is varied, the same persons are likely to assume leadership in the different groups. Certain personality characteristics, such as intelligence or verbal fluency, may be associated with leadership in a wide variety of tasks because these skills are relevant to successful performance. A characteristic apparently possessed by many task leaders is the ability to maintain emotional distance between themselves and many of their followers. The social-emotional leader, on the other hand, apparently has a strong desire to be liked by all group members. Finally, certain characteristics of followers favor those persons as leaders who can best provide high reward-cost outcomes for persons with these characteristics.

EFFECTS OF GROUP STRUCTURE ON LEADERSHIP

Our discussion so far has emphasized several points: (1) Persons exercise leadership behavior to the extent that such behavior provides favorable reward-cost outcomes to both leader and follower, (2) depending on the requirements of the situation, those with appropriate abilities, interests, and needs assume leadership functions to a greater degree than

[1]C. A. Gibb. Leadership. Reprinted by permission from G. Lindzey (Ed.), *Handbook of social psychology.* Vol. 2. Reading, Mass.: Addison-Wesley Publishing Company, Inc., 1954. P. 901.

others, and (3) where leadership is stable, it is owing to the leader's possession of characteristics with similar implications in a wide variety of situations. Were we to concern ourselves exclusively with laboratory groups, whose existence is normally of very short duration, these several factors might adequately explain why some persons manage to retain leadership over a period of time. In groups that have functioned long enough to develop stable structures and a certain routine, however, much of the stability in leader personnel can be explained in other terms. Perhaps this is best understood if we ask ourselves why the leader-follower relation that emerges in one situation continues into a new one.

In part the answer lies in the fact that the mutually rewarding pattern in the previous situation has created certain stabilities in the communication, power, and status structures that reinforce initially established leadership patterns. These stabilities of structure are established in several ways. With respect to the communication structure, Klein (1956) suggests that habits of communication used to solve a series of similar problems carry over into a situation characterized by new problems:

> Suppose now that in the history of the group the same problem has frequently arisen. In that case the sequence in which contributions to the task are made will tend to become habitual. It will become habitual for certain members to speak before others do, for Jack to wait until Joe has spoken. In this way, restrictions in free communication are brought about. The need for orderliness and predictability of behavior will further accentuate this tendency toward restricted communication. Once such a routine has become established, it tends to remain whether the task is a routine one or not. Thus the communication structure may become independent of the problem to be solved. . . . (P. 25)

As some investigators have noted, successful performance of an activity contributing to the group's goal achievement raises a person's status (Parsons, Bales, & Shils, 1953). Once a status structure is established, with high status ascribed to those exercising leadership, it is likely to be perpetuated. Because of the desire to maintain status congruence, those who initially have high status resulting from their part in one group activity will be strongly motivated to take an active role in other group activities.

The communication and status structures mutually reinforce each other and are in turn related to power, in a rather complex fashion. Status is often a resource adding to the power of the high-status person, but at the same time status may serve as a brake on power: status is endangered if power is used too freely. The relation between power, leadership and *communication centrality* (See Chapter 12) is also relevant. Klein (1956) has argued that the most central person in a communication network has greater direct and indirect access to the information others possess, and since many others must exert influence on the group through him, he can control the flow of such information to his advantage. In addition, his very centrality makes the group highly dependent on him for the performance of leadership functions. Both he and others are apt to define him as the leader. That he is so defined is supported by a number of investigations discussed in more detail in the next chapter. In these experiments the channels of communication open to members of problem-solving groups were arranged so that some persons held much more central positions than others. When the subjects were asked to indicate who was the leader in their groups, the person with the most central position was most frequently named.

Finally, occupying a particular status, either as a leader or as a follower, affects the skills and motives of each status occupant so as to maintain the existing structure. In discussing the tendency of leaders in the labor movement to perpetuate themselves, Michels (1949) notes that leaders develop skills in the exercise of leadership functions, an opportunity largely denied to followers. At the same time their greater investment in time and energy, as well as the integration of this role into the self, results in strong motivation on the part of leaders to maintain their position. The corresponding lesser involvement of a follower, often accompanied by a sense of obligation to the leader, further maintains each in his respective role.

STUDY QUESTION

17. *Indicate several ways in which aspects of group structure perpetuate the leadership of particular individuals.*

Summary: Group structure and leadership

In established groups, the formation of stable structures has much to do with maintaining certain persons as leaders over a long period of time. The mutual rewards experienced by members of a successful group create stabilities in the communication, power, and status structures that reinforce initially established leadership patterns. This occurs as a result of established habits of communication and the linkage between the communication, status, and power structures. Occupying a central position in the communication structures gives the leader an advantage over others in continuing to initiate, direct, and maintain activities. Established leaders also have the best opportunity to develop leadership skills, as well as the strongest motivation, stemming from their desire to maintain their status. The lack of opportunity for followers to develop leadership skills, their lesser involvement, and their sense of obligation to leaders further stabilize the leadership structure.

Summary and Conclusions

The current approach to leadership emphasizes leadership behavior: those actions that are functionally related either to goal achievement or to the maintenance and strengthening of the group. Such behavior is engaged in to a varying degree by all members. In virtually all groups, however, role differentiation is the rule. Certain members initiate and receive more than their share of communications, and they also direct a larger portion of their comments to the group as a whole. The content of their communications is directive in nature. These persons are recognized by other members as leaders.

Frequently leadership becomes specialized, taking different forms or roles. One of these, the task role, requires the person to organize and direct the activities of members so that they are focused on achieving group goals with maximum efficiency. The other, the social-emotional role, requires the individual to maintain group morale and release tension arising from the group's work activities. These two functions maintain a state of equilibrium, allowing the group to effectively pursue its goals. The task specialist is more emotionally distant from other members than the social-emotional specialist. In part this distance arises because it is necessary for the adequate performance of his task role.

The extent to which the two functions are carried out by different persons (as opposed to the same person) varies directly with the extent to which task functions are unrewarding or costly. Allocation of the role to different persons is especially likely where the affect, status, power, and communication structures are relatively undeveloped and where there is little consensus on values, on the appropriateness of activities, or on the facts of the situation and how these facts are to be assessed. Hostility toward the leader and consequent bifurcation of the leadership role is less likely to arise where the basis of his power is legitimate, where either task accomplishment or solving emotional problems is highly salient for all members of the group, or where the responsibility for and participation in decisions are widely distributed.

Whether a person is motivated to perform a leadership function and the degree to which he is allowed to do so depend on the reward-cost outcomes experienced by him and by others. Rewards experienced by the leader include satisfactions gained from successful achievement of group goals and satisfactions intrinsic to leadership activity itself. His costs include effort expended, anxiety over failure, criticism and blame directed toward him, and the emotional distance he is required to maintain. Rewards experienced in following a leader include goal achievement, satisfaction of dependency needs, identification with a strong leader, and freedom from the costs of assuming a leadership role. Costs of following include occupying a lower status, having less control over group activities, and forgoing rewards that a leader enjoys. Rewards and costs vary with situational requirements that call for varying skills and interests on the part of different members.

Leadership has some generality across tasks and across groups with varying membership. Those personality characteristics that relate to a wide variety of situations may characterize many leaders. Task leaders possess the ability to maintain emotional distance from most of their followers; social-emotional leaders have a strong desire to like all members strongly and equally well. Certain characteristics of followers favor those persons as leaders who can best provide high reward-cost outcomes for persons with those characteristics.

Mutual rewards experienced by members of a successful group create stabilities in the communication, power, and status structures that reinforce initially established leadership patterns. The leader's position in these established structures gives him an advantage over other members in performing the leadership function effectively. He also has the best opportunity to develop leadership skills, and he is strongly motivated to retain the status he has acquired.

chapter twelve

GROUP PRODUCTIVITY
AND SATISFACTION

One important group process has not yet been discussed: the ongoing work activity of the group aimed at accomplishing a task or solving a problem. Various names applied to this process include group decision, group problem solving, and group productivity. This aspect of group behavior pervades every part of our daily life. Probably most important decisions in human societies are made in group settings. Primitive societies have their tribal councils, and modern societies abound with such decision-making groups as legislatures, cabinets, supreme courts, juries, parole boards, corporate boards, school boards, commissions, and more informal, idiosyncratic groups such as committees, work groups, individual families, and friendship groups. Moreover, almost all the output of goods and services of human society is produced in group situations. Departments or sections of factories, offices, and institutions consist of small groups of workers who influence each other with respect to the quality and quantity of the product or service they produce.

We are interested in the process by which such groups arrive at a series of decisions concerning the various problems that confront them, as well as the conditions that give rise to member satisfaction and high productivity.

Early studies of this process in the laboratory usually assigned a problem having a single correct solution to a group of persons. In everyday situations, however, groups often arrive at consensus on issues that have no single answer. Many recent studies have assigned this kind of task to laboratory groups: illustrations are simulated committee decisions, jury decisions, or case conferences. In addition, many types of groups have been studied in actual field situations, including juries, committees, conference groups, and all kinds of work groups. Productivity in problem-solving laboratory groups has usually been defined in terms of the quality and speed of solutions to problems provided by the experimenter. In field situations, productivity is usually defined in terms of the quality and quantity of the daily work task.

Individuals versus Groups

Often behavioral scientists investigate problems that have some relation to common sense or lay beliefs. One such belief relative to thinking or problem solving is expressed in the saying "Two heads are better than one." Much early research on group problem solving was addressed to the question: Are individuals or groups better at solving problems? As research findings accumulated, it became apparent that the answer was more complicated than originally assumed. The conflicting results of numerous investigators suggested that the answer would vary depending upon the nature of the group and the means by which effectiveness in solving problems was assessed.

Although most early research showed that the group was superior, these findings can be reinterpreted in terms other than true group factors. By a *true group factor* is meant an influence on problem solving that results from *interaction among group members*. If a result can be attributed to the fact that a number of individuals are working independently on a problem, without communicating with or influencing each other, the result should not be considered a group effect. Determining whether an effect is a product of interaction is not always easy. Those effects on problem solving that appear to result from group interaction but actually do not may be termed *pseudo group effects*. Once pseudo group effects characterizing early studies were identified, it became possible to study more rigorously the effects of genuine group factors on problem solving and to determine the conditions under which they either improve or detract from the quality of a solution to a problem. Although the literature will not be reviewed in detail, an examination of these pseudo and real effects of group interaction will help to relate the discussion of group structures in earlier chapters to ongoing interaction in groups.

PSEUDO GROUP EFFECTS

One pseudo effect was recognized early (Stroop, 1932; Farnsworth & Williams, 1936) in studies where the problem was simply one of estimation of one sort or another, such as the temperature of a classroom (Knight, 1921) or the ranking of weights (Gordon, 1924). Typically, the group estimate in such studies was closer to the true measure than most individual judgments, and the larger the group, the more accurate the group estimate was. This result may be readily explained in terms of a well-known statistical principle. With increases in the number of estimates upon which some combined estimate is based, the variability of such estimates around the true measure is reduced. This would be expected to occur irrespective of any true group effects. In fact, by combining judgments made repeatedly by the *same* individuals (Stroop, 1932) or by having individuals make estimates in *isolation* (Farnsworth & Williams, 1936), later investigators found the same degree of "group superiority." This effect is a real effect: under most circumstances[1] more accurate estimates can be obtained by using a number of judgments rather than one; but it is not a true group effect.

A second pseudo effect was not recognized until more recently. This is based on the differences in the probabilities that one person or many will arrive at a solution to a problem, entirely apart from the fact that they are working together. Several investigators (see Taylor & McNemar, 1955) have developed mathematical models that account in this way for the superiority of groups found in some earlier studies — superiority that had previously been attributed to true group effects. These models indicate that the comparison of the relative success of individuals and groups is inappropriate where the nature of the problem reveals the solution to all group members if one member solves it. Superiority of the group would be expected simply because in a group there is a high probability that at least one person has the knowledge or ability to solve the problem. If ten persons in a population of sixty can solve a given problem, the chances that any one individual selected at random will be a person who can solve the problem is 1 in 6. The chances that *one or another* of three persons who happen to comprise a group will solve the problem, assuming no true group effects, is 3 out of 6, and in a four-man group, 4 out of 6. Thus, the greater the number of persons put to work on a problem, the greater the likelihood that it will be solved. But again, this probability holds even though these individuals have no contact whatsoever with each other, so that this is not a legitimate group phenomenon.

In the case of a more complicated problem requiring a variety of skills that are unlikely to be found in a single individual, additional factors enter the picture. Certainly the advantages of a group would be expected to be even more in evidence. Here too, the larger the group, the greater the advantage, since the probability is higher of getting persons whose *pooled* abilities allow for the complete solution of the problem. But this is not in the same class as other pseudo effects, since communication and cooperation among individuals is necessary if the problem is to be solved. At the same time, the advantage of the group does not arise out of interaction, as do some group effects to be reported shortly.

INTERACTION AND QUALITY OF SOLUTION

Despite the fact that the superiority of groups in many of the early studies can be accounted for by pseudo group effects, later studies cannot be explained on these grounds: group processes are involved (Gurnee,

---

[1]The effect on accuracy of increasing the number of judgments only occurs where there is some valid basis for judgment. Where there is no basis for judgment (Klugman, 1945), or where all judgments in a group are systematically biased (Farnsworth & Williams, 1936), this effect does not occur.

1937; Thorndike, 1938; Timmons, 1939, 1942). Kelley and Thibaut (1954) suggest two general ways in which properties of the situation may affect the quality of the group product. First, the individual solutions arrived at in the group situation are *qualitatively* different from those that might have been arrived at had the individuals worked alone. Second, in a group situation the individual solutions are not all weighted equally, as they would be for a number of individuals working alone.

Qualitative differences may occur as follows. Kelley and Thibaut note that the contributions of an individual may be modified through hearing the solutions of others. This may occur as a result of the ideas he hears expressed by them or as a result of their personal characteristics, particularly those that affect their power to influence an individual. Increasing the number and diversity of ideas to which an individual is exposed is likely to improve the quality of his own contributions (Dashiell, 1935). The social context apart from the influence of one person on the *ideas* of the other may also improve the quality of a group solution. Under some conditions, the presence of others may stimulate an individual to work hard at the task; under others he may drag his feet. The necessity to communicate ideas to others often results in sharpening and refining them. Ideas can remain fuzzy in our heads but must be expressed clearly when they are communicated and often errors in reasoning become apparent.

Weighting individual solutions differently is the second group factor in problem solving. This may or may not work to the advantage of the group. Suppose that individuals are given a problem and asked to arrive at a solution independently, allowed to discuss the problem, and then asked to arrive at private solutions again. If these final solutions are combined so that each is given equal weight, the difference between the initial private solutions and the final group solution would represent the effects of the discussion on the individual solutions. This situation, however, rarely occurs: the solutions arrived at by some persons will carry greater weight in determining the final product than those of others. Kelley and Thibaut suggest two reasons why: First, individuals may support the opinions of others rather than their own because of external social pressure such as that of a perceived majority or that of a more powerful person; second, a self-weighting process may occur. A person may not present his solution for consideration or may not support his solution because he feels relatively uncertain of it. If the quality of a solution is directly associated with the power of the persons supporting it, the number of persons supporting it, or the degree of certainty with which it is held by its originator, then this selective weighting would improve the quality of the group solution. Such a positive association probably exists. Nevertheless, studies of the effective use of minority opinions, to be discussed later, suggest that the quality of a group solution can be improved even more if the solutions of the minority have a chance to be considered.

These two general ways of accounting for the uniqueness of the group solution as compared with some composite of individual solutions should be kept in mind as the effects of different variables on task processes are reviewed. In the following discussion these ideas will be integrated with the discussion in earlier chapters of group structures and other emergents of interaction.

STUDY QUESTIONS

1. *Explain what is meant by true group factors and pseudo group effects in problem solving.*
2. *Explain some of the methods for determining whether or not a product of group action is a pseudo group effect or a true group effect.*
3. *What are two general ways in which the properties of a group situation may affect the quality of a group product?*

SUMMARY: INDIVIDUALS VERSUS GROUPS

By a true group factor is meant a facilitating or inhibiting influence on problem solving that results from interaction among group members. If a result can be attributed to the fact that a number of individuals are working independently on a problem, without communicating with or influencing each other, the result is not a group effect.

Pseudo group effects are those that appear to result from interaction but actually do not. Such pseudo effects often occur where the problem is based on a group estimate, or where the nature of the problem reveals the solution to all group members if one member solves it. Pseudo effects involving group estimates result from a statistical property of group estimates rather than from group interaction. In situations where all members solve the problem if one does, the superiority of the "group" solution often results from the increased probabilities of solving the problem which occur when more than one individual works on it. Where problem solution depends upon pooling varied resources of different individuals, group communication and cooperation are required for a solution, but certain other effects of group interaction may play no part in arriving at a solution.

There are two general ways in which group interaction may affect the quality of group product: (1) Individual solutions in a group situation may be qualitatively different as a result of the interaction, and (2) in a group situation, individual solutions are not all weighted equally. The first of these follows from the exposure of the individual to a larger number and greater diversity of ideas, from improved motivation, and from the clarification of his ideas which results when he has to communicate them to other persons. Differential weighting of individual solutions may or may not work to the advantage of the group. Where the individuals in the position of greatest power produce the best solutions, the group product is improved. Some evidence indicates, however, that a balance of power which prevents the minority from making contributions may be detrimental to the group product.

Group Structure and the Task Situation

The outcome of a task situation is affected by group factors if they bring about changes in any of the following: (1) the resources available to the group, (2) the application of these resources to the task, and (3) the likelihood that the task will be carried out, or at least the likelihood that agreement as to the proper approach will be achieved.

PHASES IN GROUP TASK PERFORMANCE

If task groups are observed in action, the process is seen to follow a fairly uniform sequence. Group members exchange information relevant to the problem, one or more solutions based on such information are proposed, and finally agreement is reached. In everyday situations the agreed-upon solution in most instances carries implications for change in the future behavior of the group members: they subsequently carry out the task in some manner. For example, the decisions of a work group concerning new production methods are implemented by a change in their work activities. In laboratory studies this phase of the task process is sometimes ignored or considered a part of the preceding agreement phase. All four phases should, however, be kept in mind in discussing the relation between a particular factor and the quality of the group product. This is necessary because the effects of a condition may be conducive to high quality with respect to one phase of the task but may work in the opposite direction in another phase. A particular factor affects the quality of the group product through its effects on group structures and such emergents of interaction as group frames of reference and cohesion.

With respect to a given problem-solving phase, certain structures or emotional or cognitive states are more crucial than others. In large part, the communication structure determines how effectively a group marshals resources; the power structure determines the particular combination of elements that becomes the group solution, and group cohesiveness determines how quickly a group reaches agreement and the extent to which it is motivated to carry out the solution.

STRUCTURAL EFFECTS ON EARLY PHASES

Since the importance of various features of the affect, status, communication, and power structures vary depending on the phase of the problem-solving sequence, early and late phases will be discussed separately. The early phases, discussed in this section, include the amassing of such resources as the relevant information about the problem and the environment, and the later phases, discussed in the subsequent section, refer to combining resources into some proposed course of action and implementing it by group members. Since the effects of the leadership structure have been dealt with in the research literature somewhat independently of other structural features, these will be discussed later in the chapter.

Effects of group size

The effects of size of the group provide an excellent illustration of how a condition may have a rather complex relation to the task process. One might expect that as the size of a group increases, its effectiveness would rise as a function of accumulation of resources such as ideas and information. Yet idea productivity is not linearly related to size. As Gibb (1951) has suggested, idea productivity is a *negatively accelerated* increasing function of the size of a group. This means that with each increment in size there is a progressively smaller increment in the number of ideas. In large part this appears to result from the effects of size on the *communication structure*. As noted in Chapter 9, as size increases stronger restraints against communicating appear — restraints which only a few persons seem able to overcome. Everyone has observed such effects. In small groups the rate of participation is fairly equal among members, but in large groups the bulk of the talking is done by relatively few persons, with most remaining comparatively silent. Kelley and Thibaut summarize the evidence on this point:[2]

> In sum, the available investigations of group size and participation suggest that as size increases, the most active member becomes increasingly differentiated from the rest of the group, who become increasingly similar to one another in their participation output. In addition, over the range from about two to seven, there appears to be an increase in the proportion of the group who are "undercontributors" in the sense that they account for less than their equal share of the total volume in interaction. The latter result may indicate an increase in the restraints against participation, which result in an increasingly large proportion of the group being discouraged from making overt contributions.

Thus, an increase in group size will result in an increasing fund of information, an advantage counteracted by increasing restrictions on communication. Later, some additional disadvantages experienced by large problem-solving groups, will be noted.

STUDY QUESTIONS

4. *By means of changes in what three conditions are group factors likely to bring about a change in the outcome of a task situation?*
5. *What are the four phases of a problem-solving situation?*
6. *Which of the various group structures is likely to be most critical in determining group performance in a problem-solving situation?*
7. *Describe the effects of group size on the outcome of the task situation.*

Communication structure

A major feature of communication networks is the extent to which each person has direct access to other members of the group. A person may occupy a central position, where he is able to communicate directly

[2]H. H. Kelley & J. W. Thibaut. Experimental studies of group problem solving and process. Reprinted by permission from G. Lindzey (Ed.), *Handbook of social psychology.* Vol. 2. Reading, Mass.: Addison-Wesley Publishing Company, Inc., 1954. P. 762.

with many other members, or he may be in a peripheral position, where he can communicate only indirectly through a third person with most members. Most experimental studies of the effects of communication structure on task behavior have used communication nets varying in this property of centrality-peripherality.

In one experiment, five-man groups solved a simple problem under conditions where communication was restricted in accordance with one of the four communication nets reproduced in Figure 12–1 (Leavitt, 1951). Each person was given a card containing five different symbols. The problem consisted of finding the symbol that was common to everyone's card. Group members agreed on the leader and established a stable structure most rapidly when they were organized according to the wheel, and did so progressively less rapidly for the Y, the chain, and the circle, with the last-named never obtaining a stable organization. Similarly, performance was best with the wheel and poorest with the circle. Subjects performing in a circle network wrote more messages and made and corrected more errors than the other groups. All members of a circle network enjoyed their task to a greater extent than those occupying positions of low centrality in other nets. In the other networks, persons occupying a central position were apt to enjoy their task to a great degree, while those in a peripheral position were apt to be rather dissatisfied. Leavitt (1951) presents a succinct summary:

> Patternwise, the picture formed by the results is of differences almost always in the order *circle, chain, Y, wheel.*
> We may grossly characterize the kinds of differences that occur in this way: the circle, one extreme, is active, leaderless, unorganized, erratic, and yet is enjoyed by its members. The wheel, at the other extreme, is less active, has a distinct leader, is well and stably organized, is less erratic, and yet is unsatisfying to most of its members. (P. 46)

A series of studies by other investigators helps to explain why performance and satisfaction are related to centrality. Leavitt had suggested that the relative independence of action of the person occupying a central position in contrast to the dependence of persons at the periphery leads other members to perceive him as the leader, leads him to perceive himself as a leader, and accounts for his higher satisfaction. The last part of this suggestion has received some empirical support (Trow, 1957; Shaw, 1954). The variables underlying the relative effectiveness of groups with different communication structures have not yet been clearly delineated. The relation initially found between the type of network and effectiveness has been modified in further experiments. For *complex* problems the circle may be more effective than the wheel in terms of time to complete a problem and number of errors. Shaw suggests that one of the variables underlying network differences is *saturation*. He comments (1954):

> With complex problems, then, the wheel should be slower than the circle because the central person becomes saturated (i.e. because he must do most

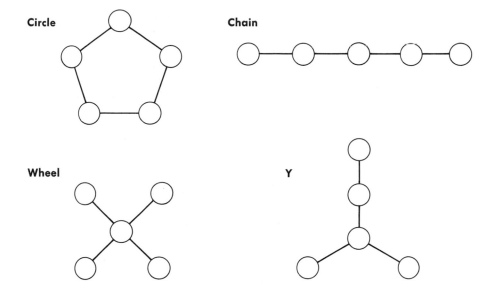

Figure 12–1

Some different communication patterns. Each line represents a communication linkage. (Adapted with permission from H. J. Leavitt. Some effects of certain communication patterns on group performance. *J. abnorm. soc. Psychol.*, 1951, **46**, 38– 50.)

of the work, either the actual solution or relaying information, the optimal output level is exceeded), and because it sometimes forces the weakest person in the group to function in the leadership role. (P. 216)

Macy, Christie, and Luce (1953) suggest two other network features that affect performance. First, where it is possible for members to receive information from two different sources, the possibility of discovering errors is increased and performance improved. Second, where communication among members is symmetric or two-way, error correction is facilitated, since members do not have to go through a third person to correct each other.

Klein (1956) has emphasized this last point in her discussion of another investigation (Heise & Miller, 1951). A series of three-man groups having the communication networks shown in Figure 12–2 solved problems of different complexity. On a complex task involving the reassembly into one list of the words from three lists, each held by a separate subject, the order of quality of performance for the numbered networks, was 1, 3, 2, 4, 5. Klein explains this finding in terms of the varying possibilities of mutual communication between members in these networks. She notes (1956) that network 2 is subject to a source of disturbance that is not encountered in networks 1 or 3.

In network 2, member B has a choice as to whom to communicate with and when he chooses C instead of A, C has to waste precious time in order to correct him through A. And if B speaks to C at the same time as A, C has to tell A to ask B to be quiet! Accordingly we find that network 2 is slower than either network 1 or 3. . . . In network 5 there is no direct communication between any two members. If A wants to check on what B said, he has to use C as an intermediary. This enlarges the possibilities of misunderstandings. All the other networks were more efficient than this one. Of the remainder, all except network 4 have more than one link through which mutual communication may pass. Network 4 is accordingly the next least efficient. To sum up so far: when two members cannot communicate mutually, the communication of the one to the other is likely to act as a disturbance and not as a help. Because in this way all messages may be delayed, both the performance of the task and the efficient organization of the group will be more difficult in networks of this kind. (P. 64)

Klein notes that the findings from the original study of Leavitt, in which the wheel, Y, chain, and circle were progressively less efficient on the fastest single trial, are also predictable on the basis of mutuality. She observes that the order of the networks reveals an increasing number of positions restricted to only one channel of communication. In the wheel, four persons are restricted to one channel, in the Y, three, and in the chain, two. No one in the circle is so restricted. In the circle, then, there is a maximum probability that a given communication will not be restricted to a sender and listener: at any one point in time one person is likely to be attempting to communicate with another while the latter is talking to a third person. Under these circumstances it is not surprising that the circle is least effective.

At first glance it might appear that this research on communication nets has little relevance to groups in everyday situations. A little reflection, however, will reveal that virtually all situations outside the laboratory involve some restrictions on communication. These situations approximate in varying degrees networks similar to the laboratory networks discussed. Whereas in typical laboratory situations all communications among members occur while all members are present, in groups outside the laboratory this is often not the case. Factors affecting the accessibility of each member to each of the other members, along with conditions affecting the motivation to communicate various kinds of information and suggestions, will close certain communication links and convert others to one-way channels. Even when group members function in a face-to-face situation where it is theoretically possible for all to hear the contributions of others, the flow of ideas may in varying degrees approximate these networks. For instance, the contributions of lower-status persons may only gain general consideration if they are attended to and relayed by certain others. In his classic study of a street-corner gang, Whyte (1943) observed that the suggestions of low-status boys rarely obtained a hearing in a discussion unless they were picked up and repeated by the higher-status members of the group.

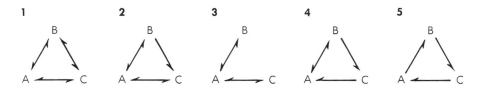

Figure 12–2

Communication networks. An arrow pointing to member *B* from member *A* signifies that *A* can speak to *B*; i.e., *B* can hear *A* speaking to him but not vice versa. Members could speak whenever they wanted to. Some members might therefore be in the unfortunate position of hearing one person speak to their right ear while another was speaking to their left! (Adapted with permission from Josephine Klein. *The study of groups.* London: Routledge & Kegan Paul, Ltd., 1956.)

Affect structure

While there is some evidence (Husband, 1940; Goodacre, 1951) that groups characterized as friendly are more productive, the relation between affect and productivity is often complicated by other variables. As noted in Chapter 9, pairs of friends communicate at a higher rate than pairs of strangers in a problem-solving situation. If we assume with Klein that the paths of communication are apt to follow friendship choices, then a sociometric structure characterized by many mutual choices would approximate a totally connected network in which everyone could communicate with everyone else. In a face-to-face discussion group where everyone is liked and consequently listened to, one might expect maximum exchange of information, resulting in a condition where the group would have available to it the greatest amount of information about the task, the situation, and possible solutions to the problem. Since sociometric choices are not equally distributed, this is an ideal which is rarely, if ever, realized. There are those who receive many choices and those who receive few or none, and there are subgroups partially or completely isolated from the other group members. Hence some persons will both possess more and provide more information than others, and their ideas will have greater circulation and be attended to more closely.

So far, problem solving has been discussed as if the communication content were always in the task area: as if people were always giving and receiving information and suggestions and reacting to these acts. This is never completely the case. Persons also communicate in the nontask or social-emotional areas and are more likely to do so when affect is high. To the degree that such communications actively divert time and energy from the task, the facilitative effects of liking will be reduced.

Status and power structure

The status and power structures partly reinforce the effects of liking on the communication structure. Differences in status both facilitate and inhibit communication among group members. Because power is usually associated with status, it appears to have similar effects; however, the effects of power need to be investigated with status held constant. So far as can be determined, no one has performed such a study.

These facilitating or interfering effects of status and power differences interact further with the content of the communication. In particular, ideas of individuals that are perceived as contrary to those of high-status persons are apt not to be communicated, at least to these persons, even though they might be ideas of high quality. A low-status person is unlikely to make a suggestion if he thinks it will be resisted by a high-status person.

Like certain conditions of affect, status and power differences may result in behaviors that divert time and energy from the task. As discussed in Chapter 9, subjects may engage in communication irrelevant to the task as a substitute for upward mobility in the status hierarchy or in an attempt to improve their status via status contagion. Similarly there is evidence to suggest that a certain amount of energy of group members will be expended in a struggle for positions of power and status. This is consistent with the previously discussed point that stability of structure is a necessary condition for speed and quality in group problem solving.

A lack of status congruency might have similar adverse effects on the number of ideas presented by members of the group. Such a condition could be expected to generate a certain amount of anxiety in each member regarding his own status and the kinds of behavior that he can expect from the others. This in turn might produce defensive behavior as well as a variety of acts designed to improve status congruency. Unfortunately, what evidence there is on the relation of status congruency to the quality of group productivity and member satisfaction suggests that the effects of status congruency are somewhat more complex. The work of Exline and Ziller (1959) and Lenski (1954) on the whole provides some support for these speculations. Similarly, a study of Air Force crews showed that status congruency was positively associated with the quality of social relations and individual emotional satisfactions (Adams, 1953). However, productivity or level of technical performance from crew to crew, after rising initially, *deteriorated* significantly with an increase in status congruency.

A more recent study suggests an interpretation of these results (Zaleznik, Christensen, & Roethlisberger, 1958). In industrial work groups it was found that status congruency affected productivity by changing the amount of interaction and the orientation to the task. Status congruency facilitates interaction—people are sure of where they stand with respect to each other. Thus it increases general satisfaction in the group, encouraging a good deal of nontask activity. It also increases conformity to group production norms—norms that frequently place limits on productivity. Lack of status congruency reduces satisfactions and may encourage more task-related activity and less adherence to group norms restricting output. On the other hand, where the norms of a group specify a high level of productivity, high status congruency may be expected to lead to high output.

STUDY QUESTIONS

8. *What is meant by positions of centrality and peripherality in a communication structure? Depict two structures that have a markedly different distribution of centrality among the positions of the group members.*

9. *In what way is the distribution of centrality among the members of a group related to (a) group effectiveness, and (b) group satisfaction? What are the various reasons offered for these relations?*

10. *What are the effects of the affect structure on group task situations?*

11. *Indicate how the status structure may both facilitate and interfere with the performance of a group task. How is status congruency related to a task situation?*

Summary: Structure and early phases

Early phases in task solution include the exchange of information and the presentation of a variety of solutions or plans of action. The relation of size of group, communication, affect, status, and power structures to these phases has been discussed. Idea productivity is a negatively accelerated increasing function of the size of a group, a function resulting largely from the effects of size on the communication structure. Larger-sized groups produce restraints against communicating which only a few persons overcome.

Problem-solving situations have been studied in groups having a variety of experimentally contrived communication nets. The primary feature of these nets is that individuals vary in the direct access they have to communication with other members and the access other members have to them. Some members occupy central positions: they can give and receive communications directly to others. Other members occupy peripheral positions: they can communicate with most other group members only indirectly through a third person or chain of persons. A given communication network may be relatively undifferentiated with respect to centrality-peripherality: all members may occupy a similar position. Or it may be quite differentiated, with some members occupying central positions and others peripheral ones. Empirical studies consistently support the conclusion that the relatively undifferentiated structure yields greater member satisfaction. For simple problems, the differentiated structure is most effective, but for complex problems, the undifferentiated structure is more effective in some instances. The differentiated structure loses its superiority for a complex problem because the persons occupying central positions become overloaded in serving as communication links.

Another property of communication structures is the degree of mutuality: the possibility of two-way communication between a member and other members. The greater the mutuality, the greater the speed and accuracy with which errors can be corrected. Empirical studies are consistent in showing a relation between the amount of mutuality in a structure and the speed and accuracy with which the group performs its task.

The affect structure has important consequences for the performance of task groups, particularly through its connection to the communication structure. Unless special restrictive conditions prevail, communication is likely to follow friendship links. A high degree of liking is apt to facilitate communication. If, however, communications occur in the social-emotional area rather than the task area, task performance is likely to be interfered with.

Status and power structures are likely to interfere with communication in a similar way. Ideas perceived as contrary to the opinions of high-status or high-power individuals are unlikely to be communicated. Instead, low-status persons may engage in communication irrelevant to the task to compensate for their low position. Some energy may be expended in a struggle for power and status that might otherwise be spent on the task. Status congruency facilitates interaction among group members, but much of this interaction may be irrelevant to the task. Where group norms specify low productivity, status congruency will lower production through increasing conformity to these norms.

STRUCTURAL EFFECTS ON LATER PHASES

In the previous section the effects of group structure on the earlier phases of problem solving were discussed. We turn now to structural effects upon the process of arriving at the solution and the effectiveness with which it is implemented.

Cohesiveness

While a high degree of attraction among members may facilitate the exchange of information, it may reduce the quality of the solution. Maximum attempts to influence others and to be influenced in turn may be expected in a highly cohesive group. If it were assumed that each person is equally likely to come up with a necessary element in the solution and that it is unlikely that any member will have all the necessary elements, then high mutual attraction should maximize the communication of information as well as receptivity to the communications of others, facilitating the joint production of an optimum solution.

Yet an important objection to this reasoning must be raised. High cohesiveness is associated with a marked degree of symmetry in the influence process (Back, 1951). Pressures toward agreement in highly cohesive groups are so strong that persons avoid the costs of resistance; they give in to keep peace. This may result in the loss of valuable elements necessary to a solution. Because of this mutual acceptance of everyone's ideas, cohesiveness should facilitate problem solving only when all members are capable of contributions of equal value. In the typical experimental situation, where problems are selected that minimize individual differences in resources and where the subjects (generally college students) are relatively homogeneous, this condition may be approximated. But it is unlikely to prevail in many situations outside the laboratory. If the group is highly cohesive but heterogeneous in ability, qualitatively poor elements are likely to be included in a solution so as not to hurt anyone's feelings. This last point is related to one means by which certain features of the status and power structures adversely affect the quality of a group's solution.

Status and power

Not only will differences in power and status affect the frequency with which various members contribute information and make suggestions, but these differences will also affect the weights assigned to contributions from different members. For two reasons, the contributions of those with high power and status will carry more weight in arriving at a final solution. The first is their relatively greater control over the reward-cost outcomes of members. The second derives from their central location in the communication structure. They have more information about the task, the environment, and the opinions and suggestions of others, and this provides them with an opportunity consciously or unconsciously to filter such information in a manner that supports their particular solution.

Whether differences in power or status improve or impair the quality of a solution depends on the degree of concentration of power and the basis of such power. One might expect that, to the degree that power in the group is a function of expertness, concentration of power would improve quality if other things affecting quality were equal. But where power is inversely associated with the quality of individual contributions, it has a detrimental effect. Instances where a group flounders because the persons with greatest power had the poorest contributions to make should be familiar to everyone. A study of Air Force crews undergoing the rigors of survival training illustrates the point: Crews relied more heavily on the aircraft commander, whose power was highest in the group but whose knowledge regarding survival techniques was meager compared to that of the survival-training instructor (Torrance, 1955).

While a final point will be discussed more fully later in this chapter, it may be noted here that although marked differences in power may under some circumstances be associated with a high-quality solution, the marked difference in degree of member participation in developing such a solution may seriously interfere with its later implementation. To the degree that persons are restrained from actively participating in the development of a solution, their resistance to its implementation is increased. A second-best solution that will be put into practice by group members is in most instances preferable to a best-possible solution that is not adopted or is inadequately implemented.

Feedback

A well-established fact is that individual learning is facilitated if a person is informed how well he is doing. Feedback of information in a group problem-solving situation should also affect performance of the group. Several experiments have investigated this hypothesis (Rosenberg & Hall, 1958; Pryer & Bass, 1959; Zajonc, 1962). In a recent investigation (Zajonc, 1962), seven-man groups were provided with confounded feedback (Rosenberg & Hall, 1958) or direct feedback pertaining to the success or failure of their speed of reaction to a stimulus. *Confounded feedback* was a condition where individual members were informed only whether the group had failed to react within a prescribed limit, and *direct feedback* was a condition where each member was informed of his own failures, those of each other member, and those of the group as a whole. The effect of these conditions on performance was that direct feedback brought about the most improvement in performance; confounded feedback resulted in only a slight improvement.

While these laboratory experiments set up artificial restrictions on communication, they nevertheless are analogous to conditions in problem-solving groups outside the laboratory. For example, in some small-group settings, the criterion of good performance is not always clear, a condition analogous to not receiving adequate feedback. In larger organizational settings, the fragmentation and division of work tasks among a large number of individuals and the inherent difficulties in communication may create a similar condition analogous to confounded feedback.

Berkowitz and Levy (1956) have noted that groups having high pride in their performance are generally productive. They suggested that this condition may derive from the members' perception of the high level of their performance: in other words, members have pride where feedback on a good performance is available. They conducted an experiment in a simulated air defense maneuver where groups of airmen were given favorable or unfavorable evaluations of the performance of their group as a whole or of the individual members. Groups receiving favorable evaluations of the group as a whole were found to have higher pride in their performance and to be more motivated than groups having unfavorable group evaluations and than groups where only individual evaluations were provided.

Thus, in one study, feedback on the performance of the group as a whole was relatively ineffective in improving performance; in the other, it was especially effective. We may conclude that feedback on performance is important to problem-solving groups, but further study is needed in order to identify the kind of feedback which is most effective for various kinds of tasks and situations.

STUDY QUESTIONS

12. *Explain why high cohesiveness in a group may reduce the effectiveness of task performance. Under what conditions is it likely to improve performance?*
13. *Under what conditions is a marked difference in power among group members likely to produce a high-quality solution to a group problem? What is the relation of this condition to putting the solution into practice?*
14. *What are the various feedback conditions and how do they affect problem-solving performance?*

Summary: Later phases

Although a high degree of cohesiveness among group members may facilitate the exchange of information, it may reduce the quality of the solution. Cohesiveness equalizes the weight given to the contributions of each member. If a group is heterogeneous in ability, this equalization is deterimental to producing a quality solution to the group problem. On the other hand, cohesiveness may contribute to effective implementation of the solution. Where group members are relatively homogeneous in ability, cohesiveness is apt to improve the effectiveness of the group.

Contributions from individuals of high power and status will be weighted more heavily because of these people's relatively greater control over the reward-cost outcomes of members and because of their central location in the communication structure. Whether this condition is detrimental or not depends upon the competence of the high-status and high-power persons. If they are especially competent, the group is more effective; if they are less competent than the average member, the power and status structures inhibit effective performance.

Neither feedback on overall group performance nor feedback on individual performance is consistently superior. Further research is needed to identify the conditions under which each type of feedback is beneficial.

LEADERSHIP STRUCTURE AND TASK PERFORMANCE

Most of the research on the effects of leadership on group functioning has been devoted to leadership style or climate. Few studies in the behavioral sciences have had greater impact than the initial studies of leadership style. Kelley and Thibaut have provided the following succinct description of the 1939 investigations by Lewin, Lippitt, and White:[3]

> Four clubs of 11-year-old boys were formed in such a way that they were equated with respect to certain personal and sociometric characteristics of their members. Four adults performed a sequence of planned leadership roles ("authoritarian," "democratic," and "laissez-faire") so that, with minor exceptions, each adult played each leadership role and each club was exposed to each style of leader. Activities were held relatively constant between the

[3]H. H. Kelley & J. W. Thibaut. Experimental studies of group problem solving and process. Reprinted by permission from G. Lindzey (Ed.), *Handbook of social psychology.* Vol. 2. Reading, Mass.: Addison-Wesley Publishing Company, Inc., 1954. P. 776.

various clubs by the device of permitting democratic and laissez-faire clubs to select an activity and then imposing the same activity on the club(s) concurrently being led by an authoritarian leader.

The results that bear most directly on problem solving can be summarized briefly. *Authoritarian* leadership appeared to induce the following characteristic reactions in the clubs: great dependency on the leader, marked intermember "irritability and aggressiveness," low frequencies of "suggestions for group action and group policy," dissatisfaction with club activities, and high quantity and low quality of productivity. . . . Under *laissez-faire* leadership, the clubs showed little dependency on the leader, great "irritability and aggressiveness" among members, high frequencies of "suggestions for group action and group policy" accompanied by great discontent about progress and achievement, considerable dissatisfaction with club activities, and apparently intermediate productivity. *Democratic* leadership produced low dependency on the leader, low incidence of intermember "irritability and aggressiveness," high frequencies of "suggestions for group action and group policy," great satisfaction with club activities, and an intermediate quantity of productivity of high quality.

Later investigations have in the main confirmed the findings. These include further experimental studies (Selvin, 1960) comparing participatory (democratic) and supervisory (laissez-faire) leaders, as well as studies in such settings as the classroom (Adams, 1945; Anderson & Brewer, 1945, 1946; Anderson, Brewer, & Reed, 1946; Robbins, 1952; Preston & Heintz, 1949) and a variety of work situations (Katz & Kahn, 1952). Some of the conclusions drawn from the initial studies, however, require qualification. In a study of decision-making groups in government and industry, a high level of member participation was associated with *low* satisfaction (Berkowitz, 1953). Presumably, in such groups the members expected and desired strong leadership, and these expectations were not met. Personality characteristics also determine the degree to which authoritarian or democratic leadership is associated with satisfaction, as noted in Chapter 11. Finally, a recent study showed that reactions to leadership styles are related in a rather complex way to such characteristics as age, marital status, and educational status (Selvin, 1960).

In spite of these qualifications of the original studies, when the vagueness of variables in the initial studies is considered, it is surprising that such confirmation has been obtained. A more systematic conceptual analysis based on the discussion of leadership in Chapter 11 and a closer look at some of these studies should provide further understanding. The following analysis will be divided into two parts, the first discussing the dependent variable, satisfaction, and the second, productivity.

Leadership and satisfaction

Satisfaction may be thought of as resulting from need gratification. In the course of problem solving, individual needs may be satisfied through task accomplishment, through the work activity itself, or through the interactions with other persons on the job. Studies such as those carried on by the Survey Research Center of the University of Michigan have shown that supervisors who did not supervise closely but allowed their subordinates a certain degree of self-determination in carrying out their activities had groups that were more satisfied with their jobs (Katz & Kahn, 1952). Presumably this situation allowed workers to satisfy needs for self-determination and self-realization.

Another study seemingly contradicts the negative effects of close supervision (Morse, 1953). Among a group of white-collar employees, freedom from close supervision was associated with dissatisfaction. This underscores the point that rewards must always be assessed against expectation. As Homans (1961) has suggested, these employees were less satisfied with their situation because the lack of close supervision led them to expect more rewards than they were in fact receiving: since they were carrying more responsibility, they felt they should be paid more than they were.

The study of supervisors revealed other differences among supervisors suggesting that they differ in the extent to which they gratify the needs of the employees under them. Thus employee-oriented supervisors, in contrast to production or company-oriented supervisors, had the more satisfied groups. Kahn and Katz (1953) comment:

> A number of supervisory characteristics which we have included in the concept of employee-orientation have important effects upon employee satisfaction, as well as productivity. This is particularly true for the foreman's giving reasons for forthcoming changes on the job, demonstrating to employees that he holds other aspects of the work situation to be as important as high productivity, and that his concept of reasonable performance is not excessive. In the tractor company, these characteristics were related to job satisfaction, satisfaction with supervision, and satisfaction with the company as a whole.
>
> A related finding appeared when each employee was asked who in the work situation took the greatest interest in him. The workers who felt that the foreman took the greatest interest in them also were getting the greatest psychological return from their employment in terms of satisfaction with job, supervisor, and company. (P. 622)

Finally, supervisors whose subordinates were more satisfied spent more time in actual supervision, in contrast to the other supervisors, who spent an appreciable portion of their time in nonsupervisory activities such as doing some of the work themselves. The investigators document this point as follows:

> The recognition by the supervisor of the importance of giving more time to his leadership role was also reflected in the morale findings. In the tractor company, for example, the men supervised by foremen who reported spending more than half their time in actual supervision not only had higher production records, but were more satisfied with the company than the men whose supervisors gave their time primarily to other aspects of the job.
>
> Moreover, in the same company the men with the highest morale as measured in terms of satisfaction with job, supervisor, and company were those

who perceived their supervisors as performing a number of broad, supportive functions. Almost all employees, of high or low morale reported that their supervisors enforced the rules and kept production up, but the high morale employees also reported that their supervisors performed such other functions as on-the-job training, recommending people for promotion and transfer, and communicating relevant information about the work and the company. (P. 615)

In short, the supervisors whose leadership style maximizes gratification of important needs in the work situation have the most satisfied employees. This finding is consistent with our treatment of leadership and group process.

STUDY QUESTIONS

15. *What is the relation between democratic leadership and satisfaction of group members? Under what circumstances does this relation fail to hold?*
16. *Which leaders have the most satisfied followers: those who supervise closely or those who exercise more indirect supervision? Why? Are there any exceptions to your answer?*
17. *Which leaders have more satisfied employees: those who focus on the leader role or those who act like one of the workers?*

Leadership and productivity

We noted previously that groups are less effective in dealing with complex problems when the communication structure has only one or a few members in central positions. The central members become overloaded or saturated with communications and are unable to handle them. Shaw (1955) suggests that the independence of members and the saturation factor interact to produce the observed effects of leadership style on morale and performance:

> To summarize, it is believed that leadership type should influence group behavior not through either independence or saturation alone, but rather through the combination of these two processes. Authoritarian leadership should decrease independence for most of its members (and hence decrease morale), and should decrease saturation effects for all group members (and hence improve performance). Nonauthoritarian leadership should increase independence for all group members (and hence increase morale), and should increase saturation for all group members (and hence lower performance). (P. 128)

These suppositions were borne out by Shaw's observations of groups having different networks and styles of leadership. As did Lippitt and White (1943), he found higher morale in the democratically led groups. His findings on performance, while consistent with the above reasoning, did differ in one respect: For the authoritarian groups, performance was better, both quantitatively in terms of time and number of messages employed, and qualitatively in terms of errors.

Leadership style could be expected to affect the quality and quantity of production in a group since it affects the quality of solutions and the motivation to implement them. We pointed out earlier that increases in group size produce a communication structure that is highly differentiated, and that this condition is detrimental to the early phases of problem solving. There is some evidence that by encouraging participation, a discussion leader can partially counteract this effect of increased size. In one investigation, thirty-four groups were provided with a leader who conducted the discussion in a permissive manner, asking questions to stimulate thinking, encouraging participation of all members, and promoting the expression of various points of view, but refraining from expressing his own opinions (Maier & Solem, 1952). The performance of these groups in solving a problem was compared with that of thirty-three groups who were provided not with a leader but with an observer who merely listened to group members while they discussed the problem. Group members privately recorded their answers before and after an eight-minute discussion. The groups did not differ appreciably in the proportion of correct answers prior to discussion, but *after* discussion the proportion of correct answers was significantly higher for the groups having discussion leaders. A further analysis revealed that this improvement appeared particularly in groups where a minority initially had the correct solution. In such instances the discussion leader served to encourage the expression and consideration of the solution. Maier and Solem (1952) conclude:

> The results are interpreted to mean that a discussion leader can function to up-grade a group's thinking by permitting an individual with a minority opinion time for discussion. In a leaderless discussion the majority dominates, and this condition releases social pressure which has an important influence on opinion. Without the right kind of leadership, therefore, a minority cannot effectively compete with the pressure of the majority. When the minority opinion is right, and there is no protection from the leader, a distinct potential contribution is lost; when it is wrong, the minority cannot convince the majority. The leader, in giving the minority a greater voice, can up-grade the end result of a discussion without running the risk of down-grading the end product. The quality of thinking in a democracy is thus dependent on the opportunities it affords minority opinions to be heard. (Pp. 287–288)

Chapter 11 noted that one consequence of the group-decision process is the increased likelihood that the decision would be carried out by group members. This appears to result from the emergence of a normative structure favoring actions in accordance with the solution and internalization of these norms on the part of the members. Under these circumstances, a solution is gradually fashioned as group members come to see and evaluate the situation in a similar manner. Through the sharing of information and exertion of social pressures by means of giving or withholding social approval, gradual consensus is achieved.

Such consensus not only facilitates cooperative action, should the implementation of the solution require it, but also reinforces individual motivation to carry out the solution. This interpretation fits the experimental studies on the effects of group decision discussed in Chapter 6, and also supports the finding that in an industrial setting changes introduced through group discussion are more successfully implemented. In the latter study, investigators varied the extent to which workers participated in the development of new work procedures. Participation ranged from no participation, through indirect participation via representatives, to direct participation (Coch & French, 1958). Productivity of the groups varied directly with the amount of participation.

In most work situations rules regarding quality and quantity of production are set up by management, an agent *external* to the work group. It has long been known that norms very rapidly arise within the group to govern the quality and quantity of production. The degree to which these norms are affected by the standards set by management will depend in part on the attitudes that group members have toward management. To the extent that the supervisor, by his style of supervision, creates favorable attitudes toward himself and management, the production rules that he represents are apt to have their effect on the group norms. This may well be an important reason why the "democratic" supervisors in the studies described earlier had groups with higher productivity (Katz & Kahn, 1952; Likert, 1961).

While our discussion has for the most part emphasized the advantages of democratic as opposed to authoritarian leadership, these advantages depend upon the demands of the situation, the distribution of skills within the group, and the group's expectations, as well as other variables. Unfortunately, as Gibb has noted, these qualifications have often been ignored:[4]

> It is common in our culture at the present time to place negative values on authoritarian leadership. Much of this attitude seems to be due to a prolonged period of ideological opposition to cultures authoritarianly organized. The tendency is to think of authoritarianism in its most extreme form of headship, and to denounce all forms of individual authority over others. Studies of groups in action reveal that in certain circumstances authoritarian leadership is highly valued. There is in the American culture an ambivalence about leadership technique, and morale is sometimes higher and satisfactions maximized when more authoritarian techniques are employed.

He further notes there are situations where a more authoritarian form of leadership is more effective:[5]

> If the group is faced with a need for emergency action, then that leader behavior is most effective which is prompt and decisive and which is perceived by the members as likely to remove quickly the threats in the situation. Authoritarian leadership is practically demanded under such circumstances.

[4]C. A. Gibb. Leadership. Reprinted by permission from G. Lindzey (Ed.), *Handbook of social psychology*. Vol. 2. Reading, Mass.: Addison-Wesley Publishing Company, Inc., 1954. P. 911.

[5]*Ibid.*

It behooves the psychologist, above all others, to recognize the facts of individual inequality. While men may be equal in rights and in the democratic ideology, they are not, in fact, equal in education, ability, or personality development. It is an axiom of group development that there is differentiation of roles along the lines of perceived individual differences. This fact alone requires that individuals be permitted differential influence if group progress is to be maximal. To admit the superior wisdom of any expert is to admit some degree of authoritarianism. It is important for the use we can make of our resources and of our groups that we recognize authoritarianism and democracy as poles of a continuum, neither of which is wholly good or wholly bad, but which represent extremes of a variable "leadership techniques" that should be adapted to all the elements of the situation — culture, personality content, structural interrelations, syntality, and task.

Some progress is being made toward distinguishing situational and other variables that are associated with the effectiveness of leadership style. Fiedler (1963) has tentatively proposed a model based on a classification of situations according to the ease with which the leader may influence performance of the group task. Three situational components are (1) the leader's personal relations with members of his group, i.e., the degree to which he is liked and respected, (2) the degree of structure in the task, ranging from highly routine, clearly spelled-out tasks to tasks that are vague and indefinite, and (3) the legitimate power and authority associated with the leader's position.

He suggests that the leader who is liked and respected by his group, who is faced with a highly structured task, and who wields considerable power by virtue of the authority invested in his position is in a relatively favorable position to influence the group. The leader who is disliked in a group faced by a vague, unstructured task and who has little formal power may encounter difficulty in wielding influence. In very favorable or very unfavorable situations a style of leadership involving active intervention and control is apt to be effective. In moderately unfavorable situations, however, a more democratic, permissive style focusing on human relations is more effective.

A wide variety of situations studied by Fiedler and his colleagues as well as other investigators appear to fit this model.

Leader's perception of coworkers

A rather sophisticated measure of person perception has been found to distinguish leaders of productive groups from leaders of less productive groups. As noted briefly in the previous chapter, effective leaders distinguish more sharply between their coworkers. This was determined by an index called the *assumed similarity of opposites* (abbreviated ASo). To provide data for obtaining this index, leaders were asked to rate on various personality traits the best coworker they had ever had and the poorest coworker they had ever had. ASo is obtained by ascertaining the degree to which these two workers are perceived by the leader as similar. The lower the index, the more different they are perceived to be. Fiedler

(1958*a;* 1958*b*) has carried on an extensive program of research relating the ASo of the leader of a team or group to various criteria of group effectiveness. His studies are notable in that they involve a great variety of groups functioning in real-life settings rather than the laboratory. His subjects include basketball teams, surveying crews, radar bombing crews, tank crews, open-hearth steelworkers, and management groups in corporations. In each instance he was interested in determining the degree of relation between the leader's ASo and criteria of group effectiveness.

In groups having a somewhat less formal structure,[6] the lower the ASo score of the informal leader, the more effective the team was. In other words, the teams winning the most basketball games or the most accurate surveying crews had leaders who perceived a considerable difference in the personalities of the person they most preferred to work with and the person they least preferred to work with. On the other hand, the leaders who did not perceive much difference between their most-preferred coworker and least-preferred coworker had less effective teams. In more formal groups, such as Navy and Army ROTC squads, no difference in the ASo scores of leaders of good and poor teams was found.

Unwilling to concede that ASo had no relation to the proficiency of formal groups, Fiedler (1958*a*) pursued the hypothesis that ASo considered together with the affect structure of the group would predict group effectiveness. He proposed further that the relation between the leader and his right-hand man (or keyman) would be important, since the keyman is an important communication link between the leader and his men. Conducting further studies, he found that the commanders of radar bombing teams who were accepted by their group and who accepted their own keyman had low ASo scores if they had effective teams. The accepted commanders who did not accept their keyman, however, had high ASo scores if they had effective teams. This result was also obtained for commanders of tank crews.

Fiedler makes sense out of this in the following way. In order for a leader of a formal group to be effective, he must maintain a certain amount of "psychological distance" between himself and his group. He must not become too emotionally involved with members of his team, a condition likely to exist if he rates the least-preferred person as relatively similar to the most-preferred. At the same time, he must maintain adequate communication with group members. He may maintain distance and adequate communication in two ways. In the first case, he may not have any particular preference for his keyman, but may be closer than the average leader to other members of the group. Thus, his distance from the group takes the form of distance from the keyman, but com-

---

[6]A group is considered to have a formal structure to the extent that the positions in it and the expected behaviors associated with these positions have been formally established, as in the case of a military unit or business organization.

munication is maintained through greater than average closeness to other group members, expressed in a high ASo. In the second case, if the successful commander does have a preference for his keyman, he maintains more distance from other group members, as expressed in a low ASo score. Communication is kept adequate through the close relation to the keyman.

In the above studies of formal groups, a necessary condition is that the leader be accepted by his group. Acceptance of him places him in a position of influence and means that effective communication is possible. Thus, among leaders who are *not* accepted, significant relations between ASo and group effectiveness are not obtained. The importance of these several factors is further emphasized by Fiedler's studies of farm cooperatives. Here the acceptance of the general manager by the board of directors as well as by his own staff was a necessary condition to obtain significant relations between his ASo score and the effectiveness of his company. The implications of these findings may be summarized in Fiedler's (1958a) words:

> Better than any of our studies, this investigation shows the interaction of the sociometric preference pattern with interpersonal perception. Neither sociometric endorsement nor the leader's interpersonal perception score by itself was here related to group effectiveness. Rather, the sociometric endorsement and acceptance should be visualized more like a pipeline through which information and attitudes can flow. By itself, the pipeline is neither "bad" nor "good." But unless there is such a pipeline available, the leader's attitudes do not have a channel through which they can reach the members of the group who directly affect performance. As shown in previous studies, being in a leadership position seems thus to be merely a license to practice. In addition one also has to have patients who are willing to be practiced on. This is indicated by the group's acceptance of the leader. Finally, having patients and a license to practice does not make one a good doctor. This depends on one's abilities and skills. In our case we find that the person who leads a task group should be a psychologically distant individual. Presumably, this type of attitude permits one to be more objective, which in turn prevents emotional involvement with one's subordinates and hence leads to better discipline and businesslike work relations. Other types of tasks such as heading a policy-making group apparently demand different attitudes on the part of the leader. (P. 256)

STUDY QUESTIONS

18. *Explain how independence and saturation of members produce certain relations between leadership style, productivity, and satisfaction.*
19. *What are the effects of having a discussion leader in large-sized groups? Why?*
20. *How does use of a group-decision process affect productivity?*
21. *Informal work-group norms exert considerable control over group productivity. Under what circumstances are these norms likely to be set at a high level of productivity?*

22. *Under what conditions is authoritarian or democratic leadership likely to be effective?*

23. *Explain what is meant by the ASo index. How does it relate to leadership?*

Summary: Leadership

Although there are some exceptions, a democratic style of leadership appears to generate more satisfaction among group members and more effective group functioning than an autocratic or a laissez-faire style. Exceptions occur when members expect strong leadership; under these circumstances they may be dissatisfied with a democratic leader.

Satisfaction has rather complex relations to a number of group variables. In industrial settings, leaders who do not supervise too closely but permit some self-determination on the part of members appear to obtain a higher level of satisfaction. But certain circumstances may provide an exception to this generalization: Freedom from supervision led to a low degree of satisfaction in one study, apparently because the greater responsibility assumed by these employees led them to expect more rewards than they were receiving. Supervisors may also obtain high satisfaction from workers if they show a particular interest in their welfare. Apparently the leaders who focus upon their leadership role instead of just being one of the workers also produce greater satisfaction.

The relation between leadership style and productivity may be explained in terms of the independence of members and the saturation or overloading of members with communications. Authoritarian leadership reduces independence and saturation; thus it is likely to produce less satisfaction but greater productivity. A discussion leader in larger groups to some extent counteracts the undesirable effects of size, increasing participation particularly on the part of the minority. This improves the quality of the group product. Participation in these circumstances and in those where the leader encourages group decisions also appears to produce a high level of motivation, increasing the likelihood that the task will be effectively carried out.

Most work situations generate informal group norms that define an appropriate production level. Leadership that fosters good attitudes toward management on the part of the workers is likely to contribute to setting a high production norm. Under most circumstances this condition is likely to prevail where leadership is democratic in style. In other circumstances, however, authoritarian leadership may be highly effective. These include emergency situations requiring rapid action and situations in which wise authoritarian leadership can make the best use of the inequalities among the members in personality, temperament, and skills. Situations where the leader is either in a very strong position or a very weak one favor an authoritarian style; a situation where the leader has a modicum amount of influence favors a democratic style.

The combined conditions of the affect structure of the group and the leader's perception of his most- and least-preferred coworkers are related to the performance of the group. The interpretation of this relation is that effective leaders are accepted by group members but are more psychologically distant from them than ineffective leaders. This social distance may take the form of a close relation to the keyman and considerable distance from other members, or a not-so-close relation to the keyman combined with a not-so-distant relation to other members.

THE PROBLEM-SOLVING PROCESS

So far group problem-solving has been considered from the standpoint of factors affecting the quality of the group product. Let us now turn to certain features of the process.

Phases of ongoing process

Certain regularities in the interactions of members in problem-solving groups have been noted in discussing communication and leadership structures. These uniformities were observed when the behaviors of group members were analyzed in terms of Bales's categories for interaction process analysis (see Chapter 9). In these accounts to be described, ongoing interaction was divided into three parts: first, middle, and final phases. When high points were compared for various major categories of behavior, it was found that in phase one, acts related to problems of *orientation* and *evaluation* had the highest relative frequencies. In the middle phase, acts related to *evaluation* increased slightly, reaching a maximum in this phase, with acts related to *orientation* dropping off appreciably. From phase to phase, acts related to problems of *control* and the relative frequencies of positive and negative responses steadily increased, reaching a maximum in the final phase. These trends are shown in Figure 12–3.

The shift from problems of orientation to those of evaluation and finally to those of control appears at first to be only as expected. It seems reasonable that when a group attempts to solve a problem, its members first exchange information about the problem and the situation, then evaluate the information, and finally make suggestions as to what should be the course of action. However, further reflection on the reasons for this sequence, along with consideration of the findings on the increase of positive and negative reactions as the group progresses from phase to phase, should uncover a number of principles previously encountered in the discussion of conformity. These principles also explain the friction frequently arising in ongoing group interaction. It has already been observed that positive and negative reactions—social approval and its withdrawal—are forms of pressure that bring about conformity in the group. Pressures toward conformity arise in a group not only because lack of conformity makes concerted action difficult, but also because the existence of conformity is gratifying in its own right. This follows from the assumption that persons have a drive to evaluate their opinions

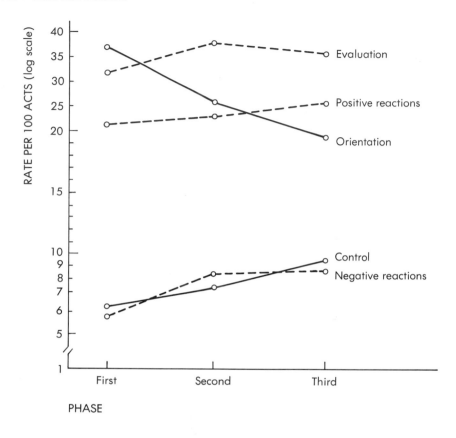

Figure 12–3

Relative frequency of acts by type and phase based upon twenty-two sessions. [Adapted with permission from R. F. Bales. Some uniformities of behavior in small social systems. In G. E. Swanson, T. M. Newcomb, & E. L. Hartley (Eds.), *Readings in social psychology.* (Rev. ed.) New York: Holt, Rinehart and Winston, Inc., 1952.]

and that, in the absence of some nonsocial criterion, they do so by comparing them with other people's opinions which are close to their own.

The increased use of negative and positive reactions from phase one to phase two reflects the increasing pressures for conformity as the group shifts from problems of orientation to those of evaluation. The facts of the situation are generally seen in the same way by different members. Indeed, the participants in Bales's groups were all given the same facts. In the evaluative phase, however, expressions of opinion about the task and situation are likely to vary from member to member unless the group shares the same values. In the problem-solving situation studied by these investigators, problems were chosen on which members were expected to differ. The differences ordinarily lead to an increase in positive and negative reactions until conformity is achieved. In fact, if too rapid movement occurs before value conformity is achieved, so that the participants begin making suggestions for action, the group will be forced back to the unresolved problem of lack of conformity. This will lead to an increase in behaviors falling into the evaluative categories and a decrease in responses classified in the categories of control. As these differences are resolved, suggestions for action will be increasingly accepted, and the frequencies in this category will increase. The group will then move into the final phase.

The higher rate of negative responses in the last phase appears to occur mostly in the early part of it and is probably a consequence of still unresolved value differences. Positive responses appear to dominate in the latter part of the final phase. This occurs not only because participants find agreement and successful control rewarding but also because group members attempt to restore the reservoir of positive feeling that was depleted as persons attempted to exert pressure on each other to change.

Attempts to influence or exercise power in such groups are based to a considerable extent on the exchange of social approval for conformity. If we assume, in the manner of Homans, that each exchange of a unit of social approval between A and B for a unit of movement toward the other's opinion results in a smaller increment of profit for both, then the likelihood that each will be able to influence the other is reduced. On each occasion the cost of the movement in terms of integrity as well as loss of reward from other like-minded persons is greater, and the reward is less because of increasing satiation. Such a situation, assuming that both persons expect to continue to interact, constitutes a threat which motivates an exchange of a considerable number of units of social approval to bring the profit level up so that each will again be disposed to make such exchanges in the future.

This principle appears to apply to many situations where individuals have drawn heavily on their reserve of power over another person. When a person as a result of his repeated demands has considerably lowered his power relative to the other, the power balance is upset, and the threat of loss of future rewards is particularly likely to motivate him to lavish rewards on the more powerful person in an attempt to restore his power to a comfortable level. The resolutions, promises, and more solicitous behavior after a lovers' quarrel illustrate the point.

This discussion of process raises a problem which hitherto has been dealt with insufficiently. As Barnard (1938) noted, every human organization must solve two problems. The first is the problem of effectiveness, which means achieving group purposes. The second is the problem of efficiency, which refers to providing satisfaction to individual members. Up to this point the second question has been largely ignored, except in the discussion of leadership. In part, the omission reflects a gap in the research literature. In the short-lived laboratory groups typically studied, efficiency is of little concern. Presumably the subjects in these studies either receive enough satisfaction to remain in the situation or, if not, find it too costly to refuse to cooperate in the study. In everyday situations, unlike the laboratory, the group must solve the problem of efficiency or it will cease to exist.

Forms of member satisfaction

As previously observed, satisfaction is generally viewed as a function of need gratification. To understand satisfaction in task groups it is useful to distinguish between needs according to the source of the rewards that lead to their satisfaction. One such source is obvious: the reward offered in exchange for task accomplishment. In industrial groups rewards for task accomplishment are largely monetary. In other groups the rewards may be status, social approval from other members, and other "psychic" rewards. A second source of rewards lies in features of task activity itself that allow for the satisfaction of such needs as those for self-expression, self-development, and self-determination. Commenting on these ego needs, Katz and Kahn (1952) note:

> In addition to the need for security and the desire to be esteemed by one's fellows, there are also the satisfactions deriving from the expression of one's abilities and talents—the self-expression and self-development recognized by modern psychiatry. Allied to this dimension of ego motivation is the need for self-determination—the satisfactions resulting from making one's own decisions and controlling one's own fate. If we consider the many studies of industrial morale we find more agreement on one type of result than any other. This type of finding is that morale and worker satisfaction are definitely related to the skill level of the job. The more varied, the more complex, the more intrinsically interesting the job, the more satisfaction workers express about what they are doing. (P. 663)

So far, the needs and rewards we have discussed are directly or indirectly related to task performance. A third class of needs and rewards is related to features of the group; these arise out of interaction above and beyond task activity. Zaleznik, Christensen, and Roethlisberger (1958) have emphasized these needs and rewards in their investigation of worker satisfaction and productivity, and refer to them as internal or group-controlled rewards to distinguish them from external or management-controlled rewards. They describe them as follows:

> The internal needs or rewards include the need for belonging to a group; for associating with other human beings; for expressing and sharing in sentiments of loyalty, friendliness and affection; for giving and receiving emotional support; for receiving the marks of group approval which we include in the ordinary terms of prestige and esteem. All these needs stem from human association and interaction in a group setting. We can think of the satisfaction of these needs, consequently, as "reward by the group" in contrast to reward by management in satisfying needs for job status. (P. 324)

Determinants of satisfaction

The satisfactions individuals receive are more than simply a function of the *amount* of rewards obtained in a group. Whether the reward is in terms of dollars, intrinsic job satisfaction, or approval, an amount that satisfies one person may not another. This is so for a number of reasons. First, individuals vary with respect to the strength of their needs. Second, they vary with respect to the number of alternatives for need gratification. The person who is receiving considerable gratification from other groups will be less dependent on a particular group for gratification, and he may be able to exact more rewards than a person who is more dependent on the group. Third, individuals differ with respect to their comparison level — in how much they feel they can *expect* from the group. Homans (1961), who has emphasized the last variable, suggests that the amount of reward the individual expects is a function of his investments. As noted in Chapter 9, in most groups members agree that persons with certain characteristics should receive more rewards than others even though their costs may be the same as those of other members, or even less. In industry most workers feel that persons with seniority, an investment, should receive higher pay. Similarly, in many quarters, it is thought only just and proper that men receive higher pay than women. Any characteristic of persons can be regarded as justifying a given distribution of costs and rewards in a group. For example, in some parts of the United States skin color is so regarded: whites expect to be paid at a higher rate than Negroes for comparable work.

When satisfaction is viewed as not only a function of how much one gets, but also how much one still desires according to some standard of a just distribution of rewards, many puzzling findings about satisfaction are cleared up. Two of a number of such findings cited by Homans may be used as illustrations. During World War II the Research Branch, Information and Education Division of the United States Army conducted a series of studies on the attitudes and behavior of the American soldier. One puzzling finding was that there was greater satisfaction with promotions in the Military Police than in the Air Force despite the fact that the actual chances of promotion were much greater in the latter. Homans (1961) notes that from the standpoint of the principle of distributive justice these findings should be expected.[7]

> Now if there is much promotion in a particular branch of the service, some men will see many of their fellows promoted while they themselves are passed over, and this will lead them to ask whether the promotions are just and whether sufficient attention has been paid to their own abilities. It will raise the question of distributive justice — justice in the distribution of rewards among men and justice, as we shall see more and more as we go along, is a principal ingredient of satisfaction. In a branch like the Military Police, on the other hand, where there has been very little promotion, the soldiers are much less apt to compare their fate with that of others and so to raise the question of justice. (P. 270)

Homans draws on a finding by Morse (1953) which would be quite

---

[7]This finding has also been explained by the concept of *relative deprivation:* Military Police not promoted feel less deprived than Air Force men not promoted (Merton & Kitt, 1950). Thibaut and Kelley's (1959) concept of comparison level is also relevant.

puzzling without this principle. In a study of satisfaction among white-collar workers, employees under *general* supervision were found to be less satisfied with pay, status, and the intrinsic content of their jobs than were employees under *close* supervision. This finding was contrary to studies in a wide variety of work situations showing that workers are less satisfied under conditions of close supervision. Again however, these findings are consistent with the principle of distributive justice. As Homans notes:

> A person under general supervision is one who takes a great deal of responsibility: he is able to decide what ought to be done without always checking back with his boss. But a man who has learned how to do a job on his own responsibility has, by that fact, made new investments, and so should get more reward. He feels he is ready for a raise in pay and a better job, even if it is also a more demanding one. If he does not get them, he will become less satisfied than his fellow workers down whose necks the boss has been breathing all the time, even though taken by itself the latter is the worse position to be in. (P. 276)

STUDY QUESTIONS

24. *What types of acts predominate in the early, middle, and late phases of the problem-solving process? Explain the reasons for these varying frequencies in different phases of the group task.*
25. *What are the three classes of satisfaction that members gain from membership in a task group?*
26. *To what extent are the various satisfactions obtained by group members a function of factors other than the rewards they receive? Explain the reasons for your answer.*

Summary: The problem-solving process

While the various phases of the problem-solving sequence include a wide variety of acts, certain actions occur at maximum frequency in different phases. In the early phase, acts related to problems of orientation and evaluation are at a maximum; in the final phase, acts related to problems of control reach their peak. An overall trend is that the relative frequencies of both positive and negative responses increase from phase to phase. The relative predominance of the various forms of action in different phases is in part related to the demands imposed by the necessity of solving a problem, but it also stems from the interaction of several other variables.

One variable underlying the relative frequencies of different acts is the need of the group to obtain conformity from its members. As the group shifts from orientation to evaluation, it reacts negatively toward those who do not conform and positively toward those who do. In the initial part of the final phase, which involves control, the high frequency of negative reactions occurs because of unresolved value differences. The later part of the final phase is characterized by many positive reactions. This apparently serves to restore positive feeling in the group, which has been depleted by the many influence attempts aimed at achieving agreement.

Satisfaction in groups takes several forms. Some satisfaction lies in the reward for task accomplishment, which may be monetary or "psychic." The latter is illustrated by the status or social approval accorded members for successful achievement. Task achievement also satisfies needs for self-expression, self-development, and self-determination. Another type of satisfaction is unrelated to task needs; it stems from the enjoyment of social interaction.

Satisfactions are not a simple function of the amount of rewards received in a group. Individuals vary with respect to the strength of their needs, the number of alternative satisfactions, and how much they expect from the group. Under certain circumstances persons receiving *less* reward may be *more* satisfied than those receiving more reward. Such puzzling findings are readily explained by concepts such as distributive justice, relative deprivation, or comparison level.

SATISFACTION AND PRODUCTIVITY

This final section will discuss a most perplexing problem: the relation between group effectiveness and efficiency, or to use the more common terms, *productivity* and *satisfaction*. Personnel policies in many organizations are formulated on the assumption that satisfied workers will be productive workers; yet a growing body of research lends little support for any simple direct relation between these two variables. Brayfield and Crockett (1955), in a critical review of this literature, conclude:

> In summary, it appears that there is little evidence in the available literature that employee attitudes of the type usually measured in morale surveys bear any simple — or, for that matter, appreciable — relationship to performance on the job. (P. 408)

They do note, however, that satisfaction or morale is related to employee absences and employment stability. Less satisfied workers have higher rates of absence and are more apt to quit their jobs. These latter findings, as Brayfield and Crockett assert, are consistent with the general principle that individuals avoid punishing situations and seek out situations which are rewarding: they stay away from a job they don't like and they try to find one that they do like.

The unexpected findings on productivity and satisfaction have prompted a closer look at the reasoning that led early investigators to expect a positive relation between productivity and satisfaction. One line of reasoning assumes that satisfaction and productivity are both a function of rewards, and hence they should vary together. The relation between productivity and rewards, however, bears further scrutiny. First, productivity is a function of many more variables than just motivation. A previous section reviewed a wide variety of factors that affect both the quality and quantity of production. But even if productivity were a function of rewards alone, there are some very good reasons why rewards, satisfaction, and productivity do not necessarily vary together in the typical work situation. As Katz and Kahn (1952) argued, not only are such rewards often removed in time and space, but they are often not administered according to a worker's productivity:

> The precise conditions which made reward and punishment effective in the laboratory are not necessarily present in the industrial situation. The rewards are removed in space and time from the productive effort desired. Nor are they administered in such a manner as to reinforce greater efforts in turning out the work. As a rule, all workers tend to benefit alike from good working conditions within the plant, from retirement systems and recreational facilities, save as these "rewards" are administered in differing degree according to very broad classifications of length of service, type of work, and similar characteristics. (P. 657)

These writers also note that such rewards will be obtained only if a worker remains in the system; hence, they may motivate a sufficient level of productivity to ensure continued employment, but a level that does not result in differences among workers within an organization.

Implicit in the argument of a direct relation between productivity and rewards is the assumption that "rewards" regarded by management as important are in fact important rewards for the worker. Brayfield and Crockett have suggested that the importance to the worker of such differential monetary rewards has been greatly overestimated. In fact, of the three kinds of rewards previously discussed — monetary rewards for task performance, rewards arising out of the task activity itself, and rewards arising out of interaction in the work situation — there is growing evidence that the latter two are much more important in explaining differences both in satisfaction and productivity. The work of Likert (1961) and his associates, as well as that of Argyris (1960), underscores satisfaction intrinsic to job activity, particularly as it is affected by the style of supervision. Rewards deriving from interaction have been emphasized by a long series of investigations under the influence of Mayo and culminating recently in the work of Zaleznik, Christensen, and Roethlisberger (1958). In fact, the latter group, in a study of satisfaction and productivity in an industrial setting, found no relation between satisfaction, productivity, and monetary rewards. Like their predecessors, these investigators found that productivity was greatly influenced by group norms which specified what was an appropriate level of productivity — a "fair day's work." Those who were dependent upon and rewarded by the group conformed to these norms.

These findings suggest another reason why productivity in work situations, unlike that in the laboratory, is not a simple function of rewards provided by an external agent. Internal rewards in the work situation may counteract the effects of external rewards. The worker who is given a monetary reward by management for high productivity may be deprived of the social-emotional rewards administered by the group because his level of productivity exceeds the group norm. For most workers, rewards of the latter type are far more important: hence we find relatively small differences in productivity between workers even though the system of payment is designed to encourage such differences. Where such differences do exist, they can be explained largely in terms of the worker's position in the group as it affects and is affected by his adherence to the group norms.

Monetary rewards are probably important in some situations. For example, in some work settings, rewards through task activity and through interaction with fellow workers may be singularly absent; monetary rewards should be important there.

So far, discussion has been based largely on differences between the laboratory situation, where productivity and rewards are related, and the work situation, where they are not. We have suggested that satisfaction and productivity are not necessarily related by being linked to rewards, because the relation between productivity and rewards is not what it has been assumed to be. Rewards in the work situation are more complex, and their administration is not uniformly and differentially related to differences in productivity. Recently Homans (1961) has presented a model on the basis of which one would not expect, except under certain conditions, satisfaction and productivity to vary directly. In fact, in most instances he would predict an *inverse* relation between the two.

The crucial variable in this model is the schedule of rewards. Perhaps an analogy between hunger satisfaction and the amount of food a person eats will help clarify the point. If a person has received very little food, he is likely to eat ravenously. As he continues, however, he eats more slowly. At the same time he becomes increasingly satisfied. An analogous situation exists with respect to reward, productivity, and satisfaction. Homans argues that if an individual receives rewards for some activity at a constant ratio, that is, in proportion to the frequency with which he emits such activity, satisfaction and productivity would be negatively related. At a point where he has received little reward, he will be working the hardest and be least satisfied. This is so because in this model, Homans assumes that the frequency with which a person emits an activity is a function of the difference between the amount of reward he has received and the amount that would satiate him. In the beginning this difference is greatest. As time goes on and the amount of reward more and more approximates the amount which would satiate him, the frequency of emitting the behavior will approach zero. The relation between reward and satisfaction, however, is the reverse. In the beginning the person is least satisfied, since the difference between the amount of reward received and the amount that will satiate the individual is at a maximum. At the end, where productivity would approach zero, satisfaction would be greatest, since a point of satiation would be reached.

Given this particular schedule of reward, then, a negative correlation between productivity and satisfaction would be expected by this model.

What kind of schedule would lead to a positive relation? Homans (1961) suggests that a positive relation would occur where an activity is infrequently rewarded until just before the point of satiation, when it is rewarded at a rapidly accelerating rate. He suggests that such a schedule does occur sometimes in life situations:

> It occurs when repeated activities that lead up to the accomplishment of some final result get rewarded very infrequently until just before the result is attained, when they begin to get rewarded in a rush. Suppose, for instance, that soldiers have been fighting a battle all day, and at dusk the enemy is just beginning to give way. Then they will put on a last big push, and their elation will mount rapidly as they get sight of victory. (P. 281)

This is a very simple model whose assumptions could probably only be met in the laboratory; yet it is instructive in suggesting that even under relatively simple conditions, the commonly held notion that high productivity and high satisfaction go together needs considerable qualification.

STUDY QUESTIONS

27. *What is the commonly assumed relation between satisfaction and productivity? To what extent is this assumption warranted?*

28. *What are the various rewards received by the worker, and what is their relative importance to him? To what extent do these rewards work together to increase his total reward?*

29. *Explain how the model presented by Homans would predict a negative correlation between productivity and satisfaction.*

Summary: Satisfaction and productivity

Two common assumptions in industry—that satisfaction and productivity are closely related and that they are a direct function of the amount of reward received by the worker—are probably both unwarranted. In the first place, rewards are seldom administered in direct proportion to the worker's productivity. Secondly, monetary rewards are usually less important than rewards arising out of task activity and out of group interaction. The latter two, along with style of supervision, appear to be more important as determinants of both productivity and satisfaction. Moreover, the several kinds of rewards available to the worker do not add up to produce a greater total reward: under some circumstances they interfere with one another. Finally, Homans has presented a model showing how, under certain conditions, satisfaction and productivity can be negatively associated.

Summary and Conclusions

This chapter has been devoted to the ongoing work activity of the group which is attempting to accomplish a task or solve a problem. Early studies comparing group and individual performance revealed a number of superiorities apparently attributable to the group. Later these were shown to be pseudo group effects resulting from statistical properties of group estimates or from the increased probabilities of solving the problem that occur when more than one individual works on it. True group effects are due to interaction among group members. Two general ways in which interaction affects the quality of a group product are: (1) Individual solutions in a group situation may be qualitatively different, and (2) in a group situation, individual solutions are not all weighted equally. The first of these follows from the exposure of the individual to a larger number and greater diversity of ideas, from improved motivation, and from the clarification which is the result of having to communicate one's ideas to other persons.

Idea productivity in the early phases of a task is a negatively accelerated increasing function of the size of a group, a function resulting largely from the restraints on communication present in a larger-sized group. Where the members of a group vary considerably in the positions of centrality they occupy, the group is likely to be effective with simple problems, but only members in positions of high centrality are likely to be satisfied. For more complex problems requiring extensive communication, a less differentiated communication structure may be more effective because it reduces the possibility of overloading members occupying positions of high centrality.

Although a high degree of liking facilitates communication, under some circumstances such communication is irrelevant to the task. Status and power differentials may interfere with effective communication, lowering the quality of task performance. Status congruency facilitates interaction among members, but much of the interaction may be irrelevant to the task. The production level set by the workers is important; status congruency facilitates adherence to this norm. For a heterogeneous group, high cohesiveness may reduce the quality of the solution because it equalizes the weight given to the contributions of each member. Contributions from individuals of high power and status are weighted more heavily. Whether this is detrimental or not depends upon their competence.

A democratic style of leadership appears to generate more satisfaction among group members and more effective group functioning than an autocratic or a laissez-faire style. Several qualifications of this generalization are necessary. Members expecting strong leadership may be dissatisfied with a democratic leader. Supervision which is not too close usually has favorable effects on satisfaction and productivity of a group, although focusing on the leader role instead of just being one of the workers is also important for a supervisor. Independence and saturation produced by different leadership styles help to explain the effects of these styles. Authoritarian leadership reduces independence and saturation; thus under appropriate circumstances it is likely to produce less satisfaction but greater productivity. In larger groups, however, democratic leadership encouraging discussion and group decision has favorable effects on both satisfaction and productivity. Leadership fostering favorable attitudes toward management may assist in setting group norms of production at a high level. Under some circumstances, authoritarian leadership is more effective. This includes emergency situations as well as those where such leadership makes effective use of the inequalities among members in personality, temperament, and skills, and situations where the leader is either in a very strong or a very weak position to influence the performance of the group task. Finally, effective leaders must be accepted by their group but are likely to be more psychologically distant from group members.

In the entire problem-solving sequence, the following types of acts reach their peak in the early, middle, and late phases, respectively: acts of orientation, acts of evaluation, and acts of control. These frequencies stem from task demands and from several other interacting variables. One important variable is the need of the group to obtain conformity from its members. This results in negative acts for nonconformity and positive acts for conformity, which increase over the entire sequence, diminishing only toward the end. A marked increase in positive acts occurs at the end, apparently in order to restore the positive feelings that have been depleted by pressures toward conformity.

Satisfactions obtained by group members include rewards for task accomplishment, exercise of the need for self-expression and self-development, and the enjoyment of social interaction. Satisfactions are not a simple function of the amount of rewards received, but depend upon the principle of distributive justice or a person's comparison level. The common assumptions in industry that satisfaction and productivity are closely related, and that they are a direct function of the amount of reward received by the worker, are probably both unwarranted. Rewards are seldom administered in direct proportion to the worker's productivity; monetary rewards, which are emphasized by management, are less important to the worker than task rewards or social-emotional satisfactions; and, finally, the several kinds of rewards do not summate: they may instead counteract one another.

chapter thirteen

INTERGROUP RELATIONS

Understanding of group behavior cannot be complete without some consideration of relations between groups and the effects of these relations upon group functioning and organization. The present chapter is devoted to a limited aspect of this topic.

One of the most intensively investigated areas of intergroup relations is attitudes toward ethnic minorities. A vast literature is devoted to prejudice toward minority groups of all types and descriptions from a great variety of countries around the world. In more recent years, attention has been increasingly focused upon more general problems of intergroup conflict and its resolution, with topics ranging all the way from factional disputes within tribes to war between nations. There are essentially three problems underlying these topics. One pertains to the conditions under which unfavorable attitudes arise toward groups. Another concerns the principles that explain the continuation of unfavorable attitudes. A third pertains to the factors that contribute to changing these attitudes in a favorable direction. Although the problems overlap to some extent, some of the answers are unique to each.

In spite of the voluminous research literature, intergroup theory is rather poorly developed. Apparently, in the earlier years of research on intergroup relations, the need for theoretical guidance of research activities was not clearly recognized. Research on prejudice suffers also from the fact that most of the empirical work has been focused on cognitions and feelings, with less attention being given to intergroup behavior. More recently, interest in intergroup theory and behavior has markedly increased. Also, the emergence of social-psychological theories now provides considerable structure for the diverse empirical findings on intergroup relations.

Nature of Intergroup Relations

This discussion focuses upon two aspects of intergroup relations: prejudice and discrimination.

PREJUDICE

As applied to intergroup relations, prejudice is an attitude that predisposes a person to think, perceive, feel, and act in favorable or unfavorable ways toward a group or its individual members. Whether or not a prejudiced individual will actually behave in accordance with his attitude depends upon situational and other factors. Thus the term *prejudice* stresses the perceptual, cognitive, and emotional content of the individual's internal predispositions and experience. It does not necessarily imply that behavior is congruent with such experience.

The perceptual-cognitive content of prejudice has already been discussed at length in Chapter 2 in the section on stereotypes. Members of a group or category of persons are seen as having certain traits or qualities that are different from those of the general population. Such stereotyping has three characteristics: (1) Persons are categorized according to certain identifying characteristics, (2) perceivers agree on the attributes that the persons in the category possess, and (3) a discrepancy exists between attributed traits and actual traits. Although some stereotypes are more definite than others, for most familiar minority groups consensus among perceivers is very much above the level that would be achieved if traits were assigned to the group at random.

The emotional content of prejudice for a particular individual is usually thought of as a point on a continuum ranging from an extremely favorable feeling to an extremely negative feeling. Thus, an individual's prejudice may be strongly unfavorable, moderately unfavorable, etc. Other emotional aspects of prejudice may be studied, such as the actual content of the emotions as expressed verbally by the individual, or the consistency with which he expresses such feelings in a wide variety of situations.

DISCRIMINATION

Discrimination is the differential treatment of individuals considered to belong to a particular social group (Williams, 1947). As Simpson and Yinger (1958) note, discrimination is ordinarily the overt or behavioral expression of prejudice: it is the categorical treatment of a person because of his membership in a particular group. In general, the individual so treated is denied some privilege or right that is accorded to other members of society who do not belong to the minority group. Simpson and Yinger also note, however, that discrimination may occur without

the accompanying feeling of prejudice—for example, where a pro-
prietor refuses to accept as patrons members of a minority group because he feels it would injure his business. He may not be prejudiced,
but feels that he must place his business before other considerations—or
he may actually be prejudiced and simply use his business as an opportunity for expressing his prejudice.

GROUP CONFLICT

Group conflict is a somewhat broader term than prejudice or discrimination. Groups may express overt hostility toward one another or may
engage in a struggle for prestige, power, or some other goal. The counterpart of group conflict is cooperation, a state where groups work together in the pursuit of common goals. In order to understand conflict,
some attention need also be given to cooperation. Because many of the
broader aspects of group conflict are only beginning to be empirically
studied, this discussion will be focused largely on the two forms of conflict most intensively investigated: prejudice and discrimination.

STUDY QUESTIONS

1. *Define the concept of prejudice. What is the nature of its cognitive component and its affective component?*
2. *What is meant by discrimination, and how is it different from prejudice?*

Origins of Prejudice and Discrimination

This section identifies the conditions under which prejudice and discrimination against a particular group arise. It is addressed to the question of why one group rather than another is singled out as an object
of prejudice and discrimination. The factors responsible for the maintenance of such prejudice and discrimination will be discussed later.

As a convenience in discussing intergroup relations, the terms
ingroup and *outgroup* will be used. An *ingroup* consists of persons who
experience a sense of belonging, a sense of having a like identity. An
outgroup, considered from the point of view of ingroup members, is
a group of persons who definitely have some distinctive characteristics
of their own that set them apart from the ingroup.

ORIGINS OF PREJUDICE

A first principle is the following: *The character of the existing relations
between ingroup and outgroup generates attitudes toward the outgroup that
are consonant with these relations.* In other words, the structure of the
relation between two groups in terms of relative status and power
produces cognitions and feelings that are appropriate to the existing
structure. For example, where a dominant group holds another group
in a condition of slavery, slaves are likely to be considered lazy, irrespon-

sible, and lacking in initiative. These beliefs emerge from the fact that slaves act upon orders from their masters and are not given an opportunity to demonstrate initiative or responsibility. Thus the beliefs about them are consonant with their behavior, which is controlled by the structure of the relation.

Another example comes from the historical development of prejudice against Jews. An image of the Jews as rich, grasping, and shrewd grew out of their occupational role as moneylenders (Simpson & Yinger, 1958). In the tenth and eleventh centuries the development of cities led to a sharply increased demand for capital in the form of money. The Church prohibited Christians from lending money at interest, but did permit Christians to borrow from Jews. Thus Jews became bankers when this occupation was extremely profitable, and the cognitive images commensurate with the role became firmly established. In addition, no doubt, competitive circumstances produced negative affect toward Jews: they were persons who refused to lend money to some and who charged more interest than borrowers thought fair, and they were envied for their wealth.

The marked change in the perception of an outgroup which occurs as a result of a change in the structure of intergroup relations may also be illustrated with some objective data collected on the dispute between India and China over the borderline between their countries (Sinha & Upadhyaya, 1960b). Stereotypes of the Chinese held by Indians were measured in February, 1959, before a state of conflict had arisen, and again in December, when tensions were strong. College students at Patna University in India were asked in February and again in December to select the five attributes from a list of eighty that most characterized members of nine countries, including China. A dramatic change occurred in characteristics assigned to the Chinese. Only three of the ten traits originally assigned to the Chinese were attributed to them during the dispute. Chinese who had been looked upon as friendly, progressive, honest, nationalistic, brave, cultured, and active before the dispute were subsequently considered to be aggressive, cheaters, selfish, warmongers, cruel, shrewd, and stupid. Only minor changes occurred in the stereotypes of the other countries. A number of other studies have shown similar changes in national stereotypes as a result of world events (Dodd, 1935; Dudycha, 1942; Seago, 1947; Buchanan, 1951).

Worth noting is the point that the attributes assigned to members of the outgroup were not limited to those deriving from the relation itself. The hostile Chinese were not only aggressive warmongers, but were also labeled as shrewd by some and stupid by others. This follows from the fact that individuals are likely to perceive status attributes as congruent with one another, a point discussed in Chapter 9.

A closely related principle, applying to beliefs instead of attitudes, may also be stated: *If a person is perceived as having a markedly different status from one's own, he is likely to be perceived as having different beliefs.* A study requiring subjects to "guess" the beliefs of various other strangers, including Negroes, demonstrated that white subjects assume a Negro to have beliefs dissimilar from their own (Byrne & Wong, 1962).

ORIGINS OF DISCRIMINATION AND CONFLICT

We have explained how prejudice is generated from a relation of unequal status between two groups. We may also examine the causal chain at an earlier point in the sequence and ask how the unequal status arises in the first place. Here a basic principle from exchange theory is relevant: Where the reward-cost outcomes of two separately bounded groups are perceived to be mutually exclusive, so that each group can improve its outcomes only at the expense of the other, the members of each group strive to protect or to increase their outcomes. *If the two groups are unequal in power, they will establish different outcomes unless prevented by norms that restrain exploitation of the weaker by the more powerful.* These different outcomes create differences in the status of the two groups.

The extent to which the members of the minority group feel discriminated against and dislike or feel hostile toward the majority group is a function of the relation between their comparison level and that of the majority group. In Chapter 7 we defined the comparison level as some minimum level of expectation or just desserts. If the minority group has the same comparison level as the majority group, it is likely to be dissatisfied and hostile. But if its comparison level is sufficiently low relative to that of the majority group, no such feelings may be experienced. Whether or not the comparison level of the majority group is likely to be used by the minority group to determine its own comparison level depends upon its past experiences, the outcomes available in alternative relations, and structural and cultural factors. For example, in a society with strong equalitarian values, differential status would be more likely to create dissatisfaction than it would in a society where a caste system is the accepted way of life.

Minority groups with rising comparison levels are likely to be very dissatisfied. For example, as long as the comparison level of the American Negro was kept very low, he did not express much overt dissatisfaction. Since World War II, however, the gains made by the Negro in partially breaking down segregation and other forms of discrimination practices have contributed to a rising comparison level, resulting in much greater dissatisfaction even though he is slightly better off than previously. Mass demonstrations, organized protests, and more violent forms of protest may be expected to increase as the comparison level, as long as it remains below that of the majority group, continues to rise.

In the previous discussion, the perceptual element is crucial. It is the *perception* that outcomes are mutually exclusive, the *perception* of one's own outcomes and those of the other group, and the *perception* of possible threats to present level of outcomes that determine behavior, not the realities of the situation.

Thus, discrimination and conflict arise from competitive situations, particularly those where one side has greater power and status than another and where comparison levels of the two groups are determined by the same considerations. This is illustrated by a laboratory experiment in which the experimenter established two levels of status for two groups of boys. They played several games in which one group was always assigned a lower status by the experimenter. The game of "human croquet" is described by the experimenter as follows (Thibaut, 1950):

> In this game the members of one team stand side by side in a line and each member bends over to form an arch or "wicket." The members of the other team then are formed in a single file and, on a signal from the experimenter, the first member crawls through the wickets and back again, at which time he touches the second member who then crawls through and back, and so on. The goodness of a team's performance depends on how long it takes all of its members to complete this procedure. (P. 257)

The point is that one team assigned to the passive role of wicket is not allowed to assume the other role of showing how it can perform in the game. Similarly, the high-status team in another game is allowed to throw beanbags at a target which is held by the low-status team, who also retrieve the beanbags. But the low-status team is not given an opportunity to toss bags at the target. Throughout the investigation, the experimenter consistently favored the high-status group. These conditions produced a good deal of hostility, particularly on the part of the low-status team toward the high-status team. The high-status team appeared to experience some triumph but also some guilty feelings arising from the norms of fair play, which restrict exploitation. Hostility is illustrated by such taunts as, "My little sister can throw better than that," and by name-calling, kicking, pushing, slapping, and hitting. In this experiment, most of the hostile feeling appeared to be expressed by the deprived, low-status group.

In a more elaborate experiment conducted in a field setting, two groups were put in competition with each other so that both sides experienced various costs (Sherif et al., 1961). Considerable hostility developed on the part of both groups. Two separate groups of boys were set up in a camp situation. For the first two days they had no knowledge of each other, and no interaction took place between them. During this period, stable group structures became established, as well as an ingroup feeling. The next stage introduced various competitive situations between the groups, such as a tug of war, won by the "Rattlers." The "Eagles" retaliated by burning the Rattlers' flag, which had been left on the backstop of the athletic field. Various other incidents multiplied, producing extreme social distance between the groups. In addition, stereotyped images arose. Such terms as *brave*, *tough*, and *friendly* were applied to members of one's own group, and *sneaky*, *smart alecks*, and *stinkers* applied to members of the outgroup. Bias was illustrated by the fact that the performance of outgroup members was underestimated; ingroup performance was overestimated.

The principle that actions of an outgroup which lower the reward-cost outcomes of the ingroup lead to discrimination and conflict is supported by other field studies. In a study of neighborhoods in Chicago and the areas immediately adjacent that had recently been occupied by Negroes, it was found that low-income whites in the area closest to them were more hostile than those in adjacent areas more remote from Negroes (Winder, 1955). On the basis of interview responses, the investigator concluded that the hostility was based on competition for dwelling units in the midst of a severe housing shortage. These white residents felt, with some justification, that they would be driven out because of the desire of their landlords to rent to Negroes, from whom they could collect a higher rent.

STUDY QUESTIONS

3. *State and explain two principles contributing to prejudice.*
4. *Explain how discrimination arises. What is the importance of the comparison level in determining whether or not hostile feelings occur?*

SUMMARY: ORIGINS

A basic principle underlying the origins of prejudice and discrimination against a particular group is the following: The character of the existing relations between ingroup and outgroup generates attitudes toward the outgroup that are consonant with these relations. In other words, the structure of the relation between two groups in terms of relative status and power produces cognitions and feelings which are appropriate to that structure. Various attributes and beliefs not directly relevant to the intergroup relation may also be perceived: If an outgroup has a status different from that of the ingroup with respect to certain attributes, its members are likely to be perceived as having other attributes and beliefs congruent with that status.

Essentially the position taken here is that discrimination and hostility arise from a relation in which two groups have unequal status. The unequal status between groups is explained in terms of exchange theory. Members of separately bounded groups engaged in interaction with each other behave so as to maximize the reward-cost outcomes accruing to themselves. If two groups are unequal in power, members of the more powerful group are likely to establish more favorable reward-cost outcomes than those in the less powerful group. To the extent that the comparison levels of the two groups are determined by the same conditions, the group having lower status is likely to feel discriminated against and to experience dislike and hostility toward the majority group.

Maintenance of Prejudice and Discrimination

To some extent, conditions that create prejudice and discrimination may be rather obvious. The factors that maintain prejudice and discrimination over a period of time are perhaps more subtle. We may view these factors as operating on three levels: the social structure, individual personality dynamics, and the culture.

FACTORS IN THE SOCIAL STRUCTURE

Conformity to the norm of prejudice

Once prejudice and discrimination against an outgroup are well established, the accompanying cognitions and feelings concerning the outgroup acquire a normative quality. They are shared by members of the ingroup; members expect each other to hold such attitudes. A good illustration comes from a housing study (Works, 1961). It was anticipated that white and Negro housewives in an integrated housing project would have more contacts with each other than white and Negro husbands, and thus the white housewives were expected to be less prejudiced than their husbands. This hypothesis was *not* substantiated. The suggested reason was that wives influenced their husbands to change their attitudes to accord with their own. Interviews with husbands provided some support for this view.

Perhaps the best evidence that social norms are an important factor in prejudice has been presented in a study of prejudice against Negroes in the southern United States and in the Union of South Africa (Pettigrew, 1958). Both of these regions are characterized by strong prejudice against the Negro. The investigation demonstrated that persons who were most likely to conform to the norms of their society were also the most prejudiced. The degree of prejudice against Africans by white South African students was determined by an attitude scale, and two groups were formed: those higher than average in prejudice, and those lower than average. Another questionnaire was scaled to measure conformity to social norms independently of prejudice. Every item of this scale was endorsed to a greater extent by the more highly prejudiced group, a result which demonstrates a direct association between conformity and prejudice. Other characteristics likely to be associated with acceptance of the social norms of prejudice were then studied. Students were found to be more anti-Negro if they were born in South Africa, if they identified with the Nationalist party, if they were upwardly mobile, and if their fathers were employed in a manual occupation.

In the southern United States, six sociocultural dimensions were considered to be associated with greater conformity to social norms and thus were considered likely to identify persons who were more prejudiced. These six dimensions, as anticipated, were all found to be associated with higher prejudice. The following were more prejudiced: females more than males, churchgoers more than nonchurchgoers, the upwardly mobile more than the nonmobile, Democrats or Republicans more than independents, the nonveteran more than the veteran, and the less educated to a greater degree than the more educated. The most crucial factor in interpreting these data is that in the northern United States, these sociocultural dimensions were either *not* associated with prejudice or they were associated to a lesser extent. This is as expected, since prejudice against the Negro is not as pervasive a social norm in the North. In conclusion, the study indicated that both in South Africa and in the southern United States, where prejudice is an important social norm, persons who show more conformity to norms are also more prejudiced. A possible alternative interpretation—that the conformers were more prejudiced because they were more authoritarian in personality—was ruled out by a statistical analysis of the measures of this characteristic obtained from the South Africans and Americans in the Southern and Northern states.

The factors underlying conformity to the norms of prejudice may be explained in terms of the varying reward-cost outcomes ensuing from conformity or nonconformity. If prejudice and discrimination against another group is the norm, then the overt expression of prejudice and the performance of acts of discrimination are likely to elicit approval from other members (Hyman & Sheatsley, 1954). Conversely, expression of a friendly attitude toward members of the minority group or failure to discriminate against them violates the norm of prejudice and is likely to be costly in bringing forth disapproval and other sanctions from group members. Pettigrew (1961) observes that a person in some Southern communities who dares to speak out in favor of integration must often bear slanderous letters and phone calls, burned crosses, and bomb threats.

One illustration of the rewards for conformity is the success of Southern politicians who have risen to power on the issue of maintaining segregation and white supremacy. For example, one study of Arkansas voting patterns has shown that *prior* to the Little Rock racial crisis involving integration in public schools, the more the voters of a county favored segregation, the less likely they were to vote for Governor Faubus (Pettigrew & Campbell, 1960). After he enacted his dramatic role as a defender of segregation, however, this condition was reversed: the counties most strongly supporting segregation cast proportionately more votes for him. Another investigation of voting patterns for J. Strom Thurmond, the Dixiecrat candidate for President, indicated that much of his support came from his emphasis on white supremacy (Heer, 1959).

The perceived costs of nonconformity to norms are widely varied and act in many ways to reinforce prejudice against minority groups. For example, officials of some universities which use quota systems to exclude all but a small proportion of minority group members plead that if their institution does not conform to the prejudices of the students and faculty, morale of the campus community will be greatly damaged (Epstein & Forster, 1958). Or a business executive argues that since Jews are not accepted as members in various exclusive clubs in which important business deals are transacted, he cannot hire them as executives in his business. This is illustrated in the following comment (Belth, 1958):

> "It is important for our business . . . that our plant managers maintain a certain status in their communities. They must join the country club and the leading city club. Today, that's where the big deals are discussed and made. They must be socially acceptable to the banking and business leaders of the town. They must be able to maintain a free and easy association with the people who count. If we promote Jewish personnel into key, sensitive positions, we run a risk of social non-acceptability. We avoid this by picking someone else." (P. 11)

The costs of nonconformity may also be illustrated by the dilemma which confronted Protestant ministers in the Little Rock, Arkansas, crisis. National Protestant leadership had come out strongly in favor of integration. Various opinion polls, however, showed that only one out of six Southerners favored desegregation. Thus, a minister who followed his church leaders and spoke out vigorously in favor of school integration was in danger of lowering both attendance and contributions to his church—and of losing members outright. A study of the behavior of Little Rock ministers faced with this dilemma showed that, although they had initially made public statements in favor of integration, their further public statements after rioting occurred at Central High School did not take a clear position on the integration issue, but simply denounced violence and stressed peace and prayer (Campbell & Pettigrew, 1959).

In all these instances, it is the *perceived* costs of conformity that determine behavior. For example, it is probable that discrimination against minority groups in business transactions is in the long run more costly than nondiscrimination, but these actual costs do not affect behavior unless they are perceived.

Interaction patterns

Prejudice and discrimination create certain interaction patterns that contribute to maintenance of the *status quo*. Several interaction patterns increase cohesion and thus strengthen the power of the group to enforce conformity to norms of prejudice and discrimination. Any factor that makes members more dependent on the ingroup is likely to increase cohesion. For example, members of the ingroup interact more frequently with each other and reduce interaction with members of the outgroup. Such interaction produces positive affect and greater cohesion among members of the ingroup, giving them more power to enforce conformity.

Interaction within the ingroup may also increase the economic dependence of members upon each other. Businessmen or professionals who deal exclusively with members of the ingroup face loss of investments and income if they refuse to side with them in any issue involving prejudice or discrimination. Also, to the extent that a group member looks to other members for validation of his attitudes and beliefs, he is more subject to conformity pressures. Finally, if interaction within each group predominates over interaction across group lines, the development of patterns of thinking, feeling, and behaving unique to each group is fostered. Such interaction patterns extend the cultural gulf that separates the two groups. For example, the segregation of the American Negro increases interactions among Negroes and among whites but reduces interaction across these racial groups. This contributes to differences in attitudes and values between these two groups.

Leadership support

Still another maintenance process is the emergence of leaders who support norms of prejudice and discrimination. Political leaders, as noted earlier, are likely to rise to power to the extent that they represent the norms characteristic of the voting populace. Persons holding attitudes at variance with the norms are not likely to be successful in elections. Thus, as these leaders acquire power, they exert further influence in support of the *status quo*. This process has probably been extremely important in the South in the past in maintaining prejudice toward the Negro. There are signs, however, that the conflict between Southern values on the one hand, and national values of equality, respect for law and order (i.e., respect for the implementation by courts of the Supreme Court desegregation decision), and the interest in industrializing the South on the other hand, are likely to lead to replacement of segregationist leaders by more moderate ones (Tumin & Rotberg, 1957).

Environmental supports for prejudice

Krech and Crutchfield (1948) have observed that where prejudice is widespread, a person can observe various features of his environment that support his prejudiced attitudes. We have noted that prejudice and discrimination arise out of a specific type of relation between an ingroup and an outgroup and that eventually attitudes toward the outgroup acquire a normative character. Ultimately these attitudes are built into the social institutions of the society in which they prevail. For example, until after World War II, attitudes toward Negroes were reflected in the practices of the military services: they assigned Negro soldiers and sailors to segregated units, thus helping to perpetuate these attitudes. In Southern states, segregation in parks, schools, restaurants, terminals, and other public facilities has been legitimatized by municipal and state laws.

Images of the various minority groups are also reflected in literature, movies, and television; minority group members in these media are often cast in a role appropriate to the minority group stereotype (Berelson & Salter, 1946). Other institutions such as the church and the educational system are no exception to this rule; only recently, as a result of the Supreme Court decision in 1954 outlawing segregation in educational institutions, have there been widespread attempts to erase the reflection of the norm of prejudice from public schools and colleges.

Finally, because of discrimination, certain objective qualities of some minority groups, such as Negroes, are in fact consistent with prejudiced attitudes. There are two categories of qualities created by discrimination. First, since Negroes as a group receive poorer educations, have lower incomes, work in menial occupations, and live in substandard housing, they are in fact different from members of the majority white group. These differences provide the prejudiced person with evidence of the "validity" of his beliefs and feelings about the Negro. Because they are most discriminated against, the Negroes best illustrate the importance of such environmental supports.

Another category of difference stems from the minority group member's reaction to discrimination. Allport (1958) has cited a number of such reactions that serve as environmental supports. For example, because of the constant anxiety over meeting a prejudiced reaction in an interpersonal situation, a member of a minority group may become oversensitized to possible prejudice. This may be used against him by prejudiced persons, who complain that he goes around with a "chip on his shoulder." An opposite mechanism may also be used as an illustration. In reaction to prejudice, members of minority groups may withdraw from contact with majority group members: they are then accused of being clannish.

STUDY QUESTIONS

5. *Cite some evidence for the principle that prejudice is in part a form of conformity to a social norm. Relate this principle to exchange theory.*
6. *Explain how interaction patterns contribute to the maintenance of prejudice and discrimination.*
7. *What is the role played by leaders in maintaining prejudice and discrimination?*
8. *What are environmental supports and how do they help to support prejudice and discrimination?*

Summary: Social structure

Once prejudice and discrimination against an outgroup are well established, the accompanying cognitions and feelings concerning the outgroup acquire a normative quality. They are shared by members of the ingroup; members expect each other to hold such attitudes. Various positive and negative sanctions are applied by the group to individual members who conform or fail to conform. Interaction patterns that accompany prejudice and discrimination contribute to the maintenance of these attitudes. Increased interaction among ingroup members increases mutual affect and dependency. Similarly, a decrease in interaction across group lines allows for the development of patterns of feeling, thought, and action unique to the ingroup and outgroup. Moreover, interaction between ingroup and outgroup on the basis of unequal status serves to support prejudice and discrimination.

The persons who most strongly support the norms of the group, which include prejudice and discrimination, are likely to rise to positions of leadership. Their influential roles contribute further to the maintenance of these attitudes and behaviors. Finally, prejudice and discrimination create their own "environmental supports," which make the members of minority groups objectively different from members of the majority group.

INDIVIDUAL PROCESSES

The social structure has much to do with determining the particular groups that become objects of prejudice and discrimination, and it also establishes various conditions that help to maintain prejudice toward these groups. Certain processes operating at the level of the individual personality should not be ignored, however. Prejudice is established and maintained in each individual through learning and other individual processes.

Frustration and aggression: Scapegoating

Freud (1915) was one of the first to emphasize and analyze in great detail the point that when a person is prevented from satisfying his needs, he is likely to engage in aggressive behavior. Early experimental work (Dollard et al., 1939) on this hypothesis provided some support for it. Often the frustrating agent is not a suitable target for hostility because of his great power. In such instances the hostility may be directed against a "scapegoat," an innocent party. Simpson and Yinger (1958) describe this process and note that minority group members may often be selected as targets:

> There is much evidence to indicate that the blocking of goal-directed behavior frequently creates hostile impulses in the individual. In many instances this hostility cannot be directed toward the source of the frustration; there may be no human agent, or the agent may be unknown, or too powerful to strike. . . . The hostility under such circumstances may be stored up, or it may be directed toward oneself or toward some substitute target that is more accessible or less able to strike back. In other words, a "free-floating," undirected hostility may result from frustration when the actual frustrating agent cannot be attacked; and the social context often favors displacement of this hostility onto minority-group members. (P. 76)

In this process of scapegoating, the true basis of the frustration is not removed. Thus the hostility is continually generated, and expressed toward the minority group. A study of feuding between clans in Morocco suggests that this social conflict is quite functional (Lewis, 1961). Under the harsh conditions of life there, enemy clans provide an outlet for a person's aggressions; moreover, the continual feuding with these clans strengthens the feeling of security that the individual experiences through membership in his own clan.

Quite a number of studies have been conducted in the attempt to test the scapegoating hypothesis experimentally.[1] Although not all the studies have supported the hypothesis, more recent investigations[2] have generally confirmed it. These have also identified some of the limitations of the experiments[3] that failed to substantiate the notion of scapegoating. Studies of scapegoating generally set up a situation in which the experimental subjects are made to fail in a task, are insulted by the experimenter, or are blocked from attaining some goal in which they are interested. Such frustration is presumed to create aggression, some of which should result in an increase in prejudice on scales administered after the frustrating experience. The investigations vary considerably, however, in the method by which subjects are frustrated, the measure of prejudice used, and the overall situation that defines the experimental context.

One of the most adequate of these studies is Weatherley's (1961). An anti-Semitism scale was administered to a large number of male college students. Two groups high in anti-Semitism and two groups low in it were chosen. One group in each category was subjected to an aggression-arousing situation: The experimenter made highly insulting remarks during the time the subjects were filling out a brief questionnaire. The control subjects, also consisting of one group high in anti-Semitism and one low, filled out the same questionnaire in a friendly, nonprovoking atmosphere. Following this session, both groups were given picture-story tests by a different experimenter, who ostensibly had nothing to do with the earlier sessions. The pictures were eight pencil sketches, two each of four different males, to whom were assigned names, ages, and occupations. Two of the names were Jewish-sounding, and two were not.

Subjects were asked to tell a story about each picture. The stories were later analyzed to determine the number of aggressive acts committed toward the characters that had been depicted in the sketches. The most significant findings of the study were (1) that the highly anti-Semitic subjects directed more aggressive responses to the Jewish characters in their stories than the low anti-Semitic subjects did, and (2) that there was no difference between high and low groups in the number of responses they assigned to non-Jewish characters. Thus, while many other studies have tested the scapegoating hypothesis that prejudiced persons have a generalized tendency to displace aggression, the present study tests the more specific notion that a highly anti-Semitic person may have a strong tendency to displace aggression toward Jews, but not necessarily toward other objects.

[1]Miller & Bugelski, 1948; Rosenblith, 1949; Lindzey, 1950; Stagner & Congdon, 1955; Cowen, Landes, & Schaet, 1958; Berkowitz, 1961; Weatherley, 1961; Berkowitz & Green, 1962.

[2]Cowen, Landes, & Schaet, 1958; Berkowitz, 1959, 1961; Weatherley, 1961; Berkowitz & Green, 1962.

[3]Zawadski, 1948; Lindzey, 1950; Stagner & Congdon, 1955.

One limitation of this study, however, is that most of the difference between high and low anti-Semitic subjects just reported was due to the fact that the *low* anti-Semitic subjects in the *experimental* group directed appreciably *fewer* aggressive actions toward the Jewish characters than did the control group. Similarly, the low anti-Semitic subjects directed *fewer* aggressive actions toward the Jewish characters than toward the non-Jewish characters. Thus, most of the result obtained in this experiment appears to be due to a positive bias toward Jews on the part of subjects low in anti-Semitism, rather than to a negative bias against Jews on the part of subjects high in anti-Semitism.

Another experiment also emphasizes the stimulus qualities of the scapegoat (Berkowitz & Green, 1962). Subjects who worked in pairs were first induced to like or dislike their partner. Subsequently, half the subjects were frustrated by the experimenter, and the other half received more pleasant treatment. In the last part of the study, the two pair members and a neutral peer, a confederate of the experimenter, were put to work on a cooperative task. According to scapegoating theory, when the subjects were later asked to evaluate their work partners, the hostility aroused by the experimenter should be displaced to the *disliked* partner rather than the neutral partner. This hypothesis was confirmed.

Economic and status gains

One might expect scapegoating to occur most frequently where competition is most severe and status is threatened. While there is no direct evidence on this point, prejudice does seem to be greatest under these conditions. A study made in a Southern county in the United States to investigate the varying attitudes of male Southerners toward desegregation identifies a "hard core" of men who would use force to oppose desegregation if necessary (Tumin, 1958). These men as a group are at the bottom of the status hierarchy; in education, income, and occupation, they have the poorest chances for improving their own position and are the most threatened by the rise of Negro status. Thus they are likely to believe that they have the most to gain by maintaining prejudice and discrimination against the Negro.

Simpson and Yinger (1958) note shifting attitudes toward the Negro in concert with changing economic periods. When there was ample work during the early years of expansion in the United States for skilled persons such as carpenters and bricklayers, the proportion of Negroes doing this type of labor was relatively high. As the amount of work available diminished, the proportion of Negroes in these trades was gradually reduced: from 1910 to 1940 it fell from 26 percent to 15 percent in the South. Presumably this made more room for lower-class whites in these occupations, resulting in an economic gain for them.

Personality needs

A variety of personality needs may support prejudice. One need that has been intensively studied is "intolerance for ambiguity." Persons differ in the extent to which they are disturbed by confusing or ambiguous situations. At one extreme, some persons like to have everything in black and white, and at the other, some are not in the least disturbed by confusing or uncertain situations. In general, persons who are more intolerant of ambiguity are also likely to be more prejudiced (Adorno et. al., 1950). Prejudice may serve such a need because it clarifies an ambiguous and confusing situation. A white laborer who has lost his job and who is having a difficult time finding another one may, for example, decide that the cause of his troubles is the influx of Negroes into his city.

Likewise, a need to achieve superior status may be supported by prejudice, which provides a group of persons lower in status than oneself. A person may feel a sense of identification with his own kind through prejudice. Allport describes clearly how a person may bolster his self-esteem by turning his attention to outgroups:[4]

> The easiest idea to sell anyone is that he is better than someone else. The appeal of the Ku Klux Klan and racist agitators rests on this type of salesmanship. Snobbery is a way of clutching at one's status, and it is as common, perhaps more common, among those who are low in the ladder. By turning their attention to unfavored out-groups, they are able to derive from the comparison a modicum of self-esteem. Out-groups, as status builders, have the special advantage of being near at hand, visible (or at least nameable), and occupying a lower position by common agreement, thus providing social support for one's own sense of status enhancement.

The need for security may be satisfied through rejection of an outgroup. Many writers (see Coser, 1956) have noted that conflict between an ingroup and an outgroup leads to increased solidarity among members of the ingroup. Such friction sharpens the boundaries between groups and reaffirms the identity of the ingroup. Two experiments previously cited support these ideas (Thibaut, 1950; Sherif et al., 1961). Thus, we may expect that discrimination and conflict with an outgroup are likely to make an individual feel more secure in his ingroup membership: he has a greater sense of belonging.

The authoritarian personality

In Chapter 2 we described a type of person having an *authoritarian personality,* a pattern of traits which shows an important relation to prejudice. This pattern, found in the adult person, appears to relate to certain aspects of family structure and discipline experienced by him as a child. His parents are thought to have exercised rigid discipline, affection being conditional upon approval of his behavior. Dominance, submission, and differential status were emphasized. Expression of hostility, particularly toward his parents or other family members, was strictly prohibited. Thus, it is thought that he develops repressive mechanisms for disguising his own hostility and controlling his impulses. This leads to some lack of

---

[4]Reprinted by permission from G. W. Allport. *The nature of prejudice.* Garden City, N.Y.: Doubleday & Company, Inc., 1958. P. 349.

insight into his own functioning and to rigid attitudes toward interaction with other persons. The values of the authoritarian personality and the manner in which he functions appear to be especially suited to forming prejudice toward outgroups. He emphasizes power, status, and dominance. He has repressed hostilities, and the prejudice toward outgroups sanctioned by his society provides an outlet for these hostilities. His rigidity and inflexibility lead him to make black-and-white discriminations among other groups of persons.

STUDY QUESTIONS

9. *What is meant by scapegoating?*
10. *To what extent is the perception of economic gain related to prejudice?*
11. *Explain how personality needs can provide support for prejudice.*
12. *What is meant by the authoritarian personality, and what is its relation to prejudice?*

Attitudinal consistency

Chapter 3 discussed at length the tendency of various attitudinal components to be consistent with one another. The individual strives for a state of consistency between affect, cognitions, and behavioral dispositions. Thus, forces toward changing any one of these components are resisted so long as the other components remain unchanged. This principle produces some distortion or misperception of the behavior of the outgroup. Given a set of cognitions and a given level of affect toward an outgroup, actions of the outgroup that are at variance with these components are likely to be misperceived in the direction of consistency with prevailing affect and cognitions. Similarly, friendly behavior toward the outgroup will be avoided because it is inconsistent with hostile affect and cognitions.

An anecdote reported by Allport illustrates distortion of cognition in the direction of prejudice:[5]

> At a session of summer school an irate lady of middle age approached the instructor saying, "I think there is a girl of Negro blood in this class." To the instructor's noncommittal reply, the lady persisted, "But you wouldn't want a nigger in the class, would you." Next day she returned and firmly insisted, "I know she's a nigger because I dropped a paper on the floor and said to her, 'Pick that up.' She did so, and that proves she's just a darky servant trying to get above her station."

Although much support for the principle of consistency was cited in Chapter 3 and 4, sufficient empirical evidence is not yet available in support of consistency among affective, cognitive, and behavioral components of *prejudice*. Moreover, forces toward consistency may in many instances be counteracted by the strong emotional anchorage of the affec-

---

[5]Reprinted by permission from G. W. Allport. *The nature of prejudice.* Garden City, N.Y.: Doubleday & Company, Inc., 1958. Pp. 162–163.

tive component. Because prejudice involves strong emotions, it should be tied to those physiological functions associated with the emotions. Such learned associations are likely to be especially resistant to change.

In several different investigations, subjects have been shown to have large galvanic skin responses (a measure of emotional response associated with the autonomic nervous system) when a complimentary statement was read about a group against whom they are strongly prejudiced (Cooper & Singer, 1956; Cooper & Siegel, 1956; Cooper & Pollock, 1959; Cooper, 1959). The most recent of these studies indicated that such responses did not occur for groups toward whom the subject had less strong feelings. Another investigation reported that prejudiced subjects gave larger GSRs to pictures of Negroes than did nonprejudiced subjects, although results varied considerably with the sex of the subject and the sex of the person in the stimulus picture (Westie & De Fleur, 1959). These studies provide support for the view that prejudice toward a minority group is likely to have a strong emotional component that makes it resistant to change.

The physiological anchorage of the affective component of prejudice may account for some of the findings that cognitions may change without comparable changes in affect. One study, in which graduate students participated in a series of discussion groups aimed at reducing prejudice, led to a reduction in cognitive aspects of prejudice, but accompanying changes in affective and behavioral components did not occur (Mann, 1960). Another investigation, purely correlational, also failed to find support for consistency on prejudice attitudes (Mann, 1959). These two studies, however, are subject to a variety of methodological criticisms that prevent them from being used as negative evidence. In fact, if the changes in cognition are purely temporary, a later test of attitude change might well show that they have returned to their original level. This fact would support consistency, not contradict it. Because of the strength of the affect component, the consistency principle would operate to maintain cognitions unchanged. The consistency principle is also compatible with the fact that, in general, investigations aimed at changing prejudice through modification of the cognitive component have not been particularly successful (Harding et al., 1954; Simpson & Yinger, 1958).

Another form of consistency pertains to consistency among different attitudes. For example, prejudice against minority groups would seem to be incompatible with belief in democracy, which stresses equal rights and justice for all. Prejudiced attitudes, more than any other kind of attitudes, appear to be especially associated with such individual processes as misperception, compartmentalization, rationalization, and the group process of developing collective beliefs such as the ideology of race relations. These mechanisms may be interpreted as devices for alleviating inconsistency between prejudice and other attitudes. They suggest further the importance of the consistency principle. Finally, Scott (1958) has noted that not all attitudes have a rational structure: the individual is not always able to state the values that are linked to the attitude and its objects and events. Presumably, prejudice has a large degree of such nonrationality, which isolates it to some extent from other attitudes.

Prejudice and belief dissimilarity

Rokeach, Smith, and Evans (see Rokeach, 1960) have proposed that, as far as individual psychological processes are involved, dissimilarity in belief is more important than ethnic or racial membership as a determinant of prejudice and discrimination. In other words, a person will be more apt to dislike another person if he thinks the person has dissimilar beliefs than he will if he thinks the person is of a different race. That dissimilarity of belief produces dislike is consistent with the theory of interpersonal attraction outlined in Chapter 7.

In order to test this hypothesis, Rokeach and his colleagues prepared a set of hypothetical descriptions of persons. In a given pair of descriptions, race was varied with belief held constant, belief was varied with race held constant, or both were varied simultaneously. For example, the following pair varies race, but holds belief constant:

> A white person who believes in God
> A Negro who believes in God

The next pair varies belief, but holds race constant:

> A white person who believes in God
> A white person who is an atheist

The investigators had subjects indicate for each description the extent to which they felt that they could be friends with such a person. A statistical analysis of the various responses indicated clearly that similarity of belief was much more important than similarity of race in the feeling of friendship expressed by the subjects. Triandis (1961), however, has criticized this study on the grounds that the measure used is one of friendship, not prejudice. His analysis of his own data, using social distance measures, finds race to be far more important (see also Rokeach, 1961).

Several other studies, however, suggest that assumed dissimilarity of beliefs may well play an important role in prejudice. One study demonstrates that prejudiced subjects do assume that Negroes have beliefs dissimilar from their own while nonprejudiced subjects do not (Byrne & Wong, 1962). It also shows that similarity of attitudes produces positive ratings of the other person and dissimilarity of attitudes produces negative ratings, regardless of the race of the other person. Another investigation anticipated that prejudiced subjects would not accept support from Negroes in an Asch-type conformity situation, where the majority makes a judgment different from that which the individual subject perceives to be correct (Malof & Lott, 1962). However, subjects high in prejudice did in fact accept support from Negro as well as white confederates of the experimenter. This experiment also suggests the greater importance of similarity of belief as compared with dissimilarity of race. Unfortunately, the experimenters did not determine whether a reduction in prejudice took place as a result of the support given by the Negro confederates.

One serious problem arises in interpreting these various studies showing an association between dislike or prejudice, on the one hand, and dissimilarity, on the other; the causal sequence is not clear. As support for a theory of prejudice, these studies suffer from the fact that the prejudice may cause the perception of dissimilarity.

STUDY QUESTIONS

13. *Explain how the tendency toward attitudinal consistency can produce misperception of the behavior of members of minority groups.*
14. *What evidence is there for the belief that the emotional component of prejudice has a strong physiological basis?*
15. *How are such mechanisms as rationalization and compartmentalization related to the consistency principle?*
16. *Explain how prejudice might arise from belief dissimilarity. To what extent is this interpretation supported by evidence?*

Summary: Individual processes

Prejudice and discrimination are established and maintained in each person through various individual processes. When an individual is prevented from satisfying his needs, for example, he is likely to engage in aggressive behavior. When the frustrating agent is not a suitable target for hostility, his aggression may be directed against a scapegoat. Experimental work generally supports this idea, although there are some exceptions.

A variety of personality needs may support prejudice. Persons least able to tolerate ambiguity may be able to resolve ambiguity in certain situations by placing blame upon a minority group. The existence of low-status groups provides an opportunity for a person to feel superior to them. Rejection of an outgroup enhances the security that an individual experiences through association with his ingroup.

Extensive empirical work has identified a type of person known as the authoritarian personality. Central values of this person are status, power, and adherence to conventional social norms. These values are developed out of childhood experience in a family exercising rigid discipline and making affection contingent upon approved behavior. Prejudice against a wide variety of outgroups is consistent with these values.

While the ultimate economic effects of discrimination may be to the disadvantage of a majority group, many studies support the idea that prejudice and discrimination lead at least to the perception of economic gain for the individual. These attitudes help to maintain differential reward-cost outcomes for the ingroup as compared with the outgroup, outcomes that are of course perceptual in nature.

The individual strives for consistency between affect, cognitions, and behavioral dispositions. Forces toward changing any one of these components are resisted so long as the others remain unchanged. Best documented is the point that this principle leads to some misperception of the minority group, causing it to be perceived in a manner consistent with the prevailing prejudice toward it. Attitudes involving prejudice have a strong affective component. Thus the consistency principle predicts that cognitive approaches to changing prejudice would not be very successful, a prediction in accordance with the facts.

Another form of consistency pertains to consistency among different attitudes. To avoid appearing inconsistent, the prejudiced individual might be expected to make extensive use of such mechanisms as rationalization and compartmentalization, and the group might be expected to develop an ideology that makes its values appear consistent. These expectations also seem to be in accord with our knowledge of prejudice and discrimination.

Belief dissimilarity has been suggested as an explanation for prejudice. Prejudiced individuals have been shown to assume that members of minority groups have beliefs different from their own. Such dissimilarity is likely to contribute to negative affect. Empirical work is somewhat contradictory in indicating the relative importance of belief dissimilarity in prejudice. Moreover, it has not been demonstrated that belief dissimilarity is a necessary antecedent condition giving rise to prejudice.

CULTURAL FACTORS

Prejudice in a society maintains itself by contributing to the development of ideologies supporting prejudice and by guaranteeing that children will be appropriately indoctrinated.

Values and prejudice

Ultimately, attitudes toward minority groups may become part of a cultural ideology: a complex system of ideas, attitudes, and beliefs that are closely associated with cultural values. For example, the Negro may be thought more apelike, more primitive, and biologically inferior in a number of other ways. Associated with these beliefs are others: that race mixture is biologically undesirable and that such traits as sexuality, irresponsibility, and violence are related to race (Frumkin & Roucek, 1959). The widespread acceptance of such ideologies helps to support prejudice and discrimination. One of the most important ways the ideologies help maintain prejudice is that they provide a means of working attitudes and values that are actually inconsistent with each other into a seemingly consistent system. For example, if one believes the Negro to be "subhuman," then discrimination against him is no longer inconsistent with a belief in equal rights for all *human* beings.

Such ideologies are often developed concerning groups that are not even a race, as in the myth in Nazi Germany that the alleged undesirable characteristics of the Jews were qualities to be expected of those not belonging to the "Aryan race." In addition, there is no conclusive evidence that the kinds of attributes generally assigned to members of various races are in any way associated with the morphological and physiological properties of race. In spite of these well-known facts, ideologies such as those illustrated above persist and provide additional support for prejudice and discrimination.

An analysis of prejudice toward three groups in three different cultures has shown how differences in values may or may not support prejudice. The Jews, the Armenians, and the Parsis each occupied the role of middleman or trader in their countries (Stryker, 1959). Two of them, the Jews and the Armenians, were objects of prejudice. The third group, the Parsis in India, was not an object of prejudice, even though they occupied a role that was considered low in status. The investigator attributed this difference to a difference in the political values of India. The other countries valued an emerging nationalism which stressed the importance of having groups conform to a national pattern; hence, groups that were 'different" were penalized. But in India internal differences among groups were not a threat to an important value; thus there was no need for prejudice against the Parsis.

A study of race relations in Panama and the Canal Zone also shows the importance of the central values of the society (Biesanz & Smith, 1951). In the Canal Zone, operated by the United States, segregation and differential status between American whites and Panamanians were practiced, while outside the Zone, in Panama, integration and equal status interaction were the rule. The investigators suggest that this condition was in part reinforced by the difference in values between the two societies. In the Zone, a premium was placed upon high technological rationality and highly developed occupational roles, whereas in Panama, life was much more casual. They suggest that because the Panamanians were ill-prepared to meet the formal requirements of life in the Zone, the formalism and discipline in the Zone supported the pattern of discrimination against them, while the informal character of life in Panama had the reverse effect.

Socialization of the child

The child is born without any prejudice. But he is born into a family that usually reflects the prevailing attitudes of society. He is dependent upon the adult members of the family for the satisfaction of his needs, and he is ultimately required to take over their attitudes and values. These socialization processes will be discussed in detail in Chapters 17 to 19; here; we are concerned only with the development of prejudice and discrimination in the child.

Prejudice develops in children at a relatively early age, in preschool or the early school years. When tested by means of pictures or hypothetical situations, they indicate some preference for associating with other members of the majority group and avoiding members of minority groups (Horowitz, 1936; Criswell, 1937). The particular groups that are objects of prejudice are determined by the prevailing prejudices in the society. Such prejudice is mild at first but becomes stronger throughout the childhood years. At an early age children are not aware of their prejudice: adults estimate that they first became prejudiced at around twelve or thirteen years of age (Allport & Kramer, 1946). Small children are also unable to give the usual reasons for prejudice; as they grow older, however, they learn the supporting ideology and recite traditional cultural reasons for prejudice (Simpson & Yinger, 1958).

That prejudice is a direct function of socialization is demonstrated clearly in a study that compares the development of prejudice toward the Negro among several groups of Tennessee school children and several groups of children in New York City (Horowitz, 1936). Prejudice was apparent in the first grade and continued to increase throughout the primary grades. There was no difference in prejudice between the Northern and Southern children, nor was there any difference between the New York children from an all-white school and New York children from a mixed school. This similarity in attitudes was anticipated, for both the Tennessee and the New York children were widely exposed to prejudice against the Negro. A striking difference was found, however, between the children living in a cooperative housing project sponsored by a Communist organization and all the others. A strong element in Communist ideology, particularly in the 1930s when the study was conducted, is a belief in the equality of all races. Thus children of Communist parents would be likely to learn this belief from their parents—an expectation consistent with the data.

In sum, attitudes toward minority groups are ultimately woven into a complex pattern of ideas, attitudes, and beliefs closely associated with cultural values. The widespread existence of such ideologies helps to support prejudice and discrimination. When prejudice and discrimination are extensive throughout a society, the socialization of the child toward acceptance of prevailing ideologies and behavior concerning minority groups is assured.

STUDY QUESTIONS

17. *What is a cultural ideology? How do ideologies pertaining to prejudice provide support for it?*
18. *What is the role of the socialization process in the development of prejudice?*

SUMMARY: MAINTENANCE

Factors maintaining prejudice and discrimination have been discussed on three levels: the social structure, individual personality dynamics, and the culture. Several structural processes contribute to maintenance of prejudice and discrimination. Once they are well established, cognitions and feelings accompanying prejudice and discrimination acquire a normative quality. Members are expected to hold such attitudes, and positive and negative sanctions are applied by the group to individual members who conform or fail to conform. Increased interaction among ingroup members increases mutual affect and dependency, and interaction between ingroup and outgroup on the basis of unequal status supports prejudice and discrimination. Interaction within the group also leads to the development and maintenance of distinctive subcultural patterns of thought and behavior which may be used to justify discrimination. The persons conforming most closely to norms that include prejudice and discrimination are likely to rise to positions of leadership and to further support prejudice and discrimination.

Individual processes supporting prejudice include the following. Aggression aroused through frustration may be displaced to minority groups. Such personality needs as intolerance of ambiguity and the need for status and security are likely to contribute. A type of individual known as the authoritarian personality is likely to be widely prejudiced. This is because prejudice is consistent with his dominant values, which include emphasis on status and power and adherence to conventional social norms. Prejudice and discrimination are likely to be perceived as contributing to economic gain. The tendency of an individual to maintain consistency among the affective, cognitive, and behavior components of prejudiced attitudes produces resistance to change. In particular, it is likely to lead to misperception of the minority group. The emotional component of prejudice makes it likely that affective-cognitive consistency will work in the direction of maintaining prejudice. This explains the wide use by prejudiced persons of a variety of mechanisms that seemingly resolve or gloss over actual inconsistencies.

The prevalence of prejudice in a society contributes to its maintenance. Persons are thus enabled to observe features of their environment that support prejudiced attitudes. Such features appear in institutional practices, the mass media, and even in the objective characteristics of the minority group members themselves. Attitudes toward minority groups are woven into a complex pattern of ideas, attitudes, and beliefs closely associated with cultural values. These ideologies appear to be self-consistent, and thus they help the individual to resolve actual inconsistencies in his attitudes and values. The widespread existence of prejudice and discrimination in a society also ensures that the child will be socialized in the direction of these prevailing attitudes.

Changing Intergroup Prejudice

An examination of the numerous studies of conditions that bring about a reduction of prejudice and discrimination—or in some cases, an increase — provides additional material which is consistent with the principles outlined so far. In addition, it gives some further insights into the nature of prejudice and discrimination.

THE INTERGROUP-CONTACT HYPOTHESIS

Early studies raised the hypothesis that the greater the contact between majority and minority groups, the more likely prejudice is to be reduced. It soon became apparent, however, that the kind of relation between the two groups is important. As we have already seen, certain types of competitive contacts may increase prejudice. Likewise, frequent contact between master and servant or between persons in other unequal status relations would do little to reduce prejudice. Our previous discussion, which indicated that prejudice emerges from relations where statuses are unequal, would lead us to believe that *reduction* of prejudice would occur as a result of relations on an equal-status basis.

Although the equal-status hypothesis appears to be fairly consistent with various studies on the reduction of prejudice and although it has been widely accepted by students of intergroup relations, we will offer a more precise hypothesis and review the evidence pertaining to it.

ATTITUDE CHANGE AND ROLE OCCUPANCY

Each instance of intergroup contact that has been studied occurs in a particular type of situation: integrated housing, military combat, crews on shipboard, and various work situations. In order to describe intergroup contact more precisely, two concepts to be discussed in more detail in Chapters 14 to 16 will be introduced here: position or role category, and role expectations. A *position* is a category of persons occupying a place in a social relation. Examples of positions which are important to the present discussion are combat infantryman, sailor, neighbor, work associate, Negro, Jew. Associated with each position or role category are *expectations* of how a person occupying that category should behave and the personal characteristics he should possess.

From the point of view of these concepts, any contact situation may be represented as follows: Because of his position as a member of a minority group, certain stereotyped characteristics are likely to be attributed to a person, and certain behaviors will be expected of him. When he occupies another role, however, such as coworker or neighbor, conflicting expectations as to his behavior and characteristics are likely to be aroused. On the one hand is the tendency to attribute to him the characteristics that are considered appropriate to members of his minority group; on the other is the tendency to attribute to him the characteristics that belong to a coworker or neighbor. In contrast to this situation where a member of a minority group clearly occupies an additional role, in situations where contact is merely casual he is likely to be perceived and behaved toward in terms of his minority group role. Also, as noted earlier in discussing environmental supports, where the minority group role is compatible with other roles, prejudice is reinforced. For example, the Negro stereotype is supported as long as the Negro is restricted to menial occupations.

We may examine the logical consequences of continued interaction with a minority group member who occupies two roles. To the extent that the behavior of a minority group member is compatible with expectations for the role category of coworker rather than the minority group category, expectations associated with the minority group category are likely to be gradually modified or abandoned. Thus if the expectation for a coworker is that he be energetic rather than lazy, and the expectation for a minority group member is that he be lazy rather than energetic, energetic behavior on the part of the coworker over a period of time is likely to lead to abandonment of the idea that he is lazy.

More generally, when contacts with minority group members involve a role that is incompatible with their minority group status, the expectations associated with the incompatible role are likely to lead to new behavior toward them and to appropriate changes in the corresponding perceptions of their characteristics. But it is important to note that the new perceptions of these individuals are associated with their occupation of a particular role category. We might expect that the modified perceptions of them are likely to be confined to situations in which they occupy the role category in question, and that under many circumstances such perceptions will not be generalized to other situations. The various contact situations may be examined from the point of view of these ideas.

Before looking at studies involving actual contact, however, the effects of occupying other role categories in addition to minority group status might be illustrated by an investigation showing the amount of social distance felt toward Negroes in various occupational roles (Westie, 1952). White respondents chosen at random in Indianapolis were interviewed in their homes. Although the lower-class whites felt most socially distant from Negroes and made little discrimination among Negroes in different occupations, the middle-class and upper-class whites indicated less social distance and showed much more variation in feeling toward Negroes in such different occupations as doctors, bankers, machine operators, and ditchdiggers. This study illustrates the point that feelings toward a minority group member are associated with other positions that he occupies.

One of the clearest illustrations of the importance of role categories comes from a study by Minard (1952) of Negro and white miners in the Pocahontas coalfields of West Virginia. He describes a situation in which the mines are completely integrated, with Negroes and whites working side by side, but community life is almost completely segregated:

> The boundary line between the two communities is usually the mine's mouth. Management assists the miners in recognizing their entrance into the outside community with its distinctions in status by providing separate baths and locker rooms. The color line, that is, becomes immediately visible as soon as the

miner's eyes accustomed to the inner darkness of the mine have accommo-
dated themselves to the light of the outside world. . . .

The white miner adjusts to these conflicting influences by adoption of a
dual role. Within the mine he assumes a role toward his fellow workers posited
upon acceptance of practical equality of status. Outside his role as member of
the white community involves an elevation of status in which he becomes a
member of a superior caste group. (P. 30)

If the role interpretation of reduction in prejudice and discrimination
is correct, quantitative data on attitudes toward minority group members
should show change for role-relevant attributes, but not for those irrelevant to the role. That is, if the minority group member is serving as a
coworker, his perceived attributes should be adjusted to be appropriate
for his role, but those attributes relevant to personal friendship, for example, should not change. Although the data from various studies is often
not sufficiently complete and is sometimes subject to alternative interpretations, taken together they weave a fairly convincing pattern consistent
with our viewpoint.

One study of two department stores where Negro workers had been
introduced is relevant (Harding & Hogrefe, 1952). White workers were
divided into the following three groups. The *equal-status* group consisted
of white persons who presently or previously worked in departments
where there was at least one Negro whose status was *equal to or higher than*
their own. The *unequal-status* group consisted of white persons who presently or previously worked in departments where all the Negroes were of
lower status than themselves. A third group consisted of those who had
never worked with Negroes. During the latter part of an interview, employees were asked the questions shown in Table 13–1. These questions
were not asked successively, but were interspersed with other questions
not pertaining to Negroes.

The percentages of persons in each group giving *favorable* responses
to each question are listed in Table 13–1. What is quite apparent is that
workers having equal-status contact with Negroes have more favorable attitudes toward them on *job-related* items, but *not* with respect to public
transportation, restaurant facilities, housing, or friendship. Thus, on
questions 1, 2, 5, and 6, which are not job-related, employees who work
with Negroes on either an equal or an unequal basis are *not* more favorable toward Negroes than those having no work contacts. But on questions 3, 4, and 7, pertaining to work relations, those perceiving the
Negro in an equal-status role have the most favorable attitudes. This
strongly suggests that the impact of the role situation has changed role-
related attitudes, but has not generalized to other situations. Although
Negroes had been employed in one store for four years and in the other
for less than one year, there was no difference between these two stores
in the prevailing attitudes toward Negroes.

A study of merchant seamen is also consistent with our interpretation, although its correlational data is subject to many interpretations

Table 13–1

Percentage of Answers Favorable to Negroes among Different Contact Groups

QUESTIONS	EQUAL-STATUS CONTACT	UNEQUAL-STATUS CONTACT	NO CONTACT
1. How do you feel about sitting next to Negroes in buses or trains:	73	71	70
2. How would you feel about sitting down at the same table with a Negro in a lunchroom or cafeteria?	51	53	51
3. How would you feel about taking a new job in which there were both Negroes and white people doing the same kind of work as you?	73	61	48
4. How would you feel about working under a Negro supervisor?	37	29	33
5. How would you feel about living in a new apartment building or housing project which contained both white and Negro families?	13	22	18
6. How would you feel about having a Negro for a personal friend?	12	16	20
7. Do you think Negroes should have the same chance as white people to get any kind of job, or do you think white people should have the first chance at any kind of job?	65	51	57
Number of respondents	82	49	79

SOURCE: Reprinted by permission from J. Harding & R. Hogrefe. Attitudes of white department store employees toward Negro co-workers. *J. soc. Issues*, 1952, **8,** (1), 22.

(Brophy, 1946). Most citations of this investigation have observed that the greater the number of times a sailor had shipped with a Negro seaman, the less prejudiced he was found to be. Thus, 43 percent of those who had shipped two or less times with a Negro were prejudiced, as compared with only 11 percent of those who had shipped three or more times. In the latter group, 84 percent had favorable attitudes toward Negro sailors, as compared with only 43 percent of those sailors who had shipped two or less times.

The investigator has not published his attitude items, so that it is not possible to tell whether differences in prejudice are related only to the job, or whether they are more general. Another finding of this study, however, probably relates to the sailor role. Professional seamen (those who had shipped prior to September 1, 1939 — that is, before the onset of hostilities in World War II) were much less prejudiced than merchant seamen whose service was limited to wartime. Thus, only 8 percent of the professional seamen were prejudiced toward Negroes, as compared with 33 percent of the wartime sailors. Of the latter group 56 percent were pro-Negro, compared with 90 percent of the professional seamen.

We would expect professional sailors to emphasize occupational role requirements more strongly than racial position in evaluating another sailor, and this would lead to consideration of each individual on his merits as a sailor rather than on the basis of his race. Unfortunately, a sailor's professional or nonprofessional status is probably highly correlated with the number of times he has shipped with Negro sailors, since it is doubtless highly correlated with his length of service. From the published data, it is not possible to separate these factors. They could both be contributing factors creating attitude differences, or one of them could be a prime cause. In addition, another finding is that membership in a seamen's union having a militant antidiscrimination policy was also associated with a lack of prejudice, as compared with membership in several other unions not having such a policy. It is not known whether professional seamen belonged to this union to a greater extent than to the other unions, although that seems unlikely, since this union was a newer union.

The importance of the demands of the role situation in bringing about acceptance is nicely illustrated by a case study of the introduction of Negro workers into a Chicago meat-packing plant. One Negro with considerable seniority was transferred to the machine shop, which hitherto had been barred to Negroes. His own report shows how pressures of the job requirements brought about limited acceptance during the first two weeks (Palmore, 1955):

> Monday morning I punched in and there was a lot of whispering and looking over at me, you know. Everybody would walk by and look me over like they'd never seen a man like me before. So I waited and a man would come up to the foreman to ask for a helper, and the foreman would look over at me and say, "He's the only helper left." So the man would decide that he didn't need a helper after all and walk away. So this went on for two days. Nobody would work with me. They put me to work by myself dismantling pumps and stuff and cleaning up around. I would go up to a man at a lathe and ask him a question and he would answer me with only one word if he'd answer at all. Finally, on the third day, they had a job that needed two men and I was the only helper available so the man accepted me and we worked together. The next day I worked with another man. Now there are five men there who I've worked with and who will come over and start a conversation with me on their own. The rest still won't talk to me unless I talk to them first. (P. 28)

In spite of their acceptance of him on the job, however, the five men who worked with him would not eat or take coffee breaks with him, again illustrating the specificity of the role relation.

Another study of employees of a trade union with militant antidiscrimination policies showed highly favorable attitudes toward Negro co-workers (Gundlach, 1956). Unfortunately, no matched control group was used; the results were compared only with other studies which had used somewhat different attitude items as well as samples of persons who were likely to differ in characteristics relevant to attitudes. Almost all the questions concerned work relations. Perhaps noteworthy is the point that these workers were *not* as favorable in responding to a question about having Negroes for neighbors as were persons living in an integrated government housing project. Again, this suggests that shifts in the work role do not extend to the neighbor role.

In an investigation of integrated children's camps, friendships appeared to occur largely with Negroes who shared one's own living cabin (Campbell & Yarrow, 1958). In larger settings, such as activity periods for swimming, games, and other recreations, small segregated groups appeared more frequently. Changes which were appropriate to role relations but which did not generalize are also reported in a postwar study of attitudes toward Japanese-Americans (Irish, 1952). They had been brought to the University of Colorado in Boulder to teach Japanese to naval personnel during World War II. Attitudes of neighbors and nonneighbors of these Japanese-Americans were compared. On questions pertaining to the neighbor role, such as whether they would rent to Nisei or whether they would care if Japanese-Americans bought homes in the neighborhood, the neighbors were more favorable than nonneighbors. In replying to a question about national policy on the Oriental Exclusion Act, however, neighbors showed no greater desire for modification of the act than nonneighbors.

Another study, conducted in World War II, examined the degree of contact between Negro and white infantrymen in combat situations and the amount of prejudice of the white infantrymen toward the Negroes. In some instances, Negro platoons (about 50 men) were assigned to white companies (about 200 men). This was the closest degree of integration. In other cases, Negro units were part of a regiment (3,000 men), a division (13,000 men), or even larger field forces varying considerably in size. The latter assignments represent progressively less contact between Negro and white soldiers, and they were associated with less favorable attitudes toward Negroes than were held in the more integrated units.

Evidence indicated that these favorable attitudes in more integrated units were to some degree confined to Negro soldiers as *combat* companions. The investigators make the following comment on this point (Star, Williams, & Stouffer, 1958):

[Many soldiers] took occasion to note that relationships were better in combat than they were in the garrison situation. Not that there was serious overt friction between Negro and white soldiers. Such instances were, as far as is known, confined to isolated cases and involved white soldiers from other units who did not know the combat record of the Negro men. There were, however, some tensions in companies stationed where friendly contact with liberated populations was possible, and there was some expression of preference for separation in garrison. . . .

Relationships in combat could be regarded as working relationships rather than social relationships. More precisely, they could be confined more narrowly to a functionally specific basis than could the contacts involved in community living. In particular, the combat situation was exclusively masculine, and issues of social relationships between men and women did not appear as they did in garrison. Far from being a "test case" in ordinary Negro-white relations, the combat setting may be regarded as a special case making for good relationships, for the sense of common danger and common obligation was high, the need for unity was at a maximum, and there was great consciousness of shared experience of an intensely emotional kind. (Pp. 598–600)

Finally, the housing studies relevant to the neighbor role may be considered (see Wilner, Walkley, & Cook, 1955). These investigations compare the attitudes of whites living in integrated housing projects with those living in segregated projects. In some cases, the degree of integration varied. The conclusions of these studies are quite consistent: Those in integrated projects show less prejudice and have more favorable attitudes toward Negroes than those living in segregated projects. Furthermore, those having more contacts with Negroes because they lived in greater proximity to them (as by living in a highly integrated project, or by having an apartment close to a Negro apartment) were found to be less prejudiced.

These studies more than any others appear to show favorable attitudes with respect to more personal relations. If we ask what constitutes the neighbor role, these findings seem to be consistent. One should be friendly and sociable toward one's neighbor, should respect him, and should help him and expect help in return. Thus, this role differs from work roles in requiring a strong element of sociability and friendliness. Where circumstances place a minority group member in a neighbor role, appropriate role expectations should lead to friendly feelings and behavior toward him. The various studies document the point that this role is important. For example, they show that in integrated projects a sizable proportion of residents indicated that they had Negroes as friends; in segregated projects no one claimed Negroes as friends.

Not too much attention has been given in these studies to testing whether changes in attitudes generalize to other roles, a crucial question for the present interpretation. One investigation did present a five-item ethnocentrism scale to tenants in a housing project (Wilner, Walkley, & Cook, 1955, p. 69). Unfortunately, results are not reported separately for each item. One item pertains to a work situation: "It would be a mistake ever to have Negroes as foremen and leaders over whites." Another item pertains to schools but also to general contact: "Negroes have their rights but it is best to keep them in their own districts and schools and to prevent too much contact with whites." The remaining three items, however, are general statements about Negroes.

It is interesting to note that when tenants who had more contacts with Negroes are compared with those who had less contact, only one of the four building projects shows a significantly different proportion of persons agreeing with the various items. This was an integrated project; attitudes were more favorable. The other integrated project and the two segregated ones show no significant difference in attitude between persons who had more contact and those who had less. The published information' is not detailed enough, however, to indicate whether the failure to get an appreciable difference is due to the presence of the non-role items mentioned above. The investigators do draw a conclusion consistent with out interpretation in that they indicate only slight generalization to nonhousing situations (Wilner, Walkley, & Cook, 1955):

> It appears, then that proximity is related to favorableness of attitude toward the *specific Negroes in the contact situation and to acceptance of the particular interracial experience* [italics supplied]. Moreover, the more favorable attitudes of the "nears" toward the specific Negroes are generalized to some extent, but by no means completely, to Negroes as a group. There is a slight tendency, too, for the greater acceptance of the particular inter-racial experience on the part of the "nears" to be generalized to acceptance of Negroes in other social situations. (P. 69)

The emphasis given to the role relation between majority and minority groups in this section should not be taken to obscure the importance of personality factors in prejudice. Our earlier discussion of individual processes in prejudice still applies: in the contact situations described, not all individuals respond in the same way. For example, in Minard's (1952) study of Negro and white miners in the Pocahontas coalfields, about 60 percent of the white miners switched their role relation to Negroes upon entering and leaving the mine, behaving on an equal-status basis in the mine and a superior-status basis outside. But 20 percent of the men remained strongly prejudiced both in and out of the mine. The remaining 20 percent maintained friendly, nonprejudiced attitudes outside the mine as well as in. In other words, we may regard 20 percent of the miners as so strongly prejudiced that they discriminate against Negroes in the mine and out of it, and another 20 percent as sufficiently favorable that they behave in a friendly manner in the community as well as the mine. The middle 60 percent may be regarded as having a moderate degree of prejudice which yields in the face of the powerful forces of the work situation but which is operative where community support is provided. Similar individual differences occur in many of the other contact situations, and these may also be attributed to the personality factors discussed earlier.

STUDY QUESTIONS

19. *What is the limitation of the hypothesis that the greater the contact with minority groups, the less the prejudice will be?*

20. *Explain how prejudiced attitudes may change when a minority group member is placed in a role category that conflicts with his minority group role.*
21. *Summarize the evidence for the role interpretation of change in prejudice.*

Summary: Role contacts

A *position* or *role category* is a category of persons occupying a place in a social relation. Associated with each position are *expectations* of how a person occupying that role category should behave and the personal characteristics he should possess. Studies of intergroup contact may be conceptualized as involving situations where outgroup members occupy two positions that may carry somewhat incompatible expectations as to their behavior and characteristics. To the extent that the minority group member is categorized in terms of expectations associated with such incompatible roles as his work role or neighbor role, rather than in terms of the stereotyped expectations associated with his minority group role, attitudes concerning the minority group category may be expected to change. To some degree, however, these changes may remain confined to the role situation under consideration. They are not likely to generalize to widely diverse roles.

An analysis of many work, housing, and other situations involving intergroup contact provided considerable support for these ideas. Attitude changes were shown to be most marked concerning the traits or behaviors pertaining directly to the role in question. Data from one investigation suggested that to the degree a role is important, as is the occupational role to a professional, members of the majority group are likely to emphasize role performance very strongly and thus to show greater changes. This hypothesis should be more extensively investigated.

DISSONANCE AROUSAL AND ATTITUDE CHANGE

In the discussion of change in attitudes due to interaction with minority group members who occupy incompatible roles, the behaviors of the minority group members were stressed. We may now examine the behavior of the majority group member in such situations and its consequences for attitude change. In Chapter 4, the arousal of dissonance as a result of engaging in attitude-discrepant behavior and the manner in which it led to attitude change was discussed at length. Such concepts appear to be relevant to the present situation.

A prejudiced person who has made a decision to move into a public housing project finds himself committed to a situation where he is to some extent required to behave in a manner contrary to his attitudes. Housewives in the project, for example, come into frequent contact with their Negro neighbors at the laundry facilities, in the backyards, in the play areas with their children, and in many other situations. The force of the neighbor role leads them to behave in a friendly and cordial manner. If the housewife is prejudiced, her friendly behavior should arouse dissonance. Ultimately we might expect that the dissonance will be resolved by modification of the aspects of her attitudes toward Negroes that are dissonant with the neighbor role. Here we again find a prediction that only the aspects of attitudes relevant to the role situation need change: these are the only elements that are likely to be dissonant. A rule for creating more general changes may be offered, however. Any conditions that make nonrole elements of the attitude relevant to the behavior in the role situation are likely to facilitate change in these nonrole elements as well.

Intergroup-contact situations need more precise study from the point of view of dissonance concepts before any firm conclusions may be drawn, however. Earlier in our general discussion of attitude change we stressed the role of commitment in contributing to dissonance. The part played by commitment in the various contact situations is not at all clear. While personal commitment to move into a housing project appears to be clearly voluntary, assignment by the authorities to an integrated or segregated project is not. In the work situations, moreover, Negro employees have been introduced by the employer, with the employee having no part in the decision. On the other hand, some form of personal commitment may still operate in such work situations. The individual worker may feel that he has a choice in whether to behave in a prejudiced or nonprejudiced manner toward his fellow worker. Those workers exhibiting reduced prejudice may well be those who made a decision to treat their Negro coworkers on equal terms. Further investigation of intergroup-contact situations is needed to verify these ideas.

SANCTIONS FOR CERTAIN ROLES

In the studies of public housing, investigators suggest that the official policy of the housing authority might be important in creating acceptance of the situation and indirectly bringing about a reduction in prejudice. The fact that each family unit was in a government housing project gave official sanction to the pattern of integrated or segregated housing established by the authority. Assignment to a particular unit was made by the authority; the individual family was not able to choose the location.

Similarly, in some of the work situations, an active nondiscriminatory policy on the part of either the employers or the union sanctioned equal-status role relations. The authoritarian structure of the military, where personnel are accustomed to taking orders from higher authorities, would also seem to foster workable integrated patterns of interaction. The argument here takes the form that such official sanctions help to establish social norms which favor interaction on an equal-status basis.

Sanctions from authorities or important reference persons or groups may also maintain or increase prejudice. In studies of white residential areas being moved into by Negroes, the areas rather rapidly become wholly Negro.[6] The rapid movement of the whites out of the area is accelerated by a variety of pressures from "authoritative" groups or persons. When Negroes move into an area, property owners fear a reduction in property values. Because of the pressure for adequate Negro housing, many Negro buyers become interested once an area is no longer segregated. Realtors thus pressure white residents to sell to Negroes, from whom they can get a better price. Lending agencies and government insuring agencies discourage prospective white buyers from buying into the area. Similar pressures arise from public school staffs, religious institutions, and property owners' associations. Thus, without some form of control it is difficult to maintain a mixed residential area. In some instances, biracial organizations have been formed in the attempt to maintain the existing integrated pattern (Sussman, 1957).

The sanctions of authority need not always bring about change in the direction advocated. Under some circumstances an attempt by officials to change norms may lead to the development of counternorms. For example, the series of Supreme Court decisions on desegregation of Negroes led to the formation of various groups that were opposed to desegregation and were active in promoting resistance to it, such as the White Citizens' Councils throughout the South. The conditions under which norms are likely to be formed or changed have been discussed at length in Chapter 10 on emerging norms and conformity. The principles outlined there are applicable to the present discussion.

COMMON FATE AND SHARED GOALS

Both experimental and field observations support the idea that a role situation involving a common fate and shared goals leads to more favorable attitudes of the participants toward each other. Two groups experience a common fate when they share an experience likely to result in similar outcomes for them. For example, this is likely to be experienced by neighbors in a housing project and by fellow workers in a business organization. Such experiences are intensified, however, if the groups are both subjected to some external threat or danger.

In the study of Negro and white infantry soldiers in combat, the experience of fighting together against a common enemy appeared to be vital in bringing about a changed attitude. The study of merchant seamen indicated that those who had been under enemy fire were less prejudiced than those who had not. In the experiment with boys' camps, in which hostilities between the Eagles and Rattlers were deliberately produced by intergroup competition, a series of threatening situations was created which required cooperation between the groups (Sherif et al., 1961). For example, the water supply was cut off, and all personnel were needed to handle the emergency adequately. Another situation

[6]Deutsch & Collins, 1951; Merton, West, & Jahoda as described in Wilner, Walkley, & Cook, 1955; Wolf, 1957; McEntire, 1957; Fishman, 1961.

involved a stalled truck, which could only be started by having both groups of boys pull together on the tow rope. Such enforced cooperative situations in the face of threat created a single goal that both groups desired to achieve, and that could only be reached through cooperation. These situations led to a marked reduction in hostility toward the out-group.

Two laboratory experiments lend further support to the efficacy of shared threat experiences in prejudice reduction (Feshbach & Singer, 1957; Burnstein & McRae, 1962). In the more recent, subjects varying in Negro prejudice were placed, under conditions of shared threat or non-threat, in groups requiring cooperation to solve the task imposed by the experimenter. One member of each group was a Negro who was a confederate of the experimenter and who had been familiarized in advance with the problem-solving task. Threat was created for members of the experimental group by informing them that the psychology department and the university were embarking on a program of evaluating students through these experimental situations. They were told that complete records of their performances would be placed on permanent file. As anticipated, measures of prejudice taken before and after the experimental situation revealed a significant drop in prejudice for the experimental group but not for the control group, which was not subjected to threat.

STUDY QUESTIONS

22. *How might dissonance theory explain reduction in prejudice as a result of living in integrated housing?*
23. *How may the sanction of authority contribute to changes in prejudiced attitudes?*
24. *Explain what is meant by common fate and shared goals, and show how they are related to changes in prejudice.*

Summary and Conclusions

This chapter has dealt with three major problems: (1) the conditions under which prejudice and discrimination toward a particular group arise, (2) the principles that explain the continuation of prejudice and discrimination, and (3) the factors that lead to changes in prejudice and discrimination. Prejudice is an attitude that predisposes a person to think, perceive, feel, and act in favorable or unfavorable ways toward a group of persons or its individual members. Discrimination is the differential treatment of individuals considered to belong to a particular social group.

A basic principle underlying the origins of prejudice toward a particular group is the following: The character of existing relations between ingroup and outgroup generates attitudes toward the outgroup that are consonant with these relations. A second principle is as follows: If an outgroup has a status different from that of the ingroup with respect to certain attributes and beliefs, its members are likely to be perceived as having other attributes and beliefs congruent with that status.

Discrimination arises through the following process: Where the reward-cost outcomes of two separately bounded groups are perceived to be mutually exclusive, the members of each group strive to protect or to increase their outcomes. If the two groups are unequal in power, they will establish different outcomes unless prevented by norms that restrain exploitation of the weaker by the more powerful. These different outcomes create differences in the status of the two groups. Feelings of being discriminated against are likely to arise where the comparison levels of the two groups are the same.

Factors maintaining prejudice and discrimination have been discussed in terms of three systems: the social system, individual personality dynamics, and the cultural system. Structural processes contributing to maintenance include the following: Prejudice acquires a normative quality, enforced by sanctions; increased interaction among ingroup members increases cohesion, which in turn strengthens conformity pressures; increased interaction within the ingroup and decreased interaction with the outgroup increases the two groups' differences in ways of thinking, perceiving, and feeling; the normative character of prejudice produces leaders who provide support for the norms of prejudice; and the environmental supports appearing in institutional practices, the mass media, and objective characteristics of minority group members themselves also provide support.

Individual processes include the following: the expression of hostility toward a minority group as a scapegoat; the economic and status gains resulting from prejudice and discrimination; the compatibility of prejudice with such personality needs as intolerance of ambiguity and the need for security; the creation of authoritarian personality types whose values are consistent with prejudice toward outgroups; the tendency of the individual to maintain consistency among the cognitive, affective, and behavioral components of his prejudiced attitudes, as well as the tendency toward consistency among different attitudes.

Cultural factors include the development of ideologies and the socialization of the child so as to support prejudice. Prejudiced attitudes become imbedded in an ideology—a complex pattern of ideas, attitudes, and beliefs closely associated with cultural values, which makes inconsistencies between prejudice and other values appear more consistent. The widespread existence of prejudice and discrimination in a society ensures that the child will be socialized in the direction of these prevailing attitudes.

The reduction of intergroup prejudice through contact may best be interpreted as arising from situations where minority group members are placed in a role that is incompatible with the stereotyped beliefs held toward them by the majority group. The role situation is structured by social factors and by the successful performance of the role by the minority group member, leading to reinforcement of the perceptions compatible with the work or neighbor role in question. Incompatible perceptions and feelings associated with the minority group role are likely to disappear. To some extent, these changes are likely to be confined to the role situation under consideration.

Several important conditions shaping role relations in intergroup contact situations are the following: the arousal of dissonance due to engaging in behavior discrepant from one's prejudiced attitudes; the degree to which particular role relations are sanctioned by authority; the extent to which ingroup and outgroup participate in cooperative endeavor toward the achievement of common goals and the extent to which their cooperative endeavors are subjected to external threats; the manner in which intergroup relations fit in with the central values of society.

PART FOUR

The Individual and the Social System

In the previous section, group structure and process have been illustrated in newly formed laboratory groups, in more stable units such as work groups, and in institutional settings such as the family. Emphasis has been placed upon an analysis of group structures in terms of affect, power, status, and communication, and the relation of these structures to certain group processes has been discussed. Using the concept of social role as the major unit of analysis, this section considers in more detail structure and process in institutional settings such as the family or the school.

Part Three discussed in some detail two processes that contribute to development of institutional structure. Chapter 10 described how social norms emerge. Chapter 11 described the process of role differentiation by tracing the development of the role of leader. It was seen that agreement among members as to who is the leader of a group emerges in a relatively short time, a fact which signifies recognition of the role category or position of leader. This group acquiescence to the initiating behavior of the leader suggests that the differentiation is accompanied by the growth of norms or expectations that the leader should direct the group's activities.

The twin processes of norm formation and role differentiation result in the elaboration of social systems, role categories, and attached expectations that guide interaction. Such systems constitute the institutional structure. Although the development of the leadership structure was observed under the highly simplified conditions of the small-group laboratory, the same processes can be observed with ease in nonlaboratory settings. As formal organizations such as a fraternity, a social club, a business enterprise, or a church are created, or as such organizations undergo marked changes, new positions and associated expectations to govern the behavior of members can be seen emerging.

The chapters in Part Four will be concerned with the consequences of such social systems for the behavior of group members. Chapter 14 will introduce the basic concepts that are used to analyze these systems. Chapter 15 will describe features of the systems as well as relations between the systems and the individual that create strains interfering with individual and group functioning. In Chapter 16, both system and individual characteristics that contribute to the resolution of these strains will be identified.

chapter fourteen

SOCIAL ROLES

This chapter and the two succeeding ones will stress the nature of interaction from a perceptual-cognitive point of view. To some extent, certain perceptual-cognitive features of interaction have already been identified in the chapters on group structure and process. First, shared perceptions have been found to develop concerning the position occupied by each person in a group structure. For example, evidence has been presented that persons who have considerable power to influence others are perceived by group members as occupying positions of power. Similarly, group members agree on who in the group has little power. Persons who most frequently initiate and direct group action are recognized by other group members as occupying positions of leadership. Those who rarely initiate action and who generally follow the lead of others are recognized as followers.

A second feature of interaction already noted is that group members agree in holding certain expectations for the behavior of persons who occupy particular positions in the group structure. A person in a position of high power is expected to influence others readily and effectively, a leader is expected to suggest constructive actions leading to achievement of group goals, and a follower is expected to refrain from offering suggestions and to agree with the leader's ideas.

A third concept developed was that of social norm, defined as a behavioral expectation shared by group members against which the validity of perceptions is judged and the appropriateness of feelings and behavior is evaluated. For the most part, norms were considered as they applied to all group members, although considerable emphasis was given to the fact that different expectations are held for leaders and followers. Major attention was devoted to the mechanisms through which norms are enforced and to conditions that maximize or minimize norm-defining and norm-enforcing processes. The present series of chapters pertains to virtually all forms of human interaction, focusing upon the concept of norm as a rule of conduct and applying it to any individual who occupies a definite position in the social structure. In this sense, social norm is more appropriately subsumed under the concept of social role.

Nature of Social Roles

TWO CHARACTERISTICS OF EXPECTATIONS

Two features of expectations are especially important for understanding the concept of social role. These are the anticipatory nature of expectations and their normative quality.

Anticipatory nature of expectations

An individual regularly expects that he will behave in a certain manner, and he usually has definite expectations concerning the behavior of persons with whom he interacts. The importance of this aspect of interaction may be readily appreciated if one recalls situations where such expectations have been at a minimum; for example, during the first day on a new and unfamiliar job. Also illustrative are the feelings of uncertainty and the resultant tentative and shifting quality of interaction that occurs in a newly formed group. These situations in which expectations are minimal may be contrasted with others where expectations are well developed; for example, the smoothly functioning, comfortable interaction occurring between two old friends.

This anticipatory quality of interaction is important because it guides the behavior of an individual. He anticipates how the other person might react to his various actions and shapes his behavior accordingly. The attitude of the other person is inferred from subtle cues provided by his appearance, expression, and posture; by his previously known and current behavior; and by the situational context within which interaction takes place. From such information, the individual draws inferences concerning what the other person feels and thinks about him and how he is likely to behave toward him. In everyday interaction, the process of anticipating the attitudes and behaviors of the other person is greatly simplified. Through long experience, a person classifies the behavior of others in various situations into categories that represent the distinctive attitudes of each class of persons-in-situations. This enables him to anticipate the attitude of the other person in each new encounter simply by placing him and the situation in the appropriate category.

These points concerning the anticipatory quality of interaction may be briefly illustrated here; later they will be discussed in more detail. Assume a situation where a host has invited guests to dinner, and after some social conversation in the living room they enter the dining room, where dinner is being served. The men will allow the women to precede them into the dining room and will assist the women in getting seated before they sit down themselves. This behavior will be carried out quite smoothly, for both the men and women will have appropriate expectations concerning their own behavior and the behavior of the opposite sex in this particular situation.

Normative quality of expectations

Because persons anticipate the behavior of others, interaction has a contingent quality. A person's behavior is contingent upon his anticipation of how the other will react toward him. When he tells a joke, he anticipates that the other will laugh or be amused; otherwise he is unlikely to tell it. If he confides a distressing personal problem, he expects some expression of sympathy; if he does not want sympathy, he keeps the problem to himself. Since many powerful social-emotional needs are satisfied only through interaction with other persons, an individual must be able to anticipate reactions of the other to his own behavior if he is to satisfy his needs. A person desiring sociable conversation must be able to anticipate what behaviors on his part will elicit responsive conversation from the other.

Usually such anticipations are correct and well established only in situations which the individual has previously encountered, where he and the others involved have certain shared experiences in common. Each party to the interaction shares expectations concerning his own and the other's behavior. Such well-established shared expectations usually have an obligatory quality. The other person is not only *expected* to behave in a certain way; he *should* behave in that way. Failure on his part to meet expectations is likely to be met with surprise, disgust, anger, or indignation. This normative quality of expectations stems from the fact that only when one is able to anticipate consistently the behaviors of others can one maximize one's reward-cost outcomes. The extent to which expectations are normative varies in proportion to the importance of the rewards and costs involved. Norms involve important rewards and costs to the extent that they are functionally integrated with the value structure of the group, a point to be discussed in more detail later.

STUDY QUESTIONS

1. *What are the ideas developed in previous chapters on group structure and process that are relevant to an understanding of social roles?*

2. *Explain what is meant by the anticipatory and the normative quality of expectations.*

In short, in the discussions of group structure and process in earlier portions of the book, several observations were made. First, persons develop common perceptions concerning the positions occupied by each person in a group structure. Second, group members agree in holding certain expectations for the behavior of persons who occupy particular positions in the group structure. Finally, the anticipatory and normative quality of expectations was stressed. These expectations are shared by group members and are used to evaluate behavior. Persons anticipate their own behavior and the behavior of those with whom they interact, and they feel that both parties *should* behave as expected. These ideas are fundamental to an understanding of the social-role concepts introduced in the next two sections.

SOME ROLE CONCEPTS

First to be discussed are the following: position or role category, role expectation, and role behavior.

Position or role category

A *position* is a category of persons occupying a place in a social relation. A position may also be referred to as a *role category*; the terms are interchangeable.[1] Thus family systems have a position occupied by a person referred to as "mother." Only those categories of persons defined in the same way by two or more persons meet the criteria for defining a position. Categories may be perceived in the same way by all members of a society, or by only a few individuals. An example of widely shared definitions is age-sex positions. Illustrations are "small boy," "small girl," "young man," "young woman," "old man," "old woman." Persons whose occupations require them to interact widely with others outside their occupation also occupy positions based on widely shared perceptions. Illustrations are surgeon, taxi driver, lawyer, professor, barber. Clearly defined categories of persons may also be shared by only a small number of persons. Most small groups have such positions. Perhaps a clear example is the "lunch-boy" mentioned by Homans (1961). The newest employee in a small group of men working in a factory was assigned to the position of lunch-boy, which required him to bring back from the plant restaurant the food ordered by his fellow workers.

Role expectations; social role

Expectations have been described in terms of the anticipatory and

[1] The term *status* is often used instead of *position*. Unfortunately, however, status has different but somewhat overlapping meanings in the behavioral sciences. Some writers use it to refer to a position in a social relation, such as that of husband in a family system. Others using it refer to a system of differential evaluations of persons, which is the meaning that we gave it in Chapter 9. A person may be placed at a point on an evaluative continuum according to the degree to which he possesses the characteristics defining that continuum. For example, in a group where wealth is a basis for differential evaluation, wealthier persons have higher status than those with less wealth. For this reason, we have chosen to use the terms *position* and *role category* in preference to *status*.

normative quality of interaction. Role expectations are expectations that are associated with a role category. As in the case of role categories, the number of persons who hold expectations with respect to a position may vary from two persons to virtually everyone in a society of millions. Expectations associated with age-sex positions illustrate culture-wide expectations.

For example, in American society expectations associated with the age-sex position "little girl" include the belief that she should like dolls and dresses, that she should cry more readily and be more affectionate than her brother, and that she should be well-mannered compared to little boys. These expectations also include beliefs concerning what she should not do: She should not be able to outbox all the boys in the neighborhood, she should not be especially interested in playing cowboys and Indians, and she should not get as dirty as little boys when she plays outside. Another example of culture-wide expectations is those associated with the position "mother."

We may also illustrate subgroup expectations: Persons in lower socioeconomic classes have somewhat distinctive expectations toward the role category of "child." To a greater extent than persons at middle socioeconomic levels, they generally expect children to obey and respect adults and to please them (Kohn, 1963). Finally, some expectations associated with a position may be relatively unique, as when a particular mother and child share the expectation that she should sing him a certain lullaby when she puts him to bed.

Role expectations associated with a given position may vary with respect to consensus. Some expectations are widely agreed upon; others are unique to particular individuals. Most people in our society would agree that a person in the role of husband should provide at least a portion of the income for his family. That the wife also should be expected to earn income by working is a belief held much less widely.

The more general term *social role*[2] (or simply *role*) is used to refer to both the position and its associated expectations. When the role of mother is referred to, both the position in a family system and its attached expectations are being designated.

Role behavior

Role behaviors are the behaviors of an actor that are relevant to the role he is performing. These behaviors may or may not conform to expectations. For example, a professor may explain some ideas very poorly.

---

[2]The term *role* has been used in more than one sense. We have defined it as the expectations that persons hold in common toward any person who falls in a particular category by virtue of his position in a social system. Others have used the concept in a much broader sense, to refer to any meaningful grouping of behaviors. While it is recognized by those who prefer the latter usage that position is a meaningful basis for grouping, this is but one of many bases. Others group behaviors according to the purpose or function of the behaviors, or according to the sentiments or values they represent (see Turner, 1956, 1962; Bates, 1956, 1962; Goffman, 1961*b*; Biddle, Rosencranz, & Rankin, 1961).

Explanation of ideas is relevant to his role and consequently this is role behavior, although it does not conform to the expectation that a professor should explain things clearly. While performing his role he also engages in behavior irrelevant to it. To illustrate, while lecturing he might light a cigarette, an act that has nothing to do with his role.

Role expectations and role behaviors should be clearly distinguished from each other. Expectations represent how actors[3] in a role category are supposed to behave; particular individuals, however, may deviate markedly from these expectations in their actual behavior. Some persons may fit the role very well; others may not. The importance of this distinction may be grasped more fully when role strain and its resolution are discussed in the following two chapters.

STUDY QUESTION
3. *Define and explain the following concepts: position • role category • role expectation • social role • role behavior*

In sum, a position or role category is a category of persons occupying a place in a social relation. Some positions are recognized on a society-wide basis, and some are relatively unique, perceived by only a few persons. Role expectations are expectations that are associated with a role category. As in the case of role categories, the number of persons who hold expectations with respect to a position may vary greatly. For a given position, some expectations are widely agreed upon, while others may yield low consensus. Social role is a more general term used to refer to both the position and its associated expectations. Finally, role behaviors are the behaviors of an actor that are relevant to the role he is performing.

The Social System

Particular social roles cannot be considered apart from their relation to other social roles. Every social role has others to which it is related. Together, related social roles make up a system or structure within which persons interact. Such interlocking social roles are commonly referred to by social psychologists as *social systems*. An example of a social system is the family—not a particular family, but the systematic relations between the positions of husband and wife, father and child, mother and child, brother and sister, etc. This section introduces a number of important system concepts.

CONCEPTS RELATING SOCIAL ROLES

Focal position, counterposition, and role partner

The expectations associated with a position specify particular behaviors toward the occupants of certain other positions. These other positions

---

[3]*Actor* is a term gaining increasing use among social psychologists to refer to the individual as a participant in a social system.

are known as *counterpositions.* The position with which they are associated is known as the *focal* position. Persons occupying the counterpositions are known as *role partners.*[4] Examples of role partners are mother and child, doctor and patient, teacher and student. A focal position may be associated with many counterpositions: role partners of a mother are not only her children, but also her children's father, teachers, playmates, neighbors, pediatrician, dentist. These persons, when acting as her role partners, relate to her as a mother of the children with whom they are interacting.

Role obligations and rights; role sectors and role sets

The intimate connections between a position and its counterposition may be more fully appreciated by considering role relations in terms of obligations and rights. Consider two role categories such as husband and wife. Associated with the position of husband are certain expectations concerning how a person occupying this position is expected to act toward his role partner, his wife, and how she is expected to behave toward him. These relations can be described from the standpoint of the husband or from that of the wife (Gross, Mason, & McEachern, 1958).

From the standpoint of the position of husband, the expectations about his behavior are referred to as *role obligations,* and expectations about the behavior of his wife as *rights* or *privileges* associated with the role of husband. From the standpoint of the position of wife these same expectations become privileges and obligations, respectively. For example, an obligation of the husband is to provide food, shelter, clothing, and the amenities of living for his wife. From her point of view this is a right or privilege she enjoys as a wife. Conversely, a husband in our society expects his wife to take care of the house and attend to such matters as shopping, cleaning, and laundry. From his point of view this is a right associated with his role; it is an obligation associated with the role of the wife. In short, the obligations of a person in a role category are the rights of his role partner; his own rights are the obligations of his role partner.

The pair of social roles, husband and wife, illustrate a *role sector,* which consists of the expectations applicable to the relation of a focal position to a single counterposition (Gross, Mason, & McEachern, 1958). Generally, however, occupancy of a particular position involves an actor in a set of relations with a number of role partners. For instance, a teacher is involved in a set of expectations with such role partners as pupil, principal, superintendent, other teachers, and many others, as partially illustrated in Figure 14–1. The set of relations with the role partners of a person in a role category has been called a *role set* by Merton (1957*a*).

STUDY QUESTIONS

4. *What is a social system?*
5. *Define the concepts of counterposition and role partner.*

---

[4]The term *role partner* was adopted from Bredemeier and Stephenson (1962).

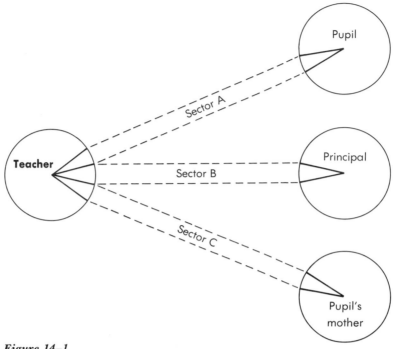

Figure 14–1
A role set and some of its role sectors.

6. *What is meant by role obligations and rights of the occupant of a position? How do these relate to the rights and obligations of his role partner?*
7. *What is a role sector and what is a role set?*

SOCIAL ROLES IN ONGOING INTERACTION

At any time an actor may simultaneously occupy a number of positions: both he and his role partners define him in terms of several role categories, and his behavior reflects the role expectations attached to these categories. Illustrations include a physician treating a member of his own family, or a teacher having her own child as a pupil in her classroom. Multiple position occupancy, as will be discussed in more detail in the next chapter, is important because in many situations an actor occupies two positions in which expectations are contradictory, leading to role strain.

At any one time, however, a person never enacts all the role categories that he occupies in the course of his daily activities. At a given moment, some of his positions are active: they are used by him and by other persons to anticipate his behavior and to judge its appropriateness. Later, other positions become active while the former become latent: he is no longer placed in those categories. This shifting from one role category to another, positions becoming active and latent as one goes about his daily life, has been vividly pictured by Linton (1945) in a classic passage:

Let us suppose that a man spends the day working as clerk in a store. While he is behind the counter, his active status is that of a clerk, established by his position in our society's system of specialized occupations. The role associated with this status provides him with patterns for his relations with customers. These patterns will be well known both to him and to the customers and will enable them to transact business with a minimum of delay or misunderstanding. When he retires to the rest room for a smoke and meets other employees here, his clerk status becomes latent and he assumes another active status based upon his position in the association group composed of the store's employees as a whole. In this status his relations with other employees will be governed by a different set of culture patterns from those employed in his relations with customers. Moreover, since he probably knows most of the other employees, his exercise of these culture patterns will be modified by his personal likes and dislikes of certain individuals and by considerations of their and his own relative positions in the prestige series of the store association's members. When closing time comes, he lays aside both his clerk and store association statuses and, while on the way home, operates simply in terms of his status with respect to the society's age-sex system. Thus if he is a young man he will at least feel that he ought to get up and give his seat to a lady, while if he is an old one he will be quite comfortable about keeping it. As soon as he arrives at his house, a new set of statuses will be activated. These statuses derive from the kinship ties which relate him to various members of the family group. In pursuance of the roles associated with these family statuses he will try to be cordial to his mother-in-law, affectionate to his wife and a stern disciplinarian to Junior, whose report card marks a new low. If it happens to be lodge night, all his familial statuses will become latent at about eight o'clock. As soon as he enters the lodge room and puts on his uniform as Grand Imperial Lizzard, in the Ancient Order of Dinosaurs he assumes a new status, one which has been latent since the last lodge meeting, and performs in terms of its role until it is time for him to take off his uniform and go home. (P. 78)

Interactional context

At any point in time, the interactional context is an important determinant of the role categories a person occupies, of the expectations applied to the role category, and of the range of permissible behavior defined by the expectations. The two features of the interactional context that determine these factors are the characteristics of the situation and characteristics of the actors.

First, persons are placed in a role category appropriate to their characteristics and behavior. How they are categorized will determine what expectations will emerge. If a person enters a bank and with passbook in hand approaches a woman who is standing behind a partition with a window grill, each will use certain information to categorize the other: he defines her as a teller, and she defines him as a customer. As soon as such categorization is made and as long as it is maintained, certain expectations and certain interactions will occur. There will be a polite exchange of greetings, the passbook will exchange hands, etc. Should he suddenly produce a gun, however, he would be categorized differently by this woman and new expectations and behavior on her part would undoubtedly occur. Similarly, if the woman behind the partition behaved in a manner which indicated that she was not a teller, he would change his expectations and behavior. This example illustrates the principle that expectations are always tied to categories of persons as well as categories of situations. Before expectations emerge, categorization must take place, and should categories shift in a given interaction situation, expectations will change.

From time to time the same role categories may have somewhat different expectations applied to them, depending upon the situation. On a military post, an enlisted man and a commissioned officer encountering each other are expected to exchange salutes. On the battlefield in sight of the enemy, such an expectation would not arise. The range of permissible behavior defined by role expectations also varies from situation to situation. Close conformity to the rules may be expected of both foreman and worker when the shop superintendent is out on the floor, but when he returns to his office the range of permissible behavior is appreciably widened.

STUDY QUESTIONS

8. *What is meant by multiple position occupancy? Under what condition does multiple position occupancy create problems?*

9. *What features of social roles are determined by the interactional context?*

SUMMARY: THE SOCIAL SYSTEM

A social system is a group of related social roles. Each position in a social system has one or more counterpositions. Persons occupying these counterpositions are known as role partners. The obligations of a person in a role category are the rights of his role partner; his own rights are the obligations of his partner. A pair of social roles consisting of the expectations associated with a position and its counterposition constitute a role sector. A role set is made up of a number of such sectors. In other words, it is the set of relations with the role partners of a person in a role category.

Individuals assume various roles at different times and on different occasions. Sometimes they simultaneously perform more than one role. When expectations associated with these multiple position occupancies are incompatible, role strain results. The role categories a person occupies, the expectations applied to the role category, and the range of permissible behavior defined by the expectations are a function of the interactional context. Two features of the interactional context that determine these factors are the characteristics of the situation and the attributes of the actors.

Social Norms and Roles

Early in the chapter, two important properties of expectations were stressed: their anticipatory and their obligatory nature. The actor is not neutral concerning whether or not his expectations are confirmed by the behavior of the other person. He not only anticipates the person's behavior, but feels that the other is *obligated* to behave in accordance with his anticipations. This is because the other is assumed to share with him common role expectations. Thus role expectations are *normative,* and in varying degrees the actor is disturbed if the other person does not conform as expected. Although group norms were discussed in Chapter 10, treatment was confined largely to pressures toward conformity and the conditions producing various degrees of conformity. This section will discuss normative expectations within a larger perspective.

PROPERTIES OF NORMATIVE EXPECTATIONS

Social norms have a variety of properties, each of which will be discussed in turn:

1. They shape behavior in the direction of shared values or desirable states of affairs.
2. They vary in the degree to which they are functionally related to important values.
3. They are enforced by the behavior of other persons.
4. They vary as to how widely they are shared; they may be society-wide, or they may belong to groups of varying sizes, even as small as a two-person group.
5. They vary in the range of permissible behavior; some norms set more stringent limits on behavior than others.

Norms and the value structure

Behavior which is contrary to expectations may arouse surprise, disgust, anger, or indignation. On the psychological level of analysis, such reactions can be explained in terms of social learning. A well-brought-up Moslem has learned to react with revulsion to the behavior of eating pork, just as we, as members of our society, would react to a serving of caterpillars. Similarly, most American middle-class males would react with feelings ranging from embarrassment to indignation to a host's suggestion that as a guest he should sleep with the host's wife. In societies where wife-lending under such circumstances is expected, a guest might well react with similar feelings if such an offer were not made.

On the sociological level of analysis, these reactions appear to be related to the value structure of the group. Just as we have noted that actors in a group share expectations with respect to one another's conduct, it can be said that members of a group share notions concerning desirable conditions or states of affairs. These conditions are called *values.* Values can be ranked in terms of how important they are to the members of a group. Prominent values among a group of students, for instance, might include such conditions or states of affairs as the possession of beauty for a girl and athletic prowess for a boy, ownership of a sports car, achievement of satisfactory grades, etc. A ranking of values would constitute the *value hierarchy* of that group. These value rankings may differ from group to group; for example, the students' ranking of values would be different from the ranking of the same values by a group of parents. Norms are functionally related to values by virtue of the fact that conforming to such rules of conduct fosters the achievement of certain desired states. For example, health is a value in our society, and the various hygienic rules are norms that direct behavior toward this valued state of affairs.

The degree of functional dependence between value and norms varies. The violation of some norms may barely endanger a value, whereas the violation of others may greatly jeopardize the achievement of a desired state of affairs. To illustrate, the norms governing cleanliness in the operating room of a hospital are functionally related to the value of health to a higher degree than the expectation that a person will cover his mouth when he sneezes in the presence of others.

Enforcement of norms

Norms are enforced by means of *sanctions.* This term refers to the actions of others or of an actor himself that have the effect of rewarding conformity and punishing nonconformity to norms by facilitating or interfering with the need gratification of the individual. Where need gratification is facilitated, we speak of *positive* sanctions. Where need deprivation is the result, we speak of *negative* sanctions. Furthermore, where the source of reward or punishment is the behavior of others, the term *external sanction* is employed. Where the source is within the actor, *internal sanction* is used.

Examples of external sanctions would be giving an employee a raise in pay or docking an employee who is late for work. Examples of internal sanctions would be a feeling of pride for having conformed to a norm in the face of strong temptations to violate it, or a feeling of guilt for having failed to conform. The strength of the sanction varies with the importance of the value and the extent to which the norm is instrumental to the achievement of the value. While external sanctions may be relied on almost exclusively to enforce norms that are of little importance, norms that relate to important values and that are highly instrumental in achieving those values are rarely if ever enforced by external sanctions alone. Groups socialize their members so that they develop strong internal sanctions for these norms. The process of socialization will be discussed in more detail in Chapters 17 to 19.

Variations in sharing normative expectations

Expectations may be shared by any number of persons, ranging from members of a large society to a two-person group. In our society, such behaviors as the handshake, the kiss, and the bowed head in prayer are regulated by society-wide norms.

Many behaviors, however, are specific to smaller groups. For example, a particular church denomination has certain ritualistic behavior which is required of its members; nonmembers do not and are not expected to participate. Small groups engaging in face-to-face interaction inevitably develop sets of social norms to guide the conduct of the members. Work groups, for example, set standards for how much work shall be done in a day, and members who violate the standards are punished. On most college campuses there are subgroups of students who maintain a norm with respect to how much time is spent in studying. Those who study too much are called such derogatory names as "grinds," "brains," or "egg-heads."

Finally, the smallest unit, a pair of persons, such as a husband and wife, may engage in behavior which is essentially normative but peculiar to them. The husband may take the dog out every morning, and the wife may drive the children to school.

Variations in limits of behavior

From our own experience we may note that some rules can be honored by a rather wide range of conduct, while others are more exacting and require a specific line of behavior. Thus, norms should be thought of as specifying the *limits* of permissible or required behavior in a particular interactional context—limits which may be relatively wide or narrow, depending on the particular norms as well as on other components in the interactional context. The range of permissible or required behavior may be illustrated by considering arrival times at a dinner party. The host usually tells his guests that the dinner party will begin at some specific hour. Few guests arrive punctually; most arrive some time after the hour. But there is a relatively narrow range of permissible or required arrival times, and when this is violated, profuse apologies from the late guests are called for. On the other hand, the range of arrival times is much greater for an evening cocktail party.

SOCIAL ROLE AS AN INTEGRATING CONCEPT

The concept of social role is one of the most central in the behavioral sciences. It serves to link three major areas of interest: social systems, personality, and culture. Sociologists, who focus on an analysis of social systems and, anthropologists, who study comparative social structure, have found it useful to conceptualize the systems of recurring interactions in a group in terms of social-role concepts. The ongoing behavior of any group can be analyzed in these terms. In a university, for instance, one may note interactions that recur from day to day. In room after room of a classroom building, certain patterned interactions take place: one person stands before a group of others; he speaks, and they write in their notebooks. The pattern can be analyzed in terms of the role behavior of those occupying the positions of teacher and student. In other buildings on campus, patterned interactions occur between occupants of other role categories, such as deans and secretaries, housemothers and cooks, members of the board of regents and administrative officials. All these patterns can be conceptualized in terms of position and role expectations and can be studied as a system—as a unity of interdependent parts. Certain large problems, such as what happens to the other parts of the social system when a particular position drops out of it or when the role expectations associated with a role category change, may be treated on this level of analysis.

In the past, social psychologists were chiefly interested in those types of roles toward the cultural end of the continuum, since their main concern was with society-wide regularities in behavior rather than with regularities common to the members of smaller subgroups. In more recent years, as social psychologists have become concerned with smaller groups, they have expressed more interest in roles toward the unique end of the continuum.

At a somewhat different level, social psychologists are also interested in features of social systems that relate to personality formation. Certainly such features of a system as the clarity of the role expectations, the amount of consensus among actors with respect to these expectations, and the integration of the expectations so that the actor does not encounter conflicting expectations, will have implications for problems in the areas of personality formation and social interaction. Part of the discussion of role in connection with personality formation must be postponed to Chapter 17 on socialization.

For the next two chapters we will be concerned with the ideas reviewed here in connection with the concept of role and how they add to our understanding of human interaction. The focus will be on certain problematic aspects of interaction, first because most of the research has concentrated on the problematic, and second because it is easier to detect the factors underlying human interaction when its normally smooth-flowing character is disrupted.

STUDY QUESTIONS

10. *What are five properties of normative expectations? Explain each of these.*
11. *How does the concept of social role serve to integrate several areas of behavioral science?*
12. *What is the particular interest of the social psychologist in social roles?*

SUMMARY: SOCIAL NORMS AND ROLES

Social norms have five properties: (1) They shape behavior in the direction of shared values or desirable states of affairs. (2) They vary in the degree to which they are related to important values. (3) They are enforced by the behavior of other persons. (4) They vary in how widely they are shared; they may be society-wide or they may belong to groups of varying sizes, even as small as a two-person group. (5) They vary in the range of permissible behavior; some norms set more stringent limits on behavior than others. Norms that relate to important values and that are highly instrumental in achieving those values are rarely, if ever, enforced by external sanctions alone.

The concept of social role is useful in linking three major areas of interest: cultural systems, social systems, and personality. Historically, social psychologists have shifted their interest from roles at the cultural end of the continuum toward those at the unique end. Social psychologists are particularly interested in features of social systems that relate to personality formation and to processes of social interaction.

Summary and Conclusions

Several observations from earlier chapters important to an understanding of social roles were reviewed. First, persons develop common perceptions concerning the positions occupied by each member in a group structure. Second, group members agree in holding certain expectations for the behavior of persons in the group structure. Finally, expectations represent the anticipatory and normative quality of interaction.

A position or role category is a category of persons occupying a place in a social relation. Role expectations are the attitudes and behaviors that persons associate with a position. Social role is a more general term used to refer to both the position and its associated expectations. Role behaviors are the behaviors of an actor that are relevant to the role he is performing.

Particular social roles cannot be considered apart from their relation to other social roles; together, a group of related roles comprise a social system. Each position in a social system has one or more counterpositions. Persons occupying these counterpositions are known as role partners. The obligations of a person in a role category are the rights of his role partner; his own rights are the obligations of his role partner. Individuals assume various roles at different times and on different occasions. An individual may simultaneously occupy several role categories. If the associated expectations are incompatible, role strain results. Various properties of the expectations associated with a position are a function of two features of the interactional context: the characteristics of the situation and the attributes of the actors.

Normative expectations have five properties: (1) They shape behavior in the direction of shared values or desirable states of affairs. (2) They vary in the degree to which they are functionally related to important values. (3) They are enforced by the behavior of other persons. (4) They vary in how widely they are shared; they may be society-wide or they may belong to small groups. (5) They vary in the range of permissible behavior.

Social role serves as a concept integrating three areas: personality, social systems, and cultural systems.

chapter fifteen

ROLE STRAIN

The previous chapter mentioned that role behavior is not always in accord with the expectations associated with a role category. Often an individual does not conform because it would place too great a strain on him to do so. This chapter analyzes the various sources of strain, and the next chapter discusses the resolution of strains.

Two terms have often been used to refer to difficulty in conforming to role expectations: *role strain* and *role conflict*. We prefer to use role strain because it is the broader of the two. The more commonly employed term role conflict is generally limited to situations where an actor is confronted with conflicting or competing expectations. Role strain covers not only those situations, but a great variety of others in which an actor experiences difficulty in meeting a role expectation.

Role strain and its resolution will be analyzed on three levels: the social system, the personality dynamics of the individual, and the cultural system. First, when human behavior is viewed in terms of the social system, recurrent interactions between individuals are focused upon and conceptualized in terms of position and role. On this level, concern is not with the characteristics of the actors themselves, but with characteristics of the system of relations between actors. Second, when the individual is focused upon, analysis takes place in terms of personality dynamics. Here, concern is with the relations between various conceptual components of the personality: needs, self conceptions, and attitudes. Finally, components of the cultural system are studied in terms of shared cognitions about the social and nonsocial world.

Sociologists as sociologists are concerned primarily with analysis on the social system level; psychologists as psychologists are concerned with analysis at the level of the individual. Anthropologists are concerned with cultural systems. Social psychologists, however, while focusing on the individual, attempt to relate his behavior to variables on all three levels. Those familiar with the work of Talcott Parsons (Parsons & Shils, 1951) will recognize in the above distinctions our indebtedness to him. In preference to direct adoption of his terminology, however, we have recast many of his ideas in terms that are more commonly employed in the field.

Social System Variables and Role Strain

Throughout this discussion the importance of expectations in the interaction process has been emphasized. Such expectations make interaction possible to the extent that they are held in common and fulfilled by the members of a group. Interaction becomes difficult or impossible to the extent that group members do not hold expectations in common or behave contrary to them. The resulting strain, considered on the level of the individual personality, involves experiencing conflicting tendencies to act and feelings of inadequacy, guilt, embarrassment, and need frustration. On the level of the social system, this strain is associated with interpersonal conflict and the failure of the system to maximize the achievement of its goals. The degree of strain is reflected in the cultural system, in terms of inconsistencies among its elements.

A common form of role strain arises in the early sessions of psychotherapy. The new patient normally comes to therapeutic sessions with the expectation that the therapist, like a physician, will provide some prescription for his problems. He expects the therapist to be extremely active—to ask him questions and to tell him how to solve his problem. The therapist, on the other hand, usually expects the patient to gradually solve his own problems through a process in which the patient is very active in reporting his feelings and thoughts and his own reactions to them, and in which he gradually arrives at a new view of himself and his place in the world. In short, the therapist expects the patient to talk a great deal and sees his own role as facilitating the patient's verbalizations, while the patient expects the therapist to do most of the talking and perceives his role as passive and dependent. How this leads to strain is illustrated by the reactions of several different patients to the inactivity of the therapist (Lennard & Bernstein, 1960):

Patient [1]: A couple of seconds ago, uh, there was a silence in which I had nothing to say or I didn't say anything. And just before you said something I thought of this fact that, uh, I wonder *who's* going to talk first and *why*.

Patient [2]: I was trying to arrive at a couple of things (*sigh*). The reaction of the analyst sitting and just staring at me, and waiting for me to say something or to think of something leads to two kinds of feelings in me. One, instead of coming forth and being able to think of things, is that I either draw a blank or, uh, have to fight to try and almost make up things to fill the void.

Patient [3]: Well, actually, I haven't found this, uh, the kind of experience that I've anticipated. It's rather frustrating. It's difficult for me to carry on a one-man conversation with myself, something I've never been able to do.

Patient [4]: I thought, uh, there would be more of a, uh, interaction, back and forth in trying to at least, get at your reactions to the kind of feeling I have. (P. 168).

CLARITY AND CONSENSUS IN ROLE EXPECTATIONS

Expectations associated with roles in a social system vary in clarity and in the degree of agreement or consensus among persons. Up to a certain point, the more explicit and specific an expectation is, the easier it is to conform to it, and the more smoothly the system functions. Where expectations are unclear, strain is produced by individual uncertainty about what is expected and by the many conflicting interpretations of what role behavior is appropriate.

Newly developed roles, in particular, often lack clarity. For example, in one study, psychiatric nurses required to enact a rather vaguely defined new role complained that, unlike their earlier role, it did not provide a clear-cut basis for action (Schwartz, 1957). The nurses had been instructed to respond to the patients as individuals, recognizing each patient's needs and attempting to satisfy them. The new role permitted extreme freedom to the patients (all of whom were chronic schizophrenics) limited only by considerations for their health and safety and the nurses' own physical and psychological comfort.

Not only did these expectations for the roles of patient and nurse conflict with the nurses' personal norms, preferences, and capabilities, with the traditional role of nurse, and with the institutional requirements of the hospital, but they also did not offer a sufficient guide to action or allow for a consistent treatment of the patients by different nurses. Schwartz comments on the lack of consensus:

> The emphasis upon responding to patients in individualized ways and the consequent reduction in shared patterns of action resulted in nurses handling the same patient behavior in different ways. Nurses who wanted privacy in the nursing office while making out reports found that other nurses permitted patients free access to the office, sometimes to their great annoyance. Some nurses wanted to remove the food cart after nourishments had been served; others preferred to leave the cart on the ward for the entire evening, even though a patient usually played with the food and threw it around the ward. (P. 412)

Schwartz notes further that the lack of clear-cut expectations left the nurses at a loss as to how to behave. One nurse, referring to the ward administrator who introduced the new role, made the following comments in an interview:

> I don't think he recognized—or he probably recognized it and was trying to break us of it—the fact that we do need and want certain very definite lines set up which we can feel our way around. Over and above that, fine—we'll be

permissive, we'll be comfortable, we'll do this, that and the other thing; but we do have to have certain anchors and guideposts. Otherwise we just feel as though the world is falling apart. . . . (P. 413)

Other studies of emerging roles similarly document the point that lack of clarity in new roles leads to role strain. Wardwell, in a study of a relatively new occupational role, that of chiropractor, also observes that a lack of clarity is a source of strain. He comments (1952):

In addition to the ambiguity in the definition of the role of any doctor, the chiropractor's role is ambiguous for several other reasons. There is vast ignorance on the part of the patients and potential patients as to what chiropractors do, and, more important, chiropractors themselves disagree on the question of what chiropractic treatment should be. The "straights" limit themselves to spinal manipulation alone, sometimes "adjusting" only upper cervical vertebrae, while the "mixers" also use heat, light, air, water, exercise, diet regulation, and electric modalities in their treatment. State laws differ as widely in the scope of practice they permit. In most states chiropractors are limited to spinal manipulation and simple hygenic measures, while in others they may perform minor surgery, practice obstetrics, and sign death certificates. . . . (P. 17)

The newness of a role is not the only cause of lack of clarity: it may also be produced by successive change in a role. A study of the roles that college women expect to adopt as adults concluded that the great changes in the role of the adult woman in recent times have given college-aged women an unclear and unrealistic picture of their adult role (Rose, 1951).

Where role expectations in a social system are unclear for whatever reason, strain in social systems leads to periodic attempts by the actors occupying positions in the system to clarify their roles. In large systems, such as business organizations, one such attempt takes the form of developing and elaborating manuals of operation that make explicit what is expected of each position occupant in the system. The same process can be observed in small systems, such as a family, or even a two-person relation like that between two lovers. One function of lovers' quarrels is to redefine their relations to each other; in our terminology, to clarify their respective roles (Waller & Hill, 1951).

Discussion so far has focused upon the *expectations* associated with positions in a given system. The positions or role categories themselves may also show lack of clarity, with similar consequences. In categorizing others, persons may use a wide variety of cues, such as dress, voice, and manner of behavior, as well as more explicit identifying information such as titles or uniforms. Using a broader conceptualization of role than is employed here, Stone (1959; 1962) has provided a penetrating analysis of the cues furnished by dress in interaction. Where such categorization cannot be made with confidence and accuracy, uncertainty and inappropriate behavior with attendant role strain will occur. All of us have had embarrassing experiences resulting from inappropriate behavior toward another person whom we wrongly identified; such experiences illustrate the point.

In sum, expectations associated with roles in a social system vary in clarity and in the degree of consensus among persons. Clarity is mainly a function of the explicitness and specificity of expectations. Newly developed roles often lack clarity and thus create role strain. Lack of clarity may also be produced by successive change in a role. Although most research has been devoted to ambiguity in *expectations,* ambiguity in the *role category* may also produce strain.

STUDY QUESTIONS

1. *What is the difference between role strain resulting from the social system and strain resulting from characteristics of the individual actor?*

2. *Explain how lack of clarity and lack of consensus in role expectations leads to role strain. Under what conditions would you expect lack of clarity and lack of consensus to characterize a system?*

Types of disagreement on role expectations

As previously noted, one consequence of lack of clarity and specificity of role expectations is that consensus is reduced. In a given system, the occupants of one or more positions may disagree. Where consensus is lacking, concerted action by the actors in that position is hindered, and they are likely to be anxious and uncertain concerning their rights and obligations. Unless their role partners are familiar with the somewhat different expectations held by each of the occupants, some difficulty in interaction will occur.

Five important forms of disagreement on expectations are the following: (1) Actors may disagree on what expectations are included in a given role. (2) Actors may disagree on the range of permitted or prohibited behavior. (3) Actors may disagree on the situations to which the role applies. (4) Actors may disagree on whether the expected behavior is mandatory or simply preferred. (5) Actors may disagree on which should be honored first when an expectation conflicts with another.

Lack of consensus on the role of wife in our society is a good example, since all five forms may be illustrated: (1) There may be lack of agreement on whether being a wife should require a woman to forgo employment. (2) A husband may disagree with his wife in believing that part-time employment is permissible, but full-time is not. (3) They may disagree in believing that she should only be employed in a case of economic necessity. (4) He may believe she absolutely should not work, and she may feel it simply would be better if she did not. (5) Finally, he may believe that her family obligations take precedence over her employment, and she may have the opposite opinion. Although these illustrations pertain to a position incumbent and his role partner, the five forms of disagreement may also apply to incumbents of the same position.

The various role partners of a position incumbent may also define his role differently from each other. Where such conflict cannot be avoided or resolved, the individual faces negative sanctions from at

least one of his partners in the form of withdrawal of affection and regard, or from the self in the form of shame or guilt. An everyday example
is the child whose parents seriously disagree on what expectations are
appropriate for his role.

Since sanctions for lack of conformity to a role expectation may be
imposed by people other than one's role partners, conflicting expectations on the part of these significant others may also be a source of
strain. A common example here is the mother-in-law who interferes
with her daughter's marital relations by attempting to redefine the role
expectations held by the young couple toward the positions of husband
and wife.

Intraposition and interposition consensus

Although the forms that lack of consensus within a system may take
follow logically from the previous discussion of the nature of interaction within systems, relatively little research has been devoted to consensus. As Gross, Mason, and McEachern (1958) have pointed out, most
role theorists until recently have assumed that the actors in a social system
agree on role expectations. This assumption has led to a dearth of information as to the determinants and consequences of varying degrees
of consensus. That a considerable range of disagreement exists for some
role expectations has recently been demonstrated by a number of re-
searchers.[1]

In a study of school superintendents, two forms of consensus were
investigated: *intraposition* and *interposition* consensus (Gross, Mason, &
McEachern, 1958). Intraposition consensus pertains to agreement among
the incumbents of a position on the expectations which apply to that
position. Interposition consensus pertains to agreement between incumbents and their role partners on the expectations which apply to
either of the two positions. For example, the extent to which school superintendents agree on the expectations attached to their own role is a
measure of intraposition consensus. The extent to which superintendents
and school board members agree on the expectations attached to the
role of superintendent, as well as to those attached to the role of school
board member, is a measure of interposition consensus. These two forms
of consensus are illustrated by Figures 15-1 and 15-2.

Two analyses, one between school systems and the other within a
particular school system, were performed. In the analysis across school
systems, a sample of incumbents of a particular position and a sample of
their role partners were taken from different school systems. Comparisons were made between the two samples and within each sample.
In the separate analyses of particular school systems, the investigators
studied consensus among the members of each school board and between
them as a group and the school superintendent.

[1]Davis, 1954; Hall, 1955; Borgatta, 1955; Rommetveit, 1955; Gross, Mason, & McEachern,
1958.

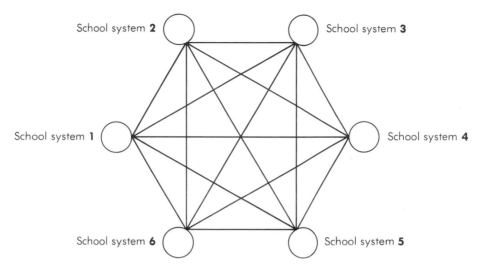

School system **2**   School system **3**

School system **1**   School system **4**

School system **6**   School system **5**

Figure 15 –1

Intraposition consensus: agreement among superintendents on the role category of superintendent. Circles represent superintendent's role.

One finding pertained to intraposition consensus among superintendents and school board members from different school systems on their respective roles. On a majority of role expectations, significant disagreement was found. Neither perfect agreement nor complete dissent was found on any item; agreement ranged between the two extremes. Agreement varied with several factors: (1) the content of the role expectation, (2) the degree of similarity in social backgrounds of the position occupants, and (3) the extent to which the position incumbents belonged to organizations of different size.

Intraposition consensus was also studied within particular school systems. By examining the consensus among school board members on their roles, it was possible to test the following hypothesis suggested by Riecken and Homans (1954): The degree of consensus in a group depends upon the similarity of the social and cultural backgrounds of the members and the length of time the members have been in interaction.

Similarities with respect to political-economic conservatism, religion, and education were related to agreement on role definitions. Also, persons who had desired to become school board members because of the political experience they would gain exhibited more consensus. On the other hand, not all kinds of similarity were associated with consensus. School board members of the same sex, those with similar attitudes about educational progressivism, and those with comparable feelings of civic duty did *not* agree more on expectations than other members who were more heterogeneous on these variables. The Riecken

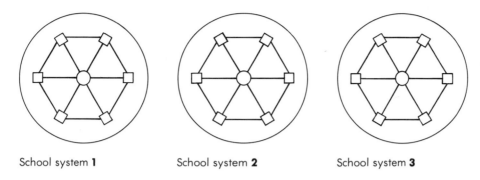

School system **1**   School system **2**   School system **3**

Figure 15–2

Interposition consensus within school systems: agreement between superintendent and board members on the role categories of superintendent and board member. Circles represent superintendent's role; squares represent board member's role.

and Homans hypothesis on degree of interaction received some support: the amount of interaction among school board members was greater when they agreed on role expectations.

Interposition consensus between school board members and their superintendents, however, was neither associated with similarity of background nor related to the amount of interaction between the board and the superintendent. Gross and his colleagues draw the following conclusion with respect to the relation between homogeneity of members of a group and their consensus on role expectations (Gross, Mason, & McEachern, 1958):

> Whether or not there is a relationship between the homogeneity of members of a group and their consensus on role expectations is dependent, first, on the characteristics on which the homogeneity measures are obtained, and second, on the positions occupied by the incumbents under examination. There have been no relationships demonstrated between the homogeneity of a superintendent and his board and consensus between them on the expectation for their two positions, so that we must conclude that there is no evidence that would support the homogeneity hypothesis for incumbents of two positions. Within the board, five significant relationships were found providing support for the hypothesis with respect to groups of incumbents of the same position. (P. 191)

The negative findings on the relation between interposition consensus and amount of interaction require further comment. They may be due to certain features of the particular social system investigated in this study. Gross and his associates note that interaction in this case was between nonprofessionals and professionals: members of a school board and the superintendent of schools. They suggest that a professional would be more likely to behave in accordance with the expectations of other professionals on school matters and would be relatively uninfluenced by the expectations of nonprofessionals. They also propose that interaction within the board is more informal than interaction between board and superintendent and suggest that informal interaction is generally more conducive to resolving conflict in role expectations than formal interaction.

The finding that homogeneity of social-cultural background was unrelated to interposition consensus may also stem from characteristics of the system studied. In fact, the reasoning that normally links those two variables may well not apply in this situation. The investigators note two ways in which homogeneity of background may be related to consensus. First, persons from similar cultural and social backgrounds will be subject to similar influences that in turn will produce more comparable role conceptions. Second, persons who are similar interact more with each other than with those who are dissimilar, and when they do interact, such similarity provides a basis for identification. Such a line of reasoning may be quite applicable to the case of school board members and may account for the relation between homogeneity and consensus for them; but the same reasoning may not apply to the interaction between a professional and a group of laymen. Even though a school superintendent is similar to his board members in such variables as sex, religion, and political-economic conservatism, he may well differ from them on educational matters by virtue of his professional training. Further, one would expect that identification, as it affects his educational views, would be with other professionals rather than with the nonprofessional members of his board.

Since the Gross, Mason, and McEachern study, a number of others have further investigated role consensus. One study of the roles of doctor, registered nurse, practical nurse, and patient in a tuberculosis sanitarium (Julian, 1962) tested three hypotheses. (1) The greater the training and preparation for a role, the greater will be the agreement among position occupants on their role and that of their role partners. In other words, because of their more extensive training, doctors and registered nurses were expected to agree more than practical nurses and patients on their own roles as well as those of their various partners. (2) Both intraposition and interposition consensus should vary according to the specificity with which the organization defines roles. Since the patients' behavior in the sanitarium was defined in more detail than the behavior of the staff, greatest agreement was expected on the patient role. (3) The position occupants who have the greatest communication and contact as determined by the organization of the social system should have the highest interposition consensus. More specifically, doctors and registered nurses should agree to a greater extent on their respective roles than doctors and practical nurses, since the chain of command in the hospital requires greater contact between the former staff members than the latter. While the data were not in complete accord with these three hypotheses, they supported them for the most part.

A study of role consensus between hospital administrators, hospital board members, and community leaders suggested that a particular role is described differently by the incumbent and his role partner to the extent that each has different linkages with other positions in the social system (Hanson, 1962). This suggestion was based on the idea that the more frequently persons interact cooperatively, the more obligated to each other they feel. To illustrate, hospital administrators are linked to and have more contact with various professional groups, including the medical staff; and board members are linked to and have more contact with community leaders. Consequently, it was found that in describing their role, administrators expressed more administrator obligations to the medical staff than did board members describing the administrator role. Similarly, hospital board members in describing their roles expressed more board-member obligations to community groups than did administrators in describing the board-member role.

Although direct studies of role consensus are relatively scarce, many of the studies of conformity to group norms discussed in Chapter 10 are probably applicable to this topic. It is likely that many factors which produce conformity also produce consensus on role expectations. For example, a study (Hall, 1955) of the aircraft commander role showed that role consensus is related to crew cohesion, and an investigation (Thomas, 1959) of role conceptions in small, medium, and large organizational units in a welfare agency found greater consensus in the smaller units.

STUDY QUESTIONS

3. *State four types of disagreement that may occur between a position incumbent and his role partner, and give examples from your own experience.*
4. *What other types of disagreement may occur?*
5. *What is meant by intraposition consensus and interposition consensus? What factors contribute to these types of consensus?*
6. *To what extent is the following hypothesis supported by evidence cited: The degree of consensus in a group depends on the similarity of the social and cultural backgrounds of the members and the length of time the members have been in interaction.*

In sum, two major types of role consensus that have been studied empirically are intraposition and interposition consensus. The former pertains to agreement among the incumbents of a position on the expectations that apply to that position. The latter pertains to agreement between position incumbents and their role partners on the expectations that apply to either of the two positions. These types of consensus have been studied most intensively with respect to the positions of school superintendents and school board members, both between school systems and within single school systems.

When comparing incumbents of the same position in different school systems, consensus was found to vary with (1) the content of the role expectation, (2) the degree of similarity in social backgrounds of the position occupants, and (3) the extent to which the position incumbents belonged to organizations of the same or different sizes. Within single school systems, similarity in certain attributes was associated with greater consensus among position incumbents, although similarity in other attributes was not. Interaction among school board members was greater when they agreed on expectations.

Interposition consensus between school board members and their superintendents was not associated with similarity of background or amount of interaction. Probably this lack of association occurs because the superintendent is oriented toward other professionals in defining role expectations for his position and those of board members. One hospital study suggested that the kinds of linkages of various positions within that social system affect the way in which role expectations are defined. In another hospital study, consensus has been found to be greater when training and preparation for a role is extensive and when roles are specifically defined by the organization; it is also greater for those positions whose occupants have the most contacts and most frequent communications with other individuals in the social system. Finally, it was suggested that many of the factors that produce conformity to group norms (see Chapter 10) also increase consensus on roles.

Consequences of various degrees of consensus

The Gross, Mason, and McEachern study also provides some empirical data on the consequences of various degrees of consensus. The findings, reported generally rather than in detail are as follows.

1. Members of school boards who have high consensus on their positions receive more gratification from their jobs. Such boards are also evaluated more favorably by their superintendents.
2. Interposition consensus between school board members and superintendent was not related to the job satisfaction of either. Interposition consensus did lead the superintendent to evaluate his school board more favorably, but it did not result in higher evaluation of the superintendent by board members.
3. In a later, different analysis, the degree to which a board conforms to the expectations held by superintendents *as a group* was associated with higher job satisfaction for the superintendent.

These findings must be evaluated against the background of the peculiarities of the system studied. The fact that members of a school board do not act as individuals but as a group would seem to underscore the need for consensus within their group. Where consensus was lacking between board members, one would expect interpersonal friction and difficulty in achieving group decisions—conditions which in other studies have been negatively associated with satisfaction in problem-solving groups. In contrast, as Gross and his associates point out, most of the functions which the superintendent carries out involve him in interaction with position incumbents other than school board members; e.g., teachers, principals, community leaders, etc. Hence his satisfaction in carrying out his duties is much less dependent on the character of his interaction with board members. The effects of interposition consensus on favorable or unfavorable evaluation of counterposition occupants, and the fact that the superintendent's satisfaction was dependent on the conformity of his board to professional expectations, again seem understandable in terms of the characteristics of school systems.

These findings support the argument that in a system involving professionals and nonprofessionals, the satisfaction of the professional is based in part on how well the nonprofessionals facilitate the achievement of professional goals. Boards within which there is agreement on educational matters and boards which conform to professional expectations on these matters would be expected to function in a manner that facilitates the achievements of goals defined by the superintendent as desirable.

Another investigation in a different social system tests the hypothesis that a high degree of interposition consensus facilitates relations between the occupant of a position and his role partner (Jacobsen, Charters, & Lieberman, 1951). Support for the hypothesis was found in a comparison of role conceptions of foremen and union stewards in industry. Foremen who saw the steward's role as the stewards did reported easy relations with their stewards. Similarly, stewards who defined the role of foreman in the same way as foremen did reported easy relations with their foremen.

STUDY QUESTION

7. *What consequences result from various degrees of consensus?*

Summary: Clarity and consensus

Expectations associated with roles in a social system vary in clarity and in the degree of consensus among persons. Clarity is mainly a function of the explicitness and specificity of expectations. Newly developed roles often lack clarity and thereby lead to role strain. Lack of clarity may also result from successive changes in a role. Although most research had been devoted to the clarity of expectations, ambiguity in the role category may also produce strain.

A position incumbent and his role partner may disagree in five ways: (1) as to what expectations are included in a given role, (2) as to the range of permitted or prohibited behavior, (3) as to the situations to which the role applies, (4) as to whether the expected behavior is mandatory or simply preferred, and (5) as to which expectation should be honored first. Disagreement on an incumbent's role may also occur between two or more of his partners or among persons outside the role set.

When incumbents of the same position in different school systems were compared, intraposition consensus was found to vary with (1) the content of the role expectation, (2) the degree of similarity in the incumbents' social backgrounds, and (3) the extent to which the incumbents belonged to organizations of the same or different sizes. Within single school systems, similarity in certain attributes was associated with greater consensus among position incumbents, although similarity in other attributes was not.

Probably because the superintendent is oriented toward other professionals in defining role expectations for his own position and for his school board, interposition consensus between board members and their superintendents was not associated with similarity of background or the amount of interaction they had. In hospital settings, consensus is greater for those roles having extensive training and preparation, for those that are specifically defined, and for those positions whose occupants interact most frequently with others. Linkages of various positions within a social system are likely to affect the way in which role expectations are defined. Many of the factors that produce conformity to group norms probably increase consensus on roles.

Satisfaction with one's role is contingent upon the type and amount of consensus, and the particular social system to which the role belongs. School board members having high consensus were more satisfied; this follows from the fact that agreement is necessary to successful performance. Interposition consensus was not associated with higher satisfaction for the school superintendent, who must relate to many role partners with diverse views. In a different social system, high interposition consensus between foremen and union stewards on their roles in industry facilitated relations between these role partners.

CONFLICTING AND COMPETING EXPECTATIONS WITHIN A ROLE

Another source of role strain lies in conflicting or competing expectations that make up a role. Such conflict or competition may exist within a particular role sector or among a number of sectors of a particular role. Conflict or competition within a role sector pertains to expectations regarding behavior toward the same role partner; an example is a mother who knows that she should not hurt her child but who also knows that she must discipline him. Conflict or competition between sectors involves different role partners: a woman with a new baby may find that his demands on her time interfere with her obligations to other family members.

Conflict arises when one expectation requires behavior which in some degree is incompatible with the behavior required by another expectation within that sector or in another sector of the particular role. The actions may be physically incompatible because one action is the opposite of the other. They may be socially incompatible because they are not expected of the same person; or finally, they may be psychologically incompatible because they require the actor to adopt opposite psychological sets (Nye, 1961). To illustrate the latter, on the occasions that a mother treats some minor accident experienced by her child, such as removing a painful splinter, she may have difficulty assuming the attitude of clinical detachment necessary for performing the operation.

Competition between expectations occurs when the actor cannot adequately honor both expectations because of limitations of time. Conflict and competition, both within a role sector and between role sectors, will be discussed below.

Conflict and competition within a role sector

Several examples of conflict and competition within a sector involve the relation of a professional person toward patients. Lee (1944) has distinguished three facets of the physician's role: (1) He is a scientist-warrior on the frontiers of knowledge, (2) he is a technician-savior of the sick, and (3) he is a small business retailer of knowledge which he has purchased at considerable cost to himself. Wardwell (1952) has noted a similar set of elements within the role of the chiropractor. While aggressive bill collecting is consistent with the small-business-retailer aspects of the doctor's role, it is inconsistent with the image of the gentle healer or the altruistic scientist.

Schulman (1958) has noted somewhat similar conflicting elements in the nursing role. He observes that on the one hand, nurses themselves, as well as the general public, expect nurses to behave as mother surrogates whose obligations run the gamut from washing a patient's feet to listening sympathetically to his innermost feelings. On the other hand, they are also defined as medical specialists or healers whose duties are to perform the technical tasks specifically necessary to combat the patient's affliction and to restore him to society. The basic conflict is between a set of expectations characterized by affect, sympathy, and emotional involvement, and another set involving restriction of these feelings. Schulman (1958) summarizes his observations on the conflict between these two facets of the nurse's role as follows:

> In terms of a single broad variable — the presence or lack of affect — the roles of mother surrogate and healer are seen to be in conflict. In its developmental or historical aspect there has been a transition from behavior expectations associated with the ancient ideal of the woman and mother toward those of the technical healing specialist, a transition never easy or simple. Each of the steps leading to the dominance of the healer role is marked by opposition, especially from nursing itself, but also from associated groups and from the lay public. In its present phase this role conflict is evidenced in repeated attempts to "redefine" nursing and the great emphasis now placed on "just

where the nurse fits" in her relations with other occupational groups and in the community. Even more, one sees the conflict in stark evidence when the question is repeated a thousandfold in American schools of nursing and at every meeting of nurse-educators: "Just where are we going?" (P. 357)

Undoubtedly an examination of the elements in other treatment roles, such as those of the clinical psychologist or the social worker, would reveal a similar configuration of conflicting elements.

Seeman (1953) cites an example concerning school superintendents which involves competition in the form of a time-allocation problem. He observed that teachers expected their superintendents to engage in public relations activities which would ensure adequate school financing and, in particular, increase the salary level of teachers. At the same time they also felt that a superintendent should spend time with teachers, visiting classrooms, etc. Superintendents felt that because of limitations of time they could not adequately meet both expectations.

Conflict and competition between role sectors

Turning to conflict and competition between expectations from different role sectors, we can again point to the role of the school superintendent. Gross, Mason, and McEachern (1958) note that a superintendent must interact with teachers, school board members, PTA members, civic leaders, etc. Often the demands of each relation raise problems of time allocation, as well as difficulties in meeting diametrically opposed expectations. One such conflict which they investigated in some detail was the conflict between the salary demands of teachers and parents on the one hand, and members of the city council and taxpayer associations on the other. Whereas a majority of the teachers and parents were perceived by the school superintendents as wanting them to fight for maximum salary increases, a majority of the members of the city council and the taxpayers associations were perceived as wanting them to "hold the line" or "be reasonable in their salary budget recommendations."

Another example of competition due to time allocation may be somewhat more familiar to the college student acquainted with university professors. The professor is expected not only to teach, but in addition to engage in scholarly research and to devote some time to community service. To the extent that all three of these expectations concerning the professor's duties are held by his dean, this is an example of competition within a single role sector. Actually, however, these demands arise in part from various role partners: his fellow professors and colleagues in his own discipline particularly expect him to do research, while members of the community in which the university is located also make direct demands upon his time.

STUDY QUESTION

8. *Give examples of and distinguish between the following: (a) conflict and competition within a role sector; (b) conflict and competition between role sectors.*

In sum, a common source of role strain lies in conflicting or competing expectations that make up a role. Conflict or competition may occur within a role sector (pertaining to only one type of role partner) or between role sectors (pertaining to more than one type of role partner). Conflict arises when one expectation requires behavior that in some degree is incompatible with another; competition occurs when an actor cannot honor two or more expectations because of limitations of time.

SIMULTANEOUS POSITION OCCUPANCY

Competition between roles

Normally an actor occupies a number of positions at any one time. His behavior is consequently subject to a number of sets of expectations. Some of these may be in conflict or competition. Gross and his colleagues have noted that school superintendents suffer strain over allocating time between their roles as husband and father and their role as head of a school system. Whereas a majority of the superintendents studied indicated that their wives expected them to spend most of their evenings with their family or friends, over half of them stated that parents and PTA groups expected them to devote most of their evenings to school and community business.

Most students do not have to go beyond their own experience to observe another illustration of competing role demands. In addition to meeting the expectations associated with the position of student, they may also encounter expectations associated with such positions as husband or wife, son or daughter, employee, sorority or fraternity member, etc. Not only does this result in strain within the individual, but it undoubtedly interferes with the effective functioning of the educational system.

Conflict between roles

Burchard's study of role conflict for military chaplains provides an excellent illustration of conflicting expectations encountered in two incompatible roles, those of a religious leader and a military officer. In particular this poses a problem in the chaplain's relations with enlisted men, with whom he mainly deals (Burchard, 1954):

> Relations with enlisted men are of great concern to chaplains, since enlisted men form the largest single audience toward which chaplains direct their behavior. All chaplains are aware that the fact that they are officers poses a barrier to primary relations with enlisted men. By and large chaplains are probably more conscious of rank than any other group of officers in the armed forces, mainly because of their ambivalent attitude toward it. The desire to become an integral part of the military heirarchy, to become accepted as one of the fellows, is very strong. On the other hand a priest, minister, or pastor is one who is set apart from the group, a leader of the flock, not just one of them. But a good leader must be accessible; he must not be too distant from his flock; he must be on good personal relations with those he is leading. A

military officer, however, must not be familiar with his men. His ability as a leader is presumed to depend, in part, on his ability to keep at a distance from his men. The chaplain, being both a military officer and a clergyman, must somehow come to grips with the problem of carrying on an effective religious ministry for enlisted personnel and at the same time of retaining his status as an officer. (P. 532)

Similar incompatibilities between the roles performed by elected public officials have been observed (Mitchell, 1958). Partisan behavior expected of the party official may conflict in letter as well as spirit with the impartial behavior expected of a judge or administrator. Another study has described a role conflict between attributes and expectations associated with the role of successful insurance agent and the role of friend within a group of agents (Wispé, 1955).

On the level of the social system, Getzels and Guba (1954) have suggested that the severity of role conflict arising from multiple position occupancy will vary with two factors: (1) the relative incompatibility of the expectations involved, and (2) the rigor with which these expectations are defined in a given situation.

For example, if we were to examine three roles, those of wife, mother, and employee, we would find that the roles of wife and mother would contain many more common expectations than either would have with the role of employee. We would expect that a woman who occupied the roles of wife and mother would experience less conflict between roles than if she were to occupy, say, the roles of wife and employee. In the latter case she would be under considerably greater strain because of the greater incompatibility of these roles. Moreover, their conflict would be accentuated if her employer and her husband held rigid expectations as to her conduct.

STUDY QUESTION

9. *Under what conditions does simultaneous occupation of more than one role category result in role strain? What factors determine its severity?*

In sum, to the extent that an actor simultaneously occupies two or more positions, he may be subject to conflicting or competing expectations. Competition occurs if the expectations place demands upon his time that cannot be met. Conflict is present if the expectations associated with the different positions are incompatible. The severity of conflict is a function of the relative incompatibility of the expectations and the rigor with which they are defined.

DISCONTINUITIES ENCOUNTERED IN STATUS PASSAGE

As previously observed, role strain arises in a particular system in part because the positions are so organized that it is possible for a person to occupy simultaneously two or more positions which subject him to conflicting expectations. Strain may arise where a system is so organized that the positions an actor *successively* occupies involve conflicting expectations. Two such forms of position shift or *status passage* may be identified: long-term and short-term.

Benedict (1938), in a now classic discussion, has illustrated the problematic aspects of the former type of shift in our society by demonstrating that role expectations associated with the position of child are often diametrically opposed in certain respects to those associated with the position of adult. She notes that the child is expected to be sexless, non-responsible, and submissive, whereas the adult role requires just the opposite traits of behavior. A person growing to maturity not only must learn new role behavior, but at the same time must unlearn opposite kinds of behavior. Certainly a great deal of strain associated with the passage from childhood to adulthood stems from such discontinuities between the two roles. A similar analysis could be made of the transition from the adult role to that of the aged, from worker to foreman, or from enlisted man to commissioned officer.

One study notes certain discontinuities experienced by the professional as he moves from the position of professional in civilian life to that of professional in the military (Bidwell, 1961). The degree of strain experienced by the actors in changing positions is dependent on more than the degree of disparity between the expectations involved. In addition, it is a function of the certainty, clarity, and abruptness of the transition, as well as the relative desirability of the positions involved.

More recently Shutler (1958) has called attention to short-term shifts leading to conflict. Examples are found in the transition from masculine aggressiveness on the ball field to dutiful obedience in the home for the ten-year-old, or the transition from aggressive career activities during the day to feminine submissiveness in the evening for the career woman.

SYSTEM ORGANIZATION AND ROLE STRAIN

One additional characteristic of social systems associated with role strain might be mentioned. Systems are so organized that the actors occupying one position are adequately rewarded for their conformity to the expectations of persons occupying other positions. This element is inherent in the previously discussed reciprocal nature of role expectations: obligations of the actors occupying a particular position are the rights of those occupying a counterposition. From the standpoint of a given position, a system may be so organized that the rights associated with the position may not be sufficiently rewarding to motivate incumbents to carry out their obligations. In such a situation the incumbents feel they are being taken advantage of, being unfairly treated, etc., and this may generate ambivalence toward meeting the expectations of the role partner. This condition is generally followed by attempts to restructure the relation in such a way as to equalize the rights and obligations associated with the two positions.

Fulfillment of role obligations is most often insufficiently rewarded where role expectations are unique, since in this type of expectation the reward for conformity stems only from the partner. In the case of widely shared expectations, the general approval of others for conforming to cultural and subcultural expectations provides some reward even when the partner does not adequately reciprocate. To illustrate, even though a wife is not meeting some of the cultural expectations associated with the position of wife, such as being an adequate homemaker, a husband is not likely to develop ambivalence about his obligation to support her, because others strongly sanction this obligation. However, strain may readily arise in connection with violation of complementary expectations unique to a particular married couple, such as the mutual expectation that a visit to one spouse's parents will be followed by a visit to the other's parents.

The possibility of similar strain occurring in connection with cultural and subcultural role expectations should not be minimized by the foregoing comments. This is particularly likely at a time when role expectations are going through a process of change. Studies of the changing roles of husband and wife have shown that college men and women overemphasize the rights associated with the marital position of their own sex and underemphasize its obligations (Kirkpatrick, 1955).

It is not always the person who receives fewer rewards in a relation who experiences role strain. Because of what has been called the *norm of reciprocity* (Gouldner, 1960), in many situations occupants of positions where obligations do not match rights may experience a certain amount of guilt, which contributes to role strain (Evan, 1962).

The above examples of role strain have been concerned with strain arising out of inequalities in role rights and obligations. Another source of strain occurs in systems where the content of the roles leads to continuous interference on the part of the occupants of one position with the goal achievement of the occupants of one or more other positions (Foskett, 1960). An example is the system of relations which provides the structure for a competitive game. In such games the expectations are that one actor will attempt to frustrate the goal achievement of another, as in bridge or football. Such conflict is intentionally built into the system of a game. Often, however, such conflicts develop in nongame systems. Few systems are so perfectly integrated as to avoid entirely strain arising from this source.

Finally, Martin (1961), in a penetrating analysis of structural strain in a psychiatric hospital, has noted a system feature resulting in strain. Where two role sets have a position in common, the stage is set for the development of coalitions of two versus one in the triads so formed. To illustrate, the patient is a role partner of both the nurse and the psychiatric resident physician. Under such circumstances, two of the three parties may combine to control or block the goal achievement of the third party, or one party may play the other two off against each other to his own advantage. This maneuver is illustrated in a family system by the child who asks his father's permission to attend a movie but prefaces it with the information that "It's okay with mother if it's all right with you."

This discussion of features of social systems which lead an individual to experience role strain should serve to emphasize that many problems in interpersonal relations are a function of the social system rather than unique features of the "personalities" of the system participants. Similarly, reduction of such strain is more than a matter of individual dynamics or processes—a point to be elaborated in the next chapter.

STUDY QUESTIONS

10. *Under what conditions does successive occupation of different roles contribute to role strain?*

11. *Enumerate several organizational aspects of social systems that contribute to role strain.*

In sum, role strain may arise when the rights associated with a position are not sufficiently rewarding to motivate actors to carry out the obligations of the position. This is most likely where role expectations lie toward the unique end of the continuum or where expectations are going through a process of change. Role strain also occurs where roles are related in such a way that conformity to the expectations of one role interferes with goal achievement by the role partner. Finally, strains may develop when the system permits interpersonal maneuvering to block the goal achievement of one or more members of the system.

SUMMARY: ROLE STRAIN AND THE SOCIAL SYSTEM

On the level of the social system, role strain results not from the characteristics of the actors themselves, but from the characteristics of the relations among actors. To the extent that expectations are held in common and enacted by the members of a group, the system is likely to function smoothly. Role strain occurs when group members do not hold expectations in common or when they behave contrary to them. It is likely to result under a number of conditions.

1. Role strain may result when expectations are unclear and consensus is low. Lack of clarity in the role category may also produce strain. A position incumbent and his role partner may disagree in five different ways: (*a*) as to what expectations are included in a given role, (*b*) as to the range of permitted or prohibited behavior, (*c*) as to the situations to which the role applies, (*d*) as to whether the expected behavior is mandatory or simply preferred, and (*e*) as to which should be honored first when an expectation conflicts with another. Two or more role partners of a position incumbent may define his role differently, creating strain for him, or persons outside the role relation may disagree with the role definitions of the incumbent and his partner. Consensus is likely to vary with the content of expectations, the similarity in the background of position occupants, the size of the organization, the amount of prepara-

tion for the position, the extent to which the organization specifically defines expectations, the frequency of interaction between position occupant and others, and the type of linkages between positions in a system. Many of the factors that produce conformity to group norms are likely to be associated with role consensus also.

2. A second source of role strain lies in the conflicting or competing expectations that make up a role. Conflict or competition may occur within a role sector, in which case it pertains to only one type of role partner, or between role sectors, in which case it pertains to more than one type of partner. Conflict arises when one expectation requires behavior that in some degree is incompatible with another; competition occurs when an actor cannot honor two or more expectations because of limitations of time.

3. Discontinuities in the successive positions occupied by an actor are a third source of strain. These may involve long-term shifts from one role to another as a result of increasing age or experience, or relative short-terms shifts occurring in day-to-day situations.

4. The simultaneous occupation of two or more positions is a fourth source of role strain. The severity of conflict resulting from multiple position occupancy is a function of the relative incompatibility of the expectations and the rigor with which they are defined. Competition occurs if the expectations place demands upon the actor that cannot be met.

5. A fifth source of role strain results from certain organizational aspects of the social system. The rights associated with a position may not be sufficiently rewarding to motivate actors to carry out the obligations of that position. This condition will lead to efforts to change the system.

6. Strain also occurs where roles are related in such a way that conformity to the expectations of one role interferes with goal achievement by the role partner.

7. Finally, strains may develop when the system permits interpersonal maneuvering to block the goal achievement of one or more members of the system.

Personality and Role Strain

So far, we have been examining the characteristics of a social system that lead to role strain and interfere with the smooth, almost automatic quality of interaction between persons. Similar disturbances may stem from characteristics of individual actors which interfere with role enactment or performance, or from the fact that a role to which an individual is assigned may be readily performed but is not suited to his needs.

Individual characteristics that lead to difficulty in meeting role expectations fall into three classes. First, the actor may lack certain abilities and attributes necessary for successful enactment of the roles involved. Second, he may have a self concept contrary to the role expectations he is supposed to enact. Finally, he may have certain attitudes and needs that interfere with the enactment of a particular role.

INDIVIDUAL ATTRIBUTES, ROLE ENACTMENT, AND ROLE STRAIN

Individual attributes that facilitate or interfere with successful role enactment may be either personal qualities such as the individual's physical characteristics, abilities, skills, or personality traits, or socially conferred attributes such as an academic degree, a license, or other evidence of certification.

These may be related to role enactment in two ways. The particular attribute may directly facilitate or interfere with the expected behavior, or it may merely be an attribute traditionally associated with a role. The latter is important because expectations that others have concerning the occupants of a particular position refer not only to behavior but to attributes of the individual as well. For instance, those who "look the part" often function more effectively in a given situation than those who do not. Consider, for example, the case of a young, boyish-looking physician. It could be argued that by virtue of his youthful vigor and his up-to-date training in medical school, he can function more effectively in his role as physician than an older colleague. Yet the fact that persons think of a physician as an older, more fatherly person may well diminish the confidence he inspires in his patients and reduce his effectiveness. Although this illustration is purely speculative, a study of the academic profession indicates that those who are judged as "looking like professors" are also judged as more successful in this role (Ellis & Keedy, 1960).

More often a given attribute may interfere directly with the role behavior itself. On this point illustrations are legion. The boy with the puny build on the football field, the student of mediocre abilities in graduate school, and the shy, retiring person in the role of a salesman are all cases in point.

As Inkeles has noted, there is considerable evidence that particular positions attract individuals whose personalities allow them to perform the role more readily, presumably with less strain (Inkeles, 1963). Students high in authoritarianism are found in greater proportions in military academies and typical Southern colleges (Stern, Stein, & Bloom, 1956). Hard-core Nazis have been found to be more given to projection, to extreme antisocial sadism, and to contempt of tenderness (Dicks, 1950). These personality traits presumably enable them to perform the Nazi role more adequately. Among Soviet Russian refugees, professional persons and administrators were found to have personality characteristics compatible with their occupations (Inkeles, Hanfmann, & Beier, 1958).

A number of studies, while not measuring role strain directly, do include a measure of role performance. If poor performance may be regarded as indicating role strain, these investigations provide some evidence concerning the contribution of personality to role strain. Two closely related investigations in a hospital setting may first be cited (Gilbert & Levinson, 1957*a*, 1957*b*). Mental hospitals long had a custodial orientation toward patients that emphasized a highly controlled setting concerned mainly with detention and safekeeping. Patients were thought of in stereotyped terms, as being categorically different from normal persons, totally irrational and unpredictable. More recently, many hospitals abandoned this orientation for a humanistic one that conceives of the hospital as a therapeutic community rather than a custodial institution. Patients are viewed in more psychological and less moralistic terms, and the attempt is made to give them more individual freedom and responsibility.

We might anticipate that a hospital aide with an authoritarian personality would find the custodial orientation more compatible than the humanistic one. This is supported by the finding that in three hospitals, measures of the extent to which each staff member subscribed to a custodial orientation correlated between .67 and .76 with his F-scale scores, a measure of his authoritarianism. Evidence was also presented that in a hospital with a humanistic orientation, those nurse's aides who had custodial orientations were rated by their supervisors as less able to relate constructively to patients.

Another investigation was concerned with the relation between the extent to which a student has an authoritarian orientation and how well he can perform in a university which emphasizes abstract analysis, relativity of values and judgment rather than fixed standards, and a personal, humanistic orientation rather than an impersonal one—all values rather incompatible with authoritarianism (Stern, Stein, & Bloom, 1956). It was found that by the end of the freshman year, 20 percent of the students high in authoritarianism had withdrawn, but none of those low in authoritarianism had done so. Complaints of the dropouts indicated that their actions were taken because of the conflict between their personalities and the requirements of the particular college they had entered.

SELF CONCEPT, ROLE ENACTMENT, AND ROLE STRAIN

As will be discussed in more detail later in the chapters on socialization, an individual attempts to behave and tries to get others to behave toward him in ways that are consistent with the picture he has of himself—his self concept. A girl who views herself as prim and proper might well have the physical characteristics, the skill, and the personality traits congenial to the role of a taxi dancehall girl. Nevertheless she might suffer considerable strain in this role because her behavior and that of her patrons would run counter to her self concept. This illustration suggests that an individual may be inhibited from enacting socially undesirable roles where such roles involve behavior contrary to his self conception. In fact, Reckless, Dinitz, and Murray (1956) have suggested that the self conceptions of "good" boys in a high-delinquency area serve as insulators against engaging in delinquent behavior. According to this study, those boys defined themselves in such a way that engaging in delinquent behavior was incompatible with the definitions. Of course, the same principle may also operate to support a socially undesirable role. The lower-class boy who defines himself as a "tough guy who knows all the angles" may well find it difficult to play the "good boy" in terms of middle-class standards.

ATTITUDES, NEEDS, ROLE ENACTMENT, AND ROLE STRAIN

We have already defined the term attitude as a predisposition to respond in a particular way toward a specified class of objects. Such tendencies to act may facilitate or hinder role enactment. A person who tends to accept the dictates of authority figures would be able to play a subordinate role without strain, while another who tends to reject authority might well suffer considerable strain in such a role. To use another illustration, a person with attitudes unfavorable to Negroes would be quite likely to feel uncomfortable in the role of host at an interracial gathering.

Finally, there are instances of role strain arising not so much because the person is unable to live up to its expectations, but because the role does not allow for the expression of his needs, does not require him to make use of his skills and abilities, or is not suited to his personality and temperament. In these instances strain does not arise from inadequacies in the individual, but from his dissatisfaction with the role. For example, a person with strong achievement needs may be frustrated by an occupational role that does not provide him with attractive opportunities for advancement. Or a person in an occupational role which allows him little contact with people may be dissatisfied because he is deprived of the social conversation which he greatly enjoys.

In sum, role strain may result from the ways in which certain characteristics of individual actors interfere with role performance, or from the fact that a role to which an individual is assigned may be readily performed but is not suited to his needs. An individual attribute may facilitate or interfere with the production of expected behavior, or it may merely be an attribute traditionally associated with a role. In the latter case, the absence of the attribute leads role partners to believe that the person cannot adequately perform the role. Role enactment may also result in strain if the role expectations are incompatible with the self concept of the incumbent.

Culture and Role Strain

In recent years there has been an increasing awareness that where the system of beliefs or ideology shared by the actors in a situation runs counter to role expectations, strain results at those points in the system. It has frequently been noted that the strong emphasis on equality in the ideology of American society places strain on role relations that involve inequality.

In the military service, for instance, a certain strain has been noted in the relations between various ranks, because military protocol involves a denial of equality. A subordinate in interaction with a superior in the military hierarchy is expected to show deference in a variety of ways. He must salute first, give way to his superior should the latter wish to pass him on a stairway, stand when the superior enters a room, and use such deferential terms as "sir" when addressing him. Persons who have not internalized the nonequalitarian ideology of the military subculture find such role behavior uncomfortable, and the discomfort often leads to subterfuges designed to avoid acts of deference. A newly enlisted soldier may frequently avoid saluting an officer by studiously looking the other way when an officer passes. A newly commissioned officer may feel somewhat sheepish about demanding deference and thus may not "notice" this intentional slight.

Such problems are not confined to the military. Because of the pervasiveness of the equalitarian element in the American ideology, almost any superior-subordinate relation will suffer some strain. Examples are the foreman-worker relation in industry, the doctor-nurse relation in medicine, the student-teacher relation in education, and the male-female and parent-child relation in the family.

When the ideology itself contains conflicting elements, some conflict between ideology and role expectations is inevitable. Individuals in occupations such as medicine, social work, the ministry, and the teaching profession are exposed to a number of ideological elements emphasizing service to humanity. Yet at the same time they share with other members of our society the ideals of materialistic success. Attempts on the part of the members of such professions to bolster their economic position are consistent with the latter ideological elements, but may be in conflict with the former.

STUDY QUESTIONS

12. *Discuss the various ways in which characteristics of individuals may produce role strain.*

13. *Under what circumstances does the ideology of a culture produce role strain?*

Summary and Conclusions

Role strain arises whenever circumstances make it difficult for an actor to conform to role expectations. Sources of strain stem from several levels: the social system, individual personality dynamics, and the culture. On the level of the social system, role strain results not from the attributes of the actors themselves, but from the characteristics of the relations among actors. Such strain occurs when group members do not hold expectations in common or when they behave contrary to them.

Role strain on the level of the social system occurs under the following seven conditions:

1. When expectations are unclear and consensus on them is low, or when the role category is unclear. Disagreement in various forms may occur between an incumbent and his role partner, between two or more partners of a position incumbent, or between persons outside the relation and the incumbents of the positions.

2. When expectations that make up a role are incompatible, or when they compete with each other. Conflict or competition may occur within a role sector, a case which pertains to only one type of role partner, or between role sectors, a case which pertains to more than one type of partner.

3. When there are discontinuities in positions successively occupied by an actor. These may involve a long-term shift from one role to another as a result of increasing age or experience, or relatively short-term shifts occurring in day-to-day situations.

4. When two or more positions containing incompatible or competing expectations are simultaneously occupied.

5. When the rights associated with a position may not be sufficiently rewarding to motivate actors to carry out the obligations of that position.

6. When roles are related in such a way that conformity to the expectations of one role interferes with goal achievement by the role partner.

7. When the social system permits interpersonal maneuvering that blocks the goal achievement of one or more members of the system.

On the level of the individual personality, role strain may result from several conditions. First, an individual attribute may facilitate or interfere with the production of expected behavior, or it may merely be an attribute traditionally associated with a role. Second, role enactment may result in strain if the role expectations are incompatible with the self concept of the incumbent. Third, a role to which a person is assigned may be within his capabilities, but not suited to his needs.

At the cultural level, strain may result where ideology runs counter to role expectations. Also, when the ideology itself contains conflicting elements, some conflict between ideology and role expectations is inevitable.

chapter sixteen

RESOLUTION OF ROLE STRAIN

So far role behavior has been analyzed from the standpoint of strain. The discussion has shown how social system, personality, and cultural variables may lead individuals in a group to experience conflict within themselves and with other actors. The picture of this aspect of human interaction would be incomplete without a description of the various mechanisms and processes that resolve internal and external conflict and that produce more smoothness in interaction than one might expect from the previous chapter. Analysis will again be made on three levels: the social system, the personality, and the culture.

Social System Variables and the Resolution of Role Conflict

MECHANISMS FOR INCREASING CONSENSUS

Role strain often builds up to a crisis which motivates the participants to seek a clarification of rights and obligations existing between them. Such attempt may range from informal "heart to heart" talks in small systems to elaborate negotiating committees in large systems. As problems of clarity and consensus increase, either because of the growing size or complexity of the system or because of rapid changes, social machinery evolves to minimize any tendency toward lack of consensus and to deal with problems related to lack of consensus when they do arise.

Such machinery takes a number of forms. First, special positions and subsystems emerge to cope with the problem of lack of consensus. This is often the major function of coordinating and liaison committees in organizations. Second, more active efforts are made to formalize relations by specifying in manuals of operation how each position occupant is to behave toward other occupants in the system. Accompanying this are techniques for ensuring the standard socialization of position occupants. Elaborate selection procedures, orientation and training programs, periodic refresher courses, etc., become a part of the system. Finally, rituals and ceremonies develop which function not only to increase identification with group goals, but which serve periodically to reinforce agreement on the rights and obligations of each person in the system.

REDUCTION OF CONFLICTING ROLE EXPECTATIONS

Social systems also have features that serve to reduce strain resulting from conflicting role expectations. These include certain structural features of the system, the establishment of priorities for different role obligations, special rules that protect actors in certain positions from sanctions, and the merging of conflicting roles.

Hierarchy of obligations

Merton (1957*a*), Parsons (1951), and Toby (1952) have pointed out that role obligations in a social system are arranged in a hierarchy. The participants in a system recognize that certain obligations take precedence over others. Where obligations have equal priorities, strain arises, as indicated in Figure 16–1. But if obligations associated with one role category take precedence, little strain arises, as indicated in Figure 16–2. In the case of a death in the family, for instance, obligations toward one's kin to aid the bereaved, to help in funeral arrangements, etc., take precedence over occupational role obligations.

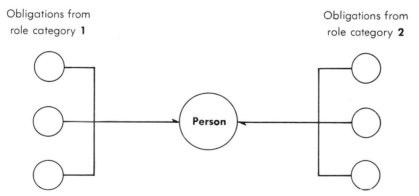

Obligations from
role category **1**

Obligations from
role category **2**

Person

Figure 16–1

An individual experiences role strain because different role obligations of equal strength orient his behavior in opposite directions.

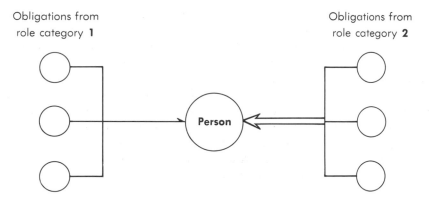

Figure 16–2
**Role strain is minimized because obliga-
tions from role category 2 are stronger
than and take precedence over those from
role category 1.**

The reader can appreciate how frequently this type of conflict resolution appears if he examines the excuses that he and others use in situations of role conflict. The commonly heard form is "I would like to but I
can't because. . . ," followed by assertion of a higher priority. Sample
excuses are "I would like to go to the dance with you but I have to study
for an exam," or "I can't be present for the exam next week because I have
to report for an Army physical." The excuse allows the individual to
resolve a conflict because both persons in these instances accept a given
order of priority. A study of the maneuvers used in role conflict situations
provides some evidence on this point (Bloombaum, 1961). Subjects frequently employed such excuses and perceived that they would not have
to conform to expectations and that they had avoided disapproval.

In part, such a hierarchy of role obligations reflects the value structure
of the group. Role obligations high in the hierarchy are functionally
related to values deemed important by the group. In part it also reflects
the fact that some roles are more resistant to modification in instances of
conflict, because to change these roles would disrupt the system to a
greater extent. To illustrate the latter, Nye (1961) has recently suggested
that the role of a woman as a wife and mother, which is in conflict with her
role as an employee, is being modified because of the relative inflexibility
of the employee role. Bates (1956) has also observed that roles vary in the
extent to which they may be modified by conflict.

Structural features that reduce strain

Several structural features of systems that reduce role strain are differences in the power of various role partners to exert sanctions, restrictions
on multiple position occupancy, and spatial and temporal separation of
situations involving conflicting role expectations.

As observed earlier, the intensity of role strain experienced by an actor may be a function of conflict in expectations between an incumbent and his role partner or conflict in expectations between two or more role partners. In many such instances an individual will experience relatively little strain because of a disparity in power between those who hold the conflicting expectations. If one of the partners is able to apply only very weak sanctions, his expectations are likely to be disregarded. The pervasiveness of power differences in most systems prevents much strain that would otherwise arise from role conflict.

Restriction on multiple position occupancy is another feature of systems that reduces role conflict which might otherwise arise. Where the expectations associated with two positions are in conflict, norms may prohibit a person from occupying both positions simultaneously. For example, nepotism rules in many organizations generally specify that no more than one person from a family may be employed within the organization or within a particular department of the organization. This prevents possible conflict between an actor's occupational and kinship obligations.

Temporal and spatial separation of situations involving conflicting role expectations is another system feature that reduces role conflict. While he is on the job during the working day, the male is exposed to the expectations associated with his occupational position. But for most occupations, these expectations do not operate in a home during the evening hours, where they might conflict with expectations associated with such positions as husband and father. Where temporal and spatial separation of such situations breaks down, however, the individual suddenly becomes aware of the conflict arising from occupancy of several positions. This appeared to be the case in a series of disasters studied by Killian (1952). He states:

> When catastrophe strikes a community, many individuals find that the latent conflict between ordinarily nonconflicting group loyalties suddenly becomes apparent and that they are faced with the dilemma of making an immediate choice between various roles. . . . The choice required of the greatest number of individuals was the one between the family and other groups, principally the employment group or the community. Especially in Texas City, many men were at work away from their families when disaster struck and presented a threat to both "the plant" and "the home." In all the communities there were individuals such as policemen, firemen, and public utilities workers, whose loved ones were threatened by the same disaster that demanded their services as "trouble shooters." Even persons who had no such definite roles to play in time of catastrophe were confronted with the alternatives of seeing after only their own primary groups or of assisting in the rescue and relief of any of the large number of injured persons, regardless of identity. Indeed, only the unattached person in the community was likely to be free of such a conflict. (Pp. 310–311)

In another disaster study, however, workers who were more spatially separated from their homes appeared to experience less strain over the potential conflict between family and work obligations than workers who were closer to their homes (White, 1962).

STUDY QUESTIONS

1. *What mechanisms exist within the system for increasing consensus on conflicting role expectations?*
2. *How does a hierarchy of role obligations reduce strain?*
3. *What are several structural features of a social system that reduce role strain?*

Protection from sanctions

An actor who is especially subject to sanctions because his position exposes him to conflicting role expectations is likely to be protected by the system. He may be insulated from observation, a special tolerance may be established for his actions, he may be protected from reprisals by those whose expectations he violates, or he may join with other occupants of the same position and develop patterns of concerted action.

Merton (1957a) has pointed out that where role partners have conflicting expectations concerning a position incumbent, the incumbent may be protected by insulating him from observation. Lawyers, physicians, ministers, and priests are often accorded the privilege of withholding from police or other authorities information given to them by their clients, patients, or parishioners. A lawyer, for instance, cannot be forced to divulge information he possesses which would indicate that his client is guilty. If he were required, as is any other citizen, to tell the court all he knows of a crime, he would find himself in conflict with the expectation appropriate to a lawyer that he act in the interest of his client. Not all factors that prevent observability have emerged because of role strain: they may originate for quite unrelated reasons. For example, in American society, teenagers and adults have different expectations for many areas of adolescent behavior. Although strain over these conflicting expectations is sometimes avoided by deliberate concealment, observability is also restricted by the pattern of association along age lines in our society. That is, much adolescent behavior takes place out of sight and hearing of adults.

Arrangements that result in high visibility, however, may win for the position occupant a special tolerance which thereby reduces strain (Merton, 1957a). Where the actors in a system are all aware that an occupant is subject to incompatible role expectations, they may tolerate his failure to meet either one or the other set of expectations, or perhaps both. Here, high visibility of a conflict may result in the individual being able to fashion a solution which is most satisfactory to himself without incurring negative sanctions from either side. Or he may avoid conflict by doing nothing, on the grounds that it is up to both sides to reconcile their differences.

Where a system is so organized that certain position occupants are especially vulnerable to conflicting expectations, patterns often emerge to protect them from reprisals. The union steward who behaves contrary to management's expectations, for instance, is normally protected from management reprisals by contract rules guaranteeing his job security. Another illustration is the pattern of social distance which usually develops to protect the superior in an organization from emotional dependence on his subordinates. For example, where a military officer or a civilian boss is forced to decide between the expectations of his superiors and those of his subordinates, the strain which might arise from withdrawal of affection and esteem by the subordinates is avoided if he has maintained social distance from them.

Finally, position occupants who are subject to conflicting expectations develop various patterns of concerted action to protect themselves (Merton, 1957a). Such protective devices range from customary reluctance to give aid to those who attack a fellow position occupant, as in the reluctance of a lawyer or physician to testify against a colleague in a malpractice suit, to the development of formal associations such as bar associations or teachers' federations, etc., which function to protect their members from conflicting role obligations. These group solutions often become normative and are sometimes formalized into written codes.

Merging of roles

Turner (1962) has hypothesized two tendencies which, operating over a period of time, result in a gradual modification of role structure in the direction or reducing conflicting expectations. With both of these tendencies, a single role emerges from two conflicting roles, either through one absorbing the other or through a merger. Turner states his hypotheses as follows:

> Whenever the social structure is such that many individuals characteristically act from the perspective of two given roles simultaneously, there tends to emerge a single role which encompasses the action. The single role may result from a merger process, each role absorbing the other, or from the development and recognition of a third role which is specifically the pattern viewed as consistent when both roles might be applicable. The parent and spouse roles illustrate the former tendency. In popular usage the sharp distinctions are not ordinarily made between parent and spouse behavior that sociologists invoke in the name of logical, as distinct from folk, consistency. The politician role exemplifies the second tendency, providing a distinct perspective from which the individual may act who otherwise would be acting simultaneously as a party functionary and as a government official. What would constitute a role conflict from the latter point of view is susceptible of treatment as a consistent pattern from the point of view of the politician role. (P. 26)

Some data in support of this mode of reducing strain are available (Perry & Wynne, 1959). The therapist-researcher in a hospital devoted entirely to clinical research frequently experienced strain arising from conflict between expectations attached to his position as therapist and his position as researcher. In some instances this conflict was resolved by role segregation. A patient would be treated in terms of one or the other role, but not both. He would be receiving therapy from one staff member and participating in a research program of some other staff member. A second way of reducing strain was redefinition of the role, creating a unique combination of obligations and rights drawn from each set of role expectations.

STUDY QUESTIONS

4. *What are the various ways in which actors in positions exposed to conflicting expectations are protected from role strain?*
5. *How may roles be reorganized so as to reduce strain resulting from conflicting expectations?*

Summary: Conflicting role expectations

Role strain is greatly limited by the presence of a hierarchy of role obligations in a social system. Any system inevitably has many conflicting expectations, but where clear priorities are established, the actor has little difficulty in deciding on the appropriate behavior. These hierarchies reflect the value structure of the group and also indicate the fact that some roles are more likely to disrupt the system than others. Such structural features as differences in the power of various role partners to exert sanctions, restrictions on multiple position occupancy, and spatial and temporal separation of situations also function to reduce strain.

Actors who are especially subject to sanctions because their position exposes them to conflicting role expectations are likely to be protected by the system. They may be insulated from observation, a special tolerance may be established for their actions, they may be protected from reprisals by those whose expectations they violate, or they may join with other occupants of the same position to develop patterns of concerted action. Finally, roles may be modified by a merger of two conflicting roles: each may absorb the other, or a third role may develop that eliminates the conflicting expectations.

REDUCTION OF STRAIN ASSOCIATED WITH CHANGES IN ROLE POSITIONS

Discussion so far has been devoted to the features of a system which increase consensus or which prevent or reduce strain arising from conflicting expectations within the system. Another source of strain noted in Chapter 15 is related to discontinuities in role positions. Here strain is largely a product of having to unlearn old patterns of behaving, thinking, and feeling, and to adopt new ones. Strain arising out of the disparity of expectations attached to positions that actors successively occupy was emphasized. Another observation was that strain is a function of certain characteristics of the transition itself; namely, its certainty, clarity, and abruptness, as well as the relative desirability of the two positions.

With respect to the certainty of the transition, one would expect less strain in systems in which status passage is dependent on the possession of certain attributes rather than on the actor's performance. Such attributes as chronological age, seniority, years in grade, etc., are gained automatically; hence there is high certainty that one will pass to the next position in the system. In systems where positions are achieved on the basis of performance, however, as where competitive examinations are used, one can expect an additional source of strain: the uncertainty of achieving the transition. Where this type of strain becomes acute, informal patterns frequently emerge which have the effect of guaranteeing the position change. In many organizations, a given position may technically be filled by anyone, but the informal practice is to choose the person who occupies a particular other position. The president in such an organization, for instance, can confidently expect to be elected to the board of directors at the expiration of his term of office.

Anthropologists have long emphasized the importance of ceremonies in connection with the degree of clarity of the transition. In many societies important transitions are given ceremonial recognition, termed *rites of passage,* which clarify for everyone the new position of the individual. These rites mark initiation into adulthood, marriage, and death, as well as entrance into various special groups. They often involve renaming of the actor. As a result, neither the new occupant nor others are in doubt as to how each should behave.

The exotic character of such ceremonies in other cultures should not blind us to the presence of the more prosaic rites of passage in our own society. They include confirmation in religious systems, graduations in educational systems, parties celebrating promotion in business, and pinning in the courtship process, to mention but a few. Bloch and Niederhoffer (1958) suggested that many features of adolescent behavior in our society are a consequence of the adolescent's attempt to clarify his position in the absence of such forms of ceremonial recognition.

With respect to the degree of abruptness in the transition, in most instances the change of position is not so abrupt as it might appear. Strauss (1959) suggests that one can denote stages of passage within each position, with the final stages serving to prepare the individual for the next position. To illustrate, most graduate students in the later stages of their training may teach a course or two, and this experience eases the transition into the professorial status which many graduate student subsequently occupy. The early stage of position occupancy often involves a certain degree of tolerance with respect to the behavior of the new position occupant. Other people realize that he needs time to get used to his new position. Such "honeymoons" are recognized not only for newlyweds but also for United States Presidents. Similar preparation for later roles has been noted by Deutscher (1962), who observed that in American society, parents are prepared for postparental life by the temporary absence of their children during the late phase of the childrearing period, as when the children leave for college, for military service, or for distant employment.

Strauss (1959) also discusses "coaching" which, in many systems, eases status passage. He uses the term to refer to the tendency for persons who have gone through a series of transitions to guide and advise those who follow. In this process, the coach interprets the neophyte's present experience and instructs him on what lies ahead, what he should be learning at each point, what he should guard against, etc. The process should be familiar to college students who are accustomed to "wising up" the entering freshman on various phases of college life that he will encounter in his roles as student, pledge, and fraternity man. At times, the coach may conspire with others to set the stage for experiences which he feels will help his protégé to develop, as when a business executive manages to give a particularly challenging assignment to one of his junior executives whom he is grooming for advancement. This and other processes which facilitate the adoption of new roles will be discussed further in Chapter 17 on socialization.

Finally, if a system is so organized that movement is normally from a position of lower desirability to one of higher, the strain is apt to be less. In some societies age-sex positions are organized in this way: the successive positions of infant, child, youth, mature adult, and elder adult are increasingly more desirable role categories. In our society, while this is the case in the early part of the sequence, it is not for the last part. Movement from the position of mature adult to that of the aged is considered undesirable. Goffman (1952) has observed a number of devices on the levels of both the individual and the system that emerge to reduce the deleterious effects of such movement on self-esteem. For instance, it is a common practice in organizations to create a new position of equal or high status for a person who is about to be demoted. Or retirement may be formally recognized by conferring a new title. With much pomp and circumstance, retiring professors at university commencements are awarded the title Professor Emeritus. In industry, employees may receive a gold watch with an appropriate inscription for faithful service, and sometimes they are given a retirement party.

IMBALANCE IN ROLE RIGHTS AND OBLIGATIONS

Where the source of strain arises out of inequality in the rights and obligations of reciprocal roles, tendencies develop within the system toward the development of a more equitable balance. Such pressures toward modification of existing role obligations occur either when the position occupants are inadequately motivated to fulfill their obligations, or when because of frustration, they engage in behaviors that interfere with the need gratification of their role partners.

For instance, where the wife is employed outside the home and the husband continues to play the traditional role of the husband, the wife finds herself saddled with full responsibility for the care of the children and the household as well as her job outside. This may result in a threat to withdraw from the relation, refusal to bear the responsibilities, or bickering, nagging, and withdrawal of emotional support from the husband. If such a state of affairs becomes painful enough for the husband, he will gradually modify his role behavior toward her (e.g., he may share in household duties, etc.), which in turn will reduce the wife's frustration to the point where a new equilibrium between the rights and obligations of their respective roles is established. Such a readjustment in rights and obligations can also be seen in larger social systems. Over the past fifty years in America, the conflict between employers and employees which arose out of inequalities in rights and obligations has gradually produced a new equilibrium between these two roles.

STUDY QUESTIONS

6. *What social system factors ease the strain produced by transitions from one role to another?*
7. *Explain the process by which an imbalance in role rights and obligations is corrected.*

SUMMARY: SOCIAL SYSTEM VARIABLES

Much of the conflict among role expectations in a social system is resolved by mechanisms built into the system or by structural arrangements that are an integral part of the system. First, various mechanisms develop to increase consensus on role expectations. These include means of facilitating communication, liaison or coordinating committees, manuals of operation, training and indoctrination of new members, and rituals or ceremonies that reaffirm the rights and obligations of the system participants.

Second are a number of features for reducing strain. Role obligations in a system are ranked in a hierarchy of priorities, so that the actor has little difficulty making a choice. Strain is also minimized by such structural features as differences in the power of various role partners to exert sanctions, restrictions on multiple position occupancy, and spatial and temporal separation of situations. Actors who are especially subject to sanctions because of their position are protected in various ways: They may be insulated from observation, they may be allowed to behave in conflicting ways, they may be protected from reprisals, or they may develop concerted action to protect themselves. Finally, conflicting role expectations may be eliminated by merging two conflicting roles.

Third, strain from discontinuities in successive role positions may be reduced by making the transition an automatic function of the possession of certain attributes, by establishing clear policies for carrying out the transition, by using rites of passage, by providing the potential position occupant with preliminary practice before assuming the role, by coaching the candidate, or by arranging the successive roles so that each is (or appears to be) more desirable than the previous one.

Fourth, where there is an imbalance of role rights and obligations, processes arise to establish a more equitable balance.

Individual Processes Leading to the Resolution of Role Strain

An individual is exposed to a multitude of expectations from the groups and from significant others with whom he interacts. Either most of these expectations are not incompatible or competing, or else social system mechanisms prevent them from producing role strain. Some, however, are in competition or conflict: time is insufficient to fulfill both of them, or they require two incompatible actions. It is assumed that an individual strives for resolution of this strain arising from being subjected to competing or conflicting expectations. In addition to the resources available to him through participation in the social system, he has at his command certain individual processes that reduce role strain.

An actor may sometimes adjust to conflicting expectations by restructuring the situation. Burchard, in his study of role conflicts among military chaplains, suggests how this is accomplished. For example, the chaplains and ex-chaplains who felt that there was no conflict between war and the Christian "turn the other cheek" philosophy justified their position by such lines of reasoning as "the individual and the nation are different" and "necessity for self-defense obviates any antiviolence teachings of Jesus" (1954, p. 34). The first of these quotations is a differentiation of the expectation so that it applies to one situation and not the other, and the second quotation nullifies one expectation by invoking another which is higher in the hierarchy of role obligations. Burchard notes that these devices have some resemblance to the familiar adjustment mechanisms of compartmentalization and rationalization, respectively.

Another study explored the ways in which subjects resolved a dilemma engendered by choosing not to fulfill a role obligation in a conflict situation (Cousins, 1951). Subjects were asked to imagine a situation where as student monitors they were to enforce an overly severe curfew rule. After they made a decision on whether or not they would report a violation on the part of a fellow student, they were presented with six reasons for their choice of action and asked to choose three. The reasons selected by students who chose not to enforce the rule reflected a reliance on a number of adjustment techniques which allowed them to cognitively restructure the situation. These included rationalization, displacement, and wish-fulfilling fantasy.

Another mode of individual resolution takes the form of reducing dependence on the group or role partner supporting one of the expectations. The individual accomplishes this by leaving the group, by redefining its value to him, or by making it irrelevant to the conflict situation. The first mode is illustrated by the older fraternity pledge who feels too much strain and gives up his intention to join the fraternity. The second is illustrated by the woman caught in a conflict between the role of wife and career woman who redefines her career as less important and accepts a less demanding job. The third mode is illustrated by the military chaplain who makes his officer rank irrelevant to his religious relations to enlisted men.

INDIVIDUAL DETERMINANTS OF CHOICE RESOLUTION

Universalistic versus particularistic bias

A number of lines of inquiry have been concerned with the determinants of choice among the various forms of role conflict resolution. The work of Stouffer and Toby has stimulated many studies on personality factors in conflict resolution. Their investigation was aimed at demonstrating that individuals have consistent orientations toward resolving role conflict in different situations. They constructed a series of hypothetical situations representing a conflict between obligations of friendship and obligations to society. Using a distinction discussed by Parsons (1949), they labeled the former *particularistic* and the latter *universalistic* obligations. One of their situations is reproduced below (Stouffer & Toby, 1951).

> You are riding in a car driven by a close friend, and he hits a pedestrian. You know he was going at least 35 miles an hour in a 20-mile-an-hour speed zone. There are no other witnesses. His lawyer says that if you testify under oath that the speed was only 20 miles an hour, it may save him from serious consequences. (P. 396)

The other situations were similar, although progressively less serious in nature. The second involved a drama critic who felt that a play invested in by a good friend was poor; yet for him to say so publicly would wipe out his friend's savings. The third concerned a doctor who examined a friend in connection with an insurance application and who was doubtful about his friend's health on one or two points. Finally, a fourth situation involved a member of a board of directors who had inside information which, if not revealed to his friend, would result in his friend's financial ruin.

These situations were presented in a questionnaire, and subjects were asked to indicate whether they felt that their friend had a definite right, some right, or no right to expect them to behave in his interest. Then they were asked whether or not they would so behave. From a statistical analysis of the responses, the authors concluded that a given individual could be placed at the same point on a dimension ranging from a universalistic orientation to a particularistic one. From knowledge of his position on this continuum, his responses to the various situations could be predicted with reasonable accuracy.

Personality correlates of particularistic-universalistic orientations

These results led others to investigate personality correlates of universalistic or particularistic orientations toward role conflict. One study hypothesized that a universalistic role orientation would be typical of the authoritarian personality (Mishler, 1953). Responses to the four situations developed by Stouffer and Toby were compared with seven personality characteristics thought to be dimensions underlying the authoritarian personality. These included whether other people are viewed with suspicion or trust, whether parents are idealized or objectively praised, whether members of the opposite sex are viewed with resentment and disrespect or affectionate respect, whether deviant behavior is condemned on a moralistic basis or viewed with permissiveness, whether demands by an authority are submitted to or rejected, and whether an individual's satisfaction is related to the achievement of external goals or individualized personal goals. (The trait mentioned first in each of these dimensions is thought to be characteristic of the authoritarian personality.) The results of the study suggest that the relation between authoritarianism and universalism is not as simple as hypothesized. It was necessary to distinguish different types of universalistic and particularistic orientations, and only some of these had a relation to authoritarian personality variables.

Another study investigated the effects on role conflict resolution of three social factors—severity of sanction, social distance, and publicity (Sutcliffe & Haberman, 1956). A series of hypothetical situations similar to those developed by Stouffer and Toby was used. Subjects were faced with the dilemma of resolving a conflict in a manner that would result in either a sanction being imposed on another person (the universalistic response) or no sanction being imposed (the particularistic response). The situations were contrived in order to vary several factors: (1) the severity of the sanctions (the seriousness of the offense ranged from murder to rudeness); (2) the degree of social distance between the subject and the other person (in some situations they were strangers, in others friends); and (3) the publicity involved (in some cases the subject's actions would become known to others, in some cases they would not).

One situation, for example, was a student usher observing another student letting off a smoke bomb in a chapel. Respondents were asked whether they would report him if they were the usher. Under one condition the student culprit was a friend of the usher; under another he was not. Also under one condition the respondent faced having others know that he had reported the culprit; under another no one would know. Analysis of the results indicated that when sanctions were weak, when the culprit was a friend, and when reporting was private, the respondent chose a particularistic response: he did not report the culprit. The opposite of these three conditions more often yielded universalistic responses.

The next part of the experiment attempted to determine whether or not a particularistic or universalistic resolution of role conflict was associated with certain personality characteristics. The investigators selected a series of ten situations in which the pressures of friendship were balanced against those of public knowledge. The seriousness of the offense was held constant. Subjects were given two items measuring the tendency to submit to authority. In addition, information on the subjects' sex, social class, religion, and political affiliation was obtained.

A statistical analysis of the data revealed, as in the previous study, that individuals were usually consistent in their response to the ten situations. Only two of the personality and background factors, however, showed an appreciable relation to the universalism-particularism bias. The authors tentatively concluded that authoritarianism was generally associated with a universalistic bias in all the ten situations, and sex-role conservatism and morality was associated with certain situations only. Opposite characteristics were associated with a particularistic bias.

In conclusion, it appears that individuals are likely to resolve role conflicts of this type in either a universalistic or particularistic manner; moreover, authoritarian persons are likely to prefer a universalistic resolution. As the findings from the experiment cited earlier suggest, however, a person with quite the opposite traits may also resolve conflict in a universalistic manner. The lack of consistent results in these two different investigations probably stems from the fact that the authoritarian personality is a multidimensional concept.

Individual role hierarchies

Burchard (1954) and Getzels and Guba (1954) have suggested that where actors are faced with conflicting expectations arising from occupying several positions, they are likely to resolve strain by choosing certain roles over others. This suggests that the individual has an established set of role hierarchies or priorities. Two determinants of the relative position of a role in such an individual hierarchy have been suggested by Getzels and Guba. One is the need structure of the individual, and the other is the legitimacy of the role expectations. To illustrate the effects of need structure, a woman with strong achievement needs who is both a mother and a career woman might be expected to honor her career obligations over those associated with her role as mother, since the former will allow greater satisfaction of her achievement needs.

By the term *legitimacy* Getzels and Guba appear to have in mind a feature of social systems previously noted; namely, the hierarchization of role obligations within a social system. Actors in a given system agree that certain obligations will take precedence over others in a case of conflict. In their study of conflict between the roles of teacher and military officer, Getzels and Guba make this comment on legitimacy (1954):

> No matter what major role an actor may select, he must face the realities of the situation in which he finds himself. He cannot long ignore the legitimate expectations of others upon him without retaliation from them. None of the Air University officer-instructors, whatever his personal predilection, may with impunity overlook the fact that he is part of a Military organization. Moreover, it is clear that he will eventually (perhaps soon) be reassigned to a military command rather than to another teaching position—at most the tour of

duty at the University is three years. That the situation is so ordered placed added legitimacy upon the officer role over and above the instructor role. (P. 174)

Ultimately, then, the particular form which a role hierarchy takes in an individual is the resultant of pressures to adopt the system of priorities prevailing in the social system and pressures of individual needs.

STUDY QUESTIONS

8. *Explain the following individual mechanisms for reducing role strain: (a) restructuring the situation; (b) changing the hierarchy of values.*
9. *Distinguish between a universalistic and a particularistic orientation. To what extent are these orientations related to personality characteristics?*

A THEORY OF ROLE CONFLICT RESOLUTION

Gross, Mason, and McEachern (1958) have developed a systematic theory of role conflict resolution. Unlike the previously cited studies, which were concerned largely with multiple position occupancy, these investigators have attempted to include the case of intrarole conflict, where an individual is subject to conflicting expectations concerning a single position.

An individual who is faced with conflicting expectations *A* and *B* may choose one of three alternatives: He may conform either to expectation *A* or to expectation *B*; he may choose to compromise by meeting both expectations in part; or finally, he may attempt to avoid conforming to either expectation. Gross and his colleagues posit that the choice an actor makes in such a situation will be a function of three variables: (1) the perceived legitimacy of the expectations, (2) the perceived strength of the sanction applied for nonconformity to each of the expectations, and (3) the orientation of the actor relative to legitimacy and sanctions.

Legitimacy

An expectation is perceived as a legitimate obligation by an actor if he believes that the occupants of a counterposition "have a right" to hold such an expectation. An expectation is perceived as illegitimate where he believes the occupants have no right to it. To illustrate, the expectation that an instructor should grade examinations in an impartial manner would be perceived by an instructor as a legitimate expectation for students to hold; i.e., he believes they have a moral right in our school system to be treated equally. However, the expectation on the part of a student that he should be given preferential treatment would be perceived by an instructor as illegitimate.

Gross and his associates assume that actors are predisposed to conform to expectations which they perceive as legitimate and to avoid conforming to expectations which they perceive as illegitimate. If for the moment we examine the effect of this variable without regard to the variables of sanction and orientation, we could, as these investigators suggest, make the following predictions: If one of the conflicting expectations is legitimate and the other illegitimate, the actor will choose to honor the legitimate one. If both are legitimate, he will compromise; and if both are illegitimate, he will avoid meeting either.

Sanctions

A sanction consists of actions toward an actor by a role partner or by the actor himself which gratify or frustrate his needs. In the case of gratification, we speak of positive sanctions; in the case of frustration, negative sanctions. A second assumption in this theory of role conflict resolution is that actors are predisposed to accept the expectations which they believe will result in the strongest negative sanctions if they fail to comply. Predicting from this variable alone, we would expect that if one of the expectations carried strong negative sanctions and the other weak sanctions, the actor would choose to honor the former. If both carried strong negative sanctions, then a compromise would be expected to occur. However, in the hypothetical situation where both expectations are perceived by the actor as being supported by weak sanctions, and where only sanctions are operative, Gross and his associates are unable to make a prediction.

In a real-life situation, of course, the variables of both legitimacy and sanctions are present. Let us examine the combined effect of the two variables. We have seen that where both expectations are associated with weak sanctions, the sanctions variable has no effect in determining the outcome. In such an instance the legitimacy variable would determine conflict resolution in the manner previously outlined. In other instances, sanctions and legitimacy dictate the same outcome; namely, the choice of either one or the other expectation, or of a compromise between them.

In everyday life, since legitimate expectations generally carry stronger sanctions for nonobservance than do illegitimate ones, sanctions and legitimacy are likely to agree on the appropriate resolution of a conflict. In fact, this marked association between sanctions and legitimacy is an important way in which social systems aid in resolving role conflicts. On occasion, however, an actor may find himself in a situation where legitimacy is balanced by sanction. Take a student in an examination situation. A legitimate expectation held by his instructor is that he will not aid another student by giving him the answers to the questions. But because of friendship, another student may expect such help, although both recognize that this is an illegitimate expectation: no student has a legitimate right to ask another to help him cheat. In this instance, the sanctions imposed for nonobservance of the illegitimate expectation, such as loss of regard from the student who expects help, may be considerably stronger than the sanctions imposed by the instructor. To handle a case like this, where sanctions and legitimacy work at cross purposes, Gross and his associates introduce a third assumption.

Orientation

The third assumption is that individuals may be differentiated according to their primacy of orientation to the legitimacy or to the sanction aspect of the expectations in the situation. The investigators posit three types of orientation to expectations.

The first gives primacy to the legitimacy dimension. Here a person would be characterized as having a *moral* orientation to expectations, and in a conflict situation he would be predisposed to fulfill the legitimate expectation and to reject the illegitimate one. If both expectations were legitimate, he would be likely to compromise; and if neither were legitimate, he would try to avoid accepting either.

A second type of individual orientation is labeled *expedient*. An individual with an expedient orientation is likely to give priority to sanctions in preference to the legitimacy of the expectations held by others. A person with such an orientation would be likely to take into account only the sanctions and to choose the expectation which carries the stronger negative sanction for nonconformity. Where nonconformity to both expectations is perceived as leading to the imposition of equally strong sanctions, an expedient orientation would lead to some sort of compromise. Where the sanctions involved are believed equally weak, there would be no basis for predicting from the variable of sanction alone, and in such a case the legitimacy variable would determine the choice.

The third type of individual orientation which Gross and his associates distinguish is the *moral-expedient* orientation. Persons with this orientation take both dimensions into account and are predisposed to adopt a course of behavior that emerges from a balancing of the two. Where both variables dictate the same line of conduct, no problem arises. Where their effects are in opposition, however, a person with a moral-expedient orientation behaves in accordance with the net balance of the two forces. For instance, if both expectations are equally legitimate but one carries a stronger sanction than the other, he conforms to the one with the stronger sanction. Where they are equally balanced, he is likely to compromise. Table 16–1 illustrates how, given information about the legitimacy or expediency of the expectations, the theory predicts the responses of a person with a moral-expedient orientation. The student should go through this table checking out predictions made on the basis of the theory.

On the basis of the theory, these investigators were able to predict the outcome for all the various combinations of legitimacy, sanctions, and orientations in instances where school superintendents were confronted with conflicting expectations. The school superintendents were presented with four structured potential role conflict situations concerning (1) hiring and promotion of teachers, (2) salary increases for teachers, (3) the priority given to financial or educational needs in drawing up a school budget, and (4) the superintendent's allocation of his after-office hours. For each situation, the respondent was asked to choose one of three alter-

Table 16–1
**Predicted Behavior for 16 Types of Role Conflicts for
Individuals with a Moral-Expedient Orientation**

TYPE	EXPECTATION	LEGITIMACY*	SANCTIONS	BEHAVIOR
1	*A*	Leg.	Strong	Compromises
	B	Leg.	Strong	
2	*A*	Leg.	Weak	Chooses *B*
	B	Leg.	Strong	
3	*A*	Leg.	Strong	Chooses *A*
	B	Leg.	Weak	
4	*A*	Leg.	Weak	Compromises
	B	Leg.	Weak	
5	*A*	Leg.	Strong	Chooses *A*
	B	Illeg.	Strong	
6	*A*	Leg.	Weak	Compromises
	B	Illeg.	Strong	
7	*A*	Leg.	Strong	Chooses *A*
	B	Illeg.	Weak	
8	*A*	Leg.	Weak	Chooses *A*
	B	Illeg.	Weak	
9	*A*	Illeg.	Strong	Chooses *B*
	B	Leg.	Strong	
10	*A*	Illeg.	Weak	Chooses *B*
	B	Leg.	Strong	
11	*A*	Illeg.	Strong	Compromises
	B	Leg.	Weak	
12	*A*	Illeg.	Weak	Chooses *B*
	B	Leg.	Weak	
13	*A*	Illeg.	Strong	Compromises
	B	Illeg.	Strong	
14	*A*	Illeg.	Weak	Chooses *B*
	B	Illeg.	Strong	
15	*A*	Illeg.	Strong	Chooses *A*
	B	Illeg.	Weak	
16	*A*	Illeg.	Weak	No choice
	B	Illeg.	Weak	

***The abbreviations used in this column are as follows: Leg—expectation perceived as legitimate;
Illeg.—expectation perceived as illegitimate.**

SOURCE: Adapted with permission from N. Gross, W. S. Mason, & A. W. McEachern.
Explorations in role analysis. New York: John Wiley & Sons, Inc., 1958. P. 294.

natives which best expressed the expectation of some eighteen relevant
groups and individuals, including local politicians, teachers, taxpayers
associations, wife, etc. To illustrate, in the hiring and promotion of

teachers one of the following three choices was to be assigned to each group by the superintendent (Gross, Mason, & McEachern, 1958):

1. Expect me to recommend the hiring and promotion of teachers and other school employees on the basis of merit only.
2. Expect me to give special consideration to their preferences in recommending the hiring and promotion of teachers and other school employees.
3. Have no expectation either way regarding whom I should recommend for hiring or for promotion. (P. 252)

Where a superintendent appeared to believe that various persons or groups held conflicting expectations for his conduct, the interviewer explored the superintendent's perception of the legitimacy of these expectations and the strength of the sanctions which the persons or groups involved could bring to bear upon him for nonconformity. This allowed each member of a pair of conflicting expectations to be labeled as legitimate or illegitimate and as carrying a strong or a weak sanction. The interviewer also explored what the respondent did in this situation, that is, whether he adhered to one or the other expectation, compromised, or avoided meeting either expectation.

To place the superintendents in the three orientation categories previously discussed, their responses to the Superintendent's Performances Instrument were analyzed. This consisted of a series of statements of expectations that could be applied to a superintendent. For each expectation the respondent was asked to indicate whether he absolutely must, preferably should, may or may not, preferably should not, or absolutely must not do the particular thing described. Those who more often chose the mandatory categories *absolutely should* or *absolutely should not* might be expected to have a moral orientation, and they were so classified. Those who more often chose the conditional response categories *preferably should, preferably should not,* or *may or may not* were classified as having an expedient orientation. Finally, those whose responses showed neither of the above patterns; i.e., were relatively inconsistent in their choice of categories, were labeled as moral-expedient.

The information obtained by these operations made it possible to predict the behavior of each of the superintendents on the basis of the theory. To illustrate, a superintendent who was classified as having a moral-expedient orientation, and who perceived that two groups held legitimate but conflicting expectations for his conduct backed by strong negative sanctions, would be expected to compromise. This prediction obtained from theory could then be compared with the interview information on how the superintendent did act. Appropriate predictions were made for all superintendents. For 264 of the 291 role conflict cases (91 percent) examined in this portion of the study, the theory led to the correct prediction. Such accuracy could be expected to occur purely by chance less than one time in one hundred.

Only in the case of competing expectations involving a time-allocation situation did the proportion of correct predictions drop below .91. In this situation, with 48 cases, the proportion was .79. It was the one case involving conflict arising from multiple position occupancy. As a husband and father, a respondent was exposed to the expectation by his family that he spend his after-office hours with them. At the same time, many groups in the community were seen by him as holding the expectation that he should devote his evenings to school and community affairs. A slight tendency on the part of the respondents to give priority to one role obligation over the other, regardless of the effects of legitimacy, sanctions, and orientation, was noted. If the theory were to include the effects of role priorities, the accuracy of prediction could probably be improved for the case of conflict arising from multiple position occupancy.

Since the theory was initially tested, one study has used it to predict role conflict resolution in four different groups (Shull & Miller, 1960). They included two groups of business executives, a group of company training directors, and a group of labor leaders. The overall accuracy of prediction was 71 percent. This percentage, while significantly above chance, was somewhat lower than that achieved by Gross and his associates. The investigators suggested that the difference might be due to the less structured measurement procedures used.

The theory has also been applied in studies of police officers and police trainees (Ehrlich, Rinehart, & Howell, 1962). While the accuracy of prediction attained was roughly comparable to that of the study just reported, it again fell considerably below the level attained by Gross and his associates. The investigators interpreted this difference as reflecting different orientations of the subjects in the populations studied. To illustrate, whereas school superintendents were considerably influenced in their resolution of conflict by the perception of the sanctions involved, patrolmen were relatively little influenced by this variable. Such differences suggest that caution should be exercised in generalizing the relative influence of legitimacy and sanctions to groups which have not been studied. In fact, Ehrlich, Rinehart, and Howell suggest that an alternative model which ignores legitimacy and sanctions and which predicts that the expectations held by an actor's most important reference group will be conformed to may provide a simpler scheme for predicting role conflict resolution. For the population they studied, at least, the predictive accuracy of this simpler model was comparable to that yielded by the theory of Gross, Mason, and McEachern.

ROLE BARGAINING

Focusing directly on the problem of role strain, Goode (1960) has recently introduced a theory based on the concept of the role bargain. His theoretical concepts are similar to and consistent with those of exchange theory. He starts from the position that an actor cannot possibly meet all the expectations involved in the relations he has with all his role partners because of competition, conflict, and related problems. Hence, the optimum allocation of his role performances is a central problem. Since he has to make decisions concerning the extent to which he will meet the expectations of his various role partners, he "shops around" to see where he can obtain the best reward-cost outcomes.

The actor does this shopping through a process of establishing a series of "role bargains" with his partners in which the "role price," or the extent to which he will meet the expectations of his partner, will be the resultant of the interaction of three factors. These are (1) his desire to carry out the activity because of such factors as the intrinsic gratification he receives from it, his commitment to it in terms of his internalized various values, etc., (2) his perception of how much the partner will reward or punish him for his role performance, and (3) the esteem or disesteem with which others who are significant to him will respond to both his performance and the attempt of the partner to make him perform adequately. With respect to the last-mentioned factor, Goode notes that this consideration places limits on a "free role" bargain. To a certain degree, there is consensus among the actors on the "going role price" or fair arrangement. Where either party drives too hard a bargain, the other persons will exert pressure to change the relation back to the going role price.

For example, assume that a woman is faced with the problem of allocating her energies with respect to two sets of expectations: those stemming from her position as an employee and her position as a wife. The role bargain that emerges between her and her husband—we will ignore for the sake of simplicity the related role bargain with her employer—will depend in part on the relative strength of her desire to fill the various expectations involved. If she enjoys her career activities much more than housework, she may prefer a role relation in which the husband is satisfied with less than full performance in the home. If in addition, because she is the least interested party in the marriage relation, her husband is able to exert only relatively weak pressures on her through manipulation of rewards and punishments, she may be in a position to drive a rather hard bargain. Conceivably she could refuse to engage in any homemaking activities—except for the operation of the third factor. That is, family members, friends, and others, oriented toward a more traditional division of labor, might well regard this condition as having gone too far and would exert pressure toward a bargain closer to the arrangements prevailing in the typical marriage relation (Thibaut & Kelley, 1959).

Goode's theory should serve as a reminder that persons have leeway to improvise and create relations more congenial to their personalities and positions. Our focus on institutional or organizational roles, as well as our attempt to bring out in bold relief these system effects on interaction, has obscured somewhat the individual efforts of the actor to reduce strain. We have focused on the individual who experiences strain in meeting certain expectations because they conflict with other expectations, because they are not commensurate with his ability, or because they run counter to his self concept or his needs. We have treated this problem as if resolution must be complete—as if until some new role emerges involving a solution, the individual must honor one set of expectations or the other and must choose either to behave or not behave in a fashion congruent with his abilities, self concept, and needs. As Goffman has noted, however, in his penetrating essay on *role distance,* the carrying out of these expectations always involves a compromise *which is allowed for by all participants.* In varying degrees, position occupants are allowed to express other aspects of the self and meet other obligations while ostensibly carrying out those of a particular position. Goffman describes the process in the following way:[1]

> Much role analysis seems to assume that once one has selected a category of person and the context or sphere of life in which one wants to consider him, there will then be some main role that will fully dominate his activity. Perhaps there are times when an individual does march up and down like a wooden soldier, tightly rolled up in a particular role. It is true that here and there we can pounce on a moment when an individual sits fully astride a single role, head erect, eyes front, but the next moment the picture is shattered into many pieces and the individual divides into different persons holding the ties of different spheres of life by his hands, by his teeth, and by his grimaces. . . .
>
> Clothing patterns provide a systematic example for analysis with a broadened conception of role and illustrate the way in which the phenomenon of role distance requires our adopting this view. Young psychiatrists in state mental hospitals who are sympathetic to the plight of patients sometimes express distance from their administrative medical role by affecting shirts open at the collar, much as do socialists in their legislative offices. Housemaids willing to wear a uniform but not to confine their hair by a cap provide a parallel example, partially rejecting their occupation in favor of their femininity. (What we have in these cases is a special kind of status symbol—a disidentifier—that the individual hopes will shatter an otherwise coherent picture, telling others not what he is but what he isn't quite.) However, it is not only organizational roles which are handled in this way. Age-sex roles are dealt with in the same manner, as when a girl dresses in a tomboy style, or a sixty-year-old man wears the brim of his hat turned up or affects a crewcut.

STUDY QUESTIONS

10. *What are legitimate expectations? What is meant by the following three orientations: moral, expedient, moral-expedient?*

11. *How may role bargaining reduce the strain experienced by an actor?*

12. *What is role distance and how does it reduce strain?*

MEANS OF RESOLVING OTHER FORMS OF ROLE STRAIN

So far in this section we have dealt largely with individual processes leading to the reduction of strain arising from a single source: exposure to competing or conflicting expectations. This treatment reflects the current research emphasis. Unfortunately, systematic research on in-

[1]Reprinted by permission from E. Goffman. *Encounters: Two studies in the sociology of interaction.* Copyright 1961 by The Bobbs-Merrill Company, Inc., Indianapolis.

dividual mechanisms of resolving strain from other sources, such as inability to play a given role and inequities in role obligations, is largely lacking. As a result, our comments in this connection are somewhat speculative and brief. Some mention has already been made of the interpersonal strategies individuals use to alter each other's behavior in a manner which leads to a tolerable balance of role rights and obligations.

Where individuals are unable to fulfill the obligations associated with the position which they occupy, they may employ the familiar adjustment mechanisms described in the clinical literature; e.g., rationalization, escape through illness, etc. Chapter 17 on socialization will treat these in somewhat more detail. Similarly, we will see in the same chapter that to a great extent, the process of role learning facilitates position change because roles are always learned in pairs. When a person learns a given role he must also learn, although perhaps to a lesser degree, the behavior involved in a counterposition. Since movement from one position to its counterposition often occurs, as in the transition from child to parent, worker to foreman, and enlisted man to officer, an actor entering the new role has already become somewhat familiar with it.

SUMMARY: INDIVIDUAL PROCESSES

Even though the social system is structured to minimize role strain, the multitude of expectations to which the individual is exposed inevitably creates some strain. Various mechanisms are available to him for reducing strain. He may restructure the situation, he may establish his own hierarchy of values, or he may use rationalization, displacement, or wish-fulfilling fantasy. An extreme solution is to leave the system.

Individuals appear to be oriented toward role conflict resolution at some point on a continuum ranging from preference for the particularistic expectation to preference for the universalistic expectation. The former is illustrated by obligations to friends; the latter by obligations to society. Attempts to relate such orientations to authoritarian personality characteristics have not been entirely successful. To some degree a universalistic orientation is associated with authoritarianism.

In a study of superintendents in a school system, some evidence was presented indicating that individuals can be classified as to whether they are oriented toward legitimate expectations, toward expectations that have strong sanctions, or toward some compromise position. An expectation is perceived as legitimate if an actor perceives that the occupants of a counterposition have a right to hold such an expectation. The responses of superintendents to a variety of situations were predicted with a high degree of accuracy by the use of such variables. The application of the theory to various other groups by different investigators yielded a considerably lower degree of accuracy.

Another process emphasizing the active contribution of the individual to resolving conflicting expectations is role bargaining. An actor establishes a series of role bargains with his partners in which the "role price," or the extent to which he will meet the expectations of his partner, will be the resultant of (1) his desire to carry out the activity because of such factors as the intrinsic gratification he receives from it, the strength of his internal commitment to it, etc., (2) his perception of how much the partner will reward or punish him for his role performance, and (3) the esteem or disesteem with which others who are significant to him will respond to both his performance and the attempt of the partner to make him perform adequately. Finally, certain types of strain, such as strain which occurs when an expectation conflicts with the self concept, may be eased by establishing some distance between oneself and the role. This is done by presenting oneself in such a way as to deny, at least in part, full acceptance of the role.

Other forms of role strain, such as inequities in role obligations, may be resolved through interpersonal strategies or alleviated by use of defense mechanisms such as rationalization. Strain resulting from inability to play a role is mitigated by processes facilitating role learning, to be discussed in the next chapter.

Cultural Variables and the Resolution of Role Strain

In the preceding discussion of individual adjustments to role strain, the tendency of actors to restructure the situation by means of such mechanisms as rationalization and compartmentalization was noted. Where many incumbents of the same role position find themselves subject to similar role strains, mutual support is present for finding a common means of resolution, and this often results in the development of a shared system of beliefs concerning appropriate forms of resolution. Such a situation may also lead to a gradual modification of the conflicting role expectations as each person troubled by the conflict supports the other in moving toward a modification of the expectations involved.

Myrdal's (1944) analysis of the historical development of the dogma of racial inequality provides an illustration of how a belief develops and becomes widely diffused when many persons in a population face a conflict. The belief that Negroes are biologically different and inferior to whites served to resolve the conflict between the American creed with its emphasis on human equality, on the one hand, and the early practice of slavery and the later forms of racial discrimination, on the other. In terms of our own role conflict schema, many persons who were both Americans and slaveholders, or later, who were Americans and members of groups which engaged in racial discrimination, could reconcile these conflicting expectations by viewing the situation in terms of this belief: "All men are created equal, but this does not include Negroes because they are biologically different from whites."

Shared belief systems may also add legitimacy to a particular role. Where position incumbents are not in agreement on the legitimacy of the expectations associated with their role, they may collectively develop a series of beliefs that rationalize the legitimacy. Wardwell (1952) in his analysis of a marginal social role, that of chiropractor, has shown how the ideology of an oppressed minority served to reduce strain. Chiropractors explained their marginal position in the healing profession as resulting from selfishly motivated persecution by the medical profession. An analysis of the belief systems of many other occupational groups would undoubtedly show that certain widely held beliefs have as a major function the reduction of role strain.

Albert Cohen (1955) has offered a theory to explain the emergence of subcultures. While his theory is not couched in the language of role analysis, it is relevant to the discussion here because it attempts to explain how new beliefs and norms emerge in response to strain. In particular, it throws light on the way individuals with similar problems of adjustment collectively facilitate the emergence of a solution involving a modification of previous role expectations. In essence, his theory suggests that when some or all members of a group face a common problem which cannot be solved by behaving in accordance with their currently held norms, members will, through a process of mutual facilitation, arrive at a new set of expectations which will allow a solution.

Although Cohen uses his theory to explain the emergence of certain norms among lower-class delinquent boys, it can be applied to other groups. For instance, an example of a shared belief system which develops to resolve role strain may be found in norms which function to restrict competition in groups. Many situations, particularly in our society, call for competition. We compete in the schoolroom, on the job, and in the courtship process, as well as in a myriad of other situations. But unlimited competition often has disastrous side effects, both for the individual and the group. It creates feelings of inadequacy and interpersonal hostility. Because of this, groups often attempt to restrict competition by developing role expectations that control competitive output or restrict the kinds of tactics which an individual may use.

To illustrate, assume that an instructor, toward the end of the semester, assigns a term paper and indicates that grades will be determined in large part by the length of the paper. This is a problem that most students can easily imagine. The solution prescribed by the traditional norms in this situation is that each should do his best in competition with the others. This, however, is not a very comfortable solution. The pressure to prepare for finals, finish other term papers, and maintain participation in a variety of extracurricular activities is great. Under these conditions, each student may begin to tentatively explore what the other is planning to do. Such questions as "How long is your paper going to be?" "How much time are you spending on your paper?" etc., will be raised. Along with these questions, each may express opinions as to the injustice of the assignment.

Through these exchanges the students encourage each other to move toward a reorientation of the situation of which each approves and which ultimately allows them to agree not to submit more than a certain number of pages. This solution, which originally found little support, now becomes established because it fits in with norms that have emerged from the process of mutual facilitation. If the students consistently behave in accordance with these newly formed expectations concerning their own role, their role partner, the instructor, is likely ultimately to revise his own expectations of the student role to fit the new formulation. The process illustrated here is a never-ending source of cultural innovation and often is initiated because of the presence of role strain.

STUDY QUESTIONS

13. *Where many individuals are placed in a position involving role strains, show how a subculture or ideology may emerge to help resolve the strain.*

14. *Explain how an ideology concerning Negroes may be used to resolve strain arising in persons who adhere to the belief in the equality of all Americans but who are prejudiced against Negroes.*

Summary and Conclusions

Processes contributing to the resolution of role strain have been discussed on three levels: the social system, the individual personality, and the culture. First, various mechanisms develop for increasing consensus on role expectations. These include means of facilitating communication, liaison or coordinating committees, manuals of operation, training and indoctrination of new members, and rituals and ceremonies that reaffirm the rights and obligations of the system participants.

Various features for reducing strain arising from conflicting expectations are also present. These include the arrangement of role obligations in a hierarchy of priorities and such structural features as differences in the power of various role partners to exert sanctions, restrictions on multiple position occupancy, and spatial and temporal separation of situations. In addition, actors who are especially subject to sanctions are protected in various ways. Finally, two roles may be merged and replaced by a single role.

Strain arising from discontinuities in successive role positions is reduced by making the transition automatic, by establishing clear policies controlling the transition, by use of rites of passage, by providing preparatory practice for a new role, by coaching a candidate, by arranging successive roles in order of increasing desirability, or by making prospective roles appear more attractive. Finally, where there is an imbalance of role rights and obligations, processes arise to establish a more equitable balance.

The individual is also very active in attempts to reduce role strain to which he is subjected. He may restructure the situations; he may establish his own hierarchy of values; he may use rationalization, displacement, or wish-fulfilling fantasy; or he may leave the system. Individuals generally have a fairly consistent orientation toward the universalistic-particularistic dimension. To some extent, the universalistic orientation is associated with authoritarianism. By classifying expectations as legitimate or illegitimate, and identifying the sanctions for conflicting expectations, and by determining whether the actor's orientation is toward the legitimate, the expedient, or some compromise position, considerable success has been attained in predicting the actor's choices in role conflict situations. To some extent, however, the degree of success depends upon the groups and situations studied. Finally, the individual may engage in role bargaining. This is a way of dealing with a multitude of expectations. He "bargains" with all his role partners and carries out the expectations of those partners who offer him the greatest reward-cost outcomes.

Certain cultural factors may contribute to the reduction of role strain. When many incumbents of the same position are subjected to similar strains, they may jointly work out a new system of beliefs which becomes a normative solution to resolving strain. These beliefs may be a restructuring of expectations, a new value hierarchy, or a whole ideology combining both of these features.

PART FIVE

Socialization

$\mathbf{S}$ocialization has been reserved as a final topic because virtually all the preceding portions of the book are relevant to it. Socialization is an interactional process whereby a person's behavior is modified to conform to expectations held by members of the group to which he belongs. Thus, it includes not only the process by which the child gradually acquires the ways of the adults around him, but also the process by which an adult takes on behaviors appropriate to the expectations associated with a new position in a group, an organization, or society at large.

Since socialization processes involve social learning in which other persons are the principal instructive agents, much of the material in Part Two on social influence and attitude change is relevant. In large part, moreover, socialization takes the form of learning role expectations associated with role categories; hence, Part Four on social roles is directly relevant.

Chapter 17, the first of three chapters on socialization, discusses processes of social learning, such as identification and role learning. Unfortunately, social learning concepts have been used in a great variety of ways by different investigators, and often research on this topic suffers from methodological shortcomings. The chapter attempts to bring some order to this confused state, but much further research is needed for a definitive statement.

Chapter 18 examines relations between variables in the social structure and variables in the individual. Some attempt is made to indicate variables that account for conscience formation and for such social motives as dependency, aggression, and achievement. Once again, firm conclusions are difficult to draw, this time because of the lack of longitudinal studies, which would overcome many of the difficulties in interpretation.

Finally, Chapter 19 asks broad questions concerning the social determinants of individual behavior, with particular emphasis on the formation on the self concept. An attempt is made to explain both stability and change in individual behavior in terms of interpersonal theory. Much stability in self and behavior stems from the constancy of the interpersonal environment. Both the individual and the social structure contribute to this constancy. Potential changes in self and behavior result from fortuitous changes in the environment or from the movement of the individual through different role categories in the social structure.

chapter seventeen

SOCIALIZATION: PROCESSES
OF SOCIAL LEARNING

One of the most significant and remarkable processes occurring in human beings is the transformation of the helpless infant into the mature adult. No other species goes through as long and as intensive a process of development, and in no other species is the contrast between infant and adult so great. As he develops, the child learns one or more languages, a wealth of empirical facts about his physical and social environment, and a variety of special skills and bodies of knowledge. He also acquires attitudes and values, some of them pertaining to moral standards and others that are ways of relating to people, such as loving or hating and helping or hurting other persons. This transformation takes place largely as a result of what have been termed *socialization processes*.

The principal agents in socialization are other persons, most notably the child's parents, teachers, siblings, playmates, and others who are significant to him. Much of what the child learns in the process of growing up is not systematically and consciously taught. Parents do not generally define themselves as teachers, yet they serve this role. Most of what they teach is not conveyed with deliberate intent; nevertheless, the child learns effectively.

Formerly, the term *socialization* had not been applied to adult learning experiences, but had been restricted to children. This traditional usage of the term was almost synonymous with the everyday phrase "bringing up the child." More recently the concept of socialization has been broadened to include aspects of adult behavior as well. Currently, socialization is thought of as an interactional process whereby a person's behavior is modified to conform with expectations held by members of the groups to which he belongs. This more inclusive definition recognizes that socialization does not stop at a certain age, but instead continues throughout life. Socialization processes are especially active each time a person occupies a new position, as when he joins a fraternity or sorority, gets promoted in a business organization, becomes a parent, or is inducted into military service.

Two aspects of socialization distinguish it from other processes of change. First, only the attitudinal and behavioral changes occurring through *learning* are relevant. Other changes, such as those resulting from growth, are not a part of the socialization process. Second, only the changes in behavior and attitude having their origins in *interaction with other persons* are considered products of socialization. The term *interaction* is here defined broadly, to include communication through the mass media, as when a student nurse reads a biography of Florence Nightingale.

Several illustrations may clarify these distinctions. Learning motor skills without tutelage by other persons, such as learning to run or jump, is not a socialization process. Learning to speak in the vernacular of one's own locality, on the other hand, is clearly a product of socialization because such learning is heavily dependent on interaction with other local inhabitants. Other illustrations of socialization include learning the folkways and customs of one's society or regional group and the religious beliefs and moral values of one's society and family.

Socialization should not be thought of as molding a person to a standard social pattern, however. Individuals are subjected to different combinations of socialization pressures, and they react differently to them. Consequently socialization processes can produce distinctive differences among persons as well as similarities.

Socialization processes receive considerable attention in such fields as developmental psychology, sociology of the child, portions of clinical psychology, certain aspects of group psychology, and culture and personality. Over the years, however, a certain division of labor has developed, reducing the overlap between these areas. In particular, social psychologists have usually limited their interest in socialization to four aspects:

1. Social learning processes such as imitation, identification, and role learning
2. The establishment by means of social learning of internal controls or conscience, the self concept, and social roles
3. The development of various behavior systems such as dependency, aggression, and affiliation and the formation of various strategies of goal achievement and defense
4. The relation of the social structure to these processes and to their effects

This chapter will focus upon the social learning process, and the remaining topics will be reserved for subsequent chapters.

A number of questions have been posed concerning socialization processes and their effects. What is the nature of the learning processes underlying socialization? How are these processes linked to their effects? What role is played by social structural and cultural factors in shaping these processes? The last two questions may be illustrated by reference to concrete behaviors. For example, what behaviors of parents will lead children to be strongly dependent upon their parents? How are these parental behaviors related to certain features of the family system, such as its size and the relation between the parents? How are they related to the cultural system, especially to the prevailing ideology of child rearing found in a particular group?

Socialization has been defined in terms of learning processes associated with interaction between persons. How does the behavior of one person affect the behavior of another? Anyone familiar with the psychology of learning will answer that one individual may influence another when he rewards or punishes him for certain responses. A parent, for example, praises his child for an action just performed or punishes him in order to eliminate its recurrence. Principles involving reward and punishment in social learning will be discussed in the following section.

STUDY QUESTIONS

1. *Explain what is meant by the concept of socialization. How does current usage of the term differ from earlier usage?*
2. *What are three major features of the socialization process that distinguish it from other forms of change?*
3. *Upon what aspects of socialization does the social psychologist focus?*

Elementary Forms of Learning

Several elementary learning principles that have been much studied in the laboratory are useful in understanding the social learning process. These include operant learning, direct tuition, incidental learning, and the effects of punishment.

OPERANT LEARNING

Extensive experimentation with animals and humans has focused upon the concept of *operant conditioning* (Skinner, 1953; Ferster & Skinner, 1957). This is also referred to as *instrumental conditioning,* and the suggestion has been made that a more appropriate term would be *operant learning* (English & English, 1958). We are interested here in the aspects of the learning process that are focused upon in such experimentation.

An *operant* is a response emitted by the organism. The term is especially appropriate for responses where the stimulus leading to the response is not easily identified, although such usage is by no means consistent. The central principle of operant learning is that when an operant is followed by reinforcement, the probability of its later occurrence is thereby increased. Reinforcement may take two forms: The operant or response leads to a rewarding stimulus, or it prevents or removes a noxious or punishing stimulus.

Experimentation on operant learning is especially concerned with the efficacy of various *schedules of reinforcement* that might be applied to operants. Also of importance is the presence or absence of various other conditions that may facilitate or interfere with learning. A schedule of reinforcement is a predetermined pattern of presentations of the rewarding or noxious stimulus following upon successive emissions of the operant. For example, if the operant is the pressing of a bar by a laboratory rat, the act of bar pressing may be connected to a mechanism delivering pellets of food according to a certain schedule or pattern. This might take the form of delivering a pellet each time the bar is pressed, delivering a pellet only once for each ten bar pressings, delivering pellets according to some random sequence, or delivering pellets once every ten minutes, regardless of the number of bar pressings which occur.

Frequently the principles of operant learning have been used to explain the behavior of human beings. A child may be thought of as emitting numerous responses, some of which are rewarded by parents or by environmental circumstances. Actions reinforced according to appropriate schedules become habitual as a result. At first one might question how new behavior could possibly be learned through operant conditioning. The response must be emitted before it can be reinforced, but if it is new, the response is not in the repertoire of the child. Skinner (1953) has noted, however, that novel responses may be acquired by *shaping* behavior through the method of successive approximation. Actions already in the repertoire of the organism that resemble the desired responses are first reinforced. Following reinforcement, these responses and similar ones resembling the desired behavior even more closely occur with increasing frequency, while responses dissimilar to the criterion are emitted less frequently. From this new set of similar responses, the experimenter again selects for reinforcement those responses that most closely resemble the desired action. In this manner, the organism is led to emit behavior that more and more closely approximates the criterion. By using this shaping process, pigeons have been taught to play ping-pong!

DIRECT TUITION

The essential characteristics of tuition are intentional guidance of behavior and the manipulation of reinforcement. Although tuition may occur among subhuman species, only man uses it extensively. The process is especially effective in human learning because of man's mastery of language. Direct tuition may be distinguished from operant learning by the fact that in direct tuition, language is used to elicit desired behaviors, whereas in operant learning, the response must be emitted by the organism. Appropriate behavior can be not only elicited but also guided and reinforced by symbols. The child, for instance, is told what to do, is guided by verbal instructions, and then is either rewarded by a verbal pat on the back or reprimanded for failing to perform the desired action. In many forms of tutored learning, feedback of information from the environment is as important as information from the tutor. For example, tutored athletic skills are in part learned through practice, which provides feedback on success or failure.

INCIDENTAL LEARNING

Operant conditioning as a form of social learning has limitations. Except where a social agent is deliberately shaping the behavior of a child, operant conditioning is distinguished by its accidental quality: action must occur before it can be reinforced. Thus it is unlikely that all the social responses found in the adult would ever have been acquired if they could only be learned in this way. Even if the trainer is interested in establishing a response in the trainee, he may have difficulty eliciting the action through tuition if it is a novel response.

Many actions not desired by the socializing agent are nevertheless learned. Operant learning is useful in explaining how such actions may be acquired. By arranging the delivery of reinforcements according to a fixed time interval, such as delivering a food pellet every ten minutes regardless of what the organism might be doing at that moment, Skinner (1948) has shown that pigeons learn to do whatever they happen to have been doing just before the reinforcement occurred. He labeled this "superstitious behavior."

Similar incidental learning occurs in humans. For example, a young child may come up with a four-letter word not used in polite society. The incongruity of this word on the lips of a child may provoke laughter from adults, which may reinforce his use of the word. Although the reinforcement is unintentional, it increases the probability that the child will repeat the undesirable word. Subsequently, he may find that repetitions of the word bring him concerned attention from his parents which he also finds reinforcing. It may well be that many aspects of behavior and experience which the parent does not intend to teach the child are acquired through operant learning.

EFFECTS OF PUNISHMENT

Americans have considerable faith in the efficacy of punishment. Children are spanked and scolded; employees are docked, fined, or criticized; and criminals are imprisoned. Used in this way, punishment is intended to eliminate undesirable behavior, not to establish some particular behavior.

A position popular with psychologists over the past few decades has been that, although punishment may temporarily suppress a particular behavior, it does not permanently weaken the motivation to perform that action. Recent reviews of the research literature by Church (1963) and by Solomon (1964), however, demonstrate clearly that this position, if it is correct at all, holds only under certain very limited conditions.

The consequences of punishment vary markedly with the conditions under which it is administered. For example, in experiments with rats, cats, and dogs, an electric shock ranging from low to high intensity has been shown to produce these effects corresponding to intensity: very low intensity strengthened behavior, moderately low intensity temporarily suppressed behavior, moderately high intensity produced partial lasting suppression, and high intensity, complete suppression. Although punishment often produces only temporary suppression, it can be dramatically effective if punishment to suppress a response is combined with reward for some alternative behavior that is incompatible with the behavior to be eliminated. For example, if puppies are swatted with a newspaper for eating horsemeat and are *at the same time* provided with an opportunity to eat food pellets instead, they develop such a strong inhibition toward horsemeat that they will starve themselves to death if presented only with horsemeat (Solomon, 1964). Thus the mere negation of a child's behavior by a parent is likely to be much less effective than negation of the behavior combined with specifying some incompatible behavior that is rewarded.

According to Solomon (1964), some additional conditions that markedly affect the consequences of punishment are: (1) whether the behavior being punished is intrinsically satisfying or a means to achieve satisfaction, (2) whether the punished behavior was originally learned through reward or punishment, (3) whether punishment is closely associated in time with the punished behavior, (4) whether punishment precedes or follows reward, (5) the strength of the behavior to be punished, (6) the extent to which punishment is familiar or unfamiliar, and (7) whether omission of the punishment strengthens behavior incompatible with the punished behavior.

Punishment frequently leads to unintentional learning. Any action that will avoid the punishment that would normally follow undesirable behavior tends to be reinforced. For example, a child may learn to deny that he acted in a certain way, or he may misrepresent his motives for misbehaving. These denials or misrepresentations are likely to become habitual if they repeatedly lead to escape from punishment. Punishment also has other consequences that will be referred to when the development of conscience is discussed in the next chapter.

Scientific knowledge of punishment is still rudimentary. Much of the research has been performed with rats, cats, and dogs, because of the understandable reluctance of experimenters to inflict punishment on humans. Generalizations from lower animals to humans are always risky. Among the many reasons for this is that, in everyday situations, the painful or noxious stimuli are readily perceived as produced by another human agent, whereas lower animals presumably perceive the painful consequences of their actions as objective properties of an environmental situation. This fact makes the human situation vastly more complicated. Indeed, it is questionable whether situations as perceived by lower animals deserve to be called *punishment,* a term which among humans, at least, implies an intentional action.

While it is useful to conceptualize socialization in terms of the learning processes just discussed, socialization has also been treated on a somewhat more complex level in terms of *learning from models.* Such concepts as imitation and identification come under this heading and are treated in the next section.

STUDY QUESTIONS

4. *Explain what is meant by operant learning. How can new responses never before performed be acquired through a process of operant learning?*
5. *What is meant by direct tuition?*
6. *What are the limitations of operant conditioning as an explanation of social learning? What are its merits?*
7. *What is incidental learning, and how is it relevant to operant conditioning?*
8. *Explain the limitations of punishment as a technique for the control of behavior.*

Learning from Models

Observers of human behavior have often called attention to the imitative nature of much human behavior, particularly the behavior of children. Children often engage in actions closely resembling those of their parents, older siblings, television and movie heroes, and others. Indeed, imitative behavior is so common that it has been thought by some early students of behavior to be instinctive (Tarde, 1903; McDougall, 1908). In more recent times a variety of learning processes have been proposed as explanations of imitation. They include identification, role practice, and role learning. These names are not entirely descriptive, for often different writers have used the same concept to describe quite different learning processes. These learning processes differ from operant conditioning in that the presence of an actual or symbolic model is crucial to learning.

OBSERVATIONAL LEARNING BASED ON MODELS

Donald Campbell (1961) has noted two forms of learning based on observation of models. In one, the learner observes the *outcomes* of the model's behavior. He learns that as a result of certain behavior, the model is rewarded or punished. For example, a young child accompanying his older brother to the corner store may learn that his brother receives candy in exchange for money. Thus he demonstrates the ability to profit from his older brother's experience.

In the other form of observational learning, the learner focuses on the observation of the *actions* of the model rather than their outcomes. Here, the *model* is not rewarded for his actions, but the *learner* is rewarded if he matches the behavior just exhibited by the model. This type of situation involves what Miller and Dollard (1941) have termed *matched-dependent* behavior. Innumerable examples could be given. The child repeating an act performed by his parent is often rewarded for "being cute"; the child is rewarded by success when he copies an acrobatic maneuver performed by his more skilled brother; with social approval the child learns new words by repeating those used by his parents. Both forms of observational learning have often been called *imitation.*

IDENTIFICATION

Identification has long been prominent in theories of socialization, since it provides a social-psychological explanation of how the child learns new behavior — and social roles in particular — as well as how he develops internal controls or a conscience. Identification has been defined in a number of ways by different writers.[1] The concept is closely related to imitation, and at times the two concepts are treated as if they were interchangeable. Some writers, on the other hand, treat identification as virtually synonymous with socialization, whereas others limit it to a specific process, such as matched-dependent learning, described in the last section.

Use of the concept of identification in this text will be severely restricted. We will focus attention upon identification as a process accounting for the *choice of one model rather than another.*

A number of principles, listed below, have been advanced by various investigators to account for choice of a model for identification. These principles are not mutually exclusive. Not only have writers proposed principles that overlap with those proposed by others, but a single theorist may employ more than one to explain identification.

1. *Secondary reinforcement.* A person is chosen as a model because he frequently rewards the learner.
2. *Vicarious reinforcement.* A person is chosen as a model because he receives rewards that are experienced vicariously by the learner.
3. *Withholding of love.* A person is chosen as a model because the learner fears that otherwise the person will withhold his love.
4. *Avoidance of punishment.* A person is chosen as a model because the learner fears that the person will otherwise injure him.
5. *Status envy.* A person is chosen as a model because he is envied as a recipient of rewards from others.
6. *Social power.* A person is chosen as a model because he has the power to reward (but does not necessarily reward the learner).
7. *Similarity to learner.* A person is chosen as a model because the learner perceives that he has a trait similar to one of his own.

[1]See Winch (1962) for a critical review of these definitions.

These basic ideas, as well as some more inclusive views of identification that combine several of these principles, are discussed in the following pages.

STUDY QUESTIONS

9. *Carefully distinguish between two major forms of observational learning. Which of these is called matched-dependent behavior?*
10. *Distinguish between imitation and identification in terms of their focus on different aspects of social learning.*
11. *State the seven reasons why a person might choose to identify with a particular model.*

Identification through secondary reinforcement

A well-known explanation of identification is the two-factor theory of "imitation" proposed by Mowrer (1950). His explanation is based upon the principle of secondary reinforcement from classical learning theory. This principle states that stimuli repeatedly associated with a stimulus that is followed by reinforcement themselves become reinforcing. For example, chimpanzees who have been taught to use poker chips to get food from a special vending machine can be made to perform other tasks by offering them chips as rewards (Wolfe, 1936).

In modeling, learning occurs as a result of repeated association of the model's behavior with rewards which the model gives the child. This association of the model's behavior with a reinforcing situation leads the behavior of the model to acquire "secondary reinforcing" properties. Thus when the child copies the model's behavior, he experiences self-administered reinforcement. For example, if the mother talks to the infant as she feeds him, her verbalizing behavior gradually acquires satisfying properties for itself alone. Eventually the infant will emit verbalizations because they have acquired reinforcing properties. Of course, the mother's verbalizations are beyond his capacity, and this example assumes that his own verbalizations are on a stimulus dimension of similarity to those of the mother. Finally, behaviors that are initially sustained because of secondary reinforcement are later maintained because they elicit positive rewards from other persons or from the environment. This process is illustrated by Figure 17–1.

An experiment with nursery school children presents some evidence in support of the secondary reinforcement interpretation of identification (Bandura & Huston, 1961). In the *nonreward* condition a female adult serving as model brought the child to the experimental room. After telling him to play with the toys on the floor, she occupied herself with paper work at a desk in a far corner of the room. In the *reward* condition, the model sat on the floor close to the child, and was positively demonstrative and rewarding during his play.

After two sessions a test of imitative learning was conducted. The model and the child played a simple "game," during which the model

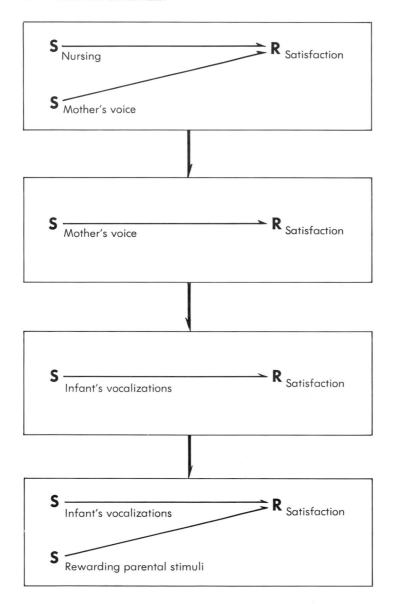

Figure 17–1
**Learning sequence in Mowrer's
two-factor theory of imitation.**

exhibited various novel verbal, motor, and aggressive behaviors totally irrelevant to the game.

When the child's "turn" in the game came, the children who had been in the reward condition showed considerably more imitative behavior than those in the nonreward condition. Children in the reward condition performed not only the behaviors necessary to play the game, but also reproduced the irrelevant actions of the model. Some of these behaviors were continued after the game as the child left the experimental room, a fact which supports the idea that they had taken on secondary reinforcing properties.

Vicarious reinforcement in identification

Bandura (1962) has pointed to evidence that when models are observed being reinforced for certain behaviors, the observer is more likely to perform these behaviors. One interpretation of these empirical findings is that the observer experiences the model's reinforcements vicariously. Bandura reports two experiments designed to test the hypothesis that rewarding the model increases the probability that the observer will adopt some of his behaviors. In one experiment, three groups of nursery school children observed child models under three different conditions: (1) an aggressive model was rewarded, (2) an aggressive model was punished, and (3) a nonaggressive model was neither punished nor rewarded. A fourth group of children had no exposure to models. As predicted, the model who had been observed being rewarded was copied to the greatest extent.

A side finding of especial significance was that even though the aggressive model was imitated, his attributes were negatively evaluated. For example, in speaking of the model, Rocky, children used phrases such as "Rocky is harsh. I be harsh like he was . . . Rough and bossy . . . Mean . . . Wicked . . . He whack people" (Bandura, 1962, p. 234). Thus the model does not have to be attractive or liked to be identified with. Postexperimental interviews with the children emphasized that the model's success in gaining and controlling the resources (toys) in the situation was the primary basis of attraction to his behavior, not inherent attractiveness of the aggressive behavior itself. An earlier study documents the point that it is the successful person who is chosen as the model, regardless of the form of behavior he uses to obtain rewards (Zajonc, 1955).

In another study, by prearrangement with the experimenter, adult subjects served as models by responding with a word whenever the experimenter pointed to them (McBreaty, Marston, & Kanfer, 1961). In accordance with their instructions, one group of subjects gave an increasing number of animal words in successive trials. The other groups, naïve concerning the purposes of the experiment, were asked to respond on each trial for the first ten trials with the first word that occurred to them. During trials ten to forty, the naïve groups simply observed the instructed group, which emitted an increasing number of animal words, reaching a rate of 50 percent animal words in the last two trials.

Two kinds of naïve observer groups were used under different conditions. One observed the models being reinforced with experimenter approval whenever they responded with animal words, and the other observed no reinforcement from the experimenter. In a subsequent test session, both kinds of observer groups were put through ten rounds to see if their rate of emitting animal words increased as a result of observation. Both groups significantly increased their responses of animal words, but the rate for those who had observed the models receiving approval was *not* significantly greater than for those who had observed the models not receiving approval. Thus, although the experiment which was previously cited supports the principle of vicarious reinforcement, this experiment does not. Here the same degree of learning occurred whether or not the models were seen to receive approval from the experimenter.

A dependency theory of identification

This theory makes use of the notions of secondary reinforcement and withholding of love. According to Sears (1957), identification occurs when the observer becomes *dependent* on the model. Because the mother initially satisfies the child's biological needs, her actions become reinforcing in their own right, making the child dependent on her. He adopts many of her actions because they are self reinforcing. Dependency is strengthened by occasional withdrawal of the mother's love from the child: when she is absent he needs to perform these actions to achieve satisfaction. Sears (1957, p. 155) notes that if the mother is always present and nurturant, the child will have little occasion to copy her action in order to obtain self reinforcement. Also, if she is not nurturant, or is disapproving or punitive, the child will not be motivated to reproduce her actions. Peak strength of the motive to identify is achieved when the child is given affection and nurturance which are periodically withdrawn, creating a situation where the child will be rewarded by reproducing the parent's behavior.

STUDY QUESTIONS

12. *Explain identification in terms of the principle of secondary reinforcement.*
13. *What is meant by vicarious reinforcement as a motive for identification?*
14. *What is the dependency theory of identification?*

A status-envy theory of identification

Whiting (1960) has offered a theory of identification in which the underlying motivation is seen as status envy. As illustrated by the following quotation, the child is motivated to identify with a parent or others by his envy of their control over resources. He is so motivated only if the person controlling the resources withholds them from him.

> If a child perceives that another has more efficient control over resources than he has, if, for example, he sees other people enjoying and consuming resources of high value to him when he is deprived of them, he will envy such a person and attempt to emulate him. . . .
> From this it follows that a child will not envy the status of the person who gives him resources because in this instance he, the child, is the consumer of the resource and already occupies the envied status. He will, on the contrary,

envy the status of those resource mediators who withhold resources from him, deprive him of resources that were formerly his, and consume or enjoy these resources in his presence. This process may be termed *envy of resource mediator*. (P. 118)

Motivation to identify with another person is produced by status envy. Actual learning to identify consists of playing the role of the envied status. Whiting (1960) further illustrates the point:

The more a child envies the status of another with respect to the control of a given resource, the more he will covertly practice that role. By covert practice we mean that he will indulge in fantasy in which he sees himself as the envied person controlling and consuming the valued resources of which he has been deprived. It is this fantasy of being someone other than himself that we would like to define as identification. . . . (P. 119)

Whiting apparently does not regard social power itself as a source of identification. In his view, control over resources does not produce identification unless the mediator of resources withholds them from the child, producing envy. The mediator who freely rewards the child is not identified with, even though he is powerful by virtue of the resources available to him. Furthermore, Whiting states that "if the resource mediator withholds a resource from a child and gives it to a third person, this third person will occupy the envied status" (p.118). Thus status envy produces identification with the recipient of rewards, not the controller of rewards, unless the controller rewards himself and deprives the observer. In the latter case he is also a recipient. The experiment described in the following section is relevant to this issue.

A comparative experiment

A recent experiment compares the effectiveness of secondary reinforcement, social power, and status envy in producing identification (Bandura, Ross, and Ross, 1962). A three-person group was established as a prototype of the family. In this study, a child observed two adults. In one experimental condition, one adult was the controller of resources and rewards, consisting of especially attractive play materials in the experimental room. He permitted another adult to play with these materials. The *social power* interpretation of identification would predict that the child would later identify with the power figure—the adult controlling the toys. The *status-envy* theory would predict, on the other hand, that the child would identify with the consumer—the adult allowed to play with the toys. A second experimental condition contained an adult controller of resources as before, but it was the child, not the other adult, who was allowed to play with the materials. According to the *secondary reinforcement* theory, the child would identify with the adult who allowed him to play with the toys.

These sessions were followed by another session in which the two adults exhibited divergent behaviors in the presence of the child, so that the experimenter might determine which of them the child would later model his behavior after. The results clearly favored social power over status envy as a basis for identification. More than twice as many imitative acts were patterned after the power figure than after the consumer. The number of imitative acts in the social power condition were also greater than those in the secondary reinforcement condition, where the child was rewarded and the other adult ignored. Rather unexpectedly, however, in the secondary reinforcement condition the ignored adult frequently served as a model, particularly when he was male. The experimenter interpreted this as reflecting sympathy for the ignored male and criticism of the power figure for being selfish.

STUDY QUESTIONS

15. *Explain identification in terms of status envy.*
16. *Distinguish between status envy and social power as bases for identification.*
17. *Describe the experiment comparing social power, status-envy, and secondary reinforcement interpretations of identification, and indicate what conclusions were drawn.*

A similarity theory of identification

Stotland (1961) has suggested a form of identification having a quite different basis from other forms discussed to this point. According to him, there is a kind of identification based on a perceptual-cognitive process, as opposed to a learning process involving motivation. He believes that identification of this nature may be particularly useful in explaining some forms of unintentional or incidental learning. Identification based on similarity occurs when a person conceives of himself and another individual as having some trait in common and further perceives that the other individual has some additional trait. He then believes himself to have the second trait and often behaves accordingly.

Particularly distinctive in this form of identification is that any two attributes that just happen to be found in another person may result in identification, if the observer possesses one of them. No meaningful relation between the attributes is required, nor does the observer need to have a motive for identifying. The model need not be an object of affection or fear, as in some of the previously discussed theories. One condition determining whether or not identification occurs is the congruence of the model's trait with one's self concept. Identification may not occur when the trait is particularly incongruent with the existing self concept.

In one of Stotland's experiments, a girl working alone was led to believe that she was a member of a three-person group. She was asked to choose the musical tune she preferred in each of eight pairs of tunes. *After* making her choice, she heard over earphones two other girls state their preferences. She then announced her own choices into a (dead) microphone. In fact, the two other girls were paid participants whose voices were transcribed. The girl was led to believe that her preferences were more similar to one of the two paid participants than to the other. She was then given another task to perform, but this time was allowed to hear the choices made by each of the paid participants *before* making her choice. The second task consisted of indicating which nonsense syllable she preferred in each of ten pairs of syllables. The purpose of this procedure, of course, was to determine whether, in choosing preferred syllables, she would favor the preferences of the paid participant who had made choices of musical tunes most similar to her own. Seventy college women participated in this experimental situation, and it was found that they did prefer the nonsense syllables chosen by the paid participant with whom they agreed more often on musical preferences, especially when the musical preferences were strong.

An extensive series of other experiments conducted by Stotland and his colleagues deals with different traits and characteristics as a basis for similarity, as well as with various situational variables that might affect the process of identification. These studies lend general support to his similarity theory of identification.

Learning to identify

Learning by identification occurs frequently because persons learn through experience to imitate successful models when they need to solve a problem. In many social situations, a person may be uncertain about how to act. One way out of the dilemma is to copy someone else's behavior. But a person does not simply choose a model at random; he has learned through experience that some models are more likely to perform the right actions than others. Thus he may choose someone who resembles previously successful models, or he may choose someone who frequently receives rewards. The observer has learned what *kind of model* generally gets what he wants; therefore it seems wise to imitate that kind of model. For example, children rapidly learn to imitate their older siblings and their parents. A boy whose older brother has a bicycle insists on having one too. In general, persons chosen as models are older, more intelligent, and possessed of special knowledge, status, or skills.[2]

Perhaps *negative identification* deserves brief discussion (Winch, 1962). On occasion a person may serve as a model for how *not* to behave. This is apt to occur where the model is disliked. Here the observer is expected to adopt behavior opposite to that displayed by the model. Little experimental work is available in support of the concept. Moreover, it is readily confused with a closely related situation that might not involve identification at all. A common observation in families is that a child, particularly in adolescence, acquires strong dislikes toward selected characteristics of one or both parents and emphasizes his distaste by behaving in an opposite fashion. For example, a son or daughter may become resentful of a mother's insistence on scrupulous tidiness and consequently may adopt

[2]Donald Campbell (1961) has a more extended discussion of this topic.

untidy habits on an extensive scale. In this instance the mother is not disliked as a person, but certain of her behaviors have become objectionable. This negative reaction may be explained in terms of operant learning, without invoking identification. Where the mother sets an impossible standard, any half-hearted attempts to comply with her demands for tidiness are met with her disapproval. This negatively reinforces tidy actions, decreasing the probability of their occurrence.

Symbolic models

Models for identification need not be actual persons. Behaviors may exist in symbolic form and for one reason or another may be copied. Thus figures in fiction or even figures created in the person's own imagination may serve as his models. The notion of an "ideal type" of person is relevant here. Moreover, a model need not be copied in his entirety; only certain elements of his behavior may be adopted. And by choosing elements of behavior from a variety of models, a person may produce original or creative behaviors.

STUDY QUESTIONS

18. *How may identification be explained in terms of similarity? What is the basic difference between this theory and all the previously discussed interpretations of identification?*

19. *What are the effects of repeated experience in identifying with models?*

20. *What is negative identification? What is a symbolic model?*

CONCLUSIONS: LEARNING FROM MODELS

Although there is general agreement that children learn by copying the behavior of models, not enough research has been conducted to appraise adequately the various theories of imitation and identification. Considerable support exists for the notion that secondary reinforcement leads to identification, and evidence from several sources supports the idea that withholding love strengthens dependency and consequent identification. But each of the various other ideas underlying identification also finds support in at least one experiment, and usually several. Moreover, none of the basic notions has been proved to be indispensable for identification to occur.

It may well be that several or all the mechanisms proposed may operate simultaneously or at different times to produce imitation and identification. For example, a model may be observed to receive rewards, may be a power person because of his control over resources, may be envied, and may have traits similar to those of the observer. In this instance several mechanisms converge to bring about identification. Identification is probably multidetermined in nearly all everyday situations.

Role Learning: Content and Process

The previous discussion presented various principles stressing differ-

ent conditions for social learning. The broader characteristics of socialization will be discussed now under the topic of role learning. Three related subjects will be covered: the content of role learning, the processes
of role learning, and the factors facilitating or interfering with role
learning.

Several concepts discussed in Chapter 14 are relevant to this section.
These are position, role expectations, role behavior, and role partner.
To recapitulate, a *position* is a category of persons occupying a certain
place in a social relation. Thus family systems have a position occupied by
a person referred to as mother. *Role expectations* are the thoughts, feelings,
and behaviors considered appropriate or inappropriate for the occupant
of a particular position. *Role behavior* is the behavior of the position occupant considered relevant to the expectations associated with the position.
Each position is linked to a number of counterpositions; in general, the
role expectations associated with a position pertain to the behavior that
the position occupant is expected to display toward persons occupying the
counterpositions. These counterposition occupants are called *role partners.*
For example, a role partner of the mother is the child.

THE CONTENT OF ROLE LEARNING

Role learning includes learning to behave, feel, and see the world in
a manner similar to other persons occupying the *same* position as oneself.
Because of the necessity for learning how to interact effectively with other
persons while playing the role, the behavior, feelings, and orientations
of role partners are also learned. The mother of a newborn infant not
only learns how it feels to be a mother, but also gradually acquires insight
into the feelings of her child. In addition, role learning is important in the
development of those perceptual-cognitive responses collectively referred
to as the *self.* The first two aspects of role learning will be discussed below;
discussion of the self will be deferred until Chapter 19.

Learning norms and values associated with the role

Fellow position occupants share an overall ideology concerning their
relations to role partners. They agree on appropriate attitudes and behavior toward counterposition occupants. The hospital intern, aspiring
to the role of physician, learns to view nurses, patients, and hospital
orderlies as other doctors view these role partners. Similarly, the fledgling
thief learns from his more professional associates appropriate ways of
viewing victims and the police (Sutherland, 1937).

The role aspirant acquires other attitudes and values shared by the
more experienced occupants of the position. The girl wants to be beautiful and popular with boys, and the boy dreams of becoming a champion
athlete. The medical student learns the attitudes of physicians toward
life and death and toward the uncertainty of medical knowledge, as well
as more mundane matters like bill collecting.

The role learner also acquires appropriate emotional responses to his own actions or those of others that conform or deviate from the values and norms he has acquired. He learns to apply sanctions to himself and to others when behavior deviates from accepted norms. These reactions of pride, approval, disgust, rage, guilt, and shame effectively shape his behavior and experience in the desired directions.

Often role expectations require that the occupant experience emotions or feelings quite different from those of persons who are in similar situations but do not occupy the same role. Young boys, for example, gradually learn not to cry in circumstances where it may be quite appropriate for young girls to cry. Learning the role of physician provides a somewhat more complex example: The male medical student must learn to inhibit responses of sexual excitement to female nudity. The female learning the role of patient similarly learns to inhibit responses of embarrassment when examined by a physician. Another emotion inhibited by physicians is like or dislike of patients. Two studies describe how physicians learn to inhibit these feelings and note that such emotions might otherwise interfere with professional obligations to accord equal interest and care to all patients (Martin, 1957; Daniels, 1960).

Role skills and techniques

Most roles have certain skills and techniques associated with them that must be learned. These are easily noted by comparing the awkward situations frequently experienced by the novice with the smoothly functioning relations to other people characterizing the experienced position occupant's behavior. These skills and techniques fall into two classes: (1) those which are directly related to the accomplishment of the tasks inherent in the role, and (2) those which deal with certain recurrent problems that position occupants face — problems which are only indirectly, if at all, related to the manifest function of the role. For example, the pickpocket must learn not only how to extract valuables from a person without detection, but also how to avoid arrest if detected. Moreover, if he is arrested, he must know how to avoid prosecution and conviction — for example, he must be competent in techniques of bribing and fabrication (Sutherland, 1937).

Another class of techniques not inherently related to a role involves the handling of stress. Those in occupations where competing emergencies constantly arise learn how to play one emergency against another so as to maintain some control over their activities. Hughes (1958), commenting on such devices, notes in part:

> The worker thinks he knows from long experience that people exaggerate their troubles. He therefore builds up devices to protect himself, to stall people off. This is the function of the janitor's wife when a tenant phones an appeal or a demand for immediate attention to a leaky tap; it is also the function of the doctor's wife and even sometimes of the professor's wife. The physician plays one emergency off against the other; the reason he can't run

right up to see Johnny who may have the measles is that he is, unfortunately, right at that moment treating a case of the black plague. (P. 55)

Perception of own role

Finally, as a result of his socialization experiences, the neophyte learns to see himself in a new way. As noted in more detail in Chapter 19, in each new role the person sees himself in ways that he imagines role partners see him, and thus he adds new elements to his self conception. To illustrate, as he progresses through medical school, the medical student who behaves and is seen by others behaving as a doctor begins to see himself as a doctor (Huntington, 1957).

STUDY QUESTIONS

21. *Perceptions, feelings, and behavior all enter into role learning. Give an example of each of these aspects of role learning.*
22. *In what respects are norms and values involved in role learning?*
23. *What are two classes of role skills and techniques that must be learned?*

ROLE LEARNING PROCESS

Role learning encompasses all the social learning principles discussed earlier in this chapter as well as all the principles that have been examined in Chapters 3 to 6 on attitude change and conformity. The only distinctive unity to role learning is that these principles combine to structure the behavior of group members in a manner appropriate for the positions they occupy. Perhaps we may gain a deeper understanding of role learning if we set up an oversimplified conception of the learning process and then note ways in which the conception inadequately portrays role learning.

One oversimplified conception of the socialization process is that the experienced position occupant teaches the new role to the candidate for the position. Such a teacher-student conception is deficient in a number of respects. First, it emphasizes the process of tuition and neglects other processes of social learning. For example, much role learning occurs through practice, in the absence of a teacher. Thus role learning will vary according to the opportunities provided for practice. Also, learning occurs as a result of encountering and arriving at solutions to problems inherent in the role. The development of appropriate emotional detachment on the part of the medical student is learned in part by role practice and tuition, but more dramatic learning occurs following the discomfort aroused when the medical student becomes too attached to a patient. One medical student asserts (Daniels, 1960):

> As a student in medical school I tended to become more emotionally identified with the patient, or at least with those who were loved ones of the patient. I had to learn to restrain myself, to see that this is just another case of something that will go on and on and never end completely, as long as there is human life and death. . . . (P. 260)

The teacher-student conception of role learning also suggests that the learner is relatively passive. In fact, however, he is active, choosing ways of playing a particular role from a permissible range of expectations. The medical student makes choices at several points: between general medicine and psychiatry, between research and clinical work, and between surgery and internal medicine. Finally, in some cases, he chooses a narrow specialty such as heart surgery or dermatology from a wide range of specialties.

The teacher-student conception also places too little emphasis on role partners. The behavior of persons who occupy counterpositions in the learner's role set contributes much to role learning. For example, the medical student's thoughts, feelings, actions, and self conceptions are modified not only through direct instruction, but also as a result of the ways in which patients, fellow medical students, nurses, and others in his role set behave toward him. The emphasis on the role of the teacher, similarly, blinds us to the important part played by peers in socialization. Fellow role learners serve as sources of reward, as instructors, and as models.

Finally, the teacher-student paradigm suggests that socialization is a series of lessons with beginnings and ends. In fact, however, many role elements are learned long before the point in time designating the beginning of the lesson. For example, certain elements in the role of the doctor are learned in a crude form even by the child as a patient.

STUDY QUESTIONS

24. *What are the limitations of the teacher-student conception of role learning?*
25. *In what ways are the following two factors important to role learning: (a) the problem situations encountered, and (b) the behavior of counterposition occupants?*

Role Learning: Facilitating and Interfering Factors

Further understanding of role learning can be gained by examining factors that facilitate or interfere with it. As in the case of bodily processes, we are seldom aware of role learning until something interferes with its normal functioning. For purposes of exposition, facilitating and interfering factors will be divided into three categories: those primarily related to characteristics of the social system through which the learner is moving, those related to features of the role learning situation, and finally, those stemming from relevant characteristics of the individual.

ROLE LEARNING AND THE SOCIAL SYSTEM

In Chapters 15 and 16 features resulting in role strain and its resolution were discussed. The same features often interfere with or facilitate learning.

Clarity and consensus

The *clarity* of the expectations attached to a position affects the ease with which it is learned. For instance, the female might be expected to have a more difficult time than the male in learning her sex role because in our society this role is not very clear (Rose, 1951). The degree of *consensus* on appropriate behavior for a position occupant might also be expected to affect learning. Where there is consensus, rewards for appropriate behaviors are more likely to be consistently applied and thus to facilitate learning.

What has been said with reference to clarity and consensus of expectations applies with equal force to positions. If one's role partner is not clear as to the position one holds, or if one's role partners do not agree on one's position, learning is more difficult. Illustrative cases are a mother who treats her grown daughter sometimes as an adult and at other times as a child, or a son who is treated by his father at an appropriate age level and by his mother as a baby.

Where cues to positions are clear, confusion is less likely. For instance, sex-role learning is undoubtedly facilitated by the obviousness of the cues to sexual identity. Because his sex is seldom mistaken, a person is rarely treated inappropriately for his role. Cues to age status are not as obvious. A twenty-one-year-old person may be treated like an adolescent in one instance and like an adult in another, an inconsistency which interferes with his learning appropriate adult behavior.

Compatibility of expectations

Compatability between simultaneously assumed roles and between successive roles will further affect role learning. Role learning is a continuous process of learning new responses and discarding old ones. A child passing from one age category to the next, a military cadet moving from one class to the next, or a medical student becoming an intern face difficulties if there are discontinuities between expectations for each successive position. Chapters 15 and 16 have dealt in some detail with these problems as well as with social system features, such as the rites of passage, which facilitate or impair the ease of transition. A somewhat analogous problem has not been dealt with, however. Roles vary in the compatibility of expectations held by occupants and nonoccupants. This has prompted some students (Simpson, 1960; Hughes, 1958) of occupational socialization to place major emphasis on the process by which the learner puts aside the lay conception of the occupation and learns to view his role as other position occupants do. Simpson (1960) has described this process for student nurses. The matriculating nursing student views the nursing role largely in terms of a humanitarian, nurturant relation to patients. After a year and a half of training, however, she sees the role in terms of specific technical skills, as do professional nurses. Although direct evidence is lacking, it is plausible to assume that the greater the difference between the lay conception of the role held by the aspirants to the position and the role expectations of those persons already socialized, the more difficulty the aspirants will have in learning the new role.

Learning prior to position entry

Many elements of a role are learned prior to the time one occupies a position. First, they can be learned by adopting a role in play or in fantasy. Before she enters nursing training, a woman has learned some of the elements in the nursing role first by playing nurse as a child and later by rehearsing this role in her daydreams. Second, learning similar roles may facilitate learning a new role. In learning and playing the role of girl scout, a woman has learned first-aid techniques that will later be part of her nursing repertory. Third, occupying positions that are related to a role provides a person an opportunity to gain some acquaintance with the roles of his partners. For example, a nursing trainee has probably occupied the counterposition of patient and as such has learned certain elements in the nursing role.

A study has provided evidence in support of the principle that through interaction with role partners one may learn elements in the role associated with a counterposition (Brim, 1958). Under certain circumstances, these elements are likely to be assimilated into one's own role. Reasoning from the general principle set forth originally by Cottrell (1942) that persons incorporate elements of the role of the other into their own roles, it was hypothesized that children with siblings of the opposite sex would possess more traits appropriate to the opposite-sex role than children with same-sex siblings would. The personality traits of 192 pairs of young siblings, rated by schoolteachers, were classified as belonging to the masculine or feminine role. Some sibling pairs consisted of brother and sister, while others were both boys or both girls.

Two hypotheses tested with respect to sex-role traits were as follows: (1) Cross-sex siblings were expected to possess more traits appropriate to the opposite-sex role, and (2) this assimilation of traits belonging to the opposite-sex role was expected to be more noticeable for the younger sibling. The reasons for the second hypothesis are that the older sibling is more likely to be a model for identification and that, being older, he is better able to differentiate his own from his sibling's role, thus resisting the assimilation of cross-sex traits.

The data, tabulated separately for each sex, consisted of frequency counts of the number of masculine and feminine traits possessed by siblings in each of the four types of sibling pairs. Both hypotheses were supported. The older girl with a younger brother had more high-masculinity traits and fewer low-masculinity traits than her counterpart, the older girl with a younger sister. Even more striking was the number of masculine traits characterizing the younger girl with the older brother. Similar results were obtained for boys, although differences were not as pronounced. In conclusion, the experiment demonstrates that under certain conditions, frequent interaction with a role partner produces some assimilation of the characteristics of the partner's role.

Role learning will be facilitated where social systems are so organized that persons normally occupy positions which are counter to those they occupy later. Where the counterposition involves behavior contrary to that expected in the position occupied later, however, this facilitating effect in part may be counterbalanced by the necessity of unlearning behavior incompatible with the new role.

A facilitating effect might also be expected where persons in late phases of a position are given the opportunity to practice the role behaviors of the position they will occupy next. Such is the case for the medical student, who in his clinical year of training is allowed to perform various aspects of the physician role. Where such practice is based on an inappropriate conception of the role, however, the neophyte may have to unlearn such responses when he does occupy the position.

Pervasiveness of a role

Roles differ in the number and variety of behaviors they encompass. Some roles include a relatively small portion of an individual's total behavior; others may be all-encompassing. The latter type takes more time and effort to learn. Contrast the occupational role of a priest, for example, with that of a carpenter. The former role pervades almost all aspects of the priest's life and requires a long, arduous period of socialization, whereas the role of carpenter is segregated from other aspects of the carpenter's life and is learned in a much shorter period.

Rewards and costs of roles

Finally, roles may be contrasted with respect to the rewards and costs of occupying a position. Persons may be highly motivated to learn one role but not another because of differences in their reward value. Age roles are a case in point. The child may be highly motivated to adopt the role of youth and the youth that of mature adult. In American society, however, persons are not motivated to adopt the role of the aged or even the middle-aged.

STUDY QUESTIONS

26. *Summarize the ways in which clarity and consensus facilitate or interfere with role learning.*
27. *Summarize the ways in which compatability of role expectations facilitates or interferes with role learning.*
28. *How may social system factors facilitate or interfere with role learning prior to entry?*
29. *How do pervasiveness of a role and the amount of satisfaction in the role contribute to learning?*

ROLE LEARNING AND SITUATIONAL CHARACTERISTICS

Socialization by some groups effects dramatic changes in the behavior of the learner, but for other groups it results in only a few superficial changes. Contrast the changes that accompany socialization by a religious order, a military academy, or even a graduate school with those that occur as the individual becomes a member of a fraternal organization, a service club, or a similar group. In some instances, these differences reflect the nature of the role itself: some roles are more encompassing than others. But also they reflect the fact that some groups operate under conditions that maximize the effectiveness of their attempts to socialize their members. In fact, where extensive changes must accompany position occupancy, the group normally commands optimum conditions for socialization. In cases of extremely effective socialization such as those occurring in the Chinese war colleges or POW camps referred to in Chapter 6, in military academies, or in professional graduate schools, a number of features that facilitate the adoption of new behavior and identities are apparent.

Conditions producing desocialization

First are factors serving to divest the neophyte of his previous roles and group allegiances. In some instances the learner is physically isolated from persons who had previously gratified his needs and who had supported his previous statuses. This isolation is illustrated in socialization of the Coast Guard cadet (Dornbusch, 1955). For the first two months the new "swab" is not allowed to leave the base or in other ways to have contact with noncadets. All clues to previous social position are suppressed so that interaction in terms of earlier statuses is discouraged, as shown in the following quotation:[3]

Uniforms are issued on the first day, and discussion of wealth and family background are taboo. Although the pay of a cadet is very low, he is not permitted to receive money from home. The role of the cadet must supercede other roles the individual has been accustomed to play. There are few clues left which will reveal social status in the outside world.

Conditions intensifying socialization

Most socializing situations do not involve strict physical isolation, but the same effects may be accomplished by monopolizing the waking time of the learner through the sheer volume of demands made. The graduate student in a professional school, for example, generally finds little time for anything but study activities that restrict his interaction almost exclusively to other students and faculty. By ensuring that he will be treated according to his new position rather than his previous ones, such monopolization strengthens the new role behavior and weakens the old. Relatively exclusive interaction within the new group fosters the growth of each member's dependency on this group for satisfaction of needs, which in turn increases the cohesiveness of the group and its consequent influence on its members. The more control that socializing groups have over

[3]Dornbusch, 1955, p. 317. Reprinted by permission from *Social Forces*, published by the University of North Carolina Press.

the total situation in which the new group member finds himself the greater their effectiveness. As noted in Chapter 6, the effectiveness of the form of socialization known as brainwashing stems in part from the extensive control over reward and punishment in the POW situation.

Rituals and ceremonies often facilitate initiation into a group role. The practice of hazing, for example, appears to have a number of effects. By emphasizing the low status of the prospective member, previous social positions are depreciated and the attractiveness of the new position is heightened. In effect, the pledge is told: "No matter who or what you were, you are nothing now but a lowly pledge; but if you successfully pass through this period you will have all the rewards of our lofty status."

The sharp contrast between the low status of the prospective member and that of the fully accepted member of the group should maximize the status envy experienced by the potential member, thus motivating him to identify with the accepted member. The worth of the new status may be increased by the discomforts experienced by the learner during hazing. On the basis of dissonance theory (see Chapter 3), persons would be expected to view the position as having increased in value in order to balance the cognitions of having willingly exposed themselves to the discomforts of hazing (Aronson & Mills, 1959).

Hazing also appears to increase cohesion among prospective members as they form a protective ingroup against the onslaughts of the socializing agents. Such cohesion will facilitate learning, providing that the group of new candidates does not develop norms opposed to those which the socializing agents are trying to inculcate. A variety of factors works against this outcome, including a curious feature of the hazing process itself; namely, a temporary reversal of roles. For a day, fraternity pledges may revolt, capture one or more active members, and subject him to some of the indignation which they experience. Dornbusch has suggested that "Gizmo Day," a variant of this practice in the Coast Guard Academy, has the effect of reducing hostility between swab and upperclassmen by teaching the swab that hazing is not a personal matter but a feature of the social system. He describes what the swab learns:[4]

> One is not being hazed because the upperclassman is a sadist, but because one is at the time in a junior status. Those who haze do not pretend to be superior to those who are being hazed. Since some of those who haze you will try to teach you how to stay out of trouble, it becomes impossible to attribute evil characteristics to those who injure you. The swab knows he will have his turn at hazing others. At most, individual idiosyncrasies will just affect the type of hazing done.
>
> This emphasis on the relativity of status is explicitly made on the traditional Gizmo Day on which the swabs and their hazers reverse roles. The swabs-for-a-day take their licking without flinching and do not seek revenge later, for they are aware that they are under the surveillance of the first-classmen. After the saturnalia, the swabs are increasingly conscious of their inability to blame particular persons for their trouble.

[4]Dornbusch, 1955, p. 319. Reprinted by permission from *Social Forces*, published by the University of North Carolina Press.

More rigorous ordeals, such as rites of passage, have additional functions: that of emphasizing for the neophyte the features of the new role which contrast with the previous role, and that of proving that he is capable of this new behavior. This fits in with the empirical finding that the greater the changes required from one age role to the next, the more intense the ordeal (Whiting, Kluckhohn, & Anthony, 1958).

Related to hazing and sometimes a part of it is the ritualistic performance of behaviors that are inconsistent with one's previous roles. Such performances range from primitive ordeals among nonliterates to public confessions of error in modern societies. Confessions were a prominent feature of socialization in the Chinese war colleges described in Chapter 6. On the basis of dissonance theory, one would expect that the practice of condemning past behavior, such as filial piety, would produce cognitive elements dissonant with the past behavior and would reduce the likelihood of its recurrence.

Conditions facilitating role learning through identification

Learning of the new role is affected by the conditions which facilitate or inhibit identification with the role model. Studies of socialization in medical school and in graduate schools have dealt with the effects of using faculty members or peers as models (Merton, Reader, & Kendall, 1957; Gottlieb, 1960; Kendall, 1960). The role of an established group member as model has already been discussed extensively. Also important, however, are peers.

Two conditions affecting the choice of models were previously noted. First, the model often possesses something that the identifier wishes to have: love, privileges, etc. Second, similarity of the model to the identifier encourages identification. Whereas established group members might serve as models because of their control over resources, peers might be expected to serve as models because of their similarity to the learner. In fact, a near-peer, a person who is somewhat further advanced in the socialization process, should be especially effective as a model. The near-peer is similar to the learner but also has obtained some of the privileges of the established group member. A child might be expected to model his behavior after a somewhat older child. An undergraduate might similarly take a graduate student as a model, and a first-year medical student a second- or third-year student.

ROLE LEARNING AND INDIVIDUAL CHARACTERISTICS

The discussion of role strain in Chapter 15 indicated that possession of appropriate abilities and personality characteristics, as well as an appropriate self conception, facilitates role performance. It follows that these characteristics also facilitate *learning* role behavior. A more detailed examination of the role of the self in this context will be deferred until Chapter 19.

STUDY QUESTIONS

30. *What is meant by desocialization? What conditions maximize this process?*

31. *Discuss the various conditions that are effective in intensifying socialization.*

32. *What factors favor choice of a near-peer as a model for identification?*

Summary and Conclusions

Although traditionally the focus of socialization has been upon child development, the current conceptualization includes any process whereby a person's behavior is modified to conform to the normative expectations held by members of groups to which he belongs.

Some social learning may be explained in terms of operant learning in which the frequency of emission of actions is modified by the occurrence of reinforcements according to some particular schedule. Much social learning is incidental or unintentional. Certain actions of the child performed accidentally are reinforced by parents or by circumstances and are thus learned. Direct tuition plays an important part in human learning. Here the training agent uses language to elicit and guide behavior in desired directions.

Much learning in humans appears to be based upon the observation of the behavior of other humans, as where a child imitates his parents. Theoretical discussion revolves around the concept of identification, focusing on the motivation for choice of model. Concepts used in explaining why a person might choose another as a model include the following: secondary reinforcement, vicarious reinforcement, withholding of love, avoidance of punishment, status envy, social power, and similarity to the learner. Sufficient research has not been carried out to draw firm conclusions about the various explanations; some empirical support seems to be available for all of them. In everyday situations, these processes probably function simultaneously.

A more general form of social learning is role learning, which includes learning to behave, feel, and see the world in a manner similar to other persons occupying the same role position as oneself. Underlying role learning are the processes of social learning discussed above. Role learning also includes acquiring an understanding of the attitudes of occupants of counterpositions and learning certain skills and techniques associated with the role. Critical elements in the role learning process include not only direct tuition by experienced occupants of the role position, but the forced learning brought about by problem situations and the behaviors of counterposition occupants.

A variety of conditions in the social system facilitates or interferes with role learning. One factor is the clarity and consensus with which positions are perceived by occupants, aspirants, and counterposition occupants. Compatibility of expectations within role sectors and within role sets is also important. To some degree, role learning may be facilitated by learning that occurs prior to position entry. This includes not only practicing the role in imaginative play or fantasy, but also learning elements of the role by occupying a counterposition. The ease with which roles may be learned varies with the extent to which they pervade many or few situations in a person's life. Extremely satisfying roles may create strong motivation, facilitating learning.

A variety of situational conditions also facilitates or interferes with role learning. Some groups operate under conditions that maximize socialization. A formal process by which the person is first desocialized is often effective. This includes his isolation from previous relations and positions, either by physical means or through monopolization of his time. The greater the control of the group over rewards and punishment, the greater the person's dependency on it and therefore the more effective the socialization process. Rituals and ceremonies such as hazing are often useful. They depreciate the current status of the prospective member and enhance the attractiveness of the position aspired to. Finally, opportunities for identification facilitate role learning.

chapter eighteen

SOCIALIZATION: INTERNALIZATION
AND THE SOCIAL STRUCTURE

The socialization processes discussed in the previous chapter produce profound changes in the individual. They establish a set of behavior standards and create a wide variety of motive patterns and associated habits. Behavior standards have their origin in the expectations that other persons hold toward the child's behavior. Gradually the child adopts these as his own, and at this point they are commonly referred to as the *conscience*.

The conscience is a system of norms that a person applies to his own acts or contemplated acts to arrive at a judgment of their rightness or wrongness. Typically, acts that are wrong according to these norms produce feelings of shame and guilt, which in turn lead to various behaviors intended to reduce guilt feelings. Actions in harmony with these norms either go unnoticed or produce positive feelings toward the self. Often psychologists and psychoanalysts refer to norms that function in this way as *internal controls*. The entire process by which the norms of the parents are adopted by the child is known as *internalization*.

Social motives include such behavior patterns as dependency, aggression, and achievement; these arise from certain socialization experiences to be described later. For example, a strong drive for achievement may be encouraged by parents who place stress on success, competition, and ways of getting ahead.

Factors in Conscience Formation

EFFECTS OF ISOLATION

A crucial first step in the socialization process is the following: *The infant must become dependent upon another person who acts as a socializing agent.* Unless acceptance by other persons is vitally important to the child, he will have little motivation for modifying his behavior in directions desired by them. The first prerequisite for the development of this dependency is the presence of another person. While children are usually born into families and cared for by them, in occasional instances a child has been relatively isolated during his early years because of parental neglect. In addition, children raised in some institutions may not experience the warm relation normally established between child and parent. These children have been studied and compared with those socialized in a typical family.

In two different cases of extreme isolation, mothers kept their infant daughters in solitude in a secluded room over a period of years, giving them only enough attention to keep them alive (Davis, 1947). When discovered around the age of six, both children were extremely retarded, exhibiting behavior resembling that of infancy. Neither could talk. One of them could not even walk. They exhibited fear of strangers and appeared unable to form a relation to other persons. Ultimately, one was placed in an institution for retarded children and died at an early age before developing very far. The other girl achieved a normal level of development.

Studies of children in institutions where individual attention from adults was extremely limited also report some physical and social retardation in a less extreme form (Spitz, 1945, 1946; Spitz & Wolfe, 1946; Dennis & Najarian, 1957). Moreover, older children who have spent their early years in an institutional environment exhibit more problem behavior, more demands for attention, and more aggression. They are retarded in speech development, mental development, and educational performance. Children of similar background who spent their early years in a foster home instead of an institution do not show these forms of retardation (Goldfarb, 1943*a*, 1943*b*).

It has been found that the home background of children with behavior problems is often characterized by extreme parental neglect (Bowlby, 1952, 1960; Redl & Wineman, 1951; Glueck & Glueck, 1950). Finally, research on animals raised from infancy in an atypical environment shows that they have abnormalities of one kind or another. Such environments either severely restrict sensory stimulation or establish some specific deficiency of environment that the investigator considers important (Fuller, 1960; Hebb, 1958; Scott & Marston, 1950). Examples of the latter include absence of the mother (Harlow, 1960) or lack of opportunity to interact with peers (Harlow & Harlow, 1962). Both conditions have striking consequences for the adult behavior of the animals who have been raised in this fashion.

From such studies, it is clear that environments involving restriction of one kind or another often affect the organism adversely. It is difficult, however, to identify the exact conditions responsible for the negative effects. Several factors have been suggested as primary causes:

1. The absence of a mother or mother substitute, resulting in lack of opportunity to form a close attachment to an adult, distorts or prevents later relations to others.

2. The restricted sensory stimulation interferes with the formation of perceptual categories, symbols, and concepts.

3. The restricted environment prevents the organism from learning how to profit from experience.

4. Infancy is a critical period during which certain stimulation and experience must be available for normal maturation. For example, a chimpanzee raised in complete darkness shows deterioration of the cells of the retina (Riesen, 1961). Apparently, without the stimulation of light the visual mechanism does not develop properly.

These interpretations are not mutually exclusive; in fact, they might all be operative.

Why adverse effects of early experience are not corrected by later learning requires explanation. In the first place, early reports probably exaggerated the extent to which such effects were permanent and irreversible (Pinneau, 1955). More thorough studies suggest that at least some degree of recovery is possible (Riesen, 1961). But there are good reasons why the effects of early experience might persist. Beach and Jaynes (1954) have suggested several:

1. Initially learned responses might interfere with learning later ones.

2. Habits learned earlier might be more persistent because of the greater strength of drives during infancy.

3. The age at which certain characteristics are acquired might be critical because of the maturation of the organism at given age periods.

The last point refers to the so-called *critical period* hypothesis. Recent evaluations of this hypothesis indicate that the range of the critical period during which learning must take place is somewhat broader than had been thought at first (Caldwell, 1961; Riesen, 1961). In fact, it has been suggested that what is more significant is not the age at which a behavior is learned, but whether or not the organism has been provided an opportunity to acquire certain experiences. At least it is clear that these essential conditions are unlikely to be met unless the child has an adequate relation to another human being.

ORIGINS OF DEPENDENCY

Dependency behavior is believed to arise according to the principle of secondary reinforcement discussed in Chapter 17. The behavior of other persons acquires reward value for the child through repeated association with satisfaction of his physical needs. As a result, he comes to desire the constant presence of the person who administers to his physical needs (normally the mother). He strives to gain her attention, help, and affection because it is rewarding. He gradually learns that if he acts in ways she approves of, he maximizes the rewards he receives from her. In addition, he learns to react with anxiety when she withdraws her support or approval. Various negative or disapproving actions on her part are signals that he might be deprived of the satisfactions she normally provides. When such situations occur, the termination of anxiety when disapproval is lifted is rewarding and probably deepens his attachment to her.

Eventually the mother becomes a "generalized reinforcing agent." Almost everyone has observed the power of a mother's comforting actions to soothe a crying, frightened child. Animal research has demonstrated that even an *inanimate* mother substitute may perform the same function under appropriate conditions. Harlow (1960) raised monkeys in the presence of dummies covered with terry cloth. The infants were observed to spend a good deal of time clinging to these terry-cloth "mothers," apparently to satisfy a primary need for contact. Later, when they were exposed to fear-arousing situations (e.g., the presence of a toy monster), the fright they exhibited appeared to be greatly appeased when they dashed over and clung to their terry-cloth mother. After a short period of such "reassurance," they often returned to inspect the frightening object, seemingly without fear.

In experimental studies of college students, it has been shown that the desire to be with others, often referred to as the *need for affiliation* (Murray, 1938), increases when the student is made anxious. Moreover, in several studies but not all of them, the strength of this form of dependency in the presence of anxiety was related to whether the person was the first-born or later-born child.[1] While the explanation of this finding may take several forms, the demonstrated relation underlines the point that early socialization experiences are significant determinants of dependency in childhood. In short, dependency appears to originate from a twofold process. The child gradually learns both that the presence and approval of the socializing agent is generally rewarding and that the absence or disapproval of the socializing agent is anxiety-arousing.

STUDY QUESTIONS

1. *Define the conscience. Explain what is meant by the following terms: (a) internal controls; (b) internalization.*

2. *Cite evidence for the fact that a dependent relation to another person is a necessary condition for adequate socialization of the child. Give several possible reasons why this is so.*

3. *Suggest some reasons why the undesirable effects of impoverished early experience are not readily overcome.*

4. *What is the origin of dependency? On what two factors does it rest?*

---

[1]Schachter, 1959; Gerard & Rabbie, 1961; Sarnoff & Zimbardo, 1961; Glass et al., 1963.

STRENGTH OF THE DEPENDENCY MOTIVE

Children vary in the strength of the dependency behavior they exhibit. In some families, children develop a very weak dependency motive and in others, an excessively strong dependency motive. A number of investigations suggest that some optimum schedule of reward and frustration of dependent responses leads to maximum strength of dependency and resultant internal controls.[2] For example, Sears, Maccoby, and Levin have attempted to relate dependency to child-rearing patterns. On the basis of interviews with mothers, they rated features of the mother's behavior and that of the child. Examining the ways in which mothers reacted to dependent actions of their children, they found that a combination of reward and punishment resulting in intermittent frustration of dependent actions produced the maximum strength of dependency in normal children. They (1957) concluded:

> When there was little reward for dependency, the amount of punishment for such behavior did not seem to make much difference in the amount of it that occurred. Only when punishment was superimposed upon a fair amount of reward was there an increase in the child's tendency to show the very behavior he was punished for. Looked at another way, reward for dependency had a tendency to increase dependency *only* when it was superimposed upon punishment for the same behavior. (P. 173)

Punishment interspersed with reward produces a stronger dependency need than reward alone. But in the absence of reward, the pain of punishment or fear of it is insufficient to produce strong dependency. Punishment from a loving parent is effective because it represents *withdrawal of love*. At the opposite extreme, a parent who greatly indulges his child, never exhibiting disapproval, would be expected to establish weaker dependency than one who frequently rewards his child and also occasionally exhibits disapproval or punishment.

Although this interpretation appears to be adequate, a well-known principle of learning may be offered as an alternate or supplemental explanation. In what is known as *variable ratio reinforcement,* reinforcement occurs aperiodically; that is, the same behavior is sometimes reinforced and sometimes not, in a pattern fixed by the experimenter but unknown to the organism. Such reinforcement produces strongly learned responses (Lewis, 1960). Behavior of parents in reinforcing their child's dependent behavior often takes a variable ratio form; this may well be an alternative interpretation for its effectiveness in producing dependency.

WARMTH, LOVE-ORIENTED DISCIPLINE, AND CONSCIENCE FORMATION

The child in interaction with other persons learns what conduct they expect from him. From their expectations, he forms a set of verbal rules

---

[2]Sears, Maccoby, & Levin, 1957; Bronfenbrenner, 1958; Hartup, 1958; Miller & Swanson, 1958; Antonovsky, 1959.

that he applies to himself. Sometimes one can directly observe these rules being applied, as when small children admonish themselves aloud. But by the time adulthood is reached, the "voice of our conscience" has become subvocal. When the child's behavior deviates from these internalized expectations, his verbal responses to it are likely to be accompanied by feelings of anxiety and guilt.

Probably all the processes of social learning described in Chapter 17 are involved in the learning of such internal controls, although the process most often emphasized is identification. When he talks to himself about his behavior, the small child can often be observed using the very tones and phrasing of his parents or other models. Internal controls will be maximized under the two conditions that maximize dependency and identification: the establishment of a warm relation between child and parent, and the use of love-oriented discipline.

Several lines of research support the view that *psychological* or *love-oriented* discipline is more effective than physical punishment in developing conscience. In psychological discipline the parent uses the affectional bond between him and the child to gain control over him. The parent performs some action threatening this bond, such as refusing to smile at him, sending him out of his presence, or telling him that he is difficult to like when he behaves "that way." Sears, Maccoby, and Levin find that maximum strength of conscience results from an alternation of acceptance and rejection, paralleling the alternation of reward and punishment in the development of dependency. Both the warmth of the relation between parent and child and the use of love-oriented techniques were independently associated to some degree with the strength of the child's conscience. When a warm relation was combined with psychological discipline, however, strength of conscience was maximized. The children having mothers who were relatively warm toward them, but who made their love contingent on the child's good behavior, appeared to have the most well-developed consciences. Another study reports that guilt arising from feelings of anger was greater among boys whose mothers used psychological punishment than among boys whose mothers used physical punishment (Allinsmith & Greening, 1955).

Cross-cultural studies also support the view that love-oriented discipline, in contrast to physical punishment or threat of punishment, produces a strong conscience. In one study comparing thirty-five primitive societies, those that made greater use of love-oriented disciplinary techniques also had a greater incidence of guilt feelings among its population than those using physical punishment (Whiting & Child, 1953). In this study, an indirect measure of guilt feelings was employed: the prevalence of the belief in the society that a person's illness was caused by his own actions. A more recent review provides further evidence for this association between love-oriented discipline and prevalence of guilt feelings (Whiting, 1959).

The very nature of human interaction in the family is likely to provide appropriate conditions for the optimum development of conscience. Almost any persons living together intimately are likely to develop strong attachments to each other and yet are also likely to frustrate each other's needs at times. Children, in particular, do not have sources of emotional support outside the family. Yet they have unsocialized needs that must be controlled by their parents. Thus the prerequisites for conscience development, warmth, and frustration of needs are present in the typical family.

Emotional warmth and love-oriented discipline are not always present in the optimum amount necessary to encourage dependency, identification, and conscience formation. Several illustrations may be given. First is the overprotective mother who, because of emotional problems of her own, is overly rewarding and seldom punitive toward the child (Levy, 1943). Thus, withdrawal of love, necessary for strong internal controls, does not occur with sufficient frequency. The case is expressed well by the everyday phrase "the spoiled child," who is self-centered, willful, and lacking in self-control because of his parents' failure to discipline him.

Second is the psychopathic parent, who is not sufficiently affectionate toward his children and who is likely to be overly punitive, weakening dependency and conscience formation. Socialization of this nature is likely to produce in the child a great deal of uncontrolled aggression and violence, along with various other forms of delinquency (Goldfarb, 1943*a*, 1943*b*). Similarly, institutionalized children, whose early years have been spent in an environment characterized by little emotional warmth, appear to develop insufficient internal controls (Bowlby, 1952).

A third condition is illustrated by the child who develops what might be thought of as an overly strong conscience. An erratic, unpredictable pattern of parental affection and withdrawal may well play an important part in this process. As a neurotic adult he suffers anxiety and guilt over minor deviations from normative expectations (Mowrer, 1950). Fourth, a review of the literature by Hoffman (1960, 1962, 1963), as well as some data of his own, suggests that the effects of love-oriented discipline are altered when parents combine it with influence techniques that rely on external pressure rather than the child's own controls. Such techniques demand an immediate change in the child's behavior, with no explanation for the demand and no attempt to compensate the child for the resulting deprivation. These techniques produce social withdrawal or internal controls based upon fear of punishment, and they engender hostility feelings toward the parents.

The conclusions may be drawn that conscience formation is a joint function of the development of a warm relation to a parent and the use of love-oriented discipline. In the absence of warmth, love-oriented discipline cannot be used, and internal controls are difficult to produce. Even when warmth is of sufficient strength, the use of physical instead of psychological punishment will impair development of the conscience.

COMPLEXITY OF CONSCIENCE FORMATION

The general view expressed by early psychoanalysts that the formation of the superego is mainly a process of incorporating parental values in early childhood has been widely accepted for many decades. Recent research, however, suggests that the conscience is *not* fully formed in early childhood, that forming it is *not* simply a process of adopting parental values, and that it is *not* a single entity.

For example, Kohlberg (1960, 1962) presents some evidence that moral development continues throughout childhood and adolescence and that interactions with other persons outside the family, particularly peers, are significant in the development of moral standards. In his view, the child passes through a series of stages of moral development, each stage representing a transformation of earlier ones. Another independent study suggests that interaction with peers in middle childhood further develops and elaborates moral notions that were primarily covert in early childhood (Maccoby, 1961). As findings accumulate from current research on moral development, it will no doubt be necessary to elaborate the principles which have been outlined here.

STUDY QUESTIONS

5. *Describe the relation between the strength of the dependency motive and certain aspects of parental behavior. In particular, comment on the roles of affection and punishment and variable ratio reinforcement.*

6. *What are the major factors in conscience formation? What conditions are unfavorable to the development of appropriate internal controls?*

7. *Comment on the possibility that the conscience may be formed simply by direct transmission of parental values to children.*

SUMMARY: DEPENDENCY AND CONSCIENCE FORMATION

Dependency of the child on other human beings is a prime condition for socialization. The initial basis for the dependency motive is the helplessness of the human infant, who is completely dependent upon adults for sustenance and shelter. Because the mother is the source of satisfaction of biological needs, behavior on her part associated with feeding and other drive-reducing activities acquires reward value through the principle of secondary reinforcement.

Dependency is further intensified through the developing relations between mother and child. Maternal warmth and affection combined with the use of love-oriented discipline appear to produce maximum dependency. Love-oriented discipline is the use of any technique that threatens the affectional tie between parent and child in order to elicit the desired behavior.

Conscience formation in turn is a function of the interaction between warmth and love-oriented discipline. Unless the child has a warm relation to another person, he will have little motivation for learning to expect from himself what others expect from him. Threats to this affectionate relation arouse anxiety, spurring him to behave in the approved manner and ultimately to adopt the standards of other persons as his own. Where affection is weak, where indulgence too great, or where physical punishment is employed in lieu of psychological punishment, internal controls are likely to be imperfectly developed.

Conscience Formation and the Social Structure

The previous discussion has shown that dependency and conscience formation are functions of the warmth of parents toward their children and the mode of discipline they use. If parents occupying different positions in the social structure differ in warmth and in forms of discipline used, dependency and internal controls appearing in their children would be expected to vary accordingly. That such differences in child rearing occur has been empirically demonstrated (Sears, Maccoby, & Levin, 1957; Bronfenbrenner, 1958; Miller & Swanson, 1958). In particular, socialization has been shown to vary with social class, family structure, and sex of the child.

SOCIAL CLASS AND DEPENDENCY TRAINING

Bronfenbrenner, in his review of the literature on social class and child rearing, notes that at present, middle-class parents are more affectionate than lower-class parents toward young children and that they frequently use withdrawal of love as a technique of punishment. Such a combination should maximize the development of internal controls. Commenting on this point, Bronfenbrenner (1958) states:

> From the point of view of our interest, these findings mean that middle-class parents, though in one sense more lenient in their discipline techniques, are using methods that are actually more compelling. Moreover, the compelling power of these practices, rather than being reduced, is probably enhanced by the more permissive treatment accorded to middle-class children in the early years of life. The successful use of withdrawal of love as a discipline technique implies the prior existence of a gratifying relationship; the more love present in the first instance, the greater the threat implied in its withdrawal. (P. 419)

The parents of lower-class children are less permissive and more frequently resort to physical punishment. Thus middle-class children should evidence greater dependency and stronger internal controls. Sears, Maccoby, and Levin (1957) support these conclusions on permissiveness and punishment, but find little difference between classes on withdrawal of love.

Various alternative interpretations are available, however. Kohlberg (1962) has pointed out that middle-class children participate more extensively in various group activities, and he has presented evidence that such participation may play an important part in producing class differences.

Another convincing interpretation has been offered by Kohn (1963). He suggests that the middle and working classes have different values because their conditions of life are different, and that these values in turn produce differences in their child-rearing practices. The essence of the difference in values, according to Kohn, is that working-class parental values center on conformity to external proscriptions, middle-class parental values on self-direction. "To working-class parents, it is the overt act that matters: the child should not transgress externally imposed rules; to middle-class parents, it is the child's motives and feelings that matter: the child should govern himself" (Kohn, 1963, p. 475).

Kohn goes on to suggest how class differences in parental values might be explained. He notes that middle-class occupations deal more with manipulation of interpersonal relations, ideas, and symbols, while working-class occupations are more concerned with the manipulation of things. Moreover, middle-class occupations entail more self-direction, while working-class occupations entail more direct supervision. Finally, getting ahead in middle-class occupations is more dependent upon one's own actions, while in working-class occupations it is more dependent upon collective action, particularly in unionized industries. Differences in education and standards of living between the two classes further reinforce the value differences.

The consequences of these differences in values are that working-class parents are more concerned with the overt act of the child, while middle-class parents focus upon the child's intent in acting as he does. For example, a child's outburst is likely to be punished by working-class parents if the furniture is damaged or the noise is intolerable, but middle-class parents will punish him only if they interpret the outburst as a loss of self-control. Moreover, because of their sensitivity to the child's internal dynamics, middle-class parents would be expected to feel a greater obligation to give their children emotional support. The primary obligation felt by the working-class parent is the need to impose constraints upon the child so that he will conform to external rules. Thus, Kohn's interpretation is consistent with our previous discussion, but provides a broader perspective on the relation between values, child-rearing practices, and consequent behaviors in the different social classes.

SEX DIFFERENCES, DEPENDENCY, AND CONSCIENCE DEVELOPMENT

Findings on sex differences are somewhat more detailed. Both Sears, Maccoby, and Levin and Bronfenbrenner report stronger internal controls for females although, contrary to expectation, they find no sex differences in dependency. In this connection, Bronfenbrenner has argued that if the trend toward applying love-oriented techniques to the male as well as the female should continue, the effect on the American male will be deleterious, since such techniques will discourage the development of independence, initiative, and self-sufficiency, traits valued for males in our culture. He comments (1961):

In short, we are suggesting that the "love-oriented" socialization techniques, which over the past twenty-five years have been employed in increasing degree by American middle class families, may have negative as well as constructive aspects. While fostering the internalization of adult standards and the development of socialized behavior, they may also have the effect of undermining capacities for initiative and independence, particularly in boys. Males exposed to this "modern" pattern of child rearing might be expected to differ from their counterparts of a quarter-century ago in being somewhat more conforming and anxious, less enterprising and self-sufficient, and, in general, possessing more of the virtues and liabilities commonly associated with feminine character structure. (P. 12)

FAMILY STRUCTURE, DEPENDENCY, AND CONSCIENCE DEVELOPMENT

Bronfenbrenner also offers evidence that the changing structure of the American family contributes to the growth of dependency at the expense of initiative (1961):

Both responsibility and leadership are fostered by the relatively greater salience of the parent of the same sex. . . . Boys tend to be more responsible when the father rather than the mother is the principal disciplinarian. . . . In short, boys thrive in a patriarchal context, girls in a matriarchal. . . . The most dependent and least dependable adolescents describe family arrangements that are neither patriarchal nor matriarchal, but equalitarian. To state the issue in more provocative form, our data suggest that the democratic family, which for so many years has been held up and aspired to as a model by professionals and enlightened laymen, tends to produce young people who "do not take initiative," "look to others for direction and decision," and "cannot be counted on to fulfill obligations." (P. 14)

If we assume that mothers use love-oriented techniques more often than fathers, the findings of Henry (1956) are relevant. He demonstrated that boys who perceived their mothers as the principal disciplinarian in the family gave self-blaming rather than other-blaming responses, a tendency suggestive of a stronger conscience. This relation between family structure and the development of dependency and internal controls in the two sexes may be augmented by the operation of an additional factor. If American values have shifted toward less emphasis on initiative and independence and more emphasis on other-directed traits (Riesman, 1950), these characteristics can be expected to develop in children as a result of both tuition and identification.

Not all the evidence is consistent with the views expressed above. Two studies of family structure and its effects on the *adolescent* suggest that the democratic family produces more independence and responsibility in the adolescent than does the more authoritarian, power-oriented family structure (Peck, 1958; Elder, 1961). In part, the variation in results from study to study may be due to the fact that some studies have focused upon early childhood and others upon adolescence. In addition, the methodology of studies of socialization has many shortcomings, as both Winch (1962) and Yarrow (1963) have noted. All too often the sole source of information is an interview with the mother, who describes her own behavior and that of the child not only as she presently sees these behaviors, but often as she recalls them from many years before. The fallibility of her memory and of her powers of observation places severe limitations on these studies.

Moreover, investigators have sometimes defined such variables as parental warmth, psychological discipline, and internal controls quite differently from one another, making it difficult to compare their studies. Finally, the immediate effects of family structure upon the young child may be quite different from the later consequences of such experiences, and the same treatment at a later age may well have a different outcome. For example, permitting the preschool child to express aggression quite freely may produce a high incidence of aggressive behavior at preschool age, but may ultimately result in a low incidence of aggression later (Sears, 1961).

Regarding conscience formation and the social structure, we may conclude that with some exceptions, the research on social class is consistent with the treatment of dependency training and conscience formation presented earlier in this chapter. In general, the greater use by middle-class parents of techniques of discipline that rest upon parental affection and approval produces greater dependency in early childhood as well as more intensive internalization of standards of behavior. The greater use of love-oriented techniques of punishment for female children likewise produces stronger internal controls. Finally, the trend in our society toward placing greater responsibility on the mother for child discipline has resulted in more warmth and more use of love-oriented techniques of punishment. Some evidence suggests that this matriarchal disciplinary pattern makes the male child less independent and less responsible than he is when the father is the predominant disciplinarian. The possibility of alternative or supplemental explanations of these findings, mainly in the form of a more direct transmission of the values of middle-class parents to their children, should not be overlooked.

STUDY QUESTIONS

8. *What are the differences in the child-rearing practices of middle-class and lower-class parents? How do these differences affect dependency and conscience formation in the two different classes?*
9. *What sex differences are there with respect to dependency and conscience formation?*
10. *What are the effects on dependency, conscience formation, and related personality characteristics when the mother is the principal disciplinarian?*

Other Social Motives

Although dependency is the most basic social motive, at least two others of great significance in our society deserve some discussion. These are aggression and achievement.

Aggressive behavior is characterized by an intent to hurt or injure someone, either physically or otherwise. In the young child, aggression often takes an obvious form, such as striking another child. Among adults, aggression may be so disguised that the perpetrator of an aggressive act may not be consciously aware of his intent. Sears, Maccoby, and Levin (1957) note:

> Aggression, as the term is commonly used, means behavior that is intended to hurt or injure someone. Most human adults have quite a repertory of acts that fit this definition. Some of these are bold and violent, others sly and attenuated. Some are accompanied by rage or annoyance; others are done coldly and seemingly, to the perpetrator, without emotion. The complexity and subtlety of adult aggression is the end product of two or three decades of socialization by the individual's parents and peers, however, and bears little resemblance to the primitive quality of the infant's action patterns, from which it developed. (P. 218)

Although the primitive rage that accompanies aggression in the infant may be unlearned, the intent and the form of aggression in the socialized individual are learned. Sears, Maccoby, and Levin have suggested that this learning falls into the following pattern. The child experiences discomfort which initially leads to rage and to behaviors that evoke *discomfort in other persons*. These behaviors also frequently lead others unintentionally to reward him by relieving his discomfort. In time, the infant learns that the expression of aggression is likely to bring about rewarding behavior from other persons.

Eventually, these investigators suggest, aggressive acts become satisfying in themselves as a result of two processes. First, as a result of punishment for aggression, the child experiences tension in connection with aggressive impulses. This tension is relieved, at least momentarily, when the aggressive act occurs. Such release of tension, subjectively experienced as "letting off steam," is rewarding. Second, since aggression frequently results in reward, either as a result of the child's tension release or because others act to relieve his frustration, and since such cues as the signs of distress in the other person are followed by reward, the infliction of discomfort on others becomes rewarding in itself. In other words, seeing distress in others has become a rewarding experience; hence the individual produces it through aggressive actions.

Rewards, frustration, and aggression

Early research on the determinants of aggression was guided by the notion that the strength of aggression was a function of the degree of frustration experienced. The first studies appeared to provide support for this notion (Dollard et al., 1939). More recent evidence suggests that the relation between these variables is not so simple. Although most of the research on aggression has been guided by the notion that aggression follows directly from frustration, aggression might alternatively be expected to result from one or more of the processes of socialization previously discussed. One way in which the child learns aggression is through operant conditioning. It is not the intention of the mother to reward such behavior; nevertheless, by continuing to be the source of frustration, and by giving such positive rewards as picking the child up and soothing him in response to aggressive behavior, she fosters the continuance of aggression. As the child grows older, tolerant or permissive attitudes toward aggression will allow the continued expression of aggression, which by now has become self-rewarding.

Direct tuition may also foster aggression. A number of studies suggest that where parents approve of aggression against agemates, it will occur (Davis & Dollard, 1940; Lesser, 1952). Finally, the processes of role learning and identification are consistent with the findings that parental aggression in the form of punishment of the child, particularly physical punishment, is associated with high aggression. This point is made clear by Sears, Maccoby, and Levin (1957) in summarizing their research on aggression and its control:

> When the parents punish—particularly when they employ physical punishment—they are providing a living example of the use of aggression at the very moment they are trying to teach the child not to be aggressive. The child, who copies his parents in many ways, is likely to learn as much from this example of successful aggression on his parents' part as he is from the pain of punishment. Thus, the most peaceful home is one in which the mother believes aggression is not desirable and under no circumstances is ever to be expressed toward her, but who relies mainly on non-punitive forms of control. The homes where the children show angry, aggressive outbursts frequently are likely to be homes in which the mother has a relatively tolerant (or careless!) attitude toward such behavior, or where she administers severe punishment for it, or both. (P. 266)

Thus, the two factors contributing to aggression stressed by these investigators are high permissiveness for aggression and much punishment of aggressive acts. Table 18–1 summarizes the data on which their conclusions are based. More recently, several other studies have reported similar familial antecedents of aggression (Bandura & Walters, 1959; Lynn, 1961; McCord, McCord, & Howard, 1961).

Social class and aggression

The overt expression of aggression is directly related to the strength of aggressive needs and inversely related to the strength of internal controls that inhibit aggression. Since lower-class parents rely more on physical punishment and express less warmth toward their children, the children may be expected to develop stronger aggressive needs and weaker internal controls. Most of the empirical evidence does support this supposition.[3] Sears, Maccoby, and Levin, however, report that in their subjects, aggression did not differ by social class. Possibly the greater per-

[3]Mussen & Conger, 1956; Sears, Maccoby, & Levin, 1957; Sewell, 1960; Walder, 1961.

Table 18–1
Association between Mothers' Behavior and Aggressiveness in Their Children

	PERCENT HIGHLY AGGRESSIVE	
MOTHERS' BEHAVIOR	Boys (N = 195)	Girls (N = 162)
Low permissiveness and low punishment	4	13
Low permissiveness and high punishment	20	19
High permissiveness and low punishment	25	21
High permissiveness and high punishment	42	38

Note — Both columns total only 91 percent because in a few cases the mother's behavior could not be classified on the basis of available interview data.

SOURCE: Reprinted by permission from R. R. Sears, Eleanor E. Maccoby, & H. Levin. *Patterns of child rearing.* New York: Harper & Row, Publishers, Incorporated, 1957.

missiveness toward aggression by the middle-class mothers in their sample may have counteracted the effect of these other conditions. But again, processes other than child-rearing practices may also account for these class differences. The differences in the value structures of social classes may well explain why the lower-class child learns aggressive behavior: higher rates of aggression for lower-class children *may* result simply from tuition, identification, and role learning.

Sex differences in aggression

Higher aggression among males also has several alternative explanations.[4] It may be attributed to different cultural expectations for each sex or to different child-rearing practices for boys and girls. Moreover, aggression may have some linkage with physiological differences between the sexes. In the animal kingdom, males are generally more aggressive than females, and experiments have demonstrated that the male sex hormone is a critical element producing this difference. Among humans, these factors may all be operative. In American society, boys are expected to be more aggressive than girls, and they are allowed or even encouraged to be so. In terms of parental handling, the more permissive attitude of parents toward aggression by the male child and the more frequent use of physical punishment for boys would lead to stronger aggressive behavior. Finally, the weaker internal controls developed by the male child as compared with the female child permit more aggression.

[4]Although Sears, Maccoby, and Levin (1957) report other evidence for greater aggression among boys, their own study found a relatively small sex difference for their five-year-olds. While it was in the expected direction, the difference was only significant at the 10 percent level. As they suggest, this small difference, contrary to the findings of others, may well have been due to the mother's tendency to take into consideration the sex of the child and to "correct" for this when reporting aggressive behavior.

STUDY QUESTIONS

11. *What is meant by aggressive behavior?*

12. *Explain how aggressive behavior may become rewarding to the aggressor.*

13. *To what extent does frustration invariably lead to aggression?*

14. *Identify the critical factors in parental behavior that produce aggression in the child.*

15. *Describe social-class differences in children with respect to aggressive behavior and the relation of this difference to variations in child-rearing practices.*

16. *What sex differences exist in aggression, and how may they be explained?*

ACHIEVEMENT

Individuals respond differently to situations where some standard of excellence might be applied to their behavior. At one extreme, persons set high standards for themselves, strive very hard to achieve them, and respond with considerable feeling to their success or failure in meeting them. At the other extreme, persons are unlikely to set such standards, exert little effort, and feel relatively indifferent about achieving the standards. These two kinds of persons are said to differ in *achievement motivation*. This behavior has been extensively investigated in recent years. Generally it has been measured either in terms of some behavioral index of over- or underachievement (Strodtbeck, 1958) or in terms of achievement themes in stories elicited by a series of pictures taken from the Thematic Apperception Test[5] (McClelland et al., 1953).

Determinants of achievement motivation

There appears to be considerable agreement as to the child-rearing practices associated with high achievement. Findings of a recent study may be summarized as follows (Rosen, 1961). Direct tuition and identification serve to establish a strong achievement orientation. First, through the behavior of significant other persons, the child is directly rewarded for trying to succeed. Second, his successful efforts are rewarded, and failures are punished. Parents teach achievement behavior through direct guidance of the problem-solving sequence. The child is encouraged to keep trying; a high standard of performance is urged. Third, the conditions that maximize identification and internalization of parental achievement standards lead to high achievement. In particular, parents of high achievers combine above-average warmth with approval or disapproval (withdrawal of love) for good or poor performance (Rosen & D'Andrade, 1959).

---

[5]The Thematic Apperception Test, devised by Murray (1938), consists of a series of pictures that show scenes subject to a variety of interpretations. The respondent makes up a story describing what he thinks the scene represents. On the assumption that he will endow the central figure with his own attributes, the clinical psychologist analyzes the respondent's personality as expressed in the collection of stories.

Achievement and the social structure

The sociocultural correlates of achievement motivation have been more extensively investigated than those of any other motivational system. Study of achievement motivation has also been extended beyond the effects of child-rearing practices to include other factors in socialization. Social classes differ markedly in achievement motivation. Whether it is appraised by some performance measure or in terms of achievement themes in fantasy, middle- and upper-class children score higher on this characteristic than lower-class children.

Variations in child-rearing practices and in values among different social classes have been examined in the attempt to account for these differences. Middle-class parents apparently place greater stress on independence training than lower-class parents (Rosen & D'Andrade, 1959). They are more likely to stress self-reliance, autonomy, and achievement in situations involving standards of excellence. They more often recognize and reward evidences of achievement, and they are more sensitive to and punitive toward failure.

Value differences between classes are also related to differential achievement (Strodtbeck, 1958; Rosen & D'Andrade, 1959). Middle-class mothers, unlike lower-class mothers, are likely to believe in the possibility of manipulating the world to their advantage, in present sacrifices for future rewards, and in individual rather than group obligations and rewards. Moreover, they generally have higher levels of aspiration for their children. Given the more effective techniques of inducing identification used by middle-class parents, one would expect strong internalization of these values and aspirations. Finally, other studies have shown that middle-class children experience success in their attempts at achievement more often than lower-class children (Veroff, Feld, & Gurin, 1962). The conclusion may be drawn that all the processes of socialization previously discussed contribute to higher achievement motivation among middle-class children.

Similar differences in achievement motivation, values, and levels of aspiration have been found among various racial and ethnic groups (Strodtbeck, 1958; Rosen & D' Andrade, 1959). Greeks and Jews are more achievement-oriented and have more achievement values than Italians, French-Canadians, and Negroes. Results are contradictory for Catholics and Protestants.

Family size, birth order, and age of mother have also been related to achievement motivation. Each is a poor predictor by itself, however, since its effect is dependent upon the effects of the other variables and on social class. Rosen (1961) has described this interdependency as follows:

> It is not very helpful in predicting an individual's achievement motivation to know his position in the birth order—indeed this information may be misleading rather than useful—unless the social class and size of his family of orientation are also known. In small middle class families, for example, the effect of ordinal position seems to be relatively unimportant: the oldest and

youngest child in a two-child, middle class family have almost identical motivation scores, but as the size of the family increases the scores for the oldest child in the middle class become higher than those for the youngest child. However, in the lower class the reverse is true: the youngest child has a higher achievement motivation score on the average than the oldest child — a position that is maintained even when the size of the family increases. Similarly, the effect of mother's age upon the child's achievement motivation varies with the size of her family and social class. Thus the hypothesis that the sons of young mothers would have higher achievement motivation than the sons of old mothers proved to be correct, but only when the family is small. As the size of the family increases, particularly in the lower class, the scores of sons of young mothers drop rapidly and are surpassed by the scores of sons of middle-aged and old mothers. (P. 585)

Finally, achievement values have been related to the power structure in the family. In families where the father's power is high relative to the power of the mother and son, the son's achievement values are low. That is, the son is less likely to believe that the world can be rationally mastered and that he should risk separation from his family (Strodtbeck, 1958).

STUDY QUESTIONS

17. *Explain what is meant by the achievement motive. How may it be measured?*
18. *What are the major aspects of parental behavior that result in differences in achievement motivation in their children?*
19. *What are the social-class differences in achievement motivation, and how are these differences to be accounted for?*
20. *What other independent variables may be related to achievement motivation?*

GAPS IN KNOWLEDGE OF SOCIAL MOTIVES

Available research on social motives has serious limitations. Almost all of it has been cross-sectional — groups of children are studied at a certain age, but rarely is the same child studied over a period of many years. Consequently knowledge of the continuity or discontinuity in the behavior of an individual child is lacking. Generally the assumption is made that the child acquires certain traits or characteristics which persist into adulthood. While this assumption may be correct, evidence in support of it is scanty.

Moreover, although parental behavior toward children of a particular age is undoubtedly dependent upon the relationship between child and parent at an earlier age, their relationship is not necessarily a consistent one. For example, a father who initially shows great enthusiasm and warmth toward his small son may be quite frustrated in his attempts to make a companion out of his son at that age. Early warmth and enthusiasm may then be replaced by a more indifferent attitude that is quite inconsistent with his earlier feelings. The following studies suggest that these qualifications concerning presently available research are justified.

A follow-up study by Sears (1961) has shown that although high punishment of preschool children produced more aggressive behavior in them at preschool age, at age twelve these same children were relatively low in antisocial aggression. At this age, however, the children exhibited more indirect forms of aggression and showed more anxiety concerning aggression. Permissiveness presented a similar problem with respect to continuity. High permissiveness toward children at preschool age, also associated with high aggression at that age, continued to be associated with high aggression at age twelve. But children whose parents were permissive exhibited less aggression in indirect forms and less anxiety over aggression at age twelve.

Some caution is necessary in interpreting these results, because at preschool age aggression was assessed by interviews with mothers, and at age twelve it was evaluated by having the children fill out a questionnaire. Also, the correlations were quite low in both studies. An independent study shows that ratings of aggressiveness in children by their parents do not correlate with ratings made by their classmates in school (Walder, 1961). The lack of correlation between peer ratings and parental ratings of aggression suggests that self ratings and parental ratings might not be comparable either.

A number of other investigations in which the same children were studied over a period of many years indicate that some characteristics prominent at one age often disappear at another. One study finds considerable stability in dependence and passivity at different ages for females but not for males (Kagan & Moss, 1960). Another reports that overdependence and seriousness were moderately correlated in early childhood and preadolescence, while selfishness, quarrelsomeness, and attention-demanding behavior had markedly different frequencies in the same children at different ages (McFarlane, Allen, & Honzik, 1954).

Another problem which deserves more study than it has received is the consistency of maternal behavior toward children. One study compares observational data collected during the first three years of life with interview data on the same children collected between the ages of nine to fourteen years (Schaefer & Bayley, 1960). Considerable maternal consistency on a dimension of love versus hostility was found between the two periods. In other words, mothers who were loving toward their small children were likely to be loving at later ages, while those who were less loving or were hostile toward them as infants were likely to have a similar attitude later. Consistency was not perfect, of course, and in many individual cases, mothers had markedly different attitudes toward their children at the two age levels.

The same investigators found little consistency on another dimension, the extent to which mothers controlled their children or allowed them independence. Maccoby (1961) has noted that one reason why very different behaviors toward the child are manifested at different ages is that a particular behavior may be more compatible with the personality and capacity of the mother at one age than at another. For example, maternal warmth toward an infant may be equated with considerable body contact, such as holding, carrying, rocking, and nursing; but toward a child of school age, warmth may mean an expression of interest in his accomplishments and pride in his independence. A mother who enjoys infants may be unable to be equally warm toward the same child when they are older.

Lois Murphy (personal communication, 1961) has called attention to marked changes that take place in children and has suggested that the conception of a fixed personality structure persisting throughout life has been overstressed:

> The concept of character in the sense of a fixed core-structure persisting through the lifetime of an individual has been so reified that it has become virtually a part of our mythology . . . it makes us regard the surprises, the dramatic changes as somehow exceptions to the rule. . . .
>
> Among the children we have observed, new interactions contribute to change at times of transition due to internal changes in the child, external changes such as a new school, neighborhood, or major changes in the pattern of family relationships and the interactions of these inner and external changes. . . .
>
> Longitudinal studies generally show tendencies to constriction preceding the adolescent blossoming, but in some individuals this phase becomes fixed into a lasting character-rigidity while with others it is outgrown. Observations in adolescence, college and post-college stages also show dramatic changes in some individuals in relations between drive, expression, control, and defense. . . .

SUMMARY: AGGRESSION AND ACHIEVEMENT

In early childhood, high permissiveness and high punishment lead to a maximum amount of aggressive behavior on the part of the child, while low permissiveness and low punishment lead to a minimum amount. By age twelve, however, the child who was punished frequently for aggression at preschool age exhibits little antisocial aggression and expresses aggression more indirectly. He also shows more anxiety over aggression than children who were treated differently when they were of preschool age.

Studies of social class and aggression suggest that the relatively greater reliance on physical punishment, as well as relatively less warmth toward children on the part of lower-class parents, results in stronger aggressive needs and less ability to inhibit aggressive impulses. Males have been shown to exhibit more aggression than females and to have weaker controls over its expression. Whether this is due to biological differences, different child-rearing practices, or different role expectations for the two sexes is not clear. Probably all these factors play some part in producing a sex difference in aggression.

The orientation to achieve a high standard of excellence and to excel others, commonly referred to as high achievement motivation, is produced by a variety of factors. Direct tuition and reward by achievement-oriented parents, as well as identification with them by the child, contribute to this orientation in him. Social classes differ markedly in achievement motivation, with middle-class parents placing more stress on self-reliance, independence, and achievement of high standards of excellence. Middle-class children more often achieve success in such pursuits and receive corresponding rewards. Variations in achievement motivation are also found in various racial and ethnic groups. In addition, certain aspects of family structure relate to achievement, including family size, birth order, age of the mother, and the power structure of the family.

Knowledge of social motives is limited because of the dearth of longitudinal studies. Little is known concerning the consistency of parental behavior over the entire developmental span. Similarly, there may be little consistency in the behavior of children at different ages. Thus, it is difficult to draw with certainty precise conclusions on the long-range effects of rearing a child in a particular way.

Socialization and Family Structure

Some effects of family structure on dependency, aggression, and achievement have already been noted. Typically, family structure variables include size of family, birth order, the relative predominance of the mother or father in the socialization process, and the existence of only children versus children with siblings. Frequently such variables have disappointingly weak relations to dependency, aggression, achievement, and other variables. This is probably due at least in part to difficulties in adequately conceptualizing social motives and family structure. With respect to family structure variables such as birth order or the existence of siblings are probably oversimplified.

For example, on the basis of his clinical experience, Toman (1961) has suggested that age and sex are the minimum characteristics that must be taken into account in considering family structure. Thus, instead of placing all first-born children in one category and later-born in another, he identifies four relations as quite distinct from each other. These are (1) older brother versus younger sister, (2) older brother versus younger brother, (3) older sister versus younger brother, and (4) older sister versus younger sister. In the discussion of role learning (see Chapter 17), a study was cited suggesting that consideration of these dyads might be important (Brim, 1958). The relevant finding was the cross-sex siblings acquire through identification more of the traits of the opposite sex than do like-sexed siblings.

Toman stresses a quite different point. He believes that the patterns of relation developed in these family dyads generalize to later relations with persons of the same and the opposite sex. For example, the person who has been an older brother might as an adult be expected to assume considerable responsibility, to be authority-oriented, to be a hard worker, and to relate well to other men. If he has had only a younger brother but not a younger sister, he might well expect his wife to have some of the qualities of his younger brother.

But family structure is more complicated than we have indicated. Toman suggests that the four dyads take one form when the age difference is approximately three to six years, another form when there is only one year's difference between the siblings, and still another when the age difference is great. A further complicating factor is the manner in which the parents relate to the sibling combinations. The sheer amount of interaction between parents and siblings will markedly affect the relation between siblings, according to Toman. If the parents assume all responsibilities themselves, an older brother is unlikely to take on responsibility as part of his role. The effects of sibling relations are likely to be optimal when parents have a laissez-faire attitude toward the children or when they reinforce the particular roles suited to the sibling configuration.

The manner in which parents relate to only children would similarly make quite a difference. The stereotype of the spoiled only child would be likely to apply where parents centered their life on the one child. But this need not occur; for example, some families may have a single child because the parents, particularly the mother, feel inadequate with children, do not wish to be "bothered" with additional children, etc.

Toman is most interested in the implications of family structure during socialization for the new adult family formed by the children when they marry. He suggests that, other things being equal, perpetuation of a role similar to that played during socialization leads to the best adjustment. Thus, an older brother of a younger sister would most readily adjust to a marriage with a woman who had been the younger sister of an older brother. Of course, if either of these earlier relations had been particularly unsatisfactory ones, the prediction would not hold.

The relation of early family structure to a new family formed by marriage, however, may be complicated in various ways by attempts to perpetuate early sibling relations in inappropriate situations. For example, Hilgard (1951) has referred to this phenomenon as "social heredity" and has given a number of case histories as illustrations. One of her examples is the case of a mother who, as the younger sister of an older brother strongly favored by her parents, had been teased and tormented by him. When she had two boys of her own, she unconsciously provoked her older son into various aggressive actions toward herself and his younger brother so that she could punish him. Thus the underlying motivation appeared to be a desire to "get even" with her older brother by casting her son in that role.

The brief discussion of family structure illustrates some of the directions that might be taken in research attempting to relate family structure during socialization to later behavior. It also illustrates the paucity of present knowledge, for the discussion has been based largely upon clinical literature rather than research studies.

STUDY QUESTIONS

21. *State several limitations of our present knowledge of socialization.*

22. *Present a concept of family structure in terms of dyads. Can you suggest other ways in which the structure of the family might be characterized?*

Summary and Conclusions

Unless the child becomes physically and emotionally dependent upon another person, socialization will be impaired. In the typical family the development of dependency is assured by the nature of family interaction, which necessarily produces strong dependencies as well as occasional frustration and conflict. In extremely atypical families, or in the case of institutionalized children, only a weak dependency may develop.

Given a warm relation between parent and child, psychological forms of discipline are effective in producing appropriate internal controls in children. Child-rearing practices vary with the position of the parents in the social structure, and the consequent effects of these variations upon child behavior are consistent with the general principles governing the establishment of dependency and internal controls.

Two highly significant social motives, aggression and achievement, have been discussed at some length. In early childhood, high permissiveness and high punishment on the part of the mother lead to maximum aggression, while low permissiveness and low punishment produce minimum aggression. Studies of social class and aggression suggest that the relatively greater reliance on physical punishment, as well as relatively less warmth toward children on the part of lower-class parents, results in stronger aggressive needs and less ability to inhibit aggressive impulses.

Strong achievement motivation, more characteristic of middle-class children than of lower-class children, is produced by direct tuition, reward, and identification with achievement-oriented parents. Variations in achievement motivation are also found in various racial and ethnic groups. Certain aspects of family structure relate to achievement, including family size, birth order, age of the mother, and the power structure of the family.

Present knowledge of socialization is limited in several ways. Most investigations study the child at a single point in time, and this cross-sectional approach has serious methodological shortcomings which limit the conclusions that may be drawn. Few longitudinal studies following the development of individual children have been carried out. For example, little is known of the consistency of a child's behavior over the entire developmental period, and information concerning consistency of parental behavior is even more scarce. Finally, improvements in the conceptualization of social motives and of family structure are required, and further research on the effects of such structure on various behaviors is needed.

chapter nineteen

SOCIALIZATION: SELF
AND PERSONALITY

To this point we have discussed processes of social learning, such as identification and role learning, the interpersonal conditions that produce effective internal controls in children, and the effects of variations in child-rearing practices upon child behavior. The conditions producing the important social motives aggression and achievement have also been discussed at some length. What is perhaps the most central, most important, and most troublesome question in socialization, however, has been reserved for this final chapter: In any given situation or series of situations, what are the factors that determine how an individual will behave, and what is the relative importance of these various determinants?

Determinants of Individual Behavior

This question has received widely varying answers which have their strong supporters. The range of answers can be illustrated by presenting two views that are at opposite extremes.

TWO EXTREME VIEWS

One view is that behavior springs fully from structured dispositions within the individual; the other is that a person's behavior is determined by the situation he is in. Below is a description of these views; following it is a discussion of the ideas that social psychologists emphasize as necessary for understanding individual differences among persons.

Behavior as individual disposition

The lay view of personality is well expressed in Heider's observation, "Persons are seen as the origins of actions." As noted in Chapter 2, it is much simpler to interpret a hostile act as a natural expression of a malevolent person than to understand the situational and circumstantial factors that led him to commit the act. The average man exaggerates the role of the person as causal agent. He fails to see the social forces that make persons act as they do in various situations. But this lay view is also held in more sophisticated and more qualified form by many clinical psychologists, personality theorists, and other students of individual behavior. Murphy (1947) has summed up their attitude succinctly in the following comment:

> The laboratory psychologist and the clinician have both conceived the individual as a system of events and tendencies carried around within the skin of the individual subject. They have both assumed that his delinquencies or his triumphs, his interests or his nervous maladjustments, result fully and simply from structured dispositions within him. (P. 877)

Essentially this conception of individual behavior assumes that the behavior patterns which characterize a person reflect intraindividual structures or mechanisms such as habits, needs, cognitive structures, or, most frequently, personality traits. Miller (1963) has described the approach in another way:

> Psychologists have traditionally limited themselves to the individual, engaging in a quest for "genetypic" traits which provide the basis for predicting the subject's behavior with many kinds of people in many situations. For example, the predisposition to anxiety has been considered a general trait. Scores on anxiety tests have been used to predict the capacities for achievement in school, for getting along socially, and for controlling physical movements. (P. 641)

Behavior as a function of the situation

Sociologists, anthropologists, and many social psychologists have taken an opposite view. They have argued that a person's behavior is mostly a reflection of the situation he happens to be in. Inherent in the situation are the social forces that shape and determine his behavior at any given moment, although it is recognized that his previous experience with such situations has predisposed him to react in certain ways in the particular circumstances. A representative approach is that of Brim (1960):

> When one looks at what is actually going on around him, he finds striking the great variation in the individual's behavior from one situation to another during the course of the day: as the individual moves, for example, from his occupational role, to his various family roles, to his roles with the neighbors in the community, and so on. Recall the familiar example of the German adult male who is meek and subservient to his superiors in his occupational role, but who changes into a domineering, hostile, and aggressive father upon returning to his home. Consider the modern executive, who in his occupational

role is autonomous, creative, and decisive but who upon going home and taking up his status as husband may become docile and dependent in family matters. What should capture the interest of the student of personality, therefore, is not the consistency of individual differences as he looks upon behavior. Rather it is the great adaptability, the truly impressive variation in response to situational demands, which characterizes man as he moves from one situation to another. (P. 137)

THE INTERPERSONAL APPROACH

Proponents of these two views are both able to marshal a fair amount of evidence in support of their positions. At first thought, it appears obvious that both views could not be correct. But careful reflection suggests that there is merit in both of these positions and, further, that they are not particularly difficult to reconcile. An approach that accomplishes this in a general way is gaining support. Most commonly it is referred to as an *interpersonal* approach to understanding individual behavior. Miller (1963) has lucidly described the distinction between the intraindividual approach and the interpersonal approach:

> Some of the most fundamental differences between intrapersonal and interpersonal conceptions originate in the questions asked. In a study of friendship, for example, the investigator who prefers intrapersonal concepts studies traits of the subject that may affect his capacity to make friends—his tolerance of frustration, his passivity, his sensitivity to another's feelings, and his hostility; he anticipates that the more the subject's traits approximate an ideal pattern— tolerance, low passivity, high sensitivity, low hostility—the more likely he is to make friends easily. Sociometric measurement often indicates significant association between such variables and popularity. Interpersonal phrasing also requires information about individual dispositions, but the information is used to throw light on the relationships between certain types of people in particular types of situations. The questions thus shifts from "How will a person with these traits be accepted by his peers" to "How well will this particular combination of people get along?" The investigator studies a particular friendship, not one person's adjustments to his friends in general; the compatibility of a particular couple, not one man's promise of realizing a successful marriage; the ways in which a son and father behave toward one another, not the boy's general adjustment. (Pp. 641–642)

To anyone who has read the preceding chapters of this book it should be obvious that much of social psychology typifies the interpersonal approach: focus is not upon individuals, but upon interactions between members of dyads or larger groups. At the same time, however, the social-psychological orientation is strongly situational and is probably not considered adequate by the clinician or personologist to explain the behavior of specific individuals. Most notably, the social psychologist has not exerted himself to explain the continuity and consistency in an individual's behavior over time and in different situations. Because of the dearth of longitudinal studies, there is no extensive information on such consistencies, although many behavioral scientists accept them as a fact.

For the present, we also will assume that consistency exists. In the remainder of the chapter we will show how an interpersonal approach can reconcile such consistency with a situational emphasis. In addition, we will examine the contribution of the interpersonal approach to explaining personality change.

In summary, the major question in this chapter is the following. In any given situation or series of situations, what are the various factors that determine how an individual will behave, and what is the relative importance of these various determinants? The range of answers is illustrated by two extreme views: (1) that behavior springs fully from structured dispositions within the individual, and (2) that a person's behavior is determined by the situation he is in. Both views have merit, and the interpersonal approach to the study of behavior appears to reconcile them. This approach focuses upon relations between individuals rather than the behavior of a single individual. It allows a place for both disposition and situation.

STUDY QUESTIONS

1. *Contrast and describe the following two views: (a) Behavior springs fully from structured dispositions within the individual. (b) A person's behavior is mostly a reflection of the situation he is in.*

2. *What is meant by the interpersonal approach to understanding individual behavior?*

Nature of the Self Concept

One consequence of being human is that a person becomes an object to himself. Because of his possession of language and a superior intelligence, man has a unique capacity for thinking about his body, his behavior, and his appearance to other persons. Each of us has a set of cognitions and feelings toward ourselves. The terms most commonly applied to this set of elements are *self* or *self concept.*

It is convenient to think of a person's attitudes toward himself as having three aspects—the cognitive, the affective, and the behavioral. The *cognitive* component represents the content of the self, illustrated by such thoughts as, "I am intelligent, honest, sincere, ambitious, tall, strong, overweight, etc." The *affective* component represents one's feelings about oneself and is more difficult to illustrate, because feelings toward oneself are usually not expressed in words. It would include a rather general feeling of self-worth, as well as evaluations of more specific cognitive aspects or other aspects of self. For example, a woman may dislike her nose, which is slightly crooked. The *behavioral* component is the tendency to act toward oneself in various ways: a person may behave in a self-deprecating or a self-indulgent manner, or he may show oversensitivity to certain of his characteristics.

SOCIAL NATURE OF THE SELF

A tradition going back to the earliest formulation on the self is the emphasis on its social nature. While *all* attitudes are rooted in social experience, self-attitudes are thought to be a product of interaction in a special sense. First, theories of self-development emphasize the individual's perception of how other persons see him. Second, they focus attention on the process by which he compares his ideas about himself with social norms, that is, with the expectations he believes other persons have concerning what he should be like. These features were stressed in one of the earliest treatments of the self by Cooley, who likened our perceptions of how others see us to the reflections of a looking glass. Referring to this "looking-glass self," Cooley (1902) noted:

> As we see our face, figure, and dress in the glass, and are interested in them because they are ours, and pleased or otherwise with them according as they do or do not answer to what we should like them to be; so in imagination we perceive in another's mind some thought of our appearance, manners, aims, deeds, character, friends, and so on, and are variously affected by it.
> A self-ideal of this sort seems to have three principal elements: the imagination of our appearance to the other person; the imagination of his judgment of that appearance, and some sort of self-feeling, such as pride or mortification. The comparison with a looking-glass hardly suggests the second element, the imagined judgment, which is quite essential. The thing that moves us to pride or shame is not the mere mechanical reflection of ourselves, but an imputed sentiment, the imagined effect of this reflection upon another's mind. (P. 152)

Miller (1963) has applied the term *subjective public identity* to the individual's perception of his appearance to a particular group. As he notes, this is comparable to Cooley's looking-glass self. An individual has many such identities—as many as there are groups which he believes see him in a distinctive way. Ultimately, however, out of his experiences with other persons, he forms an inner self, a *core*, that in James's words represents his "truest, strongest, deepest self." Included in the core are his most valued, most salient attitudes toward himself. This core develops out of social learning processes, particularly role learning and identification.

The process of identification is of particular importance in understanding the development of the self. In Chapter 17 the analysis of identification suggested a variety of reasons why another person might be chosen as a model. Once such models are chosen, a person learns to view himself as he imagines he is seen by them. He not only models his overt behavior after them, but also takes on their cognitions and feelings—in sum, takes on the *attitude of the other* (Mead, 1934). To the extent that he is the object of these attitudes, they form a constellation that represents his self concept. Thus the love and affection of parents for a child and their attitudes toward him as he grows are of tremendous importance in forming his self concept. Beyond the early years of childhood, many other persons outside his family assume an increasingly important role in forming self: teachers, classmates, playmates, and friends. In adult years, his occupational associates and his sweethearts, spouse, and children contribute further to this process.

STUDY QUESTIONS

3. *What is the self concept? What are its components?*
4. *What is meant by the looking-glass self, and what are its three components? What is meant by the term* subjective public identity?
5. *What is the role played by identification in the development of the self?*

Self and role

The process by which the self concept, particularly a person's subjective public identities, is developed through social interaction may in part be seen as the assignment of the person to a series of social roles. As an individual moves through the social structure, he is placed in various role categories. He is first a baby, later a small boy. He is a dull pupil, John's little brother, and Tommy's best friend. As he performs these roles, he learns to see himself as various role partners see him. In each, he learns the expectations that other persons associate with the category, and he forms a subjective public identity corresponding to each. In a sense, the picture he has of himself is one with many facets or aspects, each corresponding to a particular identity. As we will see later, however, they do not remain entirely independent: certain processes modify these aspects of self. Goffman has vividly described the impact of role expectations on the individual:[1]

> It is important to note that in performing a role the individual must see to it that the impressions of him that are conveyed in the situation are compatible with role-appropriate personal qualities effectively imputed to him: a judge is supposed to be deliberate and sober; a pilot, in a cockpit, to be cool; a book-keeper to be accurate and neat in doing his work. These personal qualities, effectively imputed and effectively claimed, combine with a position's title, when there is one, to provide a basis of *self-image* for the incumbent and a basis for the image that his role others will have of him. A self, then, virtually awaits the individual entering a position; he need only conform to the pressures on him and he will find a *me* ready-made for him.

When children are asked to describe themselves, the impact of their parent's definitions of them often are readily seen in the results. They have formed a rudimentary self out of the images that these significant other persons have of them. Adults, however, are likely to make a greater use of various socially defined categories. These differences are well illustrated by the work of Kuhn and his associates. They administered the Twenty Statements Test, an unstructured self-measurement instrument which asked subjects to make twenty statements in answer to the question "Who Am I?" On the following page are reproduced the responses of a fourth-grade girl and a university senior (Kuhn, 1960, p. 41). As seen, Kuhn and his associates found an increasing use of social categories with age. At seven years, only one-fourth of the twenty statements were so classified, but at twenty-four years, about half were social categories.

[1]Reprinted by permission from E. Goffman, *Encounters: Two studies in the sociology of interaction.* Copyright 1961 by The Bobbs-Merrill Company, Inc. Pp. 87–88.

RESPONSES OF A 4TH-GRADE GIRL [ORIGINAL SPELLING RETAINED]	RESPONSES OF A UNIVERSITY SENIOR
I boss to much	I am of the female sex
I get mad a my sisters	My age is 20
I am a show off	I am from (city and state)
I interupt to much	I have two parents
I talk to much	My home is happy
I wast time	I am happy
Sometimes I am a bad sport	I have been to 4 colleges
I fiddle around	I will graduate in (month and year)
I am careless at times	I have a brother
I forget	I am a (sorority name)
Sometimes I don't do what mother tells me to	I am in the Waves Officer School
I tattle on my sisters	I attend church
Sometimes I am unkind	I live a normal life
	I am interested in sports
	I am a (department major)
	I am attractive
	I have high moral standards
	I am an adjusted person
	I am of the middle class

This corresponds to the increasing number of role categories occupied as the child grows up.

A more subtle learning than that just illustrated also occurs as the individual assumes various roles: His self-regard is shaped by the feelings which other persons have toward him. As a baby and small child, he is likely to be loved, an experience that plants the rudiments of a positive self-regard. Attitudes expressed toward him by successive role partners as he proceeds through life's stages add to and develop further the affective elements in his self image.

STUDY QUESTIONS

6. *What is the importance of social roles for the development of the self?*
7. *How does this relate to the differences in responses of children and adults to the "Who Am I" test?*

SUMMARY: THE NATURE OF THE SELF

The self is acquired from the views that other persons have toward an individual. Because of their relation to him, he chooses certain other persons as models for identification. He not only copies their overt behaviors, but also takes on the attitudes that they hold toward him. Cooley suggests that an individual forms an opinion of how he appears to the other person, guesses how that person judges his appearance, and reacts with a positive or negative self-feeling to the imagined judgment. The individual's perception of his appearance to a particular group of other persons or to an especially significant other person has been termed by Miller his *subjective public identity*. An individual has as many such identities as there are groups or significant other persons who he believes see him in a distinctive way. From his experiences with other persons he also forms an inner self or *core,* representing his most central characteristics and most salient attitudes toward himself. Like other attitudes, a person's attitudes toward himself have three components: the cognitive, the affective, and the behavioral.

The development of the self concept, particularly a person's subjective public identities, may be understood in part in terms of his assignment to a series of social roles. As he moves through the social structure, he is placed in various role categories and acquires an identity associated with each. Ultimately some of the characteristics acquired in these identities may become a part of his core self. A vital aspect of this developmental process is the gradual acquisition of a general affect toward self, which for most individuals is positive.

Stability of Self and Individual Behavior

The discussion of self as a set of subjective public identities corresponding to roles pictured the individual as a relatively passive object, molded and shaped by the persons around him who are older, more powerful, wiser, and more experienced. Casual observation of small children, however, reveals that even they are not so easily molded in this fashion. In part, such resistance is due to biological characteristics of the organism, including such factors as energy level and temperament. In addition, once the self concept is established and certain behavior patterns are adopted, conditions arise that cause the individual to be less readily influenced and to resist change actively. The present section will show how the person may be immersed in a social environment of interacting forces and still behave in a distinctive manner that at many points is opposed to these forces.

This view recognizes stability over time in an individual's behavior but attempts to explain it in terms of stabilities in his relations to other persons. In part, constancies in a person's behavior result from his participation in various social systems; in part, however, they are due to individual mechanisms that stabilize his interpersonal environment. This section will deal with such mechanisms; a later section will discuss the forces in the social system which create stability—and those which lead to change.

AN INTERPERSONAL THEORY OF THE SELF

The individual is not passive, but is an *active agent* in maintaining a stable interpersonal environment. To elaborate on this point, elements from a theory published elsewhere by the writers will be introduced in somewhat simplified form (Secord & Backman, 1961). What we will attempt to show is that circumstances may put pressure on the individual to change, but active efforts on his part maintain stability of self and behavior. Certain of his characteristics contribute to this process, such as his concept of himself, his individual ways of perceiving other persons, and his learned behavior patterns.

The unit of analysis has three components, consisting of (1) an aspect of S's self, (2) S's interpretation of his behavior relevant to that aspect, and (3) his beliefs about how another person (O) behaves toward him and feels toward him with regard to that aspect. The assumption is made that S *attempts to maintain a state of congruency between these three components. A state of congruency exists when the behaviors of S and O imply definitions of self congruent with relevant aspects of his self concept.*

Two forms of congruency may be illustrated — congruency by implication, and congruency by validation. In congruency by implication, *S* may perceive that *O* sees him as possessing a particular characteristic corresponding to an aspect of his self concept. A girl who regards herself as beautiful may perceive that another person also thinks she is beautiful. In congruency by validation, the behavior or other characteristics of *O* allow or call for behavior on the part of *S* that confirms a component of self. For example, a person who regards himself as strong and protective is especially able to behave in this fashion when he interacts with a person who is dependent. These examples illustrate cognitive congruency. Later we will discuss affective congruency, a condition met when *S* perceives *O* as having the same feeling toward *S* as a whole or toward some characteristic of *S* that *S* holds toward himself.

A final point is that we may, if we wish, focus on only two of the three components. In fact, most of the following discussion will omit reference to (2), *S*'s behavior. It will consider congruency between (1), an aspect of *S*'s self concept, and (3), *S*'s view of *O*'s attitude or behavior. For the sake of simplicity, we will assume that a state of congruency exists between (1) and (2).

STABILIZING MECHANISMS IN INTERACTION

According to interpersonal congruency theory, the individual actively uses techniques or mechanisms for maintaining his interpersonal environment so as to maximize congruency. These include misperception, selective interaction, selective evaluation of the other person, selective evaluation of self, and evocation of congruent responses from the other person.

Misperception

The interpersonal environment enters into congruency only as it is seen by the individual. In instances where the actual expectations of others are not congruent with the person's self concept or behavior, it is sometimes possible for him simply to misperceive how the others see him in order to achieve congruency. A number of correlational studies have found that correspondence between self as seen by the individual and as he thinks others see him is greater than the actual correspondence between self concept and the views held by other persons.[2]

[2]Miyamoto & Dornbusch, 1956; Reeder, Donohue, & Biblarz, 1960; Backman & Secord, 1962; Moore, 1963.

The results of an experimental study illustrate some of the forms that such misperceptions take (Harvey, Kelley, & Shapiro, 1957). College subjects rated themselves and another person in their class on a variety of traits. They were then exposed to fictitious ratings of themselves which in varying degrees involved unfavorable evaluations. In different instances, they were led to believe that the ratings came from an authoritative source (a friend) or from a stranger. Some shifts in the direction of evaluating the self more negatively occurred, but in addition, subjects distorted the evaluations in a favorable direction when asked to recall them. When given the opportunity, they also dissociated the devaluations from the source by denying that those evaluations were actually made by the other persons. By and large, their reactions were more marked where the degree of devaluation was the greatest and where the ratings were perceived as coming from a friend rather than from a stranger.

Selective interaction

Another important but easily overlooked means by which an individual may maintain interpersonal congruency is through selectively interacting with certain persons and not others. More precisely, a person elects to interact with those persons with whom he can most readily establish a congruent state. For example, if he regards himself as especially intelligent, he interacts frequently with persons who respect his intelligence or who allow him to exercise it. In this manner he avoids a good deal of strain that might be placed on his self concept if he were to interact indiscriminately. By choosing such persons as friends, he creates an important and durable source of support for congruent interactions. In a study of a sorority, it was found that girls interacted most frequently with those whom they perceived as confirming their self concepts to the greatest extent (Backman & Secord, 1962).

In the discussion of role strain in Chapter 15, a number of studies were cited indicating that strain arises when a role category is incompatible with an individual's characteristics. This suggests that persons are likely to avoid entering such positions and tend to seek more compatible role categories. Several additional studies indicating that selective interaction contributes to congruency may be cited.

One study demonstrates that teachers who have been teaching for many years have smaller discrepancies between their self concept and their perception of the teacher role than do inexperienced teachers (Hoe, 1962). This did not appear to be a function of change in self or in perception of the teacher role, but was apparently owing to the tendency of those with larger discrepancies between self and the teacher role to become dissatisfied and drop out.

Studies of occupational socialization to be discussed later also support this notion of selective interaction. They suggest that selection of a particular occupation is affected by the person's conception of himself in relation to the characteristics of these occupational roles. One study of specialty choice among medical students seems most appropriate (Stern &

Scanlon, 1958). Students different in personality as reflected on the Stern Activities Index chose different specialties. The personality of the student who picked out a particular specialty was similar to the personality of practitioners in that specialty. To illustrate, among the five specialties studied, pediatricians were high on socially aggressive, assertive, and demonstrative needs, whereas obstetricians and gynecologists were more restrained, self-conscious, and diffident. If we assume that these occupational roles create conditions congenial to the prevailing personality characteristics of people found in the role, then the selection of the role by those having similar personalities creates conditions requiring little change in self.

Selective evaluation of the other person

In part, congruency is a function of the importance of the other person. Behaviors or attitudes of persons who are of no importance to the individual are not considered incongruent even though they are at variance with his self concept or his behavior. Thus a person may maximize congruency by favorably evaluating those who behave congruently toward him and devaluating those who behave incongruently. This view was supported in a study of a sorority, where it was found that girls who were liked most by a member were those whom she perceived as having the most congruent views of her and who actually had the most congruent views (Backman & Secord, 1962). This correlational finding, of course, does not demonstrate cause and effect. A number of experimental studies provide more direct support (Harvey, Kelley, & Shapiro, 1957; Howard & Berkowitz, 1958; Worchel, 1961). They demonstrate that when a person is negatively evaluated by another, he reduces his liking for that person. In a sense, he discredits the source of the negative evaluation, thereby eliminating the incongruency.

Selective evaluation of self

Congruency is also a function of the importance of the aspect of self relevant to behavior or to interaction with another person. If an *insignificant* aspect of self is at variance with a person's perception of his behavior or that of another, incongruency is minimized. Consequently, the person may maximize congruency by altering the values placed on various aspects of self so that the aspects which are in agreement with his perceptions of his behavior and that of others are most highly valued. Similarly, he may devaluate aspects of self which are not congruent with components of his behavior and the behavior of others. An example from McCandless (1961) illustrates the process with respect to self and behavior:

> Let us take, for example, a boy who has entered junior-high school, when for the first time clear choices of activity must be made, some being sacrificed so that others may be pursued. He has equally strong and equally valued conceptions of himself as an athlete and as a scholar, but must choose between two

activities: debate and basketball. He chooses debate. It might be predicted that he will sharply devalue the importance of basketball, and possibly of all sports; but will sharply upgrade the importance of debate and other types of intellectual activity. The actual *direction* of his conception of himself as an athlete may not shift, but the *value* to him of this facet of his self-concept will change in a negative direction. Conversely, the value of intellectual activities will become greater, and the importance of the intellectual facet of his self-concept will increase. (P. 201)

Response evocation

An individual may, consciously or unconsciously, intentionally or unintentionally, behave in a way that results in other persons behaving toward him in a congruent fashion. While the study of such strategies in interaction is still largely in the speculative and descriptive stage, two partially overlapping approaches may be mentioned. These involve the *presentation of self* and *altercasting*. Goffman (1959), Stone (1959; 1962), and others have noted that a person in interaction controls the cues he provides to other persons to ensure that he will be categorized in certain ways and not in others. A female may, by her behavior, her speech, her dress, and her grooming, create the impression that, while she is sexually attractive and broadminded, she is not a loose woman. Assuming that this impression coincides with aspects of her self and behavior and that it is effectively conveyed, it should evoke congruent behavior from men. They are not likely to treat her as if she were either promiscuous or prudish.

Whereas the various strategies revolving around the presentation of self indirectly affect the other person by leading him to define the situation in a certain way, altercasting is often more direct (Weinstein, 1962). A person using this strategy attempts to cast another person into a role that will bring forth the desired response. For example, if he wishes to obtain a favor by trading on friendship, he might say: "Now, Joe, as a good friend of mine, I know you would. . . ." In everyday situations, more subtle techniques of altercasting are often used.

STUDY QUESTIONS

8. *What is meant by the concept of interpersonal congruency? Describe two kinds: congruency by implication and congruency by validation. Give some examples of your own invention.*

9. *Explain how each of the following mechanisms works to establish interpersonal congruency: (a) misperception, (b) selective interaction, (c) selective evaluation of the other person, (d) selective evaluation of self, and (e) response evocation.*

Affective congruency

As noted earlier, the concept of congruency may be applied to feelings as well as to cognitive elements. A state of affective congruency exists when *S* believes that *O* feels toward him as *S* feels toward himself, either in regard to himself as a whole or in regard to some aspect of self. In another form of affective congruency, *S* has comparable feelings toward an aspect of self and his corresponding behavior. Affective congruency is maintained by the same mechanisms as those previously described for cognitive congruency. Persons may misperceive how others feel about them. They may selectively associate with and selectively evaluate other persons. They may attempt to evoke congruent feelings from other persons.

Considerable evidence suggests that persons present themselves in such a way as to evoke a positive evaluation by other persons. Because of the prevalence of this type of behavior, some theorists have suggested that people have a strong need for self-enhancement—that they continually strive to make others think well of them (Rogers, 1951; Combs & Snygg, 1959; Worchel, 1961). The difficulty with such a hypothesis is that a minority of people do not display this behavior. A fairly common type of person that most of us have encountered is the self-deprecating individual, who continually rejects expressions of favorable views of him by others. At the extreme, some neurotics have a deep sense of inferiority and worthlessness which pervades much of their behavior. This self-effacing neurotic has been well described by Horney (1950):

> He must *not* feel consciously superior to others or display any such feelings in his behavior. On the contrary he tends to subordinate himself to others, to be dependent upon them, to appease them . . . anything in the attitude of others, like admiration or recognition, that puts him in a superior position makes him uneasy. What he longs for is help, protection, and surrendering love. . . .
>
> The anxious shunning of pride, triumph, or superiority shows in many ways. Characteristic and easy to observe is the fear of winning in games. A patient . . . could at times play an excellent game of tennis or chess. As long as she was oblivious of her good position all went well. But as soon as she became aware of being ahead of her opponent she suddenly missed the ball or (in playing chess) overlooked the most obvious moves that would ensure victory. . . .
>
> Exactly the same attitude obtains in other situations. It is characteristic for this type not to be aware of being in a stronger position and not to be able to make use of it. Privileges, in his mind, turn into liabilities. He is often not aware of his superior knowledge, and at the crucial moment not able to show it. He is at sea in any situation in which his rights are not clearly defined—as for instance in relation to domestic or secretarial help. Even when making perfectly legitimate requests he feels as though he were taking undue advantage of the other person. And he either refrains from asking or does it apologetically, with a "guilty" conscience. (Pp. 215–216)

The principle of affective congruency makes unnecessary the postulation of any need for self-enhancement. Affective congruency covers both self-enhancement and self-deprecation. The prevalence of self-enhancement behavior is merely a reflection of the fact that most individuals were loved and fussed over as infants and small children. They developed positive feelings toward themselves that reflected the positive feelings held toward them by significant other persons. A small number of persons have been targets of intensely negative attitudes on the part of significant others, however, and thus are likely to have acquired a deep feeling of insecurity and worthlessness. These feelings, whether positive or negative, tend to persist because a person fashions his later experiences to maintain congruency between self, behavior, and the behavior and attitudes of other persons toward him. Thus, if his core self includes a strong feeling of worth, he will strive for behaviors congruent with that feeling, he will prefer to relate to other individuals who evaluate him similarly, and he will avoid those who do not. On the other hand, if he has negative feelings toward self, he will be attracted to others who have negative feelings toward him and will persist in behaviors that are negatively evaluated.

Various studies that demonstrate "self-enhancement" are consistent with the principle of affective congruency, if it is assumed that the great majority of the subjects in these studies had positive feelings toward themselves. In several investigations, subjects used a variety of mechanisms to protect themselves from a person who evaluated them unfavorably. For example, the person was not believed, he was disliked and discredited, his attitude was distorted in a favorable direction, or he was avoided (Harvey, Kelley, & Shapiro, 1957; Dittes, 1959; Worchel, 1961; Harvey, 1962). Another study demonstrated that when persons knew that evaluations of them on the basis of tests were going to be made public, they were more likely to distort their self-evaluations in favorable directions as a protective device (Gerard, 1961). The use of selective evaluation of other persons to maintain affective congruency has also been demonstrated (Backman & Secord, 1959). Subjects who were initially strangers in several ten-man groups engaging in face-to-face interaction were led to believe that certain others in the group liked them. They subsequently reported liking these particular persons more than they liked other members of the group.

None of the experiments cited provides a comparative test of the principles of self-enhancement and affective congruency. That is, they do not furnish positive evidence for one concept and negative evidence for the other. A really adequate experiment has yet to be conducted, although several experiments provide some tentative support for affective congruency as opposed to self-enhancement. One investigation involving failure in a group situation indicated that under one experimental condition, subjects with high self-esteem protected themselves from unfavorable evaluations by other persons better than did those with low self-esteem (Stotland et al., 1957). This result is predicted by the principle of affective congruency, but not by a postulated need for self-enhancement. A self-enhancement principle would predict that protective mechanisms would be used by persons with low esteem as well as those with high esteem.

Another investigation is somewhat relevant, since it concerns congruency between *O*'s evaluation and *S*'s behavior although it does not pertain to *S*'s self concept (Deutsch & Solomon, 1959). As noted earlier, if another person behaves congruently toward an individual, the individual should like him. A group task was manipulated so that subjects perceived their performance as good or poor. After completion of the task, they were exposed to positive and negative evaluations of their work in the form of a note, presumably from another group member. These evaluations were either congruent or incongruent with the subjects' performances. The congruency effect did occur even in instances where the evaluation was unfavorable: persons were liked if they evaluated the subject's performance as he himself did.

This result was accompanied by another effect. Persons were also liked if they evaluated an individual's performance favorably — even if he himself evaluated it poorly. Although apparently contradictory to congruency theory, this finding can be reconciled if it is assumed that when another person evaluates an individual's performance, some of his evaluation is perceived as applying to aspects of self that are positively valued. To the extent that subjects interpreted the favorable reaction of another person as applying to some aspects of self as well as to performance, they would be led to like the other person because *this* aspect of his behavior *is* congruent.

Another reason why early self conceptions persist, whether they are positive or negative, is the physiological basis of emotions that makes them resistant to modification. Our emotions are intimately associated with a variety of physiological functions that seem to serve as a support for their expression, a fact recognized in lay language by the term "gut feeling," which refers to certain basic emotions having virtually no cognitive aspect. This recognition of the separation of cognitions and feelings into different categories is as old as the ancient Greek philosophers and has been expressed in many different ways. To some extent man is an irrational being, governed by certain emotions not quite within his control. For example, there may be no particular logic in the love of one person for a particular other, no reasons that he feels really explain his love. Or a person may get angry at someone even when getting angry is not a very reasonable action. These parts of his nature are more difficult to modify than his neutral cognitions.

Affective-cognitive consistency

In Chapter 3, Rosenberg's theory of affective-cognitive consistency was discussed as it applies to attitudes in general. Since the self is a constellation of attitudes toward the person as an object, it may also be applied here. Affective-cognitive consistency of self would take the form of compatibility between cognitive and affective aspects. One operational way of defining this is that the values assigned to cognitive aspects of self should be consistent with the overall affect toward self. Thus a person with positive feelings toward himself should attribute such positively valued traits to himself as intelligence, consideration, responsibility, etc. In a review of studies of the tendency of persons to endorse socially desirable test items, Edwards (1957*b*) has shown that most people have a powerful tendency to assign to themselves positively valued personality traits. This is consistent with the assumption that most people have positive feelings toward themselves.

From the theory of affective-cognitive consistency, we would expect that if the affective component of self remains unchanged, cognitive components will also remain stable so that they continue to be consistent with the affective component. As new role categories are occupied, however, the role expectations of other persons create a force toward change in self. To the extent that these expectations conflict either with existing cognitions or with affect toward self, they will be difficult to incorporate into the self concept. But if the force toward socialization in the new role is strong enough, the new cognitions will eventually be incorporated. Where acquired cognitions clash with existing affect, conflict is created. The various congruency processes previously discussed will then lead to some form of resolution in which either the cognitions or the affect are modified so that balance is restored.

STUDY QUESTIONS

10. *What is meant by affective congruency?*

11. *What is the need for self-enhancement, and what difficulty is there in postulating that this need is universal?*

12. *Explain how the principle of affective congruency makes the postulation of a need for self-enhancement unnecessary. What is the evidence in support of this principle?*

13. *Besides congruency, what other factor contributes to maintaining a given affect toward self over a period of time?*

14. *Explain how the principle of affective-cognitive consistency may be used to explain the stability of self over time.*

Summary: Stabilizing mechanisms

The various means by which the individual may achieve congruency are the following:

1. *Misperception.* Since congruency is a perceptual-cognitive state, a person may sometimes achieve it by misperceiving the attitude of others toward him or by misinterpreting his own behavior. Empirical studies appear to be consistent with this hypothesis.

2. *Selective interaction.* The individual may also maximize congruency by electing to interact with certain persons and not others. This may be accomplished by making friends of the persons with whom he can most readily establish a congruent state, or by choosing a role that will bring forth from others behaviors and attitudes that are congruent. Several studies support this principle.

3. *Selective evaluation of the other person.* In part, congruency is a function of the importance of the other person. Thus, a person may maximize congruency by favorably evaluating those who behave congruently toward him and devaluating those who behave incongruently toward him. Correlational and experimental studies are consistent with this hypothesis.

4. *Selective evaluation of self.* Congruency is also a function of the importance of the aspect of self relevant to behavior or to the other person. Congruency may be maximized by altering the values placed on various aspects of self so that a person most values the aspects which are in agreement with his perceptions of his behavior and the behavior of others. Similarly, he devaluates aspects of self corresponding to his behaviors and behaviors of other persons that are not congruent. Experimentation is needed on this principle.

5. *Response evocation.* Consciously or unconsciously, intentionally or unintentionally, an individual may behave in a fashion that results in other persons behaving toward him in a congruent fashion. Examples are the presentation of self and altercasting. In both processes, a person in interaction controls the cues he provides to other persons to ensure that he will be categorized in certain congruent ways. Altercasting is somewhat more direct, in that the individual actively places the other person in an appropriate role by verbal or other means. Further empirical work on these ideas is needed.

6. *Affective congruency.* A state of affective congruency exists when S believes that O feels toward him as S feels toward himself. Another form of congruency exists when S has comparable feelings toward an aspect of self and his corresponding behavior. This notion of affective congruency explains the presence in most people of a "need for self-enhancement," which is the tendency to see and present oneself in a favorable light. Feelings toward self are likely to become firmly rooted as a result of early experience, particularly because of the intimate tie between such feelings and physiological functions. To the extent that a person's core self includes a strong feeling of worth (as is the case for most persons), he will use the various congruency mechanisms to create an interpersonal environment which is consistent with the feeling. Experimental evidence is compatible with these ideas.

7. *Affective-cognitive consistency.* Affective-cognitive consistency of self requires that cognitive and affective aspects of self be compatible. The high proportion of socially desirable responses given by persons on self-inventories illustrates their desire to maintain such consistency, if we assume that most persons have positive feelings toward self. To the extent that either the affective or the cognitive component is firmly stabilized, resistance to change in the other component is likely to be high because of the need to maintain affective-cognitive consistency. On this topic further empirical work which is especially relevant to self is needed.

STABILIZING EFFECTS OF THE SOCIAL STRUCTURE

This chapter has emphasized that the stability over time of an individual's self and behavior rests on constancies in his interpersonal environment. In the preceding section the means by which the individual contributes to such constancies have been enumerated. Another source of stability lies in the social structure, which contributes to maintaining a constant interpersonal environment in two ways.

First, because a person occupies a certain position in a social system, he is seen by others and sees himself in ways dictated by the role category he occupies. By this means stable relations are likely to arise and continue. Second, a person's memberships in various groups ensure a continuation of interaction with persons with whom he has already established congruent relations. They reduce the chances that he will encounter individuals whose behavior or attitudes would require drastic modification of his self concept and behavior in order to achieve congruency.

Each of these structural sources of stability may be further illustrated. With respect to participation in a social system, a person is seen by others and sees himself in ways dictated by his role category. Persons learn not only the behavioral expectations belonging to a position or role category, but also the personal attributes associated with it. By occupying certain positions they are consistently defined by others and consequently define themselves in terms of traits associated with the role category. Perhaps age-sex roles are the most obvious example. Various personality characteristics typical of maleness or femaleness in a given group are learned and maintained because males and females are consistently defined as possessing them.

With respect to group memberships, the previous discussion of the ways in which the individual contributes to stabilizing his interpersonal environment included the point that he is likely to enter groups and participate in social systems if the probability of establishing congruent relations is high. Once he has entered such groups, his participation in congruent relations is in part determined by the conditions and processes that control the groups. For long periods of his life, a person is surrounded by the same other individuals, who include family members, playmates, and friends. Even when actual individuals change, those who replace earlier associates have certain similarities to the previous ones because of the constraining effects of the social structure (a person stays in a certain socioeconomic class, in a certain occupation, etc.).

The various processes contributing to stability in individual behavior are presented in a single perspective in Figure 19–1. Starting from the left, contributions of the social structure are indicated: (1) It determines the frequencies of interaction between a person S and various other persons; (2) it places S in various role categories; and (3) it controls the behaviors of other persons toward S. Each process in turn serves to establish a certain interpersonal environment in which S moves. In interaction with this environment, S strives to establish relations that are congruent with self and behavior. The various congruency processes discussed in the previous section are employed by S to achieve congruency. Note, however, that these processes in turn act on the interpersonal environment.

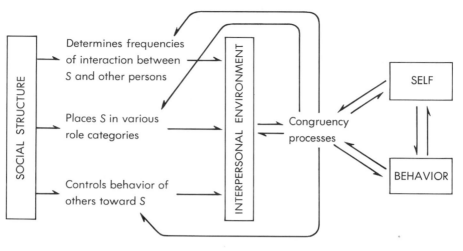

Figure 19–1

Relations between social structure, interpersonal environment, self, and behavior.

To a certain degree, *S* is able to determine the frequency with which he interacts with various other persons, the role categories he is placed in, and the behavior that others display toward him; thus he shapes the interpersonal environment to a limited extent.

Consistency in the interpersonal environment

So far, the discussion of congruency has been limited largely to interaction between an individual and one other person with regard to a single aspect of self and behavior. It would be unrealistic, of course, to consider that all such aspects of self and relations to different persons are independent of each other. In that case the person, chameleon-like, would change his self and behavior each time he interacted with a different person or each time a different aspect of self was involved. While some variability from situation to situation does occur, most students of personality believe that there is also much consistency in a person's behavior in different situations.

To the extent that different situations support similar aspects of self and behavior, these aspects may be said to support each other. Consequently, resistance to change in such components of self or behavior is apt to be especially great, and change is unlikely to be accomplished by shifts in single relations that may be fortuitously encountered. Much further theorizing and research is needed on the relations among different dyadic interactions. For the present, one experimental illustration may suffice.

An experiment was conducted to test the hypothesis that the greater the number of significant persons supporting an aspect of self, the more resistant to change that aspect is (Backman, Secord, & Peirce, 1963). College students were asked to rank themselves on a series of fifteen characteristics and also to estimate how they thought each of five persons important to them would rank them on these characteristics. They were given several personality tests for the ostensible purpose of determining how much insight they had into their own personalities. For each individual, the experimenter selected two traits for special analysis and treatment. Both traits were ranked among the highest five applying to self by each person, but one represented high perceived agreement among the five significant other persons, and the other represented low perceived agreement. The specific hypothesis was that the trait having the greater consensus would be more resistant to change than the trait having the lower consensus.

On a later occasion, a false report purportedly based upon the personality tests was presented to the subjects. Actually, the report was based upon the initial self-rankings. It contained descriptive statements very similar to those on which the subject had previously ranked himself. The rank order of traits on this report as arranged by the experimenter was the same as the subject's previous ranking, except that the two traits selected for special treatment were reported as being eight rank steps lower than the subject had ranked them.

After the subject had had time to study this report, and presumably to note the discrepancies between it and his rankings of himself, he was asked to rank himself again. On this second self-ranking, most subjects were influenced by the false report to lower the ranking of these two traits; however, the trait having low consensus was lowered to a greater extent than the trait having high consensus. Thus, the study demonstrates that the greater the number of significant other persons who are seen as defining oneself in a manner compatible with one's own definition, the more resistant to change is that self-definition.

STUDY QUESTIONS

15. *What are the two major ways in which social structure may help to maintain stability of self and behavior over time?*

16. *Describe the ways in which the social structure has an impact on the interpersonal environment of the individual, and show how this impact is related to self and behavior through congruency processes.*

17. *In terms of interpersonal congruency, what is meant by consistency in the interpersonal environment?*

Summary: Social structure

Although the social structure may under certain conditions contribute to change in individual behavior, there are two ways in which it maintains a stable interpersonal environment. First, because a person occupies a certain position in a social system, he is seen by others and sees himself in ways dictated by the role category he occupies. Thus stable relations are likely to be maintained. Second, a person's memberships in various groups ensure continuing interaction with persons with whom he has already established congruent relations. Likewise, his memberships reduce the chances that he will encounter individuals whose behavior or attitudes would require drastic modification of self and behavior in order for him to achieve congruency.

A very important topic on which little research has been done concerns the consistency among components of the interpersonal environment. To the extent that they are consistent, self and behavior should be more resistant to change. One form of consistency, perceived agreement in the attitudes of other persons toward an individual, has been studied in an experiment whose results supported this hypothesis.

SUMMARY: STABILITY OF SELF AND BEHAVIOR

Much consistency in behavior occurs because the individual responds actively to situational factors in a manner that maintains the distinctive character of his behavior. This activity was discussed in terms of interpersonal congruency theory, in which the unit of analysis consists of three components: an aspect of S's self, S's interpretation of his behavior relevant to that aspect, and his beliefs about how another person (O) behaves toward him and feels toward him with regard to that aspect. A person attempts to maintain a state of congruency between the three components. Congruency exists when the behaviors of S and O imply definitions of self compatible with relevant aspects of his self concept. In congruency by implication, S may perceive that O sees him as possessing a particular characteristic corresponding to an aspect of his self concept. In congruency by validation, the behavior or other characteristics of O allow or call for behavior on the part of S that confirms a component of self. Congruency may also be affective, as when S has the same feelings toward himself that O has toward him.

There are a number of activities on the part of the individual that contribute to stability of self by creating for him an interpersonal environment which is likely to be congruent with his self concept and behavior. These include (1) misperceiving the attitudes or behavior of other persons, or misinterpreting his own behavior, (2) selectively interacting with persons who have congruent attitudes or who behave congruently toward him, (3) positively evaluating persons who have congruent attitudes or behavior toward him, (4) evaluating most highly the aspects of self that he perceives as congruent with the attitudes and behavior of other persons, (5) evoking congruent responses from others through presenting himself in an appropriate manner or through casting the other in a congruent role, and (6) maintaining affective-cognitive consistency in self.

There are two ways in which the social structure also contributes to maintaining an interpersonal environment. *First,* as a participant in a social system, a person occupies one or more positions that have definite expectations associated with them. Thus the attitudes held toward him by his role partners and those he holds toward himself are likely to be congruent. *Second,* a person's memberships in various groups ensure a continuation of interaction with persons with whom he has already established congruent relations. They also reduce the chances that he will encounter individuals whose behavior or attitudes would require drastic modification of self and behavior in order to achieve congruency. To the extent that a person occupies positions which are relatively consistent with one another, the various social systems in which he participates support each other in maintaining a stable interpersonal environment.

Changes in Self and Individual Behavior

The social structure is not only a source of stability, but under certain conditions also induces changes in the interpersonal environment. As a person moves through the social structure, systematic changes occur in the ways he is categorized and the ways other persons behave toward him. Features of the social structure also induce changes in the personnel of his environment. In addition, various fortuitous events can produce changes. To illustrate changes arising from the social structure, the discussion below will treat the positional changes which occur with increasing age and with occupational socialization.

AGE–LINKED POSITIONS

Each society has laid out for the individual a series of role categories that he will occupy at various stages of his life. Thus, every male will occupy such categories as infant, small boy, big boy, adolescent, young man, middle-aged man, and elderly man. In addition, each person will have a certain place in his family, depending upon its structure and composition. He will have a certain birth order as the youngest, the oldest, or some middle position. He will have either no siblings, or one or more siblings. Family activities may frequently or infrequently include contacts with other relatives such as grandparents, uncles and aunts, and cousins.

Outside the family, the male will occupy certain roles in his peer groups. At adulthood he will often enter military service, and usually he will marry, acquiring the roles of husband, father, etc. His occupational role will play an important part in his life. All these roles contribute to his self concept. To the extent that they are sequential and discontinuous, with movement from one to the next requiring behavior changes, they are instrumental in bringing about certain changes in the self. Cavan (1962) provides a vivid description of the discontinuity of the role category forced upon a man at retirement, showing how, at this point in life, a new and less valued self image is thrust upon the person:

At the point of retirement, we may make a generalized picture of the male. He has a well-ingrained self-image as competent, successful at some level of work, usefully productive, self-supporting, and able to provide for his family.

This image has been built up over years of time by the favorable reactions of his family, friends, co-workers, and those segments of society whose opinion he values. He has, moreover, found a kind of work — a social role — that permits him to express his self-image satisfactorily, and he is firmly incorporated into a physical environment and a group of co-workers which make it possible for him to carry out his role.

Using the concepts employed above, let us consider what happens at the point of compulsory retirement. First, the means of carrying out the social role disappears: the man is a lawyer without a case, a bookkeeper without books, a machinist without tools. Second, he is excluded from his group of former co-workers; as an isolated person he may be completely unable to function in his former role. Third, as a retired person, he begins to find a different evaluation of himself in the minds of others from the evaluation he had as an employed person. He no longer sees respect in the eyes of former subordinates, praise in the faces of former superiors, and approval in the manner of former co-workers. The looking glass composed of his former important groups throws back a changed image: he is done for, an old-timer, old-fashioned, on the shelf. (P. 527)

Occupational socialization and the self

Several studies of occupational socialization document formative effects on the self concept as an individual passes through the social structure. These effects have been traced by comparing the frequency and the rank order in which nursing students in various stages of professional training designated themselves by an occupational self-reference (Kuhn, 1960). Only a third of those near the end of their freshman year identified themselves as nurses in one of the first three statements on the Twenty Statements Test, but more than seven out of ten students did so by the end of their junior year. This demonstrates the incorporation of the image of "nurse" into the self.

A similar trend has been noted in medical students (Huntington, 1957). Thirty-one percent of the first-year medical students reported that they felt more like a doctor than a student when dealing with patients. This figure rose to 83 percent for students finishing their fourth year of training. Whether or not students primarily saw themselves as doctors also depended on which role partner they were interacting with. When they were interacting with fellow students, faculty members, or nurses, the percent of those who saw themselves as physicians was considerably less than when they were dealing with patients.

This finding is consistent with the theoretical position that the expectations of counterposition occupants are an important determinant of how the position occupant sees his role. More students see themselves as physicians when they are interacting with patients, who are more likely than other role partners to see them as doctors. Further support stems from the finding that 39 percent of the 117 first-year students who thought their patients regarded them as doctors defined themselves as such, whereas only 6 percent of the 35 students who believed their patients defined them as students saw themselves as doctors.

Finally, one would expect students to have a rather unstable image of themselves as doctors because of the lack of consensus among the various others in their role set. Presumably, when the student physician graduates, and the other persons in his role set actually see him and are believed by him to see him as a doctor, this occupational role will become a stable part of his self image. Where the cues associated with a role category are clear and unambiguous, consensus may be expected to occur eventually and the role expectations to be ultimately associated with self. Where the cues to a role category are vague or ambiguous, as they are in the interim position of medical student, agreement among others in the role set and consequent stability of the self concept would seldom be obtained.

Learning to view oneself in a new manner involves considerably more than applying a new self-referent to oneself. One learns to see oneself in terms of the range of physical, social, and personality attributes which are characteristic of fellow position occupants, even including those attributes that are not directly concerned with the performance of the role. Recent studies showing differences between occupational groups in self-descriptions provide ample documentation of this point (Scanlon, Hunter, & Sun, 1961). Typically, such studies of occupational socialization show a gradual shift in personality characteristics in the direction of the appropriate professional image as the neophyte proceeds through training.

Occupying a new position in the social structure may also involve radical changes in the personnel in one's environment. New persons become significant, old associates drop out or fade in significance. The person who is inducted into the service or who takes a position in a strange community is suddenly surrounded by new associates. To the degree that these persons define him in an unfamiliar way, and to the extent that the effects of the new definitions are not countered by the various means of maintaining congruency previously discussed, strong forces are created toward a change in self and behavior.

Significant interpersonal relations

A presumably vital factor shaping the self concept, but one little studied by scientists, is found in the influence of a highly significant other person on the individual. Often a person forms a close tie to someone else who greatly influences his behavior. This other person may be a close friend, or he may be someone who is older and highly respected and admired. Or he could be someone who has a very special relation to the individual, as a wife or husband, a lover, or a therapist. Such persons, because of their great importance to the individual as well as their special relation to him, may well bring about marked changes in self and behavior.

These changes may work on affective or cognitive components, or both. If one component is changed, the other is likely to be modified to reestablish affective-cognitive consistency. Cognitive changes in self that have been observed to occur after a period of psychotherapy provide an example (Rogers & Dymond, 1954). Psychotherapy is a very intense emotional experience, and in client-centered therapy where cognitive changes have been clearly documented, the therapist is warm and accepting toward the patient. The therapist's attitude may lead the patient gradually to increase the amount of positive affect toward himself, which in turn is followed by the adoption of more positive self-cognitions to achieve consistency.

STUDY QUESTIONS

18. *How does a person's movement through the social structure with increasing age contribute to change in self and behavior?*
19. *Discuss typical findings from studies of occupational socialization.*
20. *How may significant interpersonal relations contribute to change in self and behavior?*
21. *Describe the processes by which the social structure changes the interpersonal environment of the individual. How do these processes relate to congruency processes involving self and behavior?*

SUMMARY: CHANGE IN SELF AND BEHAVIOR

An overall view of the processes leading to change is presented in Figure 19–2. Fortuitous factors, movement through the social structure, or both may change frequencies of interaction with other persons, may change their behavior toward the individual, may change the role categories the individual occupies, and may change the personnel with whom he interacts. This changed interpersonal environment is likely to be incongruent with some aspects of self and behavior. Congruency proc-

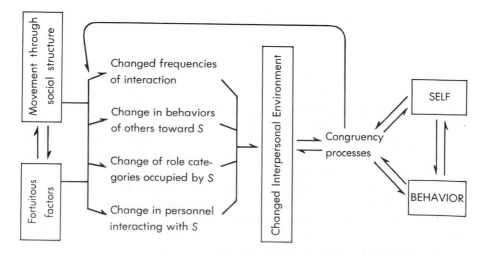

Figure 19–2
Processes leading to change in self and behavior.

esses then come into play to restore balance. If changes in the interpersonal environment have not been too great, the individual may manage to restore congruency with little change in self and behavior. With greater changes in the interpersonal environment, however, congruency is likely to be restored only through changes in self and behavior.

Summary and Conclusions

This chapter uses interpersonal theory to explain the stability and consistency of a person's behavior, as well as changes in self and behavior. A central concept is congruency, a state prevailing when the behaviors of an individual and another person imply definitions of self congruent with relevant aspects of his self concept. Congruency may be cognitive or affective; in other words, a person may believe that another person defines him in cognitive terms in the same way that he defines himself, or he may believe that another person has the same feelings toward him that he has toward himself.

A person has a set of subjective public identities, each identity appropriate to an especially significant other person or group of persons. Out of his experience with other persons he also forms an inner self or core, representing his most central characteristics and most salient attitudes toward himself. The development of the self concept, particularly a person's subjective public identities, may be understood in part in terms of his assignment to a series of social roles. As he moves through the social structure, he is placed in various role categories and acquires an identity associated with each role. Ultimately some of the characteristics acquired in these identities may become a part of the core self. An important part of the core is affect toward the self: a global feeling having a positive, negative, or ambivalent quality.

Activities by the individual that contribute to stability of self include the following: (1) misperceiving the attitudes or behavior of other persons, or misinterpreting his own behavior, (2) selectively interacting with persons who have congruent attitudes or who behave congruently toward him, (3) positively evaluating persons who have congruent attitudes or behavior toward him, (4) evaluating most highly the aspects of self that he perceives as congruent with the attitudes and behavior of other persons, (5) evoking congruent responses from others through presenting himself in an appropriate manner or through casting the other in a congruent role, and (6) maintaining affective-cognitive consistency in self.

Consistency of self and behavior is also a function of the stabilizing effects of the social structure. A stable social structure contributes to maintaining congruency in two ways. First, the various role categories in which the individual is placed dictate the attitudes and behaviors of other persons toward him as well as his own attitudes toward himself in directions that are likely to be congruent. Second, membership in groups ensures that a person will interact frequently with persons who define him in a congruent manner and ensures that his behavior will be congruent with self. To the extent that the components of the interpersonal environment are consistent with one another, self and behavior should be more resistant to change.

Changes in self and behavior occur as the interpersonal environment undergoes marked changes because of fortuitous factors, or because of the person's movement through different role categories in the social structure, or both. This changed environment is likely to involve changed frequencies of interaction with other persons, a change in the behaviors of these persons toward an individual, a change in role categories occupied by him, and a change in the personnel who interact with him. Since these changes create incongruencies, congruency processes then come into play. They either restore balance without changing self or behavior, or they reestablish congruency by modifying some aspects of self and behavior.

Bibliography

Abelson, R. P. Modes of resolution of belief dilemmas. *J. conflict Resolut.,* 1959, **3**, 343–352.

Abelson, R. P., & G. S. Lesser. The measurement of persuasibility in children. In C. I. Hovland & I. L. Janis (Eds.), *Personality and persuasibility.* New Haven, Conn.: Yale University Press, 1959. Pp. 141–166. (*a*)

Abelson, R. P., & G. S. Lesser. A developmental theory of persuasibility. In C. I. Hovland & I. L. Janis (Eds.), *Personality and persuasibility.* New Haven, Conn.: Yale University Press, 1959. Pp. 167–186. (*b*)

Adams, R. G. The behavior of pupils in democratic and autocratic social climates. *Abstracts of dissertations,* Stanford University, 1945, **20**, 83–86.

Adams, S. Status congruency as a variable in small group performance. *Soc. Forces,* 1953, **32**, 16–22.

Adorno, T. W., Else Frenkel-Brunswik, D. J. Levinson, & R. N. Sanford. *The authoritarian personality.* New York: Harper & Row, Publishers, Incorporated, 1950.

Aldington, R. (Ed.) *A book of "characters."* New York: E. P. Dutton & Co., Inc., 1924.

Alfert, Elizabeth. Two components of assumed similarity. *J. abnorm. soc. Psychol.,* 1958, **56**, 135–138.

Allinsmith, W., & T. C. Greening. Guilt over anger as predicted from parental discipline: A study of superego development. *Amer. Psychologist,* 1955, **10**, 320.

Allport, G. W. *The nature of prejudice,* Garden City, N.Y.: Doubleday & Company, Inc., 1958.

Allport, G. W., & H. Cantril. Judging personality from the voice. *J. soc. Psychol.,* 1934, **5**, 37–55.

Allport, G. W., & B. M. Kramer. Some roots of prejudice. *J. Psychol.,* 1946, **22**, 9–39.

Allport, G. W., & P. E. Vernon. *A study of values.* Boston: Houghton Mifflin Company, 1931.

Allport, G. W., & P. E. Vernon. *Studies in expressive movement.* New York: The Macmillan Company, 1932.

Altrocchi, J. Dominance as a factor in interpersonal choice and perception. *J. abnorm. soc. Psychol.,* 1959, **59**, 303–307.

Altrocchi, J., & S. Shrauger. The personality of the perceiver as a factor in person perception. *Psychol. Bull.,* 1964. In press.

Anderson, H. H., & Helen M. Brewer. Studies of teachers' classroom personalities. I. Dominative and socially integrative behavior of kindergarten teachers. *Appl. Psychol. Monogr.,* No. 6. Stanford. Calif.: Stanford University Press, 1945.

Anderson, H. H., & J. E. Brewer. Studies of teachers' classroom personalities. II. Effects of teachers' dominative and integrative contacts on children's classroom behavior. *Appl. Psychol. Monogr.,* No. 8. Stanford, Calif.: Stanford University Press, 1946.

Anderson, H. H., J. E. Brewer, & Mary F. Reed. Studies of teachers' classroom personalities. III. Follow-up studies of the effects of dominative and integrative contacts on children's behavior. *Appl. Psychol. Monogr.,* No. 11. Stanford, Calif.: Stanford University Press. 1946.

Anderson, N. H. Test of a model for opinion change. *J. abnorm. soc. Psychol.,* 1959, **59**, 371–381.

Anderson, N. H., & A. A. Barrios. Primacy effects in personality impression formation. *J. abnorm. soc. Psychol.,* 1961, **63**, 346–350.

Antonovsky, H. F. A contribution to research in the area of mother-child relationships. *Child Develpm.,* 1959, **30**, 32–51.

Argyris, C. *Understanding organizational behavior.* Homewood, Ill.: Dorsey Press, 1960.

Aronfreed, J. M., S. A. Messick, & J. C. Diggory. Reexamining emotionality and perceptual defense. *J. Pers.,* 1953, **21**, 517–528.

Aronson, E., & J. Mills. The effect of severity of initiation on liking for a group. *J. abnorm. soc. Psychol.,* 1959, **59**, 177–181.

Aronson, E., Judith A. Turner, & J. M. Carlsmith. Communicator credibility and communication discrepancy as determinants of opinion change. *J. abnorm. soc. Psychol.,* 1963, **67**, 31–36.

Asch, S. E. Forming impressions of personality. *J. abnorm. soc. Psychol.,* 1946, **41**, 258–290.

Asch, S. E. *Social psychology.* Englewood Cliffs, N. J.: Prentice-Hall, Inc., 1952.

Asch, S. E. Studies of independence and conformity: A minority of one against a unanimous majority. *Psychol. Monogr.,* 1956, **70**, No. 9 (Whole No. 416).

Asch, S. E. The metaphor: A psychological inquiry. In R. Tagiuri & L. Petrullo (Eds.), *Person perception and interpersonal behavior.* Stanford, Calif.: Stanford University Press, 1958. Pp. 86–94.

Ashley, W. R., R. S. Harper, & D. L. Runyon. The perceived size of coins in normal and hypnotically induced economic states. *Amer. J. Psychol.,* 1951, **64**, 564–572.

Back, K. W. Influence through social communication. *J. abnorm. soc. Psychol.,* 1951, **46**, 9–23.

Backman, C. W., & P. F. Secord. The effect of perceived liking on interpersonal attraction. *Hum. Relat.,* 1959, **12**, 379–384.

Backman, C. W., & P. F. Secord. Liking, selective interaction, and misperception in congruent interpersonal relations. *Sociometry,* 1962, **25**, 321–335.

Backman, C. W. & P. F. Secord. The compromise process and the affect structure of groups. *Hum. Relat.,* 1964, **17**, 19–22.

Backman, C. W., P. F. Secord, & J. R. Peirce. Resistance to change in the self-concept as a function of perceived consensus among significant others. *Sociometry,* 1963, **26**, 102–111.

Bales, R. F. A set of categories for the analysis of small group interaction. *Amer. sociol. Rev.,* 1950, **15**, 146–159.

Bales, R. F. Some uniformities of behavior in small social systems. In G. E. Swanson, T. M. Newcomb, & E. L. Hartley (Eds.), *Readings in social psychology.* (Rev. ed.) New York: Holt, Rinehart and Winston, Inc., 1952. Pp. 146–159.

Bales, R. F. The equilibrium problem in small groups. In T. Parsons, R. F. Bales, & E. A. Shils (Eds.), *Working papers in the theory of action.* New York: The Free Press of Glencoe, 1953. Pp. 111–161.

Bales, R. F., & E. F. Borgatta. Size of group as a factor in the interaction profile. In A. P. Hare, E. F. Borgatta, & R. F. Bales (Eds.), *Small groups.* New York: Alfred A. Knopf, Inc. Pp. 396–413.

Bales, R. F., & P. E. Slater. Role differentiation in small decision-making groups. In T. Parsons & R. F. Bales (Eds.), *Family, socialization and interaction process.* New York: The Free Press of Glencoe, 1955. Pp. 259–306.

Bales, R. F., & F. L. Strodtbeck. Phases in group problem solving. *J. abnorm. soc. Psychol.,* 1951, **46**, 485–495.

Bales, R. F., F. Strodtbeck, T. Mills, & Mary E. Roseborough. Channels of communication in small groups. *Amer. sociol. Rev.,* 1951, **16**, 461–468.

Bandura, A. Social learning through imitation. *Nebraska symposium on motivation.* Lincoln, Nebr.: University of Nebraska Press, 1962. Pp. 211–269.

Bandura, A., & Aletha C. Huston. Identification as a process of incidental learning. *J. abnorm. soc. Psychol.,* 1961, **63**, 311–318.

Bandura, A., Dorothea Ross, & Sheila A. Ross. A comparative test of the status envy, social power, and secondary reinforcement theories of identificatory learning. *J. abnorm. soc. Psychol.,* 1963, **67**, 527–534.

Bandura, A., & R. H. Walters. *Adolescent aggression.* New York: The Ronald Press Company, 1959.

Barnard, C. I. *The functions of the executive* Cambridge, Mass.: Harvard Univ. Press, 1938.

Bartos, O. J. Leadership, conformity, and originality. Paper presented at the American Sociol. Ass., Seattle, Washington, August, 1958.

Bass, B. M. An analysis of the leaderless group discussion. *J. appl. Psychol.,* 1949, **33**, 527–533.

Bateman, R. M., & H. H. Remmers. A study of the shifting attitude of high school students when subjected to favorable and unfavorable propaganda. *J. soc. Psychol.,* 1941, **13**, 395–406.

Bates, F. L. Position, role, and status: A reformulation of concepts. *Soc. Forces,* 1956, **34**, 313–321.

Bates, F. L. Some observations concerning the structural

aspect of role conflict. *Pacif. sociol. Rev.*, 1962, **5**, 75–81.

Bauer, R. A. Brainwashing: Psychology or demonology? *J. soc. Issues,* 1957, **13** (3), 41–47.

Bayton J. A., L. B. McAlister, & J. Hamer. Race-class stereotypes. *J. Negro Educ.*, 1956 (Winter), 75–78.

Beach, F. A., & J. Jaynes. Effects of early experience upon the behavior of animals. *Psychol. Bull.,* 1954, **51**, 239–263.

Beach, L., & M. Wertheimer. A free response approach to the study of person cognition. *J. abnorm. soc. Psychol.,* 1961, **62**, 367–374.

Beams, H. L. Affectivity as a factor in the apparent size of pictured food objects. *J. exp. Psychol.,* 1954, **47**, 197–200.

Beatty, F. S., L. E. Dameron, & J. E. Greene. An investigation of the effects of reward and punishment on visual perception. *J. Psychol.,* 1959, **47**, 267–276.

Beck, K. W. Reliability in social perception. Unpublished master's thesis, Purdue University, 1957.

Belth, N. C. Discrimination and the power structure. In N. C. Belth (Ed.), *Barriers: Patterns of discrimination against Jews.* New York: Anti-Defamation League of B'nai B'rith, 1958. Pp. 10–15.

Benedict, Ruth. Continuities and discontinuities in cultural conditioning. *Psychiatry,* 1938, **1**, 161–167.

Bennett, Edith B. Discussion,

decision, commitment, and consensus in "group decision." *Hum. Relat.,* 1955, **8**, 251–274.

Benoit-Smullyan, E. Status, status types and status interrelations. *Amer. sociol. Rev.*, 1944, **9**, 151–161.

Berelson, B. R., P. F. Lazarsfeld, & W. N. McPhee. *Voting: A Study of opinion formation in a presidential campaign.* Chicago: The University of Chicago Press, 1954.

Berelson, B. R., & Patricia J. Salter. Majority and minority Americans: An analysis of magazine fiction. *Publ. Opin. Quart.,* 1946, **10**, 168–190.

Berkowitz, L. Sharing leadership in small, decision-making groups. *J. abnorm. soc. Psychol.,* 1953, **48**, 231–238.

Berkowitz, L. Anti-Semitism and the displacement of aggression. *J. abnorm. soc. Psychol.,* 1959, **59**, 182–188.

Berkowitz, L. Anti-Semitism, judgmental processes, and displacement of hostility. *J. abnorm. soc. Psychol.,* 1961, **62**, 210–215.

Berkowitz, L., & J. A. Green. The stimulus qualities of the scapegoat. *J. abnorm. soc. Psychol.,* 1962, **64**, 293–301

Berkowitz, L., & R. C. Howard. Reactions to opinion deviates as affected by affiliation need (n) and group member interdependence. *Sociometry,* 1959, **22**, 81–91.

Berkowitz, L., & B. I. Levy. Pride in group performance and group-task motivation. *J. ab-*

norm. soc. Psychol.*, 1956, **53**, 300–306.

Berkowitz, M. I. An experiential study of the relation between group size and social organization. Unpublished doctoral dissertation, Yale University, 1958.

Bettelheim, B. Individual and mass behavior in extreme situations. *J. abnorm. soc. Psychol.,* 1943, **38**, 417–452.

Bevan, W., Jr., & W. F. Dukes. Size estimation and monetary value: A correlation. *J. Psychol.,* 1952, **34**, 43–54.

Biddle, B. J., H. A. Rosencranz, & E. F. Rankin, Jr. *Studies in the role of the public school teacher.* Columbia, Mo.: University of Missouri Press, 1961.

Biderman, A. D. Cultural models of captivity relationships. Technical report. (Proj. 339-41) (AFOSR-452) Contract AF 49 (638) 727. February, 1961.

Biderman, A. D., & H. Zimmer. (Eds.) *The manipulation of human behavior.* New York: John Wiley & Sons, Inc., 1961.

Bidwell, C. E. The young professional in the Army: A study of occupational identity. *Amer. sociol. Rev.,* 1961, **26**, 360–372.

Bieri, J. Cognitive complexity-simplicity and predictive behavior. *J. abnorm. soc. Psychol.,* 1955, **51**, 263–268.

Biesanz, J., & L. M. Smith. Race relations in Panama and the Canal Zone. *Amer. J. Sociol.,* 1951, **57**, 7–14.

Bitterman, M. E., & C. W. Kniffin. Manifest anxiety and "perceptual defense." *J. abnorm. soc. Psychol.,* 1953, **48**, 248–252.

Blake, R. R., H. Helson, & Jane S. Mouton. The generality of conformity behavior as a function of factual anchorage, difficulty of task, and amount of social pressure. *J. Pers.*, 1956, **25**, 294–305.

Blake, R. R., & Jane S. Mouton. The experimental investigation of interpersonal influence. In A. D. Biderman & H. Zimmer (Eds.), *The manipulation of human behavior.* New York: John Wiley & Sons, Inc., 1961. Pp. 216–276. (*a*)

Blake, R. R., & Jane S. Mouton. Conformity, resistance, and conversion. In I. A. Berg & B. M. Bass (Eds.), *Conformity and deviation.* New York: Harper & Row, Publishers, Incorporated, 1961. Pp. 1–37. (*b*)

Blau, P. *The dynamics of bureaucracy.* Chicago: The University of Chicago Press, 1955.

Bloch, H. A., & A. Niederhoffer. *The gang: A study in adolescent behavior.* New York: Philosophical Library, Inc., 1958.

Blood, R. O., Jr., & D. M. Wolfe. *Husbands and wives.* New York: The Free Press of Glencoe, 1960.

Bloombaum, M. Factors in the resolution of role conflict. Paper read at Amer. Sociol. Ass., St. Louis, August, 1961.

Bonney, M. E. Relationships between social success, family size, socioeconomic home background, and intelligence among school children in grades III to V. *Sociometry*, 1944, **7**, 26–39.

Bonney, M. E. A sociometric study of the relationship of some factors to mutual friendships on the elementary, secondary, and college levels. *Sociometry*, 1946, **9**, 21–47.

Bonney, M. E., R. E. Hoblit, & A. H. Dreyer. A study of some factors related to sociometric status in a men's dormitory. *Sociometry*, 1953, **16**, 287–301.

Borgatta, E. F. Attitudinal concomitants to military statuses. *Soc. Forces*, 1955, **33**, 342–347.

Borgatta, E. F., & R. F. Bales. Interaction of individuals in reconstituted groups. *Sociometry*, 1953, **16**, 302–320.

Borgatta, E. F., A. S. Couch, & R. F. Bales. Some findings relevant to the great man theory of leadership. *Amer. sociol. Rev.*, 1954, **19**, 755–759.

Bowerman, C., & B. Day. A test of the theory of complementary needs as applied to couples during courtship. *Amer. sociol. Rev.*, 1956, **21**, 602–605.

Bowlby, J. *Maternal care and mental health.* Geneva, Switzerland: World Health Organization, 1952.

Bowlby, J. Separation anxiety. *Internat. J. Psycho-Anal.*, 1960, **41**, 89–113.

Bramel, D. A dissonance theory approach to defensive projection. *J. abnorm. soc. Psychol.*, 1962, **64**, 121–129.

Bray, D. W. The prediction of behavior from two attitude scales. *J. abnorm. soc. Psychol.*, 1950, **45**, 64–84.

Brayfield, A. H., & W. H. Crockett. Employee attitudes and employee performance. *Psychol. Bull.*, 1955, **52**, 396–424.

Bredemeier, H. C., & R. M. Ste-phenson. *The analysis of social systems.* New York: Holt, Rinehart and Winston, Inc., 1962.

Brehm, J. W. Post-decision changes in the desirability of alternatives. *J. abnorm. soc. Psychol.*, 1956, **52**, 384–389.

Brehm, J. W. Increasing cognitive dissonance by a *fait accompli. J. abnorm. soc. Psychol.*, 1959, **58**, 379–382.

Brehm, J. W. Attitudinal consequences of commitment to unpleasant behavior. *J. abnorm. soc. Psychol.*, 1960, **60**, 379–383. (*a*)

Brehm, J. W. A dissonance analysis of attitude-discrepant behavior. In C. I. Hovland & M. J. Rosenberg (Eds.), *Attitude organization and change.* New Haven, Conn.: Yale University Press, 1960. Pp. 164–197. (*b*)

Brehm, J. W., & A. R. Cohen. Re-evaluation of choice alternatives as a function of their number and qualitative similarity. *J. abnorm. soc. Psychol.*, 1959, **58**, 373–378.

Brehm, J. W., & A. R. Cohen. *Explorations in cognitive dissonance.* New York: John Wiley & Sons, Inc., 1962.

Bricker, P. D., & A. Chapanis. Do incorrectly perceived tachistoscopic stimuli convey some information? *Psychol. Rev.*, 1953, **60**, 181–188.

Brigante, T. R. Adolescent evaluations of rewarding, neutral, and punishing power figures. *J. Pers.*, 1958, **26**, 435–450.

Brim, O. G., Jr. Family structure and sex role learning by children: A further analysis of

Helen Koch's data. *Sociometry,* 1958, **21,** 1–16.

Brim, O. G., Jr. Personality development as role-learning. In I. Iscoe & H. W. Stevenson (Eds.), *Personality development in children.* Austin, Tex.: University of Texas Press, 1960. Pp. 127–159.

Brodbeck, May. The role of small groups in mediating the effects of propaganda. *J. abnorm. soc. Psychol.,* 1956, **52,** 166–170.

Brodbeck, May. The influence of propaganda without social support. In Dorothy Willner (Ed.), *Decisions, values and groups.* New York: Pergamon Press, 1960. Pp. 241–245.

Broderick, C. B. Predicting friendship behavior: A study of the determinants of friendship selection and maintenance in a college population. Unpublished doctoral dissertation, Cornell University, 1956.

Bronfenbrenner, U. Socialization and social class through time and space. In Eleanor E. Maccoby, T. M. Newcomb, & E. L. Hartley (Eds.), *Readings in social psychology.* (3rd ed.) New York: Holt, Rinehart and Winston, Inc., 1958. Pp. 400–425.

Bronfenbrenner, U. Some possible effects of national policy on character development in the United States of America and the Soviet Union. Personal communication. 1960.

Bronfenbrenner, U. The changing American child: A speculative analysis. *J. soc. Issues,* 1961, **17,** 6–18.

Brookover, W. B., S. Thomas, & Ann Paterson. Self concept of ability and school achievement. *Sociol. Educ.,* 1964, **37,** 271–278.

Brophy, I. N. The luxury of anti-Negro prejudice. *Publ. Opin. Quart.,* 1946, **9,** 456–466.

Brown, J. S. *The motivation of behavior.* New York: McGraw-Hill Book Company, 1961.

Broxton, June A. A test of interpersonal attraction predictions derived from balance theory. *J. abnorm. soc. Psychol.,* 1963, **66,** 394–397.

Brozek, J., H. Guetzkow, & Marcella Baldwin. A quantitative study of perception and association in experimental semistarvation. *J. Pers.,* 1951, **19,** 245–264.

Bruner, J. S., & C. C. Goodman. Value and need as organizing factors in perception. *J. abnorm. soc. Psychol.,* 1947, **42,** 33–44.

Bruner, J. S., & H. V. Perlmutter. Compatriot and foreigner: A study of impression formation in three countries. *J. abnorm. soc. Psychol.,* 1957, **55,** 253–260.

Bruner, J. S., & L. Postman. Tension and tension-release as organizing factors in perception. *J. Pers.,* 1947, **15,** 300–308.

Bruner, J. S., & L. Postman. Symbolic value as an organizing factor in perception. *J. soc. Psychol.,* 1948, **27,** 203–208.

Bruner, J. S., & L. Postman. On the perception of incongruity: A paradigm. *J. Pers.,* 1949, **18,** 206–223.

Bruner, J. S., D. Shapiro, & R. Tagiuri. The meaning of traits in isolation and combination. In R. Tagiuri & L. Petrullo (Eds.), *Person perception and interpersonal behavior.*

Stanford, Calif.: Stanford University Press, 1958. Pp. 277–288.

Bruner, J. S., & R. Tagiuri. The perception of people. In G. Lindzey (Ed.), *Handbook of social psychology.* Vol. 2. Reading, Mass.: Addison-Wesley Publishing Company, Inc., 1954, Pp. 601–633.

Buchanan, W. Stereotypes and tensions as revealed by the UNESCO international poll. *Int. soc. Sci. J.,* 1951, **3,** 515–528.

Burchard, W. W. Role conflicts of military chaplains. *Amer. sociol. Rev.,* 1954, **19,** 528–535.

Burnstein, E., & Adie V. McRae. Some effects of shared threat and prejudice in racially mixed groups. *J. abnorm. soc. Psychol.,* 1962, **24,** 257–263.

Byrne, D., & Barbara Blaylock. Similarity and assumed similarity of attitudes between husbands and wives. *J. abnorm. soc. Psychol.,* 1963, **67,** 636–640.

Byrne, D., & J. A. Buehler. A note on the influence of propinquity upon acquaintanceships. *J. abnorm. soc. Psychol.,* 1955, **51,** 147–148.

Byrne, D., & T. J. Wong. Racial prejudice, interpersonal attraction, and assumed dissimilarity of attitudes. *J. abnorm. soc. Psychol.,* 1962, **65,** 246–253.

Caldwell, Bettye M. The usefulness of the critical period hypothesis in the study of filiative behavior. Paper read at Amer. Psychol. Ass., New York, August, 1961.

Campbell, A. Factors associated with attitudes toward Jews. In T. M. Newcomb & E. L.

Hartley (Eds.), *Readings in social psychology.* New York: Holt, Rinehart and Winston, Inc., 1947. Pp. 518–527.

Campbell, A., P. E. Converse, W. E. Miller, & D. E. Stokes. *The American voter.* New York: John Wiley & Sons, Inc., 1960.

Campbell, D. T. The indirect assessment of social attitudes. *Psychol. Bull.,* 1950, **47**, 15–38.

Campbell, D. T. Conformity in psychology's theories of acquired behavioral dispositions. In I. A. Berg & B. M. Bass (Eds.), *Conformity and deviation.* New York: Harper & Row, Publishers, Incorporated, 1961.

Campbell, E. Q. Moral discomfort and racial segregation: An examination of the Myrdal hypothesis. *Soc. Forces,* 1961, **39**, 228–234.

Campbell, E. Q., & T. F. Pettigrew. Racial and moral crisis: The role of Little Rock ministers. *Amer. J. Sociol.,* 1959, **64**, 509–516.

Campbell, J. D., & Marian R. Yarrow. Personal and situational variables in adaptation to change. *J. soc. Issues,* 1958, **14** (1), 29–46.

Caplow, T. A. A theory of coalitions in the triad. *Amer. sociol. Rev.,* 1956, **21**, 489–493.

Carpenter, B., M. Wiener, & Janeth T. Carpenter. Predictability of perceptual defense behavior. *J. abnorm. soc. Psychol.,* 1956, **52**, 380–383.

Carter, L. F. The identification of "racial" membership. *J. abnorm. soc. Psychol.,* 1948, **43**, 279–286.

Carter, L. F., W. Haythorn, & M. Howell. A further investigation of the criteria of leadership. *J. abnorm. soc. Psychol.,* 1950, **45**, 350–358.

Carter, L. F., & M. Nixon. An investigation of the relationship between four criteria of leadership ability for three different tasks. *J. Psychol.,* 1949, **27**, 245–261.

Carter, L. F., & K. Schooler. Value need and other factors in perception. *Psychol. Rev.,* 1949, **56**, 200–207.

Carter, R. F. Some effects of the debates. In S. Kraus (Ed.), *The great debates.* Bloomington, Ind.: Indiana University Press, 1962. Pp. 253–270.

Cartwright, D. Some principles of mass persuasion. *Hum. Relat.* 1949, **2**, 253–267.

Cartwright, D., & F. Harary. Structural balance: A generalization of Heider's theory. *Psychol. Rev.,* 1956, **63**, 277–293.

Cartwright, D., & A. Zander (Eds.). *Group dynamics: Research and theory.* (2nd ed.) New York: Harper & Row, Publishers, Incorporated, 1960.

Cavan, Ruth S. Self and role in adjustment during old age. In A. M. Rose (Ed.), *Human behavior and social processes: An interactionist approach.* Boston: Houghton Mifflin Company, 1962. Pp. 526–536.

Chapanis, Natalia P., & A. Chapanis. Cognitive dissonance: Five years later. *Psychol. Bull.,* 1964, **61**, 1–22.

Charters, W. W., Jr., & T. M. Newcomb. Some attitudinal effects of experimentally increased salience of a membership group. In Eleanor E. Mac-

coby, T. M. Newcomb, & E. L. Hartley (Eds.), *Readings in social psychology.* (3rd ed.) New York: Holt, Rinehart and Winston, Inc., 1958. Pp. 276–280.

Chen, T. H. E. *Thought reform of the Chinese intellectuals.* Fair Lawn, N. J.: Oxford University Press, 1960.

Chodorkoff, B. Self-perception, perceptual defense, and adjustment. *J. abnorm. soc. Psychol.,* 1954, **49**, 508–512.

Church, R. M. The varied effects of punishment on behavior. *Psychol. Rev.,* 1963, **70**, 369–402.

Cloward, R. A., & L. E. Ohlin. *Delinquency and opportunity: A theory of delinquent gangs.* New York: The Free Press of Glencoe, 1960.

Coch, L., & J. R. P. French, Jr. Overcoming resistance to change. In Eleanor E. Maccoby, T. M. Newcomb, & E. L. Hartley (Eds.), *Readings in social psychology.* (3rd ed.) New York: Holt, Rinehart and Winston, Inc., 1958. Pp. 233–250.

Cohen, A. K. *Delinquent boys, the culture of the gang.* New York: The Free Press of Glencoe, 1955.

Cohen, A. R. Need for cognition and order of communication as determinants of opinion change. In C. I. Hovland (Ed.), *Order of presentation in persuasion.* New Haven, Conn.: Yale University Press, 1957. Pp. 79–97.

Cohen, A. R. Upward communication in experimentally created hierarchies. *Hum. Relat.,* 1958, **11**, 41–53.

Cohen, A. R. Some implications

of self-esteem for social influence. In C. I. Hovland & I. L. Janis (Eds.), *Personality and persuasibility.* New Haven, Conn.: Yale University Press, 1959. Pp. 102–120.

Cohen, A. R. Attitudinal consequences of induced discrepancies between cognitions and behavior. *Publ. Opin. Quart.,* 1960, **24**, 297–318.

Cohen, A. R. An experiment described in J. W. Brehm and A. R. Cohen, *Explorations in cognitive dissonance.* New York: John Wiley & Sons, Inc., 1962. Pp. 78–81.

Cohen, A. R., J. Brehm, & B. Latane. Choice of strategy and voluntary exposure to information under public and private conditions. *J. Pers.,* 1959, **27**, 63–73.

Cohen, A. R., H. I. Terry, & C. B. Jones. Attitudinal effects of choice in exposure to counter-propaganda. *J. abnorm. soc. Psychol.,* 1959, **58**, 388–391.

Coleman, J. S. *The adolescent society.* New York: The Free Press of Glencoe, 1961.

Coleman, J. S., E. Katz, & H. Menzel. The diffusion of an innovation among physicians. *Sociometry,* 1957, **20**, 253–270.

Coleman, Janet F., R. R. Blake, & Jane S. Mouton. Task difficulty and conformity pressures. *J. abnorm. soc. Psychol.,* 1958, **57**, 120–122.

Combs, A. W., & D. Snygg. *Individual behavior: A perceptual approach to behavior.* New York: Harper & Row, Publishers, Incorporated, 1959.

Committee on Government Operations, U.S. Senate, 84th

Cong., 2nd Sess. *Hearings, Communist interrogation, indoctrination and exploitation of American military and civilian prisoners.* June 19–20, 26–27, 1956.

Cooley, C. H. *Human nature and the social order.* New York: Charles Scribner's Sons, 1902. Reprinted by The Free Press of Glencoe, New York, 1956.

Cooper, J. B. Emotion in prejudice. *Science,* 1959, **130**, 314–318.

Cooper, J. B., & D. Pollock. The identification of prejudicial attitudes by the galvanic skin response. *J. soc. Psychol.,* 1959, **50**, 241–245.

Cooper, J. B., & Helen E. Siegel. The galvanic skin response as a measure of emotion in prejudice. *J. Psychol.,* 1956, **42**, 149–155.

Cooper, J. B., & D. N. Singer. The role of emotion in prejudice. *J. soc. Psychol.,* 1956, **44**, 241–247.

Coser, L. *The functions of social conflict.* New York: The Free Press of Glencoe, 1956.

Cottrell, L. S., Jr. The analysis of situational fields in social psychology. *Amer. sociol. Rev.,* 1942, **7**, 370–382.

Cousins, A. N. Social equilibrium and the psychodynamic mechanism. *Soc. Forces,* 1951, **30**, 202–209.

Cowen, E. L., J. Landes, & D. E. Schaet. The effects of mild frustration on the expression of prejudiced attitudes. *J. abnorm. soc. Psychol.,* 1958, **58**, 33–38.

Crider, C. C., & T. E. Lasswell. The ability of listeners to estimate the social class of

speakers by listening to their voices. Paper read at Pacif. Sociol. Soc., San Francisco, April, 1960.

Criswell, Joan H. Racial cleavage in Negro-white groups. *Sociometry,* 1937, **1**, 81–89.

Crockett, W. H. Emergent leadership in small, decision-making groups. *J. abnorm. soc. Psychol.,* 1955, **51**, 378–383.

Crockett, W. H., & T. Meidinger. Authoritarianism and interpersonal perception. *J. abnorm. soc. Psychol.,* 1956, **53**, 378–380.

Cronbach, L. J. Processes affecting scores on "understanding of others" and "assumed similarity." *Psychol. Bull.,* 1955, **52**, 177–193.

Cronbach, L. J. Proposals leading to analytic treatment of social perception scores. In R. Tagiuri & L. Petrullo (Eds.), *Person perception and interpersonal behavior.* Stanford, Calif.: Stanford University Press, 1958. Pp. 353–380.

Crutchfield, R. S. Conformity and character. *Amer. Psychologist,* 1955, **10**, 191–198.

Cutlip, S. M. Content and flow of AP news: From trunk to TTS to reader. *Journalism Quart.,* 1954, **31**, 434–446.

Daniels, M. J. Affect and its control in the medical intern. *Amer. J. Sociol.,* 1960, **66**, 259–267.

Danielson, W. A. Eisenhower's February decision: A study of news impact. *Journalism Quart.,* 1956, **33**, 433–441.

Dashiell, J. F. Experimental studies of the influence of social situations on the behavior of individual human adults. In C. Murchison (Ed.), *Handbook of social psychology.* Worcester, Mass.: Clark University Press, 1935. Pp. 1097–1158.

Daston, P. G. Perception of homosexual words in paranoid schizophrenia. *Percept. mot. Skills,* 1956, **6**, 45–55.

Davis, A., & J. Dollard. *Children of bondage.* Washington, D.C.: American Council on Education, 1940.

Davis, J. Conceptions of official leader roles in the Air Force. *Soc. Forces,* 1954, **32**, 253–258.

Davis, J. M. Personality, perceptual defense, and stereoscopic perception. *J. abnorm. soc. Psychol.,* 1959, **58**, 398–402.

Davis, K. Final note on a case of extreme isolation. *Amer. J. Sociol.,* 1947, **52**, 432–437.

Davis, K. E., & E. E. Jones. Changes in interpersonal perception as a means of reducing cognitive dissonance. *J. abnorm. soc. Psychol.,* 1960, **61**, 402–410.

Dean, D. G. Alienation: Its meaning and measurement. *Amer. sociol. Rev.,* 1961, **26**, 753–758.

De Fleur, M. L., & O. N. Larsen. *The flow of information: An experiment in mass communication.* New York: Harper & Row, Publishers, Incorporated, 1958.

DeLucia, J. J., & R. Stagner. Emotional vs. frequency factors in word-recognition time and association time. *J. Pers.,* 1953, **22**, 299–309.

Dennis, W., & P. Najarian. Infant development under environmental handicaps. *Psychol.*

Monogr., 1957, **71**, No. 7 (Whole No. 436).

Deutsch, M., & Mary E. Collins. *Interracial housing.* Minneapolis: The University of Minnesota Press, 1951.

Deutsch, M., & L. Solomon. Reactions to evaluations by others as influenced by self evaluations. *Sociometry,* 1959, **22**, 93–112.

Deutscher, A. Socialization for post-parental life. In A. Rose (Ed.), *Human behavior and social processes: An interactionist approach.* Boston: Houghton Mifflin Company, 1962. Pp. 506–525.

Deutschmann, P. J., & W. A. Danielson. Diffusion of knowledge of a major news story. *Journalism Quart.,* 1960, **37**, 345–355.

Dicks, H. V. German personality traits and Nazi ideology. *Hum. Relat.,* 1950, **3**, 111–154.

Dinnerstein, Dorothy. A study of the development of certain cognitive structures. Unpublished doctoral dissertation, Graduate Faculty of Political and Social Science, New School for Social Research, 1951.

Dittes, J. E. Attractiveness of group as a function of self-esteem and acceptance by group. *J. abnorm. soc. Psychol.,* 1959, **59**, 77–82.

Dittes, J. E. & H. H. Kelley. Effects of different conditions of acceptance on conformity to group norms. *J. abnorm. soc. Psychol.,* 1956, **53**, 100–107.

Dixon, N. F. The effect of subliminal stimulation upon autonomic and verbal behavior. *J.*

abnorm. soc. Psychol., 1958, **57**, 29–36.

Dodd, S. C. A social distance test in the Near East. *Amer. J. Sociol.,* 1935, **41**, 194–204.

Dollard, J., L. W. Doob, N. E. Miller, O. H. Mowrer, & R. R. Sears. *Frustration and aggression.* New Haven, Conn.: Yale University Press, 1939.

Dornbusch, S. M. The military academy as an assimilating institution. *Soc. Forces,* 1955, **33**, 316–321.

Dow, M. E., & J. E. Gordon. The interaction of association value and stimulus configuration in size estimation. *J. exp. Psychol.,* 1957, **54**, 332–335.

Dudycha, G. J. The attitudes of college students toward war and the Germans before and during the Second World War. *J. soc. Psychol.,* 1942, **15**, 317–324.

Dulaney, D. E., Jr. Avoidance learning of perceptual defense and vigilance. *J. abnorm. soc. Psychol.,* 1957, **55**, 333–338.

Dulaney, D. E., Jr., & C. W. Eriksen. Accuracy of brightness discrimination as measured by concurrent verbal responses and GSRs. *J. abnorm. soc. Psychol.,* 1959, **59**, 418–423.

Dusenbury, D., & F. H. Knower. Experimental studies of the symbolism of action and voice. II. A study of the specificity of meaning in abstract tonal symbols. *Quart. J. Speech,* 1939, **25**, 67–75.

Edwards, A. L. *Techniques of attitude scale construction.* New York: Appleton-Century-Crofts, Inc., 1957. (*a*)

Edwards, A. L. *The social desir-*

ability variable in personality assessment and research. New York: Holt, Rinehart and Winston, Inc., 1957. *(b)*

Efron, D., & J. P. Foley, Jr. Gestural behavior and the social setting. In T. M. Newcomb & E. L. Hartley (Eds.), *Readings in social psychology.* New York: Holt, Rinehart and Winston, Inc., 1947. Pp. 33–39.

Ehrlich, Danuta, I. Guttmann, P. Schonbach, & J. Mills. Postdecision exposure to relevant information. *J. abnorm. soc. Psychol.*, 1957, **54,** 98–102.

Ehrlich, J., J. W. Rinehart, & C. Howell. The study of role conflict: Explorations in methodology. *Sociometry,* 1962, **25,** 85–97.

Eisenstadt, S. N. The place of elites and primary groups in the process of absorption of new immigrants. *Amer. J. Sociol.,* 1951, **57,** 222–231.

Eisenstadt, S. N. Processes of communication among new immigrants. *Publ. Opin. Quart.,* 1952, **16,** 42–58.

Ekman, P. Body position, facial expression, and verbal behavior during interviews. *J. abnorm. soc. Psychol.,* 1964, **68,** 295–301. *(a)*

Ekman, P. Communication through nonverbal behavior. Progress report, Grant MH 07587-01, National Institute of Mental Health, U.S. Public Health Service, February, 1964. *(b)*

Elder, G. H., Jr. Structural variations in the child rearing relationship. Personal communication. 1961.

Elliot, D. N., & B. H. Wittenberg. Accuracy of identification of Jewish and non-Jewish photographs. *J. abnorm. soc. Psychol.,* 1955, **51,** 339–341.

Ellis, R. A., & T. C. Keedy, Jr. Three dimensions of status: A study of academic prestige. *Pacif. sociol. Rev.,* 1960, **3,** 23–28.

Emerson, R. M. Deviation and rejection: An experimental replication. *Amer. sociol. Rev.,* 1954, **19,** 688–693.

Emerson, R. M. Power-dependence relations. *Amer. sociol. Rev.,* 1962, **27,** 31–41.

English, H. B., & Ava C. English. *A comprehensive dictionary of psychological and psychoanalytical terms.* New York: Longmans, Green & Co., Inc., 1958.

Epstein, B. R., & A. Forster. Barriers in higher education. In N. C. Belth (Ed.), *Barriers: Patterns of discimination against Jews.* New York: Anti-Defamation League of B'nai B'rith, 1958. Pp. 60–73.

Eriksen, C. W. Perceptual defense as a function of unacceptable needs. *J. abnorm. soc. Psychol.,* 1951, **46,** 557–564.

Eriksen, C. W. Defense against ego threat in memory and perception. *J. abnorm. soc. Psychol.,* 1952, **47,** 230–235.

Eriksen, C. W. Subception: Fact or artifact? *Psychol. Rev.,* 1956, **63,** 74–80.

Eriksen, C. W. Unconscious processes. In M. R. Jones (Ed.), *Nebraska symposium on motivation.* Lincoln, Nebr.: University of Nebraska Press, 1958. Pp. 169–227.

Eriksen, C. W. Discrimination

and learning without awareness: A methodological survey and evaluation. *Psychol. Rev.,* 1960, **67,** 279–300.

Eriksen, C. W., H. Azuma, & R. B. Hicks. Verbal discimination of pleasant and unpleasant stimuli prior to specific identification. *J. abnorm. soc. Psychol.,* 1959, **59,** 114–119.

Eriksen, C. W., & C. T. Browne. An experimental and theoretical analysis of perceptual defense. *J. abnorm. soc. Psychol.,* 1956, **52,** 224–230.

Evan, W. M. Role strain and the norm of reciprocity in research organizations. *Amer. J. Sociol.,* 1962, **68,** 346–354.

Exline, R. V., & R. C. Ziller. Status congruency and interpersonal conflict in decision-making groups. *Hum. Relat.,* 1959, **12,** 147–162.

Faison, E. W. J. Experimental comparison of the effectiveness of one-sided and two-sided mass communications on the influence of economic attitudes. Paper read at American Ass. Publ. Opin. Res., Berkeley, May, 1961.

Farnsworth, P. R., & M. F. Williams. The accuracy of the median and mean of a group of judgments. *J. soc. Psychol.,* 1936, **7,** 237–239.

Fay, P. J., & W. C. Middleton. Judgment of Spranger personality types from the voice as transmitted over a public address system. *Charact. & Pers.,* 1936, **8,** 144–155.

Fay, P. J., & W. C. Middleton. The ability to judge sociability from voice as transmitted over a public address system. *Charact. & Pers.,* 1941, **13**, 303–309.

Feather, N. T. Cognitive dissonance, sensitivity, and evaluation. *J. abnorm. soc. Psychol.,* 1963, **66**, 157–163.

Ferster, C. B., & B. F. Skinner. *Schedules of reinforcement.* New York: Appleton-Century-Crofts, Inc., 1957.

Feshbach, S., & R. Singer. The effects of personal and shared threat upon social prejudice. *J. abnorm. soc. Psychol.,* 1957, **54**, 411–416.

Festinger, L. The analysis of sociograms using matrix algebra. *Hum. Relat.,* 1949, **2**, 153–158.

Festinger, L. Laboratory experiments: The role of group belongingness. In J. G. Miller (Ed.), *Experiments in social process.* New York: McGraw-Hill Book Company, 1950. Pp. 31–46. (*a*)

Festinger, L. Informal social communication. *Psychol. Rev.,* 1950, **57**, 271–282. (*b*)

Festinger, L. A theory of social comparison processes. *Hum. Relat.,* 1954, **7**, 117–140.

Festinger, L. *A theory of cognitive dissonance.* New York: Harper & Row, Publishers, Incorporated, 1957.

Festinger, L., & J. M. Carlsmith. Cognitive consequences of forced compliance. *J. abnorm. soc. Psychol.,* 1959, **58**, 203–210.

Festinger, L., D. Cartwright, Kathleen Barber, Juliet Fleischl, Josephine Gottsdanker, Annette Keysen, & Gloria Leavitt. A study of rumor: Its origin and spread. *Hum. Relat.,* 1948, **1**, 464–486.

Festinger, L., & H. Kelley. *Chang-ing attitudes through social contacts.* Ann Arbor, Mich.: Research Center for Group Dynamics, 1951.

Festinger, L., S. Schachter, & K. Back. *Social pressures in informal groups: A study of human factors in housing.* New York: Harper & Row, Publishers, Incorporated, 1950.

Fiedler, F. E. Interpersonal perception and group effectiveness. In R. Tagiuri & L. Petrullo (Eds.), *Person perception and interpersonal behavior.* Stanford, Calif.: Stanford University Press, 1958. Pp. 243–257. (*a*)

Fiedler, F. E. *Leader attributes and group effectiveness.* Urbana, Ill.: The University of Illinois Press, 1958. (*b*)

Fiedler, F. E. The leader's psychological distance and group effectiveness. In D. Cartwright & A. Zander (Eds.), *Group dynamics: Research and theory.* (2nd ed.) New York: Harper & Row, Publishers, Incorporated, 1960. Pp. 586–606.

Fiedler, F. E. A contingency model of leadership effectiveness. Unpublished paper based on F. E. Fiedler, C. E. Osgood, L. M. Stolurow, & H. C. Triaides, Group and organizational factors influencing creativity. Technical report #10, ONR Project NR–177–472, Nonr 1834(36). July, 1963.

Fiedler, F. E., F. J. Blaisdell, & W. G. Warrington. Unconscious attitudes as correlates of sociometric choice in a social group. *J. abnorm. soc. Psychol.,* 1952, **47**, 790–796.

Fiedler, F. E., & E. L. Hoffman. Age, sex, and religious background as determinants of interpersonal perception among Dutch children: A cross-cultural validation. *Acta Psychol., Amsterdam,* 1962, **20**, 185–195.

Fishman, J. A. Some social and psychological determinants of intergroup relations in changing neighborhoods: An introduction to the Bridgeview study. *Soc. Forces,* 1961, **40**, 42–51.

Fleishmann, E. A., E. F. Harris, & H. E. Burtt. *Leadership and supervision in industry: An evaluation of a supervisory training program.* Columbus, Ohio: Ohio State University Bureau of Educational Research, 1955.

Forsyth, E., & L. Katz. A matrix approach to the analysis of sociometric data: Preliminary report. *Sociometry,* 1946, **9**, 340–349.

Foskett, J. M. Role conflict: The concept. Paper read at Pacif. Sociol. Soc., Spokane, April, 1960.

Freeman, J. T. Set or perceptual defense? *J. exp. Psychol.,* 1954, **48**, 283–288.

Freeman, J. T. Set versus perceptual defense: A confirmation. *J. abnorm. soc. Psychol.,* 1955, **51**, 710–712.

French, J. R. P., Jr. A formal theory of social power. *Psychol. Rev.,* 1956, **63**, 181–194.

French, J. R. P., Jr., H. W. Morrison, & G. Levinger. Coercive power and forces affecting conformity. *J. abnorm. soc. Psychol.,* 1960, **61**, 93–101.

French, J. R. P., Jr., & B. H. Raven. The bases of social power. In D. Cartwright (Ed.), *Studies in social power.* Ann Arbor, Mich.: University of

Michigan Press, 1959. Pp. 118–149.

French, J. R. P., Jr., & R. Snyder. Leadership and interpersonal power. In D. Cartwright (Ed.), *Studies in social power.* Ann Arbor, Mich.: University of Michigan Press, 1959. Pp. 150–165.

Freud, S. Instincts and their vicissitudes (1915). In E. Jones (Ed.), *Collected papers.* Vol. 4. London: The Hogarth Press, Ltd., 1950. Pp. 60–83.

From, F. Perception of human action. In H. P. David & J. C. Brengelmann (Eds.), *Perspectives in personality research.* New York: Springer Publishing Co., 1960. Pp. 161–174.

Fromm, E. *Escape from freedom.* New York: Holt, Rinehart and Winston, Inc., 1941.

Frumkin, R. W., & J. S. Roucek. The relationship of major ideological premises of whites and Negroes as manifested in political and social policy changes to the present and future education of Negroes in the United States: A social scientific analysis. *Negro educ. Rev.,* 1959, **10**, 141–157.

Fuhrer, M. J., & C. W. Eriksen. The unconscious perception of the meaning of verbal stimuli. *J. abnorm. soc. Psychol.,* 1960, **61**, 432–439.

Fuller, D. L. Programmed life histories and socialization of the dog. Paper read at Amer. Psychol. Ass., Chicago, September, 1960.

Gage, N. L., & L. J. Cronbach. Conceptual and methodological problems in interpersonal perception. *Psychol. Rev.,* 1955, **62**, 411–422.

Geidt, F. H. Comparison of visual, content, and auditory cues in interviewing. *J. consult. Psychol.,* 1955, **19**, 407–416.

Gerard, H. B. Some determinants of self-evaluation. *J. abnorm. soc. Psychol.,* 1961, **62**, 288–293.

Gerard, H. B., & J. M. Rabbie. Fear and social comparison. *J. abnorm. soc. Psychol.,* 1961, **62**, 586–592.

Getzels, J. W., & E. G. Guba. Role, role conflict, and effectiveness. *Amer. sociol. Rev.,* 1954, **19**, 164–175.

Gibb, C. A. Leadership. In G. Lindzey (Ed.), *Handbook of social psychology.* Vol. 2. Reading, Mass.: Addison-Wesley Publishing Company, Inc., 1954. Pp. 877–920.

Gibb, J. R. The affect of group size and of threat reduction upon creativity in a problem solving situation. *Amer. Psychologist,* 1951, **6**, 324. (Abstract)

Gilbert, Doris C., & D. J. Levinson. "Custodialism" and "humanism" in staff ideology. In M. Greenblatt, D. J. Levinson & R. H. Williams (Eds.), *The patient and the mental hospital.* New York: The Free Press of Glencoe, 1957. Pp. 20–35. (a)

Gilbert, Doris C., & D. J. Levinson. Role performances, ideology, and personality in mental hospital aides. In M. Greenblatt, D. J. Levinson, & R. H. Williams (Eds.), *The patient and the mental hospital.* New York: The Free Press of Glencoe, 1957. Pp. 197–208. (b)

Gilbert, G. M. Stereotype persistence and change among college students. *J. abnorm. soc. Psychol.,* 1951, **46**, 245–254.

Gilchrist, J. C., J. F. Ludeman, & W. Lysak. Values as determinants of word-recognition thresholds. *J. abnorm. soc. Psychol.,* 1954, **49**, 423–426.

Glass, D. C., M. Horwitz, I. Firestone, & J. Grinker. Birth order and reactions to frustration. *J. abnorm. soc. Psychol.,* 1963, **66**, 192–194.

Glueck, S., & Eleanor Glueck. *Unraveling juvenile delinquency.* New York: The Commonwealth Fund, 1950.

Goeke, J. R. The two-step flow of mass communication: The theory re-examined. Personal communication. 1961.

Goffman, E. On cooling the mark out: Some aspects of adaptation to failure. *Psychiatry,* 1952, **15**, 451–463.

Goffman, E. *The presentation of self in everyday life.* Garden City, N.Y.: Doubleday & Company, Inc., 1959.

Goffman, E. *Asylums: Essays on the social situation of mental patients and other inmates.* Chicago, Ill.: Aldine Publishing Company, 1961. (a)

Goffman, E. *Encounters: Two studies in the sociology of interaction.* Indianapolis: The Bobbs-Merrill Company, Inc., 1961. (b)

Gold, M. Power in the classroom. *Sociometry,* 1958, **21**, 50–60.

Goldberg, F. H., & H. Fiss. Partial cues and the phenomenon of discrimination without awareness. *Percept. mot. Skills,* 1959, **9**, 243–251.

Goldfarb, W. The effects of early institutional care on adolescent personalities. *J. exp. Educ.,* 1943, **12**, 106–129. (a)

Goldfarb, W. Infant rearing and problem behavior. *Amer. J.*

Orthopsychiat. 1943, **13**, 249–265. (*b*)

Goldiamond, I. Indicators of perception: 1. Subliminal perception, subception, unconscious perception: An analysis in terms of psychophysical indicator methodology. *Psychol. Bull.,* 1958, **55**, 373–411.

Goldman-Eisler, Frieda. The measurement of time sequences in conversational behavior. *Brit. J. Psychol.,* 1951, **42**, 355–362.

Gollin, E. S. Organizational characteristics of social judgment: A developmental investigation. *J. Pers.,* 1958, **26**, 139–154.

Gollin, E. S., & S. Rosenberg. Concept formation and impressions of personality. *J. abnorm. soc. Psychol.,* 1956, **52**, 39–42.

Goodacre, D. M., III. The use of a sociometric test as a predictor of combat unit effectiveness. *Sociometry,* 1951, **14**, 148–152.

Goode, W. J. A theory of role strain. *Amer. sociol. Rev.,* 1960, **25**, 483–496.

Goodnow, R. E., & R. Taguiri. Religious ethnocentrism and its recognition among adolescent boys. *J. abnorm soc. Psychol.,* 1952, **47**, 316–320.

Gordon, Kate H. Group judgments in the field of lifted weights. *J. exp. Psychol.,* 1924, **3**, 398–400.

Gottlieb, D. The socialization process in American graduate schools. Paper read at Amer. Sociol. Ass., New York, August, 1960.

Gouldner, A. W. The norm of reciprocity: A preliminary statement. *Amer. sociol. Rev.,* 1960, **25**, 161–178.

Grant, V. W. *The psychology of sexual emotion: The basis of selective attraction.* New York: Longmans, Green & Co., Inc., 1951.

Green, B. F. Attitude measurement. In G. Lindzey (Ed.), *Handbook of social psychology.* Vol 1. Reading, Mass.: Addison-Wesley Publishing Company, Inc., 1954. Pp. 335–369.

Greenbaum, M. Manifest anxiety and tachistoscopic recognition of facial photographs. *Percept. mot. Skills,* 1956, **6**, 245–248.

Greenblatt, M., R. H. York, & Esther L. Brown. *From custodial to therapeutic patient care in mental hospitals.* New York: Russell Sage Foundation, 1955.

Gross, Cecily F. Intrajudge consistency in ratings of heterogeneous persons. *J. abnorm soc. Psychol.,* 1961, **62**, 605–610.

Gross, N., W. S. Mason, & A. W. McEachern. *Explorations in role analysis,* New York: John Wiley & Sons, Inc., 1958.

Grossman, Beverly, & Joyce Wrighter. The relationship between selection-rejection and intelligence, social status, and personality amongst sixth-grade children. *Sociometry,* 1948, **11**, 346–355.

Grusky, O. A case for the theory of familial role differentiation in small groups. *Soc. Forces,* 1957, **35**, 209–217.

Guetzkow, H. Differentiation of roles in task-oriented groups. In D. Cartwright & A. Zander (Eds.), *Group dynamics: Research and theory.* (2nd ed.) New York: Harper & Row, Publishers, Incorporated, 1960. Pp. 683–704.

Guetzkow, H., & P. H. Bowman. *Men and hunger.* Elgin, Ill.: Brethren Publishing House, 1946.

Gullahorn, J. T. Distance and friendship as factors in the gross interaction matrix. *Sociometry,* 1952, **15**, 123–134.

Gundlach, R. H. Effects of on-the-job experiences with Negroes upon racial attitudes of white workers in union shops. *Psychol. Rep.,* 1956, **2**, 67–77.

Gurnee, H. A comparison of collective and individual judgments of facts. *J. exp. Psychol.,* 1937, **21**, 106–112.

Guttman, L. The problem of attitude and opinion measurement. In S. A. Stouffer, L. Guttman, E. A. Suchman, P. F. Lazarsfeld, Shirley A. Star, & J. A. Gardner (Eds.), *Measurement and Prediction.* Princeton, N.J.: Princeton • University Press, 1950. Pp. 46–59. (*a*)

Guttman, L. The basis for scalogram analysis. In S. A. Stouffer, L. Guttman, E. A. Suchman, P. F. Lazarsfeld, Shirley A. Star, & J. A. Gardner (Eds.), *Measurement and Prediction.* Princeton, N.J.: Princeton University Press, 1950. Pp. 60–90. (*b*)

Haire, M., & Willa F. Grunes. Perceptual defenses: Processes protecting an organized perception of another personality. *Hum. Relat.,* 1950, **3**, 403–412.

Hall, R. L. Social influence on the aircraft commander's role. *Amer. sociol. Rev.,* 1955, **20**, 292–299.

Halpin, A. W., & B. J. Winer. *The leadership behavior of the airplane commander.* Columbus, Ohio: Ohio State University Research Foundation, 1952.

Hanson, R. C. The systemic linkage hypothesis and role consensus patterns in hospital-community relations. *Amer. sociol. Rev.,* 1962, **27**, 304–313.

Harary, H. A criterion for unanimity in French's theory of social power. In D. Cartwright (Ed.), *Studies in social power.* Ann Arbor, Mich.: The University of Michigan Press, 1959. Pp. 168–182.

Harding, J., & R. Hogrefe. Attitudes of white department store employees toward Negro co-workers. *J. soc. Issues,* 1952, **8** (1), 18–28.

Harding, J., B. Kutner, H. Proshansky, & I. Chein. Prejudice and ethnic relations. In G. Lindzey (Ed.), *Handbook of social psychology.* Vol. 2. Reading, Mass.: Addison-Wesley Publishing Company, Inc., 1954. Pp. 1021–1061.

Hardy, K. R. Determinants of conformity and attitude change. *J. abnorm. soc. Psychol.,* 1957, **54**, 289–294.

Hare, A. P. *Handbook of small group research.* New York: The Free Press of Glencoe, 1962.

Harlow, H. F. Nature and development of the affectional systems. Personal communication. 1960.

Harlow, H. F., & Margaret Harlow. Social deprivation in monkeys *Scient. American,* 1962, **207**, 136–146.

Harsanyi, J. C. Measurement of social power, opportunity costs, and the theory of two-person bargaining games. *Behav. Sci.,* 1962, **7**, 67–80.

Hartley, E. L. *Problems in prejudice.* New York: King's Crown Press, 1946.

Hartley, E. L., & Ruth E. Hartley. *Fundamentals of social psychology.* New York: Alfred A. Knopf, Inc., 1952.

Hartmann, G. W. A field experiment on the comparative effectiveness of "emotional" and "rational" political leaflets in determining election results. *J. abnorm. soc. Psychol.,* 1963, **31**, 99–114.

Hartup, W. W. Nurturance and nurturance-withdrawal in relation to the dependency behavior of pre-school children. *Child Develpm.,* 1958, **29**, 191–202.

Harvey, O. J. An experimental approach to the study of status relations in informal groups. *Amer. sociol. Rev.,* 1953, **18**, 357–367.

Harvey, O. J. Personality factors in resolution of conceptual incongruities. *Sociometry,* 1962, **25**, 336–352.

Harvey, O. J., & G. D. Beverley. Some personality correlates of concept change through role playing. *J. abnorm. soc. Psychol.,* 1961, **63**, 125–129.

Harvey, O. J., & C. Consalvi. Status and conformity to pressures in informal groups. *J. abnorm. soc. Psychol.,* 1960, **60**, 182–187.

Harvey, O. J., D. E. Hunt, & H. M. Schroder. *Conceptual systems and personality organi-* *zation.* New York: John Wiley & Sons, Inc., 1961.

Harvey, O. J., H. H. Kelley, & M. M. Shapiro. Reactions to unfavorable evaluations of the self made by other persons. *J. Pers.,* 1957, **25**, 398–411.

Harvey, O. J., & H. M. Schroder. Cognitive aspects of self and motivation. In O. J. Harvey (Ed.), *Motivation and social interaction: Cognitive determinents.* New York: The Ronald Press Company, 1963. Pp. 95–133.

Hastorf, A. H. The perception and evaluation of behavior change. Paper presented at Western Psychol. Ass., Portland, Oregon, April, 1964.

Hastorf, A. H., S. A. Richardson, & S. M. Dornbusch. Personal communication, 1960.

Hastorf, A. H., S. A. Richardson, & S. M. Dornbusch. The problem of relevance in the study of person perception. In R. Tagiuri & L. Petrullo (Eds.), *Person perception and interpersonal behavior.* Stanford, Calif.: Stanford University Press, 1958. Pp. 54–62.

Hebb, D. O. The socialization of the child. In Eleanor E. Maccoby, T. M. Newcomb, & E. L. Hartley (Eds.), *Readings in social psychology.* (3rd ed.) New York: Holt, Rinehart and Winston, Inc., 1958. Pp. 335–340.

Heer, D. M. The sentiment of white supremacy: An ecological study. *Amer. J. Sociol.,* 1959, **64**, 592–598.

Heider, F. Attitudes and cognitive organization. *J. Psychol.,* 1946, **21**, 107–112.

Heider, F. Social perception and

phenomenal causality. In R. Tagiuri & L. Petrullo (Eds.), *Person perception and interpersonal behavior.* Stanford, Calif.: Stanford University Press, 1958. Pp. 1–21. (*a*)

Heider, F. *The psychology of interpersonal relations.* New York: John Wiley & Sons, Inc., 1958. (*b*)

Heinicke, C., & R. F. Bales. Developmental trends in the structure of small groups. *Sociometry,* 1953, **16**, 35–36.

Heise, G. A., & G. A. Miller. Problem solving by small groups using various communication nets. *J. abnorm. soc. Psychol.,* 1951, **46**, 327–335.

Henry, A. W. Family role structure and self blame. *Soc. Forces,* 1956, **35**, 34–38.

Herz, M. F. Some psychological lessons from leaflet propaganda in World War II. In D. Katz, D. Cartwright, S. Eldersveld, & A. M. Lee (Eds.), *Public opinion and propaganda.* New York: Holt, Rinehart and Winston, Inc., 1954. Pp. 543–552.

Hilgard, Josephine R. Sibling rivalry and social heredity. *Psychiatry,* 1951, **14**, 375–385.

Himmelfarb, S. Factors related to the perception of "Jewishness." Paper read at Amer. Psychol. Ass., Chicago, September, 1960.

Himmelweit, Hilda., A. N. Oppenheim, & P. Vince. *Television and the child.* Fair Lawn, N.J.: Oxford University Press, 1958.

Hobart, C. W., & Lauralee Lindholm. The theory of complementary needs: A reexamina-

tion. *Pacific sociol. Rev.,* 1963, **6**, 73–79.

Hochbaum, G. H. The relation between group members' self confidence and their reactions to group pressures to uniformity. *Amer. sociol. Rev.,* 1954, **19**, 678–687.

Hoe, Betty H. Occupational satisfaction as a function of self-role congruency. Unpublished master's thesis, University of Nevada, June, 1962.

Hoffman, L. R. Similarity of personality: A basis for interpersonal attraction? *Sociometry,* 1958, **21**, 300–308.

Hoffman, M. L. Power assertion by the parent and its impact on the child. *Child Develpm.,* 1960, **31**, 129–143.

Hoffman, M. L. Parent discipline and the child's consideration for others. Personal communication. 1962.

Hoffman, M. L. Child-rearing practices and moral development: Generalizations from empirical research. *Child Develpm.,* 1963, **34**, 295–318.

Hoisington, L. B., & Carol Spencer. Specific set and the perception of "subliminal" material. *Amer. J. Psychol.,* 1958, **71**, 263–269.

Hollander, E. P. Conformity, status, and idiosyncrasy credit. *Psychol. Rev.,* 1958, **65**, 117–127.

Hollander, E. P. Competence and conformity in the acceptance of influence. *J. abnorm. soc. Psychol.,* 1960, **61**, 365–369.

Homans, G. C. *The human group.* New York: Harcourt, Brace & World, Inc., 1950.

Homans, G. C. The cash posters.

Amer. sociol. Rev., 1954, **19**, 724–733.

Homans, G. C. *Social behavior: Its elementary forms.* New York: Harcourt, Brace & World, Inc., 1961.

Horney, Karen. *Neurosis and human growth.* New York: W. W. Norton & Company, Inc., 1950.

Horowitz, E. L. The development of attitude toward the Negro. *Arch. Psychol., Columbia University,* 1936, No. 194.

Horowitz, M. The veridicality of liking and disliking. In R. Tagiuri & L. Petrullo (Eds.), *Person perception and interpersonal behavior.* Stanford, Calif.: Stanford University Press, 1958. Pp. 191–209.

Horwitz, M. Hostility and its management in classroom groups. In W. W. Charters, Jr. & N. L. Gage (Eds.), *Readings in the social psychology of education.* Boston: Allyn and Bacon, Inc., 1963. Pp. 196–211.

Hovland, C. I. (Ed.) *The order of presentation in persuasion.* New Haven, Conn.: Yale University Press, 1957.

Hovland, C. I. Reconciling conflicting results derived from experimental and survey studies of attitude change. *Amer. Psychologist,* 1959, **14**, 8–17.

Hovland, C. I., Enid H. Campbell, & T. Brock. The effects of "commitment" on opinion change following communication. In C. I. Hovland (Ed.), *The order of presentation in persuasion.* New Haven, Conn.: Yale University Press, 1957. Pp. 23–32.

Hovland, C. I., O. J. Harvey, &

M. Sherif. Assimilation and contrast effects in reactions to communication and attitude change. *J. abnorm. soc. Psychol.*, 1957, **55**, 244–252.

Hovland, C. I., & I. L. Janis. Summary and implications for future research. In C. I. Hovland & I. L. Janis (Eds.), *Personality and persuasibility.* New Haven, Conn.: Yale University Press, 1959. Pp. 225–254.

Hovland, C. I., I. L. Janis, & H. H. Kelley. *Communication and persuasion.* New Haven, Conn.: Yale University Press, 1953.

Hovland, C. I., A. A. Lumsdaine, & F. D. Sheffield. *Experiments on mass communication.* Princeton, N.J.: Princeton University Press, 1949.

Hovland, C. I., & W. Mandell. An experimental comparison of conclusion-drawing by the communicator and by the audience. *J. abnorm. soc. Psychol.*, 1952, **47**, 581–588.

Hovland, C. I., & W. Mandell. Is there a "law of primacy in persuasion"? In C. I. Hovland (Ed.), *The order of presentation in persuasion.* New Haven, Conn.: Yale University Press, 1957. Pp. 13–22.

Hovland, C. I., & H. A. Pritzker. Extent of opinion change as a function of amount of change advocated. *J. abnorm. soc. Psychol.*, 1957, **54**, 257–261.

Hovland, C. I., & W. Weiss. The influence of source credibility on communication effectiveness. *Publ. Opin. Quart.*, 1952, **15**, 635–650.

Howard, R. C., & L. Berkowitz. Reactions to the evaluations of

one's performance. *J. Pers.*, 1958, **26**, 494–507.

Hughes, E. C. *Men and their work.* New York: The Free Press of Glencoe, 1958.

Hunter, E. C., & A. M. Jordan. An analysis of qualities associated with leadership among college students. *J. educ. Psychol.*, 1939, **30**, 497–509.

Huntington, Mary J. The development of a professional self-image. In R. K. Merton, G. G. Reader, & Patricia Kendall (Eds.), *The student-physician.* Cambridge, Mass.: Harvard University Press, 1957. Pp. 179–187.

Hurwitz, J. I., A. Zander, & B. Hymovitch. Some effects of power on the relations among group members. In D. Cartwright & A. Zander (Eds.), *Group dynamics: Research and theory.* (2nd ed.) New York: Harper & Row, Publishers, Incorporated, 1960. Pp. 800–809.

Husband, R. W. Cooperative versus solitary problem solution. *J. soc. Psychol.*, 1940, **11**, 405–409.

Hyman, H. H. The psychology of status. *Arch. Psychol., Columbia University*, 1942, No. 269.

Hyman, H. H. Reflections on reference groups. *Publ. Opin. Quart.*, 1960, **24**, 383–396.

Hyman, H. H., & P. B. Sheatsley. The authoritarian personality: A methodological critique. In R. Christie & Marie Jahoda (Eds.), *Studies in the scope and method of the authoritarian personality.* New York: The Free Press of Glencoe, 1954, Pp. 50–122.

Ichheiser, G. Misunderstanding in human relations. *Amer. J. Sociol.*, 1949, **55**, 1–70.

Inkeles, A. Sociology and psychology. In S. Koch (Ed.), *Psychology: A study of a science.* Vol. 6. *Investigations of man as socius: Their place in psychology and the social sciences.* New York: McGraw-Hill Book Company, 1963. Pp. 317–387.

Inkeles, A., Eugenia Hanfmann, & Helen Beier. Modal personality and adjustment to the Soviet socio-political system. *Hum. Relat.*, 1958, **11**, 3–22.

Irish, D. P. Reactions of Caucasian residents to Japanese-American neighbors. *J. soc. Issues*, 1952, **8** (1), 10–17.

Jackson, D. N., & S. Messick. Individual differences in social perception. *Brit. J. soc. clin. Psychol.*, 1963, **2**, 1–10.

Jacobsen, E., W. W. Charters, & S. Lieberman. The use of the role concept in the study of complex organizations. *J. soc. Issues*, 1951, **7** (2), 18–27.

Jahoda, G. Nationality preferences and national stereotypes in Ghana before independence. *J. soc. Psychol.*, 1959, **50**, 165–174.

Jahoda, Marie., M. Deutsch, & S. W. Cook. (Eds.) *Research methods in social relations.* New York: Holt, Rinehart and Winston, Inc., 1951, 2 vols.

Janis, I. L. *Air war and emotional stress: Psychological studies of bombing and civil defense.* New York: McGraw-Hill Book Company, 1951.

Janis, I. L. Personality correlates of susceptibility to persuasion. *J. Pers.*, 1954, **22**, 504–518.

Janis, I. L. Anxiety indices related to susceptibility to persuasion. *J. abnorm. soc. Psychol.*, 1955, **51**, 663–667.

Janis, I. L. *Psychological stress: Psychoanalytic and behavioral studies of surgical patients.* New York: John Wiley & Sons, Inc., 1958.

Janis, I. L., & Rosalind L. Feierbend. Effects of alternative ways of ordering pro and con arguments in persuasive communications. In C. I. Hovland (Ed.), *Order of presentation in persuasion.* New Haven, Conn.: Yale University Press, 1957, Pp. 115–128.

Janis, I. L., & S. Feshbach. Effects of fear-arousing communications. *J. abnorm. soc. Psychol.*, 1953, **48**, 78–92.

Janis, I. L., & P. B. Field. A behavioral assessment of persuasibility: Consistency of individual differences. *Sociometry,* 1956, **19**, 241–259.

Janis, I. L., & P. B. Field. Sex differences and personality factors related to persuasibility. In C. I. Hovland & I. L. Janis (Eds.), *Personality and persuasibility.* New Haven, Conn.: Yale University Press, 1959. Pp. 55–68.

Janis, I. L., & C. I. Hovland. An overview of persuasibility research. In C. I. Hovland & I. L. Janis (Eds.), *Personality and persuasibility.* New Haven, Conn.: Yale University Press, 1959. Pp. 1–28.

Janis, I. L., A. A. Lumsdaine, & A. I. Gladstone. Effects of preparatory communications

on reactions to a subsequent news event. *Publ. Opin. Quart.,* 1951, **15**, 487–518.

Janis, I. L. & D. Rife. Persuasibility and emotional disorder. In C. I. Hovland & I. L. Janis (Eds.), *Personality and persuasibility.* New Haven, Conn.: Yale University Press, 1959, Pp. 121–137.

Jennings, Helen H. *Leadership and isolation.* (2nd ed.) New York: Longmans, Green & Co., Inc., 1950.

Johnson, R. C., C. W. Thomson, & G. Frincke. Word values, word frequency, and visual duration thresholds. *Psychol. Rev.*, 1960, **67**, 332–342.

Jones, E. E. Authoritarianism and first impressions. *J. Pers.,* 1954, **23**, 107–127.

Jones, E. E., & R. deCharms. Changes in social perception as a function of the personal relevance of behavior. *Sociometry,* 1957, **20**, 75–85.

Jones, E. E., & R. deCharms. The organizing function of interaction roles in person perception. *J. abnorm. soc. Psychol.,* 1958, **57**, 155–164.

Julian, J. Some determinants of role consensus within and between organizational strata. Paper read at Pacif. Sociol. Ass., Sacramento, April. 1962.

Kagan, J., & H. Moss. The stability of passive and dependent behavior from childhood through adulthood. *Child Develpm.*, 1960, **31**, 577–591.

Kahn, R. L., & D. Katz. Leadership practices in relation to productivity and morale. In D. Cartwright & A. Zander (Eds.), *Group dynamics: Research*

and theory. New York: Harper & Row, Publishers, Incorporated, 1953. Pp. 612–628.

Kaminski, G. *Das Bild vom Anderen.* Berlin: Georg Luttke Verlag, 1959.

Kastenbaum, Alice. An experimental study of the formation of impressions of personality. Unpublished master's thesis, Graduate Faculty of Political and Social Science, New School for Social Research, 1951.

Kates, S. L. First-impression formation and authoritarianism. *Hum. Relat.*, 1959, **12**, 277–285.

Kates, S. L., & L. S. Klein. Authoritarian beliefs and perceptual recognition of emotionally charged words. *Amer. Psychologist,* 1954, **9**, 403–404.

Katz, D. The functional approach to the study of attitude change. *Publ. Opin. Quart.,* 1960, **24**, 163–204.

Katz, D., & K. W. Braly. Racial prejudice and racial stereotypes. *J. abnorm. soc. Psychol.,* 1933, **30**, 175–193.

Katz, D., & R. L. Kahn. Some recent findings in human relations research in industry. In G. E. Swanson, T. M. Newcomb, & E. L. Hartley (Eds.), *Readings in social psychology.* (Rev. ed.) New York: Holt, Rinehart and Winston, Inc., 1952, Pp. 650–665.

Katz, D., C. G. McClintock, & I. Sarnoff. Measurement of ego-defense related to attitude change. *J. Pers.,* 1957, **25**, 465–474.

Katz, D., I. Sarnoff, & C. G. McClintock. Ego-defense and attitude change. *Hum. Relat.,* 1956, **9**, 27–46.

Katz, D., & E. Stotland. A preliminary statement to a theory of attitude structure and change. In S. Koch (Ed.), *Psychology: A study of a science.* Vol. 3. *Formulations of the person and the social context.* New York: McGraw-Hill Book Company, 1959. Pp. 423–475.

Katz, E. The two-step flow of communication: An up-to-date report on an hypothesis. *Publ. Opin. Quart.,* 1957, **21,** 61–78.

Katz, E. The social itinerary of technical change: Two studies on the diffusion of innovation. *Hum. Organiz.,* 1961, **20,** 70–82.

Katz, E., P. M. Blau, M. L. Brown, & F. L. Strodtbeck. Leadership stability and social change: An experiment with small groups. *Sociometry,* 1957, **20,** 36–50.

Katz, E., & J. J. Feldman. The debates in the light of research. In S. Kraus (Ed.), *The great debates.* Bloomington, Ind.: Indiana University Press, 1962. Pp. 173–223.

Katz, E., & P. F. Lazarsfeld. *Personal influence: The part played by people in the flow of mass communication.* New York: The Free Press of Glencoe, 1955.

Kelley, H. H. The warm-cold variable in first impressions of persons. *J. Pers.,* 1950, **18,** 431–439.

Kelley, H. H. Communication in experimentally created hierarchies. *Hum. Relat.,* 1951, **4,** 39–56.

Kelley, H. H. Two functions of reference groups. In G. E. Swanson, T. M. Newcomb, & E. L. Hartley (Eds.), *Readings*

New York: Holt, Rinehart and Winston, Inc., 1952. Pp. 410–414.

Kelley, H. H. Salience of membership and resistance to change of group-anchored attitudes. *Hum. Relat.,* 1955, **8,** 275–290.

Kelley, H. H., & T. W. Lamb, Certainty of judgment and resistance to social influence. *J. abnorm. soc. Psychol.,* 1957, **55,** 137–139.

Kelley, H. H., & M. M. Shapiro. An experiment in conformity to group norms where conformity is detrimental to group achievement. *Amer. sociol. Rev.,* 1954, **19,** 667–677.

Kelley, H. H., & J. W. Thibaut. Experimental studies of group problem solving and process. In G. Lindzey (Ed.), *Handbook of social psychology.* Vol. 2. Reading, Mass.: Addison-Wesley Publishing Company, Inc., 1954. Pp. 735–785.

Kelley, H. H., J. W. Thibaut, R. Radloff, & D. Mundy. The development of cooperation in the "minimal social situation." *Psychol. Monogr.,* 1962, **76,** No. 19 (Whole No. 538).

Kelley, H. H., & E. H. Volkart. The resistance to change of group-anchored attitudes. *Amer. sociol. Rev.,* 1952, **17,** 453–465.

Kelley, H. H., & Christine L. Woodruff. Members' reactions to apparent group approval of a counter-norm communication. *J. abnorm. soc. Psychol.,* 1956, **52,** 67–74.

Kelly, G. A. *The psychology of personal constructs.* New York: W. W. Norton & Company, Inc., 1955. 2 vols.

ion change. *Publ. Opin. Quart.,* 1961, **25,** 57–78.

Kelman, H. C. The induction of action and attitude change. In S. Coopersmith (Ed.), *Personality research.* Copenhagen: Munksgaard, 1962. 81–110.

Kelman, H. C., & C. I. Hovland. "Reinstatement" of the communicator in delayed measurement of opinion change. *J. abnorm. soc. Psychol.,* 1953, **48,** 327–335.

Kendall, Patricia. Medical education as social process. Paper read at Amer. Sociol. Ass., New York, August, 1960.

Kerckhoff, A., & K. A. Davis. Value consensus and need complementarity in mate selection. *Amer. sociol. Rev.,* 1962, **27,** 295–303.

Kidd, J. W. An analysis of social rejection in a college men's residence hall. *Sociometry,* 1951, **14,** 226–234.

Killian, L. M. The significance of multiple-group membership in disaster. *Amer. J. Sociol.,* 1952, **57,** 309–313.

King, B. T. Relationships between susceptibility to opinion change and childrearing practices. In C. I. Hovland & I. L. Janis (Eds.), *Personality and persuasibility.* New Haven, Conn.: Yale University Press, 1959. Pp. 207–221.

Kipnis, D. The effects of leadership style and leadership power upon the inducement of an attitude change. *J. abnorm. soc. Psychol.,* 1958, **57,** 173–180.

Kipnis, Dorothy M. Changes in self concepts in relation to perceptions of others. *J. Pers.,* 1961, **29,** 449–465.

Kirkpatrick, C. *The family as proc-*

The Ronald Press Company, 1955.

Kissin, B., H. Gottesfeld, & R. Dickes. Inhibition and tachistoscopic thresholds for sexually charged words. *J. Psychol.,* 1957, **43**, 333–339.

Klapper, J. T. *The effects of mass media.* New York: The Free Press of Glencoe, 1961.

Klausner, S. Z. Choosing a new reference group. Paper read at Amer. Sociol. Ass., St. Louis, September, 1961.

Klein, G. S., H. J. Schlesinger, & D. E. Meister. The effect of personal values on perception: An experimental critique. *Psychol. Rev.,* 1951, **58**, 96–112.

Klein, Josephine. *The study of groups.* London: Routledge & Kegan Paul, Ltd., 1956.

Kleiner, R. Perceptual defense or perceptual set. *J. soc. Psychol.,* 1959, **49**, 95–103.

Klugman, S. F. Group judgments for familiar and unfamiliar materials. *J. gen. Psychol.,* 1945, **32**, 103–110.

Knight, H. C. A comparison of the reliability of group and individual judgments. Unpublished master's thesis. Columbia University, 1921.

Koffka, K. *Principles of Gestalt psychology.* New York: Harcourt, Brace and Company, 1935.

Kogan, N. & Florence C. Shelton. Differential cue value of age and occupation in impression formation. *Psychol. Rep.,* 1960, **7**, 203–216.

Kohlberg, L. The development of children's orientations toward a moral order. Paper read at Hum. Develpm. Sympos., University of Chicago, April, 1960.

Kohlberg, L. The role of early experience in the study of conscience. Paper read at West. Psychol. Ass., San Francisco, April, 1962.

Kohler, W. *Dynamics in psychology.* New York: Liveright Publishing Corporation, 1940.

Kohn, A. R., & F. E. Fiedler. Age and sex differences in the perception of persons. *Sociometry,* 1961, **24**, 157–164.

Kohn, M. L. Social class and parental values. *Amer. J. Sociol.,* 1959, **64**, 337–351. (*a*)

Kohn, M. L. Social class and the exercise of parental authority. *Amer. sociol. Rev.,* 1959, **24**, 352–366. (*b*)

Kohn, M. L. Social class and parent-child relationships. *Amer. J. Sociol.,* 1963, **68**, 471–480.

Kohn, M. L., & Eleanor E. Carroll. Social class and the allocation of parental responsibilities. *Sociometry,* 1960, **23**, 372–392.

Koltuv, Barbara B. Some characteristics of intrajudge trait intercorrelations. *Psychol. Monogr.,* 1962, **76**, No. 33 (Whole No 552).

Kramer, E. Judgment of personal characteristics and emotions from nonverbal properties of speech. *Psychol. Bull.,* 1962, **60**, 408–420.

Krech, D., & R. S. Crutchfield. *Theory and problems of social psychology.* New York: McGraw-Hill Book Company, 1948.

Kretschmer, E. *Physique and character.* New York: Harcourt, Brace and Company, Inc., 1925.

Ktsanes, T. Mate selection on the basis of personality type: A study utilizing an empirical typology of personality. *Amer. sociol. Rev.,* 1955, **20**, 547–551.

Kuhn, M. H. Self attitudes by age, sex, and professional training. *Sociol. Quart.,* 1960, **1**(1), 39–55.

Kurland, S. H. The lack of generality in defense mechanisms as indicated in auditory perception. *J. abnorm. soc. Psychol.,* 1954, **49**, 173–177.

Lacey, O. W., N. Lewinger, & J. F. Adamson. Foreknowledge as a factor affecting perceptual defense and alertness. *J. exp. Psychol.,* 1953, **45**, 169–174.

Lambert, W. W., R. L. Solomon, & P. D. Watson. Reinforcement and extinction as factors in size estimation. *J. exp. Psychol.,* 1949, **39**, 637–641.

Lana, R. E. Pretest-treatment interaction effects in attitudinal studies. *Psychol. Bull.,* 1959, **56**, 293–300.

Lana, R. E. Three theoretical interpretations of order effects in persuasive communications. *Psychol. Bull.,* 1964, **61**, 314–320.

Larsen, O., & R. Hill. Mass media and interpersonal communication in the diffusion of a news event. *Amer. sociol. Rev.,* 1954, **19**, 426–443.

Lazarsfeld, P. F., B. R. Berelson, & Hazel Gaudet. *The people's choice.* New York: Columbia University Press, 1948.

Lazarsfeld, P. F., & R. K. Merton. Friendship as social process: A substantive and methodological analysis. In M. Berger, T. Abel, & C. H. Page (Eds.), *Freedom and control in modern society*. Princeton, N.J.: D. Van Nostrand Company, Inc., 1954.

Lazarus, R. S., C. W. Eriksen, & C. P. Fonda. Personality dynamics and auditory perceptual recognition. *J. Pers.* 1951, **19**, 471–482.

Lazarus, R. S., & R. A. McCleary. Autonomic discrimination without awareness: A study of subception. *Psychol. Rev.*, 1951, **58**, 113–122.

Lazarus, R. S., H. Yousem, & D. Arenberg. Hunger and perception. *J. Pers.*, 1953, **21**, 312–328.

Leavitt, H. J. Some effects of certain communication patterns on group performance. *J. abnorm. soc. Psychol.*, 1951, **46**, 38–50.

Lecky, P. *Self-consistency: A theory of personality*. New York: Island Press, 1945.

Lee, A. M. The social dynamics of the physician's status. *Psychiatry*, 1944, **7**, 371–377.

Lennard, H. L., & A. Bernstein. *The anatomy of psychotherapy*. New York: Columbia University Press, 1960.

Lenski, G. Status crystallization: A nonvertical dimension of social status. *Amer. sociol. Rev.*, 1954, **19**, 405–413.

Lesser, G. S. Maternal attitudes and practices and the aggressive behavior of children. Unpublished doctoral dissertation, Yale University, 1952.

Lesser, G. S., & R. P. Abelson. Personality correlates of persuasibility in children. In C. I. Hovland & I. L. Janis (Eds.), *Personality and persuasibility.*, New Haven, Conn.: Yale University Press, 1959. Pp. 187–206.

Levine, R., I. Chein, & G. Murphy. The relation of the intensity of a need to the amount of perceptual distortion: A preliminary report. *J. Psychol.*, 1942, **13**, 283–293.

Levinger, G. The development of perceptions and behavior in newly formed social power relationships. In D. Cartwright (Ed.), *Studies in social power*. Ann Arbor, Mich.: The University of Michigan Press, 1959.

Levy, D. M. *Maternal overprotection*. New York: Columbia University Press, 1943.

Levy, L. H. Perceptual defense in tactual perception. *J. Pers.*, 1958, **26**, 467–478.

Lewin, K. *A dynamic theory of personality*. New York: McGraw-Hill Book Company, 1935.

Lewin, K. *Principles of topological psychology*. New York: McGraw-Hill Book Company, 1936.

Lewin, K. Group decision and social change. In Eleanor E. Maccoby, T. M. Newcomb, & E. L. Hartley (Eds.), *Readings in social psychology*. (3rd ed.) New York: Holt, Rinehart and Winston, Inc., 1958. Pp. 197–211.

Lewin, K., R. Lippitt, & R. K. White. Patterns of aggressive behavior in experimentally created social climates. *J. soc. Psychol.*, 1939, **10**, 271–299.

Lewis, D. J. Partial reinforcement: A selective review of the literature since 1950. *Psychol. Bull.*, 1960, **57**, 1–28.

Lewis, W. H. Feuding and social change in Morocco. *J. conflict Resolut.*, 1961, **5**, 43–54.

Libo, L. *Measuring group cohesiveness*. Ann Arbor, Mich.: Institute for Social Research, 1953.

Lifton, R. J. Thought reform of Chinese intellectuals: A psychiatric evaluation. *J. soc. Issues*, 1957, **13**(3), 5–20.

Lifton, R. J. *Thought reform and the psychology of totalism: A study of "brainwashing" in China*. New York: W. W. Norton & Company, Inc., 1961.

Likert, R. A technique for the measurement of attitudes. *Arch. Psychol., Columbia University*, 1932, No. 140.

Likert R. *New patterns of management*. New York: McGraw-Hill Book Company, 1961.

Lindzey, G. An experimental examination of the scapegoat theory of prejudice. *J. abnorm. soc. Psychol.*, 1950, **45**, 296–309.

Lindzey, G., & E. T. Borgatta. Sociometric measurement. In G. Lindzey (Ed.), *Handbook of social psychology*, Vol. 1. Reading, Mass.: Addison-Wesley Publishing Company, Inc., 1954. Pp. 405–448.

Lindzey, G., & S. Rogolsky. Prejudice and identification of minority group membership. *J. abnorm. soc. Psychol.*, 1950, **45**, 37–53.

Linton, Harriet, & Elaine Graham. Personality correlates of persuasibility. In C. I. Hovland & I. L. Janis (Eds.), *Personality and persuasibility*. New Haven, Conn.: Yale University Press, 1959. Pp. 69–101.

Linton, R. *The cultural background*

of personality. New York: Appleton-Century-Crofts, Inc., 1945.

Lipetz, M. E. The effects of information on the assessment of attitudes by authoritarians and nonauthoritarians. *J. abnorm. soc. Psychol.,* 1960, **60**, 95–99.

Lippitt, R., N. Polansky, F. Redl, & S. Rosen. The dynamics of power. *Hum. Relat.,* 1952, **5**, 37–64.

Lippitt, R., & R. K. White. The "social climate" of children's groups. In R. G. Barker, J. S. Kounin, & H. F. Wright (Eds.), *Child behavior and development.* New York: McGraw-Hill Book Company, 1943. Pp. 485–508.

Loomis, C. P. Ethnic cleavages in the Southwest as reflected in two high schools. *Sociometry,* 1943, **6**, 7–26.

Lott, A. J., & Bernice E. Lott. Group cohesiveness, communication level, and conformity. *J. abnorm. soc. Psychol.* 1961, **62**, 408–412.

Luchins, A. S. Forming impressions of personality: A critique. *J. abnorm. soc. Psychol.,* 1948, **43**, 318–325.

Luchins, A. S. On an approach to social perception. *J. Pers.,* 1950, **19**, 64–84.

Luchins, A. S. Primacy-recency in impression formation. In C. I. Hovland (Ed.), *The order of presentation in persuasion.* New Haven, Conn.: Yale University Press, 1957. Pp. 33–61. (*a*)

Luchins, A. S. Experimental attempts to minimize the impact of first impressions. In C. I. Hovland (Ed.), *The order of presentation in persuasion.* New

Haven, Conn.: Yale University Press, 1957. Pp. 62–75. (*b*)

Luchins, A. S. Influence of experience with conflicting information on reactions to subsequent conflicting information. *J. soc. Psychol.,* 1960, **51**, 367–385.

Ludlum, T. S. Effects of certain techniques of credibility upon audience attitude. *Speech Monogr.* 1958, **25**, 278–284.

Lumsdaine, A. A., & I. L. Janis. Resistance to "counterpropaganda" produced by one-sided and two-sided "propaganda" presentations. *Publ. Opin. Quart.,* 1953, **17**, 311–318.

Lundberg, G. A., & Virginia Beazley. Consciousness of kind in a college population. *Sociometry,* 1948, **11**, 59–74.

Lundberg, G. A., & Mary Steele. Social attraction patterns in a village. *Sociometry,* 1938, **1**, 375–419.

Lundy, R. M. Assimilative projection and accuracy of prediction in interpersonal perceptions. *J. abnorm. soc. Psychol.,* 1956, **52**, 33–38. (*a*)

Lundy, R. M. Self-perceptions and descriptions of opposite sex sociometric choices, *Sociometry,* 1956, **19**, 272–177. (*b*)

Lundy, R. M., W. Katkovsky, R. L. Cromwell, & D. J. Shoemaker. Self acceptability and descriptions of sociometric choices. *J. abnorm. soc. Psychol.,* 1955, **51**, 260–262.

Lynn, R. Personality characteristics of the mothers of aggressive and unaggressive children. *J. genet. Psychol.,* 1961, **99**, 159–164.

Lysak, W., & J. C. Gilchrist. Value, equivocality and goal availability. *J. Pers.,* 1955, **23**, 500–501.

McBreaty, J. F., A. R. Marston, & F. H. Kanfer. Conditioning a verbal operant in a group setting: Direct vs. vicarious reinforcement. *Amer. Psychologist,* 1961, **16**, 425. (Abstract)

McCandless, B. R. *Children and adolescents.* New York: Holt, Rinehart and Winston, Inc., 1961.

McCleary, R. A., & R. S. Lazarus. Autonomic discrimination without awareness: An interim report. *J. Pers.,* 1949, **18**, 171–179.

McClelland, D. C. *Personality.* New York: William Sloane Associates, 1951.

McClelland, D. C., & J. W. Atkinson. The projective expression of needs: I. The effects of different intensities of the hunger drive on perception. *J. Psychol.,* 1948, **25,** 205–222.

McClelland, D. C., J. W. Atkinson, R. A. Clark, & E. L. Lowell. *The achievement motive.* New York: Appleton-Century-Crofts, Inc., 1953.

McClintock, C. G. Personality syndromes and attitude change. *J. Pers.,* 1958, **26**, 479–493.

Maccoby, Eleanor E. Youth and political change. *Publ. Opin. Quart.,* 1954, **18**, 23–29.

Maccoby, Eleanor E. The choice of variables in the study of socialization. *Sociometry,* 1961, **24**, 357–371.

McConnell, J. V., R. L. Cutler, & E. B. McNeil. Subliminal stimulation: An overview, *Amer. Psychol.,* 1958, **13**, 229–242.

McCord, W., Joan McCord & A. Howard. Familial correlates of aggression in nondelinquent male children. *J. abnorm. soc. Psychol.*, 1961, **62**, 79–93.

McCurdy, H. G. Coin perception studies and the concept of schemata. *Psychol. Rev.*, 1956, **63**, 160–168.

McDavid, J., Jr. Personality and situational determinants of conformity. *J. abnorm. soc. Psychol.*, 1959, **58**, 241–246.

McDougall, W. *An introduction to social psychology.* London: Methuen & Co., Ltd., 1908.

McEntire, D. Government and racial discrimination in housing. *J. soc. Issues*, 1957, **13**(4), 60–67.

McFarlane, Jean W., Lucile Allen, & Marjorie Honzik. A developmental study of the behavior problems of normal children between 21 months and 14 years. Berkeley Calif.: University of California Press, 1954.

McGinnies, E. Emotionality and perceptual defense. *Psychol. Rev.*, 1949, **56**, 244–251.

McGuire, W. J. Order of presentation as a factor in "conditioning" persuasiveness. In C. I. Hovland (Ed.), *Order of presentation in persuasion.* New Haven, Conn.: Yale University Press, 1957. Pp. 98–114.

McGuire, W. J. A syllogistic analysis of cognitive relationships. In C. I. Hovland & I. L. Janis (Eds.), *Attitude organization and change.* New Haven, Conn.: Yale University Press, 1960. Pp. 65–111.

McGuire, W. J. The relative effi- cacy of active and passive prior defense in immunizing beliefs against persuasion. *J. abnorm. soc. Psychol.*, 1961, **63**, 326–332.

McGuire, W. J. Persistence of the resistance to persuasion induced by various types of prior belief defenses. *J. abnorm. soc. Psychol.*, 1962, **64**, 241–248.

McGuire, W. J., & D. Papageorgis. The relative efficacy of various types of prior belief defense in producing immunity to persuasion. *J. abnorm. soc. Psychol.*, 1961, **62**, 327–337.

MacKenzie, Barbara K. The importance of contact in determining attitudes toward Negroes. *J. abnorm. soc. Psychol.*, 1948, **43**, 417–441.

McNemar, Q. Opinion-attitude methodology. *Psychol. Bull.*, 1946, **43**, 289–374.

Macy, J., L. Christie, & D. Luce. Coding noise in a task-oriented group. *J. abnorm. soc. Psychol.*, 1953, **48**, 401–409.

Madden, J. M. Personal preferences and conformity. *J. soc. Psychol.*, 1960, **52**, 269–277.

Maier, N. R. F., & A. R. Solem. The contribution of a discussion leader to the quality of group thinking: The effective use of minority opinions. *Hum. Relat.*, 1952, **5**, 277–288.

Malof, M., & A. J. Lott. Ethnocentrism and the acceptance of Negro support in a group pressure situation. *J. abnorm. soc. Psychol.*, 1962, **65**, 254–258.

Mann, J. H. The effect of interracial contact on sociometric choices and perceptions. *J. soc. Psychol.*, 1959, **50**, 143–152.

Mann, J. H. The differential nature of prejudice reduction. *J. soc. Psychol.*, 1960, **52**, 339–343.

Marcus, P. M. Expressive and instrumental groups: Toward a theory of group structure. *Amer. J. Sociol.*, 1960, **66**, 54–59.

Marsh, R. C., & A. L. Coleman. Group influences and agricultural innovation: Some tentative findings and hypotheses. *Amer. J. Sociol.*, 1956, **61**, 588–594.

Martin, H. W. Structural sources of strain in a small psychiatric hospital. Paper read at Amer. Sociol. Ass., St. Louis, 1961.

Martin, W. Preferences for types of patients. In R. K. Merton, G. G. Reader, & Patricia Kendall (Eds.), *The student-physician.* Cambridge, Mass.: Harvard University Press, 1957. Pp. 189–205.

Mathews, Anne, & M. Wertheimer. A "pure" measure of perceptual defense uncontaminated by response suppression. *J. abnorm. soc. Psychol.*, 1958, **57**, 373–376.

Mausner, B. The effect of one partner's success in a relevant task on the interaction of observer pairs. *J. abnorm. soc. Psychol.*, 1954, **49**, 557–560.

Mayo, Clara W., & W. H. Crockett. Cognitive complexity and primacy-recency effects in impression formation. *J. abnorm. soc. Psychol.*, 1964, **68**, 335–338.

Mead, G. H. *Mind, self and society.* Chicago: The University of Chicago Press, 1934.

Meile, R. L. Perceptions of threat and group leadership. Paper read at Amer. Sociol. Ass., Washington, D.C., 1962.

Melikian, L. H. Authoritarianism and its correlates in the Egyptian culture. *J. soc. Issues,* 1959, **15** (3), 58–68.

Mensh, I. M., & J. Wishner. Asch on "Forming impressions of personality": Further evidence. *J. Pers.,* 1947, **16**, 188–191.

Menzel, H., & E. Katz. Social relations and innovation in the medical profession: The epidemiology of a new drug. *Publ. Opin. Quart.,* 1956, **19**, 337–352.

Merton, R. K. *Mass persuasion: The social psychology of a war bond drive.* New York: Harper & Row, Publishers, Incorporated, 1946.

Merton, R. K. Patterns of influence: A study of interpersonal influence and communications behavior in a local community. In. P. F. Lazarsfeld & F. N. Stanton (Eds.), *Communications research, 1948–1949.* New York: Harper & Row, Publishers, Incorporated, 1949. Pp. 180–219.

Merton, R. K. The role set. *Brit. J. Sociol.,* 1957, **8**, 106–120. (*a*)

Merton, R. K. *Social theory and social structure.* New York: The Free Press of Glencoe, 1957. Pp. 131–194. (*b*)

Merton, R. K., & Alice S. Kitt. Contributions to the theory of reference group behavior. In R. K. Merton & P. F. Lazarsfeld (Eds.), *Continuities in social research: Studies in the scope and method of "The American soldier."* New York: The Free Press of Glencoe, 1950. Pp. 40–105.

Merton, R. K., G. G. Reader, & Patricia L. Kendall. (Eds.) *The student-physician.* Cambridge, Mass.: Harvard University Press, 1957.

Meyers, C. E. The effect of conflicting authority on the child. In K. Lewin et al., *Authority and frustration: Studies in topological and vector psychology.* Vol. 3. Ames, Iowa: The Iowa State University Press, 1944. Pp 33–98.

Michels, R. *A summary and interpretation of political parties: A sociological study of the oligarchial tendencies of modern democracy.* New York: The Free Press of Glencoe, 1949.

Miller, D. R. The study of social relationships: Situation, identity, and social interaction. In S. Koch (Ed.), *Psychology: A study of a science.* Vol. 5. *The process areas, the person, and some applied fields.* New York: McGraw-Hill Book Company, 1963. Pp. 639–737.

Miller, D. R., & G. E. Swanson. *The changing American parent.* New York: John Wiley & Sons, Inc., 1958.

Miller K. M., W. A. Scott, & P. R. Waters. The vexing problem of perceptual defense. *Bull. Brit. Psychol. Soc.,* 1959, **38**, 30*a*.

Miller, N., & D. T. Campbell. Recency and primacy in persuasion as a function of the timing of speeches and measurements. *J. abnorm. soc. Psychol.,* 1959, **59**, 1–9.

Miller, N. E., Jr. The effect of group size on decision-making discussions. Unpublished doctoral dissertation, University of Michigan, 1951.

Miller, N. E., & R. Bugelski. Minor studies in aggression: The influence of frustrations imposed by the in-group on attitudes expressed toward outgroups. *J. Psychol.,* 1948, **25**, 437–442.

Miller, N. E., & J. Dollard. *Social learning and imitation.* New Haven, Conn.: Yale University Press, 1941.

Mills, J. Changes in moral attitudes following temptation. *J. Pers.,* 1958, **26**, 517–531.

Mills, T. M. Power relations in three person groups. *Amer. sociol. Rev.,* 1953, **18**, 351–357.

Mills, T. M. The coalition pattern in three person groups. *Amer. sociol. Rev.,* 1954, **19**, 657–667.

Mills, T. M. Developmental processes in three-person groups. *Hum. Relat.,* 1956, **9**, 343–354.

Minard, R. D. Race relationships in the Pocahontas coal field. *J. soc. Issues,* 1952, **8** (1), 29–44.

Mishler, E. G. Personality characteristics and the resolution of role conflict. *Publ. Opin. Quart.,* 1953, **17**, 115–135.

Mitchell, W. C. Occupational role strains: The American elective public official. *Admin. Sci. Quart.,* 1958, **3**, 210–228.

Miyamoto, S. F., & S. M. Dornbusch. A test of the interactionist hypothesis of self-conception. *Amer. J. Sociol.,* 1956, **61**, 399–403.

Moeller, G., & M. H. Applezweig. A motivational factor in conformity. *J. abnorm. soc. Psychol.,* 1957, **55**, 114–120.

Moore, J. A further test of interactionist hypothesis of self-conception. Paper read at

Pacif. Sociol. Ass., Portland, 1963.

Moreno, J. L. *Who shall survive?* (2nd ed.) Beacon, N.Y.: Beacon House, Inc., 1953.

Morse, Nancy. *Satisfactions in the white-collar-job.* Ann Arbor, Mich.: University of Michigan, Survey Research Center, 1953.

Morton, A. S. Similarity as a determinant of friendship: A multidimensional study. Unpublished doctoral dissertation, Princeton University, 1959.

Mowrer, O. H. *Learning theory and personality dynamics.* New York: The Ronald Press Company, 1950. Pp. 531–561.

Murdock, B. B., Jr. Perceptual defense and threshold measurements. *J. Pers.,* 1954. **22**, 565–571.

Murphy, G. *Personality: A biosocial approach to origins and structure.* New York: Harper & Row, Publishers, Incorporated, 1947.

Murphy, G., Lois B. Murphy, & T. M. Newcomb. *Experimental social psychology.* New York: Harper & Row, Publishers, Incorporated, 1937.

Murphy, Lois B. Character development in normal children: Sources of flexibility. Paper read at Amer. Psychol. Ass., New York, September, 1961.

Murray, H. A. *Explorations in personality.* New York: Oxford University Press, 1938.

Murstein, B. L. The complementary need hypothesis in newly-weds and middle-aged married couples. *J. abnorm. soc. Psychol.,* 1961, **63**, 194–197.

Mussen, P. H., & J. J. Conger, *Child development and personality.* New York: Harper & Row, Publishers, Incorporated, 1956.

Myers, G. C. A study in incidental memory. *Arch. Psychol., Columbia University,* 1913, **4**, No. 26, 1–108.

Myrdal, G. *An American dilemma.* New York: Harper & Row, Publishers, Incorporated, 1944.

Neel, A. F. Conflict, recognition time, and defensive behavior. *Amer. Psychologist,* 1954, **9**, 437.

Newcomb, T. M. *Personality and social change: Attitude formation in a student community.* New York: Holt, Rinehart and Winston, Inc., 1943.

Newcomb, T. M. An approach to the study of communicative acts. *Psychol. Rev.,* 1953, **60**, 393–404.

Newcomb, T. M. The prediction of interpersonal attraction. *Amer. Psychologist,* 1956, **11**, 575–586.

Newcomb, T. M. *The acquaintance process.* New York: Holt, Rinehart and Winston, Inc., 1961.

Norfleet, Bobbie. Interpersonal relations and group productivity. *J. soc. Issues,* 1948, **4** (2), 66–69.

Nunnally, J. C., & H. M. Bobren. Variables governing the willingness to receive communications on mental health. *J. Pers.,* 1959, **27**, 38–45.

Nye, I. F. The employed mother: Basic changes in family structure. Paper read at Amer. Sociol. Ass., St. Louis, August, 1961.

Osgood, C. E. Cognitive dynamics in conduct of human affairs. *Publ. Opin. Quart.,* 1960, **24**, 341–365.

Osgood, C. E., G. J. Suci, & P. H. Tannenbaum. *The measurement of meaning.* Urbana, Ill.: The University of Illinois Press, 1957.

Osgood, C. E., & P. H. Tannenbaum. The principle of congruity in the prediction of attitude change. *Psychol. Rev.,* 1955, **62**, 42–55.

Osler, S. F., & P. M. Lewinsohn. The relation between manifest anxiety and perceptual defense. *Amer. Psychologist,* 1954, **9**, 446.

Ostrander, E. H., & J. Steger, III. Impression formation and sequence of information presentation. Paper read at Amer. Psychol. Ass., Chicago, 1960.

Palmore, E. B. The introduction of Negroes into white departments. *Hum. Organiz.,* 1955, **14**, 27–28.

Papageorgis, D., & W. J. McGuire. The generality of immunity to persuasion produced by pre-exposure to weakened counterarguments. *J. abnorm. soc. Psychol.,* 1961, **62**, 475–481.

Parker, S. Leadership patterns in a psychiatric ward. *Hum. Relat.,* 1958, **11**, 287–301.

Parsons, T. *Essays in sociological theory: Pure and applied.* New York: The Free Press of Glencoe, 1949.

Parsons, T. *The social system.* New York: The Free Press of Glencoe, 1951.

Parsons, T., & R. F. Bales. *Family, socialization and inter-*

action process. New York: The Free Press of Glencoe, 1955.

Parsons, T., R. F. Bales, & E. A. Shils. *Working papers in the theory of action.* New York: The Free Press of Glencoe, 1953.

Parsons, T., & E. A. Shils. (Eds.) *Toward a general theory of action.* Cambridge, Mass.: Harvard University Press, 1951.

Pastore, N. Attributed characteristics of liked and disliked persons. *J. soc. Psychol.,* 1960, **52**, 157–163. (*a*)

Pastore, N. A note on changing toward liked and disliked persons. *J. soc. Psychol.,* 1960, **52**, 173–175. (*b*)

Patchen, M. A conceptual framework and some empirical data regarding comparisons of social rewards. *Sociometry,* 1961, **24**, 136–156.

Patel, A. S., & J. E. Gordon. Some personal and situational determinants of yielding to influence. *J. abnorm. soc. Psychol.,* 1960, **61**, 411–418.

Pear, T. H. *Voice and personality.* London: Chapman & Hall, Ltd., 1931.

Pear, T. H. *Personality, appearance and speech.* London: George Allen & Unwin, Ltd., 1957.

Peck, R. F. Family patterns correlated with adolescent personality structure. *J. abnorm. soc. Psychol.,* 1958, **57**, 347–350.

Pepitone, A. Attributions of causality, social attitudes, and cognitive matching processes. In R. Tagiuri & L. Petrullo (Eds.), *Person perception and interpersonal behavior.* Stanford, Calif: Stanford University Press, 1958. Pp. 258–276.

Pepitone, A., and R. Hayden.

Some evidence for conflict resolution in impression formation. *J. abnorm. soc. Psychol.,* 1955, **51**, 302–307.

Pepitone, A., & G. Reichling. Group cohesiveness and the expression of hostility. *Hum. Relat.,* 1955, **8**, 327–338.

Pepitone, A., & J. Sherberg. Cognitive factors in interpersonal attraction. *J. Pers.,* 1957, **25**, 757–766.

Perry, S. E., & L. C. Wynne. Role conflict, role redefinition, and social change in a clinical research organization. *Soc. Forces,* 1959, **38**, 62–65.

Peterson, Ruth C. *Scale of attitude toward war.* Chicago: The University of Chicago Press, 1931.

Petrovich, D. V. The apperceptive study of psychological aspects of pain. *Percept. mot. Skills,* 1960, **11**, 57–65.

Pettigrew, T. F. Personality and sociocultural factors in intergroup attitudes: A cross-national comparison. *J. conflict Resolut.,* 1958, **2**, 29–42.

Pettigrew, T. F. Social psychology and desegregation research. *Amer. Psychologist,* 1961, **16**, 105–112.

Pettigrew, T. F., & E. Q. Campbell. Faubus and segregation: An analysis of Arkansas voting. *Publ. Opin. Quart.,* 1960, **24**, 436–447.

Pinneau, S. R. The infantile disorders of hospitalism and anaclitic depression, *Psychol. Bull.,* 1955, **52**, 429–452.

Pope, L. *Millhands and preachers.* New Haven, Conn.: Yale University Press, 1942.

Pope, L. Patterns of denomina-

tional development: Churches and sects. In L. Wilson & W. L. Kolb (Eds.), *Sociological analysis.* New York: Harcourt, Brace & World, Inc., 1949. Pp. 658–673.

Postman, L. The experimental analysis of motivational factors in perception. In *Current theory and research in motivation: A symposium.* Lincoln, Nebr.: University of Nebraska Press, 1953. Pp. 59–108. (*a*)

Postman, L. On the problem of perceptual defense. *Psychol. Rev.,* 1953, **60**, 298–306. (*b*)

Postman, L., Wanda C. Bronson, & G. L. Gropper. Is there a mechanism of perceptual defense? *J. abnorm. soc. Psychol.,* 1953, **48**, 215–224.

Postman, L., & D. R. Brown. The perceptual consequences of success and failure. *J. abnorm. soc. Psychol.,* 1952, **47**, 213–221.

Postman, L., J. S. Bruner, & E. McGinnies. Personal values as selective factors in perception. *J. abnorm. soc. Psychol.,* 1948, **43**, 142–154.

Postman, L., & R. S. Crutchfield. The interaction of need, set and stimulus structure in a cognitive task. *Amer. J. Psychol.,* 1952, **65**, 196–217.

Postman, L., & G. Leytham. Perceptual selectivity and ambivalence of stimuli. *J. Pers.,* 1951, **19**, 390–405.

Postman, L., & B. Schneider. Personal values, visual recognition and recall. *Psychol. Rev.,* 1951, **58**, 271–284.

Potashin, Reva A. A sociometric study of children's friendships. *Sociometry,* 1946, **9**, 48–70.

Precker, J. A. Similarity of valuings as a factor in selection of peers and near-authority figures. *J. abnorm. soc. Psychol.*, 1952, **47**, 406–414.

Preston, M. G., & R. K. Heintz. Effects of participatory *versus* supervisory leadership on group judgment. *J. abnorm. soc. Psychol.*, 1949, **44**, 345–355.

Proctor, C. H., & C. P. Loomis. Analysis of sociometric data. In Marie Jahoda, M. Deutsch, & S. W. Cook (Eds.), *Research methods in social relations.* Vol. 2. New York: Holt, Rinehart and Winston, Inc., 1951. Pp. 561–585.

Proshansky, H., & G. Murphy. The effects of reward and punishment on perception. *J. Psychol.*, 1942, **13**, 295–305.

Prothro, E. T. Cross-cultural patterns of national stereotypes. *J. soc. Psychol.*, 1954, **40**, 53–59.

Prothro, E. T., & L. H. Melikian. Studies in stereotypes: III. Arab students in the Near East. *J. soc. Psychol.*, 1954, **40,** 237–243.

Prothro, E. T., & L. H. Melikian. Studies in stereotypes: V. Familiarity and the kernel of truth hypothesis. *J. soc. Psychol.*, 1955, **41**, 3–10.

Pryer, Margaret W., & B. M. Bass. Some effects of feedback on behavior in groups. *Sociometry,* 1959, **22**, 56–63.

Pustell, T. E. The experimental induction of perceptual vigilance and defense. *J. Pers.*, 1957, **25**, 425–438.

Rabbie, J. M., J. W. Brehm, & A. R. Cohen. Verbalization and reactions to cognitive dissonance. *J. Pers.*, 1959, **27**, 407–417.

Rabinowitz, W. A note on the social perceptions of authoritarians and nonauthoritarians. *J. abnorm. soc. Psychol.*, 1956, **53**, 384–386.

Radloff, R. Opinion evaluation and affiliation. *J. abnorm. soc. Psychol.*, 1961, **62**, 578–585.

Ramuz-Nienhuis, Wilhelmina, & Annie Van Bergen. Relations between some components of attraction-to-group. *Hum. Relat.*, 1960, **13**, 271–277.

Rasmussen, G., & A. Zander. Group membership and self-evaluation. *Hum. Relat.*, 1954, **7**, 239–251.

Raven, B. H., & J. R. P. French, Jr. Legitimate power, coercive power, and observability in social influence. *Sociometry,* 1958, **21**, 83–97. (*a*)

Raven, B. H. & J. R. P. French, Jr. Group support, legitimate power, and social influence. *J. Pers.*, 1958, **26**, 400–409. (*b*)

Reckless, W. C., S. Dinitz, & Ellen Murray. Self-concept as an insulator against delinquency. *Amer. sociol. Rev.*, 1956, **21**, 744–746.

Redl, F., & D. Wineman. *Children who hate.* New York: The Free Press of Glencoe, 1951.

Reece, M. M. The effect of shock on recognition thresholds. *J. abnorm. soc. Psychol.*, 1954, **49**, 165–172.

Reeder, L. G., G. A. Donohue, & A. Biblarz. Conceptions of self and others. *Amer J. Sociol.*, 1960, **66**, 153–159.

Richardson, Helen M. Studies of mental resemblance between husbands and wives and between friends. *Psychol. Bull.*, 1939, **36**, 104–120.

Richardson, Helen M. Community of values as a factor in friendships of college and adult women. *J. soc. Psychol.*, 1940, **11**, 303–312.

Richardson, Helen M., & N. G. Hanawalt. Leadership as related to the Bernreuter personality measures: V. Leadership among adult women in social activities. *J. soc. Psychol.*, 1943, **36**, 141–154.

Richardson, S. A., A. H. Hastorf, & S. Dornbusch. The impact of different assumptions on research in "interpersonal perception." Paper read at Amer. Sociol. Ass., New York, August, 1960.

Rickman, J. Psychodynamic notes. In H. Cantril (Ed.), *Tensions that cause wars.* Urbana, Ill.: The University of Illinois Press, 1950.

Riecken, H. W. The effect of talkativeness on ability to influence group solutions to problems. *Sociometry,* 1958, **21**, 309–321.

Riecken, H. W., & G. C. Homans. Psychological aspects of social structure. In G. Lindzey (Ed.), *Handbook of social psychology.* Vol. 2. Reading, Mass.: Addison-Wesley Publishing Company, Inc., 1954. Pp. 786–829.

Riesen, A. H. Critical stimulation and optimum period. Paper read at Amer. Psychol. Ass., New York, September, 1961.

Riesman, D. *The lonely crowd: A study of the changing American character.* New Haven, Conn.: Yale University Press, 1950.

Rigby, Marilyn K., & W. K. Rigby. Perceptual thresholds as a function of reinforcement and frequency. *Amer. Psychol.,* 1952, **7**, 321. (Abstract)

Riley, J. W., Jr., & Matilda W. Riley. Mass communication and the social system. In R. K. Merton, L. Broom, & L. S. Cottrell, Jr. (Eds.), *Sociology today: Problems and prospects.* New York: Basic Books, Inc., Publishers, 1959. Pp. 537–578.

Riley, J. W., Jr., W. Schramm, & F. W. Williams. Flight from Communism: A report on Korean refugees. *Publ. Opin. Quart.,* 1951, **15**, 274–286.

Riley, Matilda W., & R. Cohn. Control networks in informal groups. *Sociometry,* 1958, **21**, 30–49.

Riley, Matilda W., R. Cohn, J. Toby, & J. W. Riley, Jr. Interpersonal orientations in small groups: A consideration of the questionnaire approach. *Amer. sociol. Rev.,* 1954, **19**, 715–724.

Riley, Matilda W., & J. W. Riley, Jr. A sociological approach to communications research. *Publ. Opin. Quart.,* 1951, **15**, 445–460.

Robbins, Florence G. The impact of social climates upon a college class. *Sch. Rev.,* 1952, **60**, 275–284.

Rock, I., & F. S. Fleck. A reexamination of the effect of monetary reward and punishment on figure-ground perception. *J. exp. Psychol.,* 1950, **40**, 766–776.

Rodgers, D. A. Relationship between real similarity and assumed similarity with favorability controlled. *J. abnorm. soc. Psychol.,* 1959, **59**, 431–433.

Roethlisberger, F. J., & W. J. Dickson. *Management and the worker.* Cambridge, Mass.: Harvard University Press, 1939.

Rogers, C. R. *Client-centered therapy.* Boston: Houghton Mifflin Company, 1951.

Rogers, C. R., & Rosalind F. Dymond (Eds.), *Psychotherapy and personality change: Coordinated studies in the client-centered approach.* Chicago: The University of Chicago Press, 1954.

Rogers, E. C., & G. M. Beal. The importance of personal influence in the adoption of technological changes. *Soc. Forces,* 1958, **36**, 329–335.

Rokeach, M. *The open and closed mind.* New York: Basic Books, Inc., Publishers, 1960.

Rokeach, M. Belief versus race as determinants of social distance: Comment on Triandis' paper. *J. abnorm. soc. Psychol.,* 1961, **62**, 187–188.

Rommetveit, R. *Social norms and roles: Explorations in the psychology of enduring social pressures.* Minneapolis: The University of Minnesota Press, 1955.

Rommetveit, R. *Selectivity, intuition and halo effects in social perception.* Oslo, Norway: Oslo University Press, 1960.

Rommetveit, R., & R. Svalheim. Selectivity in person perception in different experimental settings. *Acta psychol., Amsterdam,* 1959, **16**, 290–301.

Rose, A. M. The adequacy of women's expectations for adult roles. *Soc. Forces,* 1951, **30**, 69–77.

Rosen, B. C. Family structure and achievement motivation. *Amer. sociol. Rev.,* 1961, **26**, 574–585.

Rosen, B. C., & R. D'Andrade. The psycho-social origin of achievement motivation. *Sociometry,* 1959, **22**, 185–217.

Rosen, S., G. Levinger, & R. Lippitt. Perceived sources of social power. *J. abnorm. soc. Psychol.,* 1961, **62**, 439–441.

Rosenberg, M. J. The experimental investigation of a value theory of attitude structure. Unpublished doctoral dissertation, University of Michigan, 1953.

Rosenberg, M. J. Cognitive structure and attitudinal affect. *J. abnorm. soc. Psychol.,* 1956, **53**, 367–372.

Rosenberg, M. J. A structural theory of attitude dynamics. *Publ. Opin. Quart.,* 1960, **24**, 319–340. (*a*)

Rosenberg, M. J. An analysis of affective-cognitive consistency. In C. I. Hovland & M. J. Rosenberg (Eds.), *Attitude organization and change.* New Haven, Conn.: Yale University Press, 1960. Pp. 15–64. (*b*)

Rosenberg, M. J. Cognitive reorganization in response to the hypnotic reversal of attitudinal affect. *J. Pers.,* 1960, **28**, 39–63. (*c*)

Rosenberg, M. J. When dissonance fails: On eliminating evaluation apprehension from attitude measurement. Technical Report No. 3, Contract Nonr 495(24). Office of Naval Research, 1964.

Rosenberg, M. J., & R. P. Abelson. An analysis of cognitive balancing. In C. I. Hovland & I. L. Janis (Eds.), *Attitude organization and change.* New Haven,

Conn.: Yale University Press, 1960. Pp. 112–163.

Rosenberg, M. J., & C. W. Gardner. Some dynamic aspects of post-hypnotic compliance. *J. abnorm. soc. Psychol.*, 1958, **57**, 351–366.

Rosenberg, S., & R. L. Hall. The effects of different social feedback conditions upon performance in dyadic teams. *J. abnorm. soc. Psychol.*, 1958, **57**, 271–277.

Rosenblith, Judy F. A replication of "Some roots of prejudice." *J. abnorm. soc. Psychol.*, 1949, **44**, 470–489.

Ruechelle, R. C. An experimental study of audience recognition of emotional and intellectual appeals in persuasion. *Speech Monogr.*, 1958, **25**, 49–58.

Sampson, E. E. Status congruence and cognitive consistency. *Sociometry*, 1963, **26**, 146–162.

Sampson, E. E., & C. A. Insko. Cognitive consistency and performance in the autokinetic situation. *J. abnorm. soc. Psychol.*, 1964, **68**, 184–192.

Sanford, F. H. Research on military leadership. In J. C. Flanagan (Ed.), *Psychology in the world emergency*. Pittsburgh, Pa.: University of Pittsburgh Press, 1952. Pp. 17–74.

Sarbin, T. R. Role theory. In G. Lindzey (Ed.), *Handbook of social psychology*. Vol. I. Cambridge, Mass.: Addison-Wesley Publishing Company, Inc., 1954. Pp. 223–258.

Sarnoff, I. Psychoanalytic theory and social attitudes. *Publ. Opin. Quart.*, 1960, **24**, 251–279.

Sarnoff, I., & P. Zimbardo. Anxi-

ety, fear, and social affiliation. *J. abnorm. soc Psychol.*, 1961, **62**, 356–363.

Scanlon, J. C., Barbara Hunter, & G. Sun. Sources of professional identity in medicine. Personal communication. 1961.

Schachter, S. Deviation, rejection, and communication. *J. abnorm. soc. Psychol.*, 1951, **46,** 190–207.

Schachter, S. *The psychology of affiliation: Experimental studies of the sources of gregariousness.* Stanford, Calif.: Stanford University Press, 1959.

Schachter, S., & R. Hall. Group-derived restraints and audience persuasion. *Hum. Relat.*, 1952, **5**, 397–406.

Schaefer, E. S., & Nancy Bayley. Consistency of maternal behavior. *J. abnorm. soc. Psychol.*, 1960, **61**, 1–6.

Schafer, E., & G. Murphy. The role of autism in a visual figure-ground relationship. *J. exp. Psychol.*, 1943, **32**, 335–343.

Schein, E. H. The Chinese indoctrination program for prisoners of war: A study of attempted "brainwashing." In Eleanor E. Maccoby, T. M. Newcomb, & E. L. Hartley (Eds.), *Readings in social psychology.* (3rd ed.) New York: Holt, Rinehart and Winston, Inc., 1958. Pp. 311–334.

Schein, E. H., I. Schneier, & C. H. Barker. *Coercive persuasion.* New York: W. W. Norton & Company, Inc., 1961.

Schellenberg, J. A., & L. S. Bee. A re-examination of the theory of complementary needs in mate selection. *Marriage fam. Liv.*, 1960, **22**, 227–232.

Schelling, T. C. *The strategy of conflict.* Cambridge, Mass.: Harvard University Press, 1960.

Schramm, W., & W. Danielson. Anticipated audiences as determinants of recall. *J. abnorm. soc. Psychol.*, 1958, **56**, 282–283.

Schramm, W., J. Lyle, & E. B. Parker. *Television in the lives of our children.* Stanford, Calif.: Stanford University Press, 1961.

Schulman, S. Basic functional roles in nursing Mother surrogate and healer. In E. G. Jaco (Ed.), *Patients, physicians, and illness.* New York: The Free Press of Glencoe, 1958. Pp. 528–537.

Schwartz, Charlotte G. Problems for psychiatric nurses in playing a new role on a mental hospital ward. In M. Greenblatt, D. J. Levinson, & R. H. Williams (Eds.), *The patient and the mental hospital.* New York: The Free Press of Glencoe, 1957. Pp. 402–426.

Scodel, A., & H. Austrin. The perception of Jewish photographs by non-Jews and Jews. *J. abnorm. soc. Psychol.*, 1957, **54**, 278–280.

Scodel, A., & Maria L. Freedman. Additional observations on the social perceptions of authoritarians and nonauthoritarians. *J. abnorm. soc. Psychol.*, 1956, **52**, 92–95.

Scodel, A., & P. Mussen. Social perceptions of authoritarians and nonauthoritarians. *J. abnorm. soc. Psychol.*, 1953, **48**, 181–184.

Scott, J. P., & Mary-Vesta Marston. Critical periods affecting the development of normal and maladjusted social behavior of puppies. *J. genet. Psychol.*, 1950, **77**, 25–60.

Scott, W. A. Rationality and nonrationality of international attitudes. *J. conflict Resolut.*, 1958, **2**, 8–16.

Seago, D. W. Stereotypes: Before Pearl Harbor and after. *J. Psychol.*, 1947, **23**, 55–63.

Sears, R. R. Identification as a form of behavioral development. In D. B. Harris (Ed.), *The concept of development.* Minneapolis: The University of Minnesota Press, 1957, Pp. 147–161.

Sears, R. R. Relations of early socialization experience to aggresion in middle childhood. *J. abnorm. soc. Psychol.*, 1961, **63**, 466–493.

Sears, R. R., Eleanor E. Maccoby, & H. Levin. *Patterns of child rearing.* New York: Harper & Row, Publishers, Incorporated, 1957.

Seashore, S. E. *Group cohesiveness in the industrial work group.* Ann Arbor, Mich.: Survey Research Center, University of Michigan, 1954.

Secord, P. F. The role of facial features in interpersonal perception. In R. Tagiuri & L. Petrullo (Eds.), *Person perception and interpersonal behavior.* Stanford, Calif.: Stanford University Press, 1958. Pp. 300–315.

Secord, P. F. Stereotyping and favorableness in the perception of Negro faces. *J. abnorm. soc. Psychol.*, 1959, **59**, 309–315.

Secord, P. F. Perception of simi-larity between self and alter. Paper presented at Western Psychological Ass., Portland, Ore., April, 1964.

Secord, P. F., & C. W. Backman. Personality theory and the problem of stability and change in individual behavior: An interpersonal approach. *Psychol. Rev.*, 1961, **68**, 21–32.

Secord, P. F., & C. W. Backman. Interpersonal congruency, perceived similarity, and friendship. *Sociometry*, 1964, **27**, 115–127.

Secord, P. F., C. W. Backman, & H. T. Eachus. Effects of imbalance in the self concept on the perception of persons. *J. abnorm. soc. Psychol.*, 1964, **68**, 442–446.

Secord, P. F., & Ellen S. Berscheid. Stereotyping and the generality of implicit personality theory. *J. Pers.*, 1963, **31**, 65–78.

Secord, P. F., & W. Bevan. Personalities in faces: III. A cross-cultural comparison of impressions of physiognomy and personality in faces. *J. soc. Psychol.*, 1956, **43**, 283–288.

Secord, P. F., W. Bevan, & W. F. Dukes. Occupational and physiognomic stereotypes in the perception of photographs. *J. soc. Psychol.*, 1953, **37**, 261–270.

Secord, P. F., W. Bevan, & Brenda Katz. The Negro stereotype and perceptual accentuation. *J. abnorm. soc. Psychol.*, 1956, **53**, 78–83.

Secord, P. F., W. F. Dukes, & W. Bevan. Personalities in faces: I. An experiment in social perceiving. *Genet. Psy-chol. Monogr.*, 1954, **49**, 231–279.

Secord, P. F., & J. E. Muthard. Personalities in faces: II. Individual differences in the perception of women's faces *J. abnorm. soc. Psychol.*, 1955, **50**, 238–242. (*a*)

Secord, P. F., & J. E. Muthard. Personalities in faces: IV. A descriptive analysis of the perception of women's faces and the identification of some physiognomic determinants. *J. Psychol.*, 1955, **39**, 269–278. (*b*)

Secord, P. F., & Ellen Saumer. Identifying Jewish names: Does prejudice increase accuracy? *J. abnorm. soc. Psychol.*, 1960, **61**, 144–145.

Secord, P. F., T. M. Stritch, & Linda Johnson. The role of metaphorical generalization and congruency in the perception of facial characteristics. *J. soc. Psychol.*, 1960, **52**, 329–337.

Seeman, M. Role conflict and ambivalence in leadership. *Amer. sociol. Rev.*, 1953, **18**, 373–380.

Selltiz, Clair, Marie Jahoda, M. Deutsch, & S. W. Cook. *Research methods in social relations.* (Rev. ed.) New York: Holt, Rinehart and Winston, Inc., 1959.

Selvin, H. C. *The effects of leadership.* New York: The Free Press of Glencoe, 1960.

Sewell, W. H. Social class and childhood personality. Paper read at Berkeley Conf. Pers. Childh., Berkeley, May, 1960.

Shapiro, D. Psychological factors in friendship, choice and

rejection. Unpublished doctoral dissertation, University of Michigan, 1953.

Shapiro, D., & R. Tagiuri. Some effects of response context on trait inferences. *J. Pers.*, 1958, **26**, 42–50.

Shaw, M. E. Some effects of problem solution efficiency in different communication nets. *J. exp. Psychol.*, 1954, **48**, 211–217.

Shaw, M. E. A comparison of two types of leadership in various communication nets. *J. abnorm. soc. Psychol.*, 1955, **50**, 127–134.

Sheldon, W. H., & S. S. Stevens. *The varieties of temperament: A psychology of constitutional differences.* New York: Harper & Row, Publishers, Incorporated, 1942.

Sheldon, W. H., S. S. Stevens, & W. B. Tucker. *The varieties of human physique: An introduction to constitutional psychology.* New York: Harper & Row, Publishers, Incorporated, 1940.

Sherif, M. *An outline of social psychology.* New York: Harper & Row, Publishers, Incorporated, 1948.

Sherif, M., & H. Cantril. The psychology of attitudes. *Psychol. Rev.*, 1945, **52**, 306–314.

Sherif, M., O. J. Harvey, B. J. White, W. R. Hood, & Carolyn Sherif. *Experimental study of positive and negative intergroup attitudes between experimentally produced groups.* Robbers Cave Study. Norman, Okla.: University of Oklahoma, 1954. (multilithed)

Sherif, M., O. J. Harvey, B. J. White, W. R. Hood, & Carolyn Sherif. *Intergroup conflict and cooperation: The robbers cave experiment.* Norman, Okla.: University Book Exchange, 1961.

Sherif, M., & C. I. Hovland. *Social judgment: Assimilation and contrast effects in communication and attitude change.* New Haven, Conn.: Yale University Press, 1961.

Sherif, M., B. J. White, & O. J. Harvey. Status in experimentally produced groups. *Amer. J. Sociol.*, 1955, **60**, 370–379.

Shils, E. A. Primary groups in the American Army. In R. K. Merton & P. F. Lazarsfeld (Eds.), *Continuities in social research: Studies in the scope and method of "The American soldier."* New York: The Free Press of Glencoe, 1950. Pp. 16–39.

Shils, E. A., & M. Janowitz. Cohesion and disintegration in the Wehrmacht in World War II. *Publ. Opin. Quart.*, 1948, **12**, 280–315.

Short, J. F., Jr. Aggressive behavior in response to status threats. Paper read at Amer. Sociol. Ass., St. Louis, August, 1961.

Shull, F. A., Jr., & D. C. Miller. Role-conflict behavior in administration: A study in the validation of a theory of role-conflict resolution. Paper read at Amer. Sociol. Ass., New York, August, 1960.

Shutler, Mary E. A reexamination of Benedict's hypothesis on the effects of discontinuous cultural conditioning. Unpublished master's thesis, University of Arizona, 1958.

Sidowski, J. B. Reward and punishment in a minimal social situation. *J. exp. Psychol.*, 1957, **54**, 318–326.

Sidowski, J. B., L. B. Wycoff, & L. Tabory. The influence of reinforcement and punishment in a minimal social situation. *J. abnorm. soc. Psychol.*, 1956, **52**, 115–119.

Simmel, G. *The sociology of Georg Simmel.* (Trans. by K. H. Wolff.) New York: The Free Press of Glencoe, 1950.

Simpson, G. E., & J. M. Yinger. *Racial and cultural minorities.* New York: Harper & Row, Publishers, Incorporated, 1958.

Simpson, Ida H. Patterns of socialization into professions: The case of student nurses. Paper read at Amer. Sociol. Ass., New York, August, 1960.

Sinha, A. K. P., & O. P. Upadhyaya. Stereotypes of male and female university students in India toward different ethnic groups. *J. soc. Psychol.*, 1960, **51**, 93–102. *(a)*

Sinha, A. K. P., & O. P. Upadhyaya. Change and the persistence in the stereotype of university students toward different ethnic groups during Sino-Indian border dispute. *J. soc. Psychol.*, 1960, **52**, 31–39. *(b)*

Skinner, B. F. Superstition in the pigeon. *J. exp. Psychol.*, 1948, **38**, 168–172.

Skinner, B. F. *Science and human behavior.* New York: The Macmillan Company, 1953.

Slater, P. E. Contrasting correlates of group size. *Sociometry*, 1958, **21**, 129–139.

Smith, A. J. Similarity of values and its relation to acceptance and the projection of similarity. *J. Psychol.*, 1957, **43**, 251–260.

Smith, D. E. P., & J. E. Hochberg. The effect of "punishment" (electric shock) on figure-ground perception. *J. Psychol.*, 1954, **38**, 83–87.

Smith, E. E. The power of dissonance techniques to change attitudes. *Publ. Opin. Quart.*, 1961, **25**, 626–639.

Smith, J. G. Influence of failure, expressed hostility, and stimulus characteristics on verbal learning and recognition. *J. Pers.*, 1954, **22**, 475–493.

Smith, K. R., G. B. Parker, & G. A. Robinson, Jr. An exploratory investigation of autistic perception. *Amer. Psychologist*, 1950, **5**, 313–314. (Abstract)

Smith, Kay H. Ego strength and perceived competence as conformity variables. *J. abnorm. Psychol.*, 1961, **62**, 169–171.

Smith, M. B. Personal values as determinants of a political attitude. *J. Psychol.*, 1949, **28**, 477–486.

Smith, M. B., J. S. Bruner, & R. W. White. *Opinions and personality.* New York: John Wiley & Sons, Inc., 1956.

Solley, C. M., & R. Lee. Perceived size: closure versus symbolic value. *Amer. J. Psychol.*, 1955, **68**, 142–144.

Solomon, R. L. Punishment. *Amer. Psychologist*, 1964, **19**, 239–253.

Solomon, R. L., & D. H. Howes. A note on McGinnies' "Emotionality and perceptual defense." *Psychol. Rev.*, 1950, **57**, 229–234.

Spence, D. P. A new look at vigilance and defense. *J. abnorm. soc. Psychol.*, 1957, **54**, 103–108.

Spitz, R. A. Hospitalism: An inquiry into the genesis of psychiatric conditions in early childhood. *The psychoanalytic study of the child.* New York: International Universities Press, 1945, **1**, 53–74.

Spitz, R. A. Hospitalism: A follow-up report. *The psychoanalytic study of the child.* New York: International Universities Press, 1946, **2**, 113–117.

Spitz, R. A., & K. M. Wolfe. Anaclitic depression: An inquiry into the genesis of psychiatric conditions in early childhood. *The psychoanalytic study of the child.* New York: International Universities Press, 1946, **2**, 313–342.

Stagner, R., & C. S. Congdon. Another failure to demonstrate displacement of aggression. *J. abnorm. soc. Psychol.*, 1955, **51**, 695–696.

Star, Shirley A., & Helen M. Hughes. Report on an educational campaign: The Cincinnati plan for the United Nations. *Amer. J. Sociol.*, 1950, **55**, 1–12.

Star, Shirley A., R. M. Williams, Jr., & S. A. Stouffer. Negro infantry platoons in white companies. In Eleanor E. Maccoby, T. M. Newcomb, and E. L. Hartley (Eds.), *Readings in social psychology.* (3rd ed.) New York: Holt, Rinehart and Winston, Inc., 1958. Pp. 596–601.

Stein, K. B. Perceptual defense and perceptual sensitization under neutral and involved conditions. *J. Pers.*, 1953, **21**, 467–478.

Steiner, I. D. Primary group influences on public opinion. *Amer. sociol. Rev.*, 1954, **19**, 260–267.

Steiner, I. D. Receptivity to supportive versus nonsupportive communications. *J. abnorm. soc. Psychol.*, 1962, **65**, 266–267.

Stephan, F. F., & E. G. Mishler. The distribution of participation in small groups: An exponential approximation. *Amer. sociol. Rev.*, 1952, **17**, 598–608.

Stern, G. G., & J. C. Scanlon. Pediatric lions and gynecological lambs. *J. med. Educ.*, 1958, **33**, Part 2, 12–18.

Stern, G. G., M. I. Stein, & B. S. Bloom. *Methods in personality assessment: Human behavior in complex social situations.* New York: The Free Press of Glencoe, 1956.

Stone, G. P. Clothing and social relations: A study of appearance in the context of community life. Unpublished doctoral dissertation, University of Chicago, 1959.

Stone, G. P. Appearance and the self. In A. M. Rose (Ed.), *Human behavior and social processes.* Boston: Houghton Mifflin Company, 1962. Pp. 86–118.

Stotland, E. Identification with persons and groups. Final report on Grant M-2423 to National Institute of Mental Health, U.S. Public Health Service, October, 1961.

Stotland, E., D. Katz, & M. Patchen. The reduction of prejudice through the arousal of self-insight. *J. Pers.*, 1959, **27**, 507–531.

Stotland, E., S. Thorley, E. Thomas, A. R. Cohen, & A. Zander. The effects of group expectations and self-esteem upon self-evaluations. *J. abnorm. soc. Psychol.*, 1957, **54**, 55–63.

Stouffer, S. A., A. A. Lumsdaine, Marion H. Lumsdaine, R. M. Williams, Jr., M. B. Smith, I. L. Janis, Shirley A. Star, & L. S. Cottrell, Jr. *Studies in social psychology in World War II.* Vol. 1. *The American soldier: Combat and its aftermath.* Princeton, N.J.: Princeton University Press, 1949.

Stouffer, S. A., E. A. Suchman, L. C. DeVinney, Shirley A. Star, & R. N. Williams. *The American soldier.* Vol. 1. *Adjustment during army life.* Princeton, N.J.: Princeton University Press, 1949.

Stouffer, S. A., & J. Toby. Role conflict and personality. *Amer. J. Sociol.*, 1951, **56**, 395–406.

Strauss, A. *Mirrors and masks: The search for identity.* New York: The Free Press of Glencoe, 1959.

Strickland, Bonnie R., & D. P. Crowne. Conformity under conditions of simulated group pressure as a function of the need for social approval. *J. soc. Psychol.*, 1962, **58**, 171–181.

Strickland, L. H. Surveillance and trust. *J. Pers.*, 1958, **26**, 200–215.

Strickland, L. H., E. E. Jones, & W. P. Smith. Effects of group support on the evaluation of an antagonist. *J. abnorm. soc. Psychol.*, 1960, **61**, 73–81.

Stritch, T. M. Experimentally induced changes in physiognomy and personality impressions. Unpublished doctoral dissertation, Emory University, 1954.

Strodtbeck, F. L. Husband-wife interaction over revealed differences. *Amer. sociol. Rev.*, 1951, **16**, 468–473.

Strodtbeck, F. L. Family interaction, values, and achievement. In D. C. McClelland, A. L. Baldwin, U. Bronfenbrenner, & F. L. Strodtbeck (Eds.), *Talent and society.* New York: D. Van Nostrand Company, Inc., 1958. Pp. 135–194.

Stroop, J. R. Is the judgment of the group better than that of the average member of the group? *J. exp. Psychol.*, 1932, **15**, 550–562.

Stryker, S. Social structure and prejudice. *Soc. Probl.*, 1959, **6**, 340–354.

Stycos, J. M. Patterns of communication in a rural Greek village. *Publ. Opin. Quart.*, 1952, **16**, 59–70.

Sullivan, H. S. *Conceptions of modern psychiatry.* Washington, D.C.: The William Alanson White Psychiatric Foundation, 1947.

Sumner, W. G. *Folkways: A study of the sociological importance of usages, manners, customs, mores, and morals.* New York: Dover Publications, Inc., 1906.

Sussman, M. B. The role of neighborhood associations in private housing for racial minorities. *J. soc. Issues*, 1957, **13**(4), 31–37.

Sutcliffe, J. P., & M. Haberman. Factors influencing choice in role conflict situations. *Amer. sociol. Rev.*, 1956, **21**, 695–703.

Sutherland, E. H. *The professional thief.* Chicago: The University of Chicago Press, 1937.

Tagiuri, R. Relational analysis: An extension of sociometric method with emphasis upon social perception. *Sociometry*, 1952, **15**, 91–104.

Tagiuri, R. Social preference and its perception. In R. Tagiuri & L. Petrullo (Eds.), *Person perception and interpersonal behavior.* Stanford, Calif.: Stanford University Press, 1958. Pp. 316–336.

Tagiuri, R. Movement as a cue in person perception. In H. P. David & J. C. Brengelmann (Eds.), *Perspectives in personality research.* New York: Springer Publishing Co., 1960. Pp. 175–195.

Tajfel, H. Value and the perceptual judgment of magnitude. *Psychol. Rev.*, 1957, **64**, 192–204.

Tajfel, H., & S. D. Cawasjee. Value and the accentuation of judged differences: A confirmation. *J. abnorm. soc. Psychol.*, 1959, **59**, 436–438.

Tajfel, H., & A. L. Wilkes. Salience of attributes and commitment to extreme judgments in the perception of people. *Brit. J. soc. clin. Psychol.*, 1964, **3**, 40–49.

Tannenbaum, A. S. An event-structure approach to social power and to the problem of power comparability. *Behav. Sci.*, 1962, **7**, 315–331.

Tannenbaum, P. H. Initial attitude toward source and concept as factors in attitude change through communication. *Publ. Opin. Quart.*, 1956, **20**, 413–426.

Tarde, G. *The laws of imitation.* (Trans. by E. C. Parsons.) New York: Henry 'Holt and Company, Inc., 1903.

Taylor, D. W., & Olga McNemar. Problem solving and thinking. *Annu. Rev. Psychol.*, 1955, **6**, 455–482.

Taylor, H. C. Social agreement in personality traits as judged from speech. *J. soc. Psychol.*, 1934, **5**, 244–248.

Taylor, Janet A. Physiological need, set, and visual duration threshold. *J. abnorm. soc. Psychol.*, 1956, **52**, 96–99.

Tharp, R. G. Psychological patterning in marriage. *Psychol. Bull.*, 1963, **60**, 97–117.

Thibaut, J. W. An experimental study of the cohesiveness of underprivileged groups. *Hum. Relat.*, 1950, **3**, 251–278.

Thibaut, J. W., & H. H. Kelley. *The social psychology of groups.* New York: John Wiley & Sons, Inc., 1959.

Thibaut, J. W., & H. W. Riecken. Authoritarianism, status, and the communication of aggression. *Hum. Relat.*, 1955, **8**, 95–120.

Thistlethwaite, D. L., H. de

Haan, & J. Kamenetsky. The effects of "directive" and "nondirective" communication procedures on attitudes. *J. abnorm. soc. Psychol.*, 1955, **51**, 107–113.

Thistlethwaite, D. L., & J. Kamenetsky. Attitude change through refutation and elaboration of audience counterarguments. *J. abnorm. soc. Psychol.*, 1955, **51**, 3–12.

Thistlethwaite, D. L., J. Kamenetsky, & H. Schmidt. Factors influencing attitude change through refutative communication. *Speech Monogr.*, 1956, **23**, 14–25.

Thomas, E. J. Role conceptions and organizational size. *Amer. sociol. Rev.*, 1959, **24**, 30–37.

Thomas, E. J., & C. F. Fink. Effects of group size. *Psychol. Bull.*, 1963, **60**, 371–384.

Thorndike, R. L. The effect of discussion upon the correctness of group decisions, when the factor of majority influence is allowed for. *J. soc. Psychol.*, 1938, **9**, 343–362.

Thornton, G. R. The effect upon judgments of personality traits of varying a single factor in a photograph. *J. soc. Psychol.*, 1943, **18**, 127–148.

Thornton, G. R. The effect of wearing glasses upon judgments of personality traits of persons seen briefly. *J. appl. Psychol.*, 1944, **28**, 203–207.

Thurstone, L. L., & E. J. Chave. *The measurement of attitude.* Chicago: The University of Chicago Press, 1929.

Timmons, W. M. Decisions and attitudes as outcomes of the discussion of a social problem.

Contrib. Educ. No. 777, Bureau of Publications, Teachers College, Columbia University, New York, 1939.

Timmons, W. M. Can the product superiority of discussors be attributed to averaging or majority influences? *J. soc. Psychol.*, 1942, **15**, 23–32.

Toby, J. Some variables in role conflict analysis. *Soc. Forces,* 1952, **30**, 323–327.

Toman, W. *Family constellation.* New York: Springer Publishing Co., 1961.

Torrance, E. P. Some consequences of power differences on decision making in permanent and temporary three-man groups. In A. P. Hare, E. F. Borgatta, & R. F. Bales (Eds.), *Small groups: Studies in social interaction.* New York: Alfred A. Knopf, Inc., 1955. Pp. 482–491.

Torrance, E. P. An experimental evaluation of "no-pressure" influence. *J. appl. Psychol.*, 1959, **43**, 109–113.

Triandis, H. C. A note on Rokeach's theory of prejudice. *J. abnorm. soc. Psychol.*, 1961, **62**, 184–186.

Trow, D. B. Autonomy and job satisfaction in task-oriented groups. *J. abnorm. soc. Psychol.*, 1957, **54**, 204–209.

Tumin, M. M. Readiness and resistance to desegregation: A social portrait of the hard core. *Soc. Forces.*, 1958, **36**, 256–263.

Tumin, M. M., & R. Rotberg. Leaders, the led, and the law: A case study of social change. *Publ. Opin. Quart.*, 1957, **21**, 355–370.

Turk, H. Instrumental and expressive ratings reconsidered. *Sociometry*, 1961, **24**, 76–81.

Turner, R. H. Role-taking, role standpoint, and reference group behavior. *Amer. J. Sociol.*, 1956, **61**, 316–328.

Turner, R. H. Role-taking process versus conformity. In A. Rose (Ed.), *Human behavior and social processes: An interactionist approach.* Boston: Houghton Mifflin Company, 1962. Pp. 20–40.

Vanderplas, J. M., & R. R. Blake. Selective sensitization in auditory perception. *J. Pers.*, 1949, **18**, 252–266.

Veness, Thelma, & Dorothy W. Brierley. Forming impressions of personality: Two experiments. *Brit. J. soc. clin. Psychol.*, 1963, **2**, 11–19.

Verba, S. *Small groups and political behavior: A study of leadership.* Princeton, N.J.: Princeton University Press, 1961.

Veroff, J., Sheila Feld, and G. Gurin. Achievement motivation and religious background. *Amer. sociol. Rev.*, 1962, **27**, 205–217.

Vinacke, W. E. Stereotyping among national-racial groups in Hawaii: A study in ethnocentrism. *J. soc. Psychol.*, 1949, **30**, 265–291.

Vinacke, W. E., & A. Arkoff. An experimental study of coalitions in the triad. *Amer. sociol. Rev.*, 1957, **22**, 406–414.

Voor, J. H. *Subliminal perception and subception.* Doctoral dissertation. Washington, D.C.: The Catholic University of America Press, 1956.

Vroom, V. H. Projection, negation, and the self concept. *Hum. Relat.*, 1959, **12**, 335–344.

Wager, W. L. Interpersonal and mass communication in an organizational setting. *Sociol. Inquiry*, 1962, **32**, 88–107.

Wagman, M. Attitude change and the authoritarian personality. *J. Psychol.*, 1955, **40**, 3–24.

Walder, L. O. Application of role and learning theories to the study of the development of aggression in children: III. An attempt at an empirical test of a theory. *Psychol. Rep.*, 1961, **9**, 306–312.

Walker, E. L., & R. W. Heyns. *An anatomy for conformity.* Englewood Cliffs, N.J.: Prentice-Hall, Inc., 1962.

Waller, W., & R. Hill. *The family.* New York: Holt, Rinehart and Winston, Inc., 1951. Pp. 186–187.

Wardwell, W. A. The reduction of strain in a marginal social role. *Amer. J. Sociol.*, 1952, **61**, 16–24.

Watson, Jeanne. Some social and psychological situations related to change in attitude. *Hum. Relat.*, 1950, **3**, 15–56.

Watts, A. F. *The language and mental development of children.* Boston: D. C. Heath, 1944.

Watts, W. A., & W. J. McGuire. Persistence of induced opinion change and retention of the inducing message contents. *J. abnorm. soc. Psychol.*, 1964, **68**, 233–241.

Weatherley, D. Anti-Semitism and the expression of fantasy aggression. *J. abnorm. soc. Psychol.*, 1961, **62**, 454–457.

Weiner, M., Janeth T. Carpenter, & B. Carpenter. External validation of a measure of conformity behavior. *J. abnorm. soc. Psychol.*, 1956, **52**, 421–422.

Weinstein, E. A. Some dimensions of altercasting. Paper read at Amer. Sociol. Ass., Washington, D.C., August, 1962.

Weiss, W. A "sleeper" effect in opinion change. *J. abnorm. soc. Psychol.*, 1953, **48**, 173–180.

Weiss, W., & B. J. Fine. Opinion change as a function of some intrapersonal attributes of the communicatees. *J. abnorm. soc. Psychol.*, 1955, **51**, 246–253.

Wertheimer, M. Experimentelle Studien uber das Sehen von Bewegung. *Z. Psychol.*, 1912, **61**, 161–265.

Wertheimer, M. Values in person cognition. In USAF Behav. Sci. Conf. Rep., University of New Mexico, 1957. *Decisions, values, and groups.* New York: Pergamon Press, 1960. Pp. 135–153.

Westie, F. R. Negro-White status differentials and social distance. *Amer. sociol. Rev.*, 1952, **17**, 550–558.

Westie, F. R., & M. L. De Fleur. Autonomic responses and their relationship to race attitudes. *J. abnorm. soc. Psychol.*, 1959, **58**, 340–347.

White, Meda M. Role conflict in disasters: Not family but familiarity first. Research report, Disaster Study Group, National Academy of Science, National Research Council, August, 1962.

Whiting, J. W. M. Sorcery, sin and the superego: A cross-cultural study of some mechanisms of social control. In M. R. Jones (Ed.), *Nebraska symposium on motivation.* Lincoln, Nebr.: University of Nebraska Press, 1959. Pp. 174–195.

Whiting, J. W. M. Resource mediation and learning by identification. In I. Iscoe & H. W. Stevenson (Eds.), *Personality development in children.* Austin, Tex.: University of Texas Press, 1960. Pp. 112–126.

Whiting, J. W. M., & I. L. Child. *Child training and personality.* New Haven, Conn.: Yale University Press, 1953.

Whiting, J. W. M., R. Kluckhohn, & A. Anthony. The function of male initiation ceremonies at puberty. In Eleanor E. Maccoby, T. M. Newcomb, & E. L. Hartley (Eds.), *Readings in social psychology.* (3rd ed.) New York: Holt, Rinehart and Winston, Inc., 1958. Pp. 359–370.

Whittaker, Edna M., J. C. Gilchrist, & Jeanne W. Fischer. Perceptual defense or response suppression. *J. abnorm. soc. Psychol.,* 1952, **47**, 732–733.

Whyte, W. F. *Street corner society: The social structure of an Italian slum.* Chicago: The University of Chicago Press, 1943.

Wiener, M., & P. H. Schiller. Subliminal perception or perception of partial cues. *J. abnorm. soc. Psychol.,* 1960, **61**, 124–137.

Williams, R. M., Jr. *The reduction of intergroup tensions.* New York: Social Science Research Council, 1947.

Williams, R. M., Jr. Friendship and social values in a suburban community: An exploratory study. *Pacific sociol. Rev.,* 1959, **2**, 3–10.

Wilner, D. M., Rosabelle P. Walkley, & S. W. Cook. Residential proximity and intergroup relations in public housing projects. *J. soc. Issues,* 1952, **8**(1), 45–69.

Wilner, D. M., Rosabelle P. Walkley, & S. W. Cook. *Human relations in interracial housing.* Minneapolis: The University of Minnesota Press, 1955.

Wilson, Bryan R. The pentacostal minister: Role conflicts and status contradictions. *Amer. J. Sociol.* 1959, **64**, 494–504.

Wilson, R. S. Personality patterns, source attractiveness, and conformity. *J. Pers.,* 1960, **28**, 186–199.

Winch, R. F. The theory of complementary needs in mate selection: A test of one kind of complementariness. *Amer. sociol. Rev.,* 1955, **20**, 52–56. (*a*)

Winch, R. F. The theory of complementary needs in mate selection: Final results on the test of the general hypothesis. *Amer. sociol. Rev.,* 1955, **20**, 551–555. (*b*)

Winch, R. F. *Mate-selection: A study of complementary needs.* New York: Harper & Row, Publishers, Incorporated, 1958.

Winch, R. F. *Identification and its familial determinants.* Indian-apolis: The Bobbs-Merrill Company, Inc., 1962.

Winch, R. F., T. Ktsanes, & Virginia Ktsanes. The theory of complementary needs in mate selection: An analytic and descriptive study. *Amer. sociol. Rev.,* 1954, **19**, 214–249.

Winch, R. F., T. Ktsanes, & Virginia Ktsanes. Empirical elaboration of the theory of complementary needs in mate selection. *J. abnorm. soc. Psychol.,* 1955, **51**, 508–514.

Winder, A. E. White attitudes towards Negro-white interaction in an area of changing racial composition. *J. soc. Psychol.,* 1955, **41**, 85–102.

Winslow, C. N. A study of the extent of agreement between friends' opinions and their ability to estimate the opinions of each other. *J. soc. Psychol.,* 1937, **8**, 433–442.

Wishner, J. Reanalysis of "impressions of personality," *Psychol. Rev.,* 1960, **67**, 96–112.

Wispé, L. G. Physiological need, verbal frequency, and work association. *J. abnorm. soc. Psychol. Rev.,* 1960, **67**, 96–111. *Psychol.,* 1954, **49**, 229–234.

Wispé, L. G. A sociometric analysis of conflicting role expectancies. *Amer. J. Sociol.,* 1955, **61**, 134–137.

Wispé, L. G., & N. C. Drambarean. Physiological need, work frequency and visual duration thresholds. *J. exp. Psychol.,* 1953, **46**, 25–31.

Witkin, H. A., R. B. Dyk, H. F. Faterson, D. R. Goodenough, & S. A. Karp. *Psychological differentiation: Studies of devel-*

opment. New York: John Wiley & Sons, Inc., 1962.

Wohlwill, J. F. Developmental studies of perception. *Psychol. Bull.,* 1960. **57,** 249–288.

Wolf, Eleanor. The invasion-succession sequence as a self-fulfilling prophecy. *J. soc. Issues,* 1957, **13**(4), 7–20.

Wolfe, J. B. Effectiveness of token-rewards for chimpanzees. *Comp. Psychol. Monogr.,* 1936, **12,** No. 60.

Woodruff, A. D. Personal values and the direction of behavior. *Sch. Rev.,* 1942, **50,** 32–42.

Woodruff, A. D., & F. J. DiVesta. The relationship between values, concepts, and attitudes. *Educ. psychol. Measmt.,* 1948, **8,** 645–660.

Worchel, P. Self-enhancement and interpersonal attraction. Paper read at Amer. Psychol. Ass., New York, August, 1961.

Works, E. The prejudice-interaction hypothesis from the point of view of the Negro minority group. *Amer. J. Sociol.,* 1961, **67,** 47–52.

Yarrow, Marian R. Problems of methods in parent-child re-search. *Child Develpm.,* 1963, **34,** 215–226.

Zajonc, R. B. Some effects of the "space" serials. *Publ. Opin. Quart.,* 1955, **18,** 367–374.

Zajonc, R. B. The effects of feedback and probability of group success on individual and group performance. *Hum. Relat.,* 1962, **15,** 149–161

Zaleznik, A., C. R. Christensen, & F. J. Roethlisberger. *Worker satisfaction and development.* Boston: Harvard University Bureau of Business Research, 1956.

Zaleznik, A., C. R. Christensen, & F. J. Roethlisberger. *The motivation, productivity, and satisfaction of workers: A prediction study.* Boston: Harvard University Bureau of Business Research, 1958.

Zander, A., A. R. Cohen, & E. Stotland. Power and the relations among professions. In D. Cartwright (Ed.), *Studies in social power.* Ann Arbor, Mich.: Research Center for Group Dynamics, University of Michigan, 1959.

Zander, A., & T. Curtis. Effects of social power on aspiration setting and striving. *J. abnorm. soc. Psychol.,* 1962, **64,** 63–74.

Zawadski, B. Limitations of the scapegoat theory of prejudice. *J. abnorm. soc. Psychol.,* 1948, **43,** 127–141.

Zelditch, M., Jr. Role differentiation in the nuclear family: A comparative study. In T. Parsons & R. F. Bales, *Family socialization and interaction process.* New York: The Free Press of Glencoe, 1955. Pp. 307–351.

Zigler, E., & L. Yospe. Perceptual defense and the problem of response suppression. *J. Pers.,* 1960, **28,** 220–239.

Zimmerman, Claire., & R. A. Bauer. The influence of an audience on what is remembered. *Publ. Opin. Quart.,* 1956, **20,** 238–248.

Zipf, Sheila G. Resistance and conformity under reward and punishment. *J. abnorm. soc. Psychol.,* 1960, **61,** 102–109.

Zuckerman, M. The effect of frustration on the perception of neutral and aggressive words. *J. Pers.,* 1955, **23,** 407ff.

Name Index

Abelson, R. P., 110, 136, 168, 172, 182 – 184
Adams, R. G., 390
Adams, S., 384
Adamson, J. F., 28
Adorno, T. W., 80, 426
Aldington, R., 54, 55
Alfert, Elizabeth, 81
Allen, Lucile, 571
Allinsmith, W., 558
Allport, G. W., 22, 30, 62, 63, 422, 426, 427, 433
Altrocchi, J., 79, 81
Anderson, H. H., 390
Anderson, N. H., 59, 143
Anthony, A., 550
Antonovsky, H. F., 557
Applezweig, M. H., 348
Arenberg, D., 19
Argyris, C., 406
Arkoff, A., 285
Aronfreed, J. M., 28
Aronson, E., 154, 192, 549
Asch, S. E., 56 – 59, 130, 327
Ashley, W. R., 39, 44
Atkinson, J. W., 18, 20, 568

Austrin, H., 30
Azuma, H., 37

Back, K. W., 244, 283, 313, 337, 338, 344, 386
Backman, C. W., 82, 86, 246, 249, 252, 271, 583 – 584, 585, 586, 589, 594
Baldwin, Marcella, 20
Bales, R. F., 310 – 314, 317, 354 – 359, 365 – 367, 369, 399 – 401
Bandura, A., 533, 535, 537, 566
Barber, Kathleen, 314
Barker, C. H., 221 – 223
Barnard, C. I., 401
Barrios, A. A., 59
Bartos, O. J., 346
Bass, B. M., 314, 388
Bateman, R. M., 142
Bates, F. L., 457, 496
Bauer, R. A., 210, 223
Bayley, Nancy, 571
Bayton, J. A., 72
Beach, F. A., 555
Beach, L., 79

Subject Index